The Island Press

BIBLIOGRAPHY OF
ENVIRONMENTAL LITERATURE

The Island Press

BIBLIOGRAPHY OF ENVIRONMENTAL LITERATURE

Compiled by

Joseph A. Miller, Sarah M. Friedman, David C. Grigsby, and Annette Huddle

The Yale School of Forestry and Environmental Studies

ISLAND PRESS

Washington, D.C. • Covelo, California

About Island Press

Island Press, a nonprofit organization, publishes, markets, and distributes the most advanced thinking on the conservation of our natural resources—books about soil, land, water, forests, wildlife, and hazardous and toxic wastes. These books are practical tools used by public officials, business and industry leaders, natural resource managers, and concerned citizens working to solve both local and global resource problems.

Founded in 1978, Island Press reorganized in 1984 to meet the increasing demand for substantive books on all resource-related issues. Island Press publishes and distributes under its own imprint and offers these services to other nonprofit organizations.

Support for Island Press is provided by Geraldine R. Dodge Foundation, The Energy Foundation, The Charles Engelhard Foundation, The Ford Foundation, Glen Eagles Foundation, The George Gund Foundation, William and Flora Hewlett Foundation, The James Irvine Foundation, The John D. and Catherine T. MacArthur Foundation, The Andrew W. Mellon Foundation, The Joyce Mertz-Gilmore Foundation, The New-Land Foundation, The Pew Charitable Trusts, The Rockefeller Brothers Fund, The Tides Foundation, and individual donors.

Copyright © 1993 Island Press

Library of Congress Cataloging-in-Publication Data

The Island Press bibliography of environmental literature / compiled
   by Joseph A. Miller . . . [et al.].
      p. cm.
   "The Yale School of Forestry and Environmental Studies."
   Includes indexes.
   ISBN 1-55963-189-9 (cloth: acid-free paper)
   1. Ecology—Bibliography. 2. Environmental literature—
—Bibliography. 3. Human ecology—Bibliography. I. Miller, Joseph
Arthur, 1933—. II. Yale University. School of Forestry and Environmental Studies.
Z5322.E2185 1992
[QH451]
33.7—dc20
                              92-14099
                              CIP

Printed on recycled, acid-free paper

Manufactured in the United States of America
10 9 8 7 6 5 4 3 2 1

HOW TO USE THIS BOOK

The Island Press Bibliography of Environmental Literature consists of 14 sections arranged in two parts of 7 sections each. (See the Table of Contents.) Within each of the 14 sections, items are subdivided into groups of 10 to 40 bibliographic references. The references in each of these groups are listed alphabetically by title.

An introduction at the beginning of each section lists the groupings of references, describes their subject content, and refers the user to related sections in the bibliography.

All items in the bibliography are numbered consecutively, beginning with Section 1. Numbers in the Author-Title and Subject indexes refer to these consecutive numbers, not to page numbers.

To Find

Subjects: Use the Quick-Reference Index, the Table of Contents, or the Subject Index, beginning on page 353.
Authors: Use the Author-Title Index, beginning on page 295.
Titles: Use the Author-Title Index, beginning on page 295.

Quick-Reference Index

This Quick-Reference Index lists general topics and leads users to the sections in the bibliography that contain the most references related to those topics or are important for understanding them. For example, references on acid rain are related to atmosphere, in Section 2; effects on plants, in Section 5; effects on trees and forests, in Section 6; law and policy, in Section 10; and air pollution control, in Section 13.

Numbers refer to sections in the Table of Contents.

CONTENTS

PREFACE

Users of reference books already know about the information problem. Information is abundant; it overflows. But getting the right kind of information when it is needed has become more difficult than ever. Here we are concerned with finding environmental information, which involves a range of subjects, from air pollution to wildlife conservation. Each of these subjects has professional, public, and scientific dimensions. In addition, many of these areas are growing rapidly: systems of management, methods and techniques of research, and concepts and ideas are changing and forming. As a result, there is a large gap between knowledge and practice.

The Island Press Bibliography of Environmental Literature is intended to bring these various subjects and academic disciplines together in one volume, to provide some picture of and access to the knowledge base underlying environment and natural resources.

Compilers of bibliographies are driven by their subjects. If the subject matter is narrow in scope or manageable in size, a bibliographer can strive for completeness. Everything else is well-intentioned, well-informed selection. We hope readers will find our selections well informed; they were certainly well intentioned. Our main criterion was to select publications issued during the 1980s. More recent information is always preferable in scientific and technical fields, though newest is not necessarily best. Ideally, the compilers would have made judicious choices among the best of the older and newer literature. But those kinds of decisions could not be made without getting the recommendations of many subject specialists. We chose to expend our efforts on looking over the items selected and judging for ourselves. We did, however, make considerable use of the expert evaluations found in book reviews and other sources. In sum, then, important older works and classics are included in this bibliography, but not necessarily all that might have been.

Our second criterion was to focus on books and journals. We chose to provide representative coverage in all subject areas. These choices were supplemented by publications giving access to additional sources of information—guides to the literature, directories, encyclopedias, dictionaries, and abstract or index publications. Selections were made from reviews in scientific, technical, and library periodicals, from publishers' announcements, from recommendations, and from the senior author's microcomputer database of environmental publications.

Most, but not all, entries were inspected. For those not inspected, bibliographic information was taken from cataloged records in Yale libraries or in libraries of the Research Libraries Information Network, mainly through their respective computerized systems.

The annotations are meant to describe, not evaluate. But since the writing and rewriting, changes, additions, and corrections were made by all the authors, occasional subjective evaluations may be found.

We did not include separate listings of organizations or computer databases. These are obviously important sources of information and initially were going to be included. But databases, organizations, and research centers are listed and described in many directories, so we decided instead to list and annotate those directories. Computer databases are noted in our annotations, however, when there is an online or CD-ROM version of an abstract or index publication.

Printed sources of information may seem almost old-fashioned in the age of literature searching in computerized databases. What the computer sources do not show, however, is the shape and form of the literature. Thus, the scheme of organization in this bibliography has a broad educational purpose. It is an attempt to show relationships, obvious and obscure, among the various subject areas. In this arrangement the literature of broad topics like *pollution* or *energy* is seen in several aspects, in different areas of human activity. Social and economic considerations are more thoroughly explored. From the compilers' point of view, the bibliography's principal value is that it gives shape and coherence to the literature of the past decade.

The Island Press Bibliography of Environmental Literature should serve a great many users in different ways: as a review of the literature, as a primer for research, or as a quick reference. It should variously appeal to professionals, managers, academics, students, environmentalists, librarians, government officials, and business people. We hope that it will lead those with questions and problems quickly to appropriate information sources.

The bibliography is in two parts: natural environment and human environment. The natural environment sections of Part I emphasize components of the biosphere or natural resources: air, water, land, plants, trees, and animals. The human environment sections of Part II emphasize components of the human environment: society, ethics and philosophy, the arts, education, law and politics, economics, health, technology and engineering, and the methods of science. The first part asserts realities of the natural world; the second part reminds us of the human context that influences, governs, or determines our actions toward the biophysical environment.

An alphabetically arranged Quick-Reference Index to the main areas of the bibliography precedes the Table of Contents. A page or two at the beginning of each section of the bibliography describes the arrangement and scope of that section and provides cross-references and guidance to related sections. Concluding the bibliography are an Author-Title Index and a Subject Index.

As already noted, the product of our labors is a well-intentioned selection. We leave it to those making use of it to judge how well we have selected and described and arranged. At the very least, the bibliography provides a kind of benchmark. Our having done this much, what is missing or inadequate may be more easily seen and corrected. And to those who would do better and are willing to try, we wish you good luck and Godspeed.

Joseph A. Miller

ACKNOWLEDGMENTS

Authors usually find themselves in a thankful mood when their projects are almost completed. We are no exception. It is a pleasure to acknowledge and extend our thanks here to many people who have helped get this bibliography into print.

First are the foundations. The Jessie Ball duPont Fund, principal donor, and the William and Flora Hewlett Foundation provided the grants to develop this bibliography. Both foundations have been exceptionally patient in waiting for the results of their philanthropy.

Charles Savitt, President of Island Press, had the idea of compiling a comprehensive bibliography and interested the foundations in supporting the project. He, too, has patiently waited longer than anticipated.

Gordon Geballe, Associate Dean at the Yale School of Forestry and Environmental Studies, was instrumental in arranging final funding.

The project has built upon bibliographic work funded during the 1980s at the Yale School of Forestry and Environmental Studies Library. Our primary and continuing sponsor is Conoco, Inc., through the ESPER Project. Other donors include the Pew Charitable Trusts, the General Reinsurance Corporation, the Andrew Mellon Foundation, the Richard King Mellon Foundation, and the General Service Foundation.

Dick Zeldin of Moseley Associates contributed his expertise on the production of reference books, along with many words of advice and encouragement. Patricia Harris contributed thoughtful and meticulous copyediting; her questions and suggestions have greatly improved the final product. Joe Ingram, executive editor of Island Press, and managing editor Beth Beisel have been understanding, encouraging, and helpful.

Patricia Shanley performed wonders of research and made sure that ethnobotanical publications were well represented. Lynn Perrigo began the whole process of bibliographic compilation as part of her graduate work in library science at Southern Connecticut State University.

Betsy Carlson, Rohit Salve, Helena Brykarz, and Vinnay Gidwani, students of the Yale School of Forestry and Environmental Studies, provided research and editorial assistance. Michael Brent entered and checked bibliographic data. Gary George wrote essential programs.

The senior author wishes

- to thank especially Sarah M. Friedman, David C. Grigsby, and Annette Huddle. They began as research assistants and became coauthors. Working with them has been personally rewarding and intellectually stimulating.

- to acknowledge the role of colleagues at Yale University: Dean John Gordon of the School of Forestry and Environmental Studies served as principal investigator for the project. William R. Burch, Jr., professor of natural resource management at the School and my longtime partner in the ESPER Project, believes in bibliographies, libraries, and information services. In the university library, Katherine Branch, Librarian for the Sciences, and the other science librarians have created a remarkably collaborative and professionally satisfying work environment. Margery Maass, my colleague at the School of Forestry and Environmental Studies Library, performed additional duties so that I could devote more time to the project.

- to mention some longtime friends whose sympathetic listening meant more than they will ever know: Harold Schofield, novelist and historian; Athena Davaki; and Jean Pablo.

- to recognize a long-term educational influence: Tom Bard Jones, professor emeritus of history, University of Minnesota, and a bibliographer himself, provoked my interest in reference work and information retrieval nearly 40 years ago.

- to record, with heartfelt appreciation, the support of his family during this long venture.

Joseph A. Miller
New Haven, Connecticut
June 1992

Part I

NATURAL ENVIRONMENT (1–1710)

Section 1

Whole Earth Systems and Conditions

At the whole earth level in this opening section are found works dealing with governing conditions and systems. First are works on the state of global resources and environment. Second are those dealing with the living and nonliving systems of the biophysical world: biology, ecology, physics, and chemistry. The living and nonliving categories anticipate and introduce the subject matter of succeeding sections.

Global Resources and Environment

Entries in this group have been chosen for global or planetary perspective, for evaluations of status and conditions, and for general reference. Readers will find that categories like natural resources, conservation, and preservation, which are often separated, are placed together here because it was not possible to subdivide them consistently.

See also:

- Section 2: Air, atmospheric environment; climate change; ozone
- Section 3: Water, hydrosphere, aquatic environment
- Section 4: Land: terrestrial ecosystems
- Section 5: Plants, agriculture
- Section 6: Trees, forests, forestry
- Section 7: Animals, wildlife
- Section 8: Society, culture, human ecology; society and environment: country studies
- Section 9: Ethics, philosophy, religion; nature writing and thought, arts
- Section 10: Law, politics, government
- Section 11: Economy, economics, business and industry
- Section 12: Health, medicine, human biology
- Section 13: Engineering, technology
- Section 14: Science, research, methods; modeling and simulation; assessment and monitoring

Environmental Management. Included here are the key periodicals and books dealing with the composite activity that is environmental management. These titles were placed at the beginning of the bibliography because they are at the general level and because each captures the interconnections of policy, planning, practice, and research. Also in this subgroup are works on environmental planning and management and on environmental professionals and careers.

See also:

- Section 8: Society and environment: country studies; environmental organizations, movements; education and communication
- Section 10: National laws and policies; U.S. politics and policies; U.S. executive agencies, administration and regulation
- Section 11: Economy, costs and benefits, valuation; industry, economic sectors
- Section 13: Environmental control technology
- Section 14: Modeling and simulation; assessment and monitoring; testing and analysis

Biological Systems

This group of entries provides a brief introduction to the literature of biology. Included are reference works, textbooks, abstract and indexing publications, and databases. For inspiration and thought, there are expositions by prominent biologists on the origins and development of life on earth.

See also:

- Section 3: Freshwater biology and ecology; marine biology and ecology
- Section 5: Plant sciences
- Section 6: Tree and forest sciences
- Section 7: Animal biology, zoology
- Section 12: Health, medicine, human biology

Ecology

Given the importance of "ecology and ecological" in this bibliography, many more conceptual and theoretical works in ecology have been included than works in other subject areas of biology.

See also:

- Section 3: Freshwater biology and ecology; marine biology and ecology
- Section 4: Land: terrestrial ecosystems
- Section 5: Plant ecology
- Section 6: Forest ecology, ecosystems
- Section 7: Animal ecology, species
- Section 8: Social and human ecology, population
- Section 14: Modeling and simulation

Ecology: Periodicals. Throughout the bibliography, periodicals, journals, and other serials are entered with books and monographs. Ecology periodicals are the exception; the key titles are entered in this subgroup.

Biodiversity. Conservation Biology. Genetics

"Biodiversity" and "conservation biology" are terms that came into prominence during the 1980s. Conceptually they represent a union of genetics, other biological sciences, and conservation, in the sense of nature conservation or preservation. Recent publications of this kind, dealing with biological diversity in general terms, are here. Also found in this group are entries on genetics and evolutionary biology.

See also:

- Section 5: Endangered plants, genetic resources
- Section 6: Trees, forests, forestry; species, genetic resources
- Section 7: Endangered species, conservation biology
- Section 8: Human evolution, history; rural communities; tribal communities
- Section 9: Ethics, philosophy, religion
- Section 10: International law and policies; U.S. politics and policies; U.S. laws and legislation, courts, disputes; U.S. executive agencies, administration and regulation

Physical and Chemical Systems

Works in this group introduce the physical world, including outer space. The bias in selection was toward imaginative explanations of physicochemical phenomena and dictionaries, encyclopedias, and other reference books.

See also:

- Section 1: Geology, earth sciences
- Section 2: Atmosphere, climate, weather; climate change; air pollution, atmospheric chemistry
- Section 3: Water: physical aspects, hydrology; marine: physical aspects
- Section 4: Soils; land degradation, erosion, reclamation
- Section 5: Plants, agriculture; soil and water relations
- Section 6: Trees, forests, forestry; air, soil, and water relations, pollution
- Section 8: Education and communication
- Section 13: Engineering, technology
- Section 14: Information sources; reference books, journals; quantification, measurement, statistics

Chemistry. Biogeochemical Cycles. Pollutants. The "grand biospheric cycles" and all the lesser ones are chemical, physical, and biological processes. In this subgroup are works presenting the fundamental aspects of these cycles, physicochemical processes of pollution, and environmental chemistry. As noted in the following list, pollution subject matter is distributed widely through the bibliography, in sections on air, water, land, plants, trees, animals, and the human environment.

See also:

- Section 2: Air pollution, atmospheric chemistry
- Section 3: Water pollution
- Section 4: Soils; land degradation, erosion, reclamation
- Section 5: Plants, agriculture; atmospheric environment, pollution, pesticides
- Section 6: Trees, forests, forestry; air, soil, and water relations, pollution
- Section 7: Animal biology, zoology
- Section 8: Society, culture, human ecology
- Section 9: Ethics, philosophy, religion
- Section 10: Law, politics, government
- Section 11: Industry, economic sectors; pollution, industrial wastes
- Section 12: Health, medicine, human biology
- Section 13: Environmental control technology
- Section 14: Modeling and simulation; assessment and monitoring; testing and analysis

Geology. Earth sciences. Selections in this subgroup introduce or provide access to the literature of geology and earth sciences; with emphasis on geomorphology, history, volcanoes, and earthquakes.

See also:

- Section 2: Atmosphere, climate, weather; climate change; air pollution, atmospheric chemistry
- Section 3: Aquatic and marine sciences; water: physical aspects, hydrology; marine: physical aspects
- Section 4: Soils; land degradation, erosion, reclamation
- Section 13: Civil engineering, construction, geotechnology

Energy. The most general works on energy and energetics are grouped here. As with other subjects in this introductory section, entries dealing with energy are found throughout the bibliography.

See also:

- Section 1: Geology, earth sciences
- Section 2: Climate change; air pollution, atmospheric chemistry
- Section 3: Water, hydrosphere, aquatic environment
- Section 8: Society and environment: country studies
- Section 10: U.S. politics and policies; U.S. laws and legislation, courts, disputes; U.S. executive agencies, administration and regulation
- Section 11: Industry, economic sectors; energy; pollution, industrial wastes
- Section 13: Air pollution control; energy technology; radioactive, nuclear

WHOLE EARTH SYSTEMS AND CONDITIONS (1–288)

Global Resources and Environment (1–38)

1. Hammond, Allen; ed. **The 1992 information please environmental almanac**. Houghton Mifflin, 1992. 606 pp., ill., index. Compiled by World Resources Institute. Comprehensive collection, compilation, and display of environmental data drawn from numerous statistical sources. In four parts: state of the planet; issues close to home (food, energy, water, waste); a national view (forests and wetlands, air pollution, recreation, green cities, state comparisons, state profiles, Canadian province profiles); a global view (greenhouse warming, tropical forests, country comparisons). The country, state, provincial, territorial, and city comparisons are based on a standard set of qualitative and quantitative measures.

2. Lovelock, James E. **The ages of Gaia: a biography of our living earth**. Norton, The Commonwealth Fund book program, 1988. 252 pp., ill., bibl., index. Answers to critics by originator of the Gaia hypothesis.

3. Mounsey, H.; ed. **Building databases for global science**. Taylor & Francis, 1988. 419 pp. Proceedings of the first meeting of the International Geographical Union Global Database Planning Project, held in May 1988. Some 50 participants discussed provision of spatial databases for dealing with complex problems on a global scale. Papers on the status of database activities, database design, problems and opportunities, and meeting recommendations. Some of the problems: data exchange, accuracy, and comparability; copyright and ownership; access and cooperation. Essential reading for would-be planetary managers.

4. Allaby, Michael. **Dictionary of the environment**. New York University Press, 3d ed., 1989. 423 pp. Definitions two to three sentences in length explain concepts, technical terms, and environmental events. Includes basic information on environmental institutions and agencies. Entries cross-referenced.

5. Ehrlich, Anne H.; Ehrlich, Paul R. **Earth**. Franklin Watts, 1987. 255 pp., ill. Companion to the British television series of the same name. Provides an overview of the current global predicament. Discusses geological history, including the evolution of life, ecosystems, and humans. Covers social and ecological consequences of overpopulation and inappropriate technology.

6. Turner, B. L., II. **The earth as transformed by human action: global and regional changes in the bio-sphere over the past 300 years**. Cambridge University Press, 1991. 713 pp. Examines changes in population, technology, institutions and culture, location of production and consumption, and urbanization. Eighteen papers discuss changes in the land, water, oceans, atmosphere, biota, and chemicals and radiation. Twelve case studies document regional transformations. Presents theories to explain human actions regarding the biosphere.

7. Woodwell, George M.; ed. **The earth in transition: patterns and processes of biotic impoverishment**. Cambridge University Press, 1990. 530 pp. Collection of case studies illustrates changes in the biosphere by humans. Discusses effects of chronic disturbances to the structure and function of forests, woodlands, grasslands, tundra, and aquatic systems.

8. Goldsmith, Edward; Hildyard, Nicholas; eds. **The earth report: the essential guide to global ecological issues**. Price Stern Sloan, 1988. 240 pp., maps, ill., index. Handbook examines major ecological issues, mostly in dictionary form. Six essays explore man and the natural order, politics of food aid, post-Chernobyl nuclear energy, clean water, acid rain, and the Gaia hypothesis. Includes a list of international environmental organizations.

9. **EER: environmental events record**. United Nations Environment Programme, 1990 to date. Gathered and prepared by UNEP from information in the media and scientific reports. Intended as a reference to and record of recent significant environmental phenomena.

10. **Environmental data report**. Basil Blackwell, 2d ed., 1989. 547 pp., maps, ill. Prepared for the United Nations Environment Programme by the GEMS Monitoring and Assessment Research Centre, in cooperation with the World Resources Institute and the Department of the Environment, UK. Presents statistics in tabular form on pollution, climate, natural resources, health, population, transport, and wastes.

11. Lovelock, James E. **Gaia: a new look at life on earth**. Oxford University Press, 1979. 157 pp., ill., bibl. Statement of the Gaia hypothesis, which contends that the biosphere acts as a feedback mechanism to regulate earth's atmosphere and other inorganic processes in order to maintain an optimal physical environment for life on the planet.

12. Myers, Norman; Nath, Uma Ram; Westlake, Melvin. **Gaia: an atlas of planet management**. Anchor Press, 1984. 272 pp., ill., bibl., index. Profusely illustrated (two-thirds photographs, graphs, charts; one-third text) introduction to global problems and interactions.

13. Council on Environmental Quality; U.S. Department of State. **The Global 2000 report to the President**. Government Printing Office, 1980. Ill., bibl., index. 3 vols. Study of probable changes in the world's population, natural resources, and environment by the century's end, commissioned by President Jimmy Carter in 1977. Vol. 1: Entering the twenty-first century. Summarizes the "disturbing" projections of population growth, diminished biological resources, and continued poverty. Declares the need for action, for international cooperation and commitment, and for "new and imaginative ideas." Vol. 2: The technical report. In four parts: projections, analysis of projection tools (U.S. government, other global models, and comparison of results. Vol. 3: Documentation on the government's global sectoral models: the government's "global model."

14. Southwick, Charles H.; ed. **Global ecology**. Sinaur, 1985. 323 pp., ill., bibl., index. Collection of reprinted articles from *Science,* the *Bulletin of atomic scientists*, and other journals giving background on global ecological trends and such human considerations as health, poverty, and overpopulation.

15. Mannion, A. M. **Global environmental change: a natural and cultural environmental history**. Wiley, 1991. 350 pp. Synopsis of how both natural and cultural agents have transformed the earth's surface over the past 3 million years, focusing on the emergence of society, industry, and agriculture and comparing these with the effects of climate change.

16. Council on Environmental Quality. **Global future, time to act: report to the President on global resources, environment and population**. Government Printing Office, 1981. 209 pp., index. Response to the Global 2000 Report and the crises it identified. Presents options and actions addressing pollution, population, biodiversity, sustainable development, and other problem areas. Participants from 19 federal agencies.

17. Repetto, Robert; ed. **The global possible: resources, development, and the new century**. Yale University Press, 1985. 538 pp., ill., bibl., index. Result of the Global Possible Conference of the World Resources Institute. Ranges over the entire spectrum of interactions—food, water, cities, poverty, energy, environment, resources.

18. Goldsmith, Edward; and others. **Imperiled planet: restoring our endangered ecosystems**. MIT Press, 1990. 288 pp., maps, ill., bibl., index. Overview of the earth's ecosystems and human impacts on them. Topics of the first section, "A World in Crisis," include forests, agricultural lands, rangelands, rivers, groundwater, wetlands and mangroves, coasts and estuaries, seas and oceans, coral reefs, islands, mountains, deserts, Antarctica, and the Arctic. The briefer second section, "The Human Dimension," discusses quality of life, future prospects, and possible solutions. Astonishing photographs.

19. Commoner, Barry. **Making peace with the planet**. Pantheon Books, 1990. 292 pp., index. Argues that current environmental problems are the result of conflict between the ecosphere and the post–World War II "technosphere." Suggests practical steps to resolve ecological, political, and economic instability.

20. Sampson, Neil; Hair, Dwight; eds. **Natural resources for the 21st century**. Island Press, 1989. 349 pp., ill., bibl., index. Compiles information from experts on population, economic trends, and climate changes and their effects on croplands, soil, water quantity and quality, forests, and wildlife.

21. Brower, Kenneth. **One earth**. Collins, 1990. 192 pp., ill. Pictures from over 80 international photographers depict severe environmental damage worldwide and various responses.

22. Silver, Cheryl Simon; DeFries, Ruth S. **One earth, one future: our changing global environment**. National Academy Press, 1990. 208 pp., index. Explains and connects the varied global changes resulting from human activities, reviewing global warming, the ozone layer, acid deposition, and rising seas. Examines economic concerns and the challenges of balancing development and environmental protection.

23. World Commission on Environment and Development. **Our common future**. Oxford University Press, 1987. 383 pp., bibl. The influential Brundtland report, outlining "a global agenda for change" to deal with the interlocking problems of economic development and environmental protection. In three sections: common concerns, common challenges, and common endeavors. Topics: population, food security, species preservation, energy consumption, industry, and human settlements.

24. Mathews, Jessica Tuchman; ed. **Preserving the global environment: the challenge of shared leadership**. The American Assembly; World Resources Institute; Norton, 1991. 362 pp., ill., index. Contributed essays focus on three areas: the impact on international relations of such global concerns as population growth, deforestation, and climate warming; workable economic policies to address global environmental problems; and strategies for achieving international cooperation.

25. Simon, Julian L.; Kahn, Herman; eds. **The resourceful earth: a response to Global 2000.** Basil Blackwell, 1984. 585 pp., ill., bibl., index. Response to the pessimistic Global 2000 report. Argues that threats to the environment are overstated and that global trends indicate continuous improvement of human health and welfare.

26. McLaren, D. J.; Skinner, B. J.; eds. **Resources and world development.** Wiley, Physical, chemical, and earth sciences research report, no. 6, 1987. 940 pp., ill., bibl., index. Papers from two 1986 conferences by 86 experts assess trends in resource availability and use over the next 50 years, covering energy, mineral, land, and water resources.

27. Rosswall, Thomas; Woodmansee, Robert G.; Risser, Paul, G.; eds. **Spatial and temporal variability in biospheric and geospheric processes.** Wiley, SCOPE, v. 35, 1988. 335 pp., ill., bibl., index. Contributors from biological and physical sciences describe the interactions between various components of the biosphere, particularly temporal and spatial links. Includes statistical and mathematical approaches and the linking of terrestrial and climate models.

28. El-Hinnawi, Essam; Hashmi, Manzur H. **State of the environment.** Butterworth, 1987. 182 pp., ill., bibl., index. Survey of world environmental problems from various United Nations Environment Programme reports. Topics include air quality and atmospheric issues; land, water, and food production; energy and transport; chemical and hazardous wastes; social and economic issues; and military activity.

29. State of the environment. Organization for Economic Cooperation and Development, 3d ed., 1991. 297 pp., maps, ill., tables. Comprehensive review of environmental conditions in the 24 OECD countries. In three parts: Part 1 details progress and concerns in the areas of air, water, marine, land, forests, wildlife, solid waste, and noise. Part 2 deals with the economic context—agriculture, industry, transport, and energy. Part 3 has chapters on managing the environment. *Environmental indicators* is a statistical companion volume.

30. Brown, Lester R.; project director. **State of the world.** Norton, 1984 to date., ill. Annual. Reports on progress toward a sustainable society. Assessment con-

sists of 10 to 12 chapters on topical issues, which change each year. Some chapters are reprints of *Worldwatch papers* (73). More of an advocacy report than *World resources: a guide to the global environment* (38), below.

31. State of the world environment, 1991. United Nations Environment Programme, 1988 to date. Updates 1989 *State of the world environment* report. Emphasizes biodiversity, water resources, and the marine environment. Some of these annual reports focus on one issue; in 1990, it was children and the environment.

32. Clark, W. C.; Munn, R. E.; eds. **Sustainable development of the biosphere.** Cambridge University Press, 1986. 491 pp., ill., bibl., index. Multidisciplinary report from an International Institute for Applied Systems Analysis research program on sustainability of development. Five sections: overview; human development; world environment; social response; and usable knowledge.

33. Young, John. **Sustaining the earth.** Harvard University Press, 1990. 225 pp., bibl., index. Identifies the roles of science and industry in modern society and in solving environmental problems. Addresses the growing diversity of environmental agendas and the need to incorporate ecological solutions with social, economic, and international concerns.

34. Thibodeau, Francis R.; Field, Hermann H.; eds. **Sustaining tomorrow: a strategy for world conservation and development.** University Press of New England, 1984. 186 pp., ill., bibl., index. Explores policy options for the World Conservation Strategy, based on sustainable use of biological systems. Outgrowth of seminars at Tufts University between international experts and local conservationists and students. Creates sense of dialogue.

35. Repetto, Robert C. **World enough and time: successful strategies for resource management.** Yale University Press, 1986. 147 pp., index. Explores practical policy initiatives, such as attending to basic needs, creating mechanisms to manage common property resources, ending subsidies on raw materials, recycling materials, pricing of resources properly, and building management capability. Based on 1984 World Resources Institute conference.

36. Holdgate, Martin W.; Kassas, Mohammed; White, Gilbert F.; eds. **The world environment 1972–1982: a report by the United Nations Environment Programme.** Tycooly International, Natural resources and the environment series, v. 8, 1982. 637 pp., ill., bibl., index. Comprehensive assessment of changes in physical and human environment. One decade after Stockholm Conference.

37. Mitchell, George J. **World on fire: saving an endangered earth.** Scribner, 1991. 247 pp., bibl., index. Discusses causes, solutions, and status of the greenhouse effect, acid rain, ozone depletion, and tropical forest destruction. Critique of U.S. leadership in addressing these global issues.

38. World resources: a guide to the global environment. Oxford University Press, 1986 to date. 384 pp., ill., bibl. Annual. Prepared by the World Resources Institute in collaboration with the United Nations Environment Programme and the United Nations Development Programme. Arranged in four parts: an overview or global prospect; 10 to 12 chapters on the state of individual resources, now termed "conditions and trends," formerly "resource reviews"; special-focus or problem issues (one or two chapters); and data tables (146 countries) corresponding to the chapters on resources. Provides authoritative facts and figures, entry into the literature, and relation of global environmental problems to social, political and economic issues. Data sets used for this compilation are available as a database diskette.

Environmental Management (39–73)

39. Ambio: a journal of the human environment. Royal Swedish Academy of Sciences; World Resources Institute, 1972 to date. 8 issues/yr. Founded at the time of the Stockholm Conference. Readable articles by international authorities examine issues or projects in a comprehensive fashion. Relates environmental research to policy, management, technology, and sustainable development. Frequent special issues on broad topics, like chlorofluorocarbons (CFCs) and stratospheric ozone in 1990.

40. Cabot, James S.; ed. **Becoming an environmental professional—1990.** CEIP Fund, 1990. 140 pp. Articles from leading environmental professionals on employment and career trends in the 1990s. Includes proceedings from the CEIP Fund's sixth annual Environmental Careers Conference, "What on Earth Can You Do?"

41. The Environmental Careers Organization. **The new complete guide to environmental careers.** Island Press, 2d ed., 1993. 362 pp., ill., bibl. Job outlook, salaries, and internship opportunities, plus case studies of projects, jobs, and organizations. In-depth interviews with more than 100 professionals.

42. Sullivan, Thomas F. P.; ed. **Directory of environmental information sources.** Government Institutes, 1988. 288 pp. Briefly describes and gives contact information for five kinds of sources: federal, state, professional and scientific, publications, and databases; gives frequency and cost of publications where applicable.

43. Earth Island journal: international environmental news. Earth Island Institute, 1986 to date. Quarterly. Regular reports on environmental issues in all countries. Intended for concerned laypeople and environmental activists. Very brief (one page or less) articles, some of them taken from speeches or reprinted from other publications. Original articles are written by environmental activists, science reporters, and journal staff writers.

44. Ecologist. MIT Press, 1970 to date. Bimonthly. Fully referenced advocacy articles target human impact on the global environment and the social, political, and economic barriers regulating this impact. Encourages philosophical understanding and world view based on respect for natural processes. Critiques large water projects, tropical deforestation, and development policies of World Bank, FAO, and other international agencies.

45. Di Castri, F.; Baker, F. W. G.; Hadley, M.; eds. **Ecology in practice. Part I: Ecosystem management. Part II: The social response.** Tycooly International, Natural resources and the environment series, v. 16.1–16.2, 1984. 395 pp., ill., bibl., index. Based on a 1981 conference. Papers on such topics as sustained production systems in the tropics, management of grazing and marginal land, ecosystem conservation, urban planning, environmental education, and information needs for land management decisions.

46. Ramade, Francois. **Ecology of natural resources.** Wiley, 1984. 231 pp., ill., bibl., index. Basic ecological concepts from the perspective of natural resources: agricultural ecosystems and food production; forests and woodlands; rangelands (savannas, steppes, grasslands); and national parks and nature reserves.

47. Environment. Heldref; Scientists' Institute for Public Information, 1969 to date. 10 issues/yr. Presents scientific information relevant to political and social issues, emphasizing the environmental effects of technology. Feature articles (at least three per issue) touch every interest and concern, often from a global viewpoint. Also contains news briefs, and reports on institutions, and "reports on reports."

48. Environment abstracts. Bowker, 1970 to date.

Monthly. Annual cumulation. Abstracts and indexes information from scientific, technical, and business journals; conferences; academic and government reports; newsletters, newspapers, and general magazines. Arranged in 21 environmental categories; 5,000 or more items per year. Indexes by subject, geographic, and industry "keyterms"; author; and source. Annual includes chronology and review of the year's events, review articles, directory of government agencies and conservation organizations, and conferences. Full text of most abstracted items are available on microfiche from the publisher. Computer database file available, online and on CD-ROM.

49. Environment international. Pergamon Press, 1978 to date. Bimonthly. For multidisciplinary professionals and researchers. Original papers on pollutants and toxicants in air, water, and soil; release and transport of pollutants; environmental technology; health, monitoring, and policy. Includes sections for letters, software exchange, and new patents.

50. Basta, Nicholas. **Environmental career guide: job opportunities with the earth in mind.** Wiley, 1991. 224 pp. Lists environmental businesses, describes professional careers, and maps out career strategies.

51. Environmental conservation. Elsevier, 1974 to date. Quarterly. Articles directed toward low-impact development, ecologically sound management and viability of global resources, enlightened policy, antipollution measures, education, and law. Contains research papers, case histories, short communications and reports, and news and notes of international events, issues, and conferences. Substantial editorial section.

52. Environmental management. Springer-Verlag, 1976 to date. Bimonthly. An international journal for decision makers and scientists. Applied ecology in the "widest sense"; cross-disciplinary, seeking a range of viewpoints and approaches. Consists of three sections. Forum: addresses, comments, and opinions about environmental matters. Profile: articles describing and evaluating case histories, events, policies, problems, or organizations. Research: scientific studies and their results.

53. Environmental periodicals bibliography. Environmental Studies Institute, 1972 to date. Bimonthly. Indexes articles from over 400 journals providing scientific and technical information on environmental topics. Available as computerized database, online and CD-ROM.

54. Baldwin, John H. **Environmental planning and management.** Westview Press, 1985. 336 pp., ill., bibl.

Advanced-level textbook covers all aspects of the field, covering such topics as managing water quality and quantity, air quality, and hazardous and solid wastes; energy; the economic cost of environmental controls; and procedures for writing and reviewing environmental impact statements. Analyzes the flow of resources, from acquisition to disposal.

55. Environmental professional. National Association of Environmental Professionals, 1981 to date. Quarterly. The Association's official journal publishes findings of interdisciplinary research, particularly those that link scientific, technological, and socioeconomic systems to effective assessment, regulation, and protection.

56. Environmental studies and practice. Yale University, Forestry and Environmental Studies Library, 1991 to date. Irregular. Contains a selection of recent publications (300–400), mostly annotated, from all subject areas of environmental sciences and management. Selections emphasize the relation between knowledge, practice, and policy. Includes journal articles and special issues of journals, books, and technical reports.

57. Environmentalist. Elsevier, 1981 to date. Quarterly. Official journal of the Institution of Environmental Sciences. Intends the publication as a bridge between industry, government, and environmental professionals, providing guidelines and frameworks for management mechanisms, and as a catalyst for environmental education at all levels. Articles, interviews, editorials, news, and commentary.

58. GeoJournal. Kluwer, 1987 to date. Monthly. Subtitle: An international journal of physical, biological, social and economic geography and applications in environmental planning and ecology.

59. Implementing sustainable development: our common future. NGO Liaison Service of the United Nations, 1988. Contains responses and recommendations generated by *Our common future*, the World Commission on Environment and Development report. Topics include sustainable agriculture, resource management, emerging technologies, indigenous peoples, human rights and development, multilateral interaction, the debt crisis, and global atmospheric changes.

60. Infoterra international directory. United Nations Environment Programme, 1977 to date. Irregular. Sources for inclusion in directory are selected by the 137 "national focal points" (NFPs) of Infoterra. The NFPs are government designated and often are part of environmental ministries or agencies. Provides access to over 6500 of these environmental information sources. Subjects represented include forests and forestry, arid lands, species conservation, energy, development, hydrometeorology, marine environment, toxic chemicals, waste management, occupational safety and health, water supply, and waste management. Issues special directories on selected subjects.

61. IUCN bulletin. International Union for Conservation of Nature and Natural Resources, 1952 to date. Quarterly. Provides news of IUCN programs, activities, and special commissions. Reports on international meetings and conferences. Contains features on parks and protected areas, threatened species, regions, pollution threats, and sustainable development.

62. Journal of environmental management. Academic Press, 1973 to date. Bimonthly. Publishes six to eight research articles per issue, generally case studies (local, regional, and global). Many papers have a mathematical or modeling background.

63. Journal of environmental systems. Baywood, 1971 to date. Quarterly. Interdisciplinary forum for the environmental professions. Links biological and physical systems with policy, economic, engineering, and social systems. Approaches practical environmental problems from a theoretical viewpoint.

64. Nature and resources. Parthenon; UNESCO, 1965 to date. Quarterly. Founded by UNESCO and a regular source of information on international scientific programs, such as Man and the Biosphere, until 1988. Resumed publication in 1990. Carries briefer articles, by scientists, focusing on sustainable development and the use of scientific information for making environmental decisions. News and literature sections.

65. Jorgensen, Sven Erik; Johnsen, I. **Principles of environmental science and technology.** Elsevier, Studies in environmental science, v. 33, 2d ed., 1989. 627 pp. Second edition of this textbook includes expanded coverage of ecotoxicology, ecological principles and concepts, agricultural waste, and ecological engineering. Also discusses problems of water, waste water, solid waste, and air pollution.

66. Dorney, Robert S.; Dorney, Lindsay C.; ed. **The professional practice of environmental management.** Springer-Verlag, Springer series on environmental management, 1989. 228 pp., ill., bibl. Discusses how a professional practitioner should operate and the processes of decision making in resolving environmental issues.

67. Renewable natural resources journal. Renewable Natural Resources Foundation, 1983 to date. Quarterly. Articles on all aspects of renewable natural resources; intended to advance public understanding and foster cooperation among professional, scientific, and educational organizations.

68. Resource conservation glossary. Soil Conservation Society of America, 3d ed., 1982. 193 pp., bibl. Brief, one- or two-sentence definitions of 4000 terms related to the technologies and sciences of resource conservation.

69. Hammond, Kenneth A.; Macinko, George; Fairchild, Wilma B.; eds. **Sourcebook on the environment: a guide to the literature.** University of Chicago Press, 1978. 613 pp., index. Broad guide to selected aspects of environmental literature, in four parts, with 28 essays by subject experts. Essays in Part 1, "Environmental Perspectives and Prospects," give a philosophical and conceptual framework on recurring themes, such as quality of life or resource scarcity. Part 2 has eight very broad "case studies" of environmental modification: industrial water pollution, human impact on wildlife and wildlands, agriculture, mining, urbanization, transportation, and solid waste. Part 3 deals with major elements of the environment: air, water, landforms and soils, vegetation, wildlife, coastal zones, human populations, and energy. Part 4 contains "research aids": periodicals, legislation, and organizations. Each essay refers to and is followed by a comprehensive listing of books, articles, government reports, and documents. A project of the Association of American Geographers.

70. Whole earth review. Point Foundation, 1974 to date. Quarterly. Continues: Co-evolution quarterly. By the publisher of the *Whole earth catalog.* Pointed commentary, reviews, features, and departments give a genuinely global perspective. Recent special issues on bioregions, plant genetic resources, and restoration ecology.

71. Women in natural resources. University of Idaho, Bowers Lab, 1979 to date. Quarterly. Continues: Women in forestry. Publishes "information for, from, and about women who work in natural resources," factual, personal, and philosophical. Articles on natural resources and career professional matters.

72. World watch. Worldwatch Institute, 1988 to date. Bimonthly. Articles identify trends, practices, and events threatening to the earth and its physical and social environment. Advocates changes in world population, energy, environmental, and food policies.

73. Worldwatch papers. Worldwatch Institute, 1975 to date. 4 or more issues/yr. Single-topic issues analyze global problems; topics include all aspects of the environment, poverty, energy, development, population, and inequality.

Biological Systems (74–100)

74. Biological abstracts. BIOSIS, 1926 to date. Semimonthly. Standard finding aid to the world literature of biology. Abstracts are arranged by categories, termed "concept headings." Bibliographic information includes addresses of authors. Four indexes: author, biosystematic (taxonomic category), generic (genus and species), and subject (keywords). Available as online computer database.

75. Biological and agricultural index. Wilson, 1964 to date. Monthly. Cumulative subject index to English-language periodicals in biology, agriculture, and related fields, including environmental sciences. Arranged in one alphabet. Computer database file available, online and on CD-ROM.

76. Jeffrey, Charles. **Biological nomenclature.** Edward Arnold, 3d ed., 1989. 86 pp., bibl., index. Describes the systematic background, purposes, codes, and ranking of scientific names; discusses principles of nomenclature and sources and consequences of instability; explains authorities and their proper citation; revised and updated to accommodate major changes in the international codes of practice.

77. Keeton, William T.; Gould, James L.; Gould, Carol Grant. **Biological science.** Norton, 4th ed., 1986. 1175 pp., ill., bibl., index. Comprehensive introduction to biology. Color illustrations and photographs.

78. Sherman, Irwin W.; Sherman, Vilia G. **Biology: a human approach.** Oxford University Press, 4th ed., 1989. 636 pp., ill., bibl., index. Focuses on human applications of biology, from the cellular and organismal level to the population level. Goes into considerable detail without sacrificing intelligibility for the general reader.

79. Englund, Paul T.; Sher, Alan; eds. **The biology of parasitism: a molecular and immunological approach.** Liss, MBL lectures in biology, v. 9, 1988. 544 pp., ill., bibl., index. Summaries of recent research in parasite biology and disease, parasite immunology, and parasite molecular biology, biochemistry, and genetics.

80. Wilson, Edward O. **Biophilia: the human bond to other species.** Harvard University Press, 1984. 157 pp., bibl. Noted biologist's reflections on the history of biological thought, the conservation ethic, and natural history. Argues the need for and capacity of humans to identify with other living things.

81. Gates, David M. **Biophysical ecology.** Springer-Verlag, Springer advanced texts in life sciences, 1980. 611 pp., ill., bibl., index. Graduate-level textbook and reference. Covers energy budgets, evaporation, and transpiration from the perspective of physics as applied to plants and animals. Contains useful equations.

82. BioScience. American Institute of Biological Sciences, 1964 to date. Monthly. Journal with readable mix of feature articles, research articles, letters, book reviews, calendar, professional news, commentary, and advertising. Covers all subdisciplines within biology. Regular features on regional and global aspects of natural resources, biodiversity, ecology, and pollution.

83. Friday, Adrian; Ingram, David S.; eds. **The Cambridge encyclopedia of life sciences.** Cambridge University Press, 1985. 432 pp., ill., bibl., index. Surveys the current state of knowledge in biology, discussing processes, organisms, environments, evolution, and the fossil record and demonstrating the linkages between biological phenomena.

84. Lincoln, Roger J.; Boxshall, G. A. **The Cambridge illustrated dictionary of natural history.** Cambridge University Press, 1987. 413 pp., ill. Brief definitions explain the essential concepts of ecological terms; other entries summarize the characteristics (number, habitat, distribution, morphological features) of organisms, down to the level of order and sometimes family; common names are cross-referenced to appropriate taxonomic categories.

85. Walker, Peter M. B. **Chambers biology dictionary.** Cambridge University Press, 1989. 324 pp., ill. Ten thousand definitions, most under 25 words, encompass botany, genetics, ecology, forestry, medicine, and zoology; 100 selected terms receive special attention, with illustrations and 200- to 300-word passages.

86. Smith, Robert Leo. **Ecology and field biology.** Harper & Row, 4th ed., 1990. 922 pp., ill., bibl., index. Revised college textbook. Sections on the ecosystem, population ecology, community ecology, and comparative ecosystem ecology (200 pages). More descriptive than analytical and theoretical, with frequent references to environmental management applications. Includes student resource manual, an introduction to ecological methods.

87. Sprent, Janet I. **Ecology of the nitrogen cycle.** Cambridge University Press, Cambridge Studies in Ecology, 1987. 151 pp. Describes general nitrogen cycle processes, showing how the cycle is modified in particular ecological and geographic circumstances; uses examples from all over the world. Discusses agriculture, forestry, and fuel combustion; emphasizes microorganisms and plants but includes examples showing the role of invertebrates in nitrogen cycles.

88. Tudge, Colin; ed. **The environment of life.** Oxford University Press, 1988. 248 pp., ill., bibl., index. In nontechnical language, surveys animal behavior, basic ecosystem functionings, the rise of humans and the development of agriculture and fisheries, threats from pollution, and conservation strategies.

89. Rambler, Mitchell B.; Margulis, Lynn; Fester, René; eds. **Global ecology: towards a science of the biosphere.** Academic Press, 1989. 204 pp., ill., bibl., index. Introductory-level interdisciplinary text; puts biogeochemical cycles within planetary perspective and connects satellite technology and applications to the earth sciences. Some topics include Gaia and geognosy, the integral biosphere, photochemistry of biogenic cases, and global ecological research and public response.

90. Mayr, Ernst. **The growth of biological thought: diversity, evolution, and inheritance.** Belknap Press, 1982. 974 pp., ill., bibl., index. Historical view of the developmental process of concepts in biology; touches on diversity, evolution, and inheritance.

91. Lawrence, Eleanor. **A guide to modern biology: genetics, cells, and systems.** Wiley, 1989. 507 pp., ill., bibl. Selective guide to current knowledge of molecular genetics and cell structure, emphasizing mammalian cells, and mammalian and human biology; assumes general knowledge of biology and biochemistry; topics include immunology, recombinant DNA technology, and animal development.

92. Henderson, I. F.; Lawrence, Eleanor; eds. **Henderson's dictionary of biological terms.** Wiley, 10th ed., 1989. 637 pp., ill. Extensively revised since the ninth edition to include terms from cell biology and molecular genetics. More than 18,000 terms. Many general or common names of species.

93. Moore, David M.; ed. **Illustrated encyclopedia of plants and earth sciences.** Marshall Cavendish, 1988. 10 vols. Ill., index. Three major sections: plants of the world, plant ecology, and earth sciences. One hundred and twenty contributors, color photos and illustrations; alphabetical and thematic indexes.

94. Wyatt, H. V.; ed. **Information sources in the life sciences.** Butterworth, Butterworths guides to information sources, 3d ed., 1987. 191 pp., bibl., index. Revised version of *The use of biological literature.* Explains biochemical sciences, microbiology (including virology, mycology, tissue culture, and use of animals), biotechnology, genetics, zoology, ecology, botany, and history of biology. Also covers reading (current awareness) and searching (abstracts and indexes, guides to the literature, computer databases).

95. Attenborough, David. **Life on earth: a natural history.** Little, Brown, 1979. 319 pp., ill., index. In an engaging, readable fashion, traces the development of plants, insects, fish, reptiles, birds, and mammals, following the "significant thread" in the history of each group; illustrates both the variety and the interconnectedness of life on earth.

96. Natural history. American Museum of Natural History, 1960 to date. Monthly. Articles and photoessays on species, ecosystems, places, landforms, peoples, and past environments, from archaeology to zoology, explaining, exploring, and depicting the natural sciences. Among the columns is "This View of Life," by Stephen Jay Gould.

97. Coe, Malcolm; ed. **The natural world.** Oxford University Press, Oxford illustrated encyclopedia, v. 2, 1985. 375 pp. Over 2500 clear and concise (100 words average) entries; representative sampling of plant and animal species worldwide, giving adaptations and feeding and reproductive habits.

98. Sprent, Janet I.; Sprent, Peter. **Nitrogen fixing organisms: pure and applied aspects.** Chapman and Hall, 1990. 256 pp., ill., bibl., index. Reviews nitrogen-fixing microbes and their processes, then addresses nitrogen fixation in agriculture, forestry, and aquatic and terrestrial ecosystems.

99. Allaby, Michael; ed. **The Oxford dictionary of natural history.** Oxford University Press, 1985. 688 pp. Covers earth and atmospheric sciences and biochemistry, besides subject areas in biology; less on ecology and evolution. Taxa of living organisms make up half the 12,000 entries.

100. Parker, Sybil P.; editor-in-chief. **Synopsis and classification of living organisms.** McGraw-Hill, 1982. Ill., bibl., index. 2 vols. Eighty-two hundred synoptic articles describe the characteristics, biology, ecology, and distribution of all taxa (except fossil groups), including viruses. Each article includes literature citations.

Ecology (101–137)

101. Myers, Alan A.; Giller, Paul S. **Analytical biogeography: an integrated approach to the study of animal and plant distributions.** Chapman and Hall, 1988. 578 pp., ill., bibl., index. Examines biogeographic patterns, focusing on species diversity; species number in relation to area, distance, and other variables; and endemism. Reviews geological processes, including adaptation, speciation, extinction, and ecological interactions. Studies methods of reconstruction, reporting on phylogenetic, cladistic, and applied historical biogeography.

102. McIntosh, Robert Patrick. **The background of ecology: concept and theory.** Cambridge University Press, Cambridge studies in ecology, 1985. 383 pp., bibl., index. Chronology and description of ecology in England and America. Discusses leading doctrines and controversies.

103. Morse, Douglass H. **Behavioral mechanisms in ecology.** Harvard University Press, 1980. 383 pp., ill., bibl., index. Brings together ecology and ethology in discussion of foraging strategy, habitat selection and territoriality, thermoregulation, competition for mates, reproduction, and social groups. Well-chosen examples, references, and graphs.

104. Drake, J.A.; and others, eds. **Biological invasions: a global perspective.** Wiley, SCOPE, v. 37, 1989. 525 pp., ill., bibl., index. Reviews types of invasions, including terrestrial and aquatic plants, plant pathogens, and vertebrates. Assesses attributes and methods of invaders, studying effects of chance and timing, and analyzing control programs.

105. Diamond, Jared; Case, Ted J.; eds. **Community ecology.** Harper & Row, 1986. 665 pp., ill., bibl., index. Approaches to the study of community ecology, in five sections: experimental methods; species introductions and extinctions; spatial and temporal scales; equilibrium and influencing factors; and forces structuring communities. Advocates a pluralistic approach of applying methods and scales most appropriate and profitable to the species and the question.

106. Kikkawa, Jiro; Anderson, Derek J.; eds. **Community ecology: pattern and process.** Blackwell Scientific, 1986. 432 pp., ill., bibl., index. A "fresh look" at the major processes and patterns of community ecology from contributors chosen by the editors (botanist and zoologist). In four sections: description, organization of communities, ecological processes, and evolutionary processes.

107. Pontin, A.J. **Competition and coexistence of species.** Pitman International Advanced Publications Program, 1982. 102 pp., ill., bibl., index. Discusses the causes of competition—exploitation and interference—coexistence, displacement, and the consequences of competition.

108. Pomerory, Lawrence R.; Alberts, James J.; eds. **Concepts of ecosystem ecology: a comparative view.** Springer-Verlag, Ecological studies, v. 67, 1988. 384 pp., ill., bibl., index. Papers honoring the ecologist Eugene Odum. Discusses methodologies for studying ecosys-

tems, state of knowledge of major terrestrial and aquatic ecosystems, and current and potential problems.

109. Botkin, Daniel B. **Discordant harmonies: a new ecology for the twenty-first century.** Oxford University Press, 1990. 241 pp., index. Argues that natural forces are in transition, not in equilibrium or harmony; in a dozen essays, illustrates with case studies and applies arguments to such issues as controlled burning in national forests, fishing and hunting quotas, and other natural resource management concerns.

110. Mooney, H. A.; Godron, M.; eds. **Disturbance and ecosystems: components of response.** Springer-Verlag, Ecological studies, v. 44, 1983. 292 pp., ill., bibl., index. Conference papers. Dynamic processes affecting the biosphere, whole landscapes, ecosystems, populations, and species. Features of organisms characteristic of disturbance habitats; effects of disturbance on the productive potential of natural systems. Compares natural and human-induced disturbances.

111. Strong, Donald R.; and others, eds. **Ecological communities: conceptual issues and the evidence.** Princeton University Press, 1984. 613 pp., ill., bibl., index. Papers from a 1981 symposium on the enormous difficulties of measuring and evaluating the interactions of species in ecological communities. Experimental, biogeographic and historical evidence; species combinations and changes in time and space.

112. Kolasa, Jurek; Pickett, Steward T. A.; eds. **Ecological heterogeneity.** Springer-Verlag, Ecological studies, v. 86, 1991. 332 pp., ill., bibl., index. Examines the concept of heterogeneity and discusses its application and implications in ecological areas; topics include physical and biological heterogeneity, managing and monitoring of ecosystems, and scaling of ecological systems under analysis.

113. Committee on the Applications of Ecological Theory to Environmental Problems; Orians, Gordon H. (chair). **Ecological knowledge and environmental problem-solving: concepts and case studies.** National Academy Press, 1986. 388 pp., maps, ill., bibl., index. Presents ecological concepts, theories, and models and reviews data and procedures common to many environmental problems. Thirteen case studies illustrate the influence, use, and results of such ecological information.

114. Walter, Heinrich; Breckle, Siegmar-W. **Ecological systems of the geo-biosphere: ecological principles in global perspective.** Springer-Verlag, 1985. 242 pp. Global approach to ecology; looks at biosphere as entity whose parts are dynamically linked.

115. Colinvaux, Paul A. **Ecology.** Wiley, 1986. 725

pp., ill., bibl., index. Designed as a teaching text; reviews ecological processes and theories using an integration approach from the individual to the community; includes recommendations for revising chapter order to fit integration or reduction approach or environmental theme.

116. Ricklefs, Robert E. **Ecology.** Freeman, 3d ed., 1990. 896 pp., ill., bibl., index. Revised college text. Strong on evolutionary ecology, analytic theory, mathematical models, and tropical ecology. Less material on population interactions and community ecology.

117. Odum, Eugene P. **Ecology and our endangered life-support systems.** Sinauer, 1989. 283 pp., ill., index. New version of the author's textbook *Ecology*, extensively rewritten for the nonscientist. Emphasizes causes and long-term solutions to the world's environmental problems.

118. Deshmukh, Ian. **Ecology and tropical biology.** Blackwell Scientific, 1986. 387 pp., ill., bibl., index. A comprehensive ecology textbook that "treats the tropics integrally, rather than as a special topic." Identifies and evaluates differences between tropical and temperate ecology and discusses human ecology in tropical countries.

119. Begon, Michael; Harper, John L.; Townsend, Colin R. **Ecology: individuals, populations, and communities.** Blackwell Scientific, 2d ed., 1990. 945 pp., ill., bibl., index. Revised college textbook. Structured about populations, which are used in discussing community ecology and autecology. Presentations of theory based more on empirical examination and uniqueness of observed patterns. Chapters on abundance, population management, islands, detritivores and decomposers.

120. Mooney, Harold A.; Drake, James A.; eds. **Ecology of biological invasions of North America and Hawaii.** Springer-Verlag, Ecological studies, v. 58, 1986. 321 pp., ill., bibl., index. Papers from a 1984 symposium discuss factors involved in biological invasions; case studies examine specific biotypes, processes affecting invasions, and the results of such changes in biotic communities.

121. Pickett, S. T. A.; White P. S.; eds. **The ecology of natural disturbance and patch dynamics.** Academic Press, 1985. 472 pp., ill., bibl., index. Conference papers intended to synthesize the literature on patch dynamics and provide some framework for examining disturbance in natural systems. Discusses the adaptation of organisms and evolution of populations in patch dynamic environments and the implications of patch dynamics for the organization of communities and functioning of ecosystems.

122. Pittock, A. Barrie; Harwell, Mark, A.; Hutchinson, Thomas C.; and others. **Environmental consequences of nuclear war.** Wiley, SCOPE, v. 28, 1986. Ill., bibl., index. 2 vols. Comprehensive examination by hundreds of scientists from 30 countries of potential consequences of nuclear war. Vol. 1: Physical and atmospheric effects. Direct effects, sources and properties of smoke and dust, atmospheric processes, meteorological and climatological effects, and radiological dose assessment. Vol. 2: Ecological and agricultural effects. Relevant ecological principles, vulnerability of ecological systems, and agricultural and human effects.

123. Crawley, Michael J. **Herbivory: the dynamics of animal-plant interactions.** University of California Press, Studies in ecology, v. 10, 1983. 437 pp., ill., bibl., index. Results of herbivory on community and population dynamics, covering demography, growth rate, fecundity, seedling establishment, plant species richness, succession, plant community structure, associational resistance, and competition and coexistence. Discusses functional and numerical responses of animals; monophagy and polyphagy; selection and preference; food quality; and plant defenses against herbivores.

124. O'Neill, R. V.; and others. **A hierarchical concept of ecosystems.** Princeton University Press, Monographs in population biology, v.23, 1986. 253 pp., ill., bibl., index. Review and critique of historical concepts and definitions of the term "ecosystem," noting inadequacy of these approaches in formulating a strong theory of ecosystems. Presents a new theory and suggests its applicability to ecological systems.

125. Ehrlich, Paul R. **The machinery of nature.** Simon & Schuster, 1986. 320 pp., ill., bibl., index. Covers physiological, population, behavioral, community, and ecosystem ecology; biogeography; predation; and competition. Emphasizes evolutionary approach.

126. Microbial ecology. Springer Verlag, 1974 to date. Bimonthly. International journal publishing research in the microbiology of natural ecosystems; ecological studies in applied microbiology; current methodological developments; and microbial processes associated with environmental pollution; and related areas.

127. Price, Peter W.; Slobodchikoff, C. N.; Gaud, William S.; eds. **A new ecology: novel approaches to interactive systems.** Wiley, 1984. 515 pp., ill., bibl., index. Highlights recent research in resources and populations, life history strategies, ecology of social behavior, and organization of communities.

128. Meilke, H. W. **Patterns of life: biogeography of a changing world.** Unwin Hyman, 1989. 370 pp., ill., bibl., index. Collection of all the basic systems and processes that contribute to evolution and make up the biosphere. Discusses the planetary and geological context of life, the biogeographic significance of such events as continental drift and ice ages; marine, freshwater, island, and terrestrial environments; and human impacts, including agriculture, fire, and urban industrialization. Lively introduction to biogeography.

129. Price, Peter W.; and others, eds. **Plant animal interactions: evolutionary ecology in tropical and temperate regions.** Wiley, 1991. 656 pp. Emphasizes tropical studies and comparative analyses of tropical temperate ecological systems; topics include mutualistic and antagonistic plant-animal relationships, plant-butterfly interactions, and community patterns in natural and agricultural systems.

130. Murray, Bertram G. **Population dynamics: alternative models.** Academic Press, Physiological ecology series, 1979. 212 pp., ill., index. Attempts to provide a theoretical framework of population dynamics that is not controlled by density-dependent factors. Includes models of variations in population growth rates, sizes, and fluctuations.

131. Begon, Michael; Mortimer, Martin. **Population ecology: a unified study of animals and plants.** Blackwell Scientific, 2d ed., 1986. 219 pp., ill., bibl., index. Introductory text examines the dynamics and interactions within single-species populations and interspecific competition and predation. Final section expands on the above with respect to individual life history strategies, the regulation and determination of population size, and the role of intra- and interpopulation interactions in determining community structure.

132. Schulze, E. D.; Zwolfer, H.; eds. **Potentials and limitations of ecosystem analysis.** Springer-Verlag, Ecological studies, v. 61, 1987. 435 pp., ill., bibl., index. Based on a 1985 symposium. Integrated treatment of abiotic cycles and their influence on process and function at the producer and consumer levels.

133. Draggan, Sidney; Cohrssen, John; Morrison, Richard E.; eds. **Preserving ecological systems: the agenda for long-term research and development.** Praeger, 1987. 191 pp., bibl., index. Eight papers from experts in government, industry, the academic community and public interest groups present findings and research recommendations in the areas of global and biosphere impacts, local ecological impacts, biological diversity, and environmental impacts of current and emerging technologies.

134. Putman, Rory J.; Wratten, S. D. **Principles of ecology.** University of California Press, 1984. 388 pp., ill., bibl., index. Textbook strong on critical analysis, quantitative methods, and integrated explanation of major ecological ideas and concepts.

135. Tilman, David. **Resource competition and community structure.** Princeton University Press, Monographs in population biology, v. 17, 1982. 296 pp., ill., bibl., index. Provides a simple, graphical theory of multispecies competition for resources, thereby answering the question of why there are so many more plant than animal species.

136. Odum, Howard T. **Systems ecology: an introduction.** Wiley, 1983. 644 pp., ill., bibl., index. Advanced graduate text presents a theory of systems ecology and complex, real-world models. Four sections cover systems and simulations, design elements, organizations and patterns, and systems of nature and humanity.

137. Burns, Thomas P.; Higashi, M.; eds. **Theoretical studies of ecosystems: the network perspective.** Cambridge University Press, 1990. 300 pp. Comprehensive overview seeks to clarify the similarities and differences between diverse viewpoints and approaches to ecology; addresses controversial issues; identifies problems for future investigations.

Ecology: Periodicals (138–150)

138. Advances in ecological research. Academic Press, 1967 to date. Annual. Reviews "in a readable but vigorous fashion" developments across the science of ecology (four to six papers per volume) that will help to maintain "the essential unity of ecology." Perhaps a greater emphasis on methodological and experimental considerations than the *Annual review of ecology and systematics* (142). Recent reviews include effects of global CO_2 concentrations on distribution of plants and animals and tree-ring measurements of past and present forest environments.

139. Advances in microbial ecology. Plenum Press, 1977 to date. Irregular. Established by the International Committee on Microbial Ecology to provide in-depth, critical reviews that show current trends in the field. About ten reviews per volume on such topics as interactions between microorganisms, biogeochemistry of atmospheric trace gases, and methods for detecting genetically engineered organisms.

140. American midland naturalist. University of Notre Dame, 1909 to date. Quarterly. Publishes research, notes, and discussion in the following areas: limnology and hydrobiology, mammalogy, ichthyology, ornithology, plant systematics and physiology, and others.

141. American naturalist. University of Chicago Press, 1867 to date. Monthly. Journal of the American Society of Naturalists; "devoted to the conceptual unification of the biological sciences." Publishes original research, particularly theoretical syntheses, discussion, criticism, and comment.

142. Annual review of ecology and systematics. Annual Reviews, 1970 to date. Annual. Critical assessments of the literature (20 or more papers per volume) across the field of ecology. Succinct statement of the problem or issue, assessment of the literature, and conclusion. Special section on global diversity and global change planned for 1992 volume.

143. Ecological applications. Ecological Society of America, 1991 to date. Quarterly. Research and discussion papers integrating the science of ecology with applications in air, water, and on land and having special relevance to environmental management and policy. Papers are broad in scope and include such subjects as global warming, biogeochemistry, conservation biology, ecotoxicology and epidemiology, fisheries and wildlife, forests, landscape, soils and hydrology. Two special issues on global change in 1991.

144. Ecological monographs. Ecological Society of America, 1931 to date. Quarterly. Publishes original research in ecology. Each issue contains three to five longer articles.

145. Ecology. Ecological Society of America, 1920 to date. Bimonthly. Publishes original research, notes, reviews, and comments on basic and applied ecology. Also contains special reports and features, such as "The Sustainable Biosphere Initiative." Most articles are specific to a species or region.

146. Ecology abstracts. Cambridge Scientific Abstracts, 1975 to date. Monthly. Continues: Applied ecology abstracts. Comprehensive abstracting service for fundamental and applied aspects of ecology, including human ecology.

147. Functional ecology. Blackwell Scientific, 1987 to date. Bimonthly. Physiological, biophysical, and evolutionary ecology, particularly the interrelationship of aquatic and terrestrial environments.

148. Global ecology and biogeography letters. Blackwell Scientific, 1991 to date. Bimonthly. Fast track publication of scientific material on historical, ecological, and applied biogeography. Consists of research letters (to 3000 words), letters (to 500 words) on conferences and matters of general interest, editorial opinions, book reviews.

149. Journal of applied ecology. Blackwell Scientific, 1964 to date. 3 issues/yr. Publishes papers on theoretical and applied work in any discipline relating to the management, control, and development of biological resources for agriculture, forestry, aquaculture, nature conservation, and leisure activities.

150. Journal of biogeography. Blackwell Scientific, 1974 to date. Bimonthly. Includes papers on all aspects of spatial, ecological, and historical biogeography.

Biodiversity. Conservation Biology. Genetics (151–186)

151. Wilson, E. O.; Peter, Frances M.; eds. **Biodiversity.** National Academy Press, 1988. 521 pp., ill., bibl., index. Some 60 papers from the 1986 National Forum on BioDiversity, which gave prominence to the subject. Inspiring, comprehensive information source on values of, threats to, and protection of biodiversity. Emphasizes tropics.

152. Biological conservation. Elsevier, 1968 to date. Quarterly. Covers what it calls "conservation ecology," the preservation of biological and allied resources around the world. Contains numerous case studies of plants and animals and their habitats. Publishes analytical studies contributing to the understanding of conservation, results of original research, and practical applications of research for land managers, landscape designers, and nature reserve managers.

153. Biological conservation newsletter. Smithsonian Institution, National Museum of Natural History, 1981 to date. Monthly. News of workshops, meetings, research, and publications. Current literature takes up more than half of its four to six pages.

154. Dawkins, Richard. **The blind watchmaker.** Norton, 1986. 332 pp., ill., bibl., index. Explains the mechanism of evolution of complex organisms, using numerous biological as well as computer examples.

155. Frankel, Otto Herzberg; Soulé, Michael E.; eds. **Conservation and evolution.** Cambridge University Press, 1981. 327 pp., ill., bibl., index. Discusses basic genetic principles for conserving wild and domestic plants and animals. Explores long-term genetic and evolutionary problems that may result without attention to these principles.

156. Soulé, Michael E.; Wilcox, Bruce A.; eds. **Conservation biology: an evolutionary-ecological per-**

spective. Sinauer, 1980. 359 pp., ill., bibl., index. Nineteen articles examine ecological principles of preservation, consequences of insularization, role of captive propagation in conservation and exploitation and preservation of species.

157. Conservation biology: the journal of the Society for Conservation Biology. Blackwell Scientific, 1989 to date. Quarterly. Forum for discussion of conservation theory and management consisting of contributed papers, editorial commentary, notes, and news. Ecosystem and habitat preservation in areas around the world are topics in every issue.

158. Soulé, Michael E.; ed. **Conservation biology: the science of scarcity and diversity.** Sinauer, 1986. 584 pp., ill., bibl., index. Essays and reviews explaining, representing, and inspiring the new field of conservation biology, from 1985 conference. Six sections: fitness and variability of populations; patterns of diversity and rarity; fragmentation effects; community processes; sensitive habitats; and interactions with the real world.

159. Western, David; Pearl, Mary C.; eds. **Conservation for the twenty-first century.** Oxford University Press, 1989. 365 pp., ill., bibl., index. Based on a 1986 conference. In five parts, each with contributed essays: demographics and socioeconomics of the future; resources and population in the next century; the biology of conservation (extinctions, genetics and populations, communities and ecosystems); conservation management (parks, biotechnology); and conservation realities (human values, national and international planning, role of developed countries). Concludes with recommendations for research and action.

160. Warren, A.; Goldsmith, F. B.; eds. **Conservation in perspective.** Wiley, 1983. 474 pp., ill., bibl., index. A British perspective on the ecological basis of conservation, ecology and conservation in practice, and issues facing conservation organizations and agencies.

161. Conservation, science and society. UNESCO; United Nations Environment Programme, Natural resource research, v. 21, 1984. Maps, ill., bibl. 2 vols. Papers from a 1983 conference discuss the biogeographic coverage of biosphere reserves; their establishment and management; their relation to other protected areas, ecological research, and global and regional modeling; and their role in world conservation, regional socioeconomic planning, and environmental education.

162. McNeely, Jeffrey A.; and others. **Conserving the world's biological diversity.** International Union for Conservation of Nature and Natural Resources, 1990.

193 pp., maps, ill., bibl., index. Urges greater research and study to appreciate the value of biological resources; seeks to identify and understand the economic forces driving resource exploitation; argues for priorities and strategies to protect species and habitats.

163. Lincoln, R. J.; Boxshall, G. A.; Clark, P. F. **A dictionary of ecology, evolution and systematics.** Cambridge University Press, 1982. 298 pp., maps, ill., tables. Provides short working definitions; appendix includes 21 relevant maps, diagrams, tables, and lists.

164. Elliott, David K.; ed. **Dynamics of extinction.** Wiley, 1986. 294 pp., ill., bibl., index. Interdisciplinary conference papers examine extinctions of Mesozoic, Quaternary, and modern times and discuss approaches to modeling extinction events.

165. Margulis, Lynn. **Early life.** Science Books International, 1982. 160 pp., ill., bibl., index. Provocative account of earth's evolutionary history by leading researcher on the origins of life.

166. Darlington, Philip Jackson. **Evolution for naturalists: the simple principles and complex reality.** Wiley, 1980. 262 pp., bibl., index. Introduces the premises and history of the current theory of evolution. Includes a chapter on human evolution.

167. Shorrocks, B.; ed. **Evolutionary ecology.** Blackwell Scientific, Symposium of the British Ecological Society, v. 23, 1984. 418 pp. Emphasizes the importance of genotypes and genetics in ecology. Sixteen papers in three areas: evolutionary concepts, single-species populations, and species interactions.

168. Forey, P. L.; ed. **The evolving biosphere.** Cambridge University Press, Chance, change, challenge, 1981. 311 pp., maps, ill., index. Twenty-one essays by biologists and evolutionists focus on three themes: the mechanisms and processes of speciation; coexistence and coevolution (the interactions between species and the evolutionary consequences); and biogeography, the study of the parameters governing the global distribution of plants and animals.

169. Stanley, Steven M. **Extinction.** Scientific American Library, Scientific American Library series, v. 20, 1987. 242 pp., ill., bibl., index. Survey of geological and paleontological evidence of mass extinctions since Precambrian times. Emphasizes climate changes.

170. Ehrlich, Paul; Ehrlich, Anne. **Extinction: the causes and consequences of the disappearance of species.** Random House, 1981. 305 pp., bibl., index. Discusses costs of extinction, reasons for endangerment of species, and policies to limit extinction.

171. Nitecki, Matthew H.; ed. **Extinctions.** University of Chicago Press, 1984. 354 pp., ill., index. Based on papers of the 1983 Field Museum Spring Systematics Symposium; addresses causes, effects, and processes of extinction; emphasis on mass extinction.

172. Schonewald-Cox, Christine M.; and others, eds. **Genetics and conservation: a reference for managing wild animal and plant populations.** Benjamin/Cummings, Biological conservation series, v. 1, 1983. 722 pp., ill., bibl., index. Addresses population dynamics, genetic principles, and techniques that can enhance species survival. Intended for both scientists and field managers.

173. Hedrick, Philip W. **Genetics of populations.** Science Books International, 1983. 629 pp., ill., bibl., index. Gives methods of estimation for population genetics parameters and other statistical tools; discusses factors affecting the extent and pattern of genetic variation from both experimental and theoretical viewpoints; reviews multilocus models and quantitative genetics.

174. Kaufman, Les; Mallory, Kenneth; eds. **The last extinction.** MIT Press, 1986. 208 pp., ill., bibl., index. Six essays on the nature of mass extinctions emphasize the role of humans in the current or "last extinction." Case studies from the Amazon rain forest and North America are presented. Also examines the role of captive breeding in conservation strategies.

175. Committee on Managing Global Genetic Resources: Agricultural Imperatives. **Managing global genetic resources.** National Academy Press, 1990–1992. Index. 5 vols. to date. Volumes in the series are The U.S. national plant germplasm system (evaluates the National Plant Germplasm System); Forest trees (assesses status of tree genetic resources and management efforts worldwide); Livestock (examines importance of animal genetic diversity and suggests strategies to conserve it at national and international levels); Fish and shellfish (describes threats to genetic diversity and uses case studies to illustrate decision making); and Agricultural crop issues and policies.

176. Donovan, Stephen K.; ed. **Mass extinctions: processes and evidence.** Columbia University Press, 1989. 266 pp., ill., index. A dozen chapters by biologists and geologists seeking to explain why extinctions take place. Indexes to subjects and species.

177. Goldsmith, Barrie; ed. **Monitoring for conservation and ecology.** Chapman and Hall, 1991. 288 pp. Summarizes current monitoring of plants and animals in North America and Europe. Topics include the rationale behind and scientific requirements of monitoring; techniques, including remote sensing and aerial photography; and data analysis methods. Includes case studies of birds, butterflies, plant populations and communities.

178. Nature conservancy magazine. Nature Conservancy, 1961 to date. Bimonthly. Continues: Nature Conservancy news. General articles and news from the Nature Conservancy, which currently owns more than 1200 preserves, the largest private system of nature sanctuaries in the world.

179. Norton, Bryan G.; ed. **The preservation of species: the value of biological diversity.** Princeton University Press, 1986. 305 pp., bibl., index. Multidisciplinary reflections on the dimensions of the endangered species problem, values and objectives in preservation, and management issues.

180. Soulé, Michael E.; Kohm, Kathryn A.; eds. **Research priorities for conservation biology.** Island Press, 1989. 97 pp., ill. Published in cooperation with the Society for Conservation Biology. Proceedings of a 1988 workshop describe the field and identify "major, compelling" priorities for research to aid in effective conservation.

181. Myers, Norman. **The sinking ark: a new look at the problem of disappearing species.** Pergamon Press, 1979. 307 pp. Discusses the implications of and reasons for species loss, focusing on the tropical moist forests; proposes a comprehensive strategy for species conservation.

182. Durrell, Lee. **State of the ark: an atlas of conservation in action.** Doubleday, 1986. 224 pp., ill., bibl., index. Treats major issues of biodiversity, acid rain, endangered species, soil erosion, and disappearing rain forests, with conservation efforts at global, regional, ecosystem, and species levels. Numerous photographs, graphs, charts, and maps.

183. Trends in ecology and evolution. Elsevier, 1986 to date. Monthly. Publishes short articles and reviews, news, and comments on current research developments in pure and applied ecology and evolutionary biology. Emphasis is on broad, speculative, or controversial topics.

184. Oldfield, Margery L. **The value of conserving genetic resources.** U.S. Department of the Interior, National Park Service, 1984. 360 pp., ill., bibl., index. Examines importance of genetic resources for food production, medicine, timber, rubber, oils, and waxes; emphasizes need for global conservation efforts.

185. Soulé, Michael E.; ed. **Viable populations for**

conservation. Cambridge University Press, 1987. 189 pp., ill., bibl., index. Recent research in conservation biology and population biology on area needed to sustain wildlife populations. Minimum viable population (MVP) varies with species, population density, and genetic material.

186. Myers, Norman. **A wealth of wild species: storehouse for human welfare**. Westview Press, 1983. 274 pp., ill., bibl., index. Reveals the major economic contributions of wild plants and animals to agriculture, medicine, and industry.

Physical and Chemical Systems (187–201)

187. Rycroft, Michael; ed. **The Cambridge encyclopedia of space**. Cambridge University Press, 1990. 386 pp., maps, ill., bibl., index. Emphasizing space exploration, topics include propulsion, space centers, satellites, solar system exploration, and industrial and military uses of space; numerous photographs and detailed illustrations.

188. Cotterill, Rodney M. J. **The Cambridge guide to the material world**. Cambridge University Press, 1985. 352 pp., ill., bibl., index. Discusses physics, chemistry, and biology of natural materials at the microscopic and atomic levels, moving from atomic structure to the structure of animal tissues. Numerous attractive and informative illustrations.

189. Wolman, Yecheskel. **Chemical information: a practical guide to utilization**. Wiley, 2d ed., 1988. 291 pp., index. Explains the use of both computer and manual research strategies for chemists, describing the CAS Online system, scientific journals, literature searches, Beilstein's handbook, chemical marketing and process information, and others.

190. Crone, Hugh D. **Chemicals and society: a guide to the new chemical age**. Cambridge University Press, 1986. 245 pp., ill., bibl., index. Intended to give nonchemists the background to understand and interpret such chemical problems as herbicides, food additives, disease, and pollution.

191. Thomson, R. H.; ed. **The chemistry of natural products**. Blackie (dist. by Chapman and Hall), 1985. 467 pp., ill., bibl., index. Gives the structural formulas of carbohydrates, aliphatic and aromatic compounds, terpenes, steroids, alkaloids, nucleosides, nucleotides and nucleic acids, amino acids, peptides and proteins, and porphyrines and related compounds. Emphasizes structure, chemistry, and synthesis.

192. Seymour, Raymond B.; Carraher, Charles E. **Giant molecules: essential materials for everyday living and problem solving**. Wiley-Interscience, 1990. 314 pp., bibl., index. Reviews polymer chemistry and physics, natural and synthetic polymers; fibers, elastomers, and coatings; treatments of thermoplastics and thermosets; engineering plastics, inorganic polymers, specialty polymers, and additives for polymers. Includes glossary.

193. Allaby, Michael; Lovelock, James E. **The greening of Mars**. St. Martin's Press, 1984. 165 pp. Biospheric fundamentals are imaginatively applied in this fictional account of converting Mars to a habitable planet. Told in first person from the vantage point of the twenty-second century.

194. Bell, Susan S.; McCoy, E. D.; Mushinsky, Henry R.; eds. **Habitat structure: the physical arrangement of objects in space**. Chapman and Hall, 1990. 420 pp., ill., index. Surveys current knowledge of habitat complexity. Individually authored chapters are divided into four sections: patterns; colonization, succession, and resource use responses; predation, parasitism, and disturbance responses; and applications (to habitat and species conservation).

195. Vogel, Steven. **Life's devices: the physical world of animals and plants**. Princeton University Press, 1988. 367 pp., ill., bibl., index. Vogel explains life from the obvious to the arcane using an engineering perspective, thereby answering such questions as why there are no wheels in nature and why starfish have five arms. Organized thematically, topics include dimensions and scaling principles, fluid mechanics, and structures and mechanisms.

196. Parker, Sybil P.; editor-in-chief. **McGraw-Hill encyclopedia of environmental science**. McGraw-Hill, 2d ed., 1980. 858 pp., ill., bibl., index. Feature articles survey broad topics. More than 250 other entries present basic scientific and technical information on specific topics in the biological, chemical, and physical sciences. Some similarities with the same publisher's *Encyclopedia of science and technology*.

197. Atkins, P. W. **Molecules**. Scientific American Library, Scientific American Library series, v. 21, 1987. 197 pp., ill., bibl., index. Nonchemist's guide to chemistry describes 160 chemicals. Some topics: fuels, fats, soaps, synthetic and natural polymers, taste, smell, pain, sight, and color.

198. Fuchs, Vivian; ed. **The physical world**. Oxford University Press, Oxford illustrated encyclopedia, v. 1,

1985. 375 pp., ill. Examines and explains the structure of the earth, from its formation to the land, oceans, and countries present today; addresses minerals, chemistry, physics, and the earth's internal and external processes.

199. Zangwill, Andrew. **Physics at surfaces.** Cambridge University Press, 1988. 454 pp., ill., bibl., index. Graduate-level introduction to the physics of solid surfaces and the atoms and molecules that interact with them; first section, on clean surfaces, reviews thermodynamics, crystal and electronic structure, phase transitions, elementary excitations, and other topics; second section, on adsorption, covers energy transfer, physisorption, chemisorption, kinetics and dynamics, and surface reactions.

200. Baker, D. James. **Planet earth: the view from space.** Harvard University Press, Frontiers of space, 1990. 192 pp., ill. Reviews remote sensing from space, noting current satellites, their instruments, and their missions (land vegetation patterns, temperature, and the atmosphere); assesses what equipment, research, and cooperation will be needed to improve our ability to model and predict global climate change.

201. Gordon, J. E. **The science of structures and materials.** Scientific American Library, Scientific American Library series, v. 23, 1988. 217 pp. Examines the mechanical properties of natural and artificial materials and structures, demonstrating the relationships between them.

Chemistry. Biogeochemical Cycles. Pollutants (202–233)

202. ACS symposium series. American Chemical Society, 1974 to date. Several volumes/yr. Symposia in this series touch on all aspects of chemicals in the environment. Authoritative information on current research and practice.

203. Schreier, H. **Asbestos in the natural environment.** Elsevier, Studies in environmental science, v. 37, 1989. 159 pp., ill., bibl., index. Effects of asbestos on soils, plants, and aquatic environments; physical and chemical properties of asbestos; quarrying, loading, and transporting asbestos.

204. Fisher, Gerald L.; Gallo, Michael A.; eds. **Asbestos toxicity.** Dekker, 1988. 183 pp., ill., bibl., index. Papers from a 1985 symposium. Examines physical, chemical, and biological activity of asbestos. Presents new theories and models of its toxicity.

205. Biogeochemistry. Nijhoff; Junk, 1984 to date.

Monthly. Publishes research on biotic controls on chemistry of the environment, interactions of element cycles, global element cycles, and the geochemical control of the structure and function of ecosystems.

206. Nriagu, J. O.; ed. **The biogeochemistry of lead in the environment. Part A: Ecological cycles. Part B: Biological effects.** Elsevier, 1978. Ill., bibl., index. 2 vols. Articles discuss lead geochemistry in soil and rock, atmosphere, and water and assess effects in humans, animals, and vegetation.

207. Bulletin of environmental contamination and toxicology. Springer-Verlag, 1966 to date. Bimonthly. Rapid publication of significant advances in air, water, soil, and food contamination and pollution.

208. Smil, Vaclav. **Carbon-nitrogen-sulfur: human interference in grand biospheric cycles.** Plenum Press, Modern perspectives in energy, 1985. 459 pp., ill., bibl., index. Attempt to synthesize information on the three biogeochemical cycles critical to biosphere functioning, particularly the consequences of fossil fuel combustion. Implications for and discussion of energy development strategies.

209. Miller, Gregory J. **Chemistry and ecotoxicology of pollution.** Wiley, 1984. 444 pp., ill., bibl., index. Examines fundamental ecological, chemical, and toxicological factors. Proposes unifying theories of the chemistry and ecology of pollution.

210. Thibodeaux, Louis J. **Chemodynamics: environmental movement of chemicals in air, water, and soil.** Wiley, 1979. 501 pp., ill., bibl., index. Reviews transport fundamentals and addresses equilibrium at interfaces; examines chemical exchange rates between air, water, and earth and within a geological phase.

211. Chemosphere. Pergamon Press, 1972 to date. Bimonthly. International journal covers environmental chemicals, their analysis, and their effects on the biosphere. Also addresses meteorology and climate, air and water pollution, atmospheric chemistry, and occupational hazards and exposure. Numerous special issues with proceedings of conferences.

212. Ecotoxicology and environmental safety. Academic Press, 1977 to date. Bimonthly. Official journal of the International Society of Ecotoxicity and Environmental Safety. Biological and toxic effects of chemical pollutants to ecosystems.

213. Levin, Simon A.; and others, eds. **Ecotoxicology: problems and approaches.** Springer-Verlag, Springer advanced texts in life sciences, 1989. 547 pp., ill., bibl., index. Emphasizes an ecosystem approach to ecotoxicology; topics include a review of the effects of chemical stress on various environments (particularly aquatic ecosystems), methods and models, and risk assessment and management.

214. Moriarty, F. **Ecotoxicology: the study of pollutants in ecosystems.** Academic Press, 2d ed., 1988. 289 pp., ill., bibl., index. Ecologist's view of ecotoxicology. Collection of essays focuses on the response of terrestrial and aquatic populations to pollutants; populations, communities, and genetics; prediction and monitoring of effects; and case studies (peregrine falcon, spruce budworm, the Thames River, and oil pollution).

215. Sheehan, Patrick J.; and others, eds. **Effects of pollutants at the ecosystem level.** Wiley, 1984. 443 pp., ill., bibl., index. Includes a survey of published results discussing the distribution of chemicals in the environment, the difficulty of detecting their effects, and the nature of these pollutants on populations, communities, and whole ecosystems. Numerous case studies presented.

216. Hallberg, R.; ed. **Environmental biogeochemistry.** Ecological Bulletins Publishing House, Ecological bulletins, v. 35, 1983. 576 pp., maps, ill., bibl. Based on papers of a 1981 symposium. Topics include biogeochemistry of sulfur, nitrogen, carbon and metals, rivers and seawater, diagenetic systems, and miscellaneous fluxes.

217. O'Neill, P. **Environmental chemistry.** Allen & Unwin, 1985. 232 pp., ill., index. Concise introductory text discusses geochemical cycles, emphasizing importance of oxygen in chemical reactions. Examines the major elements in living matter and in the earth's crust and environmental problems associated with minor elements.

218. Environmental pollution. Elsevier, 1978 to date. 2 issues/vol.; 6 vols./yr. Publishes research and review articles on the distribution and ecological effects of all kinds of pollutants, monitoring and assessment techniques, and other aspects of pollution and its control, including political, economic, social, managerial, medical, and engineering views. Regular special issues (usually proceedings of conferences) that assess pollution and its monitoring.

219. Duffus, John H. **Environmental toxicology.** Wiley, Resource and environmental sciences series, 1980. 164 pp., bibl., index. Studies the metabolism of toxic substances by animals, plants, and microorganisms. Reviews knowledge of toxicants in four categories: pesticides and herbicides, toxic metals, atmo-

spheric toxicants, and petroleum and radionuclides. Discusses difficulty of monitoring and assessing the risk of toxicants in real-world situations. Index includes many proprietary synonyms of commercial toxicants; lists full chemical names in appendix.

220. Environmental toxicology and chemistry. Pergamon Press, 1982 to date. Monthly. Divided into three sections: environmental chemistry, environmental toxicology, and hazard assessment. Articles from industry, government, and academics discuss chemical and toxin use, management, and the protection of the environment.

221. Brimblecombe, Peter; Lein, Alla Yu. **Evolution of the global biogeochemical sulphur cycle.** Wiley, SCOPE, v. 39, 1989. 241 pp., ill., bibl., index. Proceedings of a 1984 workshop. Reviews evolution of sulfur cycle starting with the Precambrian. Discusses models, the contributions of endogenous sulfur, human influences, and interactions between sulfur and carbon in modern ecosystems.

222. Draggan, Sidney; Cohrssen, John J.; Morrison, Richard E.; eds. **Geochemical and hydrologic processes and their protection: the agenda for long-term research and development.** Praeger, 1987. 210 pp., ill., bibl., index. Assesses the status and needs of research on processes and pollution of surface water and groundwater, land, soil, the atmosphere, and oceans; also covers multimedia toxic substance and hazardous waste research. Emphasizes the need for integrated, long-term research, for predictive models of different waste loading stresses, and for appropriate institutional strategies for environmental management.

223. Global biogeochemical cycles. American Geophysical Union, 1987 to date. Quarterly. Presents papers on environmental change from marine, hydrologic, atmospheric, extraterrestrial, geological, biological, and human perspectives.

224. Hutzinger, O.; ed. **The handbook of environmental chemistry.** Springer-Verlag, 1980 to date. A multivolume series begun in 1980 to compile basic information about chemical reactions in the environment. The projected volumes, each with several parts, are natural environment and biogeochemical cycles; reactions and processes; anthropogenic compounds; air pollution; water pollution; and environmental modeling.

225. Verschureren, Karel. **Handbook of environmental data on organic chemicals.** Van Nostrand Reinhold, 2d ed., 1983. 1310 pp., ill., bibl., index. Details the effects of more than 1300 organic chemicals on ecosystems, plants, humans, and other life forms; provides physical and chemical properties for each entry listed alphabetically by common name.

226. Bolin, B.; Cook, R. B.; eds. **The major biogeochemical cycles and their interactions.** Wiley, SCOPE, v. 21, 1983. 532 pp., ill., bibl., index. Individually authored sections examine carbon, nitrogen, phosphorus, and sulfur cycles; the interactions of biogeochemical cycles in forest ecosystems, grassland ecosystems, and soils and organisms; and physiochemical processes in oceans.

227. Waid, John S.; ed. **PCBs and the environment.** CRC Press, 1986 to date. Ill., bibl., index. 3 vols. Vol. 1 covers the sources, transport, and bioaccumulation of polychlorinated biphenyls (PCBs), their effects on organisms and humans, and methods to destroy or dispose of them; Vol. 2 focuses on the effects of PCBs on plants, marine animals, birds, and microorganisms; Vol. 3 discusses instances of PCBs poisoning humans and further explores PCBs' fate, destruction, and disposal.

228. Degens, Egon T. **Perspectives on biogeochemistry.** Springer-Verlag, 1989. 423 pp., ill., bibl., index. This historical geology from a physiochemical perspective concentrates on the earth's life support systems. Also covers the evolution of the cosmos and of the earth itself.

229. Nuernberg, H. W.; ed. **Pollutants and their ecotoxicological significance.** Wiley, 1985. 515 pp., ill., index. The methods and philosophy, scientific and regulatory, of dealing with toxic pollutants, in four sections: atmosphere, aquatic environment, terrestrial and human environment, regulatory and general aspects.

230. Reviews of environmental contamination and toxicology. Springer-Verlag, 1962 to date. Several vols./yr. Vol. 119 issued at beginning of 1991. Continues: *Residue reviews.* Concise review articles on advances in research on all aspects of chemical contamination of the environment.

231. Science of the total environment. Elsevier, 1972 to date. 39 issues/yr. An international journal for scientific research into the environment and its relationship to man, particularly environmental chemistry, including air, water, and soil pollution. Many issues consist of conference proceedings.

232. Likens, Gene E.; ed. **Some perspectives of the major biogeochemical cycles.** Wiley, SCOPE, v. 17, 1981. 175 pp., ill., bibl., index. Papers from a 1979 symposium promote an integrated and global view of biogeochemical cycles. Explains the individual cycles of carbon, nitrogen, and sulfur; and their interactions in land, air,

and salt and fresh water. Two papers cover the socioeconomic impacts of human activity on the sulfur and carbon dioxide cycles.

233. Water, air & soil pollution. Kluwer, 1971 to date. Bimonthly; 6 vols./yr. Content emphasizes research on pollution in all three of these environments and their interaction. Frequent special issues, particularly on the subject of acid rain.

Geology. Earth Sciences (234–273)

234. Pielou, E. C. **After the Ice Age: the return of life to glaciated North America.** University of Chicago Press, 1991. 366 pp., maps, ill. Explains how diverse plants and animals developed and were shaped by the melting ice. Reviews the process of soil being deepened and enriched by vegetation until trees could grow. Describes the varied animal types and assesses the effects of early human settlers.

235. Harris, Stephen L. **Agents of chaos: earthquakes, volcanoes, and other natural disasters.** Mountain Press, 1990. 260 pp., maps, ill., bibl., index. Recounts historical and more recent geological disasters, and identifies areas where future earthquake and volcanic activities might occur, with particular focus on the western United States. Discusses perceptions and realities of these and other natural disasters.

236. Annual review of earth and planetary sciences. Annual Reviews, 1973 to date. Annual. Critical assessments of the literature (20 or more papers per volume) across the fields of geology, earth sciences, and astrophysics. Each review article has a brief statement of the problem or issue, an assessment of the literature, and a conclusion. In the 1992 volume are reviews of tropical topography and global climate, the geochemistry of estuaries, and acid rain.

237. Bibliography and index to geology. American Geological Institute, 1969 to date. Monthly. Indexes and abstracts the earth science literature of the world. Monthly issues are arranged in 29 subject categories. Subject indexes are based on a special thesaurus of terms displayed in three levels of specificity. Available online and on CD-ROM.

238. Smith, David G.; ed. **The Cambridge encyclopedia of earth sciences.** Cambridge University Press, 1982. 496 pp., maps, ill., bibl., index. Examines the physical and chemical makeup and behavior of the earth as a whole. Studies the processes and interactions of the earth's crust, oceans, and atmosphere. Assesses methods of evaluating the earth's resources and hazards and discusses lessons from extraterrestrial geology.

239. Allaby, Ailsa; Allaby, Michael; eds. **The concise Oxford dictionary of earth sciences.** Oxford University Press, 1990. 432 pp. Over 6000 entries, mostly limited to several sentences plus cross-references; special emphasis on the history and conceptual development of the earth sciences.

240. Gregory, K. J.; ed. **The Earth's natural forces.** Oxford University Press, Illustrated encyclopedia of world geography, Vol. 1, 1990. 256 pp. Introductory section provides overview of topic from a global perspective, discussing the origin of the solar system and the earth, climate, and geology. Covers 22 regions of the world, focusing on unique aspects of each: local winds in France, earthquakes and tsunami in Japan and Korea, the Mississippi Basin, desertification in northern Africa, volcanoes in southern Europe, and acid rain in Scandinavia.

241. McNeil, Mary. **Earth sciences reference.** Flamingo Press, 1991. 709 pp., ill., bibl., index. Entries, most under 150 words, explain and define terms in the fields of ecology, energy, environment, oceanography, and other earth sciences; contains geographic name and subject indexes.

242. Eiby, George A. **Earthquakes.** Van Nostrand Reinhold, 1980. 209 pp., ill., bibl., index. Discusses all phases of earthquakes, how and where they happen, how they are recorded, earth and sea waves, and seismic geography. Also includes a discussion of differentiating between natural quakes and those induced by the explosion of atomic bombs.

243. Nierenberg, William A.; ed. **Encyclopedia of earth system science.** Academic Press, 1991. Ill., bibl., index. 4 vols. Comprehensive collection of thousands of earth science subjects treats the earth as "a system of interactive processes," examining and assessing the effects of both natural and man-made events; includes glossary, illustrations, and cross-referencing.

244. Roberts, Willard Lincoln; Campbell, Thomas J.; Rapp, George Robert, Jr. **Encyclopedia of minerals.** Van Nostrand Reinhold, 2d ed., 1990. 979 pp. Entries report on mineral properties including chemical formula, hardness, density, cleavage, and color luster; second edition adds more than 400 species and contains over 300 photographs.

245. Environmental geology and water sciences. Springer-Verlag, 1975 to date. Bimonthly. International journal devoted to all aspects of the earth sciences, including geological hazards and processes affecting

people; management of resources; natural and artificial pollutants in the geological environment; and environmental and geological aspects of mining, oil drilling, and other extraction technologies.

246. King, Philip B. **The evolution of North America.** Princeton University Press, rev. ed., 1977. 197 pp., index, bibl. This natural history of the North American continent describes and discusses its eight geological provinces. Illustrated with more than 100 maps, figures, and line drawings.

247. Explosive volcanism: inception, evolution, and hazards. National Academy Press, Studies in geophysics, 1984. 176 pp., ill., bibl. Prepared by the Geophysics Study Committee, Geophysics Research Forum, Commission on Physical Sciences, Mathematics, and Resources, National Research Council. Papers on magmaforming processes, cyclic and episodic nature of volcanism, and physics of volcanic eruptions provide the basis for recommendations on future research and planning in the United States.

248. Boulter, Clive A. **Four dimensional analysis of geological maps: techniques of interpretation.** Wiley, 1989. 296 pp., ill., bibl., index. Reviews techniques from elementary level to the complete analysis of a published map, integrating map analysis, igneous geology, and remote sensing. Topics covered: geomorphology, stratigraphy, igneous and metamorphic rocks, geometry and distribution of rock units, remote sensing, and geological history; provides introduction to stereographic projection.

249. Ward, Dederick C.; Wheeler, Marjorie W.; Bier, Robert A., Jr. **Geologic reference sources: a subject and regional bibliography of publications and maps in the geological sciences.** Scarecrow Press, 2d ed., 1981. 560 pp., index. Bibliographic guide to the significant current reference literature of the geosciences and related studies (some 4300 items). Lists bibliographic references in three categories—general, subject, and regional. Has subject and regional indexes.

250. Tiffney, Bruce; ed. **Geological factors and the evolution of plants.** Yale University Press, 1985. 294 pp., ill., bibl., index. These papers from a 1982 symposium address plant-environment interactions from a geological perspective. Topics include early development of continental ecosystems, geological factors and biochemical aspects of the origin of land plants, phytogeography and paleoclimate of the early Carboniferous, and others.

251. Goudie, Andrew; ed. **Geomorphological techniques.** Allen & Unwin, 1981. 395 pp., ill., bibl., index.

Presents and evaluates techniques useful to practicing geomorphologists, concentrating on those techniques unique to the field. Some specific topics include a full discussion of morphometry; colorimetric and spectrophotometric analysis; tests of rock strength; techniques for the measurement of surface water erosion processes on slopes; solute studies; and radiocarbon, uranium series disequilibrium, and other dating methods.

252. Short, Nicholas M.; Blair, Robert W., Jr.; eds. **Geomorphology from space: a global overview of regional landforms.** National Aeronautics and Space Administration; Government Printing Office, 1986. 717 pp., maps, ill., bibl., index. Gallery of 237 space, mostly Landsat, images arranged by geomorphic theme; each image accompanied by supplementary photographs, an index map, and commentary. Discusses evolution of geomorphic unit mapping and the usefulness of space imagery.

253. Global and planetary change. Elsevier, 1989 to date. Quarterly. A daughter journal of *Palaeogeography, palaeoclimatology, palaeoecology.* Research articles on causes, processes, and limits of change in the earth's history. Includes papers on marine chemistry, sea level variations, human geography, global ecology and biogeography, greenhouse warming, earth observation satellites, effects of catastrophic global changes, and geological records of global change.

254. Summerfield, Michael A. **Global geomorphology: an introduction to the study of landforms.** Longman Scientific & Technical, 1990. 537 pp., ill., bibl., index. Focuses on large-scale workings and features. Uses global tectonics, planetary geomorphology, climatic change, and catastrophic events to understand and explain landform formation. Employs satellite imagery and case studies for illustration and example.

255. Holocene. Edward Arnold, 1991 to date. 3 issues/yr. Fundamental scientific research on environmental change, covering geological, biological, and archaeological evidence of recent environmental change and prediction of future changes.

256. Roberts, Neil. **The Holocene: an environmental history.** Basil Blackwell, 1989. 225 pp. Survey of climate and human changes over the past 10,000 years.

257. Hardy, Joan E.; Wood, David; Harvey, Anthony P.; eds. **Information sources in the earth sciences.** Bowker/Saur, 1989. 518 pp. Essays by 20 experts cover libraries, primary and secondary literature, abstracts and indexes, computerized information services, maps and remote sensing, regional geology, paleontology, mineral-

ogy, geochemistry, petrology, structural geology, geophysics, economic geology, engineering and environmental geology, geomorphology and hydrogeology, meteorology and climatology, soil science, and history of geology.

258. Parker, Sybil P.; editor-in-chief. **McGraw-Hill dictionary of earth sciences.** McGraw-Hill, 1984. 837 pp. Over 15,000 terms fundamental to understanding the earth sciences.

259. Parker, Sybil P.; editor-in-chief. **McGraw-Hill encyclopedia of the geological sciences.** McGraw-Hill, 2d ed., 1988. 722 pp., ill., bibl., index. Five hundred sixty concise, illustrated entries.

260. Harnly, Caroline D.; Tyckoson, David A. **Mount St. Helens: an annotated bibliography.** Scarecrow Press, 1984. 249 pp., index. Provides brief annotations, primarily of studies done after the 1980 eruption, organized into 14 subject areas.

261. Goudie, Andrew. **The nature of the environment: an advanced physical geography.** Basil Blackwell, 1984. 331 pp., ill., bibl., index. Advanced-level textbook that deals well with both the general (four main world zones) and the specific (slopes, rivers, tectonic features, the hydrologic cycle, etc.). Includes case studies drawn from all over the world, with figures and photographs.

262. Cloud, Preston. **Oasis in space: earth history from the beginning.** Norton, 1988. 508 pp., maps, ill., bibl., index. Introduction to historical geology. Provides understanding of how the earth and life have come to be the way they are.

263. Skinner, Brian J.; Porter, Stephen C. **Physical geology.** Wiley, 1987. 750 pp., bibl., index. Revised version of a standard text. In five parts: planet earth and its materials (energy, matter, materials, and rock formations); time and the changing landscape (stratigraphy, weathering, groundwater, streams, deserts, wind, glaciers, and oceans); the dynamic earth (rock deformation, earthquakes, plate tectonics, evolution of landscapes, and climate change); earth's resources (energy and minerals); and beyond planet earth (solar system).

264. Publications of the U.S. Geological Survey. Government Printing Office, 1984 to date. Annual. Continues: Publications of the Geological Survey, 1879–1963. Basic finding aid to the published output of the Geological Survey.

265. Frazier, William J.; Schwimmer, David R. **Regional stratigraphy of North America.** Plenum Press, 1987. 719 pp., maps, ill., bibl., index. Provides both detailed and synoptic stratigraphy of the various regions of North America through geological time. Relevant to the sedimentary tectonics, advanced historical geology, and survey-level paleontology.

266. Roadside geology series. Mountain Press, 1975 to date. A series of books that highlight geological features encountered along major roads and interstates. Guides have been prepared for several states. Clearly written, with many maps, photographs, and drawings.

267. Costa, John E.; Baker, Victor R. **Surficial geology: building with the Earth.** Wiley, 1981. 498 pp., ill., bibl., index. Textbook discusses populations and urban studies, rock and soil mechanics, water resources planning, geomorphic processes, engineering geology, land-use planning, and societal response to disasters.

268. Decker, Robert; Decker, Barbara. **Volcanoes.** Freeman, rev. and expanded ed., 1989. 285 pp., ill., bibl., index. Discusses the processes involved in the formation of volcanoes as well as forecasting eruptions and reducing risk from them.

269. Wood, Charles A.; Kienle, Jurgen; eds. **Volcanoes of North America: United States and Canada.** Cambridge University Press, 1990. 354 pp., maps, ill., bibl., index. Catalogs over 250 geologically young (less than 5 million years) volcanoes, noting type, location, elevation, eruptive history, and composition. Provides instructions on "how to get there." Surveys regional tectonics of Alaska, Hawaii, Canada, and the United States.

270. Simkin, Tom; and others. **Volcanoes of the world: a regional directory, gazetteer, and chronology of volcanism during the last 10,000 years.** Hutchinson Ross, 1981. 232 pp., ill., bibl. Volcanoes and their eruptions are arranged regionally, chronologically, and by name (taking into account local names and variations); eruptive characteristics, such as the extent to which eruptions have destroyed arable land, are also included. Explanatory text and bibliographies included. Does not cover undersea volcanic activity.

271. Gould, Stephen Jay. **Wonderful life: the Burgess Shale and the nature of history.** Norton, 1989. 347 pp., ill., bibl., index. Collection of essays that appeared in *Natural history*. Gould explains the discovery, misinterpretation, and subsequent revisioning of the fossils as a comment on the nature of history and evolutionary theory.

272. Derry, Duncan R.; and others. **World atlas of geology and mineral deposits.** Mining Journal Books, 1980. 110 pp., maps, ill., bibl. Divides most of the world's land area into ten maps and summarizes their

geological history. Exposes and examines the distribution of mineral resources and the geological factors that affected and caused their creation and location.

273. World mineral statistics. Her Majesty's Stationery Office, 1970/1974 to date. Annual. With data collected from primary sources, this annually issued report covers the production and trade of the majority of economically important and internationally traded mineral commodities over five-year spans. Listed by mineral, with the producing countries grouped geographically; the twelfth edition documents 1983–1987.

Energy (274–288)

274. Annual review of energy and the environment. Annual Reviews, 1976 to date. Continues: Annual review of energy. Critical assessment of research on all aspects of energy—engineering, economic, ecological, and behavioral. Fifteen or more papers per volume.

275. Gates, David M. **Energy and ecology.** Sinauer, 1985. 377 pp., ill., bibl., index. Examines the world's energy resources, their use, and their effects on the environment. Introductory chapters provide an overview of the cycles and processes of ecosystems, the atmosphere, and energy. A discussion of renewable and nonrenewable energy forms, including their technology, pollutants, and impacts on ecosystems, follows. Core chapters focus on solar, biomass, nuclear, petroleum, and alternate energy sources.

276. Murphy, Earl Finbar. **Energy and environmental balance.** Pergamon Press, Pergamon policy studies on energy and environment, 1980. 281 pp., bibl., index. Discusses interrelationships of energy demand, urban sprawl, and environmental consequences, from local to international levels.

277. Keith, Lawrence H.; ed. **Energy and environmental chemistry.** Ann Arbor Science, 1982 to date. 2 vols. Papers from international authorities. Vol. 1: Fossil fuels. Covering impacts of tar sands, oil shale, oil spills at sea, hydrocarbon emissions, and coal gasification. Vol. 2: Acid rain. Covers point source effects, regional effects, and theoretical considerations.

278. Tester, Jefferson W.; Wood, David O.; Ferrari, Nancy A.; eds. **Energy and the environment in the 21st century.** MIT Press, 1991. 1006 pp., index. A collection of over 80 essays providing an international range of perspectives on future energy technology, energy policy, and the environment.

279. Odum, Howard T.; Odum, Elisabeth C. **Energy**

basis for man and nature. McGraw-Hill, 2d ed., 1981. 352 pp., ill., index. Concise statement of energy principles and the ways in which they affect natural and social systems. Uses simple diagrams that illustrate energy principles and flows of energy in preindustrial and industrial societies, between nations, and to individuals. Compares energy flows with monetary flows.

280. Schumacher, Diana. **Energy, crisis or opportunity: an introduction to energy studies.** Macmillan; Scholium, 1985. 335 pp., maps, ill., bibl., index. Focusing mostly on the United Kingdom, examines the use and development of energy sources, including oil, natural gas, coal, nuclear and solar energy, and biomass. Studies renewable land and sea energy sources, conservation, and options for the Third World.

281. Goldemberg, José; and others. **Energy for a sustainable world.** Wiley, 1988. 517 pp., ill., bibl., index. Develops detailed approach to energy planning based on achieving the goal of a sustainable world in which energy production is compatible with broader societal goals.

282. Smil, Vaclav. **General energetics: energy in the biosphere and civilization.** Wiley, Environmental science and technology, 1991. 369 pp. Uses measurements of energy, power densities, and intensities to examine all segments of energetics, from the planetary to the human level: discusses solar radiation, geomorphic processes, photosynthesis, metabolism, and thermoregulation. Examines patterns and trends of energy use today, reviewing their effect on the environment and socioeconomic considerations.

283. International journal of global energy issues. Inderscience Enterprises, 1989 to date. Quarterly. Publishes original papers, case studies, reports, news, commentary, and book reviews on energy issues. Subjects include global limits of energy production, sources of energy, policy and planning, conservation and management, and development and global change.

284. Parker, Sybil P.; editor-in-chief. **McGraw-Hill encyclopedia of energy.** McGraw-Hill, 1981. 838 pp., ill., bibl., index. Background articles on broad topics like energy consumption or energy conservation. Three hundred entries on technologies of energy discovery, development, and distribution.

285. Chapman, P. F.; Roberts, F. **Metal resources and energy.** Butterworth, Butterworths monographs in materials, 1983. 238 pp., ill., bibl., index. Summarizes past research and reviews current positions on metals and energy. Topics covered include energy and economics, recycling, politics and scarcity, and others. Utilizes a framework relating future availability of metals and the energy needed to produce them.

286. Resources and energy. North Holland, 1978 to date. Quarterly. Devoted to interdisciplinary studies in the allocation of natural resources.

287. Justi, Eduard W. **A solar-hydrogen energy system.** Plenum, 1987. 334 pp., ill., bibl., index. For serious students of world energy problems. Hydrogen energy pioneer argues advantages of hydrogen energy systems and describes solar and nuclear processes for producing hydrogen. Translated from the German original.

288. Harold, Franklin M. **The vital force: a study of bioenergetics.** Freeman, 1986. 577 pp., ill., bibl., index. Substantial textbook in a relatively new field, the study of the generation and use of energy at the level of molecules, cells, and microorganisms.

Section 2

Air. Atmospheric Environment

Often it seems environmental problems are mostly atmospheric. "Climate warming," "ozone layer," and "acid rain" have become household words during the past decade, joining the already familiar "air pollution." Each of these human impacts has the potential of becoming an atmospheric calamity, and each adds to the already considerable natural hazards of droughts, hurricanes, typhoons, monsoons, and tornadoes.

Atmospheric problems are indeed serious and enormous, but finding sources of information about them is relatively straightforward. The main books, journals, and finding aids to the literature of air pollution are in this section, along with basic works on the constitution of the atmosphere, climate dynamics, and climate change.

Atmosphere. Climate. Weather

This group has introductory and reference works on atmosphere, climate, and weather, including a handbook on meteorology (296), a world survey of climatology (309), abstracts of the literature (301), and a guide to climate data sources (306).

See also:

- Section 1: Physical and chemical systems; geology, earth sciences
- Section 3: Aquatic and marine sciences; marine: physical aspects
- Section 4: Landscape ecology; land: terrestrial ecosystems
- Section 14: Quantification, measurement, statistics

Weather and Life. Biometeorology

Entries in this group introduce the interactions of the atmosphere with plants, animals, and human beings. These interactions are covered in more detail in subsequent sections.

See also:

- Section 4: Landscape ecology; land: terrestrial ecosystems
- Section 5: Food and agriculture; plant sciences; plants, vegetation; atmospheric environment, pollution, pesticides
- Section 6: Trees, forests, forestry; air, soil, and water relations, pollution

- Section 7: Animal biology, zoology; animal ecology, species
- Section 8: Social and human ecology, population
- Section 12: Health, medicine, human biology
- Section 14: Quantification, measurement, statistics

Climate Change

The subject of climate change speaks for itself. Entered in this group are many recent surveys of climate change for the general reader, as well as more technical books, reports, and journals.

See also:

- Section 1: Global resources and environment; environmental management; geology, earth sciences
- Section 8: Education and communication
- Section 9: Ethics, philosophy, religion
- Section 10: International law and policies
- Section 11: Industry, economic sectors; energy; pollution, industrial wastes
- Section 13: Air pollution control
- Section 14: Modeling and simulation; assessment and monitoring

Air Pollution. Atmospheric Chemistry

Basic texts, recent technical studies, and sources of literature on air pollution are here. Many works on air pollution are in other sections, notably Section 13. The scientific and technical literature can be accessed from *Air Pollution Titles* (372) and other abstracting journals or indexes.

See also Acid Rain, Ozone, below.

Acid Rain. Ozone. These two aspects of air pollution are so familiar as to warrant their own subgroups.

See also:

- Section 1: Chemistry, biogeochemical cycles, pollutants
- Section 5: Plants, agriculture; atmospheric environment, pollution, pesticides
- Section 6: Trees, forests, forestry: air, soil, and water relations, pollution
- Section 10: National laws and policies; international law and policies; U.S. politics and policies, U.S. laws and legislation, courts, disputes; U.S. executive agencies, administration and regulation
- Section 11: Industry, economic sectors; energy; pollution, industrial wastes
- Section 12: Health, medicine, human biology; toxic threats, hazards; risk assessment; toxicology
- Section 13: Air pollution control
- Section 14: Modeling and simulation; assessment and monitoring

Atmosphere. Climate. Weather (289–309)

289. Hobbs, John E. **Applied climatology: a study of atmospheric resources.** Westview Press, Studies in physical geography, 1980. 218 pp., ill., bibl., index. Summarizes the structure and composition of the atmosphere, including circulation and pollutants; investigates weather's effect on societies, health, and day-to-day activities; examines ways to improve use of the atmosphere in urban planning, weather forecasting, and international cooperation.

290. Barry, Roger Graham; Chorley, Richard J. **Atmosphere, weather and climate.** Methuen, 5th ed., 1987. 460 pp., ill., bibl., index. Reference work discusses atmospheric composition, energy, and motion; air masses, fronts, and depressions; weather and climate in temperate and tropic regions; small scale climates such as urban surfaces; and trends and fluctuations in climate variability.

291. Bulletin of the American Meteorological Society. American Meteorological Society, 1920 to date. Monthly. Articles, news, book reviews, and announcements on meteorology, oceanography, hydrology, and atmospheric sciences. Dynamic processes, remote sensing, global warming.

292. Climate dynamics. Springer-Verlag, 1986 to date. Quarterly. Climate systems observations, theory, and computation, including greenhouse gases, climate change modeling, ocean circulation, oceans, cryosphere, biomass, and land surface.

293. Climate research. Inter-Research, 1991 to date. Quarterly. International and multidisciplinary journal on the interactions of climate with organisms, ecosystems, and human societies—past, present, and future.

294. The earth's electrical environment. National Academy Press, 1986. 263 pp., ill., bibl., index. Prepared by the Geophysics Study Committee, National Research Council. Papers explain lightning, cloud and thunderstorm electricity, and global and regional electrical processes.

295. Oliver, John E.; Fairbridge, Rhodes W.; eds. **The encyclopedia of climatology.** Van Nostrand Reinhold, Encyclopedia of earth sciences, v. 11, 1987. 986 pp., ill., index. Focuses on developments of the past 20 years. About 200 entries cover basic climatological aspects as well as such topics as acid rain, El Niño, satellite climatology, health and climate, art and climate, the greenhouse effect, and desertification.

296. Houghton, David D. **Handbook of applied meteorology.** Wiley, 1985. 1461 pp., ill., bibl., index. Authoritative reference to meteorological techniques and knowledge for professionals and technicians who are not meteorologists. In five sections: fundamentals (200 pages); measurements (200 pages); applications (500 pages); societal impacts (40 pages); resources—data, books and journals, research centers and libraries, directories (200 pages).

297. Phillips, D. W.; Gullett, D. W.; Webb, M. S.; compilers. **Handbook of climate data sources of the atmospheric environment service.** Canadian Government Publishing Centre, Supply & Services Canada, 1988. 206 pp., ill. Guides the user to published and unpublished data sources available from Canada's Atmospheric Environment Service. Includes sample displays of data.

298. Kessler, Edwin; ed. **Instruments and techniques for thunderstorm observation and analysis.** University of Oklahoma Press, Thunderstorms—a social, scientific, and technological documentary, v. 3, 1988. 268 pp., ill., bibl., index. Comprehensive handbook, project of the National Severe Storms Laboratory. Covers station network observation and analysis, tornado interception with mobile teams, instrumented aircraft, photogrammetry of thunderstorms and aircraft-based pictures, storm acoustics, satellite observation, and radar techniques.

299. International journal of climatology. Wiley, 1981 to date. 8 issues/yr. Publication of the Royal Meteorological Society. Continues: Journal of climatology. Global and regional studies of climate, long-range forecasting, changes of past, present, and future climate.

300. Journal of climate. American Meteorological Society, 1962 to date. Monthly. Continues: Journal of Applied Meteorology.

301. Meteorological and geoastrophysical abstracts. American Meteorological Society, 1950 to date. Monthly. Presents abstracts of current meteorological and geoastrophysical writings "gleaned from foreign and domestic literature." Arranged in four categories: environmental sciences, meteorology, astrophysics, and hydrology. Each category, particularly the largest, meteorology, is further subdivided. Contains author and subject indexes.

302. Ahrens, C. Donald. **Meteorology today: an in-**

troduction to weather, climate and the environment. West, 1988. 581 pp., ill., bibl., index. College-level introductory text.

303. Fein, Jay S.; Stephens, Pamela L.; eds. **Monsoons.** Wiley, 1987. 631 pp., ill., bibl., index. Comprehensive account of monsoons, from their meteorology to their impact on the culture, arts, and economies of past and present societies.

304. Barry, Roger G. **Mountain weather and climate.** Methuen, 1981. 313 pp., ill., bibl., index. Intended for scientists in related disciplines. Discusses geographic controls of mountain meteorological elements (latitude, topography); circulation systems; climate characteristics of mountains; case studies of mountains in different latitudinal zones; and mountain bioclimatology.

305. Harris, Stuart A. **The permafrost environment.** Barnes & Noble Books, 1986. 276 pp., maps, ill., bibl., index. Identifies features and processes of permafrost. Explores difficulties in construction and resource exploitation (oil and gas drilling, mining). Reviews agriculture, forestry, and water supply problems. Examples from North America, Siberia, Greenland, the Alps, and Tibet.

306. Hatch, Warren L. **Selective guide to climatic data sources.** U.S. Department of Commerce, National Oceanic and Atmospheric Administration, Key to meteorological records documentation, no. 4.11, 1983. 338 pp. Lists and describes published and unpublished climate data available from the National Weather Service, primarily for localities and states of the United States. Includes sample displays of data.

307. Sanderson, M.; ed. **UNESCO sourcebook in climatology for hydrologists and water resource engineers.** UNESCO (dist. by Unipub), 1990. 109 pp., maps, ill., bibl. Describes principles and theories of climatology. Discusses radiation and energy balances, atmospheric circulation, and water in the atmosphere and at the earth's surface.

308. Landsberg, Helmut E. **The urban climate.** Academic Press, International geophysics series, v. 28, 1981. 275 pp., maps, ill., bibl., index. Synthesis of research. Treats urban heat islands, wind field, and energy fluxes; urban air composition; models of urban temperature and wind fields; special aspects of urban climate (corrosion, deterioration, and noise), and other topics.

309. Landsberg, H. E.; ed. **World survey of climatology.** Elsevier, 1969–1986. Maps, ill., bibl., indexes. 15 vols. General climatology and climatology of the free atmosphere in the first four volumes. The remaining 11 volumes survey climates of the continents, polar regions, and oceans.

Weather and Life. Biometeorology (310–331)

310. Lowry, William P. **Atmospheric ecology for designers and planners.** Peavine, 1988. 435 pp., ill., bibl., indexes. Basic information and concepts about the interaction of atmosphere and things being built. Chapters on microclimate, bioclimate, environmental design, macroclimate, and air pollution. Explanatory drawings by Samuel Lowry on nearly every page. Numerous data tables.

311. Woodward, F. I. **Climate and plant distribution.** Cambridge University Press, 1987. 174 pp., bibl., index. Approaches the complex relationship from evidence of past climates, particularly oxygen isotopes in fossil records and ice cores. Translates climate variables into predictive models that link key plant physiological responses with global vegetation.

312. Rosenzweig, Cynthia; Dickinson, Robert; eds. **Climate-vegetation interactions.** University Corporation for Atmospheric Research, Office for Interdisciplinary Earth Studies, UCAR report no. OIES 2, 1986. 156 pp., ill., bibl. Proceedings of a 1986 workshop. Examines the effects of changing atmospheric composition and climate on vegetation, as well as vegetation's effects on climate.

313. Oliver, John E. **Climatology: selected applications.** Wiley, Scripta series in geography, 1981. 260 pp., maps, ill., bibl., index. Includes discussion of solar and wind energy use and the effect of climate change on world food production. Surveys various statistical and interpretive techniques for using climate data. Discusses legal problems resulting from weather modification efforts.

314. Schneider, Stephen H.; Londer, Randi. **The coevolution of climate and life.** Sierra Club Books, 1984. 563 pp., ill., bibl., index. Traces the history of earth's climate, causes of climate change, and the interactions between climate and human activity, particularly with respect to food, water, health, and energy use. Discusses potential consequences of increased CO_2 emissions and nuclear winter. Extensive references.

315. Bourdeau, Phillipe; and others, eds. **Ecotoxicology and climate: with special reference to hot and cold climates.** Wiley, SCOPE, v. 38; IPCS joint symposia, v. 9, 1989. 392 pp. Proceedings of a workshop to assess the current knowledge of environmental toxicology in climates outside the temperate zone.

316. Robinette, Gary O.; ed. **Energy efficient site design.** Van Nostrand Reinhold, 1983. 158 pp., ill., bibl. Examines natural heating and cooling, the regional adaptation of these factors, and the effects of site elements on human comfort. Includes extensive data on climate factors as well as charts, diagrams, and illustrations.

317. Dickinson, Robert E.; ed. **The geophysiology of Amazonia: vegetation and climate interactions.** Wiley, Wiley series in climate and the biosphere, 1987. 526 pp., maps, ill., bibl., index. From a 1985 conference. Contributors consider Amazonia as a planetary-scale system and seek to understand the interrelationships of climate, biota, hydrology, soils, and human activity. Chapters on deforestation, dam building, species diversity, influences of tropical vegetation on atmospheric chemistry, element cycling, micrometeorology, climatology, effects of changed land use on climate, and other topics.

318. International journal of biometeorology. Swets & Zeitlinger, 1957 to date. Quarterly. Relatively brief (four- to six-page) research papers that consider influences of climate, altitude, and pollutants on the health and performance of plants and animals; consequences of open and enclosed spaces, clothing, settlements, and transportation; and effects of electrical, magnetic, and electromagnetic fields on chemical and life processes.

319. Campbell, Gaylon S. **An introduction to environmental biophysics.** Springer-Verlag, Heidelberg science library, 1977. 159 pp., ill., bibl., index. Describes physical microenvironments, applying physical principles and heat- and mass-transfer models to the exchange processes between organisms and their surroundings.

320. Marchand, Peter J. **Life in the cold: an introduction to winter ecology.** University Press of New England, 1987. 176 pp., ill., bibl., index. Explains plant and animal adaptations to the cold on land and in water. Discusses snowpack, human reactions to the cold, and plant-animal interactions. Emphasis is on the non-Arctic.

321. Wilhite, Donald A.; Easterling, William E.; eds. **Planning for drought: toward a reduction of societal vulnerability.** Westview Press, 1987. 597 pp., ill., bibl. Emphasizes the role of long-term forecasting, monitoring, and early warning. Discusses drought's impact on agriculture and government responses.

322. Woodward, F. I.; Sheehy, J. E. **Principles and measurements in environmental biology.** Butterworth, 1983. 263 pp., ill., bibl., index. Measuring atmospherically sensitive biological mechanisms of plants and animals close to the ground: experimental design, sampling, instruments; climate variables, radiation, gas exchanges,

water. Emphasizes vegetation. Background in biology and physics helpful.

323. Monteith, J. L.; Unsworth, M. H. **Principles of environmental physics.** Edward Arnold; Routledge, Chapman & Hall, 1990. 291 pp., ill., index. Physical processes by which living organisms respond to their environment. Reviews basic physics; radiation and heat exchange; mass and momentum transfer. Applies these concepts to the heat balance of plants and animals and to the micrometeorology of crops.

324. Kessler, Edwin; ed. **The thunderstorm in human affairs.** University of Oklahoma Press, Thunderstorms—a social, scientific, and technological documentary, v. 1, 1983. 186 pp., ill., bibl., index. Extensively illustrated discussion of major social consequences of thunderstorms and related events in the United States and techniques for reducing hazards.

325. Maunder, W. J. **The uncertainty business: risks and opportunities in weather and climate.** Methuen, 1986. 420 pp., ill., bibl., index. Encourages the integration of climate and weather information into social, economic, and political decisions. Assesses the economic effects of weather on agriculture, construction, energy use, transportation, and manufacturing. Examines ways to market and communicate weather information to forecast economic activities. Most examples from New Zealand and the United States.

326. Price-Budgen, Avril; ed. **Using meteorological information and products.** Horwood (dist. by Prentice-Hall), 1990. 491 pp. From a 1987 symposium. Emphasis on weather information and its impact on agriculture, tourism, transportation, and air and water pollution control.

327. Ruffner, James A.; Bair, Frank E.; eds. **Weather almanac.** Gale Research, 6th ed., 1992. 800 pp., ill., index. Subtitle: A reference guide to weather, climate, and air quality in the United States and its key cities, comprising statistics, principles, and terminology. Includes weather and health information and safety rules for environmental hazards associated with storms, weather extremes, earthquakes, and volcanoes. Includes world climatological highlights and special features on weather, climate, and society and on ozone in the upper atmosphere.

328. Lowry, William P. **Weather and life: an introduction to biometeorology.** Academic Press, 1969. 305 pp., ill., index. Meant to assist those crossing the boundaries between the biological and atmospheric sciences. Emphasizes concepts and development of perspective. In four parts: physical environment (radiation, temperature, heat, moisture, wind); energy budgets; biological environment (plants, animals, humans); urban environment.

329. Lamb, Hubert H. **Weather, climate, and human affairs: a book of essays and other papers.** Routledge, 1988. 364 pp., ill., bibl., index. Part I gives a history of climate and its impact on humans in Europe, from the Middle Ages to the 1840s. Part II discusses the causes and mechanisms of climate and weather change.

330. Persinger, Michael A. **The weather matrix and human behavior.** Praeger, 1980. 327 pp., ill., bibl., index. Discusses the ways in which each of the major weather variables (temperature, humidity, barometric pressure, atmospheric ion density, and others) might influence human physiology and behavior; identifies the strengths and limitations of various conceptual models; summarizes results of relevant research.

331. Reifsnyder, William. **Weathering the wilderness: the Sierra Club guide to practical meteorology.** Sierra Club Books, 1980. 276 pp., ill., index. Reviews concepts necessary to forecast weather: air mass weather, mountain meteorology, microclimate, solar climate, storm cycles, and frontal systems; provides detailed climatologies for eight areas of North America.

Climate Change (332–366)

332. Trabalka, John R.; ed. **Atmospheric carbon dioxide and the global carbon cycle.** U. S. Department of Energy, Carbon Dioxide Research Division; National Technical Information Service, 1985. 315 pp., ill., bibl., index. A Department of Energy state-of-the-art report. Covers the mechanics and quantification of global carbon sources, sinks, and exchanges.

333. Bibliography on effects of climatic change and related topics. United Nations Environmental Programme, 1988. 127 pp., bibl. Product of a 1988 international meeting. Contains nearly 1400 references, most of them after 1983. Full bibliographic information and author index. Separate section lists works pertinent to the Mediterranean area.

334. Idso, Sherwood B. **Carbon dioxide and global change: earth in transition.** IBR Press, 1989. 292 pp., ill., bibl., index. Examines the many interrelated aspects of increasing atmospheric carbon dioxide; studies both the climatic and the biological results; focuses on evidence of global warming and "global vegetative stimulation."

335. Abrahamson, Dean Edwin; ed. **The challenge of global warming.** Island Press, 1989. 358 pp., ill., bibl., index. Details the nature and effects of global warming and possible policy responses. Leading scientists and policymakers have contributed chapters. Extensive guide for further reading.

336. Rowland, F. S.; Isaksen, I. S. A.; eds. **The changing atmosphere.** Wiley, Dahlem workshop reports; Physical, chemical, and earth sciences research report, v. 7, 1987. 281 pp., bibl., index. Background papers and group reports from a 1987 Dahlem workshop treat the subject under main areas: how the atmosphere has changed (concentrations of various gases); oxidizing capacity of the atmosphere; changes in the Antarctic ozone layer; trace substances and radiation balance of the earth.

337. Firor, John. **The changing atmosphere: a global challenge.** Yale University Press, 1990. 145 pp., ill., bibl., index. Addresses three atmospheric issues demanding attention: acid rain, ozone depletion, and climate warming. Emphasizes their synergistic effects and weighs options of adapting to future environmental change or changing our current practices.

338. Office of Technology Assessment, U.S. Congress. **Changing by degrees: steps to reduce greenhouse gases.** Government Printing Office, 1991. 354 pp., ill., bibl., index. Assesses possible changes in policy and procedures in the energy, building, transportation, manufacturing, forestry, and food sectors in the United States, focusing principally on reducing carbon dioxide emissions. Reviews international efforts, recommending strategies for developing nations, eastern Europe, and OECD countries.

339. Changing climate: report of the Carbon Dioxide Assessment Committee. National Academy Press, 1983. 496 pp., ill., bibl. Presents projected CO_2 emissions and concentrations, assesses possibilities of climate change, and states implications for agriculture, water supply, and sea levels.

340. Ford, Michael J. **The changing climate: responses of the natural fauna and flora.** Allen & Unwin, 1982. 190 pp., maps, ill., bibl., index. Examines the interactions between climate and habitat features and describes ways in which plants and minerals respond to climate change. Assesses difficulties and synergistic problems they face in responding to recent, relatively mild climate changes.

341. White, Margaret R.; ed. **Characterization of information requirements for studies of CO_2 effects: water resources, agriculture, fisheries, forests and**

human health. U.S. Department of Energy, Carbon Dioxide Research Division; National Technical Information Service, 1985. 235 pp., ill., bibl., index. Establishes a base of current knowledge and defines the additional data and improved methods and models needed to estimate indirect CO_2 effects in five basic areas. Includes a background chapter on climate and vegetation responses to the carbon cycle.

342. Rotberg, Robert I.; Rabb, Theodore K.; eds. **Climate and history: studies in interdisciplinary history.** Princeton University Press, 1981. 280 pp., ill., bibl. Contributions from scientists and historians assess current research on determining past climates, using botanical, chemical, tree-ring, and isotopic data as well as records of grape harvests and other unexploited written sources.

343. Wigley, T. M. L.; Ingram, M. J.; Farmer, G.; eds. **Climate and history: studies in past climates and their impact on man.** Cambridge University Press, 1981. 530 pp., ill., bibl., index. Discusses methods of determining past climates—evidence from isotopes, glaciers, plants, and archaeological finds. Case studies from North Africa, China, Greenland, India, and Maine. Essays on developing methodologies and conceptual frameworks to study climate and history.

344. Kellogg, William W.; Schware, Robert. **Climate change and society: consequences of increasing atmospheric carbon dioxide.** Westview Press, 1981. 178 pp., maps, ill., bibl., index. Potential impacts of climate change on energy supply and demand, food production, global ecology, water resources, fisheries, population settlements, and quality of life. Discusses long-range strategies to cope with these impacts.

345. Waggoner, Paul E.; ed. **Climate change and U.S. water resources.** Wiley-Interscience, Wiley series in climate and the biosphere, 1990. 496 pp. Report of the American Association for the Advancement of Science Panel on Climatic Variability, Climate Change, and the Planning and Management of U.S. Water Resources. Impacts and recommended responses for floods and droughts, irrigation, water quality, drinking water supply, recreation and wildlife, electric power generation, and water allocation.

346. Intergovernmental Panel on Climate Change. **Climate change: the IPCC response strategies.** Island Press, 1991. 272 pp., ill. Identifies and evaluates possible response strategies for limiting or adapting to potential climate change. Reviews available institutional mechanisms for implementing these strategies. Discusses limiting greenhouse gas emissions from energy, industry, ag-

riculture, and forestry. Considers effects of adapting strategies on coastal zones and natural resource management.

347. Houghton, J. T.; Jenkins, G. J.; Ephraums, J. J.; eds. **Climate change: the IPCC scientific assessment.** Cambridge University Press, 1990. 364 pp., ill., bibl. Papers from the Intergovernmental Panel on Climate Change discuss greenhouse gases and aerosols, sea level rise, historical climate change, and efforts to model and measure current climate variations and changes.

348. Climate, climatic change and water supply. National Academy of Sciences, Studies in geophysics, 1977. 132 pp., ill., bibl. Collection of papers, intended to aid U.S. policymakers. In light of climatic variability, considers methods of estimating and planning water demands, water law, and impacts of water shortages. Case studies of water resources design and practice from the Southwest and the Northeast.

349. Kates, Robert W.; ed. **Climate impact assessment: studies of the interaction of climate and society.** Wiley, SCOPE, v. 27, 1985. 625 pp., ill., bibl., index. Handbook addresses identification, study, and response to biophysical, social, and economic impacts of climate variability.

350. Kondratev, K. Ya; Kostrova, A. P., trans. **Climate shocks: natural and anthropogenic.** Wiley, 1988. 296 pp., ill., bibl., index. Summarizes and analyzes research done in the USSR and the West. Compares the impacts on climate of greenhouse gases, volcanic eruptions, and nuclear explosions.

351. Climatic change. Kluwer, 1977 to date. 8 issues/yr. An interdisciplinary, international journal devoted to the description, causes, and implications of climate change. Publishes papers from the disciplines of meteorology, anthropology, agricultural science, astronomy, biology, chemistry, economics, engineering, geology, ecology, and oceanography.

352. Oppenheimer, Michael; Boyle, Robert H. **Dead heat: the race against the greenhouse effect.** Basic Books, 1990. 268 pp., index. Reports on the political reluctance to recognize global warming and the decreasing ozone layer. Examines non–fossil fuel energy options and recommends alternate strategies for Third World development. Posits an "action plan" and paints scenarios of the year 2050 in which this plan has and has not been followed.

353. Earthquest. University Corporation for Atmospheric Research, Office for Interdisciplinary Earth Studies, 1987 to date. Quarterly. News of the U. S. Global

Change Research Program and of the International Biosphere-Geosphere Programme.

354. The effects on the atmosphere of a major nuclear exchange. National Academy Press, 1985. 193 pp., ill., bibl., index. Report to the Department of Defense by the National Research Council. Distinguishes characteristics and possible climate effects of dust, soot, and chemical reactions in the atmosphere. Uses volcanic eruptions and extraterrestrial impacts as analogs.

355. Back, Wilfirid; Pankrath, Jurgen; Schneider, Stephen H.; eds. **Food-climate interactions.** Reidel (dist. by Kluwer Boston), 1981. 504 pp., maps, ill., index. Proceedings of a 1980 workshop provide data on present and future world food demands, climate variability and food production, food supply vulnerability, and the assessment and policy implications of food-climate interactions.

356. Global change report (IGBP). International Global Biosphere Programme Secretariat, 1986 to date. Irregular. The goal of the IGBP is to describe and understand the various processes that operate within the total earth system and their relationships, so as to predict changes in the global environment. Reports are 50 to 100 pages in length.

357. Wyman, Richard L.; ed. **Global climate change and life on earth: evidence, predictions and policy.** Chapman and Hall, 1991. 288 pp. Contributed papers assess the impact of the greenhouse effect on forests, sea levels, biodiversity, water resources, population, and public health. Links energy policy to global warming and argues for changes in personal and social consumption to preserve the planet's ecosystem.

358. Global climate change digest. Center for Environmental Information, 1988 to date. Monthly. Guide to current information on greenhouse gases and ozone depletion. Reviews and excerpts from other publications examine mechanisms of change, strategies to reduce and prevent pollution, and ways of adapting to effects.

359. Schneider, Stephen Henry. **Global warming: are we entering the greenhouse century?** Sierra Club Books, 1989. 317 pp., ill., bibl. Leading climatologist explains what we know of climate and atmosphere, social and economic impacts of global warming, and the role of the scientist in making policy.

360. Bolin, Bert; and others, eds. **The greenhouse effect, climatic change, and ecosystems.** Wiley, SCOPE, v. 29, 1987. 541 pp., ill., bibl., index. Summarizes available research on past and predicted future CO_2 emissions; sources and sinks of carbon; expected emissions of other greenhouse gases; monitoring of emissions; and impacts, including sea level changes and the response of terrestrial ecosystems.

361. Lyman, Francesca. **The greenhouse trap: what we're doing to the atmosphere and how we can slow global warming.** Beacon Press, 1990. 190 pp. Explains for general reader factors contributing to global warming and the potential effects of climate change. Recommends systemic and personal steps to improve the situation. Includes appendices of helpful sources and organizations.

362. Gribbin, John R. **Hothouse earth: the greenhouse effect and Gaia.** Grove Weidenfeld, 1990. 273 pp., ill., bibl., index. Discusses past climate processes and the evolution of life. Reviews research indicating rapid global warming over the next few decades. Recommends development of alternative energy sources and conservation.

363. Grove, Jean M. **The Little Ice Age.** Routledge, 1990. 498 pp., ill., bibl., index. Synthesis of research and literature, accompanied by numerous maps and sketches, on the Little Ice Age in Scandinavia, the Alps, Asia, North America, Greenland, and the Southern Hemisphere. Discusses possible causes for this and other phases of glacier advance.

364. Mintzer, Irving M. **A matter of degrees: the potential for controlling the greenhouse effect.** World Resources Institute, 1987. 60 pp., ill., bibl. Presents model for predicting global warming as produced by six gases. Discusses implications of various policy responses on the degree of warming. Recommends both adaptive and preventive measures.

365. Policy implications of greenhouse warming. National Academy Press, 1991. 144 pp., index. Prepared by the Synthesis Panel—National Academy of Sciences, National Academy of Engineering, and Institute of Medicine. Analyzes the major issues and recommends policy. Recommendations address issues such as energy, deforestation, human population, international strategy for the United States, and needed research.

366. Glantz, Michael H.; ed. **Societal responses to regional climatic change: forecasting by analogy.** Westview Press, A Westview special study, v. 35, 1988. 428 pp. A set of ten case studies showing how various regions of North America and different levels of government have responded to extreme changes in the environment, possibly indicating likely responses to global warming. Case studies include the Mississippi River navigation system, levels of the Great Lakes, and the Ogallala Aquifer.

Air Pollution. Atmospheric Chemistry (367–391)

367. Legge, A. H.; Krupa, S. V.; eds. **Air pollutants and their effects on the terrestrial ecosystem.** Wiley, Advances in environmental science and technology, v. 18, 1986. 662 pp., ill., index. Covers the atmospheric chemistry of air pollutants, both gaseous and nongaseous; characterization and quantification; transport and deposition; and interaction with soils and terrestrial vegetation. Also discusses data acquisition, interpretation, modeling, and application. Includes government and industry regulatory perspectives and assessment of current research needs.

368. Stern, Arthur C.; ed. **Air pollution.** Academic Press, 3d ed., 1976–1986. Ill., bibl., index. 8 vols. Authoritative reference on the cause, effect, transport, measurement, and control of air pollution. Vol. 1: Air pollutants, their transformation and transport. Vol. 2: The effects of air pollution. Vol. 3: Measuring, monitoring and surveillance. Vol. 4: Engineering control of air pollution. Vol. 5: Air quality management. These five volumes, published in 1976, were supplemented by three volumes published in 1986. Vol. 6 supplements Vols. 1 and 2; Vol. 7 supplements Vols. 3 and 4; and Vol. 8 supplements Vol. 5.

369. Guderian, Robert; ed. **Air pollution by photochemical oxidants: formation, transport, control, and effects on plants.** Springer-Verlag, Ecological studies, v. 52, 1985. 346 pp., ill., bibl., index. Describes physicochemical properties of oxidants and precursors and identifies emission sources. Discusses mode of action, diagnosis, factors altering plant responses, pollutant combinations, dose-response relationships, and other topics.

370. Butler, J. D. **Air pollution chemistry.** Academic Press, 1979. 408 pp., ill., bibl., index. Covers origins of pollutants, meteorological aspects of dispersal, and removal from the atmosphere; sampling techniques and analytical methods; health factors; and atmospheric chemistry.

371. Wark, Kenneth; Warner, Cecil F. **Air pollution: its origin and control.** Harper & Row, 2d ed., 1981. 526 pp. Textbook. Assumes prior understanding of fundamentals of thermodynamics and chemical kinetics. Chapters discuss effects, sources, and dispersion of air pollutants; particulates; general control of gases; control of sulfur and nitrogen oxides; atmospheric photochemical reactions, mobile sources, and odor controls.

372. Air pollution titles. Pennsylvania State University, Center for Air Environment Studies, 1966 to date. Bimonthly. Keyword-in-context and author indexes to recent articles and technical reports. Bibliographic information includes author addresses.

373. Stonehouse, B.; ed. **Arctic air pollution.** Cambridge University Press, Studies in polar research, 1986. 328 pp., ill., bibl., index. Proceedings of a 1985 conference. Discusses composition, source areas and pathways of pollution, ecological and climate impacts, health issues, international cooperation, and national responsibilities.

374. Graedel, T. E.; Hawkins, Donald T.; Claxton, Larry D. **Atmospheric chemical compounds: sources, occurrence, and bioassay.** Academic Press, 1986. 732 pp., ill., bibl., index. Groups compounds in the stratosphere, indoor air, and the atmosphere into 13 chapters by their chemical structures and properties. Cross-indexing by chemical type, name, Chemical Abstracts Service Registry Number, and source. Includes some discussion and explanation.

375. Finlayson-Pitts, Barbara J.; Pitts, James N., Jr. **Atmospheric chemistry: fundamentals and experimental techniques.** Wiley, 1986. 1098 pp., ill., bibl., index. Comprehensive review of the field. Discusses fundamental and applied aspects of daytime photochemical processes of the lower atmosphere and experimental techniques used in studies of atmospheric reactions. Surveys knowledge of rates and mechanisms of important gas phase reactions in the troposphere. Covers the estimating of lifetimes and fates of volatile chemicals. Discusses acid deposition; sources, reactions, and sinks of primary and secondary particles; sources, atmospheric lifetimes, and chemical fates of key species in the troposphere; and the impact of tropospheric chemical processes on the stratosphere.

376. Atmospheric environment. Pergamon Press, 1966 to date. Divided into parts: Part A, General Topics (monthly) and Part B, Urban Atmosphere (3 issues/yr.). Publishes original research and reviews of all aspects of air pollution: emissions, transport, dispersion, transformation, depositions, effects, aerosols, acid rain, micrometeorology, and regional and global atmosphere. Administrative, economic, political, and other social aspects relating to the atmospheric environment are also addressed.

377. Elsom, Derek M. **Atmospheric pollution: causes, effects, and control policies.** Basil Blackwell, 1987. 322 pp., ill., bibl., index. Delineates the nature and sources of atmospheric pollution, considering particulates and gaseous pollutants, odors, noise, waste heat, acid rain, and radionuclides. Examines effects on vegetation and crops, buildings, and climate. Discusses approaches to controlling pollution in the United States and other countries as well as international collaboration on pollution control.

378. Meetham, A.R.; and others. **Atmospheric pollution: its history, origins, and prevention**. Pergamon Press, Pergamon international library of science, technology, engineering, and social studies, 4th ed., 1981. 232 pp., ill., bibl., index. Examines origins of air pollution on an international scale and the history of its control. Describes many available devices useful in its detection and prevention. Covers the variability and effects of air pollution and legal responses in England, Europe, and the United States.

379. Wayne, Richard P. **Chemistry of atmospheres: an introduction to the chemistry of the atmospheres of Earth, the planets, and their satellites**. Clarendon Press, 1985. 361 pp., ill., bibl., index. Discusses the variety of atmospheres and the physics and meteorology necessary to understand atmospheric chemistry; covers the earth's and extraterrestrial atmospheres and the evolution and change of atmospheres.

380. Warneck, Peter. **Chemistry of the natural atmosphere**. Academic Press, International geophysics series, v. 41, 1988. 757 pp., ill., bibl., index. Introduces the physical and photochemical characteristics of the atmosphere as a whole. Discusses the chemistry of the stratosphere and troposphere; the formation, chemistry, and removal of aerosol particles; nitrogen and sulfur compounds; the cycling of carbon dioxide; and the geochemical origins of the atmosphere and its major constituents.

381. Miller, E. Willard; Miller, Ruby M. **Environmental hazards: air pollution: a reference handbook**. ABC-CLIO, 1989. 250 pp. Includes chronology of events, directory of organizations, laws and legislation, audiovisual materials, and bibliography of 400 books, journal articles, and government documents. Glossary and author, title, and subject indexes.

382. Cothern, C. Richard; Smith, James E., Jr.; eds. **Environmental radon**. Plenum Press, Environmental science research, v. 35, 1987. 363 pp., ill., bibl., index. Intended as a supplementary text for public health, environmental, and health physics courses. Reviews properties, history and uses, measurement, sources, human exposure, dosimetry, health effects, mitigation, risk assessment, and policy.

383. Stern, Arthur C.; and others. **Fundamentals of air pollution**. Academic Press, 1984. 530 pp., ill., bibl., index. Textbook by chemist, meteorologist, and two mechanical engineers. In six parts: elements of air pollution; effects of air pollution; measurement and monitoring of air pollution; meteorology of air pollution; regulatory control of air pollution; engineering control of air pollution.

384. Harrison, Roy M.; Perry, Roger; eds. **Handbook of air pollution analysis**. Chapman and Hall, 2d ed., 1986. 634 pp., ill., bibl., index. Extensively revised. Fifteen chapters cover methods of monitoring, measuring, and sampling air pollution. Includes new chapters on air pollution meteorology and chemistry, physicochemical speciation techniques and rainwater analysis, reliable low-cost procedures for developing countries, and quality assurance in monitoring.

385. Indoor pollutants. National Academy Press, 1981. 537 pp., ill., bibl. Prepared by the National Research Council, Committee on Indoor Pollutants. Characterizes the quality of the indoor air environment and assesses potential health hazards of indoor pollutants, particularly airborne pollutants, including radon, combustion products, formaldehyde, tobacco smoke, odors, and others. Does not cover the industrial workplace. Also discusses the measurement and models of indoor pollution and exposure, and factors influencing pollution, such as building design and geography. Reviews control mechanisms.

386. Bodansky, David; Robkin, Maurice A.; Stadler, David R.; eds. **Indoor radon and its hazards**. University of Washington Press, 1987. 147 pp., ill., bibl., index. Essays from several authors compare radon with other radiation hazards; explore radon's effects in relation to lung cancer and probability of mortality; and cover terminology, methods of detection, sources, and modifications of houses.

387. Brookins, Douglas G. **The indoor radon problem**. Columbia University Press, 1990. 229 pp., ill., bibl. Argues for reducing exposure even if no direct causal link to lung cancer can be proved. Discusses radioactive decay, sources and mechanisms of entry, detection methods, remedial actions, economic uses of emanations, and radon risks versus other risks. Emphasizes the United States but includes a chapter on studies in other countries.

388. Herrick, Charles N.; ed. **Interim assessment: the causes and effects of acidic precipitation**. National Acid Precipitation Assessment Program; Government Printing Office, 1987. 4 vols. Interim results of multiyear,

U.S. government investigation. Contents: Vol. 1: Executive summary. Vol. 2: Emissions and control. Vol. 3: Atmospheric processes. Vol. 4: Effects of acidic precipitation.

389. Bieva, C. J.; Courtois, Y.; Govaerts, M.; eds. **Present and future of indoor air quality.** Elsevier, International congress series, v. 860, 1989. 462 pp., ill., bibl., index. Proceedings of the Brussels Conference in 1989. Two hundred scientists, representing 20 countries, contributed the 92 papers published here. Topics include risk assessment and health, passive smoking, ventilation, climatization, and prevention and guidelines for governing indoor air quality.

390. Nazaroff, William W.; Nero, Anthony V., Jr.; eds. **Radon and its decay products in indoor air.** Wiley, Environmental science and technology, 1988. 518 pp., ill., bibl., index. Covers sources and transport, physical and chemical behavior indoors, health effects and risks, and exposure control.

391. Lioy, Paul J.; Daisey, Joan M.; eds. **Toxic air pollution: a comprehensive study of noncriteria air pollutants.** Lewis, 1986. 294 pp. Provides information on ambient toxic air pollution measurements, intended for trend analysis and assessment of total exposure and indoor air pollution relationships. Chapters provide detail on the Airborne Toxic Element and Organic Substances Study (ATEOS).

Acid Rain (392–410)

392. Acid deposition and atmospheric processes in eastern North America: a review of current scientific understanding. National Academy Press, 1983. 375 pp., maps, ill., bibl. Discusses atmospheric processes, regional air quality models, evidence for source-receptor relationships, and further research needs.

393. Reuss, J. O.; Johnson, D. W. **Acid deposition and the acidification of soils and waters.** Springer-Verlag, Ecological studies, v. 59, 1986. 119 pp., ill., bibl., index. Presents conceptual model of chemical interactions in soil, focusing on solubility, absorption, and cation exchange. Chapters on the sulfur system, the nitrogen system, forest element cycling, and aquatic interface.

394. Committee on Monitoring and Assessment of Trends in Acid Deposition. **Acid deposition: long-term trends.** National Academy Press, 1986. 506 pp., ill., bibl. Examines evidence for links between pollutant emissions, deposition, and environmental effects over time, using historical, paleolimnological and other data.

395. Acid precipitation: a bibliography. U.S. Department of Energy; National Technical Information Service, 1983. 725 pp., index. Over 3100 references focusing primarily on the biological-environmental impacts of acid precipitation, with short annotations. Lists research reports, journal articles, books, patents, theses, and conference papers.

396. Acid precipitation digest. Elsevier, 1983 to date. Monthly. Reports on current policy and research, recent literature, and upcoming conferences and events; multidisciplinary, spanning atmospheric science, aquatic and terrestrial biology and chemistry, forestry, economics, law, and pollution control.

397. Overrein, Lars N.; Seip, Hans Martin; Tollan, Arne. **Acid precipitation: effects on forest and fish: final report of the SNSF project, 1972–1980.** Oslo, Research report, FR 19/80, 1980. 175 pp., maps, ill., bibl. Summarizes the work of over 150 scientists from several Norwegian research institutes on a project to establish precisely the effects of acid precipitation on soil, vegetation, and water.

398. Congressional Research Service. **Acid rain: a survey of data and current analyses.** Government Printing Office, 1984. 954 pp., maps, ill., bibl. Prepared for the Subcommittee on Health and the Environment of the Committee on Energy and Commerce, House of Representatives.

399. Raufer, Roger K.; Feldman, Stephen L. **Acid rain and emissions trading: implementing a market approach to pollution control.** Rowman & Littlefield, 1987. 161 pp., ill., bibl., index. Using economic analysis, simple modeling, and interviews, contributors analyze current weaknesses in the emissions trading program, particularly with respect to helping electric utilities cope with acid rain controls.

400. Regens, James L.; Rycroft, Robert W. **The acid rain controversy.** University of Pittsburgh Press, Pitt series in policy and institutional studies, 1988. 228 pp., ill., bibl., index. Discusses the evolution of U.S. air quality policy and briefly assesses available, potential, and theoretically possible control technologies and mitigation strategies. Covers economic aspects of environmental benefits, control costs, and allocation of emission reduction costs. Views acid rain as a political problem and reviews policy implications.

401. Yanarella, Ernest J.; Ihara, Randal H.; eds. **The acid rain debate: scientific, economic and political dimensions.** Westview Press, Westview special studies in science, technology, and public policy, 1985. 342 pp., bibl., index. Contributed essays discuss the political context of the controversy, and policy issues and alternatives, primarily in the United States. Includes the adequacy of scientific knowledge, cost distribution, the Clean Air Act, and other topics.

402. Bubenick, David V. **Acid rain information book.** Noyes, 2d ed., 1984. 397 pp. Discusses sources of pollutants, their atmospheric transport and transformation, acid deposition and its effects, monitoring and modeling procedures, and mitigative measures and regulatory options.

403. Park, Chris C. **Acid rain: rhetoric and reality.** Methuen, 1987. 272 pp., ill., bibl., index. Reviews the effects acid rain is believed to have on the environment, particularly in Europe; explores possible solutions and includes political and diplomatic perspectives.

404. Adriano, D. C.; Havas, M.; eds. **Acidic precipitation. Vol. 1: Case studies.** Springer-Verlag, 1989. 311 pp., index. Reviews the current status of long-term studies in North America and Europe. Includes nutrient cycling, changes in aquatic population, aluminum biogeochemistry, forest productivity, lake and soil acidification, and other topics.

405. Adriano, D. C.; Johnson, A. H.; eds. **Acidic precipitation. Vol. 2: Biological and ecological effects.** Springer-Verlag, 1989. 368 pp., index. Reviews recent research (through 1987) on the effects of acid precipitation on forests, crops, soils, and freshwater aquatic systems in North America and western Europe. Discusses possible toxicity mechanisms.

406. Lindberg, S.E.; Page, A.L.; Norton, S.A.; eds. **Acidic precipitation. Vol. 3: Sources, deposition, and canopy interactions.** Springer-Verlag, 1990. 332 pp., index. Discusses sources of atmospheric acidity; interactions of airborne acidic compounds with metals; use of metals as tracers to measure past deposition rates and sources of acidity; dry deposition; forest-canopy interactions; and throughfall to the forest floor. Evaluates methods for controlling acidic emissions.

407. Norton, S. A.; Lindberg, S. E.; Page, A. L.; eds. **Acidic precipitation. Vol. 4: Soils, aquatic processes, and lake acidification.** Springer-Verlag, 1990. 293 pp., index. Focuses on soil and sediment factors (including buffering mechanisms and aluminum speciation) that enable soils, lakes, and streams to neutralize acidity. Also covers the release of acidity by melting snowpacks and liming as a treatment method.

408. Bresser, A. H. M.; Salomons, W.; eds. **Acidic precipitation. Vol. 5: International overview and assessment.** Springer-Verlag, 1990. 344 pp., maps, ill., index. Summarizes recent research from Europe, Japan,

and Canada, with emphasis on the role of acid deposition in forest decline and changing lake chemistry.

409. Rodhe, Henning; Herrera, Rafael; eds. **Acidification in tropical countries.** Wiley, SCOPE, v. 36, 1988. 405 pp., index. Discusses the effects of acidification on biogeochemical cycles, terrestrial and aquatic ecosystems, and human cultural properties. Five case studies: Venezuela, Brazil, Nigeria, China, and Australia.

410. Wellburn, Alan. **Air pollution and acid rain: the biological impact.** Wiley; Longman Scientific & Technical, 1988. 274 pp., ill., bibl., index. Discusses sulfur dioxide, nitrogen-based pollutants, ozone, photochemical smog, and other pollutants. Covers sources, atmospheric chemistry, and effects on plants, animals, and humans. Contains charts and diagrams of atmospheric pollutants and their cycles.

Ozone (411–420)

411. Hobbs, Peter V.; McCormick, M. Patrick; eds. **Aerosols and climate.** Deepak, Studies in geophysical optics and remote sensing, 1988. 486 pp., ill., bibl., index. Papers from a 1987 symposium examine the characteristics, quantities, and effects of atmospheric aerosols in the troposphere and stratosphere. Includes the effects of volcanic emissions on aerosols, climate effects of nuclear war, radiation effects of atmospheric particles, aerosols in climate modeling, and other topics.

412. Lee, Si Duk; and others, eds. **Aerosols: research, risk assessment, and control strategies.** Lewis, 1986. 1221 pp., index. Papers from a 1985 international symposium cover sampling and analysis methodologies; atmospheric transport, transformation, and deposition; epidemiological studies; stationary emissions and controls; and other topics.

413. Office of Technology Assessment, U.S. Congress. **Catching our breath: next steps for reducing urban ozone.** Government Printing Office, 1989. 237 pp. Reviews potential benefits and limits of various technologies. Discusses policy options, such as promoting alternative fuels and restricting use of organic solvents.

414. Causes and effects of stratospheric ozone reduction: an update. National Academy Press, 1982. 339 pp., bibl. A report prepared for the EPA reviews scientific theories about the chemical, physical, environmental, and health consequences of ozone reduction.

415. Fishman, Jack; Kalish, Robert. **Global alert: the ozone pollution crisis.** Plenum Press, 1990. 311 pp., ill., bibl., index. Draws attention to decreasing stratospheric ozone, increasing tropospheric ozone, and rising carbon dioxide-induced global temperatures. Explains their detrimental and often synergistic effects. Argues that excess ozone in the lower atmosphere is the most damaging; recommends regulating and restricting fossil fuel emissions.

416. Roan, Sharon. **Ozone crisis: the 15-year evolution of a sudden global emergency.** Wiley, 1989. 270 pp., ill., bibl., index. Describes the science, people, politics, and media coverage of the fight to ban chlorofluorocarbons (CFCs). Includes discussion of the 1988 international treaty restricting CFC production.

417. Ozone depletion, greenhouse gases, and climate change. National Academy Press, 1989. 122 pp., ill., bibl., index. Papers from a 1988 symposium focus on the connections between stratospheric ozone depletion, increasing greenhouse gases, and resulting climate change. Some topics: the roles of halocarbons and heterogeneous chemical processes in ozone depletion, the measurement and interpretation of free radicals in the atmosphere, and historical trends in atmospheric methane.

418. Benedick, Richard Elliot. **Ozone diplomacy: new directions in safeguarding the planet.** Harvard University Press, 1991. 300 pp., index. Analysis of the policy and diplomatic processes that led to the signing, ratification, and revisions of the historic 1987 Montreal Protocol on Substances That Deplete the Ozone Layer,

written by the chief U.S. negotiator. Sees "ozone diplomacy" as the kind of new international cooperation needed to deal with global problems. Appendices give text of the Protocol, its subsequent revisions, and lists of signatories.

419. Wolff, George T.; Hanisch, John L.; Schere, Kenneth; eds. **The scientific and technical issues facing post–1987 ozone control strategies.** Air and Waste Management Association, Transactions (Air Pollution Control Association), v. TR–12, 1988. 736 pp. Transactions of an International Specialty Conference. Reviews the problems and perspectives of ozone attainment. Peer-reviewed papers on urban- and regional-scale ozone, data analysis, control measures and technology, monitoring, and compliance.

420. Scientific assessment of statospheric ozone, Vol. 1. National Aeronautics and Space Administration; Government Printing Office, World Meteorological Organization Global Ozone Research and Monitoring Project Report, 1990. 486 pp., ill., bibl. Consensus on recent research findings related to global warming and the ozone layer, by NASA and these other agencies: National Oceanic and Atmospheric Administration; United Kingdom Department of the Environment; United Nations Environment Programme; World Meteorological Organization.

Section 3

Water. Hydrosphere. Aquatic Environment

Water at the surface of the earth is mainly in the oceans. The oceans comprise a little more than 97 percent of the total, more than 316 million cubic miles of water. Water frozen in the polar ice caps adds another 2 percent, or 6 million cubic miles. The remaining fresh water is in lakes, rivers, and underground storage.

Everyone, it is said, lives downstream, and water pollution is everywhere. The very small but precious amounts of fresh water in the global water budget are obviously at risk. But even the once "limitless" oceans are seriously polluted, endangering world fisheries, coastal ecosystems, and all marine life.

Despite their critical importance, marine and freshwater problems do not command public attention in the way atmospheric problems do. The dramatic element is missing, though everyone knows sea levels will rise if global warming occurs. But alarms over the gradual deterioration of water environments are not easily heard. The hydrosphere is divided into freshwater and marine components. Interactions of land, water, and human activities are complex and diffuse.

Fortunately, the literature on the water environment is plentifully supplied with finding aids, texts, and reference books. This section begins with a group of entries on freshwater and marine resources and their uses, management, and problems. The following groups contain references to fisheries, aquatic and marine sciences, biology and ecology, hydrology and physical aspects of water, and water pollution. All but one of these groups are divided into freshwater and marine categories.

Freshwater. Marine
These two groups contain a selection of general works on water supply, marine and freshwater resources, estuaries and coastal management, water management, and water-related issues.

See also:

- Section 1: Global resources and environment
- Section 2: Atmosphere, climate, weather; weather and life, biometeorology
- Section 4: Landscape ecology; land: terrestrial ecosystems; soils; land degradation, erosion, reclamation

- Section 5: Food and agriculture; crops, cropping systems; plants, vegetation; soil and water relations
- Section 6: Trees, forests, forestry; air, soil, and water relations
- Section 7: Animal biology, zoology; animal ecology, species
- Section 8: Society and environment: country studies; social and human ecology, population
- Section 10: Law, politics, government
- Section 13: Water engineering

Fisheries

Fisheries are so closely tied in perception and practice to their marine and freshwater environments that references to fish are mostly brought together in this section rather than in Section 7, which deals with animal biology and wildlife.

See also:

- Section 3: Freshwater biology and ecology; marine biology and ecology
- Section 4: Landscape ecology; land: terrestrial ecosystems; soils; land degradation, erosion, reclamation
- Section 5: Food and agriculture; crops, cropping systems
- Section 6: Air, soil, and water relations, pollution
- Section 7: Animal biology, zoology; animal ecology, species
- Section 8: Leisure and recreation
- Section 10: Law of the sea; U.S. executive agencies, administration and regulation; water, wildlife, minerals: United States
- Section 11: Natural resource industries
- Section 13: Water engineering
- Section 14: Modeling and simulation; assessment and monitoring

Aquatic and Marine Sciences

Included here are the most general encyclopedias, abstract and indexing sources, and essential journals. Specific works on aquatic sciences follow in the rest of Section 3.

See also:

- Section 1: Physical and chemical systems; geology, earth sciences
- Section 2: Atmosphere, climate, weather; climate change
- Section 4: Land: terrestrial ecosystems
- Section 5: Plant sciences
- Section 6: Tree and forest sciences
- Section 13: Water engineering
- Section 14: Quantification, measurement, statistics

Freshwater Biology and Ecology. Marine Biology and Ecology

These two groups have technical and scientific works on freshwater and marine ecosystems in lakes, rivers, reservoirs, estuaries, bays, coasts, and coral reefs. Included are entries for zooplankton and phytoplankton.

See also:

- Section 1: Biological systems; ecology
- Section 4: Landscape ecology; land: terrestrial ecosystems
- Section 5: Plant ecology; soil and water relations
- Section 6: Forest ecology, ecosystems; air, soil, and water relations, pollution
- Section 7: Animal biology, zoology; animal ecology, species

Water: Physical Aspects. Hydrology. Marine: Physical Aspects

These two groups address physical aspects of water, including water and wave movement, overland flow, sedimentation and bottom conditions, floods, drainage, and groundwater dynamics.

See also:

- Section 1: Physical and chemical systems
- Section 2: Atmosphere, climate, weather
- Section 4: Landscape ecology; land: terrestrial ecosystems; soils; land degradation, erosion, reclamation
- Section 5: Plants, vegetation; soil and water relations
- Section 6: Trees, forests, forestry; air, soil, and water relations, pollution
- Section 10: Water, wildlife, minerals: United States
- Section 13: Water engineering
- Section 14: Modeling and simulation

Water Pollution. Groundwater Pollution. Marine Pollution

Water pollution entries are grouped in these three categories, which include works on aquatic toxicology, acid and toxic lakes, effects of land use on water, hazard assessment, nonpoint sources, agrichemicals, pollutants, field sampling, and more.

See also:

- Section 1: Chemistry, biogeochemical cycles, pollutants
- Section 4: Soils: land degradation, erosion, reclamation
- Section 10: International law and policies; law of the sea; national laws and policies; U.S. politics and policies: U.S. laws and legislation, courts, disputes; U.S. executive agencies, administration and regulation
- Section 11: Industry, economic sectors; energy; pollution, industrial wastes

- Section 12: Health, medicine, human biology; toxic threats, hazards; risk assessment; toxicology
- Section 13: Water pollution control, wastewater
- Section 14: Assessment and monitoring; testing and analysis

421. Aquatic conservation: marine and freshwater ecosystems. Wiley, 1991 to date. Quarterly. Publishes original papers on freshwater, brackish-water, and marine ecosystems, both practical studies and theoretical approaches, over a wide geographic range.

422. Banister, Keith; Campbell, Andrew; eds. **The encyclopedia of aquatic life.** Facts on File, 1985. 349 pp., ill., bibl., index. Color photographs, illustrations, and diagrams complement well-written text covering fish, aquatic invertebrates, and fully aquatic sea mammals.

423. Miller, David H. **Water at the surface of the earth: an introduction to ecosystem hydrodynamics.** Academic Press, 1977. 557 pp., ill., bibl., index. Reviews all phases of the earth's water cycle, focusing on the concept of water budgets and the role of ecosystems; discusses precipitation, reception, evaporation, percolation, and other transport processes.

424. van der Leeden, Frits; Troise, Fred L.; Todd, David Keith. **The water encyclopedia.** Lewis, 2d ed., 1990. 808 pp. Information on water-related subjects presented mostly in tabular form. Chapters on climate and precipitation, hydrologic elements, surface water and groundwater, water use and quality, environmental problems (new to this edition), water resources management, water laws and treaties, and agencies and organizations.

Freshwater (425–455)

425. Yates, Steven A. **Adopting a stream: a Northwest handbook.** Adopt-A-Stream Foundation (dist. by University of Washington Press), 1988. 116 pp., ill., bibl. Provides a detailed look at stream life, discussing fishes, insects, other stream animals, the watershed, and stream ecology as a whole. Includes advice on adopting a stream, suggesting projects, providing examples of successful programs, and recommending contacts for information and support.

426. Coyle, Kevin J. **American Rivers guide to wild and scenic river designation: primer on national river conservation.** American Rivers, 1988. 180 pp. How to get a river included in the Wild and Scenic Rivers system.

427. Echeverria, John D.; Fosburgh, Jamie. **American Rivers outstanding rivers list.** American Rivers, 2d ed., 1990. 300 pp. Rivers of notable ecological, aesthetic, recreational, or cultural significance.

428. Moore, James W. **Balancing the needs of water use.** Springer-Verlag, 1988. 267 pp., ill., bibl., index. Reviews human management of and influence on the earth's hydrologic system, through agriculture and forestry, storage, energy production, transportation, drinking water, wastewater, and fish and wildlife.

429. Reisner, Marc. **Cadillac desert: the American West and its disappearing water.** Viking Penguin, 1986. 582 pp., maps, ill., bibl., index. History of water exploitation—tactics of politicians and business interests to gain more water for Los Angeles; competition between the Bureau of Reclamation and the Army Corps of Engineers in water projects.

430. Healey, M. C.; Wallace, R. R. **Canadian aquatic resources.** Department of Fisheries and Oceans, Canada, Canadian bulletin of fisheries and aquatic sciences, v. 215, 1987. 533 pp. Contributed papers examine the amount, distribution, and projected uses of water up to the year 2011; the roles of permafrost, forests, and grasslands in Canada's hydrologic regime; water resources and native peoples; and the evolution of water management.

431. Black, Peter E. **Conservation of water and related land resources.** Rowman & Littlefield, 2d ed., 1987. 336 pp. Textbook surveys current water conservation methods, policies, organizations, and laws in the United States and reviews economic, political, and environmental factors influencing decision making in these areas.

432. Hunt, Constance Elizabeth; Huser, Verne. **Down by the river: the impact of federal water projects and policies on biological diversity.** Island Press, 1988. 266 pp., ill., bibl., index. Discusses the nature and destruction of riparian habitats by damming and channelization; focuses on the Columbia, Colorado, Missouri, and Mississippi rivers, and the rivers of the Northeast and Southeast; briefly discusses strategies to preserve or restore remaining riparian ecosystems; includes a glossary of water resources terms.

433. Palmer, Tim. **Endangered rivers and the conservation movement.** University of California Press, 1986. 316 pp., ill., bibl., index. Discusses water development policies, particularly of the twentieth century, and the emergence of a national respect for the wildlife, scenery, and recreational opportunities afforded by rivers. Appendices list and describe endangered rivers and proposed threats to them.

434. Colborn, Theodora E.; and others. **Great Lakes, great legacy?** Conservation Foundation; Institute for Research on Public Policy, 1990. 301 pp., maps, ill., index. Assesses with case studies current and historical environmental conditions of land, air, water, climate, fish, wildlife, habitats, and human health in the Great Lakes region. Recommends policies for the next decade.

435. Howell, P.; Lock, M.; Cobb, S.; eds. **The Jonglei Canal: impact and opportunity.** Cambridge University Press, Cambridge studies in applied ecology and resource management, 1988. 537 pp., ill., bibl., index. Discusses canal in the Sudan to divert Nile River waters. Presents data, mostly gathered through field-work, about the physical, biological, and anthropological features of the region. Suggests the potential hydrologic, ecological, social and economic effects.

436. Golubev, Genady N.; Biswas, Asit K.; eds. **Large scale water transfers: emerging environmental and social differences.** Tycooly International, Water resources series, v. 7, 1985. 158 pp. Using case studies, proposes a new framework for evaluating large-scale water transfer projects that incorporates analysis of water transfer types; environmental and social impacts; institutional dimensions; choice of strategies; motivation for adoption; perception and attitudes; and monitoring and evaluation.

437. The nation's water: key unanswered questions about the quality of rivers and streams. U.S. Congress, General Accounting Office, 1986. 163 pp., ill. Examines five recent studies to assess existing knowledge about water quality, changes in water, pollution sources, and effects of the Construction Grants Program.

438. Weatherford, Gary D.; Brown, F. Lee; eds. **New courses for the Colorado River: major issues for the next century.** University of New Mexico Press, 1986. 253 pp., ill., bibl., index. Essays drawn from a 1983 symposium critically assess current management institutions and predict management responses to such hypothetical stresses as protracted drought. Also treated is the relative importance of economic efficiency, equity, and environmental quality.

439. Reisner, Marc; Bates, Sarah. **Overtapped oasis: reform or revolution for western water.** Island Press, 1990. 200 pp., ill., bibl., index. Analyzes water allocation system in western United States at local, state, and federal levels. Concise history of issues, status report on water marketing in each state, proposals to change federal and state laws for more efficient use.

440. Speidel, David H.; Ruedisili, Lon; Agnew, Allen F.; eds. **Perspectives on water: uses and abuses.** Oxford University Press, 1988. 388 pp., ill., bibl. Compila-

tion of previously published papers divided into sections on water as a resource; water in the environment; water use; problems and hazards; and economics and management. Intended as a non-biased overview of the full range of water resource activities.

441. Gresswell, R. E.; and others, eds. **Practical approaches to riparian resource management: an educational workshop.** U. S. Department of the Interior, Bureau of Land Management; Government Printing Office, 1989. 193 pp. From a 1989 conference, sponsored by professional and conservation organizations and state and federal agencies. Twenty-four papers and 30 "extended abstracts" survey current practices and methods of riparian management.

442. Echeverria, John D.; Barrow, Pope; Roos-Collins, Richard. **Rivers at risk: the concerned citizen's guide to hydropower.** Island Press, 1989. 217 pp., ill., bibl. Presents strategies to stop hydroelectric projects, through participation in Federal Energy Regulatory Commission processes and other legal avenues.

443. Worster, Donald. **Rivers of empire: water, aridity, and the growth of the American West.** Pantheon Books, 1985. 402 pp., bibl., index. Historical analysis of the social and economic transformation of the American West through the development of irrigation.

444. Rivers: studies in the science, environmental policy and law of instream flow. Rivers, 1990 to date. Quarterly. Covers water resources planning, practices, and regulations in North America.

445. Goldsmith, E.; Hildyard, N. **The social and environmental effects of large dams.** Sierra Club Books, 1984. 404 pp., bibl., index. Argues that negative consequences of "superdams" often exceed projected benefits of clean power, flood control, and water supply. Reviews problems of resettlement and social and cultural destruction; increased industrial, urban, and plantation water consumption; and limited flood control capability. Examines historical, less traumatic means of irrigation.

446. Francko, David A.; Wetzel, Robert G. **To quench our thirst: the present and future status of freshwater resources of the United States.** University of Michigan Press, 1983. 148 pp., ill., bibl., index. Reviews historical water crises, explains the dynamics of fresh water, outlines the present situation, and proposes changes in attitudes and habits toward water supply that can maintain our standard of living and productivity through already existing technologies.

447. El-Ashry, Mohamed T.; Gibbons, Diana C. **Water and arid lands of the western United States.**

Cambridge University Press, 1988. 415 pp., ill., bibl. Presents alternative policy solutions to minimize conflicts and inefficiencies related to water use. Argues against more water projects and in favor of improved allocation and use of existing supplies. Refers to similar problems in other countries.

448. Wunderlich, Walter O.; Prins, J. Egbert; eds. **Water for the future: water resources developments in perspective.** Balkema, 1987. 703 pp., maps, ill., bibl. Proceedings of the International Symposium on Water for the Future, 1987. Summarizes 7000 years of water development in the world. Gives brief summaries (ten pages) of twentieth-century water management practices in all countries.

449. Droste, Ronald L.; Adamowski, Kaz; eds. **Water for world development.** International Water Resources Association, 1988. 4 vols. Proceedings of the Sixth IWRA World Congress on Water Resources. Vol. 1: Conference summary, training and education. Vol. 2: Hydrology, groundwater, climate, and energy. Vol. 3: Agriculture, irrigation, and drainage; environment, policy and strategy. Vol. 4: Water supply; socioeconomics.

450. Dunne, Thomas; Leopold, Luna B. **Water in environmental planning.** Freeman, 1978. 818 pp. Provides a background in hydrology, fluvial geomorphology, and river quality for planners. Shows with numerous examples the usefulness of such a background for understanding, among others, water supply and use, hill slope processes, and flood hazards. Includes problem sets and solutions.

451. Biswas, Asit K.; ed. **Water management for arid lands in developing countries.** Pergamon Press, Water development, supply and management, v. 13, 1980. 252 pp., ill., bibl. Proceedings of the Training Workshop on Water Management for Arid Regions in 1978. Discusses environmental effects of water management and emphasizes the need for national water plans in arid countries.

452. Viessman, Warren, Jr.; Welty, Claire. **Water management: technology and institutions.** Harper & Row, 1985. 618 pp. Text for introductory graduate course in water resources engineering.

453. Potter, Loren D.; Gosz, James R.; Carlson, Clarence A., Jr. **Water resources in the southern Rockies and high Plains: forest recreational use and aquatic life.** University of New Mexico Press, Eisenhower Consortium institutional series report, no. 6, 1984. 331 pp., ill., bibl., index. Explains in detail how such recreational demands as second homes, ski areas, campgrounds, and

fishing and hunting in the Rockies affect water quantity and quality; describes the subsequent impacts on aquatic life.

454. Powledge, Fred. **Water: the nature, uses, and future of our most precious and abused resource.** Farrar, Straus & Giroux, 1982. 423 pp., index. Highlights crisis situations across the United States brought about by pollution and overuse; exposes numerous examples of misuse and waste; demonstrates how most water projects are politically driven and poorly conceived, situated, and managed; argues that long-term solutions should begin with an awareness that water is not inherently and perpetually free, easy, and pure.

455. Marston, Ed; ed. **Western water made simple.** Island Press, 1987. 237 pp., maps, ill., bibl., index. Reprint of four special issues of *High country news.* Overview of water issues; case studies of Colorado, Columbia and Missouri river basins; intended for the nonspecialist.

Marine (456–476)

456. Silva, Maynard E.; Gately, Ellen M.; Desilvestre, Ingrid. **A bibliographical listing of coastal and marine protected areas: a global survey.** Woods Hole Oceanographic Institution, Woods Hole Oceanographic Institution technical report, no. WHOI–86–11, 1986. 156 pp. Lists over 600 references on marine parks; classifies references as theoretical, reviews and surveys, conference proceedings, and bibliographies; lists marine protected areas globally.

457. Caughman, Madge; Ginsberg, Joanne S. **California coastal resource guide.** University of California Press, 1987. 384 pp. Reference for geographers, historians, ecologists, planning officials, and agencies interested in California's coast. Contains numerous photographs (many are historical), maps, and line drawings.

458. Holing, Dwight. **Coastal alert: ecosystems, energy, and offshore oil drilling.** Island Press, 1990. 120 pp., index. Handbook explaining the environmental consequences of offshore oil drilling and the Lease Sale process by which the Department of the Interior opens coastal areas for drilling. Case study of citizen opposition to drilling off the California coast; discussion of alternatives to offshore drilling. Recommends specific measures citizens can take to oppose drilling, including sample editorials, press releases, etc.

459. Coastal management. Taylor & Francis, 1973 to date. Quarterly. Continues: Coastal zone management journal. International journal devoted to technical, legal, political, social, and policy issues pertinent to coastal resources. Articles present information on management tools and techniques and on institutions involved in coastal development and protection worldwide.

460. Daiber, Franklin C. **Conservation of tidal marshes.** Van Nostrand Reinhold, 1986. 341 pp., ill., bibl., index. Describes and evaluates historical management, uses and exploitation of tidal marshes. Discusses vegetation and water management; sewage disposal and waste treatment; dredge material for wetland restoration; insecticides; and oil pollution.

461. Backus, Richard H.; Bourne, Donald W.; eds. **Georges Bank.** MIT Press, 1987. 593 pp., maps, ill., bibl., index. Reviews the geology, meteorology, oceanography, biology, fisheries, conflicting uses, and ecological consequences of oil drilling.

462. Wind, Herman G.; ed. **Impact of sea level rise on society: report of a project-planning session.** Balkema, 1987. 191 pp., maps, ill., bibl. Climatologists, marine ecologists, economists, civil engineers, and specialists in geology, sociology, and geography assess possible impacts on the coastal environment, engineering, the economy, and social structures. Discusses remedial actions and strategies. Case studies from Europe, Asia, and the United States.

463. Thorne-Miller, Boyce; Catena, John. **The living ocean: understanding and protecting marine biodiversity.** Island Press, 1991. 180 pp., bibl., index. Explains marine biodiversity, threats to it, and limitations of national and international protective regulations. Discusses shore systems, estuaries, wetlands, coral reefs, coastal pelagic and deep-sea benthic systems, and hydrothermal vents.

464. Boesch, Donald F.; Rabalais, Nancy N.; eds. **Long-term environmental effects of offshore oil and gas development.** Elsevier, 1987. 708 pp., ill., bibl., index. Topics of 14 papers include effects on marine mammals and coastal habitats and biological effects as observed in the field and in microcosm studies. Part of a project to develop a monitoring program to assess the significance of long-term effects.

465. Ragotzkie, Robert A. **Man and the marine environment.** CRC Press, 1983. 180 pp. Uses the Great Lakes as a microcosm of the world's oceans; examines realm of human activity, focusing on the demand for and types of marine recreation and resulting costs, conflicts, and future prospects; also discusses fishing, shipping, undersea activities, coastal management, and regulation.

466. Kenchington, Richard A. **Managing marine**

environments. Taylor & Francis, 1990. 248 pp., maps, index. An introduction to the methods, principles, and issues involved in multiple-use planning and management of marine environments; many lessons drawn from the Great Barrier Reef Marine Park.

467. Salm, Rodney V.; Clark, John R. **Marine and coastal protected areas: a guide for planners and managers.** International Union for Conservation of Nature and Natural Resources, 1984. 302 pp., ill., bibl., index. Based on a 1982 workshop. Designed for planners and managers; discusses creation of protected areas, management techniques for different environments, and case studies.

468. Mangone, Gerard J. **Marine policy for America: the United States at sea.** Taylor & Francis, 2d ed., 1988. 365 pp., ill., bibl., index. Reviews all aspects of America's interactions with the seas; discusses the history and changes affecting the navy, the Merchant Marine, fisheries management, seabed minerals exploitation, and marine pollution; describes private institutions, government agencies, and congressional committees influencing marine policy.

469. Hurdle, Burton G.; ed. **The Nordic seas.** Springer-Verlag, 1986. 777 pp., ill., bibl., index. A reference text describing the oceanographic, geological, and geophysical properties of the waters between Greenland and Norway; topics include climatology, the ice cover, sound-speed characteristics, tides, topography, bathymetry, and plate tectonics.

470. Tver, David F. **Ocean and marine dictionary.** Cornell Maritime Press, 1979. 358 pp. Contemporary, historical, and scientific terms are defined—from seaweed to sailing ships.

471. Oceanus. Woods Hole Oceanographic Institution, 1952 to date. Quarterly. Feature articles for a general readership on marine research and problems. Frequent special issues on such topics as the Mediterranean, ocean engineering, the ocean as a waste disposal site, and marine education.

472. Cortright, Robert; Weber, Jeffery; Bailey, Robert. **Oregon estuary plan book.** Oregon Department of Land Conservation and Development, 1987. 126 pp., maps, ill., bibl. Covers Oregon's 17 largest estuaries: habitat type, level of development, and allowable future development. Values of estuaries and associated wetlands graphically displayed through illustrations and maps.

473. Edgerton, Lynne T. **The rising tide: global warming and world sea levels.** Island Press, 1991. 140 pp., index. Analyzes global warming trends and presents implications and effects of rising sea levels; reviews and recommends state, federal, and international policy and action options.

474. Carson, Rachel. **The sea around us.** Oxford University Press, special ed., 1989. 278 pp., ill. The 1952 National Book Award winner by the famed conservationist describing wonders of the world's oceans. Features a chapter on marine biology, bringing the scientific side up to date.

475. Couper, Alastair; ed. **The Times atlas and encyclopedia of the sea.** Times Books, 1989. 272 pp., ill., bibl., index. Examines both the ocean environment (listing its physical features, resources, inhabitants), and human uses of the seas (for transport, travel, commerce, warfare); through multicolored drawings, graphs, and illustrations, addresses topics from ocean currents to the law of the sea.

476. Horton, Tom; Eichbaum, William M. **Turning the tide: saving the Chesapeake Bay.** Island Press, 1991. 327 pp., maps, index. Reviews more than 20 years of effort to save the bay as presented by the Chesapeake Bay Foundation.

Fisheries (477–498)

477. Barnabé, Gilbert; Laird, Lindsay, trans. **Aquaculture.** Horwood (dist. by Prentice Hall), 1990. Ill., index. 2 vols. Vol. 1 covers technology, the culture of molluscs and echinoderms, and the rearing of crustaceans. Vol. 2 discusses fish rearing and worldwide aquaculture.

478. Aquaculture. Elsevier, 1972 to date. 32 issues/yr. Contains research on the exploration, improvement, and management of all aquatic food resources related both directly and indirectly to human consumption.

479. Hunter, Christopher J. **Better trout habitat.** Island Press, 1990. 320 pp., ill., index. Provides understanding of the physical, chemical, and biological needs of trout. Shows how to determine limiting factors and how to design and initiate a rehabilitation project, using such techniques and structures as stream-band protection and stabilization, dams, deflectors, and livestock crossings. Case studies of three stream types: those affected by agriculture, those in forested areas, and those in urban areas.

481. Cairns, Victor W.; Hodson, Peter V.; Nriagu, Jerome O.; eds. **Contaminant effects on fisheries.** Wiley-Interscience, Advances in environmental science and technology, v. 16, 1984. 333 pp., illus., bibl., index. Twenty papers by fisheries biologists and toxicologists

from a workshop on the effects of pollutants on wild fish populations. Emphasis is on the Great Lakes and on monitoring techniques.

482. Rothschild, Brian J. **Dynamics of marine fish populations.** Harvard University Press, 1986. 277 pp., bibl., index. Discusses traditional models, including yield-per-recruit, stock recruitment, and production models. Examines factors usually ignored, such as pollution, aquaculture, and habitat management. Develops a model describing how different fish populations respond to their own numbers during stages of their life histories, to competitor and predator density, and to other stimuli.

483. Caddy, J. F.; Sharp, G. D. **An ecological framework for marine fishery investigations.** Food and Agriculture Organization of the United Nations, FAO fisheries technical paper, no. 283, 1986. 152 pp. Discusses and develops ecological concepts to promote a "whole-system approach" to fishery management; examines the food web, environmental influences, spatial considerations, diversity, stability, and other factors affecting quantifying production in marine ecosystems.

484. Mills, Derek. **Ecology and management of Atlantic salmon.** Chapman and Hall, 1989. 351 pp., ill., bibl., index. Addresses salmon ecology and exploitation, environmental and biological hazards and their control, and conservation; discusses the impacts of rapidly escalating salmon farming, acid rain, and changing agricultural methods.

485. Lawson, Rowena M. **Economics of fisheries development.** Praeger, 1984. 283 pp., ill., bibl., index. Covers the economic theory of fisheries exploitation, management methods, economics of the fish market, fish marketing and processing, planning for fisheries development, and the effects of the Expanded Economic Zones on world fisheries.

486. Fisheries. American Fisheries Society, 1976 to date. Bimonthly. Contains feature articles, essays, profiles, and news of the American Fisheries Society. Many articles assess global fisheries.

487. Pitcher, Tony J.; Hart, Paul J. B. **Fisheries ecology.** Croom Helm; AVI, 1982. 414 pp., ill., bibl., index. Discusses fish nutrition, growth, and production; evolutionary effects of mortality; recruitment; prediction of fishery yields using surplus yield models; dynamic pool models; and fishery economics.

488. Lackey, Robert T.; Nielsen, Larry A.; eds. **Fisheries management.** Halsted Press, 1980. 422 pp., ill., bibl., index. Multiauthored volume in three sections:

characteristics of fisheries (fish populations, aquatic ecology); principles of their management (systems approach, encompassing economic, environmental, and policy issues); and fisheries management (the context of management for major habitats, harvesting strategies, aquaculture).

489. Fisheries review. U.S. Department of the Interior, Fish and Wildlife Service; Government Printing Office, 1955 to date. Quarterly. Continues: Sport fishery abstracts. Supplies fishery biologists with abstracts and assessments of writings covering sport fisheries, fishery research, and management.

490. Miles, Edward L.; ed. **Management of world fisheries: implications of extended coastal state jurisdiction.** University of Washington, Graduate School of Public Affairs, Institute for Public Policy and Management and Institute for Marine Studies, 1989. 318 pp., index.

491. Marine fisheries review. National Marine Fisheries Service, 1972 to date. Quarterly. In-depth review articles on fisheries science, engineering, and economics; commercial and recreational fisheries; marine mammal studies; aquaculture; and U.S. and foreign fisheries developments.

492. Caddy, John F. **Marine invertebrate fisheries: the assessment and management.** Wiley, 1989. 752 pp., ill., bibl., index. Thirty-one papers by 40 experts examine current practices in management and assessment of a wide range of commercial invertebrates.

493. Beddington, J. R.; Beverton, R. J. H.; Lavigne, D. M.; eds. **Marine mammals and fisheries.** Allen & Unwin, 1985. 354 pp., ill., bibl., index. Technical analysis of marine mammal and fisheries interactions, including economic aspects. Case studies from around the world—fur seals' interactions with commercial fisheries in the Bering Sea, dolphin-tuna conflicts in Japan, etc.

494. Ryman, Nils; Utter, Fred; eds. **Population genetics and fishery management.** Washington Sea Grant Program (dist. by University of Washington Press), 1987. 420 pp., bibl., index.

495. Progressive fish-culturist. American Fisheries Society, 1934 to date. Quarterly. Published by the American Fisheries Society in cooperation with the U.S. Fish and Wildlife Service. Contains research, communications, and notes on the science and practice of fish culture.

496. Hilborn, Ray; Walters, Carl J. **Quantitative fish stocks assessment: choice, dynamics and uncertainty.** Chapman and Hall, 1991. 544 pp., ill. Textbook

discusses alternative management actions and models; basic ecological concepts; and the uncertainty of estimating fish stocks. Includes computer programs on disk.

497. Transactions of the American Fisheries Society. American Fisheries Society, 1872 to date. Bimonthly. Contains basic and applied research in genetics, physiology, biology, ecology, health, population dynamics, culture, economics, and other fields as they relate to marine and freshwater finfish, exploitable shellfish, and their fisheries.

498. Busch, Briton Cooper. **The war against the seals: a history of the North American seal fishery.** McGill-Queen's University Press, 1985. 374 pp., ill., bibl., index. History of North Americans' involvement in the eighteenth through twentieth centuries, primarily in Newfoundland and Alaska but also in the Californias, Australia, New Zealand, and the Indian Ocean, using ships' logs and journals. Follows the near extinction of several species.

Aquatic and Marine Sciences (499–510)

499. Aquatic sciences and fisheries abstracts. Cambridge Scientific Abstracts, 1971 to date. Monthly. Abstracts of the scientific and technical literature on biology and ecology of aquatic organisms; exploitation of living and nonliving resources; ocean technology; pollution; and related legal, policy, and socioeconomic issues. Available also as a computer database, online and on CD-ROM.

500. Canadian journal of fisheries and aquatic sciences. Government of Canada, Fisheries and Oceans, 1980 to date. Monthly. Publishes research papers, reviews, perspectives, and comments on fisheries and aquatic sciences at the cell, organ, population, and ecosystem levels or on processes. Papers must lead to conclusions that "clearly contribute to knowledge."

501. Estuaries: journal of the Estuarine Research Federation. Estuarine Research Federation, 1978 to date. Quarterly. Contains original papers on any aspect of natural science applied to estuaries, including chemistry, microbiology, ecosystems, fish, geology, plants, and invertebrates. Also contains applications of research to management and public policy.

502. Estuarine, coastal and shelf science. Academic Press, 1981 to date. Monthly. Journal of the Estuarine and Coastal Sciences Association. Contains research on all aspects of the biology, chemistry, geology, hydrography, and human use of estuaries and other aquatic environments.

503. Charton, Barbara.; ed. **The Facts on File dictionary of marine science.** Facts on File, 1988. 325 pp. Defines terms and includes entries on subjects, issues, geographic locations and descriptions, and people; covers water chemistry, marine ecosystems, reefs, coastlines, waves, tides, water currents and their effects, and plants and animals. Appendices provide a list of international research projects, taxonomic classifications, chronology of marine history, and a geological time scale.

504. Limnology and oceanography. American Society of Limnology and Oceanography, 1956 to date. 8 issues/yr. Publishes basic and applied research on all aspects of limnology and oceanography.

505. Parker, Sybil P.; editor-in-chief. **McGraw-Hill encyclopedia of ocean and atmospheric sciences.** McGraw-Hill, 1980. 580 pp., maps, ill., bibl., index. A quick reference source of terms, concepts, and theories in oceanographic and atmospheric sciences.

506. Oceanic abstracts. Cambridge Scientific Abstracts, 1964 to date. Bimonthly. Indexes and abstracts scientific and technical literature from over 3500 journals, government reports, trade publications, and conference proceedings. Covers living and nonliving marine resources: marine biology, biological oceanography, physical oceanography, meteorology, marine geology and geophysics, marine chemistry; pollution; and ships and shipping. Available as an online computer database.

507. Sea Grant publications index. National Sea Grant Depository, University of Rhode Island, 1968 to date. Annual. Cumulative index to publications generated from the national Sea Grant program and available for loan from the National Sea Grant Depository.

508. Selected water resources abstracts. Water Resources Information Center, 1968 to date. Monthly. Indexes and abstracts monographs, journals, government and technical reports, conference proceedings, and other works. Entries are listed in categories: nature of water, the water cycle, water supply and its management and control, water quality management and protection, water resources planning, engineering works, resources data, grants and facilities. Available as a computer database, online and on CD-ROM.

509. Water resources bulletin. American Water Resources Association, 1965 to date. Quarterly. Publishes original research articles, review papers, descriptions of new techniques, and criticism and commentary relating to all aspects of water research.

510. Water resources research. American Geophysical Union, 1965 to date. Monthly. Interdisciplinary journal integrates research in the social and natural sciences of water. Publishes research, reviews, and technical notes in the fields of hydrology; the physical, chemical, and biological sciences in relation to water; and economics, systems analysis, sociology, and law.

Freshwater Biology and Ecology (511–537)

511. Seagrave, Chris. **Aquatic weed control.** Fishing News, Farnham, England, 1988. 154 pp., ill., index. Handbook designed for owners and managers of still waters and rivers; summarizes techniques, environmental weed control, and special problems.

512. Cvancara, Alan M. **At the water's edge: nature study in lakes, streams, and ponds.** Wiley, 1989. 232 pp. Explains the basics of freshwater ecology in the workings of lakes, ponds, and streams. Differences between standing and running water and between organisms on the surface, on the shore, and offshore. Over 100 illustrations.

513. Warner, Richard E.; Hendrix, Kathleen M.; eds. **California riparian systems: ecology, conservation and productive management.** University of California Press, 1984. 1035 pp., ill., bibl., index. More than 125 conference papers address structure, status, and trends in riparian systems; hydrologic features; legal issues; restoration problems and opportunities; water diversion projects; wildlife interactions; recreational uses; and management strategies.

514. Moss, Brian. **Ecology of fresh waters.** Blackwell Scientific, 2d ed., 1988. 332 pp., ill., bibl., index. Discusses the origins of fresh waters; upland streams and rivers; lowland rivers and floodplains; productivity in lakes and pools; plankton and fish in open waters; fish production in lakes; and the life cycles of natural and artificial lakes. This edition places a greater emphasis on flowing waters and applied ecology.

515. Moss, Brian. **Ecology of fresh waters: man and medium.** Blackwell Scientific, 1988. 417 pp. Covers all aspects of freshwater systems, beginning with the physical properties of water, the water cycle, upland streams, lowland rivers, floodplains, and the productivity of standing waters such as lakes and ponds. Defines human impact on freshwater systems.

516. Reynolds, C. S. **The ecology of freshwater phytoplankton.** Cambridge University Press, 1984. 384 pp., ill., bibl., index. Discusses mechanisms of suspension; the spatial and temporal distribution; photosynthetic activity; nutrients, growth, survival, and loss processes; and seasonal cycles.

517. Davies, Bryan R.; Walker, Keith F.; eds. **The ecology of river systems.** Junk, Monographiae biologicae, v. 60, 1986. 793 pp., ill., bibl., index. Ecological studies of 13 large drainage basins, mostly in Africa and South America, but including North American, Australian, and southern Asian rivers as well.

518. Payne, A. I. **The ecology of tropical lakes and rivers.** Wiley, 1986. 301 pp., ill., bibl., index. Deals with a wide range of lake and river types found in the tropics. Discusses lake and river environments, community structure and dynamics, seasonality, diversity and evolution, and use and control of biological resources.

519. Likens, Gene E.; ed. **An ecosystem approach to aquatic ecology: Mirror Lake and its environments.** Springer-Verlag, 1985. 516 pp., ill., bibl., index. Describes origin and physiographic setting of this New Hampshire lake; discusses its physical and chemical characteristics, plus the composition, distribution, population, biomass, and behavior of its species. Documents changes in the lake over time.

520. Freshwater biology. Blackwell Scientific, 1971 to date. Bimonthly. Publishes research and theoretical papers on lake and river ecology; microorganisms, algae, macrophytes, invertebrates, and fish and other vertebrates; and related physical and chemical aspects of the environment.

521. Le Cren, E. D.; Lowe-McConnell, R. H.; eds. **The functioning of freshwater ecosystems.** Cambridge University Press, International Biological Programme, v. 22, 1980. 588 pp., ill., bibl., index. Synthesizes and interprets research done by the International Biological Programme (IBP). Chapters on physical variables; chemical budgets and nutrients; primary and secondary production; organic matter and decomposers; trophic relationships; estimating productivity; and dynamic models. Includes a summary of Russian research in freshwater biological production. The first two chapters summarize work of the IBP freshwater section.

522. Petts, Geoffrey E. **Impounded rivers: perspectives for ecological management.** Wiley, Environmental monographs and symposia, 1984. 326 pp., ill., bibl., index. Documents physical, chemical, and biological effects of dams, with examples from river systems around the world.

523. Haworth, Elizabeth Y.; Lund, John W.G.; eds. **Lake sediments and environmental history: studies**

in palaeolimnology and palaeoecology in honour of Winifred Tutin.** University of Minnesota Press, 1984. 411 pp., ill., bibl., index. Critically examines the methods and techniques for studying lacustrine deposits and reconstructing the vegetation of lakes through glacial and interglacial periods. Assesses accuracy and shortcomings of nuclear geochronology methods. Reviews interrelationships of chemical stratigraphies and biostratigraphies.

524. Tilzer, Max M.; Serruya, Colette; eds. **Large lakes: ecological structure and function.** Springer-Verlag, 1990. 691 pp., index. Derived from a 1987 symposium; the work of 80 contributors from 15 countries. In four sections (36 chapters): physical features of large lakes; products and distribution of plankton; particle transport and chemical fluxes; and food web structures and trophic interactions.

525. Wetzel, R. G.; Likens, G. E. **Limnological analyses.** Springer-Verlag, 2d ed., 1990. 391 pp., ill. Series of field and laboratory exercises illustrating limnology. Demonstrates standard methods and experimental approaches to studying chemical, physical, and biological aspects of ponds and lakes.

526. Platts, William S.; and others. **Methods for evaluating riparian habitats with applications to management.** U.S. Department of Agriculture, Forest Service, Intermountain Research Station, General technical report, no. INT–221, 1987. 177 pp. Presents methods for evaluating and monitoring vegetation community types, soils, water column, banks, organic debris. Discusses use of remote sensing and historical evaluation. Emphasis on streams.

527. The Mono Basin ecosystem: effects of changing lake level. National Academy Press, 1987. 272 pp., maps, ill., bibl., index. Examines hydrology, physical and chemical systems, biological systems, shoreline and upland systems, and ecological response to changing lake levels.

528. Burgis, Mary J.; Morris, P. **The natural history of lakes.** Cambridge University Press, 1987. 218 pp., ill., bibl., index. Discusses topography, water properties, biotic communities, and seasonal changes of lakes. Gives examples of lake types: polar, mountain, deep, shallow, soda, saline, and man-made lakes. Discusses uses and abuses of lakes and lake conservation. Exceptional illustrations and photographs.

529. Lock, Maurice A.; Williams, Dudley D.; eds. **Perspectives in running water ecology.** Plenum Press, 1981. 430 pp., ill., bibl., index. Dedicated to stream ecologist Noel Hynes. In four sections (16 papers): energy inputs and transformations (the influences of light, organic matter, sediments, and nutrients in running water ecosystems); the migration and dispersal of benthos and the effects of hydrodynamics; impacts of dams and government bureaucrats; regional river ecology (examples from the high latitudes, Australia, and Africa).

530. Muirhead-Thomson, R. C. **Pesticide impact on stream fauna: with special reference to macroinvertebrates.** Cambridge University Press, 1987. 275 pp., ill., bibl., index. Discusses laboratory and field evaluation techniques. Presents case studies on insecticides, larvicides, piscicides, molluscicides, and herbicides.

531. Craig, John F.; Kemper, J. Brian; eds. **Regulated streams: advances in ecology.** Plenum Press, 1987. 431 pp., ill., bibl., index. Papers from a 1985 symposium cover fish and invertebrate ecology, physical processes and water quality.

532. Thornton, Kent W.; Kimmel, Bruce L.; Payne, Forrest E.; eds. **Reservoir limnology: ecological perpectives.** Wiley, 1990. 246 pp., maps, ill., bibl., index. Intended as an aid for system specialists. Chapters on transport and sedimentary processes, dissolved oxygen and nutrient dynamics, primary production, reservoirs as environments for zooplankton, and fish in reservoir ecosystems. Emphasizes the need for studying reservoirs as new limnological systems.

533. Goulding, Michael; Carvalho, Miriam Leal; Ferreira, Efrem G. **Rio Negro, rich life in poor water: Amazonian diversity and foodchain ecology as seen through fish communities.** SPB Academic, 1988. 200 pp. Examines the crucial role of flood plain forests in sustaining aquatic life in a major river tributary of the Amazon.

534. Livingston, Robert J. **The rivers of Florida.** Springer-Verlag, Ecological studies, v. 83, 1991. 289 pp., ill., bibl., index. Discusses the origins and functions of river ecosystems in Florida, then describes the ecological characteristics, geography, vegetation, fisheries, and responses to physical modification of seven river systems under severe development pressures.

535. Hammer, Ulrich Theodore. **Saline lake ecosystems of the world.** Junk, Monographiae biologicae, v. 59, 1986. 616 pp., ill., bibl., index. Focuses on inland saline lakes of non-marine origin; discusses conditions necessary for lake formation, chemical and physical characteristics, sediments, biota, ecology, and models of interaction, utilization, and management.

536. Barnes, James R.; Minshall, G. Wayne; eds. **Stream ecology: application and testing of general**

ecological theory. Plenum Press, 1983. 399 pp., ill., bibl., index. A collection of 13 papers arguing that stream ecology can contribute to the development and testing of general ecological theories; authors review past projects that have addressed accepted theories and suggest future experiments; several evaluate and test specific theories through stream-based research.

537. Meyers, Dewey G.; Strickler, J. Rudi; eds. **Trophic interactions within aquatic ecosystems.** Westview Press, AAAS selected symposia series, v. 85, 1984. 472 pp., ill., bibl., index. Papers discuss interactions between phytoplankton, zooplankton, and fish trophic levels in marine and freshwater environments.

Marine Biology and Ecology (538–567)

538. Longhurst, A. R. **Analysis of marine ecosystems.** Academic Press, 1981. 741 pp., ill., bibl., index. Papers assess the status of marine biology; review trophic and energetic relationships of certain ecosystems, particularly pelagic systems; discuss well-researched ecological processes; and examine and evaluate field, microcosm, and numerical techniques of analysis.

539. Daiber, Franklin C. **Animals of the tidal marsh.** Van Nostrand Reinhold, 1982. 422 pp., ill., bibl., index. Collects, synthesizes, and summarizes literature covering tidal marsh animals from protozoa to vertebrates; addresses issues of distribution, interaction with vegetation, feeding, and reproduction.

540. Baker, J. M.; Wolff, W. J.; eds. **Biological surveys of estuaries and coasts.** Cambridge University Press, Estuarine and Brackish-water Sciences Association handbooks, 1987. 449 pp., ill., bibl., index. Provides an introduction to survey techniques for salt marshes, intertidal and subtidal sediments and rocks, bacteria and fungi, plankton, fish, and birds; also discusses planning and safety considerations.

541. Wilson, James G. **The biology of estuarine management.** Croom Helm, 1988. 204 pp., ill., bibl., index. Based on premise that estuaries should be used to their fullest capacity. Explores estuarine uses and assessment of impacts. Discusses how to determine and rank estuarine quality. Covers sewage sludge and dredge spoil disposal.

542. Sherman, Kenneth; Alexander, Lewis. **Biomass yields and geography of large marine ecosystems.** Westview Press, AAAS selected symposia series, V. 111, 1989. 536 pp., ill., bibl., index. Studies recent changes in ocean biomass resulting from pollution and overexploitation. Examines the scientific, geographic, and legal aspects of large marine ecosystems as research and management units.

543. Chabreck, Robert H. **Coastal marshes: ecology and wildlife management.** University of Minnesota Press, 1988. 138 pp., ill.

544. Majumdar, Shyamal K.; Hall, Lenwood W.; Austin, Herbert M.; eds. **Contaminant problems and management of living Chesapeake Bay resources.** Pennsylvania Academy of Science, 1987. 573 pp., maps, ill., index. Papers review Chesapeake Bay ecosystems and fisheries; provide a socioeconomic overview; discuss problems and impacts; and outline needed management responses by neighboring states.

545. Wells, Susan M.; ed. **Coral reefs of the world.** International Union for Conservation of Nature and Natural Resources, 1991. Maps. 3 vols. Catalogs coral reefs, noting their geographical and ecological significance, current condition, and conservation programs.

546. Livingston, Robert J.; ed. **Ecological processes in coastal and marine systems.** Plenum Press, Marine science, v. 10, 1979. 548 pp., ill., bibl., index. Papers from a 1978 conference on production and export processes, energy transfer, and climatologic, and physiochemical influences. Other sections cover order and structures of benthic communities, and changes and interactions between estuaries and the continental shelf.

547. Mann, K.H. **Ecology of coastal waters: a systems approach.** University of California Press, Studies in ecology, v. 8, 1982. 322 pp., maps, ill., bibl., index. Reviews physical, chemical, and biological interactions affecting various communities: sea grass, marsh grass, mangroves, seaweed-based systems, phytoplankton-based systems, coral reefs, and sediment.

548. Moore, P. G.; Seed, R.; eds. **The ecology of rocky coasts: essays presented to J. R. Lewis.** Columbia University Press, 1986. 467 pp., ill., bibl. Papers on the ecology of dominant shore organisms, selected gastropods of the British Isles, and community ecology of this habitat. Reviews contributions of Lewis to the field.

549. The ecology of tidal freshwater marshes of the United States East Coast: a community profile. U.S. Department of the Interior, Fish and Wildlife Service, 1984. 177 pp., ill., bibl. Covers structural and functional aspects, including geology, hydrology, biotic components, energy, and nutrient and biomass cycling. Discusses values, alterations, and management practices; compares tidal freshwater marshes and salt marshes.

550. Longhurst, Alan R..; Pauly, D. **Ecology of tropical oceans.** Academic Press, ICLARM contribution, no. 389, 1987. 407 pp., ill., bibl., index. Intended as a gen-

eral text on tropical oceanography, biology and fisheries; focus is on structure of tropical marine habitats and on the fish inhabiting them.

551. Day, John W., Jr.; and others. **Estuarine ecology.** Wiley, 1989. 558 pp., bibl., index. Introduces and illustrates estuarine ecosystems through studies in Massachusetts, Louisiana, and Mexico; describes physical and chemical features; examines primary production by plants, the processes of microbes, and the levels of estuarine consumers; final section addresses human activities in terms of fisheries and environmental damage.

552. Stickney, Robert R. **Estuarine ecology of the southeastern United States and Gulf of Mexico.** Texas A & M University Press, 1984. 310 pp. Discussess region of greatest finfish catch and highest shellfish value of the United States. Suggests management techniques to avoid species declines. Discusses freshwater inflows, sedimentary processes, biological influences, and human impacts. Emphasizes ways in which estuaries are altered and damaged.

553. McLusky, Donald Samuel. **The estuarine ecosystem.** Blackie (dist. by Chapman and Hall), 2d ed., 1989. 215 pp., ill., bibl., index. Advanced undergraduate text outlines physical and biological factors; explains the productivity of estuaries and their lack of species diversity; assesses the impact of humans.

554. Wolfe, Douglas A.; ed. **Estuarine variability.** Academic Press, 1986. 509 pp., ill., bibl., index. Papers from a 1985 conference. Geographic, temporal, process, and spatial variability of estuaries is reviewed, including techniques for modeling variability.

555. Fasham, M. R. J.; ed. **Flows of energy and materials in marine ecosystems: theory and practice.** Plenum Press, NATO conference series, IV, Marine sciences, v. 13, 1984. 733 pp., ill., bibl., index. Proceedings of a 1982 NATO Advanced Research Institute meeting. Presentations and discussions focused on present and potential techniques of measuring neglected but critical aspects of the marine food chain for the development of models.

556. Romankevich, Evgenii A. **Geochemistry of organic matter in the ocean.** Springer-Verlag, 1984. 334 pp., ill., bibl. Uniform analysis of the principal forms of organic matter in the oceans: living, dissolved, colloidal, and suspended in bottom sediment and interstitial waters. Translated from the Russian original of 1978, with additional material.

557. Hood, Donald W.; Zimmerman, Steven T.; eds. **The Gulf of Alaska: physical environment and biological resources.** U.S. Department of Commerce, National

Oceanic and Atmospheric Administration, Office of Oceanography and Marine Assessment, Alaska Office, 1987. 655 pp.

558. Friedman, G. M.; Krumbein, W. E.; eds. **Hypersaline ecosystems.** Springer-Verlag, Ecological studies, v. 53, 1985. 484 pp., ill., bibl., index. Provides a general framework for studying hypersaline environments and their sedimentary, microbial, and biogeochemical processes, with special reference to a particular intertidal coastal salt marsh on the Red Sea. Relates this study to similar environments in other periods of earth history.

559. Boaden, Patrick J. S.; Seed, Raymond. **An introduction to coastal ecology.** Blackie (dist. by Chapman and Hall), 1985. 218 pp., ill., bibl., index. Concise advanced undergraduate text approaches coastal ecology from the perspective of habitat: rocky coasts, sediments, brackish-water environments, coral reefs, marshes and mangroves, and other topics.

560. Dawes, Clinton J. **Marine botany.** Wiley, 1981. 628 pp., ill., index. Explains marine plants and their environments, discussing several varieties of algae; geological, chemical, and physical factors; and concepts and methods of general and physiological ecology. Reviews six marine plant communities, including mangrove and sea grass communities.

561. Marine environmental research. Elsevier, 1978 to date. 8 issues/yr. Publishes original research on all aspects of marine environment and processes, with emphasis on multidisciplinary and new theoretical or conceptual approaches.

562. Austin, Brian. **Marine microbiology.** Cambridge University Press, 1988. 222 pp., ill., bibl., index. Concise introduction to current situation in marine microbiology. Chapters on microbiological methods, microbial populations, taxonomy of microorganisms, ecology, microbiology of macroorganisms, microbiology of the deep sea, beneficial and injurious organisms, and biotechnology.

563. Lobban, Christopher S.; Harrison, Paul J.; Duncan, Mary Jo. **The physiological ecology of seaweeds.** Cambridge University Press, 1985. 242 pp., ill., bibl., index. Advanced textbook discusses light and photosynthesis, temperature, salinity, water motion, nutrients, carbon metabolism, pollution, seashore communities, morphogenesis, and mariculture.

564. Sournia, A.; ed. **Phytoplankton manual.** UNESCO, Monographs on oceanographic methodology, v. 6, 1978. 337 pp., ill., bibl, index. Reviews sampling strategies and methods, preservation techniques, and ways of concentrating phytoplankton; discusses identifi-

cation problems and the principles and procedures of estimating cell numbers; includes advice on interpreting observations.

565. Sommer, Ulrich; ed. **Plankton ecology: succession in plankton communities.** Springer-Verlag, Brock/Springer series in contemporary bioscience, 1989. 369 pp., ill., bibl. Examines the roles of competition, grazers, fungal parasites, and predators in the succession of phytoplankton, zooplankton, and bacterioplankton.

566. Halstead, Bruce W. **Poisonous and venomous marine animals of the world.** Darwin Press, 2d rev. ed., 1988. 1168 pp., ill., bibl., index. Comprehensive survey of publications since antiquity, illustrated with nearly 300 color plates. Under each phylum, information is displayed by these categories: representative list of toxic species and their biology; venom apparatus; mechanism of intoxication; medical aspects, toxicology, pharmacology, and chemistry. A literature cited concludes each phylum.

567. Earll, R.; Erwin, D. G.; eds. **Sublittoral ecology: the ecology of the shallow sublittoral benthos.** Clarendon Press, 1983. 277 pp., ill., bibl., index. In the British Isles. Papers discuss light and water movement, biological interactions, and biogeography, particularly species composition in the shallow sublittoral zone.

Water: Physical Aspects. Hydrology (568–596)

568. Knox, Robert C.; and others. **Aquifer restoration: state of the art.** Noyes, Pollution technology review, v. 131, 1986. 750 pp., ill., bibl. Includes sections on groundwater pollution control through institutional measures, source control, well systems, capping and liners, in situ chemical treatment, and biological stabilization. Appendices discuss studies of aquifer restoration.

569. Lowing, M. J.; ed. **Casebook of methods for computing hydrological parameters for water projects: a contribution to the International Hydrological Programme.** UNESCO, Studies and reports in hydrology, v. 48, 1987. 324 pp., maps, ill., bibl. Hydrologic techniques, illustrated by cases: homogeneity tests, estimation of accuracy, filling in of gaps, probability distributions, aspects of distribution fitting, deterministic models, annual runoff, flood flows, low flows, and drought. Case studies: data and results applied to actual water projects in seven countries.

570. Walling, D. E.; Foster, S. S. D.; Wurzel, P.; eds.

Challenges in African hydrology and water resources. International Association of Hydrological Sciences Press, IAHS publication, no. 144, 1984. 587 pp. From a 1984 symposium. In two parts: Papers on groundwater consider the delineation of groundwater reservoirs, estimation of recharge, exploitation and management of small basins, use of isotope studies, mathematical modeling, and data organizing. Papers on soil erosion treat erosion rates, sediment yield, effects of climate and vegetation on sediment, measurement and prediction techniques, and conservation practices.

571. Brookes, A. **Channelized rivers: perspectives for environmental management.** Wiley, 1988. 326 pp., ill., bibl., index. Discusses need for channeling. Reviews conventional river engineering, relevant legislation in four western countries, and physical effects and biological impacts of channelization. Presents revised construction procedures and techniques for mitigation, enhancement, and restoration.

572. Falkenmark, Malin; Chapman, Tom; eds. **Comparative hydrology: an ecological approach to land and water resources.** UNESCO, 1989. 479 pp., bibl., index.

573. Ferronsky, V. I.; Polyakov, V. A.; Ferronsky, S. V., trans. **Environmental isotopes in the hydrosphere.** Wiley, rev. and supplemented ed., 1982. 466 pp., ill., bibl., index. Summarizes previous work on the examination and application of environmental isotopes in studying the hydrosphere. Chapters on isotopic geochemistry of natural waters, stable isotopes of oxygen and hydrogen for studying natural waters, cosmogenic radioactive isotopes in natural waters, radioactive isotopes of heavy metals in natural waters, and origin of the earth's hydrosphere in the light of isotopic composition of water.

574. **Estimating probabilities of extreme floods: methods and recommended research.** National Academy Press, 1988. 141 pp., ill., bibl., index. Assesses major scientific methodologies and recommends improvements in techniques and data.

575. Simmers, I.; ed. **Estimation of natural groundwater recharge: with special reference to arid and semi-arid regions.** Reidel; Kluwer, NATO ASI series, Series C, Mathematical and physical sciences, v. 222, 1987. 510 pp. Selected papers from a 1987 workshop discuss such problems as reliable estimation techniques and the suitability of extrapolating results from site-specific studies. Highlights deficiencies in present knowledge and recommends new research directions.

576. Beven, Keith; Carling, Paul; eds. **Floods: hy-** drological, sedimentological and geomorphologic implications. Wiley, British geomorphological research group symposia series, 1989. 290 pp., ill., bibl., index. Papers on the processes involved in floods and their interactions within the landscape. Also, interpretation of sediment deposits; hydraulics of flood channels; difficulties with models and quantitative predictions of floods; effects of natural and artificial channel changes on flood frequency.

577. Drever, James I. **The geochemistry of natural waters.** Prentice-Hall, 1982. 388 pp., ill., bibl., index. Principles and examples of weathering and water chemistry; clay minerals and ion exchange; evaporation and salinity; redox equilibria and redox conditions in natural waters; and mathematical and numerical models.

578. **Ground water.** Water Well Journal, 1963 to date. Bimonthly. Journal of the National Water Well Association. Papers, news, and commentary on all aspects of groundwater.

579. Freeze, R. Allan; Cherry, John A. **Groundwater.** Prentice-Hall, 1979. 604 pp., ill., bibl., index. Introductory text. Contents: physical and chemical properties; geology; flow nets; hydrologic cycle; chemical evolution of groundwater; groundwater resource evaluation; groundwater contamination; geotechnical and geological processes.

580. van der Leeden, Frits; ed. **Geraghty & Miller's groundwater bibliography.** Lewis, 5th ed., 1992. 507 pp. Contains some 5600 references to bibliographies, periodicals, books, and articles, both "classic" works and significant new papers in the fields of hydrogeology. Divided into 31 topical areas. Expanded coverage of groundwater contamination, modeling, and legal aspects.

581. Todd, David Keith. **Goundwater hydrology.** Wiley, 2d ed., 1980. 535 pp., ill., bibl., index. Explains groundwater movement and level fluctuation. Reviews well hydraulics, well drilling, and development methods. Discusses modeling techniques, surface and subsurface investigations, and saline intrusion.

582. Mandel, S.; Shiftan, Z. **Groundwater resources: investigation and development.** Academic Press, Water pollution series, 1981. 269 pp., maps, ill., bibl., index. Appropriate for those having a strong background in hydrogeology. Offers concise coverage of pumping tests, isotope techniques, groundwater geology, geophysical methods, and other topics.

583. **Hydrobiologia.** Kluwer; Junk, 1948 to date. 63 issues/yr. Original research relating hydrology and biology, freshwater and marine. Encompasses ecology, physiology, biogeography, methodology, and taxonomy. Numerous special issues.

584. Raudkivi, Arved J. **Hydrology: an advanced introduction to hydrological processes and modeling.** Pergamon Press, 1979. 479 pp., ill., bibl., index. Emphasizes processes and the methods of estimating the various quantities of water involved; some topics include precipitation, runoff, evaporation and transpiration, and flood routing. Intended for the graduate student in civil engineering.

585. Bras, Rafael L. **Hydrology: an introduction to hydrologic science.** Addison-Wesley, 1990. 643 pp., ill., index. Middle-ground approach to hydrologic science— between rigorous mathematical analysis and emphasis on environmental problems. Integrates atmospheric dynamics, surface water, soil moisture, groundwater, probability, and fluvial geomorphology. Includes illustrated problems.

586. Hammer, Mark J.; MacKichan, Kenneth A. **Hydrology and quality of water resources.** Wiley, 1980. 486 pp., ill., bibl., index. Covers water quality and hydrology of groundwater, flowing waters, and impounded waters.

587. Brooks, Kenneth N.; and others. **Hydrology and the management of watersheds.** Iowa State University Press, 1991. 402 pp., ill. Text and reference on solving problems of watersheds and developing watershed management programs. Parts 1 and 2 present basic hydrology; Part 3, watershed planning; and Part 4, special topics on problems in different regions of the world.

588. Keller, Reiner; ed. **Hydrology of humid tropical regions: aspects of tropical cyclones, hydrological effects of agriculture and forestry practice.** International Association of Hydrological Sciences, IAHS publication, no. 140, 1983. 468 pp. Proceedings of a 1983 symposium. Papers on hydrologic aspects of tropical cyclones, hydrologic regimes of the area, water balance, hydrologic models, and the use of inadequate data. Other papers deal with land use and hydrology.

589. Kusler, Jon A. **Innovation in local floodplain management: a summary of community experience.** Natural Hazards Research and Applications Information Center, 1982. 237 pp. Describes regulations and techniques currently in use across the United States. Analyzes legal issues and recommends changes in federal and local policies. Appendix profiles floodplain management programs of 56 inland and 18 coastal communities.

590. Journal of hydrology. Elsevier, 1963 to date. 36 issues/yr. Publishes original research and review papers on all aspects of hydrology—surface hydrology and water resources; hydrogeology and chemical hydrology; physical processes in hydrology; and systems hydrology.

591. Geiger, W. F.; and others, eds. **Manual on drainage in urbanized areas: a contribution to the International Hydrological Programme.** UNESCO, Studies and reports in hydrology, v. 43, 1987 to date. Vol. 1 of this manual deals with the planning and design of drainage systems.

592. Bruk, Stevan; ed. **Methods of computing sedimentation in lakes and reservoirs: a contribution to the International Hydrological Programme IHP, II project A.2.6.1 panel.** UNESCO, 1985. 224 pp., ill., bibl. Wider in scope than title implies. Covers technical and socioeconomic impacts of reservoir sedimentation; physical phenomena; measurement methods and instrumentation; methods of preserving reservoir capacity, with case studies; and engineering predictions.

593. Matthess, Georg; Harvey, John C., trans. **The properties of groundwater.** Wiley, 1982. 406 pp., ill., bibl., index. Compiles, summarizes, and organizes 50 years of research concerning groundwater worldwide. Discusses physical and chemical principles of water and solutions; geochemical processes, including ion exchange, oxidation and reduction; biological processes; and the effects of pollutants. Provides guidelines for the classification and assessment of groundwater.

594. Haan, Charles T. **Statistical methods in hydrology.** Iowa State University Press, 1977. 378 pp., ill., bibl., index. Explains the concepts and techniques involved in statistics, noting usefulness, strengths, and weaknesses. Topics include simple and multiple linear regression, multivariate analysis, and probability distributions.

595. Lazaro, Timothy R. **Urban hydrology: a multidisciplinary perspective.** Technomic, 1990. 264 pp., index. Examines impacts on streamflow and water quality from urban areas. Gives methods of analyzing and modeling changes in water quantity and quality. Assesses pollution and runoff control measures.

596. Black, Peter E. **Watershed hydrology.** Prentice-Hall, Prentice Hall advanced reference series, Physical and life sciences, 1991. 408 pp., ill., maps, bibl., indexes.

Marine: Physical Aspects (597–609)

597. Denny, Mark W. **Biology and the mechanics of the wave-swept environment.** Princeton University Press, 1988. 329 pp., ill., bibl., index. Reviews types of wave-swept organisms. Explains the mechanics of waves, addressing fluid dynamics, wave theories, tides, benthic layers, and the effects of turbulence and mixing. Applies wave knowledge to factors determining organism size, shape, and life span. Reviews instruments and equipment for near-shore environment study.

598. Postma, H.; Ziljstra, J. J.; eds. **Continental shelves.** Elsevier, Ecosystems of the world, v. 27, 1988. 421 pp. Covers geology and physical and chemical oceanography; biology, including plankton, benthic fauna, and fish populations; and energy flow in marine ecosystems. Examples from the Barents Sea, the North Sea, the East Coast of the United States, and the Gulf of Thailand. Assumes considerable prior knowledge.

599. Dyer, K. R.; ed. **Estuarine hydrography and sedimentation: a handbook.** Cambridge University Press, Estuarine and Brackish-water Sciences Association handbooks, 1979. 230 pp., ill., bibl., index. Methods of analysis and interpretation applicable to such topics as tidal measurement, hydrographic surveying, sediment sampling, suspended sediment, water current, temperature, salinity, and density analysis. Reviews advantages and disadvantages of techniques, with references.

600. Wolfe, Douglas A.; ed. **Estuarine variability.** Academic Press, 1986. 509 pp., ill., bibl., index. Proceedings of the 8th International Estuarine Research Conference in 1985. Papers address geographic, temporal, process, and spatial variability of estuaries and the modeling of estuarine variability.

601. McCormick, Larry R.; Neal, William J.; Pilkey, Orrin H. **Living with Long Island's south shore.** Duke University Press, 1984. 157 pp. Discusses shoreline dynamics, human response to erosion, and guidelines for buying and building homes on the shore. One of several "Living with . . . shore" books by this publisher.

602. Managing coastal erosion. National Academy Press, 1990. 182 pp., bibl., index. Prepared by the National Research Council, Committee on Coastal Erosion Zone Management. Summary report on causes, effects, and distribution of coastal erosion; management; National Flood Insurance Program; sample state programs; and shoreline change prediction.

603. Nairn, Alan E. M.; Stehli, Francis G.; eds. **Ocean basins and margins.** Plenum Press, 1973–1988. 7 vols. in 9. Nine volumes cover geology of the world's oceans. Background in geological sciences is needed to utilize this treatise. Vol. 1: The South Atlantic. Vol. 2: The North Atlantic. Vol. 3: The Gulf of Mexico and the Caribbean. Vol. 4A: The eastern Mediterranean. Vol. 4B: The western Mediterranean. Vol. 5. The Arctic Ocean. Vol. 6: The Indian Ocean. Vols. 7A, 7B: The Pacific Ocean.

604. Paleoceanography, paleoclimatology, paleoecology. American Geophysical Union, 1965 to date. Bimonthly. Research on marine sediments to determine past marine environments and global climate, in time scales of thousands and millions of years.

605. Bowden, Kenneth F. **The physical oceanography of coastal waters.** Halsted Press, 1983. 302 pp., ill., bibl., index. Reviews features and processes common to coastal waters, including tides, waves, currents, upwelling, salinity, and temperature distribution; also examines exchange, mixing, and interaction between coastal and oceanic circulations.

606. Seiboid, E.; Berger, W.H. **The sea floor: an introduction to marine geology.** Springer-Verlag, 1982. 288 pp., maps, ill., bibl., index. Surveys the tectonics and morphology of ocean basins and margins; sources, composition, and patterns of sediments; seafloor organisms; paleoceanography; and ocean floor resources.

607. Le Mehaute, Bernard; Hanes, Daniel M.; eds. **The sea.** Wiley, Ideas and observations on progress in the study of the seas, 1962–1990. Maps, ill. 9 vols. Multivolume continuing series. Some volumes have more than one part. Vol. 1: Physical oceanography. Vol. 2: The composition of sea water. Vol. 3: The earth beneath the sea. Vol. 4: New concepts of seafloor evolution. Vol. 5: Marine chemistry. Vol. 6: Marine modeling. Vol. 7: The ocean lithosphere. Vol. 8: Deep-sea biology. Vol. 9: Ocean engineering science.

608. Sea-level change. National Academy Press, 1990. 234 pp., maps, ill., bibl., index. Prepared by the Geographic Study Committee, Commission on Physical Sciences, Mathematics, and Resources, National Research Council. Discusses current scientific views on the causes and workings of sea level change. Assesses measurement techniques and suggests steps to improve understanding of the factors involved.

609. Devoy, R. J. N.; ed. **Sea surface studies: a global view.** Croom Helm; Methuen, 1987. 649 pp., ill., bibl., index. Multiauthored text reviews important processes and principles; discusses patterns of sea level change through history; covers applications such as tidal and wave power, placer deposits, and biostratigraphy.

Water Pollution (610–633)

610. Cresser, Malcolm S; Edwards, Anthony. **Acidification of freshwaters.** Cambridge University Press, 1987. 136 pp. Historical awareness of the problem, natural and artificial acidification processes, research methods and priorities.

611. Velz, Clarence J. **Applied stream sanitation.** Wiley, 1984. 800 pp., ill., bibl., index. Comprehensive, practical text on pollution sources, hydrologic and climatologic factors, self-purification, heat dissipation, and waste assimilation capacity.

612. Suffet, I. H.; MacCarthy, P.; eds. **Aquatic humic substances: influence on fate and treatment of pollutants.** American Chemical Society, Advances in chemistry series, v. 219, 1989. 864 pp., ill., bibl., index. Forty-five papers characterize humic substances and their environmental impacts and interactions with organic and inorganic contaminants. Covers treatment processes, including coagulation, sorption onto activated carbon, ozonation and chlorination, and ion-exchange and membrane processes.

613. Suter, Glenn W.; Lewis, Michael A.; eds. **Aquatic toxicology and environmental fate.** American Society for Testing and Materials, ASTM special technical publication, no. 1007, 1988. 605 pp. Based on papers presented at the 11th Symposium on Aquatic Toxicology and Hazard Assessment, 1987.

614. Nriagu, Jerome O.; Lakshminarayan, J. S. S.; eds. **Aquatic toxicology and water quality management.** Wiley-Interscience, Advances in environmental science and technology, v. 22, 1989. 292 pp., ill. Provides surveys of the research and toxicology of important aquatic pollutants. Based on papers presented at the 13th Annual Aquatic Toxicology Workshop.

615. Mason, C.F. **Biology of freshwater pollution.** Wiley, 2d ed., 1991. 336 pp. Explains and updates various pollutants; their sources; their effects on organisms, ecosystems, and humans; and techniques for assessing them both in the field and laboratory. New chapters on acidification, organochlorines, and oil.

616. Hansen, Nancy Richardson; Babcock, Hope M.; Clark, Edwin H. **Controlling nonpoint-source water pollution: a citizen's handbook.** Conservation Foundation; National Audubon Society, 1988. 170 pp., map, bibl. Practical tips for effective citizen action: how to prepare an assessment report, how to develop and implement a management program. Appendices include addresses of relevant federal and state agencies.

617. Henderson-Sellers, Brian.; Markland, H. R. **Decaying lakes: the origins and control of cultural eutrophication.** Wiley, Principles and techniques in the environmental sciences, 1987. 254 pp., ill., bibl., index. Comprehensive introduction to causes and control of eutrophication, problems resulting from fertilizer and wastewater pollution, and current scientific basis for understanding these processes.

618. McFeters, Gordon A.; ed. **Drinking water microbiology: progress and recent developments.** Springer-Verlag, 1990. 502 pp., bibl., index. Compilation of latest research from recent monographs and reviews.

619. Burby, Raymond J.; and others. **Drinking water supplies: protection through watershed management.** Ann Arbor Science, 1983. 273 pp. Advantages of watershed management over treatment in removing contaminants like viruses, heavy metals, and carcinogenic organics. Describes planning approach and action strategies for communities—regulations, capital improvement, financial incentives, and educational programs.

620. Solbé, J. F. de L. G.; ed. **Effects of land use on fresh waters: agriculture, forestry, mineral exploitation, urbanisation.** Horwood; Halsted Press, 1986. 568 pp. Draws on U.S and European research to present a wide range of problems and solutions—scientific, administrative, and political. Specific topics include sewage, wastewater treatment, highway drainage quality control, aquifer contamination below cities, coal mining, pesticides, nitrates, acidification, and gross organic pollution.

621. Mitchell, Mark K.; Stapp, William B. **Field manual for water quality monitoring: an environmental education program for schools.** William B. Stapp, Ann Arbor, MI, 1986. 150 pp., ill. Explains the meaning and procedure of nine water quality tests. Tells how to derive an overall water quality index from the resulting data. Also, how to assess the source of water quality problems and raise public awareness.

622. Andersson, F.; Olsson, B.; eds. **Lake Gardsjon: an acid forest lake and its catchment.** House of the Swedish Research Councils, Ecological bulletin, v. 37, 1985. 336 pp., ill., bibl. The topography, geology, hydrology, and meteorology of a watershed in Sweden affected by acid deposition.

623. Forstner, U.; Wittmann, G.T.W. **Metal pollution in the aquatic environment.** Springer-Verlag, 2d rev. ed., 1983. 486 pp., ill., bibl., index. Identifies sources and nature of toxic metals, using sediment analysis to assess contamination levels. Reviews effects on organisms and water purification. Describes metal transfer between solid and aqueous phases. Examples drawn from Europe, United States, and Japan.

624. Perdue, E. M.; Gjessing, E. T.; eds. **Organic acids in aquatic ecosystems: report of the Dahlem Workshop on Organic Acids in Aquatic Ecosystems.** Wiley, Dahlem workshop reports—Life sciences research report, no. 48, 1990. 345 pp., ill. Assesses current knowledge and identifies promising research areas.

625. Research journal of the Water Pollution Control Federation. Water Pollution Control Federation, 1928 to date. Continues: Journal of the Water Pollution Control Federation. Original research, reviews, and techniques in water pollution control. Annual literature review.

626. Brocksen, R. W.; Wisniewski, J.; eds. **Restoration of aquatic and terrestrial systems.** Kluwer, 1989. 512 pp. Proceedings of a 1988 conference; focuses on liming technology as a resource management tool. Sections on lake liming, stream liming, whole or partial watershed treatment, chemical and biological response to liming, and economic considerations of liming.

627. Hites, Ronald A.; Eisenreich, S. J.; eds. **Sources and fates of aquatic pollutants.** American Chemical Society, Advances in chemistry series, v. 216, 1987. 558 pp. Based on a 1985 symposium. Four sections on air-water processes, water column processes, water-sediment processes, and case studies present a holistic approach to the study of aquatic pollutant chemistry. Both marine and freshwater systems are covered.

628. Surface coal mining effects on ground water recharge. National Academy Press, 1990. 170 pp. Prepared by the National Research Council's Committee on Ground Water Recharge in Surface-Mined Areas. Evaluates hydrologic technologies for restoring surface-mined areas to premining conditions.

629. Schmidtke, Norbert, W.; ed. **Toxic contamination in large lakes.** Lewis, 1988. Ill., bibl., index. 4 vols. Papers from a 1986 conference emphasize integrated approaches to studying toxic contamination in large lakes. Social and political concerns are covered. Vol. 1: Chronic effects of toxic contaminants in large lakes Vol. 2: Impact of toxic contaminants on fisheries management. Vol. 3: Sources, fate, and controls of toxic contaminants. Vol. 4: Prevention of toxic contamination in large lakes: managing a large ecosystem for sustainable development.

630. Torno, Harry C.; Marsalek, J.; Desbordes, M.; eds. **Urban runoff pollution.** Springer-Verlag, NATO ASI series, Series G, Ecological sciences, v. 10, 1986. 893 pp., ill., bibl., index. Papers from a 1985 NATO Advanced Study Institute. Discusses field studies, runoff processes modeling, pollutant impact on receiving waters, runoff quality management, and real-time control.

631. Knight, Allen W.; Simmons, Mary Ann. **Water pollution: a guide to information sources.** Gale Research, Man and the environment information guide series, v. 9, 1980. 278 pp., index. Books, articles, reports, organizations, and dissertations.

632. Coler, Robert A.; Rockwood, John P. **Water pollution biology: a laboratory/field handbook.** Technomic, 1989. 120 pp., ill. Basic guide and reference covers indicator organisms, community structure and function, and bioassay and toxicity tests. Provides worked-out examples and calculations. Focuses on the skills involved in using benthic macroinvertebrates and plankton as indicator species.

633. Krenkel, Peter A.; Novotny, Vladimir. **Water quality management.** Academic Press, 1980. 671 pp., ill., bibl., index. Addresses physical, chemical, and biological aspects of water quality. Notes existing legislation. Explains modeling and systems analysis of lakes, reservoirs, streams, and estuaries. Discusses eutrophication, and thermal and groundwater pollution.

Groundwater Pollution (634–650)

634. Agrichemicals and groundwater: perspectives and solutions. Freshwater Foundation, 1988. Special issue of the *Journal of freshwater* gives historical perspective on agrichemicals, our dependence on groundwater, and the relationship between them. Discusses sustainable agriculture, integrated pest management, biotechnology, and state and local initiatives.

635. Agrichemicals and groundwater protection: resources and strategies for state and local management. Freshwater Foundation, 1989. 416 pp. Proceedings of a 1988 conference. Perspectives of government agencies and farmers; information sources and systems, including information programs of federal agencies; funding initiatives at the state level.

636. Agricultural chemicals and groundwater protection: emerging management and policy. Freshwater Foundation, 1988. 235 pp. Proceedings of a 1987 conference on more effective management and regulatory strategies and policies. Papers on agrichemical use; federal, state, and local policies and initiatives; perspectives from industry and farmers; management case studies.

637. Canter, Larry W.; Knox, Robert C. **Ground water pollution control.** Lewis, 1985. 526 pp. Three-part text discusses alternative technologies developed in response to public pressure and government incentives, decision-making techniques in selecting appropriate measures, and case studies and applications.

638. Canter, Larry W.; Knox, Robert C.; Fairchild, Deborah M. **Ground water quality protection.** Lewis,

1987. 562 pp., ill., bibl., index. Describes pollution sources and their evaluation, pollution control and cleanup, and water quality management. Includes chapter on groundwater information sources.

639. Groundwater contamination. National Academy Press, 1984. 179 pp., ill., bibl. Prepared by the National Research Council. Extent of groundwater contamination in the United States; processes by which contaminants move in groundwater; case study examples of nonpoint source contamination and hydrogeochemical studies at a landfill; risk assessment for contamination prevention; federal and state regulatory responsibilities.

640. Guswa, J. H.; and others. **Groundwater contamination and emergency response guide.** Noyes, Pollution technology review, v. 111, 1984. 490 pp., ill., bibl. Reviews groundwater hydrology, equipment, methods, and field techniques for identifying and responding to groundwater pollution incidents.

641. Princeton University Water Resources Program. **Groundwater contamination from hazardous wastes.** Prentice-Hall, 1984. 163 pp., ill., bibl., index. Introductory text explains mechanisms; evaluation and analysis of groundwater contamination; and siting of hazardous waste sites. Includes case studies.

642. Patrick, Ruth; Ford, Emily; Quarles, John. **Groundwater contamination in the United States.** University of Pennsylvania Press, 1987. 513 pp., ill., bibl., index. Characteristics of groundwater and its contamination; classification of aquifers; specific contaminants and their effects on human health; extent of contamination in 19 states; proposed and actual strategies for preventing and controlling contamination at federal, state, and local levels.

643. Rail, Chester D. **Groundwater contamination: sources, control, and preventive measures.** Technomic, 1989. 139 pp., ill., bibl. Describes specific contaminants and methods of control: microorganisms, liquid waste disposal systems, solid wastes, municipal and industrial wastes, disposal and injection wells, underground tanks and pipelines, saltwater intrusion, and surface spills.

644. Everett, Lorne G. **Groundwater monitoring: guidelines and methodology for developing and implementing a ground water quality monitoring program.** Genium Pub. Corp., 1987. 440 pp., ill., bibl. Groundwater monitoring within the context of a cost-effective resource allocation strategy. Describes four basic types of monitoring that address separate regulatory objectives; outlines specific methodologies; reviews groundwater data management concepts; discusses the monitoring of disposal wells.

645. Bitton, Gabriel; Gerba, Charles P.; eds. **Groundwater pollution microbiology.** Wiley, Environmental science and technology, 1984. 377 pp., ill., bibl., index. Fourteen papers deal with groundwater hydrology, pollution sources, health aspects, land disposal of sewage effluents and residues, microbial sampling, and relevant U.S. federal legislation.

646. Bar-Yosef, B.; Barrow, N. J.; Goldshmid, Y.; eds. **Inorganic contaminants in the vadose zone.** Springer-Verlag, Ecological studies, v. 74, 1989. 198 pp., ill. Papers from a 1987 conference grouped into four categories: processes and principles of pollutant behaviour in reactive porous media; behavior of specific elements; management of inorganic pollutants; case studies.

647. Page, G. William; ed. **Planning for groundwater protection.** Academic Press, 1987. 387 pp., ill., bibl., index. Reviews hydrogeologic background and institutional framework. Discusses drinking water and health; technical approaches to removing contamination; and local planning needs. Presents eight case studies from the United States.

648. Sierra Club Legal Defense Fund; Jorgensen, Eric P.; ed. **The poisoned well: new strategies for groundwater protection.** Island Press, 1989. 422 pp., ill., bibl., index. Basic information on groundwater: its processes, contamination, testing, and health effects of contamination. Explanation of federal laws and regulations. Detailed advice on how citizens can act to enforce compliance. Project of the Sierra Club Legal Defense Fund.

649. Yaron, B.; Dagan, G.; Goldshmid, J.; eds. **Pollutants in porous media: the unsaturated zone between soil surface and groundwater.** Springer-Verlag, Ecological studies, v. 47, 1984. 296 pp., ill., bibl., index. Contributed papers provide models and case studies in the following areas: behavior of organic compounds and inorganic chemicals; biological processes; pollution sources and control mechanisms in the unsaturated zone and in groundwater; modeling of pollutant transport.

650. Gerstl, Z.; and others, eds. **Toxic organic chemicals in porous media.** Springer-Verlag, Ecological studies, v. 73, 1989. 343 pp. Contains papers from a 1987 workshop, arranged in five parts: overview of groundwater pollution and hazards from toxic organic chemicals; physicochemical and biological interactions of agrichemicals; pesticides in porous media (mobility, availability, sorption, transport, degradation); petroleum hydrocarbons (transport, behavior, biochemical aspects); and restoration of the unsaturated zone and groundwater.

Marine Pollution (651–665)

651. Vernberg, F. John; and others, eds. **Biological monitoring of marine pollutants.** Academic Press, 1981. 559 pp., ill., bibl., index. Papers from a 1979 symposium present the results of applying laboratory techniques to field studies. Covers the effects of synthetic organics, heavy metals, and petroleum hydrocarbons on various indicator species like grass shrimp, barnacle larvae, mussels, and microalgae. Also discusses physiological monitoring.

652. Landner, Lars. **Chemicals in the aquatic environment: advanced hazard assessment.** Springer-Verlag, Springer series on environmental management, 1989. 415 pp., ill., bibl., index. Argues that standardized, short-term laboratory tests are insufficient for hazard assessment. Advocates community testing, microcosm, and mesocosm experiments. Emphasizes interpretation of ecotoxicological data in actual contexts, incorporating data on natural mortality distribution, the roles of keystone species, species with broad niches, and species with highly specialized niches. Uses ecological gradients in the Baltic Sea as background example.

653. Michaelis, W.; ed. **Estuarine water quality management: monitoring, modelling, and research.** Springer-Verlag, Coastal and estuarine studies, v. 36, 1990. 478 pp., ill., index. Proceedings of a 1989 symposium. Mostly European case studies address water dynamics and transport processes, sediment-water interaction, biological processes, and water chemistry.

654. Champ, Michael A.; Park, P. Kilho. **Global marine pollution bibliography: ocean dumping of municipal and industrial waste.** Information for Industry; Plenum Press, 1982. 399 pp., indexes. Seventeen hundred citations cover the following topics: municipal and industrial wastes; legislation and regulation at the international level; site selection studies and ocean dumping criteria; waste management strategies; biological, chemical, geological, and physical processes involved in dumping; engineering studies. Also covers dump sites by countries and regions. Over half of the references include abstracts.

655. MAP technical report series. United Nations Environment Programme, Mediterranean Action Plan, 1986 to date. Several reports (50 to 400 pages) issued annually cover all aspects of marine pollution and coastal zone mangement issues in the Mediterranean.

656. Clark, R. B. **Marine pollution.** Clarendon Press, 1989. 220 pp., ill., bibl., index. Describes the nature and effects of many pollutants, including sewage, oil, metals, halogenated hydrocarbons, radioactive materials, solid wastes, and heat. Discusses pollutant impacts on marine organisms and ecosystems, commercial fisheries, and human health; includes case studies of several seas.

657. Marine pollution bulletin. Pergamon Press, 1970 to date. Biweekly. International journal for marine environmentalists, scientists, engineers, administrators, politicians, and lawyers. Research reports, news, notes, and related editorial matter on marine pollution and the management and productivity of estuaries, seas, and oceans.

658. Gerlach, Sebastian A. **Marine pollution: diagnosis and therapy.** Springer-Verlag, rev. translation of Meeresverschmutzung, 1981. 218 pp., ill., bibl., index. Reviews types of domestic and industrial effluents, including pollution from ships, oil spills, waste heat, and radioactivity. Examines heavy metals and chlorinated hydrocarbons. Recommends solutions and strategies.

659. Seeliger, U.; de Lacerda, L. D.; Patchineelam, S. R.; eds. **Metals in coastal environments of Latin America.** Springer-Verlag, 1988. 297 pp., ill., bibl. Papers from a 1986 conference include surveys, metals in sediment and biota, metal transport and cycles, and monitoring.

660. Carpenter, Edward J.; Capone, Douglas G.; eds. **Nitrogen in the marine environment.** Academic Press, 1983. 900 pp., ill., bibl., index. Examines nitrogen in marine systems in terms of distribution; processes (fixation, nitrification, denitrification, uptake, metabolism, excretion, and regeneration); systems (cycling, upwelling, and symbioses); and methods of analysis. Incorporates international research results from the late 1970s and early 1980s.

661. Fisher, Diane; and others. **Polluted coastal waters: the role of acid rain.** Environmental Defense Fund, 1988. 102 pp., maps, ill., bibl. Analyzes role of acid rain in nitrogen loading of East Coast waters, focusing on Chesapeake Bay. Recommends state and federal action to reduce nitrogen oxide emission.

662. Head, P. C.; ed. **Practical estuarine chemistry; a handbook.** Cambridge University Press, Estuarine and Brackish-water Sciences Association handbooks, 1985. 337 pp., ill., bibl., index. Introduces techniques for collection and interpretation of chemical data from estuaries. Includes survey strategy, equipment for obtaining water samples, methods for measuring dissolved and particulate substances, role of specification electrodes in estuarine analysis, and methods of presenting and interpreting data.

663. Okaichi, Tomotoshi; Anderson, Donald M.; Nemoto, Takahish; eds. **Red tides: biology, environmental science, and toxicology.** Elsevier, 1989. 489 pp., ill., bibl., index. Proceedings of a 1987 international symposium. Over 100 papers on red tide in different regions and on the biology, biochemistry, toxicology, and environmental effects of red tide.

664. Giam, C. S.; Dou, H. J-M.; eds. **Strategies and advanced techniques for marine pollution studies: Mediterranean Sea.** Springer-Verlag, NATO ASI series, Series G, Ecological sciences, v. 9, 1986. 475 pp., ill., bibl., index. Proceedings of a 1984 NATO Advanced Study Institute. Presents chemical and biological approaches for marine pollution assessment.

665. Wastes in marine environments. Hemisphere, 1987. 313 pp., maps, ill., bibl., index. Over 700 references on industrial, municipal, and other wastes and their effects and management. Summarizes key legislation and regulatory relationships.

Section 4

LAND. TERRESTRIAL ENVIRONMENT

In the organizational scheme of this bibliography, a section was wanted that grouped together land and terrestrial systems so as to provide a foundation for the sections following on plants, trees, and animals. Section 4 is the result. It brings together publications in which land is considered as much for its intrinsic qualities and ecological functions as it is for its socioeconomic values.

The many facets of "land" have been grouped into four categories. The sequence proceeds from the basics of wild land to the emerging science of landscape ecology, to ecosystems by type and region, to soils, and finally to land degradation.

Lands. Reserves and Parks. Management

This opening miscellany contains works on land other than agricultural land or the built environment, including countryside, wilderness, parks, and reserves. Selections emphasize publications dealing with methods of evaluation, inventory, and management and the concept of landscape.

See also:

- Section 1: Global resources and environment; environmental management
- Section 5: Endangered plants, genetic resources; crops, cropping systems; landscaping, horticulture, gardening
- Section 6: Forests and forest resources: regions and countries; forest management, silviculture
- Section 7: Wildlife management; endangered species, conservation biology
- Section 8: Society and environment; social and human ecology, population; rural communities; leisure and recreation
- Section 9: Nature writing and thought, arts
- Section 10: U.S. executive agencies, administration and regulation; natural resources: United States; forests, parks, wilderness: United States; land preservation, trusts, state parks
- Section 11: Economy, costs and benefits, valuation; natural resource industries; agriculture and forest products
- Section 13: Civil engineering, construction, geotechnology

Landscape Ecology
Emerging in the 1980s, the study of landscape ecology comprehends all of the social and bio-physical processes affecting land and gives a conceptual basis for the study of land areas.

See also:

- Section 1: Geology, earth sciences; biological systems; ecology
- Section 5: Food and agriculture; crops, cropping systems; landscaping, horticulture, gardening
- Section 6: Forests and forest resources: regions and countries; forest management, silviculture
- Section 8: Social and human ecology, population
- Section 9: Nature writing and thought, arts; built environment, architecture, historical preservation

Land: Countries and Regions; North American Region; Terrestrial Ecosystems. In these three subgroups under landscape ecology are publications on the biophysical characteristics of particular land areas. Land is subdivided by geographic region or country and by type of ecosystem. These categories overlap considerably; sometimes a region and an ecosystem are almost the same. In general, those grouped by country will contain some social and economic information.

See also:

- Section 1: Global resources and environment; chemistry, biogeochemical cycles, pollutants
- Section 3: Freshwater biology and ecology
- Section 5: Plant ecology
- Section 6: Forest ecology, ecosystems
- Section 7: Animal ecology, species
- Section 8: Society and environment: country studies; social and human ecology, population
- Section 10: National laws and policies
- Section 14: Modeling and simulation

Soils
The basics of soils are presented in this group, which has entries on soil classification, surveys, erosion and sedimentation processes, testing and analysis, capability, and overall resources. Agricultural soils are discussed in Section 5; forest soils in Section 6.

See also:

- Section 1: Chemistry, biogeochemical cycles, pollutants; geology, earth sciences
- Section 3: Water: physical aspects, hydrology
- Section 5: Food and agriculture; crops, cropping systems; soil and water relations
- Section 6: Trees, forests, forestry; air, soil, and water relations, pollution
- Section 11: Natural resource industries; agriculture and forest products
- Section 13: Civil engineering, construction, geotechnology
- Section 14: Modeling and simulation; testing and analysis

Land Degradation. Erosion. Reclamation
Included here are entries on bioengineering, waste disposal on land, restoration and reclamation, and soil erosion.

See also:

- Section 1: Chemistry, biogeochemical cycles, pollutants; geology, earth sciences
- Section 5: Plants, agriculture; soil and water relations
- Section 6: Trees, forests, forestry; air, soil and water relations, pollution
- Section 13: Civil engineering, construction, geotechnology; solid waste, recycling; hazardous wastes

LAND. TERRESTRIAL ENVIRONMENT (666–885)

Lands. Reserves and Parks. Management (666–691)

666. World Conservation Monitoring Centre, IUCN Commission on National Parks and Protected Areas. **1990 United nations list of parks and protected areas.** International Union for Conservation of Nature and Natural Resources, 1990. 284 pp., maps. Includes World Heritage sites, biosphere reserves, and internationally significant wetlands.

667. Walters, Carl J. **Adaptive management of renewable resources.** Macmillan, Biological resource management series, 1986. 374 pp., ill., bibl., index. Proposes that dealing with uncertainty in management requires adaptive, experimental policies; provides mathematical techniques for developing policy. Includes problem sets.

668. Alternative strategies for desert development and management. Pergamon Press, Environmental sciences and applications, 3, 1982. Maps, ill. 4 vols. Proceedings of an international conference held in 1977. One hundred twenty-five papers present case studies of desert development opportunities worldwide, from social, economic, and technological perspectives. Some topics: energy; minerals; mining and industrial treatment; irrigation; botanical and fisheries resources; water quality, law, and planning; desalinization; waste disposal; tourism; and erosion control and water replenishment practices.

669. Lund, H. Glyde; and others, technical coordinators. **Arid land resource inventories: developing cost-efficient methods.** U.S. Department of Agriculture, Forest Service, General technical report, no. WO–28, 1981. 620 pp., maps, ill., bibl., index. Papers cover arid land characteristics and uses, information needs, inventory problems and planning, land classification, remote sensing, sampling schemes, resource measurement techniques, and data analysis systems. In Spanish and English.

670. Rogers, Garry F.; Malde, Harold E.; Turner, Raymond M. **Bibliography of repeat photography for evaluating landscape change.** University of Utah Press, 1984. 179 pp., ill., bibl. Over 450 entries, mostly English-language publications focusing on the western United States. Annotations provide information on subject of the cited report, location, number of photographs, and dates and time span. Includes introduction on methods, purposes, and reliability of repeat photography.

671. Conserving the natural heritage of Latin America and the Caribbean: the planning and management of protected areas in the neotropical realm. International Union for Conservation of Nature and Natural Resources, 1981. 329 pp., maps, bibl. Papers from a 1981 working session, in Spanish and English, on new concepts of protected area management, monitoring protected areas of the neotropics, developing management capacity, and international support for management.

672. McHarg, Ian L. **Design with nature.** Doubleday; Natural History Press, 1969. 197 pp., ill. The influential classic of landscape architecture and planning on ecological principles. Shows in text and illustrations the intrinsic suitability of land and water areas for certain land uses.

673. Edington, John M.; Edington, M. Ann. **Ecology, recreation, and tourism.** Cambridge University Press, 1986. 200 pp., ill., bibl., index. Discusses the reciprocal impact of recreation and tourism on the environment, particularly in cases of unwise natural resource use. Topics include wildlife observation, hunting and fishing, the enjoyment of scenery, disease hazards, insect nuisances, hazards from larger animals, and the environmental effects of tourist support facilities (roads, railways, garbage, and sewage).

674. Agee, James K.; Johnson, Darryll R.; eds. **Ecosystem management for parks and wilderness.** University of Washington Press, Institute of Forest Resources contribution, no. 65, 1988. 237 pp. Papers cover a wide range of topics, including laws governing park and wilderness lands, paleological records of climate variations and vegetation change, the relationship of succession and natural disturbance to preservation, managing ecosystems for large populations of vertebrates and large carnivores, air pollution, lake acidification, the role of economics, and management challenges in Yellowstone National Park.

675. Evaluacion de tierras y recursos para la planeacion nacional en las zonas tropicales: Land and resource evaluation for national planning in the tropics. U.S. Department of Agriculture, Forest Service, General technical report, no. WO–39, 1987. 524 pp., maps, ill., bibl. Proceedings of a 1988 international conference and workshop. Topics include defining resource information needs, resource inventory, analysis and plan development, implementation, monitoring and assessment.

676. Savory, Allan. **Holistic resource management.**

Island Press, 1988. 564 pp., ill., bibl., index. The author's extensive experience as a rancher and farmer in the United States and South Africa informs this comprehensive guide to holistic management. Offers specific practical instructions and numerous case studies.

677. Brann, Thomas B.; House, Louis O.; Lund, H. Gyde; eds. **In-place resource inventories: principles & practices.** Society of American Foresters, 1982. 1101 pp., maps, ill., bibl. Proceedings of a 1981 workshop. Reviews methods of producing reliable inventories and maps of resources. Covers remote sensing, classification, inventory standardization, and analytic and information management systems.

678. Lal, R.; Sanchez, P.A.; Cummings, R. W., Jr.; eds. **Land clearing and development in the tropics.** Balkema, 1986. 450 pp., ill., bibl., index. Papers of a 1982 international conference cover land development criteria, land-clearing techniques, ecosystem impacts of land clearing, soil management, and socioeconomic issues.

679. Davidson, Donald A.; ed. **Land evaluation.** Van Nostrand Reinhold, Van Nostrand Reinhold soil science series, 1986. 373 pp., ill., index. Covers ecological, terrain, and land capability approaches. Presents computer-based and other techniques.

680. Little, Peter D.; Horowitz, Michael M. **Lands at risk in the Third World: local-level perspectives.** Westview Press, 1987. 430 pp., bibl., index. Areas covered include arid and semiarid rangelands, tropical rain forests, mountain slopes, tropical river basins, and coastal lowlands. Focuses on two questions: how to identify land degradation processes and how to separate the human role from that of climate and other factors.

681. Landscape journal. University of Wisconsin Press, 1981 to date. Semiannual. Publishes research and technical information related to the design, planning, and management of land.

682. Mackinnon, J.; and others, compilers. **Managing protected areas in the tropics.** International Union for Conservation of Nature and Natural Resources, 1986. 295 pp., ill., bibl., index. Papers from a 1982 workshop discuss the basis for establishing protected areas, and managing and gaining support for them. Also covers selection, legislation, administration, planning, and evaluation of management. Intended for senior management level.

683. Carpenter, Richard A.; ed. **Natural systems for development: what planners need to know.** Collier Macmillan, 1983. 485 pp., ill., bibl., index. Serves as a self-teaching manual on implementing development

with conservation. Topics include conservation of species and habitats, watershed protection, erosion, soil salinization, coastal ecosystems, urban air pollution, water pollution, pest control, and others.

684. Parks: the international magazine dedicated to the protected areas of the world. Science and Technology Letters; Science Reviews, 1990 to date. 3 issues/yr. Published in association with IUCN's Commission on National Parks and Protected Areas. Discusses management and planning techniques for protected areas worldwide, particularly in developing countries. Addresses natural, historical, and cultural aspects of park protection and use.

685. Roberts, R. D.; Roberts T. M. **Planning and ecology.** Chapman and Hall, 1984. 464 pp., ill., bibl., index. Twenty-nine papers by ecologists, planners, and industry representatives attempt to identify planning procedures and ecological methods to better integrate the two fields. Some topics include baseline surveys, impact assessment methods and models, ecological considerations in rural planning and regional land use policy, and postproject environmental monitoring. Most case studies from the United Kingdom.

686. Oderwald, Richard G.; Burkhart, Harold E.; Burk, Thomas E.; eds. **Proceedings: use of auxiliary information in natural resource inventories.** Society of American Foresters, Society of American Foresters publication, no. SAF 86–01, 1986. 170 pp., ill., bibl. Proceedings of a 1985 meeting. Topics include the source and quality of auxiliary information, use of information from previous surveys, concurrent surveys, and Landsat and aerial photographs.

687. Conant, Francis; and others, eds. **Resource inventory & baseline study methods for developing countries.** American Association for the Advancement of Science, AAAS publication, no. 83–3, 1983. 539 pp., ill., bibl., index. Explains current methodologies for renewable resource inventories and environmental baseline surveys in order to assist planners with the resource conservation and environmental aspects of development assistance programs.

688. Machlis, Gary E.; Tichnell, David L. **The state of the world's parks: an international assessment for resource management, policy, and research.** Westview Press, 1985. 131 pp., bibl., index. Interdisciplinary examination of the threats to the world's parks, based on data collected from a representative sample. Proposes potential solutions to problems facing park managers.

689. Myers, Wayne L.; Shelton, Ronald L. **Survey methods for ecosystem management.** Wiley, 1980. 403

pp., ill., bibl., index. Describes nature and use of surveys of topography, soils, geology, radiant energy, air, water, weather, vegetation, and human influence. Appendix reviews descriptive statistics and sampling.

690. Hendee, John C.; Stankey, George H.; Lucas, Robert C. **Wilderness management.** International Wilderness Leadership Foundation, 1990. 546 pp., maps, ill., index. Reviews history, philosophy, principles, and international concepts of wilderness management. Addresses wildlife, fires, impact of recreational uses, and trends in use and users.

691. Hammitt, William E.; Cole, David N. **Wildland recreation: ecology and management.** Wiley, 1987. 341 pp., ill., bibl., index. Concerns strategies and methods for managing ecological resource problems resulting from recreational use of wildland areas. Discusses impacts on soil, water, vegetation, and wildlife; and visitor use and user characteristics.

Landscape Ecology (692–705)

692. Zonneveld, I. S.; Forman, R. T. T.; eds. **Changing landscapes: an ecological perspective.** Springer-Verlag, 1990. 286 pp., ill. Surveys recent developments and concepts, demonstrating the effects of time and space on perceptions of ecosystem pattern and development and linking landscape ecology with traditional biological and geographic theories.

693. Herrmann, Raymond; Craig, Terri Bostedt; eds. **Conference on science in the national parks.** Colorado State University, 1987. Ill., bibl. 2 vols. Vol. 1: Plenary sessions. Vol. 2: Wildlife management and habits. Papers from a 1986 conference discuss the role of science in management and preservation of park resources. Includes both site-specific and global examples.

694. Bradshaw, A. D.; Goode, D. A.; Thorp, E.; eds. **Ecology and design in landscape.** Blackwell Scientific, 1986. 463 pp., ill., bibl., index. Twenty-fourth Symposium of the British Ecological Society, Manchester, 1983. Papers address the interface of ecology and landscape design from the perspective of all phases of management, from approaches and principles to administration, repair, and renewal. Considers a wide array of settings, including lakes and rivers, national parks, urban areas, and roadsides.

695. Forman, Richard T. T.; Godron, Michel. **Landscape ecology.** Wiley, 1986. 619 pp., ill., bibl., index. Provides basic overview, discussing landscape structure and dynamics, heterogeneity, and management.

696. Landscape ecology. SPB Academic, 1987 to date. Quarterly. Presents fundamental and applied research dealing with the structure and functioning of landscapes and the relationships of humans to them.

697. Naveh, Zeev; Lieberman, Arthur S. **Landscape ecology: theory and application.** Springer-Verlag, Springer series on environmental management, 1984. 356 pp., ill., bibl., index. Explains development and conceptual foundations of this interdisciplinary human ecosystem science. Provides examples of tools and methods used in its application and case studies.

698. Turner, Monica Goigel; ed. **Landscape heterogeneity and disturbance.** Springer-Verlag, Ecological studies, v. 64, 1987. 239 pp., ill., bibl., index. Examines the connections between landscape pattern and disturbance. Discusses theoretical concepts and illustrates with case studies.

699. Hudson, Wendy E. **Landscape linkages and biodiversity.** Island Press, 1991. 214 pp., index. Explains the complexities and difficulties of conservation for biological diversity. Provides practical discussion of landscape preservation and creation of conservation corridors.

700. Landscape research. Landscape Research Group, 1976 to date. 3 issues/yr. Research reports, notes, and reviews on understanding landscapes; feature articles investigate and analyze aspects and interpretations of particular sites.

701. Park science; a resource management bulletin. U.S. Department of the Interior; National Park Service, 1980 to date. Quarterly. Continues: Pacific park science. Surveys recent and ongoing research in parks, explaining implications and potential consequences for park planning and management.

702. Tjallingii, S. P.; Veer, A. A. de; eds. **Perspectives in landscape ecology: contributions to research, planning and management of our environment.** Agricultural University of the Netherlands; Centre for Agricultural Publishing and Documentation, Wageningen, 1982. 344 pp., ill., bibl., index. Proceedings of an international congress in the Netherlands in 1981. Articles and discussions cover rural problems, urban-rural relations, and planning in natural areas. Sections are devoted also to review of theoretical concepts, methods, and applications.

703. Turner, Monica G.; Gardner, Robert H.; eds. **Quantitative methods in landscape ecology: the analysis and interpretation of landscape heterogeneity.** Springer-Verlag, Ecological studies, v. 82, 1990. 536 pp., ill., bibl., index. Posits a conceptual framework and possible applications for quantitative methods such as pattern analysis, spatial statistics, fractals, and extrapolation across scales.

704. Jordan, William R., III; Gilpin, Michael E.; Aber, John D.; eds. **Restoration ecology: a synthetic approach to ecological research.** Cambridge University Press, 1988. 342 pp., ill., bibl., index. Asserts that reassembling a community or ecosystem can be a true test of ecological understanding and a useful technique of basic research. Essays discuss experiences and problems in whole-field and partial restoration and explore research opportunities in restored, damaged, and artificial ecosystems.

705. Office of Technology Assessment, U.S. Congress. **Technologies to maintain biological diversity.** Government Printing Office, 1987. 334 pp., ill., bibl., index. Defines and explains the importance of biodiversity. Reviews technologies and techniques to maintain diversity of ecosystems and species. Assesses U.S. and international efforts and identifies options.

Land: Countries and Regions (706–742)

706. Lewis, Lawrence A.; Berry, L. **African environments and resources.** Allen & Unwin, 1988. 404 pp., bibl., index. Compiles information and data on Africa's physical and ecological features. Includes case studies in each ecosystem. Examines urbanization and historical climate changes.

707. Sioli, Harold; ed. **The Amazon: limnology and landscape ecology of a mighty tropical river and its basin.** Junk; Kluwer, Monographiae biologicae, v. 56, 1984. 763 pp., ill., bibl., index. Collection of papers on physical, chemical, meteorological, biological, and ecological aspects of the Amazon River and landscape.

708. Prance, Ghillean T.; Lovejoy, Thomas E.; eds. **Amazonia.** Pergamon Press, Key environments, 1985. 442 pp., ill., bibl., index. Contributed chapters discuss the physical features (soils, climate, nutrient cycling) and biological aspects (pollination, forest fishes, primates) of Amazonian ecology and examine the human impact (forestry, agriculture, overexploited and underused animals).

709. Laws, R. M. **Antarctic ecology.** Academic Press, 1984. Maps, ill., bibl., index. 2 vols. Vol. 1 addresses the terrestrial environment; plant biology; microbiology and invertebrates; introduced mammals; and inland waters. Vol. 2 reviews aspects and inhabitants of the marine environment, including flora, benthos, zooplank-

ton, fishes, seabirds, and mammals; discusses marine interaction and conservation.

710. Kerry, K. R.; Hempel, G.; eds. **Antarctic ecosystems: ecological change and conservation.** Springer-Verlag, 1990. 427 pp., ill., index. Examines both short- and long-term changes in ecosystems and communities, distinguishing between natural and human causes. Argues need for improved understanding to carry out monitoring and conservation efforts.

711. Walton, D. W. H.; ed. **Antarctic science.** Cambridge University Press, 1987. 280 pp., ill., bibl., index. Reviews the past 25 years of research in Antarctica, discussing the history and politics of exploration. Reviews the continent's geology, geography, atmosphere, ice dynamics, and ecology.

712. Bonner, W. N.; Walton, D. W. H.; ed. **Antarctica.** Pergamon Press, Key environments, 1985. 381 pp., ill., bibl., index. Describes the physical geography and environment, terrestrial and marine habitats, birds and mammals. Addresses issues of conservation and exploitation.

713. Smil, Vaclav. **The bad earth: environmental degradation in China.** Sharpe, 1984. 247 pp., ill., bibl., index. An overview of the environmental conflicts afflicting China, including deforestation, erosion, desertification, air and water pollution, and loss of species diversity.

714. Gupta, Raj Kumar. **Bibliography of the Himalayas.** Indian Documentation Service, 1981. 373 pp., bibl. Nearly 5000 entries; emphasizes works on plant resources and geology; also includes travel accounts, climate, animal resources, and human geography.

715. Stuart, Simon N.; Adams, Richard J.; eds. **Biodiversity in sub-Saharan Africa and its islands: conservation, management, and sustainable use.** International Union for Conservation of Nature and Natural Resources, 1990. 242 pp., maps, ill. Addresses political, economic, social, ecological, and biological problems. Proposes a strategy to stem the loss of biological diversity.

716. Hemming, John; ed. **Change in the Amazon Basin.** Manchester University Press, 1985. 2 vols. Papers from a 1982 symposium. Vol. 1: Man's impact on forests and rivers. Considers effects of large water projects, physical geographic aspects of change, indigenous use of forests, and other topics. Vol. 2: The frontier after a decade of colonisation. Examines results of Brazil's Programme on National Integration. Analyzes demographic change and problems of native peoples. Assesses government development agencies and presents case studies of frontier communities.

717. Janzen, Daniel H.; ed. **Costa Rican natural history.** University of Chicago Press, 1983. 816 pp., ill., bibl., index. Extensive introduction to climate, geology, soils, agriculture, plants, and animals. Includes checklists.

718. Komarov, Boris. **The destruction of nature in the Soviet Union.** Sharpe, 1980. 146 pp., bibl. A critique of Soviet mismanagement of resources and environmental pollution from the inside: a Soviet government official, writing under a pseudonym, reviews past and present abuses, and discusses the difficulty of environmental protection and improvement in a closed society.

719. Keast, Allen; ed. **Ecological biogeography of Australia.** Junk, Monographiae biologicae, v. 41, 1981. Maps, ill., bibl., index. 3 vols. Vol. 1 covers development of the Australian environment and its flora. Vol. 2 covers terrestrial invertebrates, inland fresh waters, and cold-blooded vertebrates. Vol. 3 covers warm-blooded vertebrates and the origins and ecology of aboriginals.

720. Booysen, P. de V.; Tainton, N. M.; eds. **Ecological effects of fire in South African ecosystems.** Springer-Verlag, Ecological studies, v. 48, 1984. 426 pp., maps, ill., bibl., index. Papers cover historical and current uses of fire; the nature and effects of fire in South Africa's five biomes; and fire's effects on vegetative structure and dynamics, forage production and quality, faunal composition and dynamics, soil and microclimate, and water yield.

721. Erskine, J. M. **Ecology and land usage in southern Africa: a survey of present day ties, problems and opportunities.** Africa Institute of South Africa, 1987. 60 pp., ill., bibl. Examines practices and problems of land use. Explains causes of land abuse, including the land tenure system, population pressures, and poor farming and grazing methods. Illustrates abuse with specific examples; stresses need for intraregional cooperation and suggests a framework.

722. Kitching, R. L.; ed. **Ecology of exotic animals and plants: some Australian case histories.** Wiley, 1986. 276 pp., maps, ill., bibl., index. Case studies of 13 Australian exotics, most classified as pests, including mosquito fish, cane toad, red fox, and rice weevil.

723. Whitten, Tony; Mustafa, Muslimin; Henderson, Gregory S. **The ecology of Sulawesi.** Gadjah Mada University Press, 1987. 777 pp., ill., bibl., index. Comprehensive study of the ecology of the Indonesian park. Gives detailed information about Sulawesi's seashores,

mountains, deep forests, and urban centers. Includes keys of selected plants and animals.

724. Goulding, Michael. **The fishes and the forest: explorations in Amazonian natural history.** University of California Press, 1980. 280 pp., ill., bibl., index. Examines the role of the Amazon floodplain forests as food supplier to fish; describes the features and feeding habits of over 50 commercial fishes; explains the benefits for the forest derived from the fishes' activities.

725. Perry, R.; ed. **Galapagos.** Pergamon Press, Key environments, 1984. 321 pp., ill., bibl., index. Contributed chapters discuss climate and geology; vegetation and threats to vegetation; animals and introduced species; and the contribution of the Galapagos Islands to science.

726. Geological and ecological studies of Qinghai-Xizang (Tibet) Plateau. Gordon & Breach, 1981. Maps, ill., bibl., index. 2 vols. Over 200 papers from a 1980 symposium based on research since the 1950s. Topics include the origin of the plateau, the features and development of its flora and fauna, and the evolution and differentiation of its geographic environments.

727. Le Houerou, Henry Noel. **The grazing land ecosystems of the African Sahel.** Springer-Verlag, Ecological studies, v. 75, 1989. 282 pp., ill., bibl. Describes the area's climate and geological features, flora and vegetation, wildlife, and livestock; discusses outlook for development; includes case study of the Ferlo region of northern Senegal.

728. International handbook of national parks and nature reserves. Greenwood Press, 1990. 539 pp. Brief history and administration of the parks and reserves systems of 34 countries, with descriptions of illustrative parks.

729. IUCN directory of Afrotropical protected areas. International Union for Conservation of Nature and Natural Resources, 1987. 1034 pp., maps, ill., bibl., index. Comprehensive directory of the parks, reserves and other protected areas of Africa and associated islands; provides information on countries' protected area systems and individual areas.

730. IUCN directory of neotropical protected areas. Tycooly International, 1982. 436 pp. Provides brief profiles of 350 protected areas, in English and Spanish. Includes information on protected areas systems of each country.

731. Tang, Xiyang. **Living treasures: an odyssey through China's extraordinary nature reserves.** Bantam Books; New World Press, 1987. 174 pp. Examines China's varied natural history and conservation agenda; focuses on 14 endangered species and the ambitious nature reserve program.

732. Jolly, Alison; Oberle, Philippe; Albignac, Roland; eds. **Madagascar.** Pergamon Press, Key environments, 1984. 239 pp., ill., bibl., index. Published in collaboration with the International Union for Conservation of Nature and Natural Resources. Contributed chapters by experts on the vegetation, flora, invertebrates, amphibians, reptiles, birds, mammals, insectivores, carnivores, and lemurs of Madagascar. Also discusses the interplay of economics and conservation; and lists Madagascar's nature reserves.

733. National Geographic research. National Geographic Society, 1985 to date. Quarterly. Interdisciplinary journal devoted to diffusing and increasing geographic knowledge. Publishes five to eight articles per issue, emphasizing disciplines in which fieldwork is fundamental. Also has shorter communications and letters.

734. Moss, Sanford A. **Natural history of the Antarctic Peninsula.** Columbia University Press, 1988. 208 pp., ill., index. Two chapters give thorough introduction to land and sea environments; text then discusses the high degree of specialization in various trophic relationships. Final chapter on the history and likely future problems of Antarctic politics.

735. Knystautas, Algirdas. **The natural history of the USSR.** McGraw-Hill, 1987. 224 pp., ill., bibl., index. Discusses geology, vegetation, and animal distribution in tundra, taiga, forests, mountains, steppes, deserts, and wetlands.

736. Bee, Ooi Jin; ed. **Natural resources in tropical countries.** Singapore University Press, 1983. 549 pp., ill., bibl., index. Papers from a 1981 workshop provide perspectives and information on minerals, energy, renewable resources, and resource management and development.

737. Chao, Sung-ch'iao. **Physical geography of China.** Wiley, 1986. 309 pp., maps, ill., bibl. Examines climate, geomorphological features, surface water and groundwater, soil geography, biogeography, and China's physical regionalization and land classification. Identifies the features and agricultural development potential of seven natural regions.

738. Clutton-Brock, T. H.; Ball, M. E.; eds. **Rhum: the natural history of an island.** Edinburgh University Press, Edinburgh island biology series, 1987. 159 pp., ill., bibl., index. A detailed account of the ecosystem of

one of Britain's largest nature reserves. Each chapter covers a separate aspect of Rhum, summarizing the research on its red deer, birds, and botany or describing features and history, including its volcanic and human history.

739. Cloudsley-Thompson, J. L.; ed. **Sahara desert.** Pergamon Press, Key environments, 1984. 348 pp., ill., bibl., index. Chapters by specialists on climates, geology, soils, flora and plant ecology, fauna, archaeology, and peoples of the Sahara.

740. Sinclair, A. R. E.; Norton-Griffiths, M.; eds. **Serengeti: dynamics of an ecosystem.** University of Chicago Press, 1979. 389 pp., ill., bibl., index. Synthesizes research from 1950s through 1970s on biology, soils, geology, and climate of the Serengeti. Discusses how grasslands respond to grazers; the dynamics, numbers, movement, feeding behavior, and social organization of grazing populations and predators; and interactions between herbivores and predators, and avian scavengers.

741. Forsyth, Adrian; Miyata, Kenneth. **Tropical nature.** Scribner, 1984. 248 pp., ill., bibl., index. Ecology of the lowland rain forests of Costa Rica and Ecuador for the general reader. Includes a list of suggested readings and a tropical travel guide.

742. Jolly, Alison. **A world like our own: man and nature in Madagascar.** Yale University Press, 1980. 272 pp., ill., bibl., index. Describes unique and common features of the island's rain forests, dry forests, spiny deserts, and prairies and the animals that live and have lived there. Discusses indigenous peoples and the challenges of conservation.

Land: North American Region (743–762)

743. Atlas of North America: Space Age portrait of a continent. National Geographic Society, 1985. 264 pp., maps, ill., bibl., index. Maps depict political boundaries; transportation lines; geological, climate, energy, and mineral features; and environmental stress points. Accompanying charts and text describe each region's history, features, flora, and fauna. Includes color satellite photographs.

744. Myers, Ronald L.; Ewel, John J.; eds. **Ecosystems of Florida.** University Presses of Florida, 1990. 728 pp., maps, ill., bibl., index. Thirty contributing authors describe the features and inhabitants of upland, freshwater wetland, aquatic, and coastal ecosystems. Discusses the structure and function of ecosystems and threats facing them. Examines prospects and strategies for conservation.

745. Wright, Henry A.; Bailey, Arthur W. **Fire ecology, United States and southern Canada.** Wiley, 1982. 501 pp., maps, ill., bibl., index. Intended to aid forest and range managers to use fire effectively as a management tool. Discusses temperature and heat effects, soil and water properties, small mammals, and prescribed burning. Reviews fire's effect on vegetation and many types of ecosystems.

746. Kirby, Ronald E.; Lewis, Stephen J.; Sexson, Terry N. **Fire in North American wetland ecosystem and fire-wildlife relations: an annotated bibliography.** U.S. Department of the Interior, Fish and Wildlife Service, Biological report, no. 88(1), 1988. 146 pp., ill., index. Three hundred nineteen citations provide specific research data, summaries of existing knowledge, and site-specific management advice for North America. Supplemental bibliography (942 citations) consists of all *Wildlife review* articles, 1935–1987, that mention wildlife management and ecology in the context of fire management, behavior, and effects.

747. Heyward, Patrica; Wright, R. Gerald; Krumpe, Edward E. **Glacier National Park Biosphere Reserve: a history of scientific study.** Wilderness Research Center; U.S. Department of the Interior, National Park Service, Cooperative Park Studies Unit, U.S. MAB report, no. 9, 1984. Bibl. 2 vols. Vol.1: A narrative description of scientific studies. Briefly synthesizes results of research on aquatic resources, vegetation, fire, fisheries resources, avian fauna, small and medium mammals, bear populations, ungulate species, air quality, climate, visitor studies, archaeology, soils, and geology. Vol. 2: Bibliography, subject annotations, tabular data summaries, and appendices. Appendices have checklists of flora and fauna and a summary of park collections.

748. Keiter, Robert B.; Boyce, Mark S.; eds. **The greater Yellowstone ecosystem: redefining America's wilderness heritage.** Yale University Press, 1991. 414 pp., maps, ill., index. Scientific, economic, and legal experts discuss proper resource management, reviewing the effects of the 1988 fires, elk and bison management, the restoration of wolves, and implications for the future.

749. **Isle Royale biosphere reserve.** U.S. Department of the Interior; National Park Service, Science Publications Office, U.S. MAB report, no. 11, 1985. Maps, bibl. 2 vols. Prepared by the Michigan Technological University, Department of Biological Sciences. Vol. 1 summarizes scientific studies on geology, soils, climate, vegetation, terrestrial fauna, aquatic systems, and disturbances. Vol. 2 is a bibliography of more than 500 scientific studies, published and unpublished.

750. Theberge, John B.; ed. **Legacy: the natural history of Ontario.** McClelland & Stewart, 1989. 397 pp., maps, ill. Presents the geography of Ontario and its geology, flora, and fauna; over 80 detailed maps and 200 full-color photographs.

751. Madsen, David; O'Connell, James F. **Man and environment in the Great Basin.** Society for American Archaeology, SAA papers, v. 2, 1982. 242 pp., ill., bibl., index. Collection of 13 papers provides a comprehensive synthesis of recent Great Basin archaeology, with a focus on the environmental framework for human development. Some topics include a history of Great Basin mammals during the past 15,000 years, models of climate, and five regional overviews of archaeology.

752. Forman, Richard T. T.; ed. **Pine Barrens: ecosystem and landscape.** Academic Press, 1979. 601 pp., ill., bibl., index. Forty-three contributors discuss the Pine Barrens of southern New Jersey as an ecosystem unto itself and as a complex mosaic of interconnected ecosystems. Sections cover people, geology and soils, climate and water, vegetation patterns, plants, and animals.

753. Chase, Alston. **Playing God in Yellowstone: the destruction of America's first national park.** Atlantic Monthly Press, 1986. 446 pp., bibl., index. Contends that Park Service policies and actions have avoided active park management, thus severely threatening the Yellowstone ecosystem.

754. Perry, John; Perry, Jane Greverus. **The Random House guide to natural areas of the eastern United States.** Random House, 1980. 835 pp., ill., maps, index. Describes 800 less-developed natural areas, including state and national parks, forests, and wildlife protection areas on the eastern seaboard, plus Vermont and West Virginia; specifies highway access, acreage, available recreation activities, and species (especially game species).

755. Bender, Gordon L.; ed. **Reference handbook on the deserts of North America.** Greenwood Press, 1982. 594 pp., maps, ill., bibl., indexes. Covers the Great Basin, the northern Great Basin Region, and the Mohave, Sonoran, Chihuahuan, and Arctic deserts. Includes chapters on plant and animal adaptations, riparian ecosystems, sand dunes, and research areas and facilities.

756. Beasley, Conger, Jr.; and others. **Sierra Club guides to the national parks of the Desert Southwest.** Random House, Sierra Club guides, 1984. 352 pp., ill., index. Presents the natural, geological and human history of 11 parks. Discusses plants and animals likely to be found there and provides photographs, trail guides, and facilities listings for each park.

757. Perry, Bill. **A Sierra Club naturalist's guide to**

the middle Atlantic Coast: Cape Hatteras to Cape Cod. Sierra Club Books, 1985. 470 pp., ill., bibl., index. Explains the geomorphology and ecology of barrier islands, estuaries, salt marshes, and eelgrass communities.

758. Berrill, Michael; Berrill, Deborah. **A Sierra Club naturalist's guide to the North Atlantic coast: Cape Cod to Newfoundland.** Sierra Club Books, 1981. 464 pp., ill., bibl., index. Provides an overview of the climate, geology, geography, tides, and currents; addresses in detail the region's ecology and specific plant and animal life; includes 140 drawings, maps, and photographs.

759. Tieszen, Larry L.; ed. **Vegetation and production ecology of the Alaskan arctic tundra.** Springer-Verlag, Ecological studies, v. 29, 1978. 686 pp., ill., bibl., index. Summarizes results of the U.S. Tundra Biome Program. Sections on floristics, vegetation and primary production; photosynthesis, respiration, and water relations; and growth, allocation and use of mineral and organic nutrients.

760. Groman, Hazel; and others, eds. **Wetlands of the Chesapeake: protecting the future of the Bay.** Environmental Law Institute, 1985. 389 pp. Proceedings of a conference held in 1985. Over 50 papers address nutrient retention and removal functions, agriculture and forestry, state and federal permitting, tax incentives, and more. Conclusions and recommendations for future research, management policies, and improved coordination.

761. Leopold, A. Starker. **Wild California: vanishing lands, vanishing wildlife.** University of California Press, 1985. 144 pp., ill. Large-format photographic essay; brief text describes history, ecology, and wildlife, from the deserts of southern California to the northern woods.

762. Baden, John A.; Leal, Donald; eds. **The Yellowstone primer: land and resource management in the Greater Yellowstone ecosystem.** Pacific Research Institute for Public Policy, 1990. 226 pp., bibl., index. Assesses management problems in private and public lands and suggests reforms to achieve environmental protection with planned economic growth. Cases examine difficulties of balancing human use with preservation, and discuss some of the politics involved in ecological reform.

Land: *Terrestrial Ecosystems (763–806)*

763. Sage, Bryan L. **The Arctic and its wildlife.** Facts on File, 1986. 190 pp., ill., bibl., index. Discusses topography, marine and terrestrial environments, plant and animal adaptations to Arctic life, flora, insects, breeding birds, and terrestrial and marine mammals.

764. Bruemmer, Fred. **The Arctic world.** Sierra Club Books, 1985. 256 pp., ill., index. Examines the animals, plants, and peoples of the Arctic; covers the history of exploration and resource use of the Arctic.

765. Goodall, D. W.; Perry, R. A.; eds. **Arid land ecosystems: structure, functioning and management.** Cambridge University Press, International Biological Programme, v. 16–17, 1979–1981. Bibl., index. 2 vols. Describes structure of arid ecosystems, excluding South America, analyzing climate, soils, geomorphology, and hydrology; considers the interactions of ecosystem components, specifically soil, plant, and animal processes. Discusses ecosystem modeling and human impacts.

766. Leatherman, Stephen P. **Barrier Island handbook.** U.S. Department of the Interior, National Park Service, Cooperative Research Unit; University of Massachusetts at Amherst, Environmental Institute, 1979. 101 pp., ill., bibl. Reviews barrier types and their formation, evolution and environments. Assesses the impact of recreational activities on sandy beaches, fore- and backdunes, and salt marshes. Explains methods used in failed attempts to stabilize barrier islands. Recommends development only if it is low density, low cost, and expendable.

767. Prance, Ghillean T.; ed. **Biological diversification in the tropics.** Columbia University Press, 1982. 714 pp., maps, bibl., index. Papers of a 1979 symposium examine and give evidence on the refuge theory of species distribution, focusing primarily on the tropical lowlands. Examples are given of plant, vertebrate, and invertebrate population distribution from prehistory to the present day.

768. Biotropica. Association for Tropical Biology, 1969 to date. Quarterly. Publishes original research and review papers on all aspects of tropical biology.

769. Larsen, James A. **The boreal ecosystem.** Academic Press, Physiological ecology, 1980. 500 pp., ill., bibl., index. Summarizes the history of vegetation and reviews climate and soil subsystems. Presents a broad view of boreal communities and specifics on plant communities, animal populations, nutrient cycling, and productivity. Discusses effects of resource management on boreal ecosystems.

770. Ewel, Katherine Carter; Odum, Howard T.; eds. **Cypress swamps.** University Presses of Florida, 1984. 472 pp., ill., bibl., index. Using the results of cypress wetland research and other swamp projects, the authors evaluate the symbiosis between humans and wetlands with respect to economy and ecosystems in order to determine the maximum vitality for both. Topics include ecological patterns in cypress swamps, effects of wastewater on cypress domes, and the structure and function of other swamps in eastern North America.

771. El-Baz, Farouk; ed. **Deserts and arid lands.** Nijhoff (dist. by Kluwer Boston), Remote sensing of earth resources and environment, v. 1, 1984. 222 pp., ill., bibl., index. Promotes and explains the use of aerial photography and remote sensing in desert study. Essays detail the classifications, physical features, and terrain types of semiarid, arid, and hyperarid terrains in North America, North Africa, Australia, China, India, and Arabia.

772. Tothill, J. C.; Mott, J. J.; eds. **Ecology and management of the world's savannas.** Australian Academy of Science, 1985. 384 pp., ill., maps. Sixty papers from a 1984 symposium on ecology and land use; topics include farming, pastoral use, mining and reserves, and maintaining productivity.

773. Hook, D. D.; and others. **The ecology and management of wetlands.** Croom Helm; Timber Press, 1988. Ill., bibl., index. 2 vols. Vol. 1: Ecology of wetlands. Vol. 2: Management, use, and value of wetlands. Proceedings of a 1986 symposium. Explains basic biology and ecology of wetland communities. Examines the valuation and use of wetlands systems. Applies these concepts to wetlands protection and management. Covers inventory and evaluation, restoration and regulation, and forestry and agricultural use.

774. Pomeroy, L. R.; Wiegert, R. G.; eds. **The ecology of a salt marsh.** Springer-Verlag, Ecological studies, v. 38, 1981. 271 pp., maps, ill., bibl., index. Synthesis of more than 25 years of research on Sapelo Island, Georgia. Discusses both the macrocommunity and the microbial community. Topics include the physical and chemical environment, primary production, aquatic macroconsumers, grazers on Spartina and their predators, aerobic microbes and meiofauna, anaerobic respiration and fermentation, and nitrogen and phosphorus cycles. Presents an overall model and review of results.

775. Louw, Gideon; Seely, Mary. **Ecology of desert organisms.** Longman, Tropical ecology series, 1982. 194 pp., maps, ill., bibl., index. Examines how organisms avoid the extremes of the environment and adapt their morphology, physiology, and behavior; chapters address reproduction, the structure and features of desert communities, and the effects of humans on the desert.

776. Huntley, B. J.; Walker, B. H.; eds. **Ecology of**

tropical savannas. Springer-Verlag, Ecological studies, v. 42, 1982. 669 pp., ill., bibl., index. Papers from a 1979 symposium on dynamic change in savanna ecosystems in South Africa discuss structure, determinants, function, and management.

777. Beaumont, Peter. **Environmental management and development in drylands.** Routledge, 1989. 505 pp., ill., index. Classifies human uses of drylands and gives detailed case studies of management, including dryland urban areas.

778. Goldammer, J. G.; ed. **Fire in the tropical biota: ecosystem processes and global challenges.** Springer-Verlag, Ecological studies, v. 84, 1990. 497 pp., ill., bibl., index. Papers from a 1989 symposium report on the impact of fires and burning biomass on global ecosystems and their processes.

779. Fire regimes and ecosystem properties. U.S. Department of Agriculture, Forest Service, General technical report, no. WO–26, 1981. 594 pp. Reviews the effects of fire on ecological systems and the importance of fire as a disturbance; notes the connection between decreasing fire frequency and increasing fire intensity; questions the scientific basis of management policies, particularly fire suppression.

780. Crum, Howard; Planisek, Sandra. **A focus on peatlands and peat mosses.** University of Michigan Press, 1988. 306 pp., ill., bibl., index. Describes the ecology of peatlands, covering peatland types and development, plant communities, nutrient cycling, ecophysiology of vascular plants and sphagnum, and the uses of peats; second half devoted to the structure and natural history of peat mosses.

781. Weller, Milton Webster. **Freshwater marshes: ecology and wildlife management.** University of Minnesota Press, Wildlife habitats, 2d ed., 1987. 150 pp., ill., bibl., index. General introduction to marsh ecosystems emphasizes wildlife; includes discussion of marsh management, restoration, and conservation.

782. Nabhan, Gary Paul. **Gathering the desert.** University of Arizona Press, 1985. 209 pp., ill., bibl., index. Part environmental philosophy, part ethnobotany and travelogue. Plea for preserving indigenous crops, ecosystems, and peoples of the Sonoran Desert. Illustrated with case studies of the symbolic and ecological uses of 12 edible wild species.

783. Evanari, Michael; Noy-Meir, Imanuel; Goodall, David W.; eds. **Hot deserts and arid shrublands.** Elsevier, Ecosystems of the world, v. 12A/B, 1985. Ill., bibl., index. 2 vols. Vol. 1 topics include formation of deserts, biogeography of flora, adaptations of plants and animals, structure and function of desert ecosystems, and deserts of America and Australia. Vol. 2 covers the deserts of Africa and Asia.

784. Williamson, Mark. **Island populations.** Oxford University Press, Oxford science publication, 1981. 286 pp., maps, bibl., index. Discusses the interplay between evolution and ecology. Background section reviews biology, geology, geography, and climatology; addresses species-area relationships and the strengths and weaknesses of several theories of species composition; covers microevolution, speciation, evolution on archipelagos, and the structure of island communities.

785. Chernov, Yu. I. **The living tundra.** Cambridge University Press, Studies in polar research, 1985. 213 pp., ill., bibl., index. Focusing on the Russian Arctic, covers the diversity of tundra landscapes; the role of temperature, humidity, and snow; adaptive strategies and distribution of tundra organisms; and interactions between organisms.

786. Kruger, F. J.; Mitchell, D. T.; Jarvis, J. U. M.; eds. **Mediterranean-type ecosystems: the role of nutrients.** Springer-Verlag, Ecological studies, v. 43, 1983. 552 pp., ill., bibl., index. Twenty-seven contributed papers divided into six sections cover the evolution and character of the ecosystems, plant forms and functions, nutrient cycling, plant nutrition, community patterns and diversity, and plant-animal interactions.

787. di Castri, Francesco; Goodall, David W.; Specht, Raymond; eds. **Mediterranean-type shrublands.** Elsevier, Ecosystems of the world, v. 11, 1981. 643 pp., ill., bibl., index. Discusses general physical environment, functional aspects of ecosystems, and human impacts; includes regional surveys of shrublands of each continent.

788. Gerrard, John. **Mountain environments: an examination of the physical geography of mountains.** MIT Press, 1990. 317 pp., ill., bibl., index. Drawing on research from the 1980s, chapters address weathering and mass movement, mountain hydrology and river processes, slope form and evolution, formation of mountains through glaciation and volcanism, and the interactions between biota, soil, climate, relief, and geology.

789. Mountain research and development. University of California Press, 1981 to date. Quarterly. Published for the International Mountain Society and United Nations University. Current research and case studies by authors working with mountain environments around the world, including problems of resource development and human welfare. Sections for news, notes, and reports of meetings.

790. Fuller, Margaret. **Mountains: a natural history and hiking guide.** Wiley, 1989. 255 pp. Explains the formation of mountains and the effects of erosion, heat, and water on them; discusses mountain environment and climate; describes the interdependent plants and animals that comprise mountain ecosystems and the classification of those ecosystems; includes practical information on equipment, food, and low-impact camping.

791. Price, Larry W. **Mountains and man: a study of process and environment.** University of California Press, 1981. 506 pp., maps, ill., bibl., index. Introduction to the processes and environment of high mountains; topics include climate, soils, vegetation, wildlife—especially arthropods—and agricultural settlement and land use.

792. Natural areas journal. Natural Areas Association, 1981 to date. Quarterly. Articles relating to research or management for natural areas, parks, rare species, and land preservation; theoretical approaches to natural areas work.

793. Kricher, John C. **A neotropical companion: an introduction to the animals, plants, and ecosystems of the New World tropics.** Princeton University Press, 1989. 436 pp., ill., bibl. Provides ecosystem overview, then details, of trees, plants, and animals. Comprehensive and balanced; details do not overwhelm the nonspecialist reader. Extensive bibliography.

794. Proceedings of the Conference on the Conservation of Wetlands of International Importance, especially as waterfowl habitat. Instituto Nazionale Di Biologia Della Selvaggina, Bologna, Supplement to Ricerche di Biologia della Selvaggina, v. 8, Nov. 1982, 1982. 1187 pp. Includes technical and legal reviews of the 1971 Wetlands (Ramsar) Convention, and summaries of national reports from over 25 countries; proposes criteria for selecting wetlands of international importance, and discusses wetland management; in Italian, English, and French.

795. Zlotin, Roman Isaevich; Khodashova, K. S. Lewus, William and Grant, W. E., trans. French, Norman R., trans. ed. **The role of animals in biological cycling of forest-steppe ecosystems.** Dowden, Hutchinson, & Ross (dist. by Academic Press), 1980. 221 pp., ill., bibl., index. Russian approach to ecosystem analysis; sections examine the features, influence, and impact of leaf-eating insects, herbivores, root eaters, and others; provides specific quantitative assessment of their effects on productivity and nutrient cycling.

796. Cole, Monica M. **The savannas: biogeography and geobotany.** Academic Press, 1986. 438 pp., maps, ill., bibl., index. Discusses the flora of savannas in South America, Africa, India, Southeast Asia, and Australia in detail; emphasizes the roles of geomorphology and climate factors in the formation of the savanna ecosystem.

797. West, Neil E.; ed. **Temperate deserts and semi-deserts.** Elsevier, Ecosystems of the world, v. 5, 1983. 522 pp., ill., bibl., index. Comprehensive treatment of the ecology and geology of 14 regions of Eurasia, North America, and South America.

798. Young, Steven B. **To the Arctic: an introduction to the Far Northern world.** Wiley, 1989. 354 pp., ill., bibl., indexes. Interdisciplinary account, emphasizing biology, by the director of the Center for Northern Studies. Many drawings and photographs.

799. Jordan, Carl F.; ed. **Tropical ecology.** Hutchinson Ross (dist. by Academic Press), Benchmark papers in ecology, v. 10, 1981. 356 pp., maps, ill., index. Takes as its premise that the distinguishing features of tropical ecosystems are their rich species diversity and higher process rates. Presents papers illustrating and influenced by these themes.

800. Pomeroy, D.E.; Service, M.W. **Tropical ecology.** Longman Scientific and Technical, 1986. 233 pp., ill., bibl., index. Provides information on climate, soils, vegetation, ecosystems, behavioral ecology, animal populations and their parameters, human ecology (including population increase and human impacts on ecosystems), and the scales of approach to ecology. Examples from African environments.

801. Boulière, Francois; ed. **Tropical savannas.** Elsevier, Ecosystems of the world, v. 13, 1983. 730 pp., ill., bibl., index. Comprehensive discussion of the physical environment of tropical savannas worldwide, including their vegetation, primary and secondary consumers (with emphasis on mammals), detritivores and decomposers, parasites and pathogens, dynamic change, and, to a limited extent, human impacts on them.

802. Risser, P. G.; and others. **The true prairie ecosystem.** Dowden, Hutchinson & Ross (dist. by Academic Press), US/IBP synthesis series, v. 16, 1981. 557 pp., maps, ill., bibl., index. An integrated approach to studying the true prairie, based on a site in northeastern Oklahoma; individual chapters cover producers, consumers, and decomposers; addresses origin, biota, and controlling variables (climate, soil) and reviews other types of North American grasslands.

803. Bliss, L. C.; Heal, O. W.; Moore, J. J.; eds. **Tundra ecosystems: a comparative analysis.** Cambridge University Press, International Biological Programme, v. 25, 1981. 813 pp., ill., bibl., index. Twenty-six articles discuss evolution of tundra: abiotic, floral, and faunal components; decomposition cycle; and the utilization and conservation of tundra.

804. Mitsch, William J.; Gosselink, James G. **Wetlands.** Van Nostrand Reinhold, 1986. 539 pp., ill., bibl., index. Comprehensive textbook on the science and management of coastal and inland wetland ecosystems, especially in North America. Discusses tidal salt- and freshwater marshes, mangrove wetlands, freshwater marshes, northern peatlands and bogs, southern deepwater swamps, and riparian wetlands. Covers hydrology, biogeochemistry, biological adaptations, and ecosystem development; also covers valuation, management, protection, and classification of wetlands.

805. **Wetlands.** Society of the Wetlands Scientists, 1981 to date. Quarterly. Publishes research on freshwater and estuarine wetlands. Topics include biology, ecology, hydrology, water chemistry, management, and regulations.

806. **Wetlands ecology and management.** SPB Academic, 1989 to date. Quarterly. Fundamental and applied aspects of freshwater, brackish-water, and marine wetlands. Covers pollution, conservation, management, biogeography, and floristic and faunistic analysis.

Soils (807–845)

807. **Advances in soil science.** Springer-Verlag, 1985 to date. Annual. Annual review of current research on soils (four to six papers per volume), with practical application to developed and developing agriculture. Examples of review topics are modeling of soil compaction, efficient drylands resource management systems, and behavior of herbicides in irrigated soils.

808. Campbell, I. B.; Claridge, G. G. C. **Antarctica: soils, weathering processes, and environment.** Elsevier, Developments in soil science, v. 16, 1987. 368 pp. Broad survey of Antarctic soils and glacial history.

809. Hillel, Daniel. **Applications of soil physics.** Academic Press, 1980. 385 pp., ill., bibl., index. Analyses of water movement and soil-water interactions: infiltration, surface runoff, internal drainage, flow distribution, groundwater drainage, evaporation, plant-water interactions, and water and energy balance. Also, individual chapters by experts on specialized topics: freezing, variability of soil properties, and solute transport.

810. Biology and fertility of soils. Springer Verlag, 1981 to date. Quarterly.

811. Landon, J. R. **Booker tropical soil manual: a handbook for soil survey and agricultural land evaluation in the tropics and subtropics.** Wiley, 2d ed., 1991. 474 pp. Paperback, updated edition of a leading reference work. Summarizes soil related methods and terminology to cover land evaluation; soil mapping, chemistry, physics, and salinity; and soil and land suitability. Clear guidelines for interpreting data in project planning, costing, and management.

812. Sposito, Garrison. **The chemistry of soils.** Oxford University Press, 1989. 277 pp., ill., bibl., index. Introduces soil constituents and processes, including electrochemical phenomenon, adsorption, and ion exchange. Also provides detailed applications of soil acidity, salinity, and fertility.

813. Fairbridge, Rhodes W.; Finkl, Charles W. Jr.; eds. **Encyclopedia of soil science. Part One: physics, chemistry, biology, fertility, and technology.** Dowden, Hutchinson & Ross (dist. by Academic Press), Encyclopedia of earth sciences, v. 12, 1979. 646 pp., ill., bibl., index. One hundred fifty entries by 100 authors from 20 countries. Preface indicates standard reference works and journals. Cross-references within text and to other volumes in the series.

814. **FAO soils bulletin.** Food and Agriculture Organization of the United Nations, 1965 to date. Irregular. Series of technical reports on land classification and survey techniques; particular soils; soil fertility, recycling, and fertilizer use; soil and water conservation; and soil degradation, salinity, and alkalinity.

815. Olson, Gerald W. **Field guide to soils and the environment: applications of soil surveys.** Chapman and Hall, 1984. 219 pp., ill., bibl. Comprehensive guide to soil survey interpretations; provides important information to those involved in environmental management. Includes useful soil survey techniques and leads the reader into field studies, lab work, and cartographic manipulations.

816. Hillel, Daniel. **Fundamentals of soil physics.** Academic Press, 1980. 413 pp., ill., bibl., index. Presents available knowledge on water movement in the unsaturated zone. Part 1: Characteristics of soils and properties of water. Part 2: Soil texture, particles, specific surface, and clays. Part 3: Water in the soil and the behavior of solutes. Part 4: Aeration and soil-air measurements. Part 5: Heat flow in soil and reaction of soil to compaction, consolidation, or other physical stress.

817. Boersma, L. L.; and others, eds. **Future developments in soil science research.** Soil Science Society of America, 1987. 537 pp., ill., bibl. Papers presented at a 1986 conference. Topics include soil physics, microbiology, biochemistry, fertility, genesis, morphology, and conservation.

818. **Glossary of soil science terms.** Soil Science Society of America, 1987. 44 pp. Contains 1350 acceptable terms, plus obsolete terms, tables on soil and phyllosilicates classification, guide for tillage terminology, and new terms for soil horizons and layers.

819. Frimmel, F. H.; Christman, R. F.; eds. **Humic substances and their role in the environment.** Wiley, Dahlem workshop reports, Life sciences research report, no. 41, 1988. 271 pp., maps, ill., bibl., index. Proceedings of a 1987 workshop. Topics include isolation of soil and aquatic humic substances, pathways of formation, structural hypotheses, and environmental reactions and functions of humic substances.

820. Journal of soil science. Blackwell Scientific, 1949 to date. Quarterly. Journal of the British Society of Soil Science. Publishes research on all aspects of soil science, soil properties, and soil chemistry and biology.

821. Head, K. H. **Manual of soil laboratory testing.** Wiley, 1980. Ill., bibl., index. 2 vols. Describes in detail equipment, methods, and practical applications of various tests for civil engineering purposes. Vol. 1 examines soil classifications and compaction tests; Vol. 2, permeability, shear strength, and compressibility tests.

822. Klute, A.; Page, A. L.; eds. **Methods of soil analysis.** American Society of Agronomy; Soil Science Society of America, Agronomy series, no. 9, 2d ed., 1982–1986. 2 vols. Ill., bibl., index. Part 1: Physical and mineralogical methods. Fifty chapters cover statistical subject matter, mineralogical methods and methods for evaluating soil matrix and structure, energy status of soil water, hydraulic conductivity and diffusivity, intake rate, and more. Part 2: Chemical and microbiological properties. Comprehensive, detailed handbook of 100 laboratory methods for characterizing chemical and microbiological qualities of soils.

823. Richards, B. N. **The microbiology of terrestrial ecosystems.** Longman Scientific & Technical; Wiley, 1987. 399 pp., ill., bibl., index. A systems approach to the interactions of soil microbes and plants. Designed as a textbook for undergraduate and graduate students.

824. Sillanpaa, Mikko. **Micronutrients and the nutrient status of soils: a global study.** Food and Agriculture Organization of the United Nations, FAO soils bulletin, no. 48, 1982. 444 pp., ill., bibl. Lists soil nutrient status of countries in Africa, the Near East, the Far East, Latin America, and Europe; explains common materials and methods used in study; discusses conclusions that micronutrient deficiencies are more widespread than is generally assumed.

825. Dixon, J. B.; Weed, S. B.; eds. **Minerals in soil environments.** Soil Science Society of America, Soil Science Society of America book series, v. 1, 2d ed., 1989. 1224 pp., ill., bibl., index. Reviews mineralogy, surface chemistry, mineral equilibrium, soil organic matter, and mineral occurrence. Two-thirds of book covers minerals in various chemical and structural groups. Includes discussion of titanium and zirconium minerals, as well as talc pyrophyllites, and zeolites.

826. Brady, Nyle C. **The nature and properties of soils.** Collier Macmillan, 10th ed., 1990. 621 pp., ill., bibl., index. Standard text. Covers physical, chemical, and biological properties; soil formation; classification and use; plant nutrients; and management of soils.

827. Broughton, W.J.; ed. **Nitrogen fixation.** Clarendon Press, 1981. 306 pp., ill, bibl., index. Contributed essays focus mostly on nitrogen fixation in natural ecosystems. Discusses microorganisms, root-nodule symbioses, environmental physiology, nitrogen fixation in aquatic and terrestrial environments.

828. Harrison, A. F.; Ineson, P.; Heal, O. W.; ed. **Nutrient cycling in terrestrial ecosystems: field methods, application and interpretation.** Elsevier, 1990. 454 pp., ill., bibl., index. Discusses methods of estimating nutrient levels and processes. Sections address inputs, losses, turnover, and uptake of nutrients; each section includes keynote and summary chapter.

829. Hillel, Daniel. **Out of the earth: civilization and the life of the soil.** Free Press, 1990. 321 pp., bibl., index. Interprets the history of civilization in the context of soil mismanagement. Analyzes current global problems, including dust bowls, saline seeps, deforestation, desertification, and pollution in historical perspective.

830. Szegi, J.; ed. **Proceedings of the 9th International Symposium on Soil Biology and Conservation of the Biosphere.** Akademiai Kiado; Stillman, 1987. 2 vols. Papers deal with nitrogen fixation and fertility, interactions between pesticides and soil organisms, the role of soil organisms in decomposition and the synthesis of organic matter, the relationships between higher plants and soil organisms, and fertilization's effects on soil biological processes.

831. Mulders, M. A. **Remote sensing in soil science.** Elsevier, Developments in soil science, v. 15, 1987.

379 pp., ill. Emphasizes applications to soil survey and landscape analysis. Topics include physical concepts of electromagnetic radiation; radiation emitted by minerals, leaves, soil materials, and plants; photographic and non-photographic techniques; image processing; basic image characteristics, aerial photography, and mapping; use of air photos, airborne line scanning, and space-borne scanning; and thermal and microwave radiation.

832. Soil biology and biochemistry. Pergamon Press, 1969 to date. Bimonthly. Leading journal for publication of research on soil biochemistry.

833. Paul, Eldor Alvin; Clark, F. E. **Soil microbiology and biochemistry.** Academic Press, 1989. 273 pp., ill., index. Explains nutrient cycling and fundamental soil processes through a process-oriented approach. Reviews carbon and nitrogen cycles and microbe-driven reactions involving sulfur, phosphorus, and metals.

834. Marshall, T. J.; Holmes, J. W. **Soil physics.** Cambridge University Press, 2d ed., 1988. 345 pp., ill., bibl., index. Examines soil-water relations. Covers deformation of soil, measurement of water content and potential, and use of isotopes and other tracers in groundwater studies.

835. Jenny, Hans. **The soil resource: origin and behavior.** Springer-Verlag, Ecological studies, v. 37, 1980. 377 pp., ill., bibl. Examines soil formation, reviewing water regimes of plants and soils, interactions of organic and inorganic particles, transformation of minerals to clay, and the creation of humus. Discusses soil variation, ecosystem classification, and the effects of such factors as time, original material, topography, and climate.

836. Soil science. Williams & Wilkins, 1916 to date. Monthly. Publishes original research on soil and soil-plant science.

837. Harpstead, Milo I.; Hole, Francis D.; Bennett, William. **Soil science simplified.** Iowa State University Press, 2d ed., 1988. 196 pp., ill., index. Presents the basics of soil science in nontechnical language. Explains and illustrates soil organisms, erosion, plant nutrition, and many soil processes.

838. Soil Science Society of America journal. Soil Science Society of America, 1936 to date. Bimonthly. Continues: Proceedings of the Soil Science Society of America. Publishes original research findings in all phases of soil science—soil physics, chemistry, microbiology, mineralogy, fertility, nutrition, classification, management, and soils of forest and rangeland.

839. Soil survey and land evaluation. Allen & Unwin, 1981 to date. 3 issues/yr. Publishes original research, review papers, technical notes, country reports, and editorial matter. Intended to link professionals involved in all aspects of soil surveys, land evaluation, land-use planners, engineers and designers, and other specialists.

840. Reybold, W. U.; Petersen, G. W.; eds. **Soil survey techniques.** Soil Science Society of America, SSSA special publications, no. 20, 1987. 98 pp., ill., bibl. Based on a 1985 symposium. Describes techniques making use of video image analysis, ground penetrating radar, microcomputers, digital elevation model data, and spectral data.

841. Brown, J. R.; ed. **Soil testing: sampling, correlation, calibration, and interpretation.** Soil Science Society of America, SSSA special publication, no. 21, 1987. 144 pp., ill., bibl. Papers from a 1985 symposium set forth basic principles of soil testing and report on progress of soil-testing research.

842. Soils and fertilizers. Commonwealth Agricultural Bureaux, 1938 to date. Monthly. Abstract journal covering the world literature.

843. Bouwman, A. F.; ed. **Soils and the greenhouse effect: the present status and future trends concerning the effects of soils and their cover on the fluxes of greenhouse gasses, the surface energy balance, and the water balance.** Wiley, 1990. 575 pp. Topics include geographic quantification of soil properties involved in fluxes of greenhouse gases; measurement of fluxes and extrapolation to smaller scales; remote sensing of land use; and regional estimation of evaporation and energy fluxes.

844. Glazovskaya, M. A. **Soils of the world.** Amerind, 1983. Maps, ill., bibl. 2 vols. Vol. I: Soil families and soil types. Vol. II: Soil geography. Presents theory of soil formation, description of principal soil families and types, and maps of distribution. Translated from the 1972 Russian edition.

845. Wetland soils: characterization, classification, and utilization. International Rice Research Institute, 1985. 559 pp., ill., bibl. Proceedings of a 1984 workshop; covers processes in wetland soils, fertility, taxonomy, and regional studies.

Land Degradation. Erosion. Reclamation (846–885)

846. Gray, Donald H.; Leiser, Andrew T. **Biotechnical slope protection and erosion control.** Van Nostrand Reinhold, 1982. 271 pp., maps, ill., bibl., index.

Reviews general principles and advantages of biotechnical slope protection systems, which combine structural-engineering and vegetative measures. Describes certain measures in detail, including contour wattling, brush layering, live staking, brush matting, plantings, and types of walls.

847. Salomons, W.; Foerstner, Ulrich; eds. **Chemistry and biology of solid waste: dredged material and mine tailings.** Springer-Verlag, 1988. 305 pp., aps., ill., bibl., index. Provides review of solution-solid interactions of metal, microbial processes, and behavior of vegetation, followed by in-depth studies of biological and chemical characteristics of mine tailings and dredged materials.

848. Overcash, Michael R.; ed. **Decomposition of toxic and nontoxic organic compounds in soils.** Ann Arbor Science, 1981. 455 pp. Translated articles taken from 30 non–English language journals covering several organic chemicals and their effects on the soil and the environment.

849. Biswas, Margaret R.; Biswas, Asit K.; eds. **Desertification: associated case studies prepared for the United Nations Conference on Desertification.** Pergamon Press, Environmental sciences and applications, v. 12, 1st, 1980. 523 pp., maps, ill., bibl. From a 1977 conference. Case studies focus on human causes of desertification and efforts to halt the process in six countries, including Israel, the USSR, the United States, and China.

850. Sears, Paul Bigelow. **Deserts on the march.** Island Press, Conservation classics, 1988. 241 pp., index. Classic work on desertification, published in 1935, during the Dust Bowl years. Reviews the history of deforestation and desertification worldwide and articulates basic principles of land use more sensitive to soil conservation.

851. Majumdar, Shyamal K.; Miller, E. Willard; Sage, Louis E.; eds. **Ecology and restoration of the Delaware River Basin.** Pennsylvania Academy of Science, 1988. 431 pp., maps, ill., index. Symposium papers give comprehensive account of biological, physical, and chemical characteristics and trends in the Delaware River basin. Also reviews contaminants, impacts, and restoration; management, legislative, and socioeconomic issues.

852. Webb, Robert H.; Wilshire, Howard G.; eds. **Environmental effects of off-road vehicles: impacts and management in arid regions.** Springer-Verlag, 1983. 534 pp., ill., bibl., index. Contributed papers assess physical and biological effects, rehabilitation potential, and management strategies. Presents case histories from Utah and southern Australia.

853. .Chadwick, M.J.; Highton, N.H.; Lindman, N.; eds. **Environmental impacts of coal mining and utilization.** Pergamon, rev. ed., 1987. 332 pp., ill., bibl., index. Revision of *Environmental implications of expanded coal utilization.*

854. Salomons, W; Foerstner, U.; eds. **Environmental management of solid waste: dredged material and mine tailings.** Springer-Verlag, 1988. 396 pp., ill., bibl., index. Examines the difficulties of aquatic versus terrestrial disposal. Discusses prediction of pollution effects and results of treatment. Reviews revegetation and restoration programs and recommends management strategies.

855. Berger, John J.; ed. **Environmental restoration: science and strategies for restoring the earth.** Island Press, 1990. 398 pp., ill., bibl., index. Results of four-day conference of restoration experts at University of California. Fifty-seven papers provide overview and site-specific case studies, representing current thinking of scientists and practitioners.

856. Goldman, Steven J.; Jackson, Katherine; Bursztynsky, Taras A. **Erosion and sediment control handbook.** McGraw-Hill, 1986. 375 pp., ill., bibl., index. Topics include evaluating a site's erosion potential and estimating soil loss and runoff volume; preparing and assessing erosion control plans; and low-cost techniques for trapping sediment and repairing common failure points in erosion control measures.

857. Hooke, J.M.; ed. **Geomorphology in environmental planning.** Wiley, British Geomorphological Research Group symposia series, 1988. 336 pp. Contributed papers discuss information needs and policy considerations involved in applying knowledge of geomorphological processes to a variety of contexts. Topics include soil erosion of lowlands, land stability, quarry restoration, river channelization, coastal protection, and upland afforestation.

858. Bender, F.; ed. **Geo-resources and environment.** Schweitzerbart'sche VerlagsBuchhandlung, 1986. 144 pp. Papers presented at a 1986 symposium review problems created by the exploitation of mineral resources in terms of soil and water, hazardous waste disposal, and regional policy and planning. Draws on research in Great Britain, Sweden, Norway, and Germany.

859. Sidle, Roy C.; Pearce, Andrew J.; O'Loughlin, Colin L. **Hillslope stability and land use.** American Geophysical Union, Water resources monograph series, v. 11, 1985. 140 pp., ill., bibl. Examines the major types of soil mass movement and their economic and environmental significance. Analyzes slope stability, influence of

natural forces, and effects of land management, with emphasis on logging, vegetation conversion, road construction, and mining.

860. Helms, Douglas; Flader, Susan L.; eds. **The history of soil and water conservation.** Agricultural History Society, 1985. 244 pp. Symposium papers focus on American experiences in soil and water conservation. Other topics include the anthropology of soil conservation (needs and culture of those being served), soil conservation in colonial Africa, and technical papers on soil erosion by wind and water.

861. Carlson, Claire L.; Swisher, James H.; eds. **Innovative approaches to mined land reclamation.** Southern Illinois University Press, 1987. 752 pp., ill., bibl., index. Proceedings of a 1986 conference. Papers on earthworks, soil reconstruction, and handling of overburden; acid water treatments; wetlands creation; and slope stability. Also addresses the use of waste products like municipal sludge and refuse, fly ash, and slurry in place of soil cover and the amelioration of such products for reclamation work.

862. Journal of soil and water conservation. Soil and Water Conservation Society, 1946 to date. Bimonthly. Feature articles and research reports on new techniques and research in soil conservation and on related agricultural programs.

863. Land degradation and rehabilitation. Wiley, 1989 to date. Quarterly. International journal concerned with the recognition, management, and rehabilitation of degraded land. Publishes research exploring processes, causes, perceptions, impacts, and avoidance of land degradation.

864. Chisholm, Anthony; Dumsday, Robert; eds. **Land degradation: problems and policies.** Cambridge University Press, 1988. 424 pp., ill., bibl., index. Twenty-nine experts from the physical, biological, and social sciences discuss a broad range of problems and suggest solutions.

865. Siderius, W.; ed. **Land evaluation for land-use planning and conservation in sloping areas.** International Institute for Land Reclamation and Improvement, ILRI publication, no. 40, 1986. 334 pp., ill., bibl. Proceedings of a 1984 international workshop. Topics include potential and limitations of the FAO Framework for Land Evaluation and erosion and conservation problems as a function of land characteristics.

866. Blunden, John. **Mineral resources and their management.** Longman, 1985. 302 pp., ill., bibl., index. Reviews the complex relationships between minerals, economic development, and environmental concern at local, regional, and international levels; discusses the impact of government mineral policy, taxation, and international financing on world mineral supply; and covers the utilization of mine and quarry wastes. Includes case histories of mining and environmental problems and solutions.

867. Harris, DeVerle P. **Mineral resources appraisal: mineral endowment, resources, and potential supply: concepts, methods, and cases.** Clarendon Press, Oxford science publications, Oxford geological sciences series, 1984. 445 pp., ill., bibl., index. Brings together models and approaches from economics, geology, statistics, and technology, explaining the concepts, assumptions, and mathematics of numerous methods of resource appraisal.

868. Kelly, Martyn. **Mining and the freshwater environment.** Elsevier, 1988. 231 pp. Assesses current knowledge, focusing on nickel, copper, zinc, and lead. Discusses the accumulation and toxicity of heavy metals in plants and animals in field and laboratory studies and the use of certain groups of organisms as pollution indicators. Also reviews acid mine drainage and placer gold mining.

869. Williams, R. Dean; Schuman, Gerald E.; eds. **Reclaiming mine soils and overburden in the western United States: analytic parameters and procedures.** Soil Conservation Society of America, 1987. 336 pp. Over 60 contributors provide a base collection of all soil-testing knowledge, detailing and evaluating methods and procedures, from electrical conductivity to particle size distribution.

870. Schaller, Frank W.; Sutton, P.; eds. **Reclamation of drastically disturbed lands.** American Society of Agronomy, 1978. 742 pp., ill., bibl., index. Proceedings of a symposium, with emphasis on North America. Covers reclamation techniques; characteristics and extent of disturbed lands; chemical, physical, and social factors in disturbance and reclamation; and legal aspects.

871. Hossner, Lloyd. **Reclamation of surface-mined lands.** CRC Press, 1988. 250 pp., ill., bibl., index. Contributed chapters discuss all phases and problems of reclamation, including chemical problems (salinity, infertility, toxic substances, and acidity) and physical problems (consolidated materials, compaction, and excessively sandy or clayey texture). Also discusses revegetation options, water quality evaluation and control, and the evaluation and management implications of spatial variability.

872. Allen, Edith B.; ed. **The reconstruction of disturbed arid lands: an ecological approach.** Westview Press, 288 pp. Contributed chapters on the problems and principles of reconstruction of hot and cold deserts, grasslands, and shrublands affected by natural and artifical disturbances. Many perspectives represented, including physiology and population, community, and ecosystem ecology.

873. Cairns, John, Jr.; ed. **Rehabilitating damaged ecosystems.** CRC Press, 1988. Ill., bibl., index. 2 vols. Presents ecological, social, political, and economic considerations for developing cost-effective rehabilitation management practices for existing and potential problems. Many case studies, most from the United States, focus on abandoned mines, wetlands and salt marshes, plant stress, and Mount St. Helens.

874. Restoration & management notes. University of Wisconsin, Madison Arboretum, 1981 to date. Semi-annual. Articles on restoration strategies and experiences from ecologists, land reclamationists, park managers, naturalists, engineers, and landscape architects; also abstracts of proceedings from relevant conferences.

875. Bradshaw, Anthony David; Chadwick, M. J. **The restoration of land: the ecology and reclamation of derelict and degraded land.** University of California Press, Studies in ecology, v. 6, 1980. 317 pp., ill., bibl., index. Theory and practice of many kinds of land restoration, including strip mines, quarries, and industrial waste and heavy metal sites. Also covers plant and soil interactions.

876. Troeh, Frederick R.; Hobbs, J. Arthur; Dohahue, Roy L. **Soil and water conservation for productivity and environmental protection.** Prentice-Hall, 1980. 718 pp., maps, ill., bibl., index. Twenty chapters cover water erosion and sedimentation, cropland drainage, soil and water pollution, cropping systems, tillage practices, and vegetation mining and construction sites.

877. Lal, R.; Stewart, B. A.; eds. **Soil degradation.** Springer-Verlag, Advances in soil science, v. 11, 1990. 345 pp., ill. Reviews the main processes of soil degradation in various ecological regions, assesses their effects on agricultural production, and suggests techniques for prevention and restoration.

878. El-Swaify, S.A.; Moldenhauer, W. C.; Lo, A.; eds. **Soil erosion and conservation.** Soil Conservation Society of America, 1985. 793 pp., ill., bibl., index. Reports from a 1983 international conference cover the magnitude and extent of erosion worldwide; the impacts, prediction, and control of soil erosion; and conservation programs.

879. Kral, David M.; Hawkins, Sherri; eds. **Soil erosion and conservation in the tropics: proceedings of**

a symposium. American Society of Agronomy; Soil Science Society of America, ASA special publication, no. 43, 1982. 149 pp., ill., bibl. Proceedings of a symposium. Covers available information on the erosion problem, its components and impacts, and experiences in planning and implementing conservation in tropical areas.

880. Morgan, R. P. C.; ed. **Soil erosion and its control.** Van Nostrand Reinhold, Van Nostrand Reinhold soil science series, 1986. 311 pp., ill., bibl., index. Contributors bring together basic and applied research. Chapters on defining erosion; the universal soil loss equation; field and laboratory methods; wind and water erosion; and policy and management suggestions.

881. Lal, R.; ed. **Soil erosion research methods.** Soil and Water Conservation Society, 1988. 244 pp. Proposes standardized methods to enable consistent and verifiable data collection and interpretation. Covers methodologies, design, models, monitoring methods, impact assessment, and wind erosion.

882. Tate, Robert L., III; Klein, Donald A. **Soil reclamation processes: microbiological analyses and applications.** Dekker, Books in soils and the environment, 1985. 349 pp., ill., bibl., index. Focuses on the roles of microbiology and biochemistry in reclamation and pre-

sents basic principles and practical techniques for reclamation planning.

883. Devinny, Josephy S.; and others, eds. **Subsurface migration of hazardous wastes.** Van Nostrand Rienhold, 1990. 387 pp., index. Topics include underground movement of waste; monitoring; soil coring; biological, physical, and chemical alterations of waste; and techniques to control waste migration.

884. Goudie, A.; ed. **Techniques for desert reclamation.** Wiley, Environmental monographs and symposia: a series in environmental science, 1990. 304 pp. Evaluates technological solutions for dealing with desert degradation, wind erosion, soil salinity, irrigation and water erosion, plant conservation, and management of animal resources.

885. Kusler, Jon A.; Kentula, Mary E.; eds. **Wetland creation and restoration: the status of the science.** Island Press, 1990. 594 pp., maps, ill., bibl. Sixteen contributed essays document fieldwork involved in creating and restoring wetlands. Perspectives on such technical aspects as information needs, terminology, project evaluation, waterfowl management, and vegetation dynamics.

Section 5

Plants. Agriculture

Plants, agriculture, and civilization have been associated for thousands of years. But present-day systems of agriculture have produced, besides greater crop yields, soil erosion, pesticide pollution, excessive dependence on oil for energy and fertilizer, loss of genetic diversity, and disappearing rural landscapes. Agriculture has become a prime environmental concern.

There has never been a shortage of publications on agricultural practices and research nor means of access to that literature. Thus, our problem is one of selection from abundance. The bibliography contains publications concerning environmental aspects of agriculture. But it also provides access to agricultural guides, indexes, and abstract/index journals. From these, the information seeker will be able to find any agricultural publication relating to environmental concerns.

The first group of selections in Section 5 has entries on general aspects of plants, agriculture, and food. There follows a more specific group of works on cropping systems, subdivided by landscape architecture and range management or pastoral systems.

Plant sciences are arranged in groups proceeding from biological to physical sciences: plants and vegetation, plant ecology, genetic resources, pests and diseases, atmospheric environment and pesticides, and soil and water relations.

Food and Agriculture
This group contains bibliographies and works dealing with food plants and resources, agricultural products, farming in general, and world agriculture.

See also:

- Section 1: Global resources and environment
- Section 2: Weather and life, biometeorology; climate change
- Section 3: Freshwater; fisheries
- Section 4: Soils
- Section 5: Plant sciences; endangered plants, genetic resources
- Section 6: Forest management, silviculture; tropical forest management
- Section 7: Animal biology, zoology

- Section 8: Rural communities; tribal communities
- Section 10: Law, politics, government; international law and policies; national laws and policies
- Section 13: Biotechnology

Diseases and Pests

Entries on plant diseases, pests, pest management, integrated and biological control, and weeds are grouped here.

See also:

- Section 1: Environmental management; biological systems; ecology
- Section 6: Forest management, silviculture; tree and forest sciences; air, soil, and water relations, pollution
- Section 7: Animal ecology, species; invertebrates
- Section 13: Biotechnology

Soil and Water Relations

Physical aspects of plants are presented in this group and the following group. Soil and water relationships, erosion, water quality, agricultural wastes, soil conditions and management, and water stress are some of the topics covered.

See also:

- Section 1: Chemistry, biogeochemical cycles, pollutants; geology, earth sciences
- Section 2: Atmosphere, climate, weather
- Section 3: Water: physical aspects, hydrology
- Section 4: Soils; land degradation, erosion, reclamation
- Section 5: Food and agriculture; crops, cropping systems; plant sciences
- Section 6: Trees, forests, forestry; air, soil, and water relations, pollution

Atmospheric Environment. Pollution. Pesticides

This group includes entries on the atmospheric environment, air pollution injuries, crop losses, natural pesticides, and chemical pesticides and herbicides.

See also:

- Section 1: Chemistry, biogeochemical cycles, pollutants
- Section 2: Weather and life, biometeorology; air pollution, atmospheric chemistry
- Section 6: Trees, forests, forestry; air, soil, and water relations, pollution
- Section 13: Environmental control technology; air pollution control; hazardous wastes

PLANTS. AGRICULTURE (886–1194)

Food and Agriculture (886–919)

886. ACCIS guide to United Nations information sources on food and agriculture. Food and Agriculture Organization of the United Nations, ACCIS guides to United Nations information sources, no. 1, 1987. 124 pp., bibl., index. The Advisory Committee for the Co-ordination of Information Systems lists sources on plant production and protection, animal production and health, and food and nutrition.

887. Fisher, Rita C.; and others, eds. **Agricultural information resource centers: a world directory.** International Association of Agricultural Librarians and Documentalists, 1990. 641 pp. Provides addresses and fax and telephone numbers from over 4000 agriculture libraries and document centers worldwide; includes information on subject and size of collections, types and materials, available services (including database searches), and in-house databases.

888. Agricultural research centres: a world directory of organizations and programmes. Longman (dist. by Gale Research), 10th ed., 1990. 1100 pp. Guide to organizations conducting or financing research in agriculture, horticulture, forestry, botany, and other relevant disciplines; lists contact information, scope of research activities, current projects, and publications.

889. Douglass, Gordon K.; ed. **Agricultural sustainability in a changing world order.** Westview Press, Westview special studies in agriculture, science, and policy, 1984. 282 pp., ill., bibl., index. Multidisciplinary analyses on the impact of rapid population growth, technology, environmental degradation, and resource scarcity on sustainability of agricultural systems.

890. Alternative agriculture. National Academy Press, 1989. 460 pp., ill., index. Examines scientific and economic aspects of alternative systems designed to keep U.S. farm exports competitive while reducing damaging environmental consequences. Some topics include integrated pest management, crop rotation, and animal management systems; presents 11 case studies from all over the country.

891. Hecht, Susanna. **Amazonia, agriculture and land-use research.** Centro Internacional do Agricultura Tropical, CIAT series, no. O3E–3, 1982. 428 pp., ill., bibl. Proceedings of an international conference sponsored by the Rockefeller Foundation. Reviews Amazon region development plans and policies and assesses agricultural potential of six major Amazonian countries. Reports on forestry and agroforestry research, land uses and soil management, ecosystem research, pasture and animal production, and annual and perennial crops.

892. Bibliography of agriculture with subject index. Oryx Press, 1942 to date. Monthly. Citations to articles, documents, technical reports, proceedings, and other nonbook materials on the literature of agriculture and allied sciences worldwide. Books are indexed in the National Agricultural Library catalog, published separately. Items in the bibliography and the catalog are available as an online computer database.

893. Cutler, Horace G.; ed. **Biologically active natural products: potential use in agriculture.** American Chemical Society, ACS symposium series, v. 380, 1988. 483 pp., ill., bibl., index. Based on a 1987 symposium. Thirty papers discuss natural products derived from microorganisms and higher plants that have potential agricultural uses.

894. Molnar, Joseph J.; Kinnucan, Henry.; eds. **Biotechnology and the new agricultural revolution.** Westview Press, AAAS selected symposium, v. 108, 1989. 288 pp.

895. Ceres: the FAO review. Food and Agriculture Organization of the United Nations, 1968 to date. Bimonthly. Short articles and news of FAO activities and agricultural issues around the world.

896. Facciola, Stephen. **Cornucopia: a source book of edible plants.** Kampong, 1990. 677 pp., bibl., index. Lists plants by family, describes edible product and how it is used; provides information on features, origin, and days to maturity. Gives contact information on some 1300 firms supplying these plants.

897. Stanhill, G.; and others, eds. **Energy and agriculture.** Springer-Verlag, Advanced series in agricultural sciences, v. 14, 1984. 192 pp., ill., bibl., index. Analyzes energy flow in agriculture and assesses the economic impact of energy costs. Examines renewable and nonrenewable energy sources and evaluates energy use in EEC, Australian, and U.S. agriculture.

898. Strange, Marty. **Family farming: a new economic vision.** University of Nebraska Press, 1988. 311 pp., ill., bibl., index. Based on author's experiences working with Nebraska farmers in the Center for Rural Affairs. Discusses the cultural and historical context of family farming. Counters myths that work against the long-term interests of family farming and presents policy choices.

899. FAO documentation: current bibliography. Food and Agriculture Organization of the United Nations, 1972 to date. Bimonthly. Lists publications of the FAO. Provides full bibliographic information, followed by author, subject, geographic, and project indexes in English, French, and Spanish.

900. Body, Richard. **Farming in the clouds.** Temple Smith, 1984. 161 pp. Identifies five major groups of victims of agricultural policies in Britain that protect and subsidize high-input, high-output farming methods. These victims include some farmers, consumers, other countries, developing countries, and the unemployed.

901. Robinson, John R.; ed. **Farmland preservation directory: Northeastern United States.** Natural Resources Defense Council, 1986. 180 pp. Lists federal, state, and private organizations that can provide cost-effective help for land preservation and improved farming practices. Describes services and programs.

902. Groh, Trauger M.; McFadden, Steven S. H. **Farms of tomorrow: community supported farms, farm supported communities.** Biodynamic Farming and Gardening Association, 1990. 169 pp. Explains the theory of community supported agriculture (CSA), based on organic and biodynamic farming and social and economic considerations. Lists resources, contacts, and examples of CSA communities.

903. Nriagu, Jerome O.; Simmons, Milagros S.; eds. **Food contamination from environmental sources.** Wiley-Interscience, Advances in environmental science and technology, v. 23, 1990. 785 pp., index. Contamination in the food chain by accumulated biological and chemical toxins, including heavy metals, pesticides, and fungal and viral toxins.

904. Tudge, Colin. **Food crops for the future: the development of plant resources.** Basil Blackwell, 1987. 225 pp., ill., bibl., index. Surveys food plants, noting crops with development potential, and explains genetics and the basic features of plant breeding; describes successful breeding programs and problems caused by nitrogen fertilization; addresses issues of food production in developed and developing countries.

905. Hansen, Art; McMillan, Della E.; eds. **Food in sub-Saharan Africa.** Rienner, Food in Africa series, 1986. 410 pp., ill., bibl., index. Twenty-two papers provide a general overview of the environmental and cultural situation, food production, postharvest technologies, and potential solutions to food problems.

906. Busch, Lawrence; Lacy, William B.; eds. **Food security in the United States.** Westview Press, A Westview replica edition, 1984. 430 pp., ill., bibl., index. Contributed essays discuss such issues of food security as soil erosion, nutrition and food processing, transportation and marketing, farm worker health and safety, energy availability, and equity of access to food by the entire population.

907. MacFadyen, J. Tevere. **Gaining ground: the renewal of America's small farms.** Holt, Rinehart and Winston, 1984. 242 pp., bibl., index. Engaging and strong arguments for preserving small-scale farming as a productive and economic alternative to large-scale, high-technology farming.

908. Murphy, Josette; Sprey, Leendert H. **Monitoring and evaluation of agricultural change.** International Institute of Land Reclamation and Improvement, ILRI publication, no. 32, 1982. 314 pp., ill., bibl. Guidelines on how to design and conduct a monitoring and evaluation program on agricultural change, with emphasis on the semiarid tropics.

909. Natural resources and the human environment for food and agriculture in Africa. Food and Agriculture Organization of the United Nations, FAO environment and energy paper, no. 6, 1986. 83 pp., ill., bibl. Assesses the state of natural resources in Africa and problems facing food and agricultural production, including deforestation, desertification, soil erosion, and fertilizer and pesticide pollution.

910. Heiser, Charles Bixler, Jr. **Of plants and people.** University of Oklahoma Press, 1985. 237 pp., ill., bibl., index. The origin, importance, and development of various domesticated plants; the interactions between humans and natural selection in domestication.

911. Lewington, Anna. **Plants for people.** Oxford University Press, 1990. 232 pp., ill. Shows the nearly universal dependence of people on plants: the ingredients essential to modern industrial products and uses of plants by native peoples for shelter, clothing, transportation, and medicine.

912. Office of Technology Assessment, U.S. Congress. **Plants: the potentials for extracting protein, medicines, and other useful chemicals.** Government Printing Office, 1983. 252 pp., ill., bibl. Workshop proceedings. Opportunities and limitations of commercial development; research and development; recommendations for government's role in the area.

913. Schnidman, Frank; Smiley, Michael; Woodbury, Eric G. **Retention of land for agriculture: policy, practice, and potential in New England.** Lincoln Institute of Land Policy, 1990. 358 pp. Presents a history of private and public action to preserve land for agriculture. Considers aesthetic, economic, and environmental aspects.

914. Kahn, Ely Jacques. **The staffs of life.** Little, Brown, 1985. 310 pp., index. The major crop plants in human culture and contemporary agriculture—maize, potatoes, wheat, rice and soybeans—in five chapters. Combines mythology, philology, literature, anecdotes, and botany.

915. The state of food and agriculture, 1989. Food and Agriculture Organization of the United Nations, FAO agriculture series, no. 22, 1989. 171 pp., ill., index. Presents worldwide information and data on the economic environment, agricultural production and trade, fisheries, and forestry; examines regionally the problems and performances of world agriculture; assesses strategies for sustainable development and resource management in developing countries.

916. Lockeretz, William; ed. **Sustaining agriculture near cities.** Soil and Water Conservation Society, 1987. 295 pp., ill., bibl., index. Papers from a 1986 meeting address four main issues; adapting to the metropolitan farming environment, political and social issues, changing uses of land and water, and farmland preservation strategies; case studies from California, Oregon, Maryland, and elsewhere.

917. Tools for agriculture: a buyer's guide to appropriate equipment. Intermediate Technology Publications; GTZ/GATE, 1985. 264 pp., ill., index. Lists hundreds of hand, animal-powered, and small-engine tools, with illustrations. Provides addresses for 1200 manufacturers and distributors in 70 countries.

918. Widdowson, R. W. **Towards holistic agriculture: a scientific approach.** Pergamon Press, 1987. 187 pp. Describes alternative agriculture, covering sources of plant nutrients, diseases and pests, crop rotation, grassland management, and animal husbandry and nutrition; appendix gives the chemical composition of foodstuffs, fodder crops, and compostable materials.

919. Alexandratos, Nikos; ed. **World agriculture: toward 2000: an FAO study.** New York University Press, 1988. 338 pp., ill., bibl., index. From a 1987 conference; sections on food and agriculture in the mid–1980s, food and agriculture to 2000, sustainable growth, forestry, fisheries, international trade, policy issues, rural poverty, technology, and environmental aspects. Appendices provide data on prediction methodologies, production and agriculture labor force, agricultural growth rate, and demand and self-sufficiency ratios.

Crops. Cropping Systems (920–945)

920. Manassah, Jamal T.; Briskey, Ernest J.; eds. **Advances in food producing systems for arid and semi-arid lands.** Academic Press, 1981. Ill., bibl. 2 vols. Proceedings of a 1980 symposium. Discusses biotechnology, water management, environmental tolerance, and range management.

921. Agricultural compendium for rural development in the tropics and subtropics. Elsevier, 1981. 739 pp., ill., bibl., index. Extensive, practical guide for field-workers, providing concise information on climate, soil and land classification, geodesy, water control, land improvement, agriculture, animal production and fisheries, economics, and sociology. Numerous tables, charts, and graphs.

922. American journal of alternative agriculture. Institute for Alternative Agriculture, 1986 to date. Quarterly. The Institute encourages low-cost, resource-conserving, and environmentally sound farming methods. Articles, news, reviews, and upcoming events.

923. Biological agriculture and horticulture. A B Academic, 1984 to date. Irregular. International journal concerned with biological-organic husbandry and sustainable food production. Publishes scientific papers and brief sections of news and reviews.

924. Crop research. Scottish Academic Press, 1982 to date. Semiannual. Continues: Horticultural research. Contains original research in experimental agronomy; plant breeding, genetics, physiology, and pathology; biometrics; and other disciplines as they pertain to the improvement of crops and crop production.

925. Crop science. Crop Science Society of America, 1961 to date. Bimonthly. Publishes research on such topics as crop physiology and metabolism; crop ecology, production, and management; seed physiology, production, and technology; crop quality and utilization; and cell biology and molecular genetics. Also covers the registration of cultivars, germ plasm, parental lines, and genetic stocks.

926. Singh, R. P.; Parr, J. F.; Stewart, B. A.; eds. **Dryland agriculture: strategies for sustainability.** Springer-Verlag, Advances in soil science, v. 13, 1990. 336 pp., ill. Presents productive, profitable, and environmentally sound strategies for sustainable dryland farming in the United States and developing nations. Chapters on tillage systems, nutrients, diseases, soil biodiversity, wind erosion, crop residues, water use, and technologies for increasing productivity.

927. Vandermeer, John H. **The ecology of inter-**

cropping. Cambridge University Press, 1989. 237 pp., ill., bibl., index. Applies classic ecological principles to intercropping; examines the competitive production principle and facilitation from theoretical and mechanistic viewpoints; explores specialized topics (perennials, weeds, and intercrop variability); and discusses the design and evaluation of intercropping systems.

928. Norman, Michael John Thornley; Pearson, C. J.; Searle, P. G. E. **The ecology of tropical food crops.** Cambridge University Press, 1984. 369 pp., ill., bibl., index. Textbook covers roles of farming systems, climate, and soils in ecology of cereals, legumes, and noncereal energy crops.

929. Arden-Clark, C. **The environmental effects of conventional and organic/biological farming systems.** Political Ecology Research Group, Research report, no. RR–16, RR–17, 1988. 2 vols. Part I: Soil structure and erosion. Part II: Soil ecology, fertility, and nutrient cycles. Part III: Pest control strategy impacts on the crop ecosystem. Part IV: Farming systems impacts on wildlife and habitat.

930. Experimental agriculture. Cambridge University Press, 1965 to date. Quarterly.

931. Ruthenberg, Hans. **Farming systems in the tropics.** Clarendon Press, 3d ed., 1980. 424 pp., ill., bibl. Describes the major farming systems. Notes their physical, biological, economic, social, and political dimensions and constraints.

932. Wilken, Gene C. **Good farmers: traditional agricultural resource management in Mexico and Central America.** University of California Press, 1987. 302 pp., ill., bibl., index. Describes traditional techniques of managing soils, slopes, field surface, water, climate, and space. Evaluates the prospects for traditional resource management in the future.

933. Little, Charles E. **Green fields forever: the conservation tillage revolution in America.** Island Press, 1987. 192 pp., ill., bibl., index. States the case for conservation tillage. Describes variations of no-till practices, evaluates costs and benefits, and presents case studies.

934. Whyte, William Foote; Boynton, Damon; eds. **Higher-yielding human systems for agriculture.** Cornell University Press, 1984. 342 pp. Evaluates past efforts to improve productivity for small-scale farmers; examines nonhuman elements of farm systems and encourages the integration of sociocultural factors into reorganization and innovation plans.

935. Richards, Paul. **Indigenous agricultural revo-lution: ecology and food production in West Africa.** Hutchinson, 1985. 192 pp., ill., bibl., index. Examines agricultural research and development policies of the colonial period and the ecology of small farming systems in Africa. Concludes that research must support and enhance local initiatives.

936. Steiner, Kurt G. **Intercropping in tropical smallholder agriculture with special reference to West Africa.** Deutsche Gesellschaft für Technische Zusammenarbeit, Schriftenreihe der GTZ, 2d ed., 1984. 304 pp., ill., bibl. Examines the agronomic aspects of intercropping, noting yield advantages, fertilizer use, and pest and weed management. Evaluates socioeconomic effects of intercropping, and argues for increased research and use of traditional cropping and intercropping systems.

937. Francis, Charles A.; ed. **Multiple cropping systems.** Collier Macmillan, 1986. 383 pp., ill., bibl., index. Discusses ecological, physical, and agronomic principles, economic and sociocultural issues, management strategies, and research needs.

938. New farm. Rodale Institute, 1979 to date. Irregular. Periodical for commercial farmers about improving soil fertility, promoting conservation, reducing costs, and exploring alternative crops. Includes membership in the Regenerative Agricultural Association.

939. Phillips, Ronald E.; Phillips, Shirley H.; eds. **No-tillage agriculture: principles and practices.** Van Nostrand Reinhold, 1984. 306 pp., ill., bibl., index. Reviews the principles involved in no-till agriculture and addresses the application of technology to practical production schemes. Many disciplines and topics, from soil properties to equipment, are included. Applies principles to large commercial producers as well as small farmers.

940. Mollison, Bill. **Permaculture: a practical guide for a sustainable future.** Island Press, 1990. 579 pp., ill., index. Explains concepts, themes, and methods of design of this permanent agricultural system. Considers climate factors, trees, soils, and water. Reviews options for various environments, including humid tropics and drylands, and discusses aquaculture. Well illustrated with drawings, photographs, charts, and checklists.

941. Regenerative farming systems: a workshop report. Rodale Institute, Regenerative Agriculture Association, 1985. 216 pp., ill. Papers from a 1985 workshop on resource-efficient farming systems, program implementation, agricultural policy, research and information needs, the potential for regenerative farming in Africa, and other topics.

942. Sillitoe, Paul. **Roots of the earth: crops in the highlands of Papua New Guinea.** Manchester University Press, 1983. 285 pp., ill., bibl., index. Examines how the Wola of Papua New Guinea classify, cultivate, and use crop plants. Compares their gender-based classification system with Western approaches. Provides data on crop occurrence and consumption and Wola botanical terms.

943. Edwards, Clive A.; and others. **Sustainable agricultural systems.** Soil and Water Conservation Society, 1990. 696 pp., maps, ill., bibl. Based on a 1988 conference. Forty contributions address historical and social aspects of sustainable agriculture, its ecological benefits, components of sustainable systems, integration into farming systems, applications in the tropics, and policy development for low-input programs.

944. Francis, C. A.; Flora, C.; King, L.; eds. **Sustainable agriculture in temperate zones.** Wiley-Interscience, 1990. 496 pp. Addresses biodiversity, stewardship, mixed food systems and other means of limiting environmental damage and promoting economic viability and stability; focuses on U.S. agriculture.

945. **World crops: the journal of international agriculture.** Agraria Press, 1949 to date. Bimonthly.

Landscaping. Horticulture. Gardening
(946–964)

946. **The BioCycle guide to yard waste composting.** Rodale Press, 1989. 197 pp. Practical advice for planning and initiating programs to collect and compost "green debris": explains principles of composting and reviews necessary techniques and equipment; includes sections on private management and marketing of compost programs.

947. Wright, Michael; Minter, Sue; Carter, Brian. **The complete handbook of garden plants.** Facts on File, 1984. 544 pp., ill., index. Briefly describes over 9000 species and varieties of flowering plants, trees, and shrubs. Includes hardiness chart and color illustrations of over 2500 plants.

948. Doward, Sherry. **Design for mountain communities: a landscape and architectural guide.** Van Nostrand Reinhold, 1990. 399 pp., ill., bibl., index. Evaluates environmental factors that can affect design, including altitude, climate, topography, soils, and vegetation. Examines strategies and guidelines for building entire communities and individual structures that are compatible with their mountain setting.

949. Hirshberg, Gary; Calvan, Tracy; eds. **Garden-ing for all seasons: the complete guide to producing food at home 12 months a year.** Brick House, 1983. 309 pp., ill., bibl., index. Practical information on indoor, outdoor, and greenhouse gardening; food-producing trees; chicken, egg, and fish production; and food preservation.

950. Jabs, Carolyn. **The heirloom gardener.** Sierra Club Books, 1984. 310 pp., ill., bibl., index. Describes efforts by gardeners to save plant varieties. Includes advice on how individuals can help, providing directions on pollination, harvest, storage, and seed exchanges.

951. **Landscape architecture.** American Society of Landscape Architects, 1910 to date. Bimonthly.

952. Feucht, James R.; Butler, Jack D. **Landscape management: planting and maintenance of trees, shrubs and turfgrasses.** Van Nostrand Reinhold, 1988. 179 pp., ill., bibl., index. Reviews basic concepts and facts regarding plant responses to their environment, placement, and care; addresses growth and development, irrigation, planting and pruning procedures, and disease and insect diagnosis; explains principles and steps for establishing a management program.

953. Flint, Harrison L. **Landscape plants for eastern North America: exclusive of Florida and the immediate Gulf Coast.** Wiley, 1983. 677 pp., ill., index. Lists 500 primary and 1000 secondary species; provides information on each species' range, function, size and habit, adaptability, seasonal interest, and problems and management.

954. Henderson, Carrol L. **Landscaping for wildlife.** Minnesota Department of Natural Resources, 1987. 144 pp., ill. Gives detailed descriptions of landscaping techniques for backyards, farmsteads, and woodlands to provide habitat for up to 100 wildlife species. Addressed specifically to northern Midwest areas but is more widely useful.

955. Hightshoe, Gary L. **Native trees, shrubs, and vines for urban and rural America: a planting design manual for environmental designers.** Van Nostrand Reinhold, 1987. 819 pp., ill., bibl., index. Tables classify 250 woody plant species by visual, ecological, and cultural features and needs. Two-page entries for each plant include descriptions, range maps, and illustrations of its flowers, leaves, and fruit.

956. Smyser, Carol A. **Nature's design: a practical guide to natural landscaping.** Rodale Press, 1982. 390 pp., ill., bibl., index. Detailed guide explains site analysis, plant selection, landscape construction, landscape creation, and maintenance. Many illustrations.

957. Everett, Thomas H. **The New York Botanical Garden illustrated encyclopedia of horticulture.** Garland STPM Press, 1980. Ill. 10 vols. Discusses the characteristics of major plant families and provides technical information on the use and cultivation of thousands of species, including vegetables, fruits, herbs, and ornamentals; applicable to the United States and Canada.

958. Organic gardening. Rodale Publishing, 1942 to date. Monthly. Continues: Organic gardening and farming. Full color, accessible and slightly humorous monthly reports on all facets of organic gardening. Articles tend toward explanation and advice: framing a garden, choosing seeds, buying a wood chipper, and so on.

959. Martin, Franklin M.; Campbell, Carl W.; Ruberte, Ruth M. **Perennial edible fruits of the tropics: an inventory.** U.S. Department of Agriculture, Agricultural Research Service; Government Printing Office, Agriculture handbook, no. 642, 1987. 247 pp. Provides common and scientific names, descriptions, nutritional value, and location where grown; photographs further explain fruits and their cultivation.

960. Ball, Jeff; Ball, Liz. **Rodale's landscape problem solver: a plant-by-plant guide.** Rodale Press, 1989. 439 pp., ill., bibl., index. Describes popular varieties and gives detailed care requirements for trees, shrubs, lawns, and other landscape plants; covers common cultivation problems, pests, and diseases, emphasizing prevention and organic solutions.

961. Hudak, Joseph. **Shrubs in the landscape.** McGraw-Hill, McGraw-Hill series in landscape and landscape architecture, 1984. 291 pp., ill., bibl., index. Reviews the basic requirements of plants and discusses the planting and handling of shrubs; includes landscape design guidelines and a catalog of shrubs adaptable and available in the United States and southern Canada.

962. Harris, Charles W.; Dines, Nicholas T.; eds. **Time-saver standards for landscape architecture: design and construction data.** McGraw-Hill, 1988. 960 pp., ill., bibl., index. Comprehensive professional reference source of techniques, processes, and materials for altering the landscape. Individual topics cross-referenced for easy use.

963. DeChiara, Joseph; Koppelman, Lee E. **Time-saver standards for site planning.** McGraw-Hill, 1984. 849 pp., ill., index. By an architect and a landscape architect and urban planner. Covers site investigation and analysis, design criteria, layout, site details and plans, and plan alternatives.

964. Craft, Mark A. **Winter greens: solar greenhouses for cold climates.** Firefly Books, Renewable energy in Canada, 1983. 262 pp. Explains the design and construction of greenhouses, particularly as extensions to existing houses; provides information on their successful management and presents and evaluates eight actual greenhouse projects.

Range Management. Pastoral Systems (965–984)

965. Pearson, C. J.; Ison, R. J. **Agronomy of grassland systems.** Cambridge University Press, 1987. 169 pp. Treats the biology and management implications of grassland agronomy, including generation, vegetative growth, mineral uptake and distribution, flowering and seed production, herbage quality and animal uptake, and the use of modeling as a problem-solving technique.

966. Cole, Harold Harrison; ed. **Animal agriculture: the biology, husbandry, and use of domestic animals.** Freeman, A series of books in animal science, 2d ed., 1980. 739 pp., ill., bibl., index. Reviews animal agriculture worldwide and describes the classification, grading, and marketing of livestock products; the principles and applications of genetics to animal improvement; animal physiology and nutrition; and the management of various species. New to this edition: aquatic species.

967. Butterworth, M. H.; and others. **Beef cattle production from tropical pastures: a descriptive bibliography.** International Livestock Centre for Africa, 1985. 112 pp., index. Brief annotations of some 600 works. Emphasizes improvement of nutritional status and weight gain in grazing cattle.

968. James, Lynn F.; Ralphs, Michael H.; Nielsen, Darwin B.; eds. **The ecology and economic impact of poisonous plants on livestock production.** Westview Press, 1988. 428 pp. Covers all aspects of both acute and less obvious herbivore poisoning by plants in the pastures and rangelands of the western United States; assesses the effects of such plants on land values and grazing privileges.

969. Heath, Maurice E.; Barnes, R. F.; Metcalf, D. S.; eds. **Forages: the science of grassland agriculture.** Iowa State University Press, 1984. 643 pp. Standard handbook since 1951. One hundred seven contributors, 63 chapters. Includes sections on grasses and legumes; production practices; evaluation and utilization; and forage-animal relationships.

970. Holmes, W.; ed. **Grass: its production and utilization.** British Grassland Society; Blackwell Scientific, 2d ed., 1989. 306 pp. Comprehensive textbook discusses developments in grassland husbandry and use, including the role of grassland management in wildlife conservation.

971. Vallentine, John F. **Grazing management.** Academic Press, 1990. 533 pp., ill., index, tables. Principles and techniques that can be applied to all grazing lands, including native or seeded rangelands and temporary pastures. Topics include grazing effects, patterns, inventory, seasons, and capacity; plant selection; animal nutrition, and kinds and mixes of grazing animals.

972. Gudmundsson, Olafur; ed. **Grazing research at northern latitudes.** Plenum Press, NATO ASI series, Series A, Life sciences, v. 108, 1986. 374 pp., ill., bibl., index. Proceedings of a 1985 workshop. Reviews primary productivity of rangelands and ecosystem reaction to grazing. Examines plant-animal interactions and nutrient intake; identifies optimal stocking rates and factors affecting pasture utilization.

973. Marten, G. C.; ed. **Grazing research: design, methodology, and analysis.** Crop Science Society of America, CSSA special publication, no. 16, 1989. 136 pp. Proceedings of a 1988 symposium, sponsored by professional organizations concerned with grazing, range management, and animal science.

974. Strange, L. R. N. **An introduction to African pastureland production: with special reference to farm and rangeland environments of Eastern Africa.** Food and Agriculture Organization of the United Nations, FAO pasture and fodder crop studies, v. 6, 1980. 192 pp., ill., bibl. Provides an overall analysis of pastureland production and an introduction to pasture plants. Emphasis on arid and semiarid regions.

975. Journal of range management. Society of Range Management, 1948 to date. Bimonthly. Publishes articles and technical notes on the study, management, and use of rangelands and their resources. Topics include measurement and sampling techniques, plant-animal interactions, rangeland improvement, economics, plant physiology, hydrology, and soils.

976. Snaydon, R. W.; ed. **Managed grasslands.** Elsevier, Ecosystems of the world, v. 17, 1987. 285 pp. Describes types of managed grassland around the world; discusses primary and secondary productivity, nutrient cycling, and systems management, focusing on temperate grasslands.

977. Sandford, Stephen. **Management of pastoral development in the Third World.** Wiley, A Wiley series on public administration in developing countries, 1983. 316 pp., bibl., index. Discusses such factors of pastoral life as water supplies, range management, land allocation, land productivity, animal health, and marketing and processing. Offers general methods of administrative and economic organization to improve pastoral development.

978. Stubbendieck, James L.; Hatch, Stephan L.; Hirsch, Kathie J. **North American range plants.** University of Nebraska Press, 3d ed., 1986. 465 pp., ill., bibl., index. Historical, food, and medicinal uses and forage value estimates of 200 species of North American range plants selected for their abundance, desirability, or undesirability. Species descriptions include nomenclature, life span, origin, growth season, and flowering and vegetative growth characteristics.

979. O'Rourke, James T.; ed. **Proceedings of the 1986 International Rangeland Development Symposium.** Society for Range Management; Winrock International Institute for Agricultural Development, 1986. 146 pp., ill., bibl. Held in 1986. Twenty brief papers report new and innovative approaches to successful projects or constraints on rangeland management. International in scope.

980. de Ridder, N.; Stroosnijder, L.; and others, compilers. **Productivity of Sahelian rangelands: a study of the soils, the vegetation and the exploitation of that natural resource.** Agricultural University of the Netherlands; Centre for Publishing and Documentation, Wageningen, 1982. Ill., bibl. 2 vols. Vol. 1: Theory. Vol. 2: Exercises. Designed as a coursebook for mid- to high-level officials involved in animal husbandry. Discusses crop physiology, water balance, and nutrient elements to explain the effects of animal husbandry on the Sahelian ecosystem and its primary production.

981. Vallentine, John F. **Range development and improvements.** Academic Press, 3d ed., 1989. 524 pp., ill., bibl., index. Discusses plant control through biological, mechanical, and herbicidal means; assesses the effects of range burning and reviews the planning and management of range seeding; examines methods of rodent and insect control and range animal handling.

982. Cook, C. Wayne; Stubbendieck, James L.; eds. **Range research: basic problems and techniques.** Society for Range Management, 1986. 317 pp., ill., bibl., index. Includes assessment of habitat factors, vegetation study, herbage measurement, livestock management, and rangeland hydrology.

983. Crowder, L.V.; Chheda, H.R. **Tropical grassland husbandry.** Longman, Tropical agriculture series, 1982. 562 pp., ill., bibl., index. Surveys literature and developments related to the introduction, improvement, breeding, and management of plants in tropical grasslands.

984. World animal review. Food and Agriculture Organization of the United Nations, 1972 to date. Quarterly. Feature articles on developments in animal production, animal health, and animal products worldwide.

Plant Sciences (985–1015)

985. Advances in agronomy. Academic Press, 1949 to date. Annual. Review papers on agricultural sciences, including biochemical genetics and plant breeding; crop husbandry and physiology; plant nutrition; soil chemistry, physics, and biology; and soil conservation.

986. Schubert, L. Elliot; ed. **Algae as ecological indicators.** Academic Press, 1984. 434 pp., bibl., index. Discusses use of algal bioassays to indicate ecological change in freshwater, marine, and terrestrial ecosystems; includes separate sections on toxic substances and heavy metals and industrial applications.

987. Rice, Elroy H. **Allelopathy.** Academic Press, 1984. 422 pp., ill., bibl., index. Introduction to the ecological roles of allelopathy, or the biochemical interactions between plants.

988. Annual review of plant physiology and plant molecular biology. Annual Reviews, 1988 to date. Annual. Twenty or more review papers per volume in subject areas like biochemistry and biophysics; genetics and molecular biology; cell differentiation; tissue, organ, and whole-plant physiology; and acclimation and adaptation.

989. Tolbert, N. E.; ed. **The biochemistry of plants: a comprehensive treatise.** Academic Press, 1980 to date. Ill., bibl., index. 16 vols. Among the subjects covered in this projected 16-volume work are plant cells; metabolism and respiration; structure and function of carbohydrates and lipids; amino acids and derivatives; proteins and nucleic acids; secondary plant products; photosynthesis; molecular biology; and intermediary nitrogen metabolism.

990. McKell, Cyrus M.; ed. **The biology and utilization of shrubs.** Academic Press, 1989. 656 pp., ill., bibl., index. Reviews genetic variability, physiological adaptations, and plant responses to environmental influences; provides advice and economic analysis on establishing shrub plantations and using shrubs for livestock fodder, wildlife habitat, erosion control, and fuel.

991. Lobban, Christopher S.; Wynne, Michael J.; eds. **The biology of seaweeds.** Blackwell Scientific, Botanical monographs, v. 17, 1981. 786 pp., maps, ill., bibl., index. Covers the red, brown, and green seaweeds; discusses their structure and reproduction, ecology, physiology and biochemistry, and commercial cultivation and use.

992. Chapman, A. R. O. **Biology of seaweeds: levels of organization.** University Park Press, 1979. 134 pp., ill., bibl., index. Reviews seaweed taxonomy, physiology, morphology, and ecology from the levels of cells and organisms to populations and communities.

993. Botanical review. New York Botanical Garden, 1935 to date. Quarterly. Review articles on the state of knowledge and research in all subject areas of botany.

994. Tomlinson, Philip Barry. **The botany of mangroves.** Cambridge University Press, Cambridge tropical biology series, 1986. 413 pp., ill., bibl., index. Briefly reviews ecology, floristics, biogeography, shoot and root systems, water relations and salt balance, flowering, seeds, and utility; presents detailed descriptions by family.

995. Christie, B. R.; ed. **CRC handbook of plant science in agriculture.** CRC Press, 1987. Ill., index. 2 vols. Vol. 1 covers genetics, botany, and growth of crop plants; Vol. 2, crop production and utilization for carbohydrates, oils, protein, fiber, drugs, and forage.

996. Critical reviews in plant sciences. CRC Press, 1983 to date. Quarterly. Articles review and synthesize significant research in all areas of plant sciences, including crop genetics and genetic engineering.

997. Wagner, H.; Hikino, Hiroshi; Farnsworth, Norman R.; eds. **Economic and medicinal plant research. Vol. 1.** Academic Press, 1985. 295 pp., ill., bibl., index. Vol. 1 identifies research into medicinally or economically significant natural plant products, including the immunostimulatory properties of fungi and higher plants, ginseng as an adaptogen, and gossypol as a male contraceptive. Vol. 5 of this series was published in 1991.

998. Economic botany. New York Botanical Garden, 1947 to date. Quarterly. Journal of the Society for Economic Botany; publishes research on applied botany and plant utilization, past and present.

999. Fitter, A. H.; Hay, R. K. M. **Environmental physiology of plants.** Academic Press, 2d ed., 1987. 423 pp., ill., bibl., index. Physiology text written from an ecological perspective. Covers response of plants to their environment; specifically, photosynthetic pathways, soil-plant water systems, extreme temperatures, and effects of acid deposition, ultraviolet radiation, and gaseous toxicity.

1000. Davis, Elizabeth. **Guide to information sources in the botanical sciences.** Libraries Unlimited, Reference sources in science and technology series, 1987. 175 pp., bibl., index. Annotated bibliography that emphasizes English-language printed material and computerized databases.

1001. Blanchard, J. Richard; Farrell, Lois; eds. **Guide to sources for agricultural and biological research.** University of California Press, 1981. 735 pp., index. Describes and evaluates important sources of information in both fields, with the emphasis on agriculture. Chapters cover agriculture and biology in general; plant sciences; crop protection; animal sciences; physical sciences; food science and nuturition; environmental sciences; social sciences; and computerized databases. Within chapters, entries are grouped by type of source (abstracts and indexes, government publications, directories, etc.). Lengthy annotations and full bibliographic information.

1002. Schenck, N. C.; ed. **Methods and principles of mycorrhizal research.** American Phytopathological Society, 1982. 244 pp., ill., bibl., index. Presents procedures for identification, morphological studies, isolation, culture, and assay of endo- and ectomycorrhizae.

1003. Böhm, Wolfgang. **Methods of studying root systems.** Springer-Verlag, 1979. 188 pp., ill., bibl., index. Describes, assesses, and illustrates field methods in the study of plant roots in different soils; methods covered include excavation, monolith, auger, profile wall, glass wall, container, and others. Also covers root washing and measurement.

1004. Harley, J. L.; Smith, S. E. **Mycorrhizal symbiosis.** Academic Press, 1983. 483 pp., ill., bibl., index. Interpretive synthesis of research primarily from the 1970s and early 1980s; reviews common kinds of mycorrhiza and their anatomy, development, and growth; includes essays on biological aspects, including specificity and recognition in symbiotic systems, metabolite transfer, and the causal anatomy of ectomycorrhizae.'

1005. Kramer, Paul J.; Kozlowski, Theodore T. **Physiology of woody plants.** Academic Press, 1979. 811 pp., index. Explains woody plant structure and processes by which plant tissues and organs are formed, including the environmental influences affecting physiological processes. Has chapters on photosynthesis, carbohy-drates, nitrogen metabolism, translocation, and transpiration.

1006. Steward, Frederick Campion; ed. **Plant physiology: a treatise.** Academic Press, 1959 to date. Ill., bibl., index. Ongoing, comprehensive work covers basic metabolic functions, growth, development, water and solute balance, and other topics.

1007. Huxley, Peter A.; ed. **Plant research and agroforestry.** International Council for Research in Agroforestry, 1983. 617 pp., ill., bibl., index. Proceedings of a consultative meeting held in Nairobi, April 1981. Papers present research results of plant use in agroforestry, analysis of agroforestry systems, and applications of plant science to agroforestry.

1008. Smith, C.M. **Plant resistance to insects: a fundamental approach.** Wiley, 1986. 286 pp., index. Reports on the effects of plant resistance on insect behavior and biology and of plant growth on resistance; locates sources of resistance, discusses the inheritance of it, and explains techniques to measure resistance; examines insect biotypes that have successfully adapted.

1009. Wickens, G. E.; Goodin, J. R.; Field, D. V.; eds. **Plants for arid lands.** Allen & Unwin, 1985. 452 pp., ill., bibl., index. Proceedings of the Kew International Conference on Economic Plants for Arid Lands, held in 1984. Ethnobotanical reviews of drought-hardy plants around the world. Papers on climate, nitrogen fixation, insect resistance, seed banks, halophytes, and soil improvement.

1010. Loveless, A. R. **Principles of plant biology for the tropics.** Longman, 1983. 532 pp., ill., bibl., index. A basic botany book, covering the structure and physiology of flowering plants, plant kingdoms, and ecology and genetics, which draws its examples from tropical plants.

1011. Priestley, David A. **Seed ageing: implications for seed storage and persistence in the soil.** Comstock Publishing Associates, 1986. 304 pp., ill., bibl., index. Reviews the vast body of literature on seed aging from a physiological and biochemical perspective, covering the loss of seed quality in storage; the longevity of seeds stored under dry conditions or in the soil; and the morphological, structural and biochemical changes of aging seeds.

1012. Murray, David R.; ed. **Seed physiology.** Academic Press, 1984. Ill., bibl., index. 2 vols. Vol.1: Seed development and grain legume nutrition; seed reserves of nitrogen, phosphorus, saccharides, and storage lipids; and toxic compounds in seeds. Vol. 2: Seed germination;

cell biology and metabolic regulation in seeds and seedlings.

1013. Meeuse, Bastiaan; Morris, Sean. **The sex life of flowers.** Facts on File, 1984. 152 pp., ill., bibl., index. Clearly describes floral structures and illustrates with drawings and full-color photographs. Emphasizes the advantages and mechanisms of cross-pollination. Discusses adaptation and coevolution of flowers and their pollinators.

1014. Vegetatio. Kluwer, 1949 to date. Monthly (6 vols./yr). Original articles, notes, and review articles on geobotany, particularly descriptions of vegetation (including classification and mapping techniques), population analyses, and functional aspects of plant communities.

1015. Schultes, Richard Evans. **Where the gods reign: plants and peoples of the Colombian Amazon.** Synergetic Press, 1988. 306 pp., ill., bibl. One hundred thirty-nine photographs taken by the author between 1941 and 1954, with accompanying text. Schultes collected over 24,000 plant specimens in the Amazon; unique view of Amazonian ecology.

Plants. Vegetation (1016–1037)

1016. Groves, R. H.; ed. **Australian vegetation.** Cambridge University Press, 1981. 449 pp., ill., bibl., index. Detailed descriptions and species lists of Australia's many vegetation types and plant communities, including grasslands, heathlands, rain forests, eucalyptus forests, and desert vegetation.

1017. Frohne, Dietrich. **A colour atlas of poisonous plants: a handbook for pharmacists, doctors, toxicologists, and biologists.** Wolfe, 1984. 284 pp., ill., bibl., index. Explains toxicological makeup and mechanisms of various plants and discusses symptoms and treatment of poisoning; color photographs aid in identification.

1018. Willis, John Christopher. **A dictionary of the flowering plants and ferns.** Cambridge University Press, 8th ed., 1973. 1245 pp. Lists generic names published from 1753 on, family names published from 1789 on, and supra- and intrafamilial classifications not based on family or generic names.

1019. Tiner, Ralph W. **A field guide to coastal wetland plants of the northeastern United States.** University of Massachusetts Press, 1987. 285 pp., ill., bibl., index. Provides descriptions and illustrations of common coastal plants, including helpful identification keys; lists

places to observe coastal wetlands from Maine to Maryland.

1020. McGregor, Ronald L.; Barkley, T. M.; Brooks, Ralph E.; eds. **Flora of the Great Plains.** University Press of Kansas, 1986. 1392 pp., bibl., index. Comprehensive reference for vascular plants; includes keys to families, followed by systematic descriptions containing keys to genus and species.

1021. Takhtajan, Armen; Crovello, Theodore J., trans.; Cronquist, Arthur, ed. **Floristic regions of the world.** University of California Press, 1986. 522 pp., maps, bibl., index. Defines and characterizes six floristic kingdoms, 35 regions, and 153 provinces, noting their origins, history, and degree of endemism; includes detailed information on Soviet Eurasia, reviewed by Soviet botanists.

1022. Magee, Dennis W. **Freshwater wetlands: a guide to common indicator plants of the Northeast.** University of Massachusetts Press, 1981. 245 pp., ill., bibl., index. Photographs of major wetland habitats and line drawings of 182 species, giving their range and distinguishing characteristics.

1023. Roosmalen, Marc G. M. van. **Fruits of the Guianan flora.** Agricultural University of the Netherlands, Centre for Agricultural Publishing and Documentation, Wageningen, 1985. 483 pp., ill., index. Expanded volume describes and illustrates 99 families, 546 genera, and 1727 species. Notes on vernacular names, dispersal ecology, and occurrence have also been added.

1024. Uhl, Natalie W.; Dransfield, John. **Genera palmarum: a classification of palms based on the work of Harold E. Moore, Jr.** L. H. Bailey Hortorium International Palm Society, 1987. 610 pp., ill., bibl., index. Reviews and evaluates the basis for classifying palms, examining morphology, anatomy, the fossil record, geography, and ecology. Describes and illustrates 200 genera.

1025. Huxley, Anthony Julian. **Green inheritance: the World Wildlife Fund book of plants.** Anchor Press, 1985. 193 pp., ill., index. The values of plants presented to the general reader, enhanced by many color photographs and drawings.

1026. Frodin, D. G. **Guide to standard floras of the world: an annotated, geographically arranged systematic bibliography of the principal floras, enumerations, checklists and chorological atlases of different areas.** Cambridge University Press, 1985. 619 pp., ill., bibl., index. Extensively annotated bibliography of vascular plant flora, arranged by regions of the world.

1027. Polunin, Oleg; Walters, Martin. **A guide to the vegetation of Britain and Europe.** Oxford University Press, 1985. 238 pp., ill., bibl., index. Intended for the nonecologist; describes those plant communities of Europe likely to be seen by the traveler.

1028. Schultes, Richard Evans; Raffauf, Robert F. **The healing forest: medicinal and toxic plants of the northwest Amazonia.** Dioscorides Press, Historical, ethno- & economic botany series, v. 2, 1990. 484 pp., ill., bibl., index. Describes almost 1500 species and variants, half of which have had little investigation into their chemical and pharmacological properties; plant families are arranged alphabetically, as are their genera and species; also describes their medicinal usage, the preparation of medicinals, native name, and associated tribe. Makes a strong case for ethnobotanical conservation.

1029. Davis, Peter Hadland; Cullen, J. **The identification of flowering plant families, including a key to those native and cultivated in north temperate regions.** Cambridge University Press, 3d ed., 1989. 133 pp., ill., bibl., index. Compact guide; includes illustrated discussions of floral structure and terminology; description of families based on Cronquist's sequence.

1030. Leeuwenberg, A.; compiler. **Medicinal and poisonous plants of the tropics.** PUDOC, 1987. 152 pp., ill., bibl., index. Papers from a 1987 symposium report on the analysis and potential and current medicinal uses of plants in China, Africa, the West Indies, Mexico, and South America.

1031. Vankat, John L. **The natural vegetation of North America: an introduction.** Wiley, 1979. 261 pp., ill., bibl., index. Provides a broad introduction to the study of vegetation in North America, then describes and explains the seven major vegetation types of the continent.

1032. Barbour, Michael G.; Billings, William D.; eds. **North American terrestrial vegetation.** Cambridge University Press, 1988. 434 pp., ill., bibl., index. Focuses on major vegetation types of North America; discusses vegetation structure, response to disturbance, community and environment interactions, nutrient cycling, effects of dominant species, and management issues.

1033. Ritchie, James Cunningham. **Past and present vegetation of the far west of Canada.** University of Toronto Press, 1984. 251 pp., ill., bibl., index. Discusses the physical setting, vascular plant floristics, modern and historical vegetation, paleoenvironmental reconstruction, current problems, and future trends.

1034. Mabberley, D. J. **The plant-book: a portable dictionary of the higher plants.** Cambridge University Press, 1987. 706 pp. Gives generic, family, and commonly used English names of flowering plants; also gives number of species within the genus; distribution; and botanical, horticultural, agricultural, medicinal, and economic uses. Includes gymnosperms, ferns, and other pteridophytes.

1035. Ellenber, Heinz; Strutt, Gordon, K., trans. **Vegetation ecology of central Europe.** Cambridge University Press, 4th ed., 1988. 731 pp., ill., bibl., index. Describes and interprets central Europe's major plant communities, noting environmental requirements, climatic tolerances, and ecological physiology of major species.

1036. Symoens, J. J.; ed. **Vegetation of inland waters.** Kluwer, Handbook of vegetation science, v. 15/1, 1988. 385 pp., ill. Eleven contributed papers describe inland water plant communities and their structure and function; also discuss methods of studying and analyzing them.

1037. Gopal, Brij. **Waterhyacinth: biology, ecology and management.** Elsevier, Aquatic plant studies, v. 1, 1987. 484 pp., maps, ill., bibl., index. Reviews distribution, structure, and reproductive biology. Examines effects of environment, nutrients, and competition on growth. Studies all measures of controlling the plant and of using it for food, paper, energy, and pollution control.

Plant Ecology (1038–1075)

1038. Tivy, Joy. **Agricultural ecology.** Wiley, 1990. 288 pp., maps, ill., bibl., index. Analyzes the differences between agriculturally managed systems and unmanaged ecosystems with respect to types of organisms, soils, nutrient cycling, productivity, livestock production, and land capability. Discusses the ecological characteristics of agricultural systems strongly limited by soil and climate conditions, such as rice paddies and dryland agriculture.

1039. Lowrance, Richard; Stinner, Benjamin R.; House, Garfield J.; eds. **Agricultural ecosystems: unifying concepts.** Wiley, 1984. 233 pp., ill., bibl., index. Presented initially at a symposium in 1982, held during the Ecological Society of America meetings.

1040. Agriculture, ecosystems and environment. Elsevier, 1974 to date. 8 issues/yr. Publishes original papers, review articles, and commentary on the ecology of agriculture production methods and their interaction with the air, water, and soil environments. Includes policy issues of agricultural change and development. Recent special issues on techniques in soil ecology and on mycorrhizae.

1041. Carroll, C. Ronald; Vandermeer, John H.; Rosset, Peter; eds. **Agroecology.** McGraw-Hill, 1990. 641 pp., maps, ill., index. Overview of this new field that is emerging from agricultural sciences, ecology, anthropology, and rural sociology.

1042. Gliessman, Stephen R.; ed. **Agroecology: researching the ecological basis for sustainable agriculture.** Springer-Verlag, Ecological studies, v. 78, 1989. 380 pp., ill., bibl. Covers basic ecological concepts in agroeconomic systems; topics include crop diversification, insect movement and regulation, shifting cultivation systems, ants as a model for biological control, and intercropping. Also discusses agroeconomic system design and management; uses examples from India, China, Veracruz, the United States, and the Netherlands.

1043. Edwards, Clive A.; and others, eds. **Biological interactions in soil.** Elsevier, 1988. 380 pp. Proceedings of a workshop covering interactions between soil-inhabiting invertebrates and microorganisms in relation to plant growth and ecosystem processes.

1044. Teas, H. J.; ed. **Biology and ecology of mangroves.** Junk; Kluwer Boston, Tasks for vegetation science; 8, 1983. 188 pp., ill., bibl. Proceedings of a 1980 symposium. Topics include mangrove zonation, development of a climax community, mangrove fishes, invertebrates and decomposing fungi, and human impacts.

1045. Smith, A. J. E.; ed. **Bryophyte ecology.** Chapman and Hall, 1982. 511 pp., ill., bibl., index. Textbook on the important bryophytes in each of the earth's major climate regions; one chapter on Sphagnum.

1046. Gray, A. J.; Crawley, M. J.; Edwards, P. J.; eds. **Colonization, succession, and stability.** Blackwell Scientific, Symposium of the British Ecological Society, v. 26, 1987. 481 pp., bibl., index. Symposium of the British Ecological Society, held jointly with the Linnean Society of London. Twenty-one papers present theory and research findings on such topics as modeling successional processes; the roles of seed characteristics and herbivory in successional processes; and the interaction of mating strategy, speciation, and phenotypes and genotypes in colonizing success.

1047. Luken, James O. **Directing ecological succession.** Chapman and Hall, 1990. 192 pp., bibl., index. Outlines a model of successional management, applying it to such management techniques as changing resource and propagule availability; discusses long-term effects of such techniques on community development

and information systems for prediction and decision making.

1048. Howe, Henry, F.; Westley, Lynn C. **Ecological relationships of plants and animals.** Oxford University Press, 1988. 273 pp., ill., bibl., index. Reference text that synthesizes research on herbivory, pollination, seed dispersal, and pest protection of plants.

1049. Groves, R. H.; Burdon, J. J.; eds. **Ecology of biological invasions.** Cambridge University Press, 1986. 166 pp., ill., bibl., index. Based on a 1984 symposium in Australia. Papers on the physiology, genetics, and ecology of invading species; the extent to which a disturbed community is susceptible to invasion; the economics of managing harmful invaders; and the use of fire and quarantine measures as management tools. Summarizes the ecology of biological invasions in Australia.

1050. Vickery, Margaret L. **Ecology of tropical plants.** Wiley, 1984. 170 pp., ill., bibl., index. Introductory textbook on various aspects of the physical environment of tropical plants, including soil, water, radiation, atmospheric gases, other plants, animals, and humans; describes several habitats: rain, deciduous, and montane forests; deserts and swamps; and salt lakes.

1051. Rosenthal, Gerald A.; Janzen, Daniel H.; ed. **Herbivores: their interaction with secondary plant metabolites.** Academic Press, 1979. 718 pp., ill., bibl., index. Eight chapters on ecological and evolutionary processes (the evolution of plant chemical defense against herbivores and herbivore defense mechanisms against such chemicals); 12 chapters survey wide variety of plant defense chemicals.

1052. Miller, James R.; Miller, Thomas A.; eds. **Insect-plant interactions.** Springer-Verlag, Springer series in experimental entomology, 1986. 342 pp., ill., bibl., index. Surveys current approaches and methods for studying the developmental, electrophysiological, and behavioral responses of insects to plants and plant products.

1053. Chapman, Valentine Jackson. **Mangrove vegetation.** Cramer, 1976. 447 pp., ill., bibl., index. Describes mangroves throughout the world; also discusses biogeography, ecological factors, physiology, morphology, embryology, and economic uses.

1054. Holzner, W.; Werger, M. J. A.; Ikusima, I.; eds. **Man's impact on vegetation.** Junk; Kluwer, Geobotany, v. 5, 1983. 370 pp., ill., bibl., index. Collection of articles discusses general aspects of human impact, impacts in various vegetation zones, and areas of long-term and severe impact.

1055. Bonham, Charles D. **Measurements for ter-**

restrial vegetation. Wiley, 1989. 338 pp., ill., bibl. Describes sampling techniques for quantifying plant communities, reviewing frequency and cover, biomass, and
density; illustrations and figures further explain equipment and methods; includes chapter bibliographies.

1056. Bilderback, David E.; ed. **Mount St. Helens,
1980: botanical consequences of the explosive eruptions.** University of California Press, 1987. 360 pp.,
maps, ill., bibl., index. A collection of papers presented
at a 1981 symposium on the biological effects of the
Mount St. Helens eruption. Provides important baseline
data on the vegetation and soils found on Mount St. Helens after the eruption.

1057. Chabot, Brian F.; Mooney, Harold A.; eds.
**Physiological ecology of North American plant com-
munities.** Chapman and Hall, 1985. 351 pp., ill., bibl.,
index. Twenty-five physiological ecologists survey available literature on 14 plant communities; enphasizes desert, Arctic, and alpine regions.

1058. Larcher, W.; Beiderman, M. A., trans. **Physiological plant ecology.** Springer-Verlag, 2d rev. ed., 1980.
252 pp., ill., bibl., index. Chapters on physical environment, radiation and temperature, carbon utilization,
minerals, and water relations. No references to ecosystems, in order to focus more on physiological relationships.

1059. Osmond, C.B.; Bjorkman, O.; Anderson, D.J.
**Physiological processes in plant ecology: toward a
synthesis with Atriplex.** Springer-Verlag, Ecological
Studies, v. 36, 1980. 468 pp., ill., bibl., index. Contributed chapters treat the systematic and geographic status
of Atriplex and discuss genecological differentiation, regional environments, and termination and seedling establishment; also summarizes studies on ion and nutrient
absorption, water relations, photosynthesis, and productivity.

1060. Abrahamson, Warren G.; ed. **Plant-animal
interactions.** McGraw-Hill, 1989. 480 pp., ill., bibl., index. Provides a general overview of the topic, then addresses pollination biology, seed dispersal by animals,
ant-plant interactions, carnivorous plants, herbivorous
insects, herbivorous mammals, and plant communities
as animal habitats.

1061. Crawley, Michael J.; ed. **Plant ecology.** Blackwell Scientific, 1986. 496 pp., ill., bibl., index. Textbook
stresses an experimental approach to plant dynamics,
emphasizing the importance of differences in individual
fitness in population and community development.

1062. Sauer, Jonathan D. **Plant migration: the dynamics of geographic patterning in seed plant spe-

cies.** University of California Press, 1988. 282 pp., ill.,
bibl., index. Brief case studies of microenvironments,
from the tropics to the subarctic, illustrate trends in plant
migration.

1063. Pearcy, R. W.; and others, eds. **Plant physiological ecology: field methods and instrumentation.**
Chapman and Hall, 1989. 457 pp., ill., bibl. Reviews and
evaluates classic and state-of-the-art approaches to field
data acquisition for processes like transpiration, leaf conductance, and photosynthesis.

1064. Doust, Jon Lovett; Doust, Lesley Lovett; eds.
Plant reproductive ecology: patterns and strategies.
Oxford University Press, 1988. 344 pp. Papers on standard topics in the field, such as life history strategies,
herbivory, pollination, competition, and dispersal. Emphasizes the application of ideas from sociobiology.

1065. Tilman, David. **Plant strategies and the dynamics and structure of plant communities.** Princeton
University Press, Monographs in population biology, v.
26, 1988. 360 pp., ill., bibl., index. Arguments relating
to productivity, disturbance, habitat, and growth rates as
they affect competition.

1066. Grime, John Philip. **Plant strategies and vegetation processes.** Wiley, 1979. 222 pp., ill., bibl., index. Explains processes that control the structure and
composition of vegetation derived from correlative, direct, and comparative types of research. In two parts:
plant strategies (primary, secondary, regenerative) and
vegetation processes (dominance, succession, coexistence).

1067. Greig-Smith, P. **Quantitative plant ecology.**
University of California Press, Studies in ecology, v. 9, 3d
ed., 1983. 359 pp., ill., bibl., index. Reviews the theories
and methods of quantitative vegetation description and
analysis; topics include sampling and comparison, association between species, species distribution and habitat
factors, and classification and ordination.

1068. Woodwell, George M.; ed. **The role of terrestrial vegetation in the global carbon cycle: measurement by remote sensing.** Wiley, SCOPE, v. 23, 1984.
247 pp., ill., bibl., index. Based on a 1979 conference.
Discusses classification of plant communities, measurement of soil organic matter, and remote sensing by satellite and aircraft.

1069. Lauenroth, W. K.; Laycock, W. A.; eds. **Secondary succession and the evaluation of rangeland
condition.** Westview Press, Westview special studies in
agriculture science and policy, 1989. 163 pp., bibl.,
index. Describes the origin, development, and current
concepts of rangeland conditions used by government

agencies in Australia and the United States. Criticizes these concepts and recommends alternative evaluation methods.

1070. Murray, David R.; ed. **Seed dispersal**. Academic Press, 1986. 322 pp., ill., bibl., index. Discusses the roles of wind, water, fruit-eating birds and mammals, rodents, and fire in the dispersal of seeds, fruits, spores, and pollen. Also covers the evolution of dispersal mechanisms.

1071. Fenner, Michael. **Seed ecology**. Chapman and Hall, Outline studies in ecology, 1985. 151 pp., ill., bibl., index. Concise work includes discussion of plant reproductive strategies, predispersal hazards, dispersal, soil seed banks, dormancy, germination, seedling establishment, and regeneration and diversity. Many references are to studies done in tropical areas.

1072. Barbour, Michael G.; Burk, Jack H.; Pitts, Wanna D. **Terrestrial plant ecology**. Benjamin/Cummings, 2d ed., 1987. 634 pp., ill., bibl., index. Gives historical overview of the field; discusses autecology and synecology and the roles of light, temperature, fire, soil, and water in each; describes the major vegetation types of North America.

1073. Kuechler, A. W.; Zonnefeld, I. S.; eds. **Vegetation mapping**. Kluwer, Handbook of vegetation science, v. 10, 1988. 635 pp., ill., index. Covers the cartographic considerations, the methods and procedures, and the applications of vegetation mapping; discusses different schools of mapping, including the editors' comprehensive method.

1074. Walter, Heinrich; Muise, Owen, trans. **Vegetation of the earth and ecological systems of the geobiosphere**. Springer-Verlag, Heidelberg science library, 3d ed., 1985. 318 pp., ill., bibl., index. Brief but comprehensive worldwide survey of the earth's vegetation and ecosystems. Explains regional variations of plants and plant communities in terms of climate and geology.

1075. Jones, Gareth. **Vegetation productivity**. Longman, Topics in applied geography, 1979. 100 pp., ill., bibl., index. Examines the nature of plant growth, factors affecting productivity, and methods to measure that growth; focuses on forest ecosystems and covers grassland and agricultural systems.

Endangered Plants. Genetic Resources (1076–1106)

1076. Doyle, Jack. **Altered harvest: agriculture, genetics and the fate of the world's food supply**. Pen-

guin Books, 1986. 502 pp., bibl., index. Traces changes in agriculture, particularly economic and ecological vulnerability, resulting from increased use of biotechnology,

1077. Jain, S. K.; Rao, R. R.; eds. **An assessment of threatened plants of India**. Botanical Survey of India; Department of Environment, 1983. 334 pp., bibl. Papers from a 1981 seminar grouped geographically; brief entries identify threatened species and describe their features, domain, scarcity, and any special notes.

1078. Synge, Hugh; ed. **The biological aspects of rare plant conservation**. Wiley, 1981. 558 pp., ill., bibl., index. Proceedings of a 1980 conference. Papers cover surveying and assessment, tropical forests as conservation priority, understanding and monitoring rarity, ecological studies of rare plants, and introductions and reintroductions.

1079. Bramwell, D.; Hamann, O.; Heywood, V.; and others, eds. **Botanic gardens and world conservation strategy**. Academic Press, 1987. 367 pp., ill., bibl. Proceedings of a 1985 conference. Topics include botanical gardens and communities, research and rescue, botanical gardens for sustainable development, and development of a worldwide network.

1080. Christiansen, M. N.; Lewis, Charles F.; eds. **Breeding plants for less favorable environments**. Wiley, 1982. 459 pp., maps, ill., bibl., index. Contributors report on plant responses to temperature, mineral toxicity and deficiency, waterlogging, drought, and air pollution. Papers on genetic engineering and plant breeding for resistance to diseases, insects, nematodes, and environmental stresses.

1081. Witt, Steven C. **BriefBook: biotechnology and genetic diversity**. California Agricultural Lands Project, 1985. 145 pp., maps, ill., bibl. Creative, offbeat introductory guide to biotechnology, its role in modern agriculture, and government, judicial, and international responses to it. Provides extensive references to people and published materials.

1082. Holden, J. H. W.; Williams, J. T.; eds. **Crop genetic resources: conservation and evaluation**. Allen & Unwin, 1984. 296 pp., ill., bibl., index. Discusses seed storage and methods for monitoring and quantifying deterioration; means of achieving and maintaining seed variability; and progress in in vitro preservation.

1083. Solbrig, Otto T.; ed. **Demography and evolution in plant populations**. Blackwell Scientific (dist. by University of California Press), Botanical monographs, v. 15, 1980. 222 pp., ill., bibl., index. Eight contributed chapters cover the genetic structure of and demographic factors in plant populations, the role of demography in natural selection, mating patterns and vegetative reproduction, plant demography in agricultural systems, and demographic problems in tropical systems.

1084. **Diversity: a news journal for the global plant genetic resources community.** Genetic Resources Communications Systems, 1985 to date. Quarterly. Information exchange by, for, and about the international plant genetic resources community. Publisher is a nonprofit organization, sustained and governed by leading plant genetic organizations, public and private.

1085. Nabhan, Gary Paul. **Enduring seeds: Native American agriculture and wild plant conservation.** North Point Press, 1989. 225 pp., bibl., index. Emphasizes the connection between cultural and biological diversity; argues against industrial-scale agriculture and in favor of local crops and traditional farming practices appropriate to a region's soil, climate, and organisms.

1086. Plucknett, Donald L.; and others. **Gene banks and the world's food.** Princeton University Press, 1987. 247 pp., ill., bibl., index. Argues that gene banks are necessary given the world's increasing population; examines modern farming strategies, and the history of germ plasm preservation and exchange; discusses modern advances in both biotechnology and germ plasm collection for many crops; focuses on the agricultural applications of gene banks.

1087. Soderstrom, Thomas R.; and others, eds. **Grass systematics and evolution.** Smithsonian Institution Press, 1987. 473 pp., ill., bibl., index. Chapters provide a review of current agrostological research, covering structural and biochemical diversity, reproductive biology, and systematics of the main groups.

1088. Evans, David A.; and others, eds. **Handbook of plant cell culture.** McGraw-Hill, 1983 to date. Irregular: vol. 6, 1990. Vol. 1: Techniques for propagation and breeding. Vols. 2 and 3: Crop species. Vol. 4: Techniques and applications. Vol. 5: Ornamental species. Vol. 6: Perennial crops. Vols. 1–4 were published by Macmillan.

1089. Pierik, R. L. M. **In vitro culture of higher plants.** Nijhoff; Kluwer; Academic Press, 1987. 344 pp., ill., bibl., index. Combination practical handbook and textbook, explains lab set-up, media preparation, isolation, and subculture, then discusses various applications, such as embryo culture, orchid propagation, production of disease-free plants, and genetic manipulation.

1090. Lucas, Gren; Synge, Hugh; and others, compilers. **The IUCN plant red data book.** International Union for Conservation of Nature and Natural Resources, 1978. 540 pp., bibl., index. Case studies of 250 plants threatened worldwide; includes distribution, population, habitat and ecology, scientific interest and potential value, threats and conservation measures.

1091. Bajaj, Y. P. S.; ed. **Medicinal and aromatic plants.** Springer-Verlag, Biotechnology in agriculture and forestry, v. 4, 1988 to date. 545 pp., ill., bibl., index. Reviews biotechnological methods used to exploit medicinal plants for their secondary substances; many case histories document the production and human uses of secondary metabolites.

1092. Rindos, David. **The origins of agriculture: an evolutionary perspective.** Academic Press, 1984. 325 pp., ill., bibl., index. Develops a theoretical basis for understanding plant domestication and the origin of agriculture. Focus is on the coevolution of humans and plants, with emphasis on processes and mechanisms. Subdivides the evolutionary development into incidental, specialized, and agricultural domestication.

1093. Felger, Richard Stephen; Moser, Mary Beck. **People of the desert and sea: ethnobotany of the Seri Indians.** University of Arizona Press, 1985. 435 pp., ill., bibl., index. Wealth of ethnobotanical material accumulated over two decades, through interaction with the Seri tribe of northwestern Mexico. Example of interdisciplinary research on traditional plant knowledge of a hunting, gathering, and seafaring people.

1094. Yeatman, Christopher W.; Kafton, David; Wilkes, Garrison. eds. **Plant genetic resources; a conservation imperative.** Westview Press, AAAS selected symposia series, v. 87, 1984. 164 pp., ill., bibl. Papers of a 1981 symposium. Topics include history and policy development in agriculture, genetic resources in forest and wildlife management, and genetic conservation in breeding of crop plants.

1095. Briggs, David; Walters, S. M. **Plant variation and evolution.** Cambridge University Press, 2d ed., 1984. 412 pp., ill., bibl., index. Summarizes the history, genetics, morphology, and ecology of plant evolution; explains pre-Darwinian approaches to species evolution and reviews recent theories regarding speciation, reproduction, and variation.

1096. Kyte, Lydiane. **Plants from test tubes: an introduction to micropropagation.** Timber Press, 1987. 160 pp., ill., bibl., index. Provides detailed description of necessary facilities, media preparation and propagation techniques. Includes culture guide for selected species.

1097. Davis, Stephen D.; and others. **Plants in danger: what do we know?** International Union for Conservation of Nature and Natural Resources, 1986. 461 pp., ill., bibl., index. Guide to the literature on endangered or threatened plants around the world. Provides the following information on each of 414 countries and islands: plant species and vegetation types, published flora checklists and field guides, relevant laws, botanical gardens and organizations involved in plant conservation, and literature on the botany and conservation of that region.

1098. Macdonald, A. Bruce. **Practical woody plant propagation for nursery growers.** Timber Press, 1986 to date. 669 pp., ill., bibl., index. Comprehensive, detailed handbook discusses basic principles, facilities and tools, rooting, layering, grafting, and micropropagation. Numerous photographs and drawings.

1099. Mantell, S. H.; Matthews, J. A.; McKee, R. A. **Principles of plant biotechnology: an introduction to genetic engineering in plants.** Blackwell Scientific, 1985. 269 pp., ill., bibl., index. Introduction to techniques of gene manipulation and tissue culture for crop improvement and development.

1100. Dirr, Michael A.; Heuser, Charles W., Jr. **The reference manual of woody plant propagation: from seed to tissue culture.** Varsity Press, 1987. 239 pp., ill. A practical guide and reference to over 1000 woody species, arranged alphabetically; includes the best techniques to use in seed, cutting, grafting, and tissue culture propagation.

1101. McMullen, Neil. **Seeds and world agricultural progress.** National Planning Association, 1987. 263 pp., ill., bibl. Discusses seed industry, seed policies of developing countries, and policies for industry development.

1102. Fowler, Cary; Mooney, Pat. **Shattering: food, politics, and the loss of genetic diversity.** University of Arizona Press, 1990. 278 pp., maps, ill., bibl., index. Discusses the value of plant genetic diversity and its loss due to the farming practices of industrialized nations. Documents the rise of biotechnology and the resulting impacts on Third World farmers.

1103. Some medicinal forest plants of Africa and Latin America. Food and Agriculture Organization of the United Nations, FAO forestry paper, no. 67, 1986. 252 pp. Discusses 40 medicinal trees and shrubs, describing botany, silvics, chemical properties, and pharmaceutical and traditional uses.

1104. Brown, A. H. D.; and others, eds. **The use of plant genetic resources.** Cambridge University Press, 1989. 382 pp., ill., bibl. Examines use, size, and structure of collections; discusses evaluation techniques in various systems; assesses technological and scientific innovations affecting resource use, including in vitro conservation and disease resistance screening.

1105. Bruecher, Heinz. **Useful plants of neotropical origin and their wild relatives.** Springer-Verlag, 1989. 296 pp., ill., bibl., index. Describes current theories regarding the domestication, cultivation, and evolution of these plants and biotechnological methods for improving their productivity; encompasses protein and oil plants, aromatics, narcotics, stimulants, spices, timber, and carbohydrate sources.

1106. Mohlenbrock, Robert H. **Where have all the wildflowers gone? a region-by-region guide to threatened or endangered U.S. wildflowers.** Collier Macmillan, 1983. 239 pp., ill., index. Provides accounts of the plants that have been or probably will be placed on the U.S. endangered species list, presented by region.

Diseases and Pests (1107–1138)

1107. Annual review of phytopathology. Annual Reviews, 1963 to date. Annual. Each issue contains 20 to 25 review papers on current research in plant diseases and injuries. Covers pathogens, hosts, epidemics, diagnosis, control measures, action of toxicants and chemicals, molecular biology, and other topics.

1108. Dhingra, Onkar D.; Sinclair, James B. **Basic plant pathology methods.** CRC Press, 1985. 355 pp., ill., bibl., index. Comprehensive handbook explains sterilization, pathogen culture and storage, inoculum detection and estimation, disease establishment, resistance testing, soil microorganisms, chemical and biological control, and histological techniques.

1109. Hedin, Paul A.; Menn, Julius J.; Hollingwoth, Robert M. **Biotechnology for crop protection.** American Chemical Society, ACS Symposium series, v. 379, 1988. 471 pp., ill., bibl., index. Based on a 1987 symposium. Examines the uses of biotechnology for weed, plant disease, and insect control; genetically engineered microbial pesticides; immunochemical applications; and regulatory and monitoring issues.

1110. Horn, David J. **Ecological approach to pest management.** Guilford Press, 1988. 285 pp. Textbook. Practical insect control techniques that incorporate ecological approaches, illustrated through examples.

1111. Lundholm, B.; Stackrud, M.; eds. **Environ-**

mental protection and biological forms of control of pest organisms. Swedish Natural Science Research Council, Ecological bulletins, no. 31, 1980. 171 pp., ill., bibl., index. Proceedings of a 1979 international workshop. Authors address problems and areas of study related to the use of biological pest control techniques instead of chemical pesticides.

1112. Holm, LeRoy G.; Pancho, Juan V.; Herberger, J.; and others. **Geographical atlas of world weeds.** Wiley, 1979. 391 pp. Lists over 7000 weeds, the countries in which they occur, and their degree of importance. Introduction is in ten languages.

1113. Grainge, Michael; Ahmed, Saleem. **Handbook of plants with pest-control properties.** Wiley, 1988. 470 pp., bibl. Briefly catalogs 2400 species with pest control properties and lists 800 pests and the plants that control them, plus an additional 1000 plants that are poisonous or reported to control human or animal disease.

1114. Cavalloro, R.; ed. **Integrated and biological control in protected crops.** Balkema, 1987. 251 pp., ill., bibl., index. Discusses principal disease threats to greenhouse plants, integrated pest control in various European countries, effectiveness of biological techniques, and useful organisms for pest control.

1115. Metcalf, Robert L.; Luckmann, William H.; eds. **Introduction to insect pest management.** Wiley, Environmental science and technology, 2d ed., 1982. 577 pp., maps, ill., bibl., index. Addresses ecological and economic aspects of pest management; reviews use of insect pathogens, insecticides, and genetic control; examines sampling and modeling techniques and pest management involving cotton, corn, and forage crops.

1116. Flint, Mary Louise; Van den Bosch, R. **Introduction to integrated pest management.** Plenum Press, 1981. 240 pp., ill., bibl., index. Reviews history of pest control and associated costs; explains integrated pest management philosophy and practical procedures; presents nine brief case histories.

1117. Fraser, R. S. S.; ed. **Mechanisms of resistance to plant diseases.** Nijhoff; Junk; Kluwer, Advances in agricultural biotechnology, 1985. 462 pp., ill., bibl., index. Discusses genetic bases of plant resistance and mechanisms of induced resistance to viruses, fungi and bacteria.

1118. Cook, R. James.; Baker, Kenneth F. **The nature and practice of biological control of plant pathogens.** American Phytopathological Society, 1983. 539 pp., ill., bibl., index. Companion volume to the authors' *Biological control of plant pathogens* (1974). How biologi-

cal control works and how it can be achieved in practice, with many examples, explained from the varying perspectives of pathogen, host, soil ecosystem, and pathogen antagonists. Emphasizes the biocontrol possibilities in slight environmental modifications.

1119. Huffaker, Carl B.; ed. **New technology of pest control.** Wiley, 1980. 500 pp., ill., bibl., index. Describes the use and advantages of many pest control methods (parasites, predators, pheromones, chemical pesticides, and selective breeding) as used on various crops, including soybeans, alfalfa, and cotton.

1120. Musselman, Lytton J.; ed. **Parasitic weeds in agriculture.** CRC Press, 1987. 328 pp. Contributed chapters focus on factors influencing the growth and development of witchweeds; the haustorium; field research techniques; and control methods, including quarantine, chemical and biological control, and breeding for resistance.

1121. Pesticide resistance: strategies and tactics for management. National Academy Press, 1986. 471 pp., ill., bibl., index. Prepared by the Committee on Strategies for the Management of Pesticide Resistant Pest Populations, Board on Agriculture, National Research Council. Papers cover genetic, biochemical, and physiological mechanisms of resistance; population biology of resistance; detection, monitoring, and risk assessment; and tactics for prevention, management, and implementing management.

1122. Flint, Mary Louise. **Pests of the garden and small farm: a grower's guide to using less pesticide.** University of California, Division of Agriculture and Natural Resources, Statewide Integrated Pest Management Project (Dist. by ANR), 1990. 276 pp., bibl., index. Reviews the overall principles and goals of integrated pest management; covers wide range of problems, including diseases, arthropods, snails and slugs, weeds, and nematodes; geared toward California but applicable elsewhere.

1123. Thresh, J. M.; and others, eds. **Pests, pathogens, and vegetation; the role of weeds and wild plants in the ecology of crop pests and diseases.** Pitman International Advanced Publications Program, 1981. 517 pp., ill., bibl., index. Some topics: plant pathogenic viruses, bacteria, and fungi; soilborne fungi, nematodes, and nematode-borne viruses; arthropod and vertebrate pests; and the impact of weeds and weed control practices on crop pests and diseases. Some contributions are comprehensive reviews, while others are shorter.

1124. **Phytopathology.** American Phytopathological

Society, 1911 to date. Monthly. Publishes research on the nature and spread of plant diseases, losses inflicted by them, and measures to control them.

1125. Mukerji, K. G.; Bhasin, Jayanta. **Plant diseases of India: a source book.** Tata McGraw-Hill, New Delhi, 1986. 468 pp., ill., bibl., index. Index of 5000 pathogens afflicting almost 3000 plant species. Includes viruses, microplasms, viroids, bacteria, actinomycetes, nematodes, and insects; emphasis on fungi, listed by host plant.

1126. Dickinson, C. H.; Lucas, J. A. **Plant pathology and plant pathogens.** Wiley, Basic microbiology, v. 6, 3d ed., 1992. 256 pp., ill., bibl., index. Focuses on the interactions of plant pathogens (fungi, bacteria, viruses) with crop plants and the environment; discusses disease management, molecular genetic techniques, pathogenicity, and host-pathogen relations.

1127. Smith, C. M. **Plant resistance to insects: a fundamental approach.** Wiley-Interscience, 1989. 286 pp. Offers an assessment and update of pest resistance and control, including coverage of molecular biological methods and transgenic plants.

1128. Fry, William E. **Principles of plant disease management.** Academic Press, 1982. 378 pp., ill., bibl., index. Derives methods of disease forecasting, control, and management from epidemiology; explains management strategies for reducing inoculum and the rate of epidemic development; case studies illustrate applications in five agroecosystems.

1129. Manners, J.G. **Principles of plant pathology.** Cambridge University Press, 1982. 264 pp., ill., bibl., index. Reviews causes of plant disease; provides insight into the physiology of host-parasite relationships and the genetics of host-pathogen interactions; examines epidemiology and the control of plant diseases through chemical and nonchemical means.

1130. Review of plant pathology. Commonwealth Mycological Institute, 1970 to date. Monthly. Abstracts of the scientific literature on plant diseases and injuries.

1131. Engelhard, Arthur W.; ed. **Soilborne plant pathogens: management of diseases with macro- and microelements.** APS Press, 1989. 217 pp., ill., bibl. Contributed chapters bring together important information on the relationship between plant nutrition and soilborne diseases, presenting case studies of applications to disease management.

1132. Hance, R. J.; Holly, K.; eds. **Weed control handbook: principles.** Blackwell Scientific, 8th ed., 1990. 582 pp. Reviews concepts involved in weed control, surveys characteristics and considerations of various weeds, and provides practical information on the formulation and application of herbicides; includes new chapter on ecological aspects of weed control methods.

1133. Radosevich, Steven R.; Holt, Jodie S. **Weed ecology: implications for vegetation management.** Wiley, 1984. 265 pp., ill., bibl., index. Discusses both the ecology of weeds and the theory and techniques of their control. Topics include weed evolution; reproduction, dispersal, germination, and survival; competition and parasitism; limiting factors and weed-crop dynamics.

1134. Weed science. Weed Science Society of America, 1970 to date. Bimonthly. Publishes research on weed biology, physiology, chemistry, and ecology, as well as on weed control and herbicide technology.

1135. Weed technology: a journal of the Weed Science Society of America. Weed Science Society of America, 1987 to date. Quarterly. Publishes research papers on weed control technology.

1136. Muenscher, Walter Conrad. **Weeds.** Comstock Publishing Associates, 2d ed., 1980. 586 pp., ill., bibl., index. Key to 571 North American weed species; descriptions and nonchemical control methods listed by scientific names of species.

1137. Lorenzi, Harri J.; Jeffery, Larry S. **Weeds of the United States and their control.** Van Nostrand Reinhold, 1987. 355 pp., ill., bibl., index. Full-page descriptions of over 300 weeds, including discussion of habitat, range map, and control techniques. Color photograph of each plant.

1138. Holm, LeRoy G.; and others. **The world's worst weeds: distribution and biology.** University Press of Hawaii, 1977. 609 pp., ill., bibl., index. Describes the principal weeds of major world crops. Brief essays discuss distribution, seriousness, and biology of 90 species, supplemented by range maps and line drawings. Briefly describes 16 major crops and their weeds.

Soil and Water Relations (1139–1167)

1139. Agricultural and forest meteorology. Elsevier, 1964 to date. Quarterly. International journal publishes research on the relation of agriculture and forestry to climatology and meteorology worldwide, with emphasis on practical applications of research.

1140. van Hoorn, J. W.; ed. **Agrohydrology: recent developments.** Elsevier, 1988. 550 pp. Papers from a 1987 international symposium present applied research in four fields: Effects of Drainage on Crops and Farm Management, Water Conservation, Hydrology of Natural

Reserves, and Reuse and Disposal of Drainage Waters from Irrigated Areas.

1141. Gasser, J. K. R.; ed. **Composting of agricultural and other wastes.** Elsevier, 1985. 320 pp. Papers from a 1984 seminar attended by the members of the EEC review the production of compost, mechanization, heat production, composting and crop production, earthworm culture, odor control, and pathogen survival.

1142. Moldenhauer, W. C.; Hudson, N. W.; eds. **Conservation farming on steep lands.** Soil and Water Conservation Society, 1988. 296 pp., ill., index. Proceedings of a 1987 workshop. Case studies of successful attempts to counter erosion on steep lands. Suggests means of planning and implementing programs. Includes country reports from Africa, Latin America, Taiwan, and Australia.

1143. Moldenhauer, W. C.; and others. **Development of conservation farming on hillslopes.** Soil and Water Conservation Society, 1991. 332 pp. Based on 1989 conference in Taiwan. Problems of agriculture, conservation, and strategies for development of hill slopes. Emphasis on successful commercial use of hill slopes and concepts to guide integration of conservation into agricultural development plans.

1144. Hurt, R. Douglas. **The Dust Bowl: an agricultural and social history.** Nelson-Hall, 1981. 214 pp., maps, ill., bibl., index. Describes dust storms of the 1930s on the Great Plains, their effects, and contributing causes. Discusses technical and social measures adopted to combat soil erosion and what happened to them by the 1950s.

1145. Clark, Edwin H., II; Haverkamp, Jennifer A.; Chapman, William. **Eroding soils: the off-farm impact.** Conservation Foundation, 1985. 252 pp. Summarizes extent of nonpoint pollution damage, focusing on the significant percentage caused by agriculture; evaluates in-stream and off-stream sediment and chemical contamination; suggests specific solutions through improved farming techniques and more efficient and effective application of government education, technical, and cost-sharing programs.

1146. FAO irrigation and drainage paper. Food and Agriculture Organization of the United Nations, 1971 to date. Irregular. Comprehensive series of technical reports—50 to 300 pages—on irrigation. Some are proceedings of conferences; many provide basic design and methods information, such as a report on water-lifting devices.

1147. Fairchild, Deborah M.; ed. **Ground water quality and agricultural practices.** Lewis, 1987. 402 pp., maps, ill., bibl., index. Reviews groundwater use and reports on the use of pesticides and fertilizers in agriculture. Evaluates groundwater pollution and its sources, focusing mostly on agrochemicals but also on saltwater intrusion and sewage effluents. Suggests protection and management techniques, including programs used in Iowa, Pennsylvania, and Delaware.

1148. Journal of environmental quality. American Society of Agronomy, 1972 to date. Quarterly. Contains technical reports, reviews and analyses, and short communications on environmental quality in natural and agricultural ecosystems, including plant-environment interactions, soil processes and chemical transport, water quality, and waste management.

1149. Journal of irrigation and drainage engineering–ASCE. American Society of Civil Engineers, 1983 to date. Quarterly. Publishes research and news of technical advances in all phases of irrigation, drainage, and other water management strategies; also covers water laws, water quality, weather modification, and project formulation for systems.

1150. Plant and soil. Kluwer, 1948 to date. 18 issues/yr. International journal focuses on fundamental and applied aspects of plant nutrition, soil fertility, plant-microbe associations, soil microbiology, soilborne plant diseases, soil and plant ecology, agrochemistry, and agrophysics.

1151. Faulkner, Edward H. **Plowman's folly and a second look.** Island Press, Conservation classics, 1987. 193 pp. Reprint of classic originally published in 1943. Argues that use of the moldboard plow has never been scientifically justified, buries useful organic matter under the subsoil, and is responsible for major soil erosion.

1152. Rendig, Victor V.; Taylor, Howard M. **Principles of soil-plant interrelationships.** McGraw-Hill, 1989. 275 pp., ill., bibl., index. Reviews recent findings on plants' water and mineral needs, root growth and distribution, soil nutrients, and the relationship between mineral nutrients and plant growth and composition; presents models of water and ion uptake; discusses water and mineral uptake and plant growth in special conditions.

1153. Sanchez, Pedro A. **Properties and management of soils in the tropics.** Wiley, 1976. 618 pp., ill., bibl., index. Focuses on specific soil-plant relationships related to physical and chemical properties, organic matter, nutrients, and methods of soil fertility evaluation; then integrates these concepts in terms of four soil management systems common to the tropics: shifting cultivation, rice culture, multiple cropping, and pasture production.

1154. Wild, Alan; ed. **Russell's soil conditions and plant growth.** Longman Scientific & Technical; Wiley, 1988. 991 pp., ill., bibl., index. Contributed chapters discuss soil properties as they affect crop growth; topics include soil formation, the behavior of water in soil, how plant roots function, soil temperature and structure, soil organisms and their effects, and the application of soil science to management.

1155. Staples, R. C.; Toenniessen, G. H.; eds. **Salinity tolerance in plants: strategies for crop improvement.** Wiley, 1984. 443 pp., ill., bibl., index. Examines the cytological and physiological aspects and mechanisms of salt tolerance; discusses successes and failures of crop selection, and ways of improvement including genetic engineering and cell culture; evaluates the alternative of controlled environment agriculture; economically analyzes improvement strategies.

1156. Soil conservation: assessing the national resources inventory. National Academy Press, 1986. Ill., bibl. 2 vols. Prepared by the National Research Council, Committee on Conservation Needs and Opportunities. Vol. 1 presents concise tables of data collected from the 1982 National Resources Inventory (NRI), documenting trends in land use and soil loss and the effects of cropping and conservation practices on different classes of land erosion. Vol. 2 papers assess the NRI from the perspectives of analytical results and methods, specific applications, and resource policy and decision making.

1157. Follett, R. F.; Stewart, B. A.; eds. **Soil erosion and crop productivity.** American Society of Agronomy, 1985. 533 pp. Conference papers present information on specific aspects of erosion, including nutrient supplies, water infiltration, tilth and aeration, and rooting depth; other topics included erosion rates around the United States, political and sociological causes of erosion, the economic costs of erosion, and conservation practices.

1158. Boardman, J.; Dearing, J. A.; Foster, I. D. L.; eds. **Soil erosion on agricultural land.** Wiley, British Geomorphological Research Group Symposia Series, 1990. 400 pp. General review articles and focused research papers from 1989 conference cover such topics as erosion processes, assessment and prediction, and policy.

1159. Soil fertility and organic matter as critical components of production systems. Soil Science Society of America; American Society of Agronomy, SSSA special publication, no. 19, 1987. 166 pp., ill., bibl. Proceedings of a 1985 symposium. Discusses roles of soil, climate, and management in nutrient availability and use and controls on both nutrient cycling and dynamics of organic matter.

1160. Cook, Ray L.; Ellis, Boyd G. **Soil management: a world view of conservation and production.** Wiley, 1987. 413 pp., ill., bibl., index. Discusses general issues of soil management for production and provides further material on management for conventional farming, shifting cultivation, multiple cropping, and organic farming.

1161. Dalzell, H. W.; and others. **Soil management: compost production and use in tropical and subtropical environments.** Food and Agriculture Organization of the United Nations, FAO soils bulletin, no. 56, 1987. 177 pp. Intended for the small landholder. Principles of composting; materials for composting; uses of compost; environmental, economic, and social aspects; and the education and training of farmers and extension workers in composting skills.

1162. Lal, R.; Pierce, F. J.; eds. **Soil management for sustainability.** Soil and Water Conservation Society, 1991. 189 pp., index. Reviews policy issues and priorities, management options, and basic processes associated with enhancing soil quality and improving its life support capabilities. Topics include soil structure and compaction, the effects of soil erosion on crop productivity, conservation tillage, and organic wastes.

1163. Jeffrey, David W. **Soil-plant relationships: an ecological approach.** Croom Helm; Timber Press, 1987. 295 pp., ill., bibl., index. Discusses responses of plants to ions and water in soil, soil characteristics, and case studies of soil-plant interactions.

1164. Lal, R. **Tropical ecology and physical edaphology.** Wiley, 1987. 732 pp., ill., bibl., index. Comprehensive review by leading authority of the characteristics, potential, and limitations of major agroecological regions in the tropics. Emphasizes relationship of soil physical properties, ecological environment, and crop production. In four parts: tropical ecology, ecological factors and physical properties, man as an ecological factor, and improvement in tropical agriculture.

1165. Kozlowski, Theodore Thomas; ed. **Water deficits and plant growth. Vol. VI: Woody plant communities.** Academic Press, 1981. 571 pp. Discusses water relations at coniferous, temperate hardwood, and tropical forests, apple and citrus orchards, and tea plantations.

1166. Kramer, Paul Jackson. **Water relations of plants.** Academic Press, 1983. 489 pp., ill., bibl., index.

Introductory text. Describes factors that control plant-water balance, showing how they affect physiological processes that determine quantity and quality of growth. Topics include cell-water relations, measurement and control of soil water, root system development, water absorption, conductivity systems, and transpiration.

1167. Simpson, G. M. **Water stress on plants.** Praeger, 1981. 324 pp., maps, ill., bibl., index. Traces the development of water deficits in plants and examines plant responses to drought. Reviews research and knowledge of drought-stress physiology and their application to plant breeding and crop production.

Atmospheric Environment. Pollution. Pesticides (1168–1194)

1168. Daessler, H.-G.; Boertitz, S.; eds. **Air pollution and its influence on vegetation: causes, effects, prophylaxis, and therapy.** Junk; Kluwer, Tasks for vegetation science, v. 18, 3d ed., 1988. 223 pp. Covers the measurement of air pollution, effects, methods of diagnosis and damage assessment, protection procedures, and methods to reduce emission effects in agriculture, horticulture, and forestry.

1169. Treshow, Michael; ed. **Air pollution and plant life.** Wiley, Environmental monographs and symposia, 1984. 486 pp., ill., bibl., index. Reference source of direct and indirect effects of air pollution, from chemical level of action to organismal and ecological effects.

1170. Schulte-Hostede, Sigurd; and others, eds. **Air pollution and plant metabolism.** Elsevier, 1988. 381 pp., ill., bibl. Proceedings of the 2nd International Symposium on Air Pollution and Plant Metabolism, held in 1987. Presents current research. Includes discussion of effects of air pollutants on plant pathogens and mycorrhizae; interactions between air pollutants and cold and water stress; and the deposition, uptake, and residence of pollutants.

1171. Taylor, H. J.; Ashmore, M. R.; Bell, J. N. B. **Air pollution injury to vegetation.** IEHO, 1986. 68 pp., ill., index. Field guide; describes the effects of different air pollutants and discusses the environmental factors that can affect plant sensitivity to such pollutants; illustrates mimicking symptoms caused by other stresses; also discusses diagnosis, chemical analysis, and yield effects.

1172. MacKenzie, James J.; El-Ashry, Mohamed T. **Air pollution's toll on forests and crops.** Yale University Press, 1989. 367 pp., maps, ill., index. Eight papers review evidence of air pollution damage to trees and crops in Europe, California, and northeastern and southeastern United States. Shows benefits of pollution reduction. Editors summarize issues and recommend policies.

1173. Heck, Walter W.; Taylor, O. Clifton; Tingey, David T.; eds. **Assessment of crop loss from air pollutants.** Elsevier, 1988. 552 pp. Proceedings of a 1987 conference; papers discuss modeling techniques, field applications, and data interpretation and extrapolation; review physiological processes; note the numerous variables involved in crop loss assessment, and discuss economic policy implications.

1174. Ridgway, Richard L.; and others, eds. **Behavior-modifying chemicals for insect management: application of pheromones and other attractants.** Dekker, 1990. 761 pp., ill., bibl., index. Principles of application, chemistry, and efficient delivery systems. Case studies of practical applications against insects affecting horticultural and field crops, forests, stored products, and animals. Information on commercial pheromone and related product suppliers worldwide and applicable domestic and foreign regulations.

1175. Mandava, N. Bhushan; ed. **CRC handbook of natural pesticides: methods.** CRC Press, 1985–1990. Ill., bibl., index. 6 vols. Some volumes have more than one part. Vol. 1: Theory, practice, and detection. Vol. 2: Isolation and identification. Vol. 3: Insect growth regulators. Vol. 4: Pheromones. Vol. 5: Microbial insecticides. Vol. 6: Insect attractants and repellents.

1176. Pimentel, David, ed. **CRC handbook of pest management in agriculture.** CRC Press, 1981. 3 vols. Vol. 1 describes losses due to pests, the potential of nonchemical controls, and the impact of pesticides. Vol. 2 discusses the application of pesticides and biological pest control and examines problems associated with livestock pests, bee pollinators, and human poisoning. Vol. 3 gives information on the chemistry, mode of action, toxicity, and mobility of the major types of pesticides.

1177. Crop protection chemicals reference. Wiley, 6th ed., 1990. 2072 pp., index. Gives contents, directions for use, application and storage information, and safety and precautionary measures for over 560 products; fully indexed; includes contact information for product inquiries.

1178. Unsworth, M. H.; Ormrod, D. P.; eds. **Effects of gaseous air pollution in agriculture and horticulture.** Butterworth, 1982. 532 pp., maps, ill., index. Conference papers review the physiological and biochemical responses to pollutants, discuss the interactions between air pollutants and both plant diseases and mineral nutrition, and identify and assess the effects of air pollutants on the growth and quality of crops; some papers put pollution in perspective, covering evolutionary responses and future research directions.

1179. Dahlsten, Donald L.; Garcia, Richard; eds. **Eradication of exotic pests: analysis with case histories.** Yale University Press, 1989. 296 pp., ill., bibl. Presents 12 case studies (Dutch elm disease, citrus blackfly, gypsy moth, Japanese beetle, and others). Evaluates the problems engendered by the use of toxic substances in pest control from social, government, economic, and scientific perspectives.

1180. Herbicide handbook of the Weed Science Society of America. Weed Science Society of America, 5th ed., 1983. 515 pp., ill., indexes.

1181. LeBaron, Homer M.; Gressel, Jonathan; eds. **Herbicide resistance in plants.** Wiley, 1982. 401 pp., ill., bibl., index. Reviews the origin, taxonomy, physiology, mechanisms, and consequences of herbicide-resistant biotypes in weeds, examining possible applications to crop species.

1182. Mitchell, Everett R.; ed. **Management of insect pests with semiochemicals: concepts and practice.** Plenum Press, 1981. 514 pp., ill., indexes. Proceedings of an international symposium presented jointly by the Insect Attractants, Behavior, and Basic Biology Research Laboratory, U.S. Department of Agriculture, and the Department of Entomology and Nematology, University of Florida, held in 1980.

1183. MSDS reference for crop protection chemicals. Chemical and Pharmaceutical Press (prod. and dist. by Wiley), 3d ed., 1990. 2 vols. Intended to help pesticide manufacturers, distributors, and retailers comply with new OSHA and EPA laws requiring them to acquire, update, and maintain material safety data sheets on agricultural products.

1184. Hedin, Paul A.; ed. **Naturally occurring pest bioregulators.** American Chemical Society, ACS symposium series, v. 449, 1991. 456 pp., ill., bibl., index. Identifies natural chemicals and mechanisms, grouping them into five categories: insect bioregulation, allelochemical insect control, phytoalexins and phytotoxins in plant pest control, plant mechanisms for insect resistance, and allelochemical plant disease control.

1185. Scopes, N.; Ledieu, M.; eds. **Pest and disease control handbook.** Inkata Press, 2d ed., 1983. 672 pp. Information about and recommendations for the use of insecticides and fungicides on a wide range of crops.

1186. Rice, Elroy L. **Pest control with nature's chemicals: allelochemics and pheromones in gardening and agriculture.** University of Oklahoma Press, 1983. 224 pp., bibl., index. Discusses the results and effects of chemically triggered plant-plant, plant-nematode, plant-insect, plant-animal, and insect-insect interactions; examines ways of using these natural chemicals and interactions in agriculture and gardening, particularly in controlling insects.

1187. Worthing, Charles; Hance, Raymond J.; eds. **The pesticide manual: a world compendium.** British Crop Protection Council; Blackwell Scientific, 9th ed., 1991. 1141 pp. Gives molecular and structural formulas, Wiswesser line-formula notation, development, properties, uses, toxicology, formulations, and methods of analysis for over 650 chemical compounds and microbial agents used as active ingredients in products to control pests and diseases. Four indexes: Chemical Abstracts Service Registry numbers, code numbers from manufacturers, common and chemical names, and trademarks.

1188. Pesticides documentation bulletin. Network Information Services, 1970 to date. Quarterly.

1189. Ware, George Whitaker. **Pesticides: theory and application.** Freeman, 1983. 308 pp. Explains the properties of chemicals used to control invertebrates, vertebrates, plants, and microorganisms. Discusses biological and environmental interactions, usage and storage, and determination of the risk-benefit ratio in chemical controls. Updated version of *The pesticide book* (1978).

1190. Hale, Maynard G.; Orcutt, David M. **The physiology of plants under stress.** Wiley, 1987. 206 pp., ill., bibl., index. Examines effects of drought, temperature, nutrition, salt, irradiation, and allelochemicals. College-level text with study questions.

1191. Treshow, Michael; Anderson, Franklin K. **Flant stress from air pollution.** Wiley, 1989. 283 pp., ill., bibl., index. Intended for the nonspecialist; provides background in botany, air pollution, plant stress, and the history of relevant research; discusses sulfur dioxide, fluorides, heavy metals, ozone, and plant responses at the molecular, organismal, and ecosystem levels.

1192. Grace J.; Ford, E. D.; Jarvis, P. G.; eds. **Plants and their atmospheric environment.** Blackwell Scientific, Symposium of the British Ecological Society, v. 21, 1981. 419 pp., ill., bibl., index. Based on a symposium; 23 chapters represent the state-of-the-art understanding of plant-atmosphere interactions as of 1979; covers such topics as stomatal behavior, plant water potentials, particulate and gaseous exchange, and acclimation.

1193. Bohmont, Bert L. **Standard pesticide user's guide: revised and enlarged**. Prentice-Hall, 1990. 498 pp., ill. Notes developments in regulation, equipment, and application and transportation, storage, and disposal techniques; offers updated information covering effects on soil, groundwater, and endangered species.

1194. Winner, William E.; Mooney, Harold A.; Goldstein, Robert A.; eds. **Sulfur dioxide and vegetation: physiology, ecology, and policy issues**. Stanford University Press, 1985. 593 pp., ill., bibl., index. Papers discuss the effects of SO_2 on plant biochemistry, physiology, and growth, as well as on community structure, function, and productivity. Reviews methods and techniques of air pollution research. Section on issues of pollution management.

Section 6

Trees. Forests. Forestry

In America, the conservation movement grew up around the practice and profession of forestry, and forest conservation has been the heart of natural resource conservation. More than ever, trees and forests are recognized for their roles in protecting watersheds, holding soil, nurturing wildlife, preserving biological diversity, sustaining human cultures, providing fuel and food, providing lumber and paper, providing amenities, and storing carbon dioxide.

Because of these roles, public opinion registers alarm as forests disappear or seem to disappear. Tropical rain forests and old-growth forests in the Pacific Northwest are the most celebrated instances, but fear of deforestation is widespread. With that fear has come lack of confidence in the objectives and techniques of forest management. But, as the entries in this section will show, much is known about growing, maintaining, and improving forests. Legitimate differences over the goals of forest management should not keep us from utilizing the art and science of forestry in solving environmental problems.

The section begins with general accounts of forests and forest resources by region and country. The forest management group then introduces some essential works on forestry and silviculture. These are further broken down into subgroups on tree planting (arboriculture, afforestation) and tropical forest management. The remainder of the section presents the subject matter of tree and forest sciences, including forest ecology and ecosystems, tree species and genetic resources, and the physical components of air, water, and soil.

Forests and Forest Resources: Regions and Countries
The entries of this first group introduce world forest resources and cover topics like deforestation, assessment of forest lands, forest land management, and forest conditions of temperate and tropical areas.

See also:

- Section 1: Global resources and environment
- Section 4: Landscape ecology; land: countries and regions; land: North American region; land: terrestrial ecosystems
- Section 5: Plants, agriculture

- Section 8: Society and environment: country studies
- Section 9: Nature writing and thought, arts
- Section 10: Law, politics, government; national laws and policies; international law and policies; U.S. politics and policies; land preservation, trusts, state parks
- Section 11: Natural resource industries; agriculture and forest products

Forest Management. Silviculture
The selections in this group are essential texts on forest management and silviculture.

See also:

- Section 5: Crops, cropping systems
- Section 8: Social and human ecology, population
- Section 10: U.S. executive agencies, administration and regulation; natural resources: United States; forests, parks, wilderness: United States
- Section 11: Natural resource industries; agriculture and forest products

Tree Planting. Afforestation. Arboriculture. This subgroup on tree planting focuses on the growing, tending, and planting of individual trees, which brings together entries on afforestation and arboriculture, the large-scale and small-scale modes of tree planting.

See also:

- Section 5: Landscaping, horticulture, gardening; plant sciences; plant ecology
- Section 8: Social and human ecology, population; tribal communities; rural communities; urban communities
- Section 9: Built environment, architecture, historical preservation

Tropical Forest Management. This subgroup refers to all aspects of tropical forest practices and utilization, not just to formal management. There are some entries on nontropical forest management taking place in developing countries. Agroforestry and forest farming are placed in this section rather than under agriculture in Section 5.

See also:

- Section 1: Biological systems; ecology
- Section 5: Crops, cropping systems; landscaping, horticulture, gardening; plant sciences; plant ecology
- Section 7: Wildlife management; animal biology, zoology; animal ecology, species
- Section 8: Tribal communities; rural communities
- Section 10 International law and policies
- Section 11: Natural resource industries; agriculture and forest products
- Section 13: Civil engineering, construction, geotechnology

Tree and Forest Sciences
In this group are entries on biology, physiology, tree growth and form, forest entomology, and social sciences aspects.

See also:

- Section 1: Biological systems; ecology
- Section 2: Atmosphere, climate, weather; weather and life, biometeorology
- Section 3: Aquatic and marine sciences
- Section 5: Plant sciences
- Section 7: Animal biology, zoology
- Section 14: Science, research, methods

Forest Ecology. Ecosystems
This group has selections on the science of forest ecology and on types of forest ecosystems around the world.

See also:

- Section 1: Biological systems; ecology
- Section 3: Freshwater biology and ecology
- Section 4: Landscape ecology; land: terrestrial ecosystems
- Section 5: Plant ecology
- Section 7: Animal ecology, species
- Section 8: Social and human ecology, population
- Section 14: Modeling and simulation

Tropical Forest Ecosystems. This subgroup was established to bring together the main recent works on tropical rain forests and other tropical forest ecosystems.

See also Tropical Forest Management, above.

Species. Genetic Resources
Works on individual tree species are placed here with those on genetics and endangered species.

See also:

- Section 1: Biodiversity, conservation biology
- Section 4: Landscape ecology; land: terrestrial ecosystems
- Section 5: Endangered plants, genetic resources
- Section 7: Endangered species, conservation biology

Air, Soil, and Water Relations. Pollution

This group contains entries on forest soils, forests and climate, fires, air pollution effects, pesticides, and nutrient cycling.

See also:

- Section 1: Chemistry, biogeochemical cycles, pollutants
- Section 2: Atmosphere, climate, weather; air pollution, atmospheric chemistry; weather and life, biometeorology
- Section 3: Water: physical aspects, hydrology
- Section 4: Soils
- Section 5: Plants, agriculture; soil and water relations; atmospheric environment, pollution, pesticides

1195. Perlin, John. **A forest journey: the role of wood in the development of civilization.** Norton, 1989. 445 pp., maps, ill., bibl., index. Chronicles the recurring cycle of forest use, prosperity, deforestation, and population movement from the origins of civilization to late nineteenth-century United States.

1196. Mather, Alexander S. **Global forest resources.** Timber Press, 1990. 341 pp., maps, ill., bibl., index. Survey of world forest resources, historical perspectives on use, control and management practices, uses of forests, environmental aspects and people and policies. Numerous maps and graphics.

1197. Westoby, Jack. **Introduction to world forestry.** Basil Blackwell, 1989. 240 pp. Current state of the world's forests; background information; comparison of forest management around the world.

1198. **Unasylva.** Food and Agriculture Organization of the United Nations, 1947 to date. Quarterly. Illustrated articles for the general reader report on forests and forestry around the world, particularly the work of the FAO.

1199. Richards, John F.; Tucker, Richard P. **World deforestation in the twentieth century.** Duke University Press, 1988. 309 pp. Proceedings of a symposium at Duke University. Papers by historians, political scientists, and foresters cover examples of deforestation in Asia, Africa, Russia, and the Americas. Focuses on the role of developed countries in exploiting tropical hardwoods.

1200. **World wood.** Miller Freeman, 1960 to date. Bimonthly. Provides international coverage of the forest products industry, including machinery and equipment, harvesting techniques, forestry practices, new technologies and management techniques, and environmental concerns.

Forests and Forest Resources: Regions and Countries (1201–1226)

1201. Anderson, Anthony B. **Alternatives to deforestation: steps toward sustainable use of the Amazon rain forest.** Columbia University Press, 1990. 281 pp., ill., index. Contributed papers critically review past management practices and the use of cleared forestland for cattle ranching. Encourages replanting of forests on abandoned pastures. Suggests sustainable alternative uses, including extracting rubber, cocoa, and medicines.

1202. **American forests.** American Forestry Association, 1895 to date. Monthly. Promoting and serving the cause of forests and forestry since the 1890s. Tree planting and urban trees and forests are current issues.

1203. Williams, Michael. **Americans and their forests: a historical geography.** Cambridge University Press, 1989. 599 pp., ill., bibl., index. Describes changes to forests since European settlement. Examines the effects on forests of timber cutting, agricultural expansion, shipbuilding, railroads, industrial expansion, and increased population.

1204. Norse, Elliott A. **Ancient forests of the Pacific Northwest.** Island Press, 1990. 327 pp., ill., bibl., index. Discusses the biological value of old-growth forests and the ecological impacts of traditional timber operations. Proposes sustainable forestry practices to save some of the remaining forests.

1205. Qureshi, Alta H.; ed. **Assessing tropical forest lands: their suitability for sustainable uses.** East-West Center, Environment and Policy Institute, 1980. 69 pp., ill., bibl. Report of the Conference on Forest Land Assessment and Management for Sustainable Uses in 1979. Part I develops a methodology for determining land use at the micro and macro levels: examines the planning process, land capability classification, and suitability assessment. Part II papers review classification concepts and methods in various settings and present case studies from the Third World and Australia.

1206. Collins, N. Mark; Sayer, Jeffrey A.; Whitmore, Timothy C.; eds. **The conservation atlas of tropical forests: Asia and the Pacific.** Simon & Schuster, 1991. 256 pp., indexes, maps, ill. Seventeen country studies, more than 50 color maps and current statistics from government agencies, the United Nations, and the World Bank.

1207. Cowell, Adrian. **The decade of destruction: the crusade to save the Amazon rain forest.** Holt, 1990. 215 pp., maps, ill. Accounts by a documentary filmmaker and friend of Chico Mendes of trips to various parts of the Amazon that began in 1958. His focus is on the "holocaust" of deforestation occurring in the 1980s and in Xingu National Park. This chronicle of rain forest destruction shows a rare understanding of the Amazonian settler.

1208. Hamilton, A. C. **Deforestation in Uganda.** Oxford University Press, 1984. 92 pp., maps, ill., bibl., index. Explains how the country's history, geography, population, and past and present forestry policies have all contributed to the destruction of Uganda's forests.

1209. Pearson, Henry A.; Hecht, Susanna B.; Downing, Theodore E.; eds. **Development or destruction: the conversion of forest to pasture in Latin America.** Westview Press, 1989. 416 pp., index. Analyzes ecological and social costs of cattle production from the perspectives of anthropology, animal science, environmental sciences, forestry, and natural resource economics. Discusses alternatives to cattle production.

1210. Barr, Brenton M.; Braden, Kathleen E. **Disappearing Russian forest: a dilemma in resource management.** Rowman & Littlefield, 1988. 252 pp., ill., bibl., index. Economic and geographic analysis of Russian forests. Reviews history of forest use in industry, society, and international trade.

1211. Eden, Michael J. **Ecology and land management in Amazonia.** Belhaven Press (dist. by Columbia University Press), 1990. 269 pp., bibl., index. Addresses the rain forest as a global resource, the particular needs of rain forest countries, and strategies to ensure rain forest conservation.

1212. Hecht, Susanna B.; Cockburn, Alexander. **The fate of the forest: developers, destroyers, and defenders of the Amazon.** Verso, 1989. 266 pp., maps, ill., bibl. Puts the exploitation of the Amazonian rain forest in a larger context, discussing the ecology of the area and its history of exploration and exploitation by Europeans.

1213. The forest resources of the ECE region: Europe, the USSR, North America. Food and Agriculture Organization of the United Nations, 1985. 223 pp., ill. Provides general forest inventory data and volume and mass estimates of woody biomass. Analyzes role of forests in providing nontimber goods.

1214. Richardson, S.D. **Forests and forestry in China: changing patterns of resource development.** Island Press, 1990. 352 pp., maps, ill., bibl., index. Updates the author's *Forestry in communist China* (1966). Discusses the social and political forces shaping forestry and natural resource management in China. Topics include forest industries and trade, production practices, and administration, policy, and law. Appendices contain sections of applicable forestry laws in China.

1215. Caufield, Catherine. **In the rainforest: report from a strange, beautiful, imperiled world.** University of Chicago Press, 2d ed., 1991. 310 pp., map. Introduction to the world's rain forests from historical, political, economic, and biological perspectives.

1216. Dwyer, Augusta. **Into the Amazon: the struggle for the rain forest.** Sierra Club Books; Random House, 1991. 264 pp., maps, ill., bibl., index. Firsthand report emphasizes the environmental aspects.

1217. Poffenberger, Mark; ed. **Keepers of the forest: land management alternatives in Southeast Asia.** Kumarian Press, 1990. 289 pp. Argues that government bureaucracies are responsible for forest destruction in Southeast Asia and calls for collaboration with local people in forest management. Case studies from the Philippines, Indonesia, and Thailand.

1218. Collins, Mark; ed. **The last rain forests: a world conservation atlas.** Oxford University Press, 1990. 200 pp., maps, ill., index. Deals with over 50 rain forest countries. Explains rain forests, their benefits (including biodiversity, forest products, and the global environment), and their complex ecosystems. Identifies conservation issues and efforts relevant to particular countries and regions. Includes 200 full-color photographs and maps.

1219. Head, Suzanne; Heinzman, Robert; eds. **Lessons of the rainforest.** Sierra Club Books, 1990. 275 pp. Contributed essays on the causes of rain forest destruction, from cutting by local farmers and ranchers to consumption by developed nations. Articulates the spiritual and ecological benefits of saving rain forests and suggests strategies for doing so. Sections include bioregional history and examples of good and bad management.

1220. Gillis, R. Peter; Roach, Thomas R. **Lost initiatives: Canada's forest industries, forest policy, and forest conservation.** Greenwood Press, Contributions in economics and economic history, no. 69, 1986. 326 pp., maps, ill., bibl., index. Discusses the relationship between government and the timber industry in the 19th century, the origins of the conservation movement, and the history of forestry in Quebec, Ontario, British Columbia, and New Brunswick. Chronicles early and continuing failures to develop an effective national forestry policy.

1221. Fahl, Ronald J.; compiler. **North American forest and conservation history: a bibliography.** ABC-CLIO, 1977. 408 pp., index. Broad coverage, from popular magazine articles to scholarly works on the history of human-forest interactions. Brief annotations; entries arranged by author, with subject index.

1222. Gradwohl, Judith; Greenberg, Russell. **Saving the tropical forests.** Island Press, 1988. 214 pp., maps, ill., bibl., index. Based on a 1985 conference. Thirty-eight case studies focus on lowland tropical moist forests around the world. Surveys methods of saving forests compatible with economic development: forest reserves, sustainable agriculture, natural forest management, and tropical forest restoration.

1223. Cox, Thomas R.; and others. **This well-wooded land: Americans and their forests from colonial times to the present.** University of Nebraska Press, 1985. 325 pp., ill., bibl., index. Survey history. Emphasizes the reciprocal relationship of forests and the expanding economy.

1224. Committee on forest development in the tropics. **Tropical forestry action plan.** Food and Agriculture Organization of the United Nations, 1985. 159 pp. Proposals and conceptual framework for saving tropical forests. Covers land use, forest-based industries, fuelwood, institutions, and other topics.

1225. Newman, Arnold. **Tropical rainforest: a world survey of our most valuable endangered habitat with a blueprint for its survival.** Facts on File, 1990. 256 pp., maps, ill., bibl., index. Reveals the complexity and interconnectedness of rain forest plant and animal life and the risks to it from logging and slash-and-burn agriculture. Suggests a range of steps and options to halt the destruction.

1226. Irland, Lloyd C. **Wildlands and woodlots: the story of New England's forests.** University Press of New England, 1982. 217 pp., ill., bibl, index. Changes in the forests and their shifting role in New England's economy. Defines uses and future of five forest types: suburban, rural, recreational, industrial, and wilderness.

Forest Management. Silviculture (1227–1257)

1227. Appropriate wood harvesting in plantation forests. Food and Agriculture Organization of the United Nations, FAO forestry paper, no. 78, 1987. 266 pp., maps, ill., bibl. Lectures given at a 1986 training course in Zimbabwe. Discusses appropriate techniques and approaches for efficient wood harvesting in developing countries.

1228. Brett, Richard M. **Country Journal woodlot primer: the right way to manage your woodland.** Country Journal, 1983. 134 pp., ill., index. Straightforward, practical advice for the small woodlot owner on improving woodlots for timber, wildlife, and recreation.

1229. Robinson, G. **The forest and the trees: a guide to excellent forestry.** Island Press, 1988. 257 pp., ill., bibl., index. Excellent forestry here means a return to uneven-aged management.

1230. Davis, Lawrence S.; Johnson, K. Norman. **For-est management.** McGraw-Hill, 1986. 790 pp., ill., bibl., index. Presents models and methods for timber production, decision analysis, valuation, and forest management planning. Includes numerous questions and problems with answers.

1231. Avery, Thomas Eugene; Burkhart, Harold E. **Forest measurements.** McGraw-Hill, 1983. 331 pp., ill., bibl., index. Explains methods employed in many types of measurement: land measurements, cubic volume, cord measure, weight scaling, log rules scaling practice, aerial photography, volumes and weights of standing trees, 3P sampling, and growth and yield models.

1232. Forest operations in politically and environmentally sensitive areas: a proceedings of the Council on Forest Engineering. Council on Forest Engineering, 1985. 162 pp., ill., bibl. Papers from a 1985 meeting organized into sections on planning aspects, cable-harvesting techniques, specialized solutions, use of machines such as hydraulic excavators or feller-bunchers, and others.

1233. Jaygreen, John G.; Howyer, Jim L. **Forest products and wood science: an introduction.** Iowa State University Press, 2d ed., 1989. 500 pp., ill., bibl., index. Chemical and structural nature of wood, its physical properties, and major forest products, including manufacturing processes.

1234. Forest products journal. Forest Products Research Society, 1951 to date. Monthly. Publishes applied research on wood and wood products.

1235. Douglass, Robert W. **Forest recreation.** Pergamon Press, 3d ed., 1982. 336 pp. An introduction to recreation area planning, development, and administration. Assesses supply of recreation areas, public pressures, and legislative responses. Reviews site selection, water supply, and sanitation. Covers operation and management of developed areas and addresses water-oriented recreation development.

1236. Leuschner, William A. **Forest regulation, harvest scheduling, and planning techniques.** Wiley, 1990. 281 pp. Covers classic and neoclassic forest regulation techniques, including mathematical programming models. Examines FORPLAN, used by the U.S. Forest Service, and multiple objectives techniques.

1237. Singh, A. K.; and others. **Forest resource, economy and environment.** Concept Publishing, New Delhi, 1987. 124 pp., maps, ill., bibl., index. Analyzes the role of the forest in shaping the economy and environment of Uttar Pradesh, India, a region of major deforestation.

1238. Walstad, John D.; Kuch, Peter J.; eds. **Forest vegetation management for conifer production.** Wiley, 1987. 522 pp., ill., index. Discusses the history and likely futures of forest weed management in major production regions of North America. Covers conifer response to various weed management strategies and economic and ecological aspects of management options.

1239. Nyland, Ralph D.; Larson, Charles C.; Shirley, Hardy L. **Forestry and its career opportunities.** McGraw-Hill, 1983. 381 pp., ill., bibl., index. Introduction to forestry and land management. Brief chapters on forest ecosystems, soils, water, timber, rangeland, properties of wood, and other topics.

1240. Forestry chronicle. Canadian Institute of Forestry, 1925 to date. Bimonthly. Professional and technical periodical of Canadian forestry.

1241. Sim, D.; Hilmi, H. A. **Forestry extension methods.** Food and Agriculture Organization of the United Nations, FAO forestry paper, no. 80, 1987. 155 pp., ill., bibl. Practical guide for extension field-workers. Covers general principles of forestry extension; communication and audiovisual aids; individual, group and, mass extension programs; and program monitoring and evaluation.

1242. Wenger, Karl F.; ed. **Forestry handbook.** Wiley, 1984. 1335 pp., ill., bibl., index. For the practicing field forester; reorganized and rewritten edition provides a reference book of data and methods in all phases of forestry and allied fields.

1243. Carlson, Les W.; Shea, Keith R.; eds. **Increasing productivity of multipurpose lands.** International Union of Forestry Research Organization, 1986. 333 pp., maps, ill., bibl. Proceedings of a 1986 workshop. Topics addressed include development of natural regeneration techniques, management of indigenous trees and shrubs, genetic improvement of indigenous and exotic woody species, and establishment of fuelwood plantations.

1244. Leuschner, William A. **Introduction to forest management.** Wiley, 1984. 298 pp., ill., bibl., index. Undergraduate-level text. Discusses forest valuation, taking into account inflation, taxation, and risk. Presents methods for rotation, determining allowable cut, and regulating even- and uneven-aged forests. Reviews mathematical programming in harvest scheduling and principles and practices of multiple-use management.

1245. Young, Raymond A.; ed. **Introduction to forest science.** Wiley, 1982. 554 pp., ill., bibl., index. Surveys the composition and location of forests worldwide, especially in North America. Explains processes of forest biology at individual tree and stand levels. Reviews methods of silviculture, forest measurement, and multiple-use management. Some material on range, timber, watershed management, recreation, fires, and forest products.

1246. Journal of forestry. Society of American Foresters, 1902 to date. Monthly. Journal advancing the science, technology, education, and practice of professional forestry. Editorial features, peer-reviewed articles, news of the Society, and forest policies.

1247. Pearce, John Kenneth; Stenzel, George; Walbridge, Thomas A., Jr.; and others. **Logging and pulpwood production.** Wiley, 2d ed., 1985. 358 pp., ill., bibl., index. Comprehensive text covers timber acquisition, planning a logging operation, road engineering and construction, skidding, yarding, loading and hauling.

1248. Edmonds, Robert L. **Lumber from local woodlots.** Northeast Regional Agricultural Engineering Service; Cornell University, 1988. 42 pp. Walks through the lumber production process, giving practical advice to woodlot owners. Reviews woodlot evaluation, management, and harvest techniques. Follows cut logs to the sawmill, discussing equipment and methods. Describes seasoning options.

1249. O'Loughlin, Jennifer; Pfister, Robert D.; eds. **Management of second-growth forests: the state of knowledge and research needs.** University of Montana, Montana Forest and Conservation Experiment Station, 1983. 269 pp., ill., bibl. Papers from a 1982 symposium discuss basic economic resources, multiresource inventory, productivity, and management.

1250. Smith, David M. **The practice of silviculture.** Wiley, 8th ed., 1986. 527 pp., ill., index. Standard textbook, with emphasis on North America. In three parts: tending and intermediate cutting, regeneration, and silvicultural systems.

1251. Matthews, John D. **Silvicultural systems.** Clarendon Press, Oxford science publications, 1989. 284 pp., ill., bibl. Relates silviculture to forest management. Addresses the protective and beneficial functions of managed forests, and some of the problems faced in protecting forests from damage. Examines techniques and features of many silvicultural systems, including clear cutting, irregular shelterwood, selection, and the coppice system. Most references from the United Kingdom and Europe.

1252. Burns, Russell M.; compiler. **Silvicultural systems for the major forest types of the United States.** U.S. Department of Agriculture, Forest Service; Government Printing Office, Agriculture handbook, no.

445, 1983. 191 pp., bibl., index. Presents biologically feasible silvicultural systems for 48 major forest types in the United States.

1253. Falardeau, Helene. **Successful forestry: a guide to private forest management.** Canadian Forestry Service, 1988. 133 pp. Twelve illustrated sections provide instruction on the techniques and methods of proper silviculture on private woodlots.

1254. Hakkila, Pentti. **Utilization of residual forest biomass.** Springer-Verlag, Springer series in wood science, 1989. 568 pp., ill., bibl. Synthesis of scientific literature and practical developments. Discusses quantity and properties of biomass, harvesting, transport, ecological consequences of biomass recovery, and uses.

1255. Hunter, Malcolm L., Jr. **Wildlife, forests, and forestry: principles of managing forests for biological diversity.** Prentice-Hall, 1990. 400 pp. Employs a macro and micro approach to discuss forest landscapes and stands. Topics include species composition, spatial heterogeneity, age structure, dead trees, vertical diversity, and intensive silviculture. Appendices include review of U.S. national policies regarding forest biodiversity and techniques to gauge diversity.

1256. Brandle, J. R.; Hintz, D. L.; Sturrock, J. W.; eds. **Windbreak technology.** Elsevier, 1988. 598 pp. Proceedings of a 1986 symposium. Addresses windbreak planting, establishment, and management. Provides advice on tree and shrub species for arid, semiarid, temperate, and tropical areas. Reviews plant, crop, wildlife, and livestock responses to windbreaks.

1257. Peterken, George Frederick. **Woodland conservation and management.** Chapman and Hall, 1981. 328 pp., ill., bibl., index. Discusses the origins of British woodlands, their ecological characteristics, and management history. Classifies Britain's seminatural woodlands and examines the goals and priorities of nature conservation in this context. Emphasizes the need to balance timber production with wildlife conservation and other uses.

Tree Planting. Afforestation. Arboriculture (1258–1276)

1258. Patch, D.; ed. **Advances in practical arboriculture.** Her Majesty's Stationery Office, Forestry Commission bulletin, no. 65, 1987. 196 pp. Proceedings of a 1985 seminar. Chapters on plant production, tree establishment, the mature tree, and protection.

1259. Arboricultural journal: the international journal of urban forestry. A B Academic, 1977 to date. Quarterly. Official journal of the Arboricultural Association, United Kingdom.

1260. Food and Agriculture Organization of the United Nations (Rome). **Eucalypts for planting.** Food and Agriculture Organization of the United Nations, Forestry series, no. 11, 1979. 677 pp., ill., bibl., index. Reviews the botanical and growth characteristics of eucalypts and all aspects of their cultivation and use. Also discusses fire protection, yield, and use or potential use of eucalypts in over 90 countries. Descriptions of over 100 species.

1261. Duryea, Mary L.; Landis, Thomas D.; eds. **Forest nursery manual: production of bareroot seedlings.** Nijhoff, 1984. 385 pp., ill., bibl., index. Handbook of practice and research. Topics include selecting and preparing a site, assuring seed quality, managing soil and water, culturing seedlings, harvesting, and outplanting.

1262. Binkley, Dan. **Forest nutrition management.** Wiley, 1986. 290 pp., ill., bibl., index. Topics include nutrient cycles, forest nutrient assessment, fertilization, biological nitrogen fixing, harvesting, site preparation, and regeneration, primarily in temperate forests.

1263. Zobel, Bruce; van Wyk, Gerrit; Stahl, Per. **Growing exotic forests.** Wiley, 1987. 508 pp., ill., bibl., index. Discusses choice of proper species and establishment, growth, and utilization in tropical, subtropical, and temperate regions.

1264. Journal of arboriculture. International Society of Arboriculture, 1975 to date. Bimonthly. Devoted to the dissemination of knowledge in the science and art of growing and maintaining amenity trees.

1265. New forests. Nijhoff, 1986 to date. Quarterly. Publishes research on the biology, biotechnology, and management of afforestation and reforestation.

1266. Nitrogen fixing trees: a training guide. Food and Agriculture Organization of the United Nations; Regional Office for Asia and the Pacific, RAPA publication, no. 1987/15, 1987. 171 pp., ill., bibl. Structured lessons for a ten-day training session for mid-level managers.

1267. Shepherd, Kenneth R. **Plantation silviculture.** Nijhoff; Kluwer, Forestry sciences, 1986. 322 pp., ill., bibl., index. Undergraduate text based on experience in New Zealand and Australia. Chapters on seed production and handling, nursery practice, plantation and land use, even-aged crops, planting, site preparation and maintenance, pruning and thinning.

1268. Weber, Fred R.; Stoney, Carol; and Crouch,

Margaret, ed. **Reforestation in arid lands.** Volunteers in Technical Assistance, 2d ed., 1986. 335 pp., ill., bibl. Comprehensive reference manual explains the environmental and political framework needed for a reforestation project. Reviews project design, soil properties, and site and species selection. Explains nursery and planting site management and methods of designing agroforestry and soil conservation systems.

1269. Albrecht, Jean; Weicherding, Patrick J.; compilers. **Second supplement to Urban forestry: a bibliography.** University of Minnesota, Agricultural Experiment Station, Miscellaneous publication, no. 53–1988, 1988. 67 pp., index. Categories include the social, economic, and physical benefits of urban forests; culture and protection; and removal and utilization. Also provides sources for urban forest planning, management, and research programs.

1270. Moll, Gary; Ebenreck, Sara. **Shading our cities: a resource guide for urban and community forests.** Island Press, 1989. 333 pp., ill., bibl., index. Brief articles on urban forestry from a wide spectrum of viewpoints provide practical information and future visions for community leaders and forestry professionals. Includes measures to save existing trees, advice on starting an urban forestry program, and profiles of successful projects in many cities.

1271. Wiersum, K. F.; ed. **Strategies and designs for afforestation, reforestation and tree planting.** PUDOC, 1984. 432 pp., ill., bibl. Twenty-five papers from 50 countries discuss aims and objectives of forestation and development; present case studies of forestation systems in Brazil, the Sahel, Upper Volta, and Thailand; cover diagnostic methodologies; and analyze specific design components of forestation.

1272. Smith, J. Russell. **Tree crops: a permanent agriculture.** Island Press, Conservation classic, c. 1950, 1987. 408 pp., ill., index. Classic work, originally published in 1928, promotes sustainable agriculture and soil conservation through tree crops, particularly on hillsides and in mountainous regions. Explains the attributes, benefits, and needs of various trees, especially nut trees, and the potential for profit through managed harvest.

1273. Pirone, P. P.; and others. **Tree maintenance.** Oxford University Press, 6th ed., 1988. 528 pp., ill. Applies mainly to North America. Includes techniques for site and tree selection; planting, pruning, and protecting trees; and diagnosis and control of diseases and pests. Covers such problems as air pollution, sunscald and leaf scorch, and construction damage.

1274. Felker, Peter; ed. **Tree plantings in semi-arid regions.** Elsevier, 1986. 444 pp., ill., bibl., index. Proceedings of a 1985 symposium. Technical papers on soil, water, nutrients, physical and chemical properties of trees, asexual propagation, nursery and field practices, and genetics. Regional papers on Latin America, Asia, and Africa.

1275. Shigo, Alex L. **Tree pruning: a worldwide photo guide.** Shigo & Trees, 1989. 186 pp., ill., bibl., index. Discusses and illustrates tree anatomy in detail, explaining the virtues and techniques of proper pruning; shows how incorrect pruning damages trees.

1276. Grey, Gene W.; Deneke, Frederick J. **Urban forestry.** Wiley, 1986. 299 pp., ill., bibl., index. Discusses distribution, composition, environment, benefits, management, and values of urban forests. Presents information on education and training programs, urban forestry programs, and support organizations.

Tropical Forest Management (1277–1312)

1277. Steppler, Howard A.; Nair, P. K. Ramachandran; eds. **Agroforestry: a decade of development.** International Council for Research in Agroforestry, 1987. 335 pp., ill. Seventeen papers define agroforestry; present ecological, institutional, and developmental perspectives; discuss agroforestry practices in Africa, India, and Central America; and review research in systems, nutrient enrichment, germ plasm evaluation, and tree-component improvement.

1278. Agroforestry abstracts. CAB International, 1988 to date. Quarterly. Abstracts of research and developments in agroforestry systems, components, and processes.

1279. MacDicken, Kenneth G.; Vergara, Napoleon T.; eds. **Agroforestry: classification and management.** Wiley, 1990. 382 pp., ill., bibl., index. Describes agroforestry systems and practices from the major agroecological zones of the world, covering both their benefits and their drawbacks. Presents research and design strategies useful in establishing new techniques and studies implementation of experimental methods.

1280. Kerkhof, Paul; Barnard, Geoffrey and Foley, Gerald, eds. **Agroforestry in Africa: a survey of project experience.** Panos Books, Panos technical series, 1990. 216 pp., maps, ill., bibl., index. Surveys 21 agroforestry projects in 11 countries; includes successful and failed projects in a wide range of ecosystems.

1281. Gholz, Henry L.; ed. **Agroforestry: realities,**

possibilities and potentials. Nijhoff; International Council for Research in Agroforestry; Kluwer, 1987. 227 pp., ill., bibl., index. Based on a 1985–1986 seminar series. Papers provide general review, regional analyses, and case histories, ranging from palm tree plantations to "living fences."

1282. Agroforestry review. International Council for Research in Agroforestry, 1979 to date. Monthly. Continues: ICRAF newsletter. Multidisciplinary international journal providing for rapid publication of research and practical experience in agroforestry and for critical reviews of sustainable land management systems. Covers all aspects of agricultural systems involving trees and forests, with particular reference to their role in rural development.

1283. Nair, P. K. Ramachandran. **Agroforestry species, a crop sheets manual.** International Council for Research in Agroforestry, 1980. 336 pp., ill., bibl. Descriptions of 90 crops suitable for use in agroforestry, arranged by their economic uses.

1284. Agroforestry systems. Nijhoff; Junk (dist. by Kluwer), 1982 to date. Quarterly. Reports on fundamental and applied research into agroforestry systems, often in the tropics, including methods, policies, multidisciplinary land-use planning, rural development, and sustainable management.

1285. Hoekstra, D.; Kuguru, F. M.; eds. **Agroforestry systems for small-scale farmers.** International Council for Research in Agroforestry, 1983. 283 pp., ill. Proceedings of a 1982 workshop. Provides some general introduction to agroforestry. Emphasizes agroforestry techniques for African tobacco farmers.

1286. Nair, P. K. R.; ed. **Agroforestry systems in the tropics.** Kluwer, Forestry sciences, 1989. 664 pp., ill., bibl. Describes and classifies more than 25 tropical and subtropical agroforestry systems worldwide and discusses their productive and protective roles; reviews technological innovations in agroforestry.

1287. Montagnini, Florencia; Prevetti, Laurel; Thrupp, Lori A. **[Agroforestry systems: principles and applications in the tropics.]** Organizacion para Estudios Tropicales, Centro Agronomico Tropical do Investigacion y Enseanza, 1986. 818 pp., ill., bibl., index. Spanish-language text for the design, management, and evaluation of agroforestry systems. Appendices present five detailed case studies, an annotated bibliography, a review of institutions wordwide involved in agroforestry work, an index of plant species being used in Latin America, and a catalog of Latin American agroforestry systems.

1288. Raintree, J. B.; ed. **D & D user's manual: an introduction to agroforestry diagnosis and design.** International Council for Research in Agroforestry, 1987. 110 pp., ill., bibl. Basic principles and procedures of diagnosis and design. Focuses on useful and adaptable procedures. Illustrated by case study in Kenya.

1289. Douglas, James Sholto; de J. Hart, Robert A. **Forest farming: towards a solution to problems of world hunger an conservation.** Intermediate Technology Publications, 1984. 207 pp. Index. Discusses theories and practical steps of integrating crop-yielding trees into global agriculture. Describes requirements and harvests of various trees and suggests strategies for farming unexploited areas.

1290. Forestry and the development of rural areas in Third World countries. Deutsche Gesellschaft für Technische Zusammenarbeit, Schriftenreihe der GTZ, no. 186, 1986. 186 pp. Describes forestry and forest industries development projects financed by the German government, in German and English. For each entry, objectives, schedules, personnel, and funding.

1291. Joshi, S. C. **Forestry handbook of Bhutan.** International Book Distributors, 1986. 145 pp., ill. Brief reference work covers silviculture of certain species, afforestation, forest management, fire control, volume tables, logging, surveying and engineering, and policy.

1292. Tewari, D. N. **Forestry in national development.** Jugal Kishore, 1986. 256 pp., bibl. Examines the role of Indian forests and forestry in wildlife preservation, environmental stability, energy production, industry, rural development, and the survival of indigenous peoples.

1293. Hamilton, Lawrence S.; Snedaker, Samuel C.; eds. **Handbook for mangrove area management.** East-West Center, Environment and Policy Institute, 1984. 123 pp., ill., bibl. Summarizes current information on mangrove resources and provides guidelines for sustainable multiple-use management, incorporating economic considerations. Presents strategies for developing national management plans.

1294. Emrich, Walter. **Handbook of charcoal making: the traditional and industrial methods.** Reidel; Kluwer, Solar Energy R&D in the European Community, Series E, Energy from biomass, v. 7, 1985. 278 pp., bibl. Discusses traditional methods, technology for industrial production, uses of pyrolysis oil, raw materials, and markets.

1295. Negi, Sharad Singh. **Handbook of social forestry.** International Book Distributors, 1986. 177 pp., bibl. Outlines objectives and methods of urban, commercial, farm, noncommercial farm, and community forestry. Evaluates social land allocation projects. Discusses the traditions and economic benefits of social forestry, and describes some ideal species for farm and community forestry in India.

1296. Intensive multiple-use forest management in the tropics: analysis of case studies from India, Africa, Latin America and the Caribbean. Food and Agriculture Organization of the United Nations, FAO forestry paper, no. 55, 1985. 180 pp., maps, ill., bibl. For each area, describes the forest, its management, and the ecological, socioeconomic, political, and administrative factors influencing forest management.

1297. Shepherd, K. R.; Richter, H. V.; eds. **Managing the tropical forest.** Australian National University, Development Studies Centre, 1984. 341 pp., ill., bibl. Papers from a workshop held in Australia in 1983. Includes land-use planning, forest management, control of harvest, rain forest dynamics, and alternatives to natural management.

1298. Manual of forest inventory: with special reference to mixed tropical forests. Food and Agriculture Organization of the United Nations, FAO forestry paper, no. 27, 1981. 200 pp., ill., bibl.

1299. Philip, Michael S. **Measuring trees and forests: a textbook written for students in Africa.** University of Dar Es Salaam, Division of Forestry, 1983. 338 pp., ill., bibl. Comprehensive text covers land measurement, measurements of cut wood and standing trees, sampling and estimation, forest inventories, and other topics.

1300. Slade, R. H.; Campbell, J. Gabriel. **Monitoring and evaluation of social forestry in India: an operational guide.** Food and Agriculture Organization of the United Nations, FAO forestry paper, no. 75, 1986. 218 pp., ill. Designed for use by all social forestry and related programs in India. Covers monitoring and evaluation of farm forestry, village woodlots, and other activities.

1301. Mergen, Francois; Vincent, Jeffrey R.; eds. **Natural management of tropical moist forests: silvicultural and management prospects of sustained utilization.** Yale University, School of Forestry and Environmental Studies, 1987. 212 pp., bibl. Papers discuss problems and potential of silvicultural systems and treatments. Evaluates economic, social, and political aspects of natural management.

1302. Evans, Julian. **Plantation forestry in the tropics.** Clarendon Press, 1982. 472 pp., ill., bibl., in-

dex. Overview of tropical silviculture; includes consideration of land, social, and economic factors and the integration of plantation forestry with other land uses. Topics treated in some detail include forest nurseries, stand growth, thinning, and pruning.

1303. Zulberti, Ester.; ed. **Professional education in agroforestry: proceedings of an international workshop.** International Council for Research in Agroforestry, 1987. 378 pp., ill., bibl. Proceedings of a 1982 international workshop. Assesses needs for professional education, appropriate forms of teaching, and existing materials and courses.

1304. Westoby, Jack. **The purpose of forests: follies of development.** Basil Blackwell, 1987. 343 pp., bibl., index. Collection of speeches and essays by former FAO official, 1962 to 1985, on the role of foresters in socioeconomic development and the extent to which forestry development has lived up to its potential as an agent of change.

1305. Douglas, James J. **A re-appraisal of forestry development in developing countries.** Nijhoff; Junk; Kluwer, Forestry sciences, v. 8, 1983. 178 pp., bibl. Discusses issues in economic development and the role of forestry. Suggests that recent trends in development theory are poorly linked to the design and implementation of forestry projects.

1306. Graaf, N.R. de. **A silvicultural system for natural regeneration of tropical rain forest in Suriname.** Agricultural University of the Netherlands, Centre for Agricultural Publishing and Documentation, Wageningen, Ecology and management of tropical rain forests in Suriname, v. 1, 1986. 250 pp., ill., bibl. Discusses the basic concepts and practical aspects of a silvicultural system adopted by the Centre for Agriculture Research in Suriname, which has proved economically and ecologically feasible. Summarizes the results of over 15 years of experiments.

1307. Simple technologies for charcoal making. Food and Agriculture Organization of the United Nations, FAO forestry paper, no. 41, 1983. 154 pp., ill., bibl. Basic manual of labor-intensive techniques for charcoal production, storage and transport.

1308. Strategies, approaches and systems in integrated watershed management. Food and Agricultural Organization of the United Nations, FAO conservation guide, v. 14, 1986. 232 pp., bibl. Papers from a 1985 meeting cover development of policy and strategies, planning, watershed management, economics, community involvement, and management in areas of shifting cultivation and grazing.

1309. Denevan, William M.; Padoch, Christine; eds. **Swidden-fallow agroforestry in the Peruvian Amazon.** New York Botanical Garden, Advances in botany, v. 5, 1988. 107 pp., ill., bibl. Shows how indigenous peoples manage their forests without apparent loss of species or soil quality. What seem abandoned fields turn out to be highly managed agroforestry systems.

1310. Mergen, Francois. **Tropical forests: utilization and conservation.** Yale University, School of Forestry and Environmental Studies, 1981. 199 pp., bibl. Proceedings of the International Symposium on Tropical Forests Utilization and Conservation, held in 1980. In three parts: status of conditions; economic and sociopolitical aspects; ecological and environmental implications. Summary of situation and knowledge just as tropical forest issues were coming to the fore.

1311. Nwoboshi, Louis Charles. **Tropical silviculture: principles and techniques.** Ibadan University Press, 1982. 333 pp., ill., bibl., index. Intended for tropical forestry schools; covers principles of silviculture, tropical forests and their regeneration, and nursery and plantation practices.

1312. Opeke, Lawrence K. **Tropical tree crops.** Wiley, 1982. 312 pp., bibl., index. Discusses basic principles and practices of tree crop cultivation and provides detailed information on ten major crops. Intended as text for undergraduates in tropical Africa.

Tree and Forest Sciences (1313–1336)

1313. Bormann, F. Herbert; Berlyn, Graeme; eds. **Age and growth rate of tropical trees: new directions for research.** Yale University, School of Forestry and Environmental Studies, Bulletin, no. 94, 1981. 137 pp., ill., bibl. Proceedings of a 1980 workshop. Chapters discuss difficulties of determining age and growth in tropical trees. Group reports address and apply disciplines of wood anatomy, wood chemistry, radioisotopes, and biometry.

1314. Stary, Bohumil; and others. **Atlas of insects beneficial to forest trees.** Elsevier, 1976 to date. Vol. 2 was published in 1988. Discusses the biology and economic importance of such predators and parasites as ants, scale bugs, predatory beetles, tachnid flies, and many others.

1315. Cannell, M. G. R.; Jackson, J. E.; eds. **Attributes of trees as crop plants.** Institute of Terrestrial Ecology; Natural Environment Research Council, 1985.

592 pp., ill., bibl., index. Papers from a 1984 conference that assembled research workers in forestry, horticulture, and agroforestry to review progress and problems in utilizing tree crops. Sections on genetics and breeding; vegetative structure; roots, symbionts, and soils; flowering and fruiting; trees in stands; and economic aspects of timber growing.

1316. Canadian journal of forest research. National Research Council of Canada, 1971 to date. Monthly. Leading international journal publishes articles, notes, discussions, reviews, and rapid communications on any aspect of forest research.

1317. Sinclair, Wayne A.; Lyon, Howard H.; Johnson. Warren T. **Diseases of trees and shrubs.** Comstock Publishing Associates, 1987. 574 pp., ill., bibl., index. Surveys disorders caused by pathogens and environmental factors affecting over 260 North American species. Describes biology, ecology, and nonchemical control methods.

1318. Speight, Martin R.; Wainhouse, David; eds. **Ecology and management of forest insects.** Oxford University Press, 1990. 374 pp., bibl., index.

1319. Coulson, Robert N.; Witter, John A. **Forest entomology: ecology and management.** Wiley, 1984. 669 pp., ill., bibl., index. Introductory section reviews general entomology. Includes an illustrated key to insect damage. Discusses principles and methods of integrated pest management and describes the habits of major forest insect feeding groups.

1320. Forest research: a mandate for change. National Academy Press, 1990. 84 pp., ill., bibl., index. Prepared by the Board on Biology, Board on Agriculture, Committee on Forestry, National Research Council. Argues for a "massive revitalization" of forestry research, in breadth and depth, to create the knowledge required to protect forests and make them more productive. Makes specific recommendations on funding and research areas.

1321. Forest science. Society of American Foresters, 1955 to date. Quarterly. Publishes original research; notes on techniques, methods, and procedures; and literature review articles.

1322. Forestry abstracts. Commonwealth Agricultural Bureaux, 1939/40 to date. Monthly. Abstracts the world literature on forestry and forest science. Available as a computer database, online and on CD-ROM.

1323. Rayner, A. D. M.; Boddy, Lynne. **Fungal decomposition of wood: its biology and ecology.** Wiley-Interscience, 1988. 587 pp., ill., bibl., index. Discusses wood as a growth environment for fungi, covering fungal biology, physiology, and life histories. Notes the role of fungi in natural and artificial ecosystems.

1324. Wilson, Brayton F. **The growing tree**. University of Massachusetts Press, 1984. 138 pp., ill., bibl., index. Clearly written explanation of form and growth of trees.

1325. Martineau, René. **Insects harmful to forest trees**. Multiscience; Canadian Forestry Service; Canadian Government Publishing Centre, Supply and Services Canada, 1984. 261 pp., ill., bibl. Discusses insect pests of spruce, larch, pine, fir, arborvitae, birch, oak, maple, elm and poplar. Numerous color photos.

1326. Insects of eastern forests. U.S. Department of Agriculture, Forest Service; Government Printing Office, Miscellaneous publications, no. 1426, 1985. 608 pp., ill., bibl., index. Focus is on insects west of the 100th meridian and north of Mexico. Insects are arranged by orders and families; for each species there is information on biology, life history, and damage caused. Text is supplemented by numerous photographs of insects and damages to hosts. There are indexes of common and scientific insect names, common and scientific names of host plants, and insects by host plants.

1327. Barbosa, Pedro; Wagner, Michael. **Introduction to forest and shade tree insects**. Academic Press, 1989. 639 pp., ill., bibl., index. Discusses the actions and impacts of shade tree insects on trees, in the context of the insects' role in forest ecology. Evaluates damage commercially and economically, and in terms of effects on tree physiology and growth. Describes forest insect control through chemical, biological, direct, and silvicultural methods.

1328. Shigo, Alex L. **A new tree biology dictionary: terms, topics, and treatments for trees and their problems and proper care**. Shigo & Trees, 1986. 132 pp., ill., bibl., index. Over 130 definitions cover such topics as tree anatomy, pathogens and pests, biological processes, and treatment methods.

1329. Shigo, Alex L. **A new tree biology: facts, photos, and philosophies on trees and their problems and proper care**. Shigo & Trees, 1989. 618 pp., ill., bibl., index. Detailed captions explain numerous photographs of trees on both the micro and macro levels. Topics range from structure and defense mechanisms to pathogens and pruning.

1330. Sundberg, U.; Silversides, C. R.; eds. **Operational efficiency in forestry. Vol. 1: Analysis**. Kluwer, Forestry sciences, v. 29, 1988. 219 pp., ill., bibl. Presents concepts and mathematical tools necessary to an understanding of the impact of physical factors on forestry activities in order to increase efficiency. Topics include transport systems, ergonomics, and energy analysis.

1331. Tauer, C. G.; Henessey, T. C.; eds. **Physiologic and genetic basis of forest decline**. Oklahoma State University, 1986. 321 pp., ill., bibl., index. Proceedings of a 1986 workshop. Topics include seed and seedling physiology, tree responses to stress, forest genetics, nursery culture, seed orchards, and biochemical factors in growth.

1332. Raghavendra, A. S.; ed. **Physiology of trees**. Wiley-Interscience, 1991. 512 pp. Comprehensive review of knowledge on tree physiology, particularly research of the past two decades.

1333. Castner, James L. **Rainforests: a guide to research and tourist facilities at selected tropical forest sites in Central and South America**. Feline Press, 1990. 416 pp., maps, ill., index. Countries, sites, and facilities take up one-half of the book; the three other chapters are rain forest information sources, "hands-on" organizations, and sources of funding.

1334. Vries, Pieter G. de. **Sampling theory for forest inventory: a teach-yourself course**. Springer-Verlag, 1986. 399 pp., ill., bibl., index. Gives the mathematical and statistical background necessary to a critical understanding of many sampling techniques. Assumes background in algebra, calculus, elementary statistics, and vectors. Topics include simple random sampling, parameters, ratio estimation, regression, and personal bias.

1335. Social sciences in forestry. University of Minnesota, Forestry Library, 1963 to date. Quarterly. Continues: Forestry economics bibliography. Comprehensive listing of the literature, in broad categories, with author index.

1336. Desch, H. E. **Timber: its structure, properties and utilisation**. Timber Press, 6th ed., 1987. 410 pp., ill., bibl., index.

Forest Ecology. Ecosystems (1337–1360)

1337. Harris, Larry D. **Biogeography, old-growth islands and wildlife in the Western Cascades**. University of Florida, School of Forest Resources and Conservation, Research report, v. 32, 1982. 309 pp., maps, ill., bibl. Provides basic background; applies biogeographic principles to develop and assess alternative management approaches.

1338. Gordon, John C.; Wheeler, C. T.; eds. **Biological nitrogen fixation in forest ecosystems: foundations and applications.** Nijhoff; Junk (dist. by Kluwer Boston), Forestry sciences, v. 9, 1983. 342 pp., ill., bibl., index. Advantages and disadvantages of using nitrogen fixation to enhance wood production. Topics include morphology of nitrogen fixers and their natural occurrence; biochemical, physiological, and environmental aspects of symbiotic nitrogen fixation; and the isolation and culture of nitrogen-fixing organisms.

1339. Larsen, James A. **Ecology of the northern lowland bogs and conifer forests.** Academic Press, 1982. 307 pp., maps, ill., bibl., index. Discusses how these ecosystems became established and briefly describes their plant species. Other topics include nutrients and plant communities, soil conditions and microbiology, and community development.

1340. Kimmins, J.P. **Forest ecology.** Macmillan, 1987. 531 pp., ill., bibl., index. Discusses the forest as a functional system, the genetic and evolutionary features of ecosystems, the physical and biotic environment, and temporal changes in ecosystem structure and function. Addresses the application of ecological information in forest management, covering classification, mapping, and the renewability of resources.

1341. Spurr, Stephen Hopkins; Barnes, Burton V. **Forest ecology.** Wiley, 3d ed., 1980. 687 pp., ill., bibl., index. An introductory textbook explaining the ecological processes of trees, forest communities, and forest ecosystems. Discusses species diversity, environmental influences, competition for resources, disturbance, and other factors affecting forest development and distribution.

1342. Forest ecology and management. Elsevier, 1976 to date. Quarterly. Publishes original research on biology, ecology, and social aspects of forest management and conservation. International in scope.

1343. Waring, Richard H.; Schlesinger, William H. **Forest ecosystems: concepts and management.** Academic Press, 1985. 340 pp., ill., bibl., index. Basic introduction to forest ecosystems; covers carbon balance, tree-water balance and hydrology, productivity and succession, nutrient cycling, and decomposition and soil development. Examines response to natural disturbances and connections to aquatic ecosystems and global ecology.

1344. Grodzinski, W.; Weiner, J.; Maycock, P. F.; eds. **Forest ecosystems in industrial regions: studies on the cycling of energy, nutrients, and pollutants in the Niepotomice Forest, southern Poland.** Springer-Verlag, Ecological studies, v. 49, 1984. 277 pp., ill., index. Based on a study of a forest ecosystem functioning under air pollution stress in southern Poland. Examines production, decomposition, energy, and nutrient flow. Proposes concepts for forest management in industrial regions.

1345. Van Cleve, K.; and others, eds. **Forest ecosystems in the Alaska taiga: a synthesis of structure and function.** Springer-Verlag, Ecological studies, v. 57, 1986. 230 pp., ill., bibl., index. Examines the nature of taiga environment, covering climate, ecosystem distribution, and fire; reviews environmental controls over organism activity (nitrogen fixation, microbial activity, and mineral availability) and ecosystem processes.

1346. Burgess, Robert L.; Sharpe, David M.; eds. **Forest island dynamics in man-dominated landscapes.** Springer-Verlag, Ecological studies, v. 41, 1981. 310 pp., ill., bibl., index. The first large-scale attempt to study regional ecological processes in terms of forest fragments. Models of island biogeography, the edge effect, colonization and seed dispersal, and succession are applied and tested.

1347. Oliver, Chadwick D.; Larson, Bruce C. **Forest stand dynamics.** McGraw-Hill, 1990. 624 pp., ill., bibl., index. How trees behave and how they form stand patterns, inductively determined from innate growth habits interacting with physical surroundings and competing plants. Chapters on tree architecture and growth, disturbances, tree invasions, stand initiation, exclusion stage, single- and multicohort stands, understory reinitiation, edges and gaps, quantifying stand development, and forest patterns over long times and large areas.

1348. West, Darrell C.; Shugart, Herman H.; Botkin, Daniel B.; eds. **Forest succession: concepts and application.** Springer-Verlag, Springer advanced texts in life sciences, 1981. 517 pp., ill., bibl., index. Based on a 1980 conference. Explains the theories and concepts of succession, examining possible causes of variations in patterns in different settings and over varied time scales. Discusses successes and limits of simulation models; includes numerous case studies documenting and interpreting succession, mostly in North American forests.

1349. Lugo, Ariel E.; Brinson, Mark; Brown, Sandra; eds. **Forested wetlands.** Elsevier, Ecosystems of the world, v. 15, 1990. 527 pp., ill., bibl., indexes. Contributed papers from 15 authorities on the structure, function, and variation of forested wetlands—riverine, fringe, and basin—around the world.

1350. Walker, Laurence C. **Forests: a naturalist's**

guide to trees and forest ecology. Wiley, 1990. 288 pp., ill., bibl. Explains how to distinguish many species of trees, noting their growth habits, reproductive strategies, associated animals, and the characteristics and uses of their wood. Includes suggestions for projects requiring no special equipment for amateur naturalists.

1351. Harris, Larry D. **The fragmented forest: island biogeographic theory and the preservation of biotic diversity.** University of Chicago Press, 1984. 211 pp., ill., bibl., index. Applies the theory of island biogeography to develop a forest management concept designed to preserve species diversity. Based on an analysis of the Western Cascades.

1352. Delcourt, Paul A; Delcourt, Hazel R. **Long-term forest dynamics of the temperate zone: a case study of late-quaternary forests in eastern North America.** Springer-Verlag, Ecological studies, v. 63, 1987. 439 pp., maps, ill., bibl., index. Discusses the nature of long-term vegetational changes. Uses quantifications of modern pollen-vegetation relationships to reconstruct past forests. Uses models to examine the role of competition in structuring past forest communities.

1353. Bormann, F. Herbert; Likens, Gene E. **Pattern and process in a forested ecosystem: disturbance, development, and the steady state based on the Hubbard Brook ecosystem study.** Springer-Verlag, 1979. 253 pp., ill., bibl., index. Long-term experiment on watershed in New Hampshire to quantify the structure and functions of natural ecosystems. Emphasizes the role of biological processes in controlling destabilizing forces affecting ecosystems and interrelationships of animate and inanimate components. Reviews steady state models. Discusses energetics, biomass, hydrology, and biogeochemistry and traces the development of vegetation following clear cutting.

1354. Landsberg, J.J. **Physiological ecology of forest production.** Academic Press, Applied botany and crop science, 1986. 198 pp., ill., bibl., index. Examines the effects of weather on physiological processes. Reviews stand structure and microclimate and the carbon balances of leaves and trees. Explains nutrient dynamics and water relations; assesses the value and limitations of models.

1355. Persson, T.; ed. **Structure and function of northern coniferous forests: an ecosystem study.** Swedish Natural Science Research Council, Ecological bulletins, no. 32, 1980. 609 pp., ill., bibl., index. Thirty-seven papers from an eight-year study of Sweden's coniferous forests detail study sites and data procedures and

examine abiotic processes, soil processes, and simulation models and theories for understanding forest functions.

1356. Ovington, J. D.; ed. **Temperate broad-leaved evergreen forests.** Elsevier, Ecosystems of the world, v. 10, 1983. 241 pp., maps, ill., bibl., index. Forests in South America, New Zealand, Australia, North America, the Mediterranean and Middle East, Japan, the Indian subcontinent, and Africa south of the Sahara are described in chapters of varying length. Provides basic information on ecology and environment.

1357. Arno, Stephen F. **Timberline: mountain and arctic forest frontiers.** Mountaineers Books, 1984. 304 pp., ill., bibl., index. Explains basic timberline ecology, then surveys conditions and tree species of timberlines in several mountain ranges.

1358. Walker, Laurence C. **Trees: an introduction to trees and forest ecology for the amateur naturalist.** Prentice-Hall, Phalarope books, 1984. 306 pp., ill., bibl., index. Facts and folklore about trees in the United States; how trees adapt to their environment; the role of trees in America's economy and history.

1359. Clark, J.R.; Benforado, J.; eds. **Wetlands of bottomland hardwood forests.** Elsevier, Developments in agricultural and managed-forest ecology, v. 11, 1981. 401 pp., ill., bibl. Proceedings of a Workshop on Bottomland Hardwood Forest Wetlands of the Southeastern United States, held in 1980. Papers discuss hydrology, fauna, soils, forests, agriculture, and ecology. Evaluates current management and conservation practices. Assesses effects of clearing, draining, and levee building. Provides technical advice for research and policymaking.

1360. Cannell, Melvin G. R.; compiler. **World forest biomass and primary production data.** Academic Press, 1982. 391 pp., bibl., index. Tables present data on stand structure and biomass production, abstracted from 600 papers on 1200 stands in 46 countries.

Tropical Forest Ecosystems (1361–1373)

1361. Jordan, Carl F.; ed. **Amazonian rain forests: ecosystem disturbance and recovery—case studies of ecosystem dynamics under a spectrum of land use intensities.** Springer-Verlag, Ecological studies, v. 60, 1987. 133 pp., maps, ill., bibl., index. Presents ten case studies of disturbance in the Amazon, including shifting cultivation and clearing for pastures, agriculture, forestry, and large-scale development.

1362. Leigh, Egbert G.; Rand, A. S.; Windsor, Donald M.; eds. **The ecology of a tropical forest: seasonal rhythms and long-term changes.** Smithsonian Institution Press, 1982. 468 pp., ill., bibl. Results of 15 years of research on Barro Colorado Island, Panama. Sections on the physical setting; biotic setting; seasonal rhythms in plants; frugivores; insects of tree crowns; litter arthropods; and long-term changes.

1363. Gentry, Alwyn H.; ed. **Four neotropical rainforests.** Yale University Press, 1990. 627 pp., ill,. bibl. Discussing site histories, floristics, birds, mammals, amphibians and reptiles, and forest dynamics, the text covers rain forest sites in Costa Rica, Panama, Peru, and Brazil. Compares and contrasts the four areas, noting species diversity, soil quality, accessibility, and human disturbance.

1364. Perry, Donald R. **Life above the jungle floor.** Simon & Schuster, 1986. 170 pp., ill., bibl., index. Personalized, anecdotal account of a research biologist's exploration of Costa Rican jungle canopy. Describes treetop ecology and specialized adaptations in the context of overall forest ecology; includes color photographs.

1365. Martin, Claude; Tsardakas, Linda, trans. **The rainforests of West Africa: ecology, threats, conservation.** Birkhaeuser, 1991. 235 pp., illus. An integral presentation of West African rain forests, based on the author's extensive experience with World Wildlife Fund International. Covers cultural, economic, and biological aspects.

1366. Role of tropical forests on the world carbon cycle: a symposium held at the Institute of Tropical Forestry, Puerto Rico. U. S. Department of Energy, Office of Health and Environmental Research, Carbon dioxide effects research assessment program, no. 007, 1980. 156 pp. Symposium held at the Institute of Tropical Forestry, Puerto Rico.

1367. Longman, K. A.; Jenik, J. **Tropical forest and its environment.** Wiley, Tropical ecology series, 2d ed., 1987. 347 pp., ill., bibl., index. Focuses on plant ecology and whole-plant physiology. Covers the influences of climate, soils, and biotic factors in forest composition and dynamics. Includes recent findings about nutrient cycling, flowering phenology, and seed dormancy.

1368. Jacobs, Marius. **The tropical rain forest: a first encounter.** Springer-Verlag, 1988. 295 pp., ill., bibl., index. Comprehensive discussion of biological, ecological, and human aspects of the world's rain forests.

1369. Sutton, S. L.; Whitmore T. C.; Chadwick, A. C.; eds. **Tropical rain forest: ecology and management.** Blackwell Scientific, British Ecological Society,

Special publication, no. 2, 1983. 498 pp., maps, ill., bibl., index. Papers of the 1982 Leeds Symposium cover community structure and diversity, plant and animal interactions, nutrient cycling and resource management.

1370. Lieth, H.; Werger, M. J. A.; eds. **Tropical rain forest ecosystems: biogeographical and ecological studies.** Elsevier, Ecosystems of the world, v. 14B, 1989. 713 pp., ill., bibl., index. Assesses the condition and future of the three main tropical forest regions. Discusses the physical environment, noting the effects of climate and covering tree architecture, taxonomy, and classification. Reviews plant and animal categories, highlighting interactions and symbiotic relationships contributing to the forests' complexity.

1371. Golley, F. B.; ed. **Tropical rain forest ecosystems: structure and function.** Elsevier, Ecosystems of the world, v. 14A, 1983. 381 pp., ill., bibl., index. Twenty-two contributions list and explain the structural elements (trees, vegetation, animals) of the forest and processes (productivity, nutrient cycling, plant-animal interactions) occurring within it. Chapters examine the physiological and behavioral aspects of forest biology and assess the effects of human settlement and resource exploitation.

1372. Chadwick, A. C.; Sutton, S. L.; eds. **Tropical rain-forest: the Leeds Symposium.** Leeds Philosophical and Literary Society, Special publication, 1984. 335 pp., ill., bibl., index. Papers on community structure and evolution, nutrient cycling, ecophysiology, animal interactions, maintenance of diversity, and resource management. Companion volume to *Tropical rain forest: ecology and management* (Special publication no. 2, British Ecological Society, 1983).

1373. Whitmore, Timothy Charles. **Tropical rain forests of the Far East.** Clarendon Press, Oxford science publications, 2d ed., 1984. 352 pp., ill., bibl., index. Critical synthesis of ecological work in rain forests of the Far East. In five parts: geological history, climate and seasonality, growth of the forest (silviculture, physiology), forest types, and human impact on the forest.

Species. Genetic Resources (1374–1393)

1374. Zobel, Bruce; Talbert, John. **Applied forest tree improvement.** Wiley, 1984. 505 pp., ill., bibl., index. Major concepts and methods of forest genetics and tree breeding, emphasizing practical operational aspects. Applicable to temperate and tropical zones.

1375. Little, Elbert L. **Audubon Society field guide**

to North American trees. Knopf, 1980. 714 pp., ill., index. Describes 364 species found east of the Rockies. Includes photographic keys to leaves, flowers, cones and fruit, and autumn foliage.

1376. Wang, Dajun; Shen, Shao-Jin. **Bamboos of China.** Timber Press, 1987. 167 pp., ill., index. Provides keys and descriptions and information on culture and propagation; describes handicrafts and decorative uses.

1377. Bonga, J. M.; Durzan, Don J.; eds. **Cell and tissue culture in forestry.** Nijhoff; Kluwer, 1987. Ill., bibl., index. 3 vols. Covers academic and practical aspects of tree biotechnology. Vol. 1: General principles and biotechnology. Vol. 2: Specific principles and methods: growth and development. Vol. 3: Case histories: gymnosperms, angiosperms, and palms.

1378. Gelderen, D. M. van. **Conifers.** Timber Press, 1986. 375 pp. Over 1180 color photographs cover all species and some varieties and cultivars; includes a systematic outline of the gymnosperms and a summary of their characteristics.

1379. Databook on endangered tree and shrub species and provenances. Food and Agriculture Organization of the United Nations, FAO forestry paper, no. 77, 1986. 524 pp., bibl. Summarizes distribution, ecology, biology, silviculture, current or potential uses, genetic status and suggested conservation measures for 81 species.

1380. Kricher, John C. **Field guide to eastern forests: North America.** Houghton Mifflin, 1988. 368 pp., ill., index. Describes and illustrates with drawings and photographs 27 biotic communities east of the Rockies. Summarizes recent ecological research in question-and-answer format. Topics include ecological succession and the biological adaptations of many organisms.

1381. National Research Council. **Firewood crops: shrub and tree species for energy production.** National Academy Press, 1980–1983. Ill., bibl., index. 2 vols. Provides advice and recommendations for implementing and managing fuelwood programs. Lists 60 fuelwood species suited for the humid tropics, tropical highlands, and arid and semiarid regions. Includes botanical and common names and information on features, environmental needs, planting methods, and uses.

1382. Campbell, David G.; Hammond, H. David; eds. **Floristic inventory of tropical forests: the status of plant systematics, collections, and vegetation, plus recommendations for the future.** New York Botanical Garden, 1989. 545 pp., ill., bibl., index. Description and inventory of tropical flora essential to understanding of tropical ecosystems. State of plant taxonomy in each tropical region, background information, detailed inventories. Joint project of Arnold Arboretum, Missouri Botanical Garden, New York Botanical Garden, and World Wildlife Fund.

1383. Boland, D. J.; and others. **Forest trees of Australia.** Thomas Nelson Australia; Commonwealth Scientific and Industrial Research Organization, 4th ed., 1984. 687 pp., maps, ill. Provides general overview of the development of Australian tree species and describes regional climate and environmental factors affecting growth and distribution. Species descriptions, grouped into gymnosperms, monocotyledons, and dicotyledons, list a tree's form, size, features and other botanical information; numerous photographs accompany the text.

1384. Krussmann, Gerd. **Manual of cultivated broad-leaved trees and shrubs.** Timber Press, 1984. Maps, ill., bibl. 3 vols. Manual for botanists, horticulturists, and foresters provides descriptions, illustrations, and species range maps.

1385. den Ouden, P.; Boom, B. K. **Manual of cultivated conifers: hardy in the cold- and warm-temperate zone.** Nijhoff (dist. by Kluwer Boston), Forestry sciences, 1982. 520 pp., ill., index. Lists 600 species and over 2000 cultivars, entries provide information on appearance, features, distribution, and environmental and cultural considerations.

1386. Rehder, Alfred. **Manual of cultivated trees and shrubs hardy in North America.** Timber Press, Biosystematics, floristic & phylogeny series, v. 1, c. 1927, 1987. 1026 pp. Reprint of a classic. This reference text inventories over 450 genera, 2500 species, and 2600 varieties of 113 families of trees, shrubs, and vines.

1387. Turnbull, John W.; ed. **Multipurpose Australian trees and shrubs: lesser-known species for fuelwood and agroforestry.** Australian Centre for International Agricultural Research, ACIAR monograph, no. 1, 1986. 316 pp., ill., bibl., index. Describes 100 species and their potential uses for fuelwood and agroforestry in developing countries. Emphasizes tropical and subtropical species adapted to infertile soils. Includes introductory chapters on Australian ecology, species introduction, and plant propagation techniques.

1388. Miller, Howard A.; Lamb, Samuel H. **Oaks of North America.** Naturegraph, 1985. 327 pp., maps, ill., bibl., index. Gives history of oaks in North America; discusses silvics and taxonomy.

1389. Myers, Norman. **Primary source: tropical forests and our future.** Norton, 1984. 399 pp., ill., bibl., index. Leading authority discusses the status of deforestation in tropical forests, their contributions to our welfare, and the scope and global significance of their destruction. Presents a conservation blueprint.

1390. Sponberg, Stephen A. **A reunion of trees: the discovery of exotic plants and their introduction into North American and European landscapes.** Harvard University Press, 1990. 270 pp., ill., bibl. Examines the transformation of North American and European urban and suburban landscapes by the spread of non-native trees and shrubs. Reviews quests of explorers and travelers to locate exotic species. Addresses the evolving role and meaning of woody plants in human existence.

1391. Burns, Russell M.; Honkala, Barbara H.; technical coordinators. **Silvics of North America.** U. S. Department of Agriculture, Forest Service; Government Printing Office, Agriculture handbook, no. 654, 1990. Ill. 2 vols. Vol. 1: Conifers. Vol. 2: Hardwoods. Describes some 200 tree species, the principal commercial species, most of them native to North America. For each species, there is a map showing range; information on habitat, life history, and genetics; and a list of principal references. Supersedes *Silvics of North American forest trees* (1965).

1392. Benson, Lyman David; Darrow, Robert A. **Trees and shrubs of the southwestern deserts.** University of Arizona Press, 3d ed., 1981. 416 pp., maps, ill., index. Includes color plates, black and white photographs, drawings, and range maps. Covers the taxonomy of vines, succulents, and low bushes of deserts, and gives floristic and topographic descriptions of deserts and adjacent arid regions.

1393. Holm-Nielsen, L. B.; Nielsen, I. C.; Balslev, H.; eds. **Tropical forests: botanical dynamics, speciation and diversity.** Academic Press, 1989. 380 pp. Proceedings of a 1988 conference. Papers on tree distribution, flood tolerance, canopy structure, and landscape patterns. Some authors examine and explain the development of particular species; others, the diversity found in particular regions.

Air, Soil, and Water Relations. Pollution (1394–1416)

1394. Binkley, Dan; and others, eds. **Acidic deposition and forest soils: context and case studies of the southeastern U. S.** Springer-Verlag, Ecological studies, analysis and synthesis, v. 72, 1989. 149 pp., maps, ill., bibl., index. Examines soil-mediated effects of acid deposition; provides general introduction, then discusses deposition patterns, soils, and nutrient cycles in the

southern United States. Includes results of computer modeling.

1395. Smith, William H. **Air pollution and forests: interaction between air contaminants and forest ecosystems.** Springer-Verlag, Springer series on environmental management, 2d ed., 1990. 618 pp., ill., bibl., index. Examines the forest ecosystem as a source and sink for contaminants. Discusses the impact of varying levels of pollution on trees and forest ecosystems with respect to tree reproduction, nutrient cycling, metabolism, and predisposition to insect outbreaks and disease. Each section includes a summary and references.

1396. Garner, Willa Y.; Harvey, John, Jr.; eds. **Chemical and biological controls in forestry.** American Chemical Society, ACS symposium series, v. 238, 1984. 406 pp., bibl., indexes. Based on a symposium held at the American Chemical Society annual meeting in 1983.

1397. MacIver, D. C.; Street, R. B.; Auclair, A. N.; eds. **Climate applications in forest renewal and forest production.** Canadian Forestry Service, 1989. 307 pp., ill., bibl. Proceedings of a 1986 symposium-workshop. Addresses the impact of climate on forest management problems. Presents climate techniques and product demonstrations relevant to many forest-climate applications.

1398. Pyne, Stephen J. **Fire in America: a cultural history of wildland and rural fire.** Princeton University Press, 1982. 654 pp., ill., bibl. Begins with lightning fires, fire behavior, and fire ecology. Covers Indian use of fires; fire histories of all regions of the United States; and policy, management, equipment, and research in the Forest Service.

1399. Chandler, Craig; and others. **Fire in forestry.** Wiley, 1983. Ill., bibl., index. 2 vols. Vol. 1: Forest fire behavior and effects. Vol. 2: Forest fire management and organization. Explains the effects of fire on soil, water, air, wildlife, and vegetation, emphasizing fire as a natural process in forests, shrublands, and grasslands. Discusses ways to limit fire damage and to use fire as a resource management tool, addressing policy, prevention, suppression, equipment, and prescribed fires.

1400. Cole, Dale W.; Henry, Charles L.; Nutter, Wade L.; eds. **The forest alternative for treatment of municipal industrial wastes.** University of Washington Press, Institute of Forest Resources contribution, no. 56, 1986. 582 pp., ill., bibl., index. Symposium addresses applications of municipal waste to North American (mostly U.S.) forests. Reviews both biological aspects and program development and presentation steps. Numerous and varied case studies.

1401. Riedl, O.; Zachar, D. **Forest amelioration.** Elsevier, Developments in agricultural and managed-forest ecology, v. 14, 1984. 624 pp., ill., bibl. Comprehensive treatment of principles and techniques for improving drainage conditions, preventing erosion by water and wind, regulating forest soil-water balance, and improving microclimatic conditions.

1402. Hutchison, B. A.; Hicks, B. B.; eds. **The forest-atmosphere interaction.** Reidel; Kluwer, 1985. 684 pp., ill., bibl., index. Proceedings of a 1983 conference. Papers explain forest environment characteristics, plus the equipment and methods needed to assess variations, disturbances, and influences. Also examines effects and aspects of wind turbulence above and within forest canopies.

1403. Hennessey, Thomas C.; Dougherty, Phillip M.; Tauer, Charles G.; eds. **Forest decline: assessing impacts of a changing environment on forest productivity.** Heron Publishing, 1987. 102 pp., ill, bibl. Proceedings of workshop on forest biology; reviews environmental stress factors suspected of causing forest decline.

1404. Fuller, M. **Forest fires: an introduction to wildland fire behavior, management, firefighting, and prevention.** Wiley, 1991. 256 pp. Includes discussion of forest fuels, the effects of weather, fire ecology, and fire's effects on flora and fauna. Covers new firefighting techniques (minimum impact, compressed-air foam). Reviews history of fire policy in the United States.

1405. Lee, Richard. **Forest hydrology.** Columbia University Press, 1980. 349 pp., ill., bibl., index. Covers the following topics as they pertain to forests and forestry: water yield and quality, precipitation disposal, subsurface water, and vaporization processes. Emphasizes water budget relationships, water movement, and water storage capabilities of forest vegetation.

1406. Shands, William E.; Hoffman, John S.; eds. **The greenhouse effect: climate change and U.S. forests.** Conservation Foundation, 1987. 304 pp., maps, ill. Contributed chapters present evidence of global warming and assess methods and models for predicting change. Examines potential effects of carbon dioxide–induced climate change on forests and reviews management options for the forest products industry.

1407. Newton, Michael; Knight, Fred B. **Handbook of weed and insect control chemicals for forest resource managers.** Timber Press, 1981. 213 pp., ill., bibl., index. Discusses forest vegetation and forest insect management, briefly reviewing alternative methods but focusing mostly on appropriate herbicides, insecticides, and pesticides and their proper use. Describes application technology and options; explains risks and precautions in handling and applying these chemicals.

1408. Pyne, Stephen J. **Introduction to wildland fire: fire management in the United States.** Wiley, 1984. 455 pp., ill., bibl., index. Explains wildland combustion and the effects of fuel and geography on fire behavior; briefly reviews U.S. fire history. Describes the theories, objectives, and techniques of fire management, addressing fire suppression and the use of prescribed burning.

1409. Mello, Robert A. **Last stand of the red spruce.** Island Press, 1987. 199 pp., ill., bibl., index. Vermont trial lawyer evaluates scientific evidence for effects of acid rain on this tree species.

1410. Jordan, Carl F. **Nutrient cycling in tropical forest ecosystems: principles and their application in management and conservation.** Wiley, 1985. 190 pp., ill., bibl., index. Describes the climate and biological factors that control and conserve nutrients. Examines variations in nutrient retention over environmental gradients (altitude, moisture, soil fertility). Discusses patterns in nutrient cycling and changes due to disturbances; assesses management options.

1411. Pritchett, William L.; Fisher, Richard F. **Properties and management of forest soils.** Wiley, 2d ed., 1987. 494 pp., ill., bibl., index. For the advanced student and practicing forester. In two parts. Part 1: Properties and dynamic processes (soil types, forest floor, soil biology, physical properties, soil water, roots, mycorrhizae, nutrient cycling, and productivity). Part 2: Management and its consequences (classification, silviculture, nurseries, problem soils, nutrients and fertilizers, effects of fire, intensive management, and productivity). Compares U.S. Soil Taxonomy System with Canadian, French, and FAO and UNESCO systems.

1412. Wilde, S. A.; Voigt, G. K.; and others. **Soil and plant analysis for tree culture.** Oxford & IBH, 5th rev. ed., 1979. 224 pp., ill., bibl. Presents techniques for analyzing the physical, chemical and biological properties of soil; also plant tissue, groundwater, forest stands, and nursery stock.

1413. Hamilton, Lawrence S.; King, Peter N. **Tropical forested watershed: hydrological and soils response to major uses or conversions.** Westview Press, 1983. 168 pp., ill., bibl. Synthesizes current knowledge of 12 human effects on various tropical soil and water phenomena.

1414. Prance, Ghillean T.; ed. **Tropical rain forests and the world atmosphere.** Westview Press, AAAS selected symposium, v. 101, 1986. 105 pp., ill., bibl. Papers from a 1984 symposium discuss the rate of destruction of the rain forest, the forest's interaction with the atmosphere, and potential atmospheric effects of deforestation.

1415. Williamson, D. R. **The use of herbicides in the forest.** Forestry Commission, United Kingdom (dist. by Her Majesty's Stationery Office), Field book, no. 8, 1989. 151 pp., index. Reviews safety precautions, equipment, and pesticide legislation in the United Kingdom.

Discusses the control of weeds common in British forestry: grasses, bracken, heather, gorse, and rhododendron.

1416. Williams, Julia; Hamilton, Lawrence S. **Watershed forest influences in the tropics and subtropics: a selected, annotated bibliography.** East-West Center, Environment and Policy Institute, 1982. 217 pp. Forest hydrology literature arranged under 33 subject headings. Emphasizes publications reporting research results.

Section 7

Animals. Wildlife

Selections for wildlife in this bibliography were particularly difficult to make, owing to the abundance of suitable titles. New books on animal biology and ecology and wildlife management appear continuously. Organizations dealing with wildlife and animal protection are the fastest-growing components of the environmental movement.

The groups and subgroups in this section, therefore, tend to be more representative than comprehensive. But all the major wildlife conservation and animal protection issues are covered, particularly those of endangered species, conservation biology, habitats, hunting, and wildlife in urban areas. The section also contains the principal technical and professional works on major species, wildlife management, and animal biology and ecology. It begins with more than a dozen general titles that pertain to every subdivision of the section.

Wildlife Management
Entries in this group address wildlife management and practices, including wildlife utilization and game ranching. Works dealing with specific aspects of wildlife management are found in the subgroups on species.

See also:

- Section 1: Global resources and environment; environmental management
- Section 3: Fisheries
- Section 4: Lands, reserves and parks, management
- Section 5: Food and agriculture; crops, cropping systems; range management, pastoral systems
- Section 6: Forest management, silviculture
- Section 8: Rural communities; tribal communities
- Section 9: Nature writing and thought, arts
- Section 10: Law, politics, government; national laws and policies; international laws and policies; U.S. executive agencies; administration and regulation; natural resources: United States; water, wildlife, minerals: United States; forests, parks, wilderness: United States
- Section 11: Economy, costs and benefits, valuation; natural resource industries; agriculture and forest products

Animal Rights. Protection

Fewer entries were selected for this group because of the already existing *Keyguide to Information Sources in Animal Rights* (1464)

See also:

- Section 5: Food and agriculture; range management, pastoral systems
- Section 8: Individuals and environment
- Section 9: Ethics, philosophy, religion; nature writing and thought, arts
- Section 10: Law, politics, government; national laws and policies; international law and policies
- Section 11: Economy, costs and benefits, valuation; natural resource industries; agriculture and forest products
- Section 14: Science, research, methods

Animal Biology. Zoology

This group introduces the categories that follow on wildlife ecology, animal species, and conservation biology. Included are journals and reference publications that function as entry points into the enormous literature of animal biology. Special mention should be made of *Wildlife Review* (1494), which covers both management and biology, and *Zoological Record* (1496), which is the principal scientific record.

See also:

- Section 1: Biological systems; ecology
- Section 2: Weather and life, biometeorology
- Section 3: Aquatic and marine sciences; freshwater biology and ecology; marine biology and ecology
- Section 5: Plant sciences
- Section 6: Tree and forest sciences

Animal Ecology. Species

This group contains works on behavior, habitat, ethology, sociobiology, social evolution, and populations. More specialized works on animal ecology are located in the following subgroups on species.

Mammals: Guides, General; Species, Regions; Aquatic and Marine; Primates; Birds: Guides and Lists, Species and Families; Amphibians and Reptiles; Fish; Invertebrates. Works on species have been placed with animal ecology because social and population aspects of species are inseparably linked to individual characteristics. Balance and representation were the guiding principles in selection except that entries for mammals are the most numerous.

See also:

- Section 1: Biological systems; ecology
- Section 3: Freshwater biology and ecology; marine biology and ecology
- Section 4: Landscape ecology; land: terrestrial ecosystems
- Section 5: Plant ecology
- Section 6: Forest ecology, ecosystems
- Section 8: Social and human ecology, population; human evolution, history
- Section 14: Modeling and simulation; assessment and monitoring

Endangered Species. Conservation Biology

The field of conservation biology is closely associated with wildlife and animal ecology. Certainly in the public mind, endangered species are animal species. Works dealing with overall threats to animal life are entered in this group. Works on threatened or endangered individuals are found in the preceding subgroups on species.

See also:

- Section 1: Biodiversity, conservation biology, genetics
- Section 5: Endangered plants, genetic resources
- Section 6: Trees, forests, forestry; species, genetic resources
- Section 8: Human evolution, history; social and human ecology, population; rural communities; tribal communities
- Section 9: Nature writing and thought, arts
- Section 10: Law, politics, government; national laws and policies; international laws and policies; U.S. executive agencies, administration and regulation; natural resources: United States; water, wildlife, minerals: United States; forests, parks, wilderness: United States
- Section 11: Economy, costs and benefits, valuation; natural resource industries; agriculture and forest products
- Section 14: Modeling and simulation; assessment and monitoring

1417. Anthrozoos: a multidisciplinary journal on the interactions of people, animals, and environment. University Press of New England, 1987 to date. Quarterly. Articles on human attitudes and interactions with their pets, work animals, and wild animals.

1418. DiSilvestro, Roger L. **Audubon perspectives: fight for survival.** Wiley, 1990. 304 pp., ill. Companion to the Audubon television specials; explains the history, habits, and ecological functions of various species and ecosystems. Examines factors contributing to the destruction of these animals and areas and efforts to conserve and restore them. Exposes development and poaching problems. Suggests strategies individuals can follow to promote the protection of wildlife and habitat.

1419. Audubon wildlife report, 1989–1990. Academic Press, 1985 to date. Irregular: 1989–1990 issued in 1989. Comprehensive report on wildlife policy and management issues, since 1985. One section of each report deals with federal agencies having management responsibilities. Another section, "Species Account," has essays on problems of threatened species.

1420. DiSilvestro, Roger L. **Endangered kingdom: the struggle to save America's wildlife.** Wiley, 1989. 241 pp., ill., bibl. Chronicles the history of management and mismanagement of game and well-known endangered species, such as the gray wolf, grizzly bear, bowhead whale, and California condor; assesses the interplay between wildlife managers and hunters; discusses current policy options.

1421. Adams, Lowell W.; Leedy, Daniel L.; eds. **Integrating man and nature in the metropolitan environment.** National Institute for Urban Wildlife, 1987. 249 pp., maps, ill, bibl. Proceedings of a national symposium held in 1986. More than 50 papers on the design, protection, and preservation of natural areas for wildlife in developed areas.

1422. International wildlife. National Wildlife Federation, 1971 to date. Monthly. Illustrated popular articles on wild species around the world. Regular coverage of habitat destruction and digest of news, trends, and issues.

1423. Fitzgerald, Sarah. **International wildlife trade: whose business is it?.** World Wildlife Fund, 1989. 459 pp., ill., bibl. Examines international and national trade controls, legal and illegal trade, and environmental and economic effects of exploiting particular plants and animals. Suggests alternative strategies to manage trade for long-term survival and economic gain.

1424. National wildlife. National Wildlife Federation, 1962 to date. Bimonthly. Illustrated popular articles, primarily about animals and their habitats but also about plants, nature, and conservation.

1425. Robinson, John G.; Redford, Kent H.; eds. **Neotropical wildlife use and conservation.** University of Chicago Press, 1991. 512 pp., ill. Argues that neotropical wildlife should be considered a resource having economic as well as aesthetic value. Assesses the significance of wildlife to people, the impact on animal populations from use, and the possibility of sustainable use.

1426. Wildlife conservation. New York Zoological Society, 1897 to date. Bimonthly. Continues: Animal kingdom. Popular articles, news, columns, and letters on wildlife conservation worldwide.

1427. Usher, Michael B.; ed. **Wildlife conservation evaluation.** Chapman and Hall, 1986. 394 pp., ill., bibl., index. How to evaluate areas suitable for plant and animal conservation. Looks at general principles and specific habitats and organisms. Shows approaches used in different parts of the world.

1428. Adams, Lowell W.; Dove, Louise E. **Wildlife reserves and corridors in the urban environment: a guide to ecological landscape planning and resource conservation.** National Institute for Urban Wildlife, 1989. 91 pp., ill., bibl. Reviews knowledge of urban area wildlife habitat. Guidelines intended to harmonize wildlife conservation and protection with urban planning and economic development.

Wildlife Management (1429–1449)

1429. Prescott-Allen, Christine; Prescott-Allen, Robert. **The first resource: wild species in the North American economy.** Yale University Press, 1986. 529 pp., ill., bibl., index. An overall economic valuation of wild plants and animals in the North American economy based on the dependence of natural resources on wild species and gene pools.

1430. Hawkins, A. S.; and others, eds. **Flyways: pioneering waterfowl management in North America.** U. S. Department of the Interior, Fish and Wildlife Service; Government Printing Office, 1984. 517 pp., maps, ill., index. The evolution of the U.S. waterfowl management program, revealed in brief articles by those who were part of it.

1431. Leopold, Aldo. **Game management.** University of Wisconsin Press, c. 1933, 1986. 481 pp., ill., index. Reprint of Leopold's classic text, which formuated the first concepts of wildlife management in the United States.

1432. Bothma, J. du P. **Game ranch management: a practical guide on all aspects of purchasing, planning, development, management and utilisation of a game ranch in southern Africa.** J. L. Van Schaik, 1989. 672 pp., ill., bibl. Eighteen contributors provide information on diseases and parasites of most-used species; capture, holding, and transport of game; meat and trophy processing; feeding and carrying capacity; and marketing strategies.

1433. Smith, Loren M.; Pederson, Roger L.; Kaminski, Richard M.; eds. **Habitat management for migrating and wintering waterfowl in North America.** Texas Tech University Press, 1989. 560 pp., ill., bibl. State-of-the-art contributions on habitat management in the Atlantic, Mississippi, Central, and Pacific flyways of North America.

1434. Kozicky, Edward L. **Hunting preserves for sport or profit.** Caesar Kleberg Wildlife Research Institute, 1987. 210 pp. Information on such essentials as the behavior of captive-reared game birds; the rearing, handling, and releasing of common hunting preserve species; habitat, guides, and dogs; predator control; and hunter safety.

1435. Marks, Stuart A. **The imperial lion: human dimensions of wildlife management in Central Africa.** Westview Press, 1984, 196 pp., ill., bibl., index. Describes a cultural approach to wildlife management more in keeping with local needs and practices and the realities of rural areas.

1436. Owen-Smith, R. Norman. **Management of large mammals in African conservation areas.** HAUM Educational Publishers, Pretoria, 1983. 297 pp., ill., bibl., index. Proceedings of a symposium held in Pretoria, South Africa, in 1982. Papers discuss the consequences of intervention or nonintervention management strategies toward large mammals in national parks of southern and eastern Africa.

1437. Belanger, Dian Olson. **Managing American wildlife: a history of the International Association of Fish and Wildlife Agencies.** University of Massachusetts Press, 1988. 247 pp., ill., bibl., index. Focuses on conservation efforts at the state level and the debate over federal versus state jurisdiction in wildlife management. Topics include migratory bird policy, game and fish propagation, water conservation, and Native American rights controversies.

1438. North American furbearers: a contempo- **rary reference.** International Association of Fish and Wildlife Agencies, 1983. 217 pp., maps, ill. Describes features, behavior, location, number, and status of 30 fur-bearing animals, with range maps, photographs, and charts.

1439. Gilbert, Frederick F.; Dodds, Donald G. **The philosophy and practice of wildlife management.** Krieger, 1987. 279 pp. Uses a biopolitical approach to examine wildlife management in North America. Topics include the biological basis of management, species management, endangered species, international wildlife, and cultural attitudes toward wildlife.

1440. Timm, Robert M.; ed. **Prevention and control of wildlife damage.** University of Nebraska at Lincoln, Great Plains Agricultural Council, Wildlife Resources Committee and Nebraska Cooperative Extension Service, Institute of Agriculture and Natural Resources, 1983. 680 pp. Describes and illustrates wildlife damage and control measures such as fences, traps, and pesticides. Focuses on more than 60 animals, including rodents, primarily in an agricultural setting.

1441. Jewell, Peter A.; Holt, Sidney; eds. **Problems in management of locally abundant wild animals.** Academic Press, 1981. 361 pp., ill., bibl., index. Proceedings of a 1980 workshop. Case studies discuss and illustrate problems arising from animal overabundance. Examines ways of identifying overabundance and assessing and determining control methods.

1442. Kallman, Harmon; and others, eds. **Restoring America's wildlife, 1937–1987: the first 50 years of the Federal Aid in Wildlife Restoration (Pittman-Robertson) Act.** U.S. Department of the Interior, Fish and Wildlife Service; Government Printing Office, 1987. 394 pp. Accomplishments of the Pittman-Robertson Wildlife Restoration Act.

1443. Peek, James M. **A review of wildlife management.** Prentice-Hall, 1986. 486 pp., ill., bibl., index. Reviews major aspects of wildlife management in the written record of the preceding 50 years. Chapters on legislation, food habits, habitat relationships, wildlife and snow, wildlife and fire, competition and predation, pesticides and herbicides, population exploitation, waterfowl management, and management in parks and wilderness areas.

1444. Riney, Thane. **Study and management of large mammals.** Wiley, 1982. 552 pp., ill., bibl., index. A practical guide for the design and implementation of field research programs, plus advice on the successful management, harvest, and conservation of large mammals.

1445. Transactions of the North American Wildlife and Natural Resources Conference. Wildlife Management Institute, 1935 to date. Annual conference attended by professionals from government agencies and nongovernment organizations. Each conference has several sessions of three to six papers, reporting on wildlife management topics and other natural resource issues. A principal source of information on management of public lands.

1446. Novak, Milan; and others, eds. **Wild furbearer management and conservation in North America.** Ontario Trappers Association, under the authority of the Ontario Ministry of Natural Resources, 1987. 1150 pp., ill., bibl., index. Comprehensive treatment of North American furbearers and the industry. Information on management principles and techniques, biology and management of over 30 species, the trapper, pelts and the fur industry, harvest techniques, and regional management programs.

1447. Corfield, Timothy. **The wilderness guardian: a practical guide to fieldwork related to wildlife conservation.** The David Sheldrick Wildlife Appeal; Nairobi Space Publications, 1984. 621 pp., ill., bibl., index. Handbook designed for African field wardens. Covers travel, camping, human and veterinary medicine, natural history, and more. Numerous illustrations.

1448. Sigler, William F. **Wildlife law enforcement.** Brown, 3d ed., 1980. 403 pp. Discusses enforcement techniques, relevant legislation, Native American hunting and fishing rights, the use of side arms, the antihunting movement, and other topics related to wildlife law enforcement.

1449. Hudson, R. J.; Drew, K. R.; Baskin, L. M.; eds. **Wildlife production systems: economic utilization of wild ungulates.** Cambridge University Press, Cambridge studies in applied ecology and resource management, 1989. 469 pp., ill., bibl., index. Chronicles the economic exploitation of wild ungulates by subsistence, recreational, and commercial hunting; game ranching and farming; and other experimental systems on several continents. Reviews methods, ecological impacts, and socioeconomic implications.

Animal Rights. Protection (1450–1469)

1450. Singer, Peter. **Animal liberation.** Avon Books, 2d ed., 1990. 320 pp., ill., bibl., index. Touchstone of the animal rights movement, arguing that animals are entitled to ethical consideration. Focuses on laboratory experiments and factory farming. Chronicles the development of the animal rights movement since the first edition in 1975.

1451. Reece, Kathleen A.; ed. **Animal organizations and services directory.** Animal Stories, 1984 to date. Annual. Gives access to hundreds of organizations and periodicals—national, state, and local.

1452. Ryder, Richard D. **Animal revolution: changing attitudes towards speciesism.** Basil Blackwell, 1989. 385 pp., ill., bibl., index. Recounts past human attitudes toward nonhuman animals from the ancient world to 1960. Focuses on different aspects of the animal rights movement: factory farming, laboratory testing, wildlife protection, and the Animal Liberation Front. Concludes with a philosophical justification for animal rights.

1453. Rollin, Bernard E. **Animal rights and human morality.** Prometheus Books, 1981. 182 pp., bibl. Philosophical discussion of moral theories and legal rights for the general reader. Applies theories to animal research and pet ownership. Does not discuss animals for food.

1454. Griffin, Donald Redfield. **Animal thinking.** Harvard University Press, 1984. 237 pp., bibl., index. Explores evidence and arguments for animal consciousness in the work of ecologists, psychologists, and philosophers.

1455. Animals and their legal rights: a survey of American laws from 1641 to 1990. Animal Welfare Institute, 1990. 441 pp., bibl.

1456. Kress, Stephen W. **The Audubon Society guide to attracting birds.** Scribner, 1985. 377 pp., ill., bibl., index. Using a habitat management approach, discusses and illustrates landscaping for birds, pools and ponds, nesting structures, and supplemental feeding.

1457. Magel, Charles R. **A bibliography of animal rights and related matters.** University Press of America, 1981. 602 pp., index. Over 3200 references, from antiquity to about 1980, arranged chronologically and by subject. Sources include books, journals, government documents, films, organizations, conferences, and university courses. Includes publications on attitudes toward animals; animals and religion, civilization, and culture; ethics; treatment, capture, restraint, transportation, and domestication of animals; spectator entertainment; animals and law, literature, art, and music.

1458. Kellert, Stephen R.; Berry, Joyce K. **A bibliography of human/animal relations.** University Press of America, 1985. 200 pp., index. Nearly 4000 citations cover social, psychological, behavioral, human impact, and regulatory dimensions of human-animal relations; also includes section on individual species and animal types.

1459. Tuan, Yi-Fu. **Dominance and affection: the making of pets**. Yale University Press, 1984. 193 pp., ill., bibl., index. Discusses animals as pets and the development of specialized breeds, the control of nature (in the form of elaborate pleasure gardens), and the use of humans as pets (dwarves, court fools, slaves, women, and children).

1460. Wynne-Tyson, Jon; compiler. **The extended circle: a commonplace book of animal rights**. Paragon House, 1989. 436 pp.,bibl. Quotes, excerpts, complete texts from several hundred sources, arranged alphabetically by writer.

1461. Allen, Robert D.; Westbrook, William H.; eds. **The handbook of animal welfare—biomedical, psychological, and ecological aspects of pet problems and control**. Garland STPM Press, 1979. 251 pp., bibl., index. Examines problems caused by irresponsible pet owners, presents research on pet behavior and pet-human interactions, and discusses techniques for communities to use to deal with pet problems.

1462. Singer, Peter. **In defense of animals**. Basil Blackwell, 1985. 224 pp., bibl., index. Contributed essays on practical and philosophical issues, including commercial animal experimentation, factory farming, and the moral sense of animals; includes an essay by Singer putting the animal liberation movement in historical perspective.

1463. Serpell, James. **In the company of animals: a study of human-animal relationships**. Basil Blackwell, 1986. 215 pp., ill., bibl., index. Examines the history of human-animal interactions from the early Holocene to the present, focusing on the modern paradox of brutality toward livestock accompanied by the affection (in some cases, extravagance) accorded pets. Presents the case both for and against pets.

1464. Magel, Charles R. **Keyguide to information sources in animal rights**. Mansell; McFarland, 1989. 267 pp., bibl., index. In three parts: Part 1 is an overview of animal rights literature, under broad topics: philosophy, science and medicine, education, law, religion, and vegetarianism. Part 2 is an annotated bibliography of 335 items favoring or historically important to animal rights, mostly English-language, arranged chronologically. The annotations are intended to describe the works and also to serve as a conceptual guide to animal rights literature. Contains a directory of 181 animal rights and welfare or-

ganizations worldwide. There is a "Literature Cited," section for works mentioned in Part 1, and appendices listing audiovisuals, periodicals, and products that have not been tested on animals or have not been made from animal ingredients.

1465. Clark, Stephen R. L. **The moral status of animals**. Oxford University Press, 1984. 221 pp., bibl., index. Detailed philosophical discussion of animal rights, based on premise that it is wrong to cause avoidable pain.

1466. Clark, Stephen R. L. **The nature of the beast: are animals moral?**. Oxford University Press, 1984. 127 pp., bibl., index. Examines evidence for animal intelligence and morality; analyzes human assumptions about relationship of human and animal natures.

1467. Rowan, Andrew N. **Of mice, models, and men: a critical evaluation of animal research**. State University of New York Press, 1984. 323 pp., bibl., index. A reasoned examination of the animal research debate; presents background on biomedical research, analyzes general and specific issues of debate, examines toxicity testing in detail, and provides alternatives and suggestions for the future.

1468. **Recognition and alleviation of pain and distress in laboratory animals**. National Academy Press, 1991. 175 pp., index. Prepared by the National Research Council Committee on the Recognition and Alleviation of Pain and Distress in Laboratory Animals. Comprehensive review of current knowledge. Discusses lab settings and their effects on animals; the physiology of pain and distress; and euthanasia (decision, methods, and emotional effects on lab technicians). Includes a listing by species of dosages and side effects of anesthetics, analgesics, and tranquilizers.

1469. Rollin, Bernard E. **The unheeded cry: animal consciousness, animal pain, and science**. Oxford University Press, Studies in bioethics, 1989. 308 pp., ill., bibl., index. Contends that denial of subjective states in animals is a historical aberration, not a necessary feature of science, and has prevented scientists from being morally responsible. Discusses the ideology of and research into animal consciousness and pain.

Animal Biology. Zoology (1470–1496)

1470. **American zoologist**. American Society of Zoologists, 1961 to date. Quarterly. Publishes papers derived from symposia covering animal behavior, genetics, neurobiology, and developmental biology.

1471. Lamb, D. W.; Kenaga, E. E.; eds. **Avian and**

mammalian wildlife toxicology. American Society for Testing and Materials, ASTM special technical publication, no. 757, 1981. 164 pp. Proceedings of a 1980 conference. Addresses the difficulties of deriving accurate data on the hazards of chemicals. Discusses the use of isolated laboratory results and the complexity of natural field exposures.

1472. Nielsen, L.; and others, eds. **Chemical immobilization of North American wildlife**. Wisconsin Humane Society, 1982. 447 pp., ill., bibl. Proceedings of a 1982 symposium. Provides technical overview of equipment and drugs and species-specific techniques for capture and handling.

1473. Fish and Wildlife Reference Service. **Fish and wildlife reference service newsletter**. MAXIMA Corporation, 1967 to date. Irregular. Lists published and unpublished research reports conducted under the Sport Fish and Wildlife Restoration Acts, which are distributed by the Fish and Wildlife Service.

1474. Knutson, Roger M. **Flattened fauna: a field guide to common animals of roads, streets, and highways**. Ten Speed Press, 1987. 88 pp., ill., bibl., index. How and where to identify and study a wide variety of squished species, including reptiles (special chapter on snakes), amphibians, birds, and mammals. Includes illustrations of flattened silhouettes.

1475. Villee, Claude A.; Walker, Warren F., Jr.; Barnes, Robert D. **General zoology**. Saunders College Publishing, 6th ed., 1984. 856 pp., ill., bibl., index. Textbook with glossary, illustrations, and summaries. Sections begin with "Animal Cells and the Organism," and progress through "Continuity of Animal Life," "Diversity of Animals," and "Their Environment."

1476. Hayes, Wayland J., Jr.; Laws, Edward R., Jr.; eds. **Handbook of pesticide toxicology**. Academic Press, 1991. Ill., bibl., index. 3 vols. Profiles the toxicology of over 250 insecticides, herbicides, and fungicides; characterizes classes of pesticides; describes each compound by identity, properties, uses, and toxicity to laboratory animals and humans; covers diagnosis, treatment, injury prevention, and effects on domestic animals and wildlife.

1477. Haegele, M. A.; Hudson, R. H.; Tucker, Richard K. **Handbook of toxicity of pesticides to wildlife**. U.S. Department of the Interior, Fish and Wildlife Service; Government Printing Office, 2d ed., 1984. Provides toxicity estimates of almost 200 chemicals and chemical formulations. Lists acute symptoms observed in test animals.

1478. Davis, John W.; Karstad, Lars H.; Trainer, Daniel O.; eds. **Infectious diseases of wild mammals**. Iowa State University Press, 2d ed., 1981. 446 pp. Reference text for professionals, revised and expanded from 1970 edition.

1479. **Journal of wildlife diseases**. Wildlife Disease Association, 1965 to date. Quarterly. Publishes original research on the effects and management implications of environmental contamination and on infectious, parasitic, toxic, physiological, developmental, and neoplastic diseases of free-living and captive wild animals.

1480. **Journal of wildlife management**. Wildlife Society, 1937 to date. Quarterly. Publishes research on population dynamics, habitat use, genetics, physiology, systematics, research techniques, and theory and methods.

1481. Whitfield, Philip; ed. **Macmillan illustrated animal encyclopedia**. Macmillan, 1984. 600 pp., ill. Catalogs the features and characteristics of vertebrates, grouping them at the family level and illustrating with specific species examples (range, habitat, size). Notes species conservation status.

1482. Burton, Maurice; Burton, Robert; eds. **Marshall Cavendish international wildlife encyclopedia**. Marshall Cavendish, 1989. Ill., index. 24 vols. Twelve hundred articles cover scientific and geographic classifications of species throughout the world. Topical articles on evolution, endangered species, zoos and refuges. Twenty-seven hundred illustrations, most of them in color.

1483. Lutts, Ralph H. **The nature fakers: wildlife, science and sentiment**. Fulcrum, 1990. 255 pp., ill., bibl., index. Chronicles the "war of the naturalists," the early twentieth-century debate over the appropriateness of sentimentality and the role of science in understanding and protecting wildlife.

1484. Leopold, A. Starker; Gutierrez, Ralph J.; Bronson, Michael T. **North American game birds and mammals**. Scribner, 1981. 198 pp., maps, ill., bibl., index. Intended as a companion to a field guide. Focuses on the natural history, geographic distribution, and ecological status of 74 birds and 70 mammals.

1485. Smith, G. R.; Hearn, J. P.; eds. **Reproduction and disease in captive and wild animals**. Oxford University Press, Symposia of the Zoological Society of London, v. 60, 1988. 209 pp., ill., bibl., index. Proceedings of a 1988 symposium. Nine articles discuss fertility suppression, gamete production, growth and reproduction, hormones, embryo manipulation, use of ultrasound, immunoassays, anaerobic bacteria and viruses as pathogens on a variety of species.

1486. Studies on neotropical fauna and environment. Swets & Zeitlinger, 1976 to date. Quarterly. Publishes papers on the ecology, systematics, and distribution of neotropical fauna, usually in English but sometimes in Spanish, Portuguese, French, or German.

1487. Cossins, Andrew R.; Bowler, K. **Temperature biology of animals.** Chapman and Hall, 1987. 339 pp., ill., bibl., index. Discusses thermal energy and environment, direct effects of temperature change; rate compensations and capacity adaptations; thermal injury and death; and effects on reproduction, development, and growth.

1488. Norberg, U. M. **Vertebrate flight: mechanics, physiology, morphology, ecology and evolution.** Springer-Verlag, Zoophysiology, v. 27, 1990. 291 pp., ill, bibl., index. Reviews basic aerodynamics and the physiological aspects of flight before examining the dynamics, mechanics, and power requirements of gliding, soaring, hovering, and forward flight. Studies evolution of and morphological adaptations for flight.

1489. Tributsch, Helmut; Langner, Paul, trans. **When the snakes awake: animals and earthquake prediction.** MIT Press, 1982. 248 pp., maps, bibl. Reviews evidence and anecdotal accounts of unusual events said to precede earthquakes. Focuses mostly on aberrant animal behavior and its possible electrostatic causes. Also examines changes in well water, fog in clear weather, and earthquake light phenomena.

1490. Dasmann, Raymond Fredric. **Wildlife biology.** Wiley, 2d ed., 1981. 212 pp., ill., bibl., index. Short, nonmathematical introductory text; covers functioning of ecosystems, distribution of biotic communities, population structure, natality and mortality, territoriality, carrying capacity, and declining diversity.

1491. Robbins, Charles T. **Wildlife feeding and nutrition.** Academic Press, Animal feeding and nutrition, 1983. 343 pp., ill., bibl., index. Applies basic principles of nutrition to wild mammals and birds. Discusses protein, water, mineral, and vitamin needs, reproductive and productive costs, gastrointestinal anatomy, digestion, and nutrient metabolism.

1492. Schemnitz, Sanford D.; ed. **Wildlife management techniques manual.** Wildlife Society, 4th ed., 1980. 686 pp., ill., bibl., index. Concerned with planning the investigative or management project. In seven sections (32 chapters): basic research, working with wild animals, studying wildlife populations, studying the en-

vironment, management, administration and policy, and specialized techniques. Numerous illustrations.

1493. Wildlife monographs. Wildlife Society, 1958 to date. Irregular. Contains papers of greater detail and longer length (usually over 80 pages) dealing with wildlife ecology and management.

1494. Wildlife review. U.S. Department of the Interior, Fish and Wildlife Service; Government Printing Office, 1935 to date. Bimonthly. Index of wildlife-related literature drawn from 1300 journals, periodicals, and other sources. Author, subject, and taxonomic indexes. Available as an electronic database on CD-ROM.

1495. Wildlife society bulletin. Wildlife Society, 1973 to date. Quarterly. Publishes research and opinion papers on all aspects of wildlife management, including law enforcement, economics, education, administration, philosophy, and contemporary wildlife problems.

1496. Zoological record. Zoological Society of London, 1870 to date. Annual. Index to zoological literature published worldwide. Each of 25 sections covers a different animal group. Also covers general zoological literature and lists new generic and subgeneric names. Has author, subject, geographic, palaeontological, and systematic indexes. Available as an online computer database.

Animal Ecology. Species (1497–1530)

1497. Brown, Luther. **Analyses in behavioral ecology: a manual for lab and field.** Sinauer, 1988. 194 pp., ill., bibl. Suggested problems, hypotheses, and techniques are presented in four main areas: sensory capabilities, feeding patterns, spacing patterns, and reproduction.

1498. Animal behaviour. Bailliere-Tindall, 1953 to date. 8 issues/yr. Publishes research in behavioral ecology.

1499. Stonehouse, Bernard; ed. **Animal marking: recognition marking of animals in research.** University Park Press, 1978. 257 pp., ill., bibl., index. Proceedings of a 1977 conference. Reviews various marking methods used by researchers and animal keepers, with most attention given to birds, seals, whales, bats, snakes, fish, and primates.

1500. Remmert, Herman. **Arctic animal ecology.** Springer-Verlag, 1980. 250 pp., ill., index, Bibl. Examines ecological factors, characteristics shared by many Arctic animals, peculiarities of the systems, and Arctic climates; presents case studies of different Arctic areas.

1501. Behavioral ecology and sociobiology. Springer-Verlag, 1976 to date. Monthly. Publishes quantitative, empirical, and theoretical studies of animal behavior at all levels (individual, population, and community).

1502. Sibly, R. M.; Smith, R. H.; eds. **Behavioural ecology: ecological consequences of adaptive behaviour.** Blackwell Scientific, Symposium of the British Ecological Society, v. 25, 1985. 620 pp., maps, bibl., index. Papers of a 1984 symposium discuss the interactions of population dynamics with feeding, spacing, breeding, and social behavior.

1503. Cole, D. J. A.; Brander, G. C.; eds. **Bioindustrial ecosystems.** Elsevier, Ecosystems of the world, v. 21, 1986. 295 pp., ill., bibl., index. Examines domestic livestock ecosystems, primarily in England. Discusses domestication of animals, physiological aspects of production, breeding, disease, and control of the physical environment.

1504. Mangel, Marc; Clark, Colin W. **Dynamic modeling in behavioral ecology.** Princeton University Press, Monographs in behavior and ecology, 1988. 308 pp., ill., bibl., index. Introduces principles of stochastic dynamic programming and applies them to various biological problems—hunting by lions, insect reproductive strategies, migrations of plankton, parental care in birds, and dispersal in spiders and raptors.

1505. Kunz, Thomas H.; ed. **Ecological and behavioral methods for the study of bats.** Smithsonian Institution Press, 1987. 533 pp., ill., bibl., index. Exhaustive review of field study techniques in each chapter by experts, many applicable to studies of other small mammals and birds. Covers capture, marking, censusing, recording vocalizations, radiotelemetry, dietary analysis, training, measuring of metabolism, and more.

1506. Rubenstein, Daniel; Wrangham, Richard, W.; eds. **Ecological aspects of social evolution: birds and mammals.** Princeton University Press, 1986. 551 pp., ill., bibl., index. Many case studies illustrate monogamous and polygynous behavior patterns in a wide variety of birds and mammals, including humans.

1507. Carwardine, Mark. **The encyclopedia of world wildlife: a survey of animals and their habitats.** Chartwell Books, 1987. 160 pp. Organized by ecosystem type; describes and illustrates hundreds of animal species.

1508. Hoelldobler, Bert; Lindauer, Martin; eds. **Experimental behavioral ecology and sociobiology.** Sinauer, 1985. 488 pp., ill., bibl., index. Discusses orientation and learning, communication signals, communication and reproductive behavior, and social organization in vertebrates and invertebrates.

1509. Lorenz, Konrad; Lorenz, Konrad Z. and Kickert, Robert Warren, trans. **The foundations of ethology.** Springer-Verlag, 1981. 380 pp., ill., bibl., index. Describes the theoretical position of classic ethology, defined here as the study of behavior in its context.

1510. Mech, L. David. **Handbook of animal radio-tracking.** University of Minnesota Press, 1983. 107 pp., ill., bibl., index. Practical manual for researchers considering a radio-tracking project; text discusses equipment, techniques, and the variety of data and information that can be gathered.

1511. Lehner, Philip N. **Handbook of ethological methods.** Garland STPM Press, Garland series in ethology, 1979. 403 pp., ill., bibl., index. Includes design and delineation of research, observation and data collection, interpretation procedures, and presentation of results.

1512. Bekoff, Marc; Jamieson, Dale. **Interpretation and explanation in the study of animal behavior.** Westview Press, 1990. Ill., index. 2 vols. Vol. 1: Interpretation, intentionality, and communication. Vol. 2: Explanations, evolution, and adaptation. Collection of essays examines the structure and limits of understanding animal minds, assessing cognition and emotion, consciousness and its significance, the role of anthropomorphism, and ethical issues.

1513. Begon, Michael. **Investigating animal abundance; capture-recapture for biologists.** University Park Press, 1979. 97 pp., ill., bibl. Presents a variety of models, reducing their mathematical derivations to commonsense explanations; stresses biological assumptions of models; discusses practical aspects of capture-recapture censusing.

1514. Trager, William. **Living together: the biology of animal parasitism.** Plenum Press, 1986. 467 pp., ill., bibl., index. Focuses on the parasites common to humans and other vertebrates, how parasites select and enter hosts and locate particular tissues and organs, the parasite-host interface, nutrient uptake, energy metabolism, and modification of hosts by parasites.

1515. Benyus, Janine M. **Northwoods wildlife: a watcher's guide to habitats.** NorthWord Press, 1989. 453 pp. Describes 18 types of wetlands, forests, and open spaces of Minnesota, Wisconsin, and Michigan and the wildlife likely to be found in each.

1516. McFarland, David; ed. **Oxford companion to animal behaviour.** Oxford University Press, 1987. 685

pp., ill., bibl., index. Reprint of the 1982 edition, with corrections and a new index.

1517. Cockburn, Andrew. **Social behavior in fluctuating populations.** Croom Helm, Studies in behavioural adaptation, 1988. 239 pp., ill., bibl., index. Examines traits characteristic of fluctuating populations and relates them to the evolution of life history and social behavior. Examples of rodents, with some discussion of snow hares, grouse, and ptarmigan.

1518. Trivers, Robert. **Social evolution.** Benjamin/Cummings, 1985. 462 pp., ill., bibl., index. An introduction to sociobiology, with theoretical reflections and insights, by a founder of the field. The first chapters explain Darwinian evolution and genetics in relation to behavior and learning, followed by principles of social evolution—kinship, parent-offspring relations, and reproductive altruism. Concludes with material on sexual selection, the sex ratio, sex, social cooperation, deceit, and self-deception. Exceptional use of drawings, photographs, graphs, and tables to illustrate the text.

1519. Sociobiology. California State University, Chico, 1975 to date. 2 or 3 issues/yr. Publishes research results, review articles, or translations of classic papers on any aspect of the biology of social animals.

1520. Wilson, Edward O. **Sociobiology: the new synthesis.** Belknap Press, 1975. 697 pp. Ill., index. Founding work in the field of sociobiology, or the biological basis of social behavior. In three parts: social evolution, social mechanisms, and social species.

1521. Brownie, Cavell; and others. **Statistical inference from band recovery data; a handbook.** U.S. Department of the Interior, Fish and Wildlife Service; Government Printing Office, Resource publication, no. 156, 2d ed., 1985. 305 pp., bibl. Focusing on bird-banding studies, presents models for analysis of age-dependent banding data. Includes reprints of ten important papers. Assumes knowledge of applied statistics and differential calculus.

1522. Huntingford, Felicity Ann. **The study of animal behaviour.** Chapman and Hall, 1984. 411 pp., ill., bibl., index. Introductory textbook. Reviews all subject areas; strong on the role of behavior in evolution.

1523. Dawkins, Marian Stamp. **Unravelling animal behaviour.** Wiley; Halsted Press, 1986. 159 pp., ill., bibl., index. Collection of ten essays addressing and clarifying conceptual problems in animal behavior—adaptation, optimality, inclusive fitness, genetic basis of behavior, nature-nurture controversy, animal communication, and sexual selection.

1524. Rodiek, Jon E.; Bolen, Eric G.; eds. **Wildlife and habitats in managed landscapes.** Island Press, 1991. 216 pp., ill., bibl., index. Presents case studies of integrated management approaches that incorporate wildlife habitat into landscape design. Topics include power line corridors in Appalachian forests, deer habitats (assessing winter nutrition, managing juniper woodlands in eastern Texas), and landscape-level management of the American marten.

1525. Robinson, William L.; Bolen, Eric G. **Wildlife ecology and management.** Macmillan, 1989. 574 pp., maps, ill., bibl., index. General introduction covers wide variety of topics, including wildlife diseases; hunting and trapping; wildlife, water, and soils; designing and maintaining wildlife habitats in conjunction with farmland, rangelands, and forests; the economics of wildlife; and urban and exotic wildlife.

1526. Roth, Charles E. **The wildlife observer's guidebook.** Prentice-Hall, 1982. 239 pp., ill., bibl., index. Discusses techniques for taking notes, making blinds, livetrapping and identifying animals, and tracking; encompasses the study of insects, fish, reptiles, amphibians, and mammals.

1527. Wagner, Frederic H. **Wildlife of the deserts.** Abrams, Wildlife habitat series, 1980. 231 pp., ill., index. Describes and illustrates with numerous color photographs the world's many types of deserts, their wildlife, and such aspects of desert ecology as predator-prey relationships and adaptations to extreme heat.

1528. Lazell, James D., Jr. **Wildlife of the Florida Keys: a natural history.** Island Press, 1989. 253 pp., ill., index. Anecdotes accompany brief descriptive essays of the often continental, temperate zone fauna to be found in this tropical ecosystem. Discusses habitats, habits, and conservation status of mammals, birds, reptiles, amphibians, and many insects. Land development threatens critical habitat. Special attention to endangered species.

1529. Ray, Carleton. **Wildlife of the polar regions.** Abrams, Wildlife habitat series, 1981. 232 pp., maps, ill., index. Describes and illustrates the life forms, from unicellular and higher plants to birds and mammals, of each of the major topographical features of polar regions; includes glossary.

1530. Kenward, Robert. **Wildlife radio tagging: equipment, techniques, and data analysis.** Academic Press, Biological techniques series, 1987. 222 pp., ill., bibl., index. Intended for wildlife biologists at all levels of experience; covers basic equipment, building of transmitters, tag assembly and attachment, tracking, fixed stations and analysis techniques.

Mammals: Guides. General (1531–1547)

1531. Genoways, Hugh. **Current mammalogy, Vol. 1.** Plenum, 1987. 519 pp., ill., bibl., index. First volume in a new series intended to provide a forum for research in mammalogy outside existing journals.

1532. Fowler, Charles W.; Smith, Tim D. **Dynamics of large mammal populations.** Wiley-Interscience, 1981. 477 pp., ill., index. Based on papers at a conference in 1978. Authories from six countries provide a detailed synthesis of population dynamics in general, single-species populations, multispecies interactions, management implications of population modeling, and other topics.

1533. Stoddart, D. Michael; ed. **Ecology of small mammals.** Chapman and Hall; Wiley, 1979. 386 pp., ill., bibl., index.

1534. Macdonald, David; ed. **The encyclopedia of mammals.** Facts on File, 1984. 895 pp., ill., bibl., index. Arranged under the broad categories of carnivores, sea mammals, primates, small and large herbivores, and insect eaters and marsupials. Sections introduce an order's characteristics, ecology, behavior, and evolution. Three- to four-page entries detail the physical features, distribution, habits, and social dynamics particular to each species, emphasizing larger and better known species.

1535. **Grzimek's encyclopedia of mammals.** McGraw-Hill, 1990. Ill., bibl., index. 15 vols. Organized by subclasses and orders. Provides information on biology, physiology, nutrition, behavior, and evolution of groups and individual species. Standardized charts facilitate comparison. Lists French, German, and English common names; 3500 photographs.

1536. **Journal of mammalogy.** American Society of Mammalogists, 1919 to date. Quarterly. Publishes research on mammal classification, evolution, and ecology.

1537. Honacki, James H.; Kinman, Kenneth E.; Koeppl, James W.; eds. **Mammal species of the world: a taxonomic and geographic reference.** Allen Press; Association of Systematics Collections, 1982. 694 pp., bibl., index. Taxonomic checklist of 4170 species; includes type, locality, distribution, protected status, and International Species Inventory System numbers.

1538. Chepko-Sade, B. Diane; Halpin, Zuleyma Tang; eds. **Mammalian dispersal patterns: the effects of social structure on population genetics.** University of Chicago Press, 1987. 342 pp., ill., bibl., index. Identifies dispersal patterns of mammals, noting various consequences on the genetic structures of populations and seeking to estimate effective or neighborhood population sizes; also discusses dispersal and demography in two human populations.

1539. Smith, Michael H.; Joule, James; eds. **Mammalian population genetics.** University of Georgia Press, 1981. 380 pp., ill., bibl., index. Papers presented at a symposium held in 1978 examine genetic variability in insular populations; connections among environmental, morphological, and genetic variability; and the use of genetics to determine phylogeny.

1540. Eisenberg, John Frederick. **The mammalian radiations: an analysis of trends in evolution, adaptation, and behavior.** University of Chicago Press, 1981. 610 pp., maps, ill., bibl., index. Discusses the radiations of many mammalian orders throughout time; other topics include macrophysiology and adaptation, the genetic basis and classification of behavior, and the structure and classification of mammalian social organization.

1541. Putnam, Rory J.; ed. **Mammals as pests.** Chapman and Hall, 1989. 271 pp. Papers drawn from a 1987 symposium discuss the current status of such pests as deer, rabbits, badgers, squirrels, and moles in the United Kingdom and Europe, as well as forms of management.

1542. Lever, Christopher. **Naturalized mammals of the world.** Longman, 1985. 487 pp., maps, ill., bibl., index. Describes the circumstances of the red-necked wallaby, the crab-eating macaque, the sambar, and other species introduced into foreign ecosystems, and now living in self-maintaining and self-perpetuating populations. Includes distribution maps.

1543. Anderson, Sydney; Jones, J. Knox; eds. **Orders and families of recent mammals of the world.** Wiley, 1984. 686 pp., ill., bibl., index. Provides concise summaries of 21 orders and 131 families of living or recently extinct mammals. Includes distribution maps and simple illustrations. Useful quick reference.

1544. Finerty, James Patrick. **The population ecology of cycles in small mammals: mathematical theory and biological fact.** Yale University Press, 1980. 234 pp., ill., bibl., index. Examines the abundant literature on cycles and asks: do cycles exist, and if they do, what causes them? Uses time-series analysis on Hudson Bay Company fur records. Links theoretical and field ecology.

1545. Nowak, Ronald M. **Walker's mammals of the world.** Johns Hopkins University Press, 5th ed., 1992.

Ill., bibl., index. 2 vols. Standard guide, revised and updated. Provides information on more than 1100 genera and 4000 species. Species are arranged within genus from simpler to advanced life forms. Some 2000 photographs, mostly of live animals. Includes data on number and distribution, physical traits, habitat, daily and seasonal activity, population dynamics, home range, social life, reproduction, and longevity. Particular attention is given to endangered species and species of exceptional economic importance.

1546. Merritt, Joseph F.; ed. **Winter ecology of small mammals.** Carnegie Museum of Natural History, Special publication, no. 10, 1984. 380 pp., ill., bibl. Proceedings of a 1981 colloquium; presents 37 papers from a variety of disciplines, including animal and plant biology, ecology, physiology, ethology, and others.

1547. Corbet, G. B.; Hill, J. E. **A world list of mammalian species.** British Museum of Natural History; Comstock Publishing Associates, 1980. 226 pp., bibl., index. Provides Latin (and English, where applicable) names and brief statement of habitat and range for each of the world's 4000 or so mammals. Arranged by orders and families. Indicates endangered and domesticated species.

Mammals: Species. Regions (1548–1570)

1548. Sukumar, R. **The Asian elephant: ecology and management.** Cambridge University Press, 1990. 251 pp., bibl., index.

1549. Whitaker, John, Jr. **The Audubon Society field guide to North American mammals.** Knopf, 1980. 745 pp., ill., index. Pocket-sized guide includes color photographs, range maps, and life history information and, for some, track markings. Animals grouped by appearance, not taxonomically.

1550. Martinka, Clifford J.; McArthur, Katharine L.; eds. **Bears—their biology and management.** Bear Biology Association, Bear Biology Association conference series, v. 3, 1980. 375 pp., ill., bibl. Papers of a 1977 conference in Kalispell, Montana. Sixty papers discuss biology, ecology and management of grizzly and polar bears and of brown bear populations in the United States, Japan, and Europe.

1551. Chadwick, Douglas H. **A beast the color of winter: the mountain goat observed.** Sierra Club Books, 1983. 208 pp., ill., bibl., index. Lively prose illuminates data collected in all seasons over more than a decade.

1552. Wemmer, Christen M.; ed. **Biology and management of the Cervidae.** Smithsonian Institution Press, Research symposia of the National Zoological Park, 1987. 577 pp., ill., bibl. Proceedings of a 1982 conference in Front Royal, Virginia. Forty-five papers on theoretical issues, case studies of exotic deer, and management in the wild and in captivity.

1553. Gauthier-Pilters, Hilde; Dagg, Anne Innis. **The camel: its evolution, ecology, behavior, and relationship to man.** University of Chicago Press, 1981. 208 pp., ill., bibl., index. Describes camels in their natural habitat in the northwestern and western Sahara, discussing habitat, feeding, drinking, adaptations, and locomotion and loads; also concentrates on nomadic "camel men" and their role in desert ecology.

1554. Gittleman, John L.; ed. **Carnivore behavior, ecology, and evolution.** Comstock Publishing Associates, 1989. 620 pp. Review papers and original research by 30 leading authorities. In three parts: ecology, behavior, and evolution.

1555. Strahan, Ronald; ed. **Complete book of Australian mammals.** Angus & Robertson, 1984. 530 pp., maps, ill., bibl. Color photographs and authoritative text summarize the habitat, ecology, reproduction, and behavior of 273 species; includes distribution maps.

1556. Dixon, Alexandra; Jones, David; eds. **Conservation and biology of desert antelopes.** Croom Helm, 1989. 238 pp.

1557. Eltringham, S. K. **The ecology and conservation of large African mammals.** Macmillan, 1979. 286 pp., ill., bibl., index. Biology and ecology, with emphasis on social organization, comprise three-fourths of the volume; conservation and management take up the remainder.

1558. Delaney, M. J.; Happold, D. C. D. **Ecology of African mammals.** Longman, 1979. 434 pp., ill., bibl., index. Reference textbook. In four parts: mammal fauna, ecology in the biotic zones, ecological perspectives, and interactions with man.

1559. Kunz, Thomas H.; ed. **Ecology of bats.** Plenum Press, 1982. 425 pp., ill, bibl., index. International authorities on aspects of bat ecology not previously well documented.

1560. Thomas, Jack Ward; Toweill, Dale E.; eds. **Elk of North America, ecology and management.** Wildlife Management Institute; Stackpole Books, 1982. 698 pp., ill., bibl., index. Comprehensive presentation of elk biology and ecology, historical values, and modern management.

1561. Schaller, George B.; et al. **The giant pandas of Wolong.** University of Chicago Press, 1985. 298 pp., ill., bibl., index. Reports on the panda's feeding, movement, and activity patterns; examines population dynamics, communication, and reproductive and social behavior; addresses the controversy over the giant panda's relation to the raccoon and the bear.

1562. Grizzly bear compendium. National Wildlife Federation; Interagency Grizzly Bear Committee, 1987. 540 pp. Sourcebook of published and unpublished research, designed for students, researchers, and managers. Includes detailed narrative summaries of morphology, physiology, mortality, behavior, population characteristics, interspecific relationships and management.

1563. Boyce, Mark S. **The Jackson elk herd: intensive wildlife management in North America.** Cambridge University Press, 1989. 306 pp., bibl., index. Analyzes changes in management of an elk herd at Jackson Hole, Wyoming, over the past 75 years, based on research done by the federal-state Cooperative Elk Studies Group. After a historical overview, there are chapters on migration and seasonal distribution; elk population, habitat ecology, and winter feeding; management on national forests and national parks and by the Wyoming Fish and Game Department; public interests in elk management; and conclusions and recommendations.

1564. Eisenberg, John Frederick **Mammals of the neotropics. Vol. 1: The northern neotropics.** University of Chicago Press, 1989. 449 pp., ill., index. Covers Panama, Colombia, Venezuela, Guyana, Suriname, and French Guiana. Large-format volume includes concise descriptions, range and habitat, and natural history notes for all species in each mammalian order.

1565. Emmons, Louise H. **Neotropical rainforest mammals: a field guide.** University of Chicago Press, 1990. 281 pp., maps, ill., bibl., index. Covers mammals of Central and South American lowland rain forests; entries, most at the level of species, recount common names, normal size, identifying features, range, natural history, and endangered or threatened status; includes discussion on classification, study, and conservation of rain forest mammals.

1566. Penny, Malcolm. **Rhinos: endangered species.** Facts on File, 1988. 116 pp. Examines the natural history of five species of rhinoceros (the black, the white, the great Indian one-horned, the Javan, and the Sumatran), reasons for their decline, and conservation efforts.

1567. Fleming, Theodore H. **The short-tailed fruit bat: a study in plant-animal interactions.** University of Chicago Press, 1988. 365 pp., maps, ill., bibl., index. Study illustrates the key role of fruit-eating bats in neotropical ecosystems.

1568. Tilson, Ronald L.; Seal, Ulysses S.; eds. **Tigers of the world: the biology, biopolitics, management, and conservation of an endangered species.** Noyes, 1987. 510 pp., ill., bibl., index. Proceedings of a 1986 symposium. Discusses systematics and taxonomy, status in the wild and in captivity, reproductive biology, captive management, white tiger politics, and conservation strategies.

1569. Halls, Lowell K.; ed. **White-tailed deer: ecology and management.** Stackpole Books, 1984. 870 pp. Extensive discussion of whitetail biology and ecology, population management, population, and habitats in North America and where introduced.

1570. Dhapman, Joseph A.; Feldhamer, George A.; eds. **Wild mammals of North America: biology, management, and economics.** Johns Hopkins University Press, 1982. 1147 pp., maps, ill., bibl., index. Provides detailed information about distribution, description, physiology, reproduction, ecology, food habits, habitat behavior, mortality, age determination, economic status, current research, and management needs as well as literature citations for 57 economically important species.

Mammals: Aquatic and Marine (1571–1582)

1571. Payne, R.; ed. **Communication and behavior of whales.** Westview Press, AAAS selected symposium, v. 76, 1983. 643 pp., ill., index, bibl. First collection of essays on live whales in their natural habitat.

1572. VanBlaricom, G. R.; Estes, J. A.; eds. **The community ecology of sea otters.** Springer-Verlag, Ecological studies, v. 65, 1988. 247 pp., ill., index, bibl. Expanded from a 1985 symposium. Papers from 13 experts, dealing in particular with the effects of reintroducing sea otters on shallow subtidal zones of the West Coast of North America.

1573. Gaskin, D.E. **The ecology of whales and dolphins.** Heinemann, 1982. 459 pp., maps, ill., bibl., index. Comprehensive discussion of evolution, ecology, and distribution from a global perspective.

1574. Lavigne, David M.; Kovacs, Kit M. **Harps & hoods: ice-breeding seals of the Northwest Atlantic.** University of Waterloo Press, 1988. 174 pp. Discusses life cycles and special adaptations, including thermoregulation, water balance, and reproductive strategies, of harp and hooded seals; also covers the history and controversy of seal hunts.

1575. Chanin, Paul. **The natural history of otters.** Facts on File, 1985. 179 pp., ill., bibl., index. Discusses physical characteristics, food and feeding behavior, relations with other animals, social organization and communication, life history, and effects of humans on the various otter species.

1576. Evans, Peter G. H. **The natural history of whales and dolphins.** Facts on File, 1987. 343 pp., ill., bibl., index. Reviews cetacean evolution, anatomy, and habits; describes taxa, systematics, zoogeography, and distribution; discusses such aspects of life histories as reproduction, migration, social organization, feeding, and aging.

1577. Mason, C. F.; Macdonald, S. M. **Otters: ecology and conservation.** Cambridge University Press, 1986. 236 pp., ill., bibl., index. Focuses on the European otter, describing its life history, details of survey methods, and the state of populations throughout the range.

1578. King, Judith E. **Seals of the world.** British Museum (Natural History); University of Queensland Press, 2d ed., 1983. 240 pp., ill., bibl., index. Initial sections provide information on distribution, description, breeding, feeding, predators, and exploitation of numerous seals, sea lions, and walruses; later parts present detailed discussion of pinniped biology.

1579. Slijper, Everhard Johannes; Pomerans, A. J., trans. **Whales.** Cornell University Press, 2d ed., 1979. 511 pp., ill., bibl., index. First published in English in 1962, this second edition revises only the concluding chapter and bibliography (by Richard J. Harrison). Examines locomotion, behavior, feeding, migration, evolution and many other whale processes and activities. More than 200 figures and photographs.

1580. Baker, Mary L. **Whales, dolphins, and porpoises of the world.** Doubleday, 1987. 224 pp., ill., bibl. Introductory text describes and illustrates 39 genera and 75 species.

1581. Bonner, Nigel. **Whales of the world.** Facts on File, 1989. 191 pp., ill., bibl., index. Introductory chapter reviews whale evolution and common anatomy, characteristics, and behavior; eight following chapters present the features, habits, and distribution of great whales, humpbacks, sperm whales, oceanic dolphins, killer whales, and others.

1582. Minasian, Stanley M.; Balcomb, Kenneth C., III; Foster, Larry A. **The world's whales.** Smithsonian Exposition Books (dist. by Norton), 1984. 224 pp., ill.,

bibl., index. General introduction to cetaceans is followed by attractive color photographs and illustrations of almost every cetacean species, accompanied by brief accounts of appearance, feeding habits, mating and breeding, and distribution.

Primates (1583–1593)

1583. Strum, Shirley. **Almost human: a journey into the world of baboons.** Random House, 1987. 294 pp., ill., index, bibl. A charming and satisfying look at baboon society. Strum was the first to contend the notion that aggression reigns supreme in groups of baboons.

1584. Tuttle, Russell H. **Apes of the world: their social behavior, communication, mentality, and ecology.** Noyes, Noyes series in animal behavior, ecology, conservation, and management, 1986. 421 pp., ill., bibl., index. Presents accounts of the behavioral ecology of gibbons, orangutans, chimpanzees, gorillas and others; notes communication, nesting, tool use, and cognition; indicates areas requiring further research.

1585. Goodall, Jane. **The chimpanzees of Gombe: patterns of behavior.** Belknap Press, 1986. 673 pp., ill., index, bibl. Life histories of some 50 animals carefully described and analyzed over a period of 25 years. Shows similarities between humans and chimpanzees in cognitive abilities and emotional situations.

1586. Kavanagh, Michael. **A complete guide to monkeys, apes, and other primates.** Cape, 1983. 224 pp., ill., bibl., index. Brief essay descriptions of each genus of prosimians, New and Old World monkeys, and the tailless primates are accompanied by distribution maps and color photographs.

1587. Marsh, Clive W.; Mittermeier, Russell A.; eds. **Primate conservation in the tropical rain forest.** Liss, 1987. 365 pp., ill., bibl., index. Examines threats to primates and practical conservation remedies. Proposes frameworks for conservation in the neotropics, the African rain forests, Madagascar, and the Asian moist tropical forests.

1588. Else, James G.; Lee, Phyllis C.; eds. **Primate ecology and conservation.** Cambridge University Press, Selected proceedings of the Tenth Congress of the International Primatological Society : v. 2, 1986. 393 pp., ill., bibl., index. Selected proceedings of a 1984 conference in Nairobi, Kenya. Papers discuss feeding behavior, nutrition, mating systems, conservation, and conflict with humans.

1589. Dunbar, Robin Ian MacDonald. **Primate so-**

cial systems. Cornell University Press, 1988. 373 pp., ill., bibl., index. Presents basic principles of primate biology, with new perspectives on primate sociality. Shows the need for mathematical models to refine and develop hypotheses and field evidence to test them. Gives examples of models and field data yielding alternative explanations.

1590. Smuts, Barbara B.; and others, eds. **Primate societies.** University of Chicago Press, 1987. 578 pp., ill., bibl., index. Forty-six contributors provide synthesis of knowledge about social lives of nonhuman primates. In five sections: evolution of social diversity, socioecology, group life, communication and intelligence, and prospects for research.

1591. Richard, Alison F. **Primates in nature.** Freeman, 1985. 558 pp., ill., bibl., index. Discusses primate distribution, diets, reproduction, demography, social organization, and roles in communities, frequently using other animals for comparison or illustration.

1592. Tattersall, Ian. **The primates of Madagascar.** Columbia University Press, 1982. 382 pp., ill, bibl., index. Lists and explains the living and extinct species of Madagascar's primates; discusses lemur morphology, adaptation, and phylogeny, plus their behavior and ecology.

1593. Wolfheim, Jaclyn H. **Primates of the world: distribution, abundance, and conservation.** University of Washington Press, 1983. 831 pp., maps, ill., bibl. For each species, presents information on distribution, range, habitat, factors affecting wild populations, and conservation efforts.

Birds: Guides. Lists (1594–1608)

1594. Harrison, Colin. **An atlas of the birds of the western Palaearctic.** Princeton University Press, 1982. 322 pp., ill., bibl., index. Covers all 639 species of the western Palearctic as well as 167 species of Africa or the eastern Palearctic. Maps show summer and winter ranges and migration patterns. Discusses each bird's habitats.

1595. Root, Terry Louise. **Atlas of wintering North American birds: an analysis of Christmas bird count data.** University of Chicago Press, 1988. 312 pp., maps, ill., bibl., index. Maps show the abundance and distribution of 346 bird species as counted by the National Audubon Society's annual cooperative volunteer bird counts; 162 other species also discussed; transparent overlays show such factors as temperature, precipitation, humidity, elevation, and vegetation.

1596. Terres, John K. **Audubon Society encyclo-**

pedia of North American birds. Knopf; Random House, 1980. 1109 pp., ill., bibl. Presents biographies of over 800 birds arranged by family; entries for each species provide information on size, features, differences between the sexes, calls or songs, flight speed, feeding habits, breeding habits, lifetime, and summer and winter ranges; also lists brief biographies of noted ornithologists and naturalists; contains many color photographs and is cross-referenced.

1597. Ehrlich, Paul R.; Dobkin, David S.; Wheye, Daryl. **The birder's handbook: a field guide to the natural history of North American birds.** Simon & Schuster, 1988. 785 pp., ill., bibl., index. Complements standard field guides by describing the breeding and feeding biology of 646 species, covering their breeding habitat, brood number, displays, and conservation status; about 250 essays discuss a wide range of topics: avian longevity, sexual selection, copulation, promiscuity, aerodynamics, flight, environmental acoustics, and many others.

1598. Ridgely, Robert S.; Tudor, Guy. **The birds of South America.** University of Texas Press, 1989 to date. Maps, ill., bibl., index. Multivolume series grouped by genera. Vol. 1: The oscine passerines. Species entries explain identification, habitat, behavior, range, and similarity to other species; color plates illustrate sample species and note distinguishing marks and variations.

1599. Broke, M.; Birkhead, T.; eds. **The Cambridge encyclopedia of ornithology.** Cambridge University Press, 1991. 362 pp., ill., index.

1600. Campbell, Bruce; Lack, Elizabeth; eds. **A dictionary of birds.** Buteo Books, 1985. 670 pp., ill., bibl. Revised edition of *A new dictionary of birds* (1964). An encyclopedia of avian biology, primarily at the family level.

1601. Perrins, Christopher M.; Middleton, Alex L.; eds. **Encyclopedia of birds.** Facts on File, 1985. 445 pp., ill., bibl., index. Organized by family; presents physical features, distribution, behavior, and relationship to humans. Includes numerous color photographs, scale drawings, and maps.

1602. Peterson, Roger Tory. **A field guide to the birds: a completely new guide to all the birds of eastern and central North America.** Houghton Mifflin, 4th ed., 1980. 384 pp., ill., index. Species descriptions and illustrations on facing pages, providing data on size, voice, range, habitat, and plumages by age, sex, and season; birds grouped by visual categories.

1603. Pratt, H. Douglas; Bruner, Phillip L.; Berrett, Delwyn G. **A field guide to the birds of Hawaii and the**

tropical **Pacific**. Princeton University Press, 1987. 409 pp., ill., bibl., index. Describes appearance, vocalizations, behavior, and distribution of native and introduced birds. Includes 45 color plates of birds regularly nesting or migrating through the area.

1604. Peterson, Roger Tory. **A field guide to western birds: a completely new guide to field marks of all species found in North America west of the 100th meridian and north of Mexico.** Houghton Mifflin, 3d ed., 1990. 432 pp. Standard guide, first published in 1941. Illustrations by the author.

1605. Cramp, Stanley; ed. **Handbook of the birds of Europe, the Middle East, and North Africa: the birds of the Western Palearctic.** Oxford University Press, 1977. Ill., bibl., index. 5 vols. Provides information at the family level on taxonomy, plumage identification, external morphological characteristics, world distribution and habitat, food and feeding habits, social patterns and behavior, vocalization, and biology.

1606. Long, John L. **Introduced birds of the world: the worldwide history, distribution and influence of birds introduced into new environments.** Universe Books, 1981. 528 pp., ill., bibl., index. Covers birds successfully and unsuccessfully introduced; provides brief descriptions of general characteristics, original and introduced distribution, and general habits, as well as range maps, notes on introduction and damage, and line drawings.

1607. Lever, Christopher. **Naturalized birds of the world.** Longman Scientific & Technical; Wiley, 1987. 615 pp., ill., bibl., index. Explains natural versus naturalized distribution of many bird species, providing specific information on when, how many, and by whom the birds were released; includes line drawings and an index of geographic areas and their naturalized species.

1608. Jones, John Oliver. **Where the birds are: a guide to all 50 states and Canada.** William Morrow, 1990. 400 pp., bibl. Guide to some 2000 birding areas in the United States and Canada. Contains lists of areas, bird charts by state, index, and key to related field guides.

Birds: Species and Families (1609–1640)

1609. Biology and conservation of northern forest owls. U.S. Department of Agriculture, Forest Service, USDA Forest Service general technical report, no. RM-142, 1987. 309 pp., ill. Proceedings of a 1987 symposium in Winnipeg, Canada. Papers discuss behavior, food habits, and habitats of six genera of owls. Brief discussion of research and management techniques.

1610. Burton, R. **Bird behavior.** Knopf; Random House, 1985. 224 pp., ill., index. Discusses flight, senses, intelligence, feeding, communication, social life, courtship, mating, rearing of young, and migration. Numerous color photographs.

1611. Jackson, Jerome A.; ed. **Bird conservation, 3.** University of Wisconsin Press; International Council for Bird Preservation, 1988. 177 pp., ill., bibl. Irregular series for the International Council for Bird Preservation. Chapters in this volume relate changes in bird populations to changes in seven North American forest ecosystems, beginning with the time before first settlement. Previous volumes in this series have had as subjects North American raptors and island birds throughout the world.

1612. Keast, A.; and others, eds. **Birds of eucalypt forest and woodlands: ecology, conservation management.** Surrey Beatty; Royal Australasian Ornithologists Union, 1985. 38 pp., ill., bibl., index. Reviews forest and woodland bird communities and examines the ecology and adaptations of several bird types; assesses the impact of humans and discusses ways to protect and promote bird communities.

1613. Newton, Ian; ed. **Birds of prey.** Facts on File, 1990. 240 pp., ill. Essays from 50 biologists and other experts. In three parts: raptors of the world; raptor biology; and raptor-human relations. More than 200 color photographs.

1614. McIntyre, Judith W. **The common loon: spirit of northern lakes.** University of Minnesota Press, 1988. 228 pp., ill., bibl., index. Examines loon breeding and family structure; studies behavioral ecology, social behavior, and communications; reviews classifications, anatomy, and plumage; includes assessment of human effects on loons and efforts to protect and promote loons.

1615. Johnsgard, Paul A. **Cranes of the world.** Indiana University Press, 1983. 257 pp., ill., bibl., index. Examines the comparative biology of cranes and provides natural histories of the 14 crane species.

1616. Goodwin, Derek. **Crows of the world.** University of Washington Press, 2d ed., 1986. 299 pp., ill., index. Describes and illustrates crows, choughs, nutcrackers, and magpies worldwide; introduction reviews nomenclature, adaptive radiation, coloration and plumage, maintenance and social behavior, display, nesting and parental care, voice and mimicry, escape, mobbing, and other antipredator behavior.

1617. Bellrose, Frank Chapman. **Ducks, geese and swans of North America.** Stackpole Books, 1980. 540 pp., maps, ill., bibl., index. Fifty-five species accounts provide information on identification, population, distribution, migration, breeding, and feeding habits; briefly reviews factors affecting waterfowl, including conservation efforts, hunting regulations, and disease.

1618. Grant, Peter R. **Ecology and evolution of Darwin's finches.** Princeton University Press, 1986. 458 pp., ill., bibl., index. The results of long-term field studies. Assesses the extent to which adaptive radiation of finches can be treated as a model of evolutionary diversification.

1619. Hudson, Peter J.; Rands, Michael R. W.; eds. **Ecology and management of gamebirds.** Blackwell Scientific, 1988. 263 pp., ill. Contributors relate theoretical principles of ecology to the management of game birds. Chapters on population changes, population biology and life history, predators, parasites, habitat quality, harvesting, and population models.

1620. Woolfenden, Glen E.; Fitzpatrick, John W. **The Florida scrub jay: demography of a cooperative-breeding bird.** Princeton University Press, Monographs in population biology, 20, 1984. 406 pp., ill., bibl., index. Summarizes the habits of the Florida scrub jay, examining the characteristics and activities of breeding pairs and helpers; discusses territory, dispersal, and the breeding cycle; provides data on survivorship and hypothesizes benefits and motivations for cooperative breeding.

1621. Scott, J. Michael; and others. **Forest bird communities of the Hawaiian Islands: their dynamics, ecology and conservation.** Cooper Ornithological Society, Studies in avian biology, no. 9, 1986. 429 pp., ill., bibl. Provides basic information on the distribution, abundance, habitat response, and limiting factors for 40 native and 33 introduced species. Discusses community ecology and recommends conservation strategies for each of the islands studied.

1622. Cody, Martin L.; ed. **Habitat selection in birds.** Academic Press, 1985. 558 pp., ill., bibl., index. Discusses the habitat selection of selected species (flycatcher, certain warblers, raptors); habitat selection in various temperate and tropical habitats (shrub-steppe, northern hardwood forests, grasslands); frugivorous and nectarivorous birds; physiological, morphological, and behavioral aspects of habitat selection; the difficulties of migration; and theoretical aspects.

1623. Johnsgard, Paul A. **Hummingbirds of North America.** Smithsonian Institution Press, 1983. 303 pp., ill., bibl., index. Presents comparative biology of all hummingbirds. For North American species, supplies range, measurements, description, habitats, and behavior. Includes color plates.

1624. Keast, Allen; Morton, Eugene S.; eds. **Migrant birds in the neotropics: ecology, behavior, distribution, and conservation.** Smithsonian Institution Press, Symposia of the National Zoological Park, v. 5, 1980. 576 pp., ill., bibl. Based on a symposium held at the Smithsonian Institution in 1977. Papers bring together and give shape to a considerable body of knowledge on migration studies. In sections: conservation, migration of taxonomic groups, regional studies, implications of overwintering in the tropics, and integrations.

1625. Johnsgard, Paul A. **North American owls: biology and natural history.** Smithsonian Institution Press, 1988. 295 pp., ill., bibl., index. Comparative section on owl evolution, classification, ecology, morphology, physiology, and behavior; specific species accounts detail all 19 North American owls, including conservation status.

1626. Heinrich, B. **One man's owl.** Princeton University Press, 1987. 224 pp., ill., bibl., index. Chronicles the behavior of an individual great horned owl and its relationship with the author.

1627. Poole, Alan F. **Ospreys: a natural and unnatural history.** Cambridge University Press, 1989. 246 pp., ill., bibl., index. First full monographic life history; covers phylogeny, migration and wintering ecology, breeding, and population decline due to pesticides.

1628. Voous, Karel Hendrik. **Owls of the northern hemisphere.** MIT Press, 1989. 320 pp., ill., bibl., index. Discusses the distribution; structure, hearing, and vision; ecological hierarchy; movements and population dynamics; behavior; breeding habitats; feeding habits; and relationships to humans of 47 species. Illustrated by 50 full-color plates.

1629. Cade, Tom J.; and others, eds. **Peregrine falcon populations: their management and recovery.** Peregrine Fund, 1988. 949 pp., ill., bibl., index. Proceedings of a 1985 conference. Topics include status of populations since 1965 in North America, Europe, and elsewhere, DDT and other chemical threats, migration and banding studies, captive propagation and reintroduction, population dynamics and ecology, geographic variation, and human interaction.

1630. Hill, David; Robertson, Peter. **The pheasant: ecology, management, and conservation.** Blackwell

Scientific, 1988. 281 pp., ill. Ecological management of the most widely distributed game bird in the world. Early chapters portray the bird's life cycle through the year; later chapters cover the role of predation, the releasing of artificially raised birds, effects of hunting on populations, and the role of pheasant management in countryside conservation.

1631. Newton, Ian. **Population ecology of raptors.** Buteo Books, 1979. 399 pp., ill., bibl., index. Synthesis of current knowledge on 287 species—population regulation, social behavior, dispersion, numbers, movements, breeding, and mortality.

1632. Johnsgard, Paul A. **The quails, partridges, and francolins of the world.** Oxford University Press, 1988. 264 pp., maps, ill., bibl., index. Discusses comparative biology (taxonomy, phylogeny, zoogeography; reproductive biology, population dynamics, the growth and development of individuals, vocalization); species accounts cover identification and measurement, biology and ecology, social behavior, reproductive biology, evolutionary relationships and conservation. Includes distribution maps.

1633. Schreiber, Rudolf L.; and others. **Save the birds.** Houghton Mifflin, 1989. 384 pp., ill., index. Discusses threatened species worldwide, the biotopes important to birds and dangers facing birds; describes birds of tropical and temperate forests and wetlands as well as those of cities and agricultural lands and shows the importance of bird conservation for whole ecosystems.

1634. Furness, R. W.; Monaghan, P. **Seabird ecology.** Chapman and Hall, 1987. 164 pp., ill., index, bibl. Presents brief introduction to life histories and feeding ecology, then discusses population regulation, interaction with fisheries, marine environment monitoring, seabirds as pests, and conservation needs.

1635. Nelson, Bryan. **Seabirds: their biology and ecology.** A & W, 1979. 219 pp., ill., bibl., index. Topics include seabirds of the world, food and feeding behavior, breeding behavior and biology, movement and distribution, populations, and interactions with humans.

1636. Blake, Tupper Ansel. **Tracks in the sky: wildlife and wetlands of the Pacific flyway.** Chronicle Books, 1987. 166 pp., ill., index. Illustrates the life history of geese and describes long-term studies on waterfowl food supply, migration staging areas, and breeding grounds.

1637. Madge, Steve; Burn, H. **Waterfowl: an identification guide to the ducks, geese and swans of the world.** Houghton Mifflin, 1988. 298 pp., ill., bibl., index. Color plates with facing distribution maps and brief text, followed by species accounts providing field identification notes, vocalizations, descriptions of major plumage stages, measurements, geographic variations, habitats, and populations; brief discussion of habits useful for identification.

1638. Owen, Myrfyn; Black, Jeffrey M. **Waterfowl ecology.** Blackie (dist. by Chapman and Hall), 1990. 194 pp., bibl., index. Explains the feeding, breeding, social, and sexual behavior of waterfowl and discusses their migration, management, and conservation; cites mostly European literature.

1639. Ratti, John T.; Flake, Lester D.; Wentz, W. Alan; compilers. **Waterfowl ecology and management: selected reading.** Wildlife Society, 1982. 1328 pp., ill., bibl. Extensive collection of brief papers, suitable as a textbook or reference book. Covers reproductive and feeding ecology, population influences, movements, evolution, and management.

1640. The wonder of birds. National Geographic Society, 1983. 280 pp. Describes bird activity in spring, summer, fall, and winter, discussing behavioral characteristics, the origin and structure of bird diversity, and how each species has adapted to its environment; also assesses conservation efforts.

Amphibians and Reptiles. Fish (1641–1657)

1641. Berra, Tim M. **An atlas of distribution of the freshwater fish families of the world.** University of Nebraska Press, 1981. 197 pp., maps, ill., bibl., index. Provides distribution maps and brief descriptions of 157 freshwater fish families; includes list of rivers and lakes, drainage maps, articles on fishes, and glossary.

1642. King, F. Wayne; Behler, John L. **The Audubon Society field guide to North American reptiles and amphibians.** Knopf, 1979. 719 pp., ill., index. Includes full-color plates, descriptions, and information on breeding, habitat, range, voice, and subspecies.

1643. Bjorndal, Karen A.; ed. **Biology and conservation of sea turtles.** Smithsonian Institution Press, 1981. 583 pp., ill., bibl. Proceedings of a 1979 conference. Topics include sea turtle biology, population status, conservation theory, technology, and law.

1644. Bone, Q.; Marshall, N. B. **Biology of fishes.** Blackie (dist. by Chapman and Hall), Tertiary level biology, 1982. 253 pp., ill., bibl., index. Topics include swimming and buoyancy, anatomy and physiology, reproduction and life histories, and communication.

1645. Spellerberg, Ian F. **Biology of reptiles: an ecological approach**. Blackie (dist. by Chapman and Hall), Tertiary level biology, 3, 1982. 158 pp., maps, ill., index. Topics include classification, origins, and radiation of reptilian species; morphology and function; distribution and abundance; reproduction and development; physical and biotic environments; behavior; and interactions with humans.

1646. Copeia. American Society of Ichthyologists and Herpetologists, 1913 to date. Quarterly. Publishes research papers of varying lengths on fishes, reptiles, and amphibians.

1647. Ross, Charles A.; ed. **Crocodiles and alligators**. Facts on File, 1989. 240 pp., ill., bibl., index. Discusses the place of crocodilians in the world today and their evolution, structure, and function. Covers food and feeding, mortality and predators, social behavior, reproduction, and habitats. Reviews art, literature, mythology and religion, attacks on humans, crocodile-skin products, farming and ranching, and conservation and management.

1648. Burnham, Kenneth P.; and others. **Design and analysis methods for fish survival experiments based on release-recapture**. American Fisheries Society, American Fisheries Society monograph, v. 5, 1987. 437 pp., ill., bibl., index. Provides general introduction to use of capture-release data, detailed discussion of protocols for different types of studies, importance of replication, properties of procedures, planning experiments, application and extension of theory, and computer software.

1649. Environmental biology of fishes. Kluwer, 1962 to date. Monthly.

1650. Sigler, William F.; Sigler, John W. **Fishes of the Great Basin: a natural history**. University of Nevada Press, Max C. Fleischmann series in Great Basin natural history, 1987. 425 pp., ill., bibl., index. Reviews general characteristics, behaviors, and values of fish, then provides life histories of 90 species, degree of detail depending on the species' economic and ecological importance.

1651. Nelson, Joseph S. **Fishes of the world**. Wiley, 2d ed, 1984. 523 pp., ill., bibl., index. Authoritative guide to the classification of fishes, down to the family level. Brief descriptions and some line drawings. Many references cited; conflicting conclusions synthesized.

1652. Hart, C. W., Jr.; Clark, Janice. **An interdisciplinary bibliography of freshwater crayfishes (Astacoidea and Parastacoidea) from Aristotle through 1985**. Smithsonian Institution Press, 1989. 498 pp.

More has been written about crayfishes than one might initially suspect. Comprehensive bibliography includes a supplement on literature up to 1987. Organized alphabetically by author, with subject indexes.

1653. Groombridge, Brian; Wright, L.; compiler. **The IUCN amphibia-reptilia red data book**. International Union for Conservation of Nature and Natural Resources, 1982. 426 pp. Case studies of 83 threatened taxa, crocodiles among them, including distribution, population, habitat, ecology, threats, conservation measures, and captive breeding.

1654. Smith, Hobart M.; Brodie, Edmund D., Jr. **Reptiles of North America: a guide to field identification**. Golden Press, The Golden field guide series, 1982. 240 pp., ill., bibl., index. Includes descriptions of species and subspecies, range maps, and color illustrations; discusses evolution, reproduction, growth and longevity, dormancy, enemies and defense, human interactions, and reptiles as pets.

1655. Williams, Kenneth L.; Wallach, V. **Snakes of the world. Vol. 1: Synopsis of snake generic names**. Krieger, 1989. 234 pp., bibl. Lists all known generic, valid, and disputed names for living and extinct snakes.

1656. Murty, A. S. **Toxicity of pesticides to fish**. CRC Press, 1987. 2 vols. Review of all available information; 1700 references from 1944 to present.

1657. Ernst, Carl H.; Barbour, Roger W. **Turtles of the world**. Smithsonian Institution Press, 1989. 313 pp., ill., bibl. Provides keys to families, genera, and species; discusses species karyotype, appearance, range, habitat, and natural history. Numerous black-and-white photographs, 16 color plates.

Invertebrates (1658–1688)

1658. Annual review of entomology. Annual Reviews, 1956 to date. Annual. Review of current research areas in entomology and related sciences.

1659. Holldobler, Bert; Wilson, Edward O. **The ants**. Harvard University Press, 1990. 732 pp., ill., bibl., index. Exhaustive treatment of ant taxonomy, evolution, life history, communication, and behavior; chapters on army ants, fungus growers, harvesting ants, and weaver ants; includes discussion of collecting, culturing, and observing ants.

1660. Eisenbeis, Gerhard; Wichard, Wilfried. **Atlas on the biology of soil arthropods**. Springer-Verlag, 1987. 427 pp., ill., bibl., index. Presents systematic descriptions of a large number of arthropods of the classes

Crustacea, Arachnida, Myriapoda, and Insecta. Includes over 1000 black-and-white scanning electron micrographs.

1661. Milne, Lorus; Milne, Margery. **The Audubon Society field guide to insects and spiders.** Knopf, The Audubon Society field guide series, 1980. 989 pp., ill., index. Provides 702 color photographs, mostly of arachnids, and brief comments.

1662. Vane-Wright, R. I.; Ackery, P. R.; eds. **The biology of butterflies.** Academic Press, Symposia of the Royal Entomological Society of London, v. 11, 1984. 429 pp., ill., bibl., index. Papers from a 1981 symposium of the Royal Entomological Society of London, organized into the following sections: systematics, populations and communities, food, genetic variation and speciation, sex and communication, migration and seasonal variation, and conservation.

1663. Crawford, Clifford S. **Biology of desert invertebrates.** Springer-Verlag, 1981. 314 pp., ill., bibl., index. Discusses in detail the life history patterns, communities, and adaptations of desert arthropods and other invertebrates.

1664. Bell, William J.; Carde, Ring T.; eds. **Chemical ecology of insects.** Sinauer, 1984. 524 pp., ill., bibl., index. Information on perceptual mechanisms; odor dispersion and chemo-orientation mechanisms in walking and flying insects; plant-herbivore relationships; predators, parasites, and prey; chemical protection; chemical-mediated spacing; and sociochemicals of bees, ants, and termites.

1665. Collins, N. M.; Thomas, J. A.; eds. **The conservation of insects and their habitats.** Academic Press, 1991. 432 pp., index. Symposium proceedings report on the progress of insect conservation programs throughout the world. Examines some of the special problems faced in insect conservation and the use of insects as environmental indicators.

1666. Satchell, J. E.; ed. **Earthworm ecology: from Darwin to vermiculture.** Chapman and Hall, 1983. 495 pp., ill., bibl., index. Symposium proceedings consider earthworm ecology in various regions, including polluted and cultivated soils; chapters examine the application of earthworm cultures for waste disposal and as a protein source and also review earthworm evolution, distribution, and taxonomy.

1667. Lee, Ken E. **Earthworms: their ecology and relationships with soils and land use.** Academic Press, 1985. 411 pp. Synthesis of research on earthworms over 40 years—biology, ecology, environment, and biotech-

nology. Emphasis on potential of earthworms in agriculture, revegetation, and managing wastes.

1668. Huffaker, Carl B.; Rabb, Robert L.; eds. **Ecological entomology.** Wiley, 1984. 844 pp., ill., bibl., index. Comprehensive text discusses basic biological and ecological adaptations and processes, natural control of insect populations, role of insects in ecosystems, and application of ecology to pest management.

1669. **Ecological entomology.** Blackwell Scientific, 1976 to date. Quarterly. Publishes original research on insect ecology, including migration and dispersal, adaptations, and integrated control of pest populations.

1670. Resh, Vincent H.; Rosenbery, David M.; eds. **The ecology of aquatic insects.** Praeger, 1984. 625 pp., ill., bibl., index. Overview textbook that highlights research needs in the field. Some topics include responses to pollution; hypothesis testing in ecological studies; the role of aquatic insects in nutrient cycling; and life histories.

1671. Fenchel, Tom. **Ecology of protozoa: the biology of free-living phagotrophic protists.** Science Tech, Brock/Springer series in contemporary bioscience, 1987. 197 pp., ill., bibl., index. Covers the historical view of protozoa; their motility, feeding, and bioenergetics; niche diversification, food chain dynamics, and other ecological principles; and protozoan communites in marine, freshwater, and terrestrial habitats.

1672. Environmental entomology. Entomological Society of America, 1972 to date. Bimonthly. Research on the interaction of insects with their environment, including topics in physiological and chemical ecology, community and ecosystem ecology, population ecology, pest management and sampling, and biological control. Reports on new entomological techniques.

1673. Blum, Murray S.; ed. **Fundamentals of insect physiology.** Wiley, 1985. 5998 pp., ill., bibl., index. Comprehensive, multiauthored textbook covers traditional topics such as digestion, excretion, respiration, circulation, metabolism, and the musculatory, exocrine, and nervous systems.

1674. Seeley, Thomas. **Honeybee ecology: a study of adaptation in social life.** Princeton University Press, 1985. 201 pp., ill., bibl., index. Some topics include the annual cycle of colonies, reproduction, nest building, food collection, temperature control, and colony defense. Separate chapter on the behavioral ecology of tropical honeybees.

1675. Stehr, Frederick W.; ed. **Immature insects.** Kendall/Hunt, 1987. 754 pp., ill., bibl., index. Provides keys for identifying nymphs and larvae, and discusses their biology and ecology.

1676. New, T.R. **Insect conservation: an Australian perspective**. Junk, Series entomologica, v. 32, 1984. 184 pp., ill., bibl., index. Examines causes of insect decline using Australian examples; discusses taxonomic and inventory challenges, habitat- and species-oriented approaches, and the scope of conservation.

1677. Price, Peter W. **Insect ecology**. Wiley, 2d ed., 1984. 607 pp., ill., bibl., index. Advanced undergraduate-graduate text; integrates behavioral and evolutionary ecology in examining insect ecology. New to this edition: chapters on insect parasites and mutualists and modeling insect population dynamics.

1678. Barbosa, Pedro; Shultz, Jack C.; eds. **Insect outbreaks**. Academic Press, 1987. 578 pp., ill., bibl., index. Contributed papers offer a synthesis of recent selected research; sections on defining and classifying pests and outbreaks, the community structure of natural and manipulated ecosystems, biotic and abiotic factors in outbreaks, and the evolutionary consequences of outbreaks.

1679. Insect science and its application. ICIPE Science Press, 1980 to date. Bimonthly. Published by the International Centre of Insect Physiology and Entomology.

1680. Strong, Donald R.; Lawton, J. H.; Southwood, Richard. **Insects on plants: community patterns and mechanisms**. Harvard University Press, 1984. 313 pp., ill., bibl., index. Discusses evolution of phytophagous insects, determinants of diversity, community patterns through time, species interaction, and coevolution. Includes brief classification of phytophagous insects.

1681. Chapman, R.F. **The insects: structure and function**. Harvard University Press, 3d ed., 1982. 919 pp., ill, bibl., index. Insect descriptions are organized by function, not by classification, thereby integrating morphology, physiology, and natural history. Includes many references and numerous clear line drawings.

1682. Higgins, Robert P.; Thiel, Hjalmar; eds. **Introduction to the study of meiofauna**. Smithsonian Institution Press, 1988. 488 pp., ill., bibl., index. Summarizes the history of meiofaunal research; discusses current research methods; and gives characteristics, habitats, and collection and processing methods for meiofaunal taxa.

1683. Young, Allen M. **Population biology of tropical insects**. Plenum Press, 1982. 511 pp., ill, bibl., index. Summarizes pertinent literature of the previous 50 years. Brings together concepts and studies that explain patterns of insect diversity in the tropics. Emphasis on New World tropics; nearly 800 bibliographical references.

1684. Ruppert, Edward E.; Fox, R. **Seashore animals of the Southeast: a guide to common shallow-water invertebrates of the southeastern Atlantic Coast**. University of South Carolina Press, 1988. 429 pp., ill., bibl., index. Field guide to 740 organisms found in water of wading depth between Cape Hatteras, North Carolina, and Cape Canaveral, Florida. Includes simple key, species descriptions, and 360 line drawings and photographs.

1685. Brian, M. V. **Social insects: ecology and behavioural biology**. Chapman and Hall, 1983. 377 pp., ill., bibl., index. Specialist volume brings together widely scattered literature on social insects, emphasizing the themes of evolutionary trends and comparative ethology. Topics include foraging by individuals and by groups; cavities, burrows, and nests; defense mechanisms; food processing and distribution; maturation, and reproduction; societies, colonies, and communities; and the comparative ecology of species.

1686. Ebeling, Walter. **Urban entomology**. University of California, Division of Agricultural Sciences, 1978. 695 pp., ill., bibl., index. Covers insects, many arthropods, and some vertebrates, Chapters are organized by the preferred food and habitats of pests. Entries provide information on distribution, habits, ecology, and biology of the pest species and advice on species-specific prevention and extermination techniques.

1687. Wings. Xerces Society, 1997 to date. 3 issues/yr. Dedicated to the protection of habitats for butterflies and other invertebrates. Publishes brief articles and news.

1688. Dethier, Vincent G. **The world of the tent-makers: a natural history of the eastern tent caterpillar**. University of Massachusetts Press, 1980. 148 pp., ill., bibl. Seventeen chapters present fictionalized accounts of the life phases of the eastern tent caterpillar; discusses technical concepts such as supercooling and host preference accessibility.

Endangered Species. Conservation Biology (1689–1710)

1689. World Conservation Monitoring Centre. **1990 IUCN red list of threatened animals**. International Union for Conservation of Nature and Natural Resources, 1990. 228 pp. As recognized by the International Union for Conservation of Nature and Natural Resources, notes extinct, endangered, rare, or indeterminate status of internationally threatened species.

1690. Hearn, J. P.; Hodges, J. K.; eds. **Advances in animal conservation.** Oxford University Press, Symposia of the Zoological Society of London, no. 54, 1985. 282 pp., ill., bibl., index. Proceedings of a symposium held at the Zoological Society of London in 1984. Seventeen papers discuss conservation in the wild and in captivity, conservation and reproductive medicine, and the role of government in conservation.

1691. Hoage, R. J.; ed. **Animal extinctions: what everyone should know.** Smithsonian Institution Press, National Zoological Park symposia for the public series, 1985. 192 pp., ill. Twelve papers derived from a 1982 symposium present information on the theory and application of conservation biology and discusse techniques for preserving species in the wild, sustainable exploitation, economic value of species, and genetics.

1692. Collar, N. J.; Andrew, P. **Birds to watch: the ICBP world checklist of threatened birds.** Smithsonian Institution Press, ICBP technical publication, no. 8, 1988. 303 pp., bibl., index. Brief annotations for each threatened species; appendices list birds by country and order.

1693. Woodburne, Michael O.; ed. **Cenozoic mammals of North America: geochronology and biostratigraphy.** University of California Press, 1987. 336 pp., ill., bibl., index. In North America, the evolution and dispersal of fossil mammals define the intervals of the Cenozoic era (the last 60 million years); here, contributed chapters synthesize data on recognizing and refining mammal ages and the boundaries between them.

1694. Luoma, Jon R. **A crowded ark: the role of zoos in wildlife conservation.** Houghton Mifflin, 1987. 209 pp., ill., bibl., index. Discusses the role of zoos in the preservation of threatened species, focusing on captive breeding programs; topics include genetic inbreeding, frozen gamete banks, return of captive animals to the wild, habitat conservation, and the political, social, and ethical pressures facing zoos.

1695. Defenders. Defenders of Wildlife, 1925 to date. Monthly. Continues: Defenders of Wildlife magazine. Illustrated feature articles on preservation of wildlife in all its forms.

1696. Nilsson, Greta. **The endangered species handbook.** Animal Welfare Institute, c. 1983, 1986. 245 pp., ill., bibl. Designed for high school students and teachers; addresses causes and consequences of extinc-

tions, wild animal trade, relevant legislation, and international treaties; includes classroom projects and lists of recommended films and books.

1697. Moseley, Charles; Lowe, David; eds. **Endangered species photo locator.** Beacham, 1990. 73 pp., ill., index. Grouped by organism and indexed by scientific and common name; provides lists of photographers and photograph sources.

1698. Baker, Sylva. **Endangered vertebrates: a selected, annotated bibliography, 1981–1988.** Garland, Garland reference library of social science, 480, 1990. 197 pp., index. International in scope; considers wide range of publications, including books, technical reports, monographs, symposia, journal and magazine articles, government documents, and dissertations. Introduction gives advice about conducting research in this field.

1699. Ali, Salim. **The fall of a sparrow.** Oxford University Press, 1985. 265 pp. Last book of India's most celebrated field biologist.

1700. King, Warren B.; compiler. **The ICBP/IUCN red data book. Part I: Threatened birds of Africa and related islands.** International Council for Bird Preservation: International Union for Conservation of Nature and Natural Resources, 3d ed., 1985. 761 pp., ill. Lists threatened birds on a zoogeographical-geopolitical basis. Data sections ordered by family provide information on endangered status, distribution, population, habitat, and conservation methods, both attempted and proposed.

1701. Wells, Susan M.; Pyle, Robert M.; Collins, N. M.; and others, compilers. **The IUCN invertebrate red data book.** International Union for Conservation of Nature and Natural Resources, 1983. 632 pp., ill., bibl., index. Case studies of threatened invertebrates; includes distribution, habitat, and ecology, potential value and scientific interest, and threats and conservation measures.

1702. Lowe, David W.; and others, eds. **The official World Wildlife Fund guide to endangered species of North America.** Beacham, 1990. Ill., bibl., index. 2 vols. Provides information on habitat, appearance, behavior, biology, conservation efforts, present status, and date added to the threatened or endangered list. Vol. 1 covers plants and mammals; Vol. 2 deals with birds, reptiles, amphibians, fishes, insects, and others.

1703. Oryx: journal of the Fauna and Flora Preservation Society. Fauna Preservation Society; Blackwell Scientific Publications, 1950 to date. Articles on species, habitat, and preservation techniques. Extensive news coverage of international wildlife conservation efforts.

1704. Austin, C. R.; Short, R. V.; eds. **Reproductive fitness.** Cambridge University Press, Reproduction in mammals, v. 4, 2d ed., 1985. 241 pp., ill., bibl., index. Examines differing reproductive strategies and mechanisms among species; assesses genetic, environmental, behavioral, and immunological factors in reproductive fitness.

1705. Clutton-Brock, T. H.; ed. **Reproductive success: studies of individual variations in contrasting breeding systems.** University of Chicago Press, 1988. 538 pp., ill., bibl., index. Twenty-five studies examine reasons for and extent of individual differences in breeding success between males and females in natural populations, emphasizing birds and mammals but also discussing insects and amphibians.

1706. Groves, R. H.; Ride, W. D. L.; eds. **Species at risk: research in Australia.** Springer-Verlag, 1982. 216 pp., ill., bibl., index. Contributed papers cover the conservation status of Australian plants and mammals, such as the koala, with case histories and discuss the role of genetics in conserving rare species.

1707. Little, Colin. **The terrestrial invasion: an ecophysiological approach to the origins of land animals.** Cambridge University Press, Cambridge studies in ecology, 1990. 304 pp., ill., bibl., index. Discusses sources and types of evidence for understanding the origin of terrrestrial animals; through case studies arranged by environment (the sea, salt marshes, fresh water), considers several evolutionary paths.

1708. Benirschke, Kurt; Warhol, Andy. **Vanishing animals.** Springer-Verlag, 1986. 99 pp., ill., bibl. Silkscreen over collage illustrations by Andy Warhol of some dozen critically endangered species accompany Benirschke's explanation of their natural history, habits, and status. Emphasis is on lesser-known species such as the okapi, mouse armadillo, and Komodo monitor.

1709. Terbough, John. **Where have all the birds gone? essays on the biology and conservation of birds that migrate to the American tropics.** Princeton University Press, 1989. 207 pp., bibl., index. Divided between North American breeding areas and tropical wintering grounds. Investigates causes and solutions for the dwindling number of tropical migrant species. Discusses population monitoring, fragmentation and its consequences, and migration evolution.

1710. Yeager, Rodger; Miller, Norman N. **Wildlife, wild death: land use and survival in eastern Africa.** State University of New York Press, 1986. 173 pp., maps, ill., bibl., index. Shows the interdependence of agricultural land use and wildlife conservation in Kenya and Tanzania. Gives recommendations for research and policy.

Part II

HUMAN ENVIRONMENT (1711–3084)

Section 8

Society. Culture. Human Ecology

Part II of this bibliography, human environment, begins with the present section on society, culture, and human ecology. The entries in this section deal with society-environment relationships in populations, countries, organizations, communities, families, and among individuals. The organizing principle is from larger, more inclusive entities to smaller, less inclusive ones. The emphasis is on the ecology of human populations, on where people live and how they live, as affected by the natural environment and by values, beliefs, education, and communication.

We have placed in this broad "social" section environmental problems and issues that are often described as socioeconomic, sociocultural, sociopolitical, or some combination of these. More specific aspects of the human environment as it relates to the natural environment are placed in the sections following: ethics, literature, and art; law and politics; economics; health and medicine; engineering and technology; and science and research.

Society and Environment
Compared with the whole earth perspective of Section 1 and the terrestrial ecosystem perspective of Section 4, society-environment entries in this group are concerned with continuing issues of social life: equity among classes, areas, and generations; formation of social policies; institutions and organizations, impacts and effects of policies; development in the broad sense; futures; and civilization.

See also:

- Section 1: Global resources and environment; environmental management
- Section 2: Climate change
- Section 3: Freshwater; marine; fisheries
- Section 4: Lands, reserves and parks, management
- Section 5: Food and agriculture
- Section 6: Forests and forest resources: regions and countries
- Section 7: Wildlife management; animal rights, protection
- Section 9: Ethics, philosophy, religion
- Section 10: Law, politics, government
- Section 11: Economy, economics, business and industry; development

- Section 12: Health, medicine, human biology
- Section 13: Engineering, technology

Society and Environment: Country Studies; United States. These two subgroups encompass the environmental problems of countries, nation-states, regions, and provinces. As noted above, these are social in the broadest sense. Also included here are geographic and statistical data on countries.

See also:

- Section 1: Global resources and environment
- Section 4: Land: countries and regions
- Section 6: Forests and forest resources: regions and countries
- Section 10: International law and policies; national laws and policies
- Section 11: Economy, costs and benefits, valuation; industry, economic sectors; development

Social and Human Ecology. Population

The entries in this group introduce human ecology—in particular, population trends, bioregionalism, and land-use planning. Specific topics in human ecology are addressed in the following subsections on human evolution and tribal, rural, and urban communities.

See also:

- Section 4: Land: countries and regions; landscape ecology; land: terrestrial ecosystems
- Section 9: Nature writing and thought, arts; built environment, architecture, historical preservation
- Section 10: Law and policies: state and local, regional
- Section 12: Health, medicine, human biology
- Section 14: Quantification, measurement, statistics

Human Evolution. History. Included here are entries on human evolution, prehistory, historical geography, archaeology, emigration, and environmental impacts of human communities over the ages.

See also:

- Section 7: Animal ecology, species
- Section 9: Ethics, philosophy, religion
- Section 12: Health, medicine, human biology

Tribal Communities. Works on the lifeways of indigenous peoples from the Amazon to the Arctic are grouped here. Note particularly the periodical *Cultural Survival* (1835), which covers these communities around the world.

See also Rural Communities, below.

Rural Communities. The entries in this subgroup cover rural appraisal and development, appropriate technology, community involvement and participation, rural social systems, communal resources, land tenure, biocultural adaptation, and traditional resource management.

See also Rural Communities: United States and Europe, below.

Rural Communities: United States and Europe. This subgroup presents selections on rural communities in developed countries. Topics include rural data, economic growth and planning, community development, countryside and farmland preservation, and maintenance rural communities.

See also:

- Section 1: Biodiversity, conservation biology, genetics
- Section 3: Fisheries
- Section 4: Lands, reserves and parks, management; land: countries and regions; landscape ecology; land: terrestrial ecosystems
- Section 5: Food and agriculture; crops, cropping systems
- Section 6: Tropical forest management
- Section 8: Individuals and environment
- Section 11: Economy, costs and benefits, valuation; natural resource industries; agriculture and forest products
- Section 12: Public health, medicine

Urban Communities. Works on the built environment of cities and towns are in this subgroup, including design, planning, and construction; suburbs; parks and open spaces; city form; growth management; and urban ecology.

See also:

- Section 4: Land: countries and regions; landscape ecology; land: terrestrial ecosystems
- Section 5: Landscaping, horticulture, gardening
- Section 6: Tree planting, afforestation, arboriculture
- Section 9: Built environment, architecture, historical preservation
- Section 10: Law and policies: state and local, regional
- Section 11: Economy, costs and benefits, valuation; development
- Section 13: Environmental control technology; civil engineering, construction, geotechnology

Environmental Organizations. Movements
Entries relating to the nonprofit and nongovernmental organizations that make up the environmental movement are in this group, together with works on leaders, leadership, and volunteers.

See also:

- Section 1: Global resources and environment; environmental management
- Section 8: Society and environment: country studies
- Section 9: Ethics, philosophy, religion; nature writing and thought, arts
- Section 10: Law, politics, government

Individuals and Environment

Combined in this group are guides to individual involvement and advocacy and works on behavior change, risk perception, family and gender, basic needs, psychological impacts of pollution, human dimensions of energy use and conservation, alternative lifestyles, social indicators, and public opinion.

See also:

- Section 1: Environmental management
- Section 9: Ethics, philosophy, religion
- Section 10: Law and policies: state and local, regional
- Section 12: Public health, medicine; toxic threats, hazards; risk assessment; health protection, safety, emergencies

Education and Communication. Entries for audiovisual directories, environmental education, environmental journalism, nature interpretation, teaching trends, and public relations are included here.

See also:

- Section 1: Environmental management
- Section 9: Ethics, philosophy, religion; nature writing and thought, arts
- Section 14: Science, research, methods

Behavior and Psychology. This subgroup has works on human responses to the built and natural environments, including sociobiology, environmental design, human factors, experience of place, and spatial orientation.

See also:

- Section 1: Biological systems; ecology
- Section 7: Animal ecology, species
- Section 8: Social and human ecology, population
- Section 9: Built environment, architecture, historical preservation; nature writing and thought, arts
- Section 12: Health, medicine, human biology

Leisure and Recreation. The selections here refer to outdoor recreation, recreation management, tourism, and park management and planning.

See also:

- Section 1: Environmental management
- Section 4: Lands, reserves and parks, management
- Section 6: Forests and forest resources: regions and countries
- Section 7: Wildlife management
- Section 9: Nature writing and thought, arts
- Section 10: U.S. executive agencies, administration and regulation; forests, parks, and wilderness: United States

SOCIETY. CULTURE. HUMAN ECOLOGY (1711–2076)

Society and Environment (1711–1740)

1711. Alternatives: perspectives on society, technology and environment. Trent University, Peterborough, Ontario, 1971 to date. Quarterly. Independent, innovative, environmental journalism from the faculty and students of Trent University. Critiques of pollution in all its forms and detailed proposals for ecologically sound changes in society, economy, and government.

1712. Price, David H. **Atlas of world culture: a geographical guide to ethnographic literature.** Sage Publications, 1989. 156 pp., bibl., index. Thirty-five hundred cultural groups identified on 40 numbered maps and linked by an index to some 1200 classic ethnographic studies that describe the cultural groups.

1713. Brown, Lester Russell. **Building a sustainable society.** Norton, 1981. 433 pp., ill., bibl., index. Focuses on the modern erosion of our resource base with respect to topsoil, forests, grasslands, fisheries, and oil. Two-thirds of the book describes a sustainable society and how to achieve it, analyzing such issues as population growth, renewable energy, means of transition, and institutional challenges.

1714. Ehrlich, Paul R.; Holdren, John P.; eds. **The Cassandra Conference: resources and the human predicament.** Texas A & M University Press, 1988. 330 pp., ill., bibl., index. Papers from a 1985 symposium featuring well-known analysts like Garrett Hardin, Herman Daly, Anne and Paul Ehrlich, and Donella Meadows. Papers review such topics as development and agriculture, rain forests, acid rain, toxic substances, the ecology of nuclear war, and the steady state economy.

1715. Jeske, Walter E.; ed. **Economics, ethics, ecology: roots of productive conservation.** Soil Conservation Society of America, 1981. 454 pp., ill., bibl. Topics include land planning, water management, and the energy squeeze on them; resource conservation technology; conservation education; restoring and maintaining living space; energy challenges to resource values; protecting finite land base; and water quantity and quality.

1716. Levinson, David; editor-in-chief. **Encyclopedia of world cultures.** G.K. Hall, 1991–1993. Maps, bibl., index. 10 vols. Projected ten-volume set will provide basic data on 1500 cultures around the world. Entries in each volume will contain culture name; alternate ethnic names for the culture; orientation (location, linguistic affiliation, and so forth); history and cultural relations; economy; kinship; marriage and family; sociopolitical organization; religion and expressive culture; and bibliography and filmography.

1717. Bradshaw, Jonathan; Harris, Toby; eds. **Energy and social policy.** Routledge & Kegan Paul, 1983. 189 pp., ill., bibl., index. Assesses potential effects on individuals and society of rising energy costs. Examines possible policy responses (fuel allowances, debt and disconnection prevention, and insulation and energy conservation) and the factors hindering policymakers.

1718. Yanarella, Ernest J.; Yanarella, Ann-Marie. **Energy and the social sciences: a bibliographic guide to the literature.** Westview Press, 1982. 347 pp. Extensive bibliography lists works on energy and politics, economics, society, environment, energy future, conventional fuels, alternative energy sources, and international perspectives on energy policy.

1719. Milbrath, Lester W. **Envisioning a sustainable society: learning our way out.** State University of New York Press, SUNY series in environmental public policy, 1989. 403 pp., ill., bibl., index. Explains the philosophical underpinnings of a sustainable society, noting how contemporary society differs. Shows how human institutions and activities must mirror the workings of natural systems, discussing employment, agriculture, quality of life, and technology.

1720. Geoforum. Pergamon Press, 1970 to date. Quarterly. Multidisciplinary journal dealing with management of the human environment, defined as urban and regional planning, industrial development, resource allocation, and management of physical environmental systems. Encourages papers on applications, housing, effects of agriculture on the environment, and deforestation. Includes studies of remote-sensing and decision support systems.

1721. Global environmental change: human and policy dimensions. Butterworth-Heinemann, 1990 to date. Quarterly. Addresses the human ecological and public policy dimensions of deforestation, desertification, soil degradation, species extinction, sea level rise, destruction of the ozone layer, atmospheric warming, and other environmental changes. Contains articles, papers, and conference reports.

1722. Calder, Nigel. **The green machines.** Putnam's Sons, 1986. 205 pp., bibl. Utopian vision and a blueprint, written in past tense from the perspective of the twenty-first century explains the virtues of biotechnology in a world of small-scale, cooperative villages.

1723. Canter, Larry W; Atkinson, S.F.; Leistritz, F. L. **Impact of growth: a guide for socio-economic impact assessment and planning.** Lewis, 1985. 533 pp., ill., bibl., index. Provides systematic approach to assessing impacts. Discusses selection of economic-demographic models; social, fiscal, and public service impacts; quality of life, importance weighting; and decision making.

1724. Reader, John. **Man on earth.** University of Texas Press, The Corrie Herring Hooks series, v. 10, 1988. 255 pp., maps, ill., bibl., index. Result of four years' traveling, observing, and photographing cultures worldwide. Portrays each culture as a unique response and adaptation to a particular set of environmental factors and considerations.

1725. Burch, William R., Jr.; DeLuca, Donald R. **Measuring the social impact of natural resource policies.** University of New Mexico Press, 1984. 216 pp., ill., bibl., index. Provides basic information for those interested or involved in the social dimensions of environmental impact assessment. Methods covered include time budget studies, life cycle analyses, adoption of innovations, community and regional studies, social surveys, and social indicators. Examples focus on energy systems.

1726. McNeely, Jeffrey A.; Miller, Kenton R.; eds. **National parks, conservation and development: the role of protected areas in sustaining society.** Smithsonian Institution Press, 1984. 825 pp., ill., bibl. Proceedings of the World Congress on National Parks in 1982. Discusses world coverage of protected areas, management issues, and developing international support. Presents case studies from each of the world's biogeographic realms.

1727. Foell, Wesley K.; Hervey, Loretta A.; eds. **National perspectives on management of energy/environment systems.** Wiley, International series on applied systems analysis, v. 11, 1982. 343 pp., ill., bibl., index. Experts from the United States, the USSR, Japan, and Europe describe planning and management of energy-environment systems in their countries. Part II reviews results of a comparative study involving four sites in Europe and the United States. Discusses results with respect to energy use, socioeconomic patterns, possible energy futures, environmental implications, and planning and policy design.

1728. Dahlberg, Kenneth A.; Bennett, John W.; eds. **Natural resources and people: conceptual issues in interdisciplinary research.** Westview Press, Westview special studies in natural resources and energy management, 1986. 394 pp., ill., bibl., index. Assesses research on human–natural resource interactions. Discusses conceptual approaches that will improve understanding.

1729. Catton, William Robert. **Overshoot: the ecological basis of revolutionary change.** University of Illinois Press, 1980. 298 pp., bibl., index. Examines human life in an ecological context, arguing that we have already exceeded the earth's carrying capacity. Contends that our faith in technology is unfounded and only a major shift in thinking will ensure our survival with dignity.

1730. PAIS bulletin. Public Affairs Information Service, 1915 to date. Monthly. Indexes publications relating to "public affairs," hence an excellent source of information on environmental problems and issues. Available as a computer database, online or CD-ROM.

1731. Nash, Hugh; ed. **Progress as if survival mattered: a handbook for a conserver society.** Friends of the Earth, 1981. 456 pp., ill., bibl. Revised edition of this anthology, containing 22 articles by prominent environmentalists—many of them classics—promoting a world order based on decentralization, independence, human welfare, justice, and stewardship.

1732. Carley, Michael J.; Bustelo, Eduardo S. **Social impact assessment and monitoring: a guide to the literature.** Westview Press, Social impact assessment series, 7, 1984. 250 pp., ill., bibl., index. In four sections: general and overview; social impact assessment; Third World social impact assessment; and periodicals and other bibliographies.

1733. Miller, Marc L.; Gale, Richard P.; Brown, Perry J.; eds. **Social science in natural resource management systems.** Westview Press, Social behavior and natural resources series, 1987. 265 pp., ill., bibl., index. Asserts the need for more use of social science approaches in resource management decision making. Examines applications in specific cases; evaluates behavior and processes of management bureaucracies. Examples from the United States, Canada, and New Zealand cover forests, fisheries, parks, wilderness, and wildlife.

1734. Society & natural resources: an international journal. Taylor & Francis, 1988 to date. Quarterly. Applies social science theory and methods to natural resource development and use. Reviews current research and discusses its policy implications.

1735. Unseld, Charles T.; and others, eds. **Sociopolitical effects of energy use and policy.** National Academy of Sciences, Study of nuclear and alternative energy systems, Supporting paper, no. 5, 1979. 511 pp., bibl.

Reports to the Sociopolitical Effects Resource Group, Risk and Impact Panel of the Committee on Nuclear and Alternative Energy Systems, National Research Council. Collection of papers examining local, regional, institutional, political, and international impacts of energy systems; includes agenda for future social science research.

1736. Watt, Kenneth E. F. **Understanding the environment.** Allyn & Bacon, 1982. 431 pp., ill., bibl., index. Examines economic, political, and cultural causes of environmental problems. Discusses social and political consequences of environmental damage; suggests legal, institutional, and economic solutions.

1737. Weigel, Van B. **A unified theory of global development.** Praeger, 1989. 263 pp. Develops, justifies, and assesses a theory of basic human needs and a basic needs imperative. Discusses them in terms of human responsibility, the population explosion, the nuclear arms race, economic systems, and international law.

1738. World development. Pergamon Press, 1973 to date. Monthly. Multidisciplinary international journal devoted to the study and promotion of world development, defined as a process of change occurring in different ways at all levels. Seeks papers with constructive ideas and analyses that highlight the lessons to be learned from the experiences of all peoples.

1739. World development report. Oxford University Press, 1978 to date. Annual. Survey, analysis, data, and synthesis on the state of economic and social development worldwide.

1740. Hughes, Barry B. **World futures: a critical analysis of alternatives.** Johns Hopkins University Press, 1985. 243 pp., ill., bibl., index. Provides background data and a conceptual structure from which to understand and evaluate forecasts of the future, involving such factors as population, economics, and technology.

Society and Environment: Country Studies (1741–1763)

1741. 1990 Directory of country environmental studies. World Resources Institute, 1990. 171 pp., index. Gives bibliographic data, abstracts, and ordering information on some 240 studies of environmental and natural resource conditions in developing countries. Covers 110 countries in Africa, Latin America, Asia, and Oceania.

1742. Timberlake, Lloyd. **Africa in crisis: the causes, the cures of environmental bankruptcy.** International Institute for Environment and Development;

Earthscan, 1985. 233 pp., maps, ill., bibl. Argues that widespread famine in Africa, triggered by drought, is caused by environmental mismanagement. Explains the relationships between agricultural systems, political priorities, environmental damage, and human suffering.

1743. Muller, George P.; compiler. **Comparative world data: a statistical handbook for the social sciences.** Greenwood Press, 1988. 504 pp. Provides statistical data from the 1970s from 128 countries on their societies, politics, and economics. Organized so that empirical regularities can be discovered without the use of computers.

1744. Current geographical publications. American Geographical Society; University of Wisconsin–Milwaukee, 1938 to date. 10 issues/yr. References to books, articles, pamphlets, government documents, maps, and atlases in the AGS collection.

1745. Mossman, Jennifer; ed. **Encyclopedia of geographic information sources.** Gale Research, 4th ed., 1987. Index. 2 vols. International Volume presents sources on 81 cities, in 75 countries and in 6 regions worldwide. U.S. Volume provides references in over 300 metropolitan areas.

1746. Environment, development & natural resource crisis in Asia & the Pacific. Sahabat Alam Malaysia (Friends of the Earth Malaysia), 1984. 422 pp., maps, ill., bibl. Proceedings of 1983 symposium; papers on forestry, fisheries, mineral and energy resources, human settlements, food and agriculture, toxics, and non-governmental organizations (NGOs).

1747. Enyedi, Gyorgy; Gijswijt, August J.; Taylor, Barbara Rhode.; eds. **Environmental policies in East and West.** Taylor Graham, London, 1987. 401 pp. Written by 14 social scientists in eastern and western Europe to understand European environmental problems and compare approaches.

1748. Ziegler, C. E. **Environmental policy in the USSR.** University of Massachusetts Press, 1987. 195 pp., ill., bibl., index. Analyzes Soviet perceptions of the environment, the development of environmental law and its administration, and Soviet-American cooperation on environmental protection.

1749. Singleton, Fred; ed. **Environmental problems in the Soviet Union and Eastern Europe.** Rienner, 1987. 208 pp., ill., bibl., index. Selected papers from the Third World Congress for Soviet and East European Studies, held in 1985.

1750. Grenon, Michel; Batisse, Michel; eds. **Futures for the Mediterranean basin: the Blue Plan.** Oxford

University Press, 1989. 279 pp. Identifies geographic and demographic characteristics unique to the Mediterranean Basin. Formulates five scenarios for the years 2000 and 2025 under various population and economic assumptions. Discusses possible development trends and analyzes their effects on land, water, and sea. Suggests action at national and local levels.

1751. Kurian, George Thomas; ed. **Geo-data: the world geographical encyclopedia.** Gale Research, 2d ed., 1989. 544 pp. Part I gives physical profiles and geographic essays of 204 nations. Part II provides information on continents, climates, oceans, seas, and gulfs, as well as 204 country maps.

1752. Harris, Chauncy D.; and others, eds. **A geographical bibliography for American libraries.** Association of American Geographers, 1985. 437 pp. Annotated entries are divided into categories covering general sources; history, philosophy, and methodology of geography; fields of physical and human geography; applied and regional geography; and publications for school libraries.

1753. Index to international statistics: IIS. Congressional Information Service, 1983 to date. Monthly. Catalogs, describes, and indexes the English-language statistical publications of approximately 95 intergovernmental organizations. Covers economic, demographic, industrial, and social concerns. Indexed by subject, title, publication number, and geographic area. Quarterly and annual cumulations.

1754. National geographic. National Geographic Society, 1888 to date. Monthly. Journal of the National Geographic Society. Illustrated articles about ecosystems, regions, cultures, archaeological sites, and conservation efforts around the world.

1755. Kidron, Michael; Segal, Ronald. **The new state of the world atlas.** Simon & Schuster, 2d ed., 1987. 176 pp., maps. Color-coded maps illustrate the state of the world by revealing issues traditionally ignored in the media: state control over the oceans, women's control over their own reproduction, calories available per capita per day, economic dependence and diversity, refugee migrations, and availability of education.

1756. OECD environmental data compendium 1991. Organization for Economic Cooperation and Development, 1991. 338 pp., maps, ill., tables. Statistical information from the OECD countries on air pollution, water use and quality, land-use changes, agriculture, protected areas, forests, wildlife, municipal and industrial wastes, waste treatment, energy consumption, industrial activity, population, and other categories. Updates 1985, 1987, and 1989 publications.

1757. Kurian, George Thomas. **Sourcebook of global statistics.** Longman, 1985. 413 pp. Provides information on 209 publications that have statistical information on the world or its principal regions. For each publication, there is complete bibliographic information, a table of contents, scope, sources of data, time period covered, updating, availability as a computer database, and evaluation.

1758. Agarwal, Anil; Narain, Sunita. **The State of India's environment 1984–1985: the second citizens' report.** Ravu Chiora Centre for Science and Environment, 1985. 393 pp., ill. Extensive report of environmental activities and concerns in India. Produced with cooperation of numerous Indian nongovernment organizations.

1759. Bird, Peter M.; Rapport, David J. **State of the environment report for Canada.** Environment Canada, 1986. 263 pp. Describes the status of farmlands, water, forests, wildlife, and other natural resources. Discusses legislation, expenditures, and public attitudes toward the environment.

1760. Statistical reference index: a selective guide to American statistical publications from private organizations and state government sources. Congressional Information Service, 1980 to date. Monthly, with annual cumulation. Provides annotated entries of statistical information sources from associations, businesses, independent research organizations, universities, and state governments.

1761. Statistics sources. Gale Research, 1962 to date. Annual: 15th ed., 1992. A subject guide to data on industrial, business, social, educational, financial, and other topics for the United States and other nations.

1762. Towards greater environmental awareness: an environmental report. Sahabat Alam Malaysia (Friends of the Earth Malaysia), 1983. 96 pp., ill., bibl. Produced by a citizen's group working to stop environmental deterioration in Malaysia. Assesses changes in various areas, from agriculture and forestry to urban environment and occupational health.

1763. Directorate of Intelligence, U.S. Central Intelligence Agency. **The world factbook: handbook of the nations.** Gale Research, 1981 to date. Annual: 10th ed., 1991. Ill. Originally published by the Central Intelligence Agency as the *World factbook, 1990.* Provides concise information on the people, government, economy, communications, defense forces, land, and infrastructure of the world's nations. Data taken from the CIA and other U.S. government agencies.

Society and Environment: United States (1764–1781)

1764. Petulla, Joseph M. **American environmentalism: values, tactics, priorities.** Texas A & M University Press, Environmental history series, v. 1, 1980. 239 pp., bibl., index. Critical reflection on qualities and values of the environmental movement. Presents history, problems, successes, critical issues, and emerging priorities.

1765. Amicus journal. Natural Resources Defense Council, 1979 to date. Quarterly. Promotes public interest and advocacy on behalf of the environment through editorials, essays, and poetry. Articles profile activists and cover international and national environmental affairs.

1766. Mason, Robert J.; Mattson, Mark T. **Atlas of United States environmental issues.** Macmillan, 1991. 252 pp., maps, ill. Presents data on natural resources, energy, agriculture, and urban centers. Background essays address coastal zone management, toxic substances, nonfuel minerals, noise and light pollution, and other topics. Focus maps offer case studies of issues and policies surrounding such events as the Yellowstone fires of 1988, Love Canal, and the *Exxon Valdez* oil spill.

1767. Audubon. National Audubon Society, 1941 to date. Monthly. Features outstanding photography and articles on environmental problems, politics, and the natural world.

1768. Buzzworm: the environmental journal. Buzzworm, Boulder, CO, 1988 to date. Quarterly. Articles and features aim to provoke environmental awareness. Covers international and national issues. Regular sections on green consumerism, children and the environment, and urban ecology.

1769. Kreissman, Bern. **California: an environmental atlas and guide.** Bear Klaw Press, 240 pp., maps, bibl., index. Lists environmentally significant sites and geographic features throughout California, identifying government-designated recreation, protected, and restored areas as well as experimental and research sites. Explains legislative basis for these areas, and includes contact information.

1770. E: the environmental magazine. Earth Action Network, 1990 to date. Bimontly. Seeks to connect readers with the environmental movement of the 1990s. Feature articles on issues and policies; interviews with

noted environmentalists; news of events and publications; ecologically sound products and services.

1771. Environmental action. Environmental Action, 1970 to date. Bimonthly. Founded at the time of Earth Day. Features news notes and commentary on environmental problems, including political action. Theme section in most issues, such as children and the environment, wasteful packaging, or religion and the environment.

1772. deHaven-Smith, Lance. **Environmental concern in Florida and the nation.** University Presses of Florida, 1991. 144 pp., maps, ill., bibl., index. Based on national and Florida-wide surveys. Shows that the public's environmental awareness is often superficial and parochial.

1773. Petulla, Joseph M. **Environmental protection in the United States: industry, agencies, environmentalists.** San Francisco Study Center, 1987. 200 pp., bibl., index. Presents history of groups and institutions. Discusses specifics of working in environmental protection, based on interviews and questionnaires.

1774. Council on Environmental Quality. **Environmental quality: the annual report of the Council on Environmental Quality.** Government Printing Office, 1970 to date. Annual: 22d, 1991. Uses differing organizational formats over the years but always includes chapters on status of environmental protection, special reports on environmental issues and policies, and data and trends. An authoritative, inexpensive, and encyclopedic source of information.

1775. Council on Environmental Quality. **Environmental trends.** Government Printing Office, 1981. 346 pp., maps, ill., bibl., index. Council on Environmental Quality. Presents charts, maps and text recording key changes in the environment and in related social conditions from the 1960s and 1970s. Includes primary sources, brief explanation of data, and full subject index.

1776. Piasecki, Bruce; Asmus, Peter. **In search of environmental excellence: moving beyond blame.** Simon & Schuster, 1990. 203 pp. Approaches to solving environmental problems in different sectors of society—business, government, and general public.

1777. Northwest environmental journal. Institute for Environmental Studies, 1985 to date. Monthly. Science and policy issues covering the Pacific Northwest region of North America.

1778. Sierra. Sierra Club, 1893 to date. Bimonthly. Publication from the Sierra Club; covers the preservation group's activities and agenda; articles focus on conservation and recreational uses of natural resources, both domestically and internationally.

1779. State of the environment: a view toward the nineties. Conservation Foundation, 1987. 614 pp., ill., bibl., index. Reviews the United States' progress in managing its natural resources. Discusses developments in population, economy and public opinion; solid waste, air and water pollution, and toxic and hazardous waste; land, water, and energy use; and protection and preservation of critical areas, wildlife, and biodiversity.

1780. State of the environment: an assessment at mid-decade: a report from the Conservation Foundation. Conservation Foundation, 1984. 586 pp., ill., bibl., index. Describes immediate environmental conditions, trends, and progress. Examines longer-term issues: efforts to identify and assess future environmental problems, an integrated approach to pollution control, and the workings of intergovernmental relations and policy implementation.

1781. State of the environment 1982: a report from the Conservation Foundation. Conservation Foundation, 1982. 464 pp., ill., bibl., index. Discusses U.S. environmental condition, trends, prospects, and issues; analyzes institutional changes and options affecting policy.

Social and Human Ecology. Population (1782–1811)

1782. Todd, Nancy Jack; Todd, John. **Bioshelters, ocean arks, city farming: ecology as the basis of design.** Sierra Club Books, 1984. 210 pp., ill., bibl., index. From building interiors and city sidewalks to hydroponic gardens and energy-efficient farms, promotes designs that reflect bioregionality, are based on renewable energy sources, help heal the environment, and follow the "laws of life." Includes examples.

1783. Sale, Kirkpatrick. **Dwellers in the land: the bioregional vision.** Sierra Club Books, 1985. 217 pp., bibl., index. An introduction to the basics of bioregionalism. Traces its conceptual roots in Western culture and explains its values.

1784. Environment & planning. Pion, 1974 to date. Published in sections, with separate subscriptions. Environment and planning: A, urban and regional planning; B, planning and design; C, government and policy; and D, society and space.

1785. Ellen, Roy F. **Environment, subsistence and system: the ecology of small-scale social formations.** Cambridge University Press, Themes in the social sciences, 1982. 324 pp., ill., bibl., index. Reviews and assesses several models that have been used to explain the relationship between human behavior and the environment, including determinism, possibilism, cultural ecology, systems ecology, and others. Also reviews recent ethnographic literature in this light and suggests a model of social institutions and ecosystems compatible with social theory.

1786. Cutter, Susan L.; Renwick, Hilary Lambert; Renwick, William H. **Exploitation, conservation, preservation: a geographic perspective on natural resource use.** Rowman & Allanheld, 1985. 448 pp., ill., bibl., index. Integrates physical, economic, social, and political aspects of natural resource conservation. Provides range of interpretation and opinion.

1787. Gregory, K. J.; Walling, D. E. **Human activity and environmental processes.** Wiley, 1987. 466 pp., ill., index. Focuses on processes of the physical environment and how they are affected by human activities. The processes are presented in five parts, corresponding to major divisions of the environment: atmosphere, hydrosphere, geosphere, pedosphere, and biosphere. All contributors are physical geographers or geologists.

1788. Human ecology. Plenum, 1972 to date. Quarterly. An interdisciplinary forum for papers on all aspects of the interaction between people and the physical environment.

1789. Sargent, Frederick, II. **Human ecology: a guide to information sources.** Gale Research, Health affairs information guide series, v. 10, 1983. 293 pp., index. Annotated bibliography of books, journals, reports, conference proceedings, abstracts, and indexes. Covers abiotic and biotic environment, human biology and behavior, human-environment interactions and manipulations, environmental quality, community health, and disease control.

1790. Sale, Kirkpatrick. **Human scale.** Coward, McCann & Geoghegan, 1980. 558 pp., bibl., index. Advocates people-sized, low technology responses to planning problems.

1791. Drabek, Thomas E. **Human system responses to disaster: an inventory of sociological findings.** Springer-Verlag, Springer series on environmental management, 1986. 509 pp., bibl., index. Culmination of an extensive literature search. Analyzes and categorizes over 1000 publications on disaster with respect to planning, warning, evacuation, postimpact actions, restoration, reconstruction, hazard perceptions, and attitudes toward and adoption of adjustments. Considers individual, group, organization, community, society, and international responses.

1792. Smith, Sheldon; Reeeves, Ed; eds. **Human systems ecology: studies in the integration of political economy, adaptation, and socionatural regions.** Westview Press, 1988. 252 pp., maps, ill. Nine case studies of people-environment interactions with respect to agriculture and food distribution and adaptation to environmental, economic, and political constraints.

1793. Ross, John A.; ed. **International encyclopedia of population.** Macmillan; Free Press, 1982. Ill., maps. 2 vols. One hundred forty-two articles covering demographics, policies, family planning, aging, migration patterns, and other population issues worldwide.

1794. Patricios, Nicholas, N.; ed. **International handbook on land use planning.** Greenwood Press, 1986. 679 pp., ill., bibl., index. Contributed essays from over 20 countries in Asia, Africa, Europe, the Americas, and Australia on the historical development and current status of land-use planning, institutional and land ownership frameworks, approaches to land-use planning, and discernible trends.

1795. Hewitt, K.; ed. **Interpretations of calamity from the viewpoint of human ecology.** Allen & Unwin, Risks & hazards series, 1983. 304 pp., ill., index, bibl. Chapters on climate changes, crop failures, and other natural disasters.

1796. Schultz, Theodore William. **Investing in people: the economics of population quality.** University of California Press, The Royer lectures; 1980, 1981. 173 pp., bibl., index. Argues for emphasizing human capital rather than physical resources in development work and recognizing the role of markets in improving economic well-being, particularly of the agrarian poor.

1797. Steiner, F. R; Van Lier, H. N.; eds. **Land conservation and development: examples of land-use planning projects and programs.** Elsevier, Developments in landscape management and urban planning, v. 6B, 1984. 481 pp. A project of the International Study-group on Multiple Use of Lands (ISOMUL). Examples of several kinds of plans, from new towns to nature reserves and industrial sites. Contributors are practicing planners, consultants, academics, and others from Western Europe and North America.

1798. Blaikie, P.; Brookfield, H.; and others. **Land degradation and society.** Methuen, 1987. 296 pp., ill., bibl., index. Eight case studies from Nepal, North America, Indonesia, the Pacific, China, India, and Europe are used to show a "regional political ecology" approach toward problems of land management and degradation.

1799. Jackson, Richard H. **Land use in America.** Winston, Scripta series in geography, 1981. 226 pp., ill., bibl., index. Reviews the history of land use regulations, noting their development and evolution, plus the growing role of federal and state government controls. Focuses on the original land-use base, the factors that affect land distribution, and concerns about growing cities, dwindling farmland, and current land use.

1800. Fabos, Julius Gy. **Land-use planning: from global to local challenge.** Chapman and Hall, 1985. 223 pp., ill., bibl., index. Views planning as a creative, not a regulatory, process. Reviews technology, science, and findings of ecologists to conclude that diversity strengthens the cultural landscape. Discusses the changes wrought by automated mapping and electronic data manipulation, as well as land-use planning issues at local, regional, and national levels.

1801. **Natural hazards observer.** University of Colorado, Natural Hazards Research and Applications Center, 1981 to date. Bimonthly. Funded by several federal agencies, the Center disseminates information among researchers, individuals, and organizations concerned with mitigating the effects of natural disasters.

1802. **Population and environment.** Human Sciences Press, 1980 to date. Quarterly. Journal sponsored by the American Psychological Association's Division of Population and Environmental Psychology.

1803. Boserup, Ester. **Population and technological change: a study of long-term trends.** University of Chicago Press, 1981. 255 pp., bibl., index. Studies the interactions between population density and technological developments, covering the transition from hunting and gathering to early agriculture, early urbanization, and early industrial societies.

1804. **Population and vital statistics report.** United Nations Statistical Office, 1949 to date. Annual. Provides latest worldwide demographic statistics.

1805. **Population bulletin.** Population Reference Bureau, 1945 to date. Bimonthly. Series of reports examining trends in population, mainly in the United States.

1806. **Population bulletin of the United Nations.** United Nations, 1951 to date. Irregular: no. 31, 1991. Publishes population research of the UN. Seeks to promote scientific understanding of population questions and to provide a global perspective on demographic issues.

1807. Ehrlich, Paul R.; Ehrlich, Anne H. **The population explosion.** Simon & Schuster, 1990. 320 pp., bibl., index. An update of the *The population bomb* (1968). Expounds thesis that current environmental and ecological problems stem from an increasing population using finite resources. Asserts that solutions must be political, cultural, and ethical.

1808. Population index. Princeton University, Woodrow Wilson School of Public and International Affairs, 1937 to date. Quarterly. Abstracts of books, monographs, periodicals, and other literature on population and related topics arranged by subject category, with author and geographic indexes. Routine statistical works on population are cited in special issues.

1809. Davidson, Donald A. **Soils and land use planning.** Longman, Topics in applied geography, 1980. 129 pp., maps, ill., bibl., index. Drawing on examples from many countries, presents a methodology for evaluating economically and socially sound uses of different kinds of soils.

1810. Lundqvist, Jan; Lohm, Ulrik; Falkenmark, Malin; eds. **Strategies for river basin management: environmental integration of land and water in a river basin.** Reidel; Kluwer, 1985. 346 pp. Papers from a 1984 seminar present case studies from developed and undeveloped countries on obstacles to coordinated land and water conservation management; legal and administrative tools as incentives or disincentives in integrated planning; problems due to growing urban systems; and the river basin as an ecosystem.

1811. Simon, Julian L. **The ultimate resource.** Princeton University Press, 1981. 415 pp., ill., bibl., index. Seeks to undermine and discredit neo-Malthusian arguments by discounting potential scarcity of natural resources and emphasizing the benefits of an increasing population.

Human Evolution. History (1812–1832)

1812. Foley, Robert. **Another unique species: patterns in human evolutionary ecology.** Wiley, 1987. 313 pp., ill., bibl., index. Discusses patterns of hominid evolution in terms of their ecological basis. Organized thematically, not chronologically. Topics include hominids as tropical animals, as large mammals, as terrestrial primates, and as colonizing animals.

1813. Butzer, Karl W. **Archaeology as human ecology: method and theory for a contextual approach.** Cambridge University Press, 1982. 364 pp., ill., bibl., index. Methods and theory for incorporating environmental studies within the study of archaeology.

1814. Simmons, I. G. **Changing the face of the earth: culture, environment, history.** Basil Blackwell, 1989. 487 pp. Traces the accidental and intended impacts of humans on nature throughout history. Examines the behavior and effects of humans from hunting and gathering through the agricultural, industrial, and nuclear ages.

1815. Wilson, Peter J. **The domestication of the human species.** Yale University Press, 1988. 201 pp., ill., bibl., index. Argues that domestication, rather than agriculture and pastoralism, was the primary cultural innovation in human evolution. Explains how institutions such as economics and politics must be understood in this light.

1816. Kelso, William M.; Most, Rachel. **Earth patterns: essays in landscape archaeology.** University Press of Virginia, 1990. 319 pp., ill., bibl. Eighteen case studies of using archaeological excavation to decipher the structure and evolution of past landscapes. Four sections cover country gardens in Virginia, early U.S. urban landscapes, ancient gardens and landscapes, and landscape science.

1817. Crosby, Alfred W. **Ecological imperialism: the biological expansion of Europe, 900–1900.** Cambridge University Press, 1986. 368 pp., ill., bibl., index. Explores biogeographic reasons for historic European emigrations. Shows impacts of European plants and animals in several areas, notably New Zealand.

1818. Hughes, J. Donald. **Ecology in ancient civilizations.** University of New Mexico Press, 1975. 181 pp. Examines ecosystems of the ancient world and human impacts on them. Discusses attitudes toward nature and resources and the influence of religion on environmental ethics.

1819. Tattersall, Ian; Delson, Eric; Van Couvering, John; eds. **Encyclopedia of human evolution and prehistory.** Garland, Garland reference library of the humanities, v. 768, 1988. 638 pp., ill. Over 1200 topics in human evolution, paleontology, and archaeology. Gives principal sites and their specimens. Essays on concepts and methods cover the entire range of approaches to studying human prehistory.

1820. Environmental history review. American Society for Environmental History, 1976 to date. Quarterly. Continues: Environmental review. Seeks understanding of the human experience of the environment, emphasizing the perspectives of history and the humanities.

1821. Mead, Jim I.; Meltzer, David J.; eds. **Environments and extinctions: man in late glacial North America.** University of Maine at Orono, Center for the Study of Early Man, Peopling of the Americas, Edited volume series, 1985. 209 pp., ill., bibl., index. Essays focus on recent discoveries in the study of late Pleistocene human adaptations in North America.

1822. Hooke, Janet M.; Kain, R. J. P. **Historical change in the physical environment: a guide to sources and techniques.** Butterworth, Studies in physical geography, 1982. 236 pp., ill., bibl., indexes.

1823. Grim, Ronald E.; ed. **Historical geography of the United States: a guide to information sources.** Gale Research, Geography and travel information guide series, v. 5, 1982. 291 pp., index. Covers material published since 1965. Provides cartographic sources, archival and other historical sources, and selected literature in historical geography.

1824. Goudie, Andrew. **The human impact on the natural environment.** MIT Press, 1986. 338 pp., ill., bibl., index. Describes human impacts through the ages on vegetation, animals, soil, water, landforms, and climate. Numerous illustrations.

1825. Taylor, Ralph B. **Human territorial functioning: an empirical, evolutionary perspective on individual and small group territorial cognitions, behaviors, and consequences.** Cambridge University Press, 1988. 351 pp., ill., bibl., index. Microscale study using a conceptual model applied to varied settings of indoor and outdoor residential spaces. Discusses territorial functioning in relation to resource conservation.

1826. Lewin, Roger. **In the age of mankind: a Smithsonian Institution book of human evolution.** Smithsonian Institution Press, 1988. 255 pp., ill., index. Past and current scholarship on the evolution of *Homo sapiens*, including the roots of language and consciousness and the origins of villages, cities, and civilizations.

1827. Mitchell, Robert D.; Groves, Paul A.; eds. **North America: the historical geography of a changing continent.** Rowman & Littlefield, 1987. 468 pp., maps, ill., bibl., index, tables. A collection of essays arranged chronologically from the time of European exploration and colonization to the present. Discusses regional formation and growth, expanding frontiers, cultural transfer, resource exploitation, and national integration. Many maps, tables, and figures.

1828. Thomas, Elizabeth Marshall. **Reindeer moon.** Houghton Mifflin, 1987. 338 pp., ill., bibl. Ethnobiological novel in which archaeology, paleozoology, paleo-

botany, and historical climate studies come to life in the words of a woman, Yanan, member of a hunter-gatherer tribe in what is now Siberia, some 20,000 years ago.

1829. Grupe, Gisela; Herrmann, Bernd; eds. **Trace elements in environmental history.** Springer-Verlag, 1988. 174 pp., ill., bibl., index. Contains papers of 1987 symposium. Interdisciplinary approach to using trace chemical analysis of prehistoric skeletal material to evaluate past ecological features and human-environment relationships.

1830. Sheets, Payson D.; Grayson, Donald K.; eds. **Volcanic activity and human ecology.** Academic Press, 1979. 644 pp., ill., bibl., index. Reviews dating, chronology, stratigraphy, and types of volcanic activity and their effects on animals, plants, humans, and the environment. Relates volcanic activity to other factors (social customs, climate change, disease) that affect human behavior. Examples from prehistoric times to the present.

1831. Boyden, Stephen Vickers. **Western civilization in biological perspective: patterns in biohistory.** Clarendon Press, 1987. 370 pp., ill., bibl., index. Western civilization portrayed as human adaptation to ecological circumstances. Applies this new understanding to modern problems and potential survival options.

1832. Ehrenberg, Margaret R. **Women in prehistory.** University of Oklahoma Press, Oklahoma series in classical culture, v. 4, 1989. 192 pp., ill., bibl., index. Brings archaeology and feminism together. Discusses sources and methodologies. Reconsiders the evidence to examine the lives, social roles, and status of prehistoric women from the Paleolithic to the Iron Age, mostly in Europe. Discusses earliest communities, foraging societies, and the discovery and expansion of agriculture.

Tribal Communities (1833–1851)

1833. Hemming, John. **Amazon frontier: the defeat of the Brazilian Indians.** Macmillan, 1987. 647 pp., maps, ill., bibl., index. Social-economic history of the Amazon, stressing the period from 1755 to the early twentieth century. Discusses the work of natural history explorers and recounts the effects of European exploitation on the people, politics, and development of the Amazon region.

1834. Vecsey, Christopher; Venables, Robert W.; eds. **American Indian environments: ecological issues in native American history.** Syracuse University Press, 1980. 208 pp., maps, ill., bibl. Ten essays compare European and Indian beliefs about nature, land use, and sovereignty. Discusses the consequences of uprooting and relocation on Indian peoples in historical and contemporary settings.

1835. Cultural survival. Cultural Survival, 1976 to date. Quarterly. Articles, news, and commentary address issues of immediate and long-term concern to the indigenous peoples of the world.

1836. McNeeley, Jeffrey A.; Pitt, David; eds. **Culture and conservation: the human dimension in environmental planning.** Croom Helm, 1985. 308 pp. Discusses value of utilizing knowledge and practice of indigenous and traditional peoples in conservation and environmental planning. Numerous case studies.

1837. Conklin, Harold C. **Ethnographic atlas of Ifugao: a study of environment, culture, and society in Northern Luzon.** Yale University Press, 1980. 116 pp., maps, ill., bibl., index. Large-format volume (41 x 46 cm) provides wealth of data on Ifugao culture, focusing on resource management and environmental adaptation throughout the agricultural year. Many photographs and map plates.

1838. Hall, Sam. **The fourth world: the heritage of the Arctic and its destruction.** Knopf, 1987. 240 pp., ill., bibl., index. A survey of the indigenous peoples of the Arctic, their historical way of life, and destructive impacts of encroaching Western civilization. Chronicles the emerging politicization of Arctic peoples.

1839. Sturtevant, William C.; ed. **Handbook of North American Indians.** Government Printing Office, 1978 to date. Ill., bibl., index. Ongoing series describes cultures from the Arctic and Subarctic, California, the Northeast, and the Southwest. Accounts for historical, environmental, and ecological factors. Volumes planned for the Great Basin, Plateau, Plains, and Southeast cultures. Introductory volumes discuss the history of Indian-White relations and Indians in contemporary society.

1840. Anderson, Robert S.; Huber, Walter. **The hour of the fox: tropical forests, the World Bank, and indigenous people in Central India.** University of Washington Press, 1988. 158 pp. Documents a failed forestry project financed by the World Bank and the Indian Government. Focuses on the social problems encountered in development, highlighting the limited consideration given to tribal forest dwellers and their interests.

1841. Fearnside, Philip M. **Human carrying capacity of the Brazilian rainforest.** Columbia University Press, 1986. 293 pp., ill., bibl., index. Examines rain forest ecology, human settlement, and agriculture to develop a methodology for modeling human carrying capacity on the Transamazon Highway.

1842. Harris, David R.; ed. **Human ecology in savanna environments.** Academic Press, 1980. 522 pp., ill., bibl., index. Twenty-three papers from 1978 conference discuss past and present human adaptations to and uses of tropical savanna environments worldwide.

1843. Winterhalder, Bruce; Smith, Eric Alden; eds. **Hunter-gatherer foraging strategies: ethnographic and archeological analyses.** University of Chicago Press, 1981. 268 pp., ill., bibl., index. Papers examine hunter-gatherer subsistence strategies on their own merits, emphasizing ecological theory, microeconomics, and evolutionary biology. Uses archaeological and ethnographic case studies from Alaska, Michigan, and Australia.

1844. Ingold, T.; Riches, D.; Woodburn, J.; eds. **Hunters and gatherers. Vol.1: History, evolution and social change.** Berg (dist. by St. Martin's Press), Explorations in anthropology, 1988. 331 pp., ill., bibl., index. From a 1986 conference. Topics include hunters and gatherers and outsiders; flux, sedentism, and change; historical and evolutionary transformations; and theoretical and comparative approaches. Reflects the shift in concern from ecological adaptation to issues of social change, particularly with respect to the internal dynamics of communities.

1845. Clay, Jason W. **Indigenous peoples and tropical forests: models of land use and management from Latin America.** Cultural Survival, Cultural survival report, no. 27, 1988. 116 pp., ill., bibl. Analyzes land-use practices in various tropical ecosystems (gathering, hunting, fishing, and swidden and permanent agriculture) with respect to modifications by indigenous peoples in response to economic, social, population, and political pressures. Also discusses indigenous attempts to establish large-scale, sustainable resource management systems in Colombia, Ecuador, and Panama.

1846. Denslow, Julie Sloan; Padoch, Christine; eds. **People of the tropical rain forest.** University of California Press, 1988. 231 pp., ill., bibl., index. Discusses the prehistory and the modern ways of life of several tropical rain forest peoples, including natives of the Amazonian forest, northern Thailand, and the Congo River basin in Zaire. The impact of government policies and the arrival of big business and migrants in rain forests worldwide are also covered.

1847. Williams, Nancy M.; Hunn, Eugene S.; eds.

Resource managers: North American and Australian hunter-gatherers. Australian Institute of Aboriginal Studies, AAAS selected symposium, v. 67, 1982. 267 pp., ill., bibl., index. Papers consider the roles of religion, fire, social organization, sharing, jural rights, and seasonal mobility in resource management in 11 hunter-gatherer societies.

1848. Bandhu, Desh; Garg, R. K.; eds. **Social forestry and tribal development.** Indian Environmental Society; Natraj, 1986. 162 pp., bibl. Collection of 17 papers from two workshops organized by the Indian Environmental Society, discussing the role of social forestry in the development of India's tribal groups.

1849. Hodgins, Bruce W.; Benidickson, J. **The Temagami experience: recreation, resources, and Aboriginal rights in the northern Ontario wilderness.** University of Toronto Press, 1989. 370 pp., ill., bibl., index. Chronicles the use of this resource by the Temagami Indians, the Hudson Bay Company, lumber companies, railroads, and second-home recreationists, particularly since 1901, when the Temagami Forest Reserve was created.

1850. Morauta, Louise; Pernetta, John; Heaney, William; eds. **Traditional conservation in Papua New Guinea: implications for today.** Institute for Applied Social and Economic Research, Monograph/Institute of Applied Social and Economic Research, v. 16, 1982. 392 pp., ill., bibl. Proceedings of a 1980 conference. Discusses traditional conservation methods for soil, vegetation, minerals, wildlife, forests, and freshwater and marine resources.

1851. Davis, Shelton H. **Victims of the miracle: development and the Indians of Brazil.** Cambridge University Press, 1977. 205 pp., maps, bibl., index. Case study details how the Brazilian government's economic development policies have resulted in suffering to the Indians and damage to their appropriated resources.

Rural Communities (1852–1891)

1852. Mortimore, Michael J. **Adapting to drought: farmers, famine and desertification in West Africa.** Cambridge University Press, 1989. 299 pp., ill., bibl., index. Examines adaptations to the droughts of northern Africa in the 1970s and 1980s. Suggests policy changes to take advantage of local insights. Examples drawn mostly from northern Nigeria.

1853. Hallsworth, E. G. **Anatomy, physiology and psychology of erosion.** Wiley, IFIAS monograph, v. 1, 1987. 176 pp. Based on an international survey of more than 10,000 farmers in the tropics and subtropics. Covers the processes of soil formation, its potential for erosion, and the role of vegetation in preventing erosion. Describes attitudes of farmers and presents reasons why they treat the land as they do.

1854. Appropriate technology. Intermediate Technology Publications, 1974 to date. Quarterly. Provides development workers with news, articles, and reports from the field. Articles describe practical technologies and fieldwork situations.

1855. Darrow, Ken; Saxenian, Mike. **Appropriate technology sourcebook: a guide to practical books for village and small community technology.** Volunteers in Asia, 1986. 800 pp., ill., index. Comprehensive sourcebook gives brief descriptions of over 1000 books, all of which can be purchased in microfiche format.

1856. Building rural communities: the experiences of the Indian rural reconstruction movement. International Institute of Rural Reconstruction, 1987. 250 pp. Provides a history of this private, indigenous movement, which has served as a model for government and nongovernment agencies in South Asia.

1857. Montgomery, John Dickey. **Bureaucrats and people: grassroots participation in Third World development.** Johns Hopkins University Press, Johns Hopkins studies in development, 1988. 140 pp., bibl., index. Drawing examples from Asia, Africa, and Latin America, Montgomery discusses what role bureaucrats can play in encouraging and guiding populism, how individual bureaucrats can benefit from such a policy, how citizens can organize themselves, and the ethical limits of government interference in individual action.

1858. Anderson, David; Grove, R.; eds. **Conservation in Africa: people, policies, and practice.** Cambridge University Press, 1987. 355 pp., ill., bibl., index. Based on a 1985 workshop. Papers by historians, anthropologists, and ecologists examine the relation of conservation practices and policies to rural development and social change.

1859. Moran, Emilio F. **Developing the Amazon.** Indiana University Press, 1981. 292 pp., ill., bibl., index. Shows the importance of micro-level analyses in policymaking by exploring the impacts of development on the Amazonian rain forest and its homesteaders in the Altamira region.

1860. Rambo, A. Terry; Gillogy, Kathleen; Hutterer, Karl; eds. **Ethnic diversity and the control of natural resources in Southeast Asia.** Center for South and

Southeast Asian Studies, Michigan Papers on South and Southeast Asia, v. 32, 1988. 229 pp., ill., bibl. Based on a 1984 conference. Promotes an evolutionary approach to study the mutual cause-and-effect relationships between ethnic differences and the possession and control of local natural resources. Includes essays on groups in Malaysia, Thailand, China, Indonesia, and the Philippines.

1861. Pratt, Brian; Boyden, Jo; eds. **The field directors' handbook: an Oxfam manual for development workers.** Oxford University Press, 1985. 512 pp., ill., bibl. Guidelines for implementing small-scale community development programs. Reviews major principles of development and programs in social and economic development, agriculture, health, and disaster prevention.

1862. Blair, Harry W.; Olpadwala, Porus D. **Forestry in development planning: lessons from the rural experience.** Westview Press, 1988. 205 pp., ill., index. Reviews relationship between forestry and rural development. Focus is on rural institutions and development strategies. Case histories show how good forest management supports rural development.

1863. van Staveren, J. M.; van Dusseldorp, D. B. W. M.; eds. **Framework for regional planning in developing countries: methodology for an interdisciplinary approach to the planned development of predominantly rural areas.** International Institute for Land Reclamation and Improvement, Publication, no. 26, 1980. 345 pp., ill., bibl. Specifies the stages and steps that form a detailed interdisciplinary study. Recommends reporting procedures and structures of reports. Includes advice on coordinating and integrating all needed information to insure an encompassing and inclusive framework.

1864. Harrison, P. **The greening of Africa: breaking through in the battle for land and food.** Penguin Books, 1987. 380 pp., ill., bibl., index. Journalist's account of successful agroforestry, windbreaks, natural forest management, and other natural resource projects in Africa; reviews environmental and developmental difficulties while highlighting successes.

1865. Conroy, Czech; Litvinoff, Miles; eds. **The greening of aid: sustainable livelihoods in practice.** Earthscan, 1988. 302 pp. Contributed essays deal with various aspects of development (technology, planning, institutions, and human settlements) and present examples of successful projects, including land classification and appraisal, fishing, and cement manufacturing.

1866. Smith, Valene L.; ed. **Hosts and guests: the anthropology of tourism.** University of Pennsylvania Press, 2d ed., 1989. 341 pp., ill., bibl., index. Discusses the nature and types of tourism and what impacts tourism has on local cultures. Based on field research by anthropologist authors; includes case studies.

1867. Schumann, Debra A.; Partridge, William L.; eds. **The human ecology of tropical land settlement in Latin America.** Westview Press, Westview special studies on Latin America and the Caribbean, 1989. 470 pp., ill., bibl. Twelve case studies illuminate the dynamics of land settlement, discussing equity; land access; labor shortages; health, nutrition, and population; the role of market linkages; and the effects of colonization on indigenous peoples.

1868. Allan, Nigel J. R.; and others, eds. **Human impact on mountains.** Rowman & Littlefield, 1989. 308 pp. Essays on mountain people around the world and methods of studying environmental interactions.

1869. De Camino Velozo, Ronnie. **Incentives for community involvement in conservation programmes.** Food and Agriculture Organization of the United Nations, FAO conservation guide, v. 12, 1987. 159 pp., ill., bibl. Discusses value of using incentives; classifies, defines, and analyzes incentives and presents methods of applying them at national and project levels.

1870. Kumar, Jyoti. **Integrated rural development: perspectives and prospects, 1952–82.** Mittal, 1987. 229 pp., bibl., index. Assesses the Indian Community Development Programme, Small Farmers Development Agency, Drought Prone Areas Programme, and Command Area Development Agency.

1871. International yearbook of rural planning. Geo Books, 1987 to date. Annual. Includes descriptions of notable events, publications, and legislation; articles discuss topical issues. Applies to North America, the United Kingdom, and Europe.

1872. Rambo, A. Terry; Sajise, Percy E.; eds. **An introduction to human ecology research on agricultural systems in southeast Asia.** East-West Center, 1984. 327 pp., ill., bibl. Introduces the human ecology perspective and systems analysis in the study of tropical agroecosystems. Uses case studies from Malaysia, Java, Thailand, and the Philippines.

1873. Donner, Wolf. **Land use and environment in Indonesia.** C. Hurst, 1987. 368 pp., maps, ill., bibl., index. Provides a survey of environmental impacts in Java and the Outer Islands due to agricultural and nonagricultural land uses.

1874. MacDonald, Andrew S. **Nowhere to go but down? peasant farming and the international devel-**

opment game. Unwin Hyman, 1989. 224 pp., bibl. Discusses demographic, technological, bureaucratic, and international constraints on the development of subsistence agriculture. Critique of the "international agricultural development game" and recommendations for change.

1875. Grossman, Lawrence S. **Peasants, subsistence ecology and development in the highlands of Papua New Guinea.** Princeton University Press, 1984. 302 pp., ill., bibl., index. Village-level case study of the ways in which the international commercial economy impacts rural communities in developing countries.

1876. Shah, S. L. **Planning and management of natural and human resources in the mountains: a micro level approach with special reference to central Himalaya.** Yatan, 1986. 259 pp., maps, bibl., index. Discusses ecological and cultural settings and existing and anticipated pressures. Analyzes strategies for management of agriculture, forestry, pastures, water, and human resources.

1877. Proceedings of the 1985 International Conference on Rapid Rural Appraisal, Khon Kaen University. Rural Systems Research Project and Farming Systems Research Project, Thailand, 1987. 357 pp., maps, ill., bibl. Contains summary report plus chapters on specific rapid rural appraisal (RRA) concepts, methods, and applications. Includes recommendations for training and institutionalization.

1878. McCay, Bonnie J.; Acheson, James M.; eds. **The question of the commons: the culture and ecology of communal resources.** University of Arizona Press, Arizona studies in human ecology, 1987. 439 pp., ill., bibl., index. The institution of the commons is examined from the perspective of conservation, community, and economics using case studies. In three sections: hunters and fishermen of the Far North and Amazon; farming, pastoral, and marine communal institutions; and marine fisheries management by governments, user groups, and local communities.

1879. Chambers, Robert. **Rural development: putting the last first.** Longman Scientific & Technical, 1983. 246 pp., bibl., index. Describes the complex nature of rural poverty in the Third World. Exposes and explains the attitudes, intentions, practices, and preconceptions of many outside relief and development professionals. Suggests methods and processes for setting priorities and defining goals, recommending greater emphasis on local knowledge and practical solutions.

1880. Stone, David R.; ed. **A selection of unpublished World Wide Fund for Nature (WWF) project reports on microfiche.** Leiden, 1990. Microfiche copies of 47 project reports, worldwide, 1970s to 1989. reports per year. Reports cover ecological, resource management, and conservation issues. Accompanying printed guide contains a list of titles, an abstract for each report, and indexes by geographic region, author, and subject.

1881. Powelson, John P. **The story of land: a world history of land tenure and agrarian reform.** Lincoln Institute of Land Policy, 1988. 347 pp., bibl., index. From Mesopotamia to the twentieth century, reviews land policies and reforms in differing eras and societies. Examines the shifting set of rights and obligations that land ownership entails. Attempts to understand why land reforms failed and why the same mistakes can be and are repeated today.

1882. Chambers, Robert; Saxena, N.C.; Shah, Tushaar. **To the hands of the poor: water and trees.** Intermediate Technology, 1989. 273 pp., ill., bibl., index. Discusses lift irrigation and trees as possible solutions to rural poverty, focusing in each case on group and community initiatives, private rights and markets, and policy implications.

1883. Marten, Gerald G.; ed. **Traditional agriculture in Southeast Asia: a human ecology perspective.** Westview Press, 1986. 358 pp., ill., bibl., index. Agronomists, ecologists, and social scientists analyze traditional agricultural methods and find that stability, sustainability, resilience, and efficiency are more important than high yield. Case studies from the Philippines, Thailand, and Indonesia.

1884. Glennie, Colin. **Village water supply in the decade: lessons from field experience.** Wiley, 1983. 152 pp., ill., bibl., index. Firsthand, detailed account of successful rural water supply project in Malawi, East Africa. Chronicles each step of the project and the management of manpower and community participation.

1885. Therkildsen, O. **Watering white elephants: lessons from donor funded planning and implementation of rural water supplies in Tanzania.** Scandinavian Institute of African Studies, Uppsala, Centre for Development Research Publications, no. 7, 1988. 225 pp. Case studies of projects in Tanzania since the 1970s by donor agencies in Denmark, Holland, Finland, and Sweden and by the World Bank. The lessons: too much emphasis on data collection, regional master water plans, and quick results; too little host country participation and project monitoring. Argues for experimental and adaptive projects that will strengthen institutional capabilities of host countries.

1886. Maclachlan, Morgan D. **Why they did not starve: biocultural adaptation in the South Indian village.** Institute for the Study of Human Issues, 1983. 296 pp., ill., bibl., index. Analyzes the adaptations of one village that enabled its residents to avoid starving during a prolonged drought.

1887. Jain, S. C.; ed. **Women and technology.** Rawat, 1985. 200 pp., bibl., index. Papers of an Indian workshop. Emphasizes need for appropriate technology to improve the quality of life for women. Discusses technology currently available and techniques for implementing it.

1888. ISIS Women's International Information & Communication Service. **Women in development: a resource guide for organization and action.** New Society, 1984. 225 pp., ill., bibl. Guide to recent thought and literature containing a feminist perspective on issues of food, water, and economic development. Discusses multinationals, rural development, appropriate technology, health, education and communication, and migration and tourism. Gives contact information for relevant groups, organizations, and institutions.

1889. Wood fuel surveys. Food and Agriculture Organization of the United Nations, Forestry for local development programmes, no. GCP/INT/365/SWE, 1983. 202 pp. Papers address the necessity of designing wood fuel surveys that incorporate local participation and that help solve rural energy problems; the interrelationship of social, agricultural, and forest ecosystems in Indian villages; urban demands on wood fuel supplies; and technical advice for conducting surveys.

1890. World agricultural economics and rural sociology abstracts. Commonwealth Agricultural Bureaux, 1959 to date. Monthly. Abstracts of the world's published literature in agricultural economics and rural sociology arranged by subject category. Contains author and subject indexes and annual cumulations. Available as an online computer database.

1891. Klee, Gary A.; ed. **World systems of traditional resource management.** V. H. Winston; Wiley, Scripta series in geography, 1980. 290 pp., ill., bibl., index. Reviews means of conserving and managing resources distinct from Western, energy-intensive strategies. Explains and evaluates traditional methods and presents general principles regarding scale, decision making, application, and long-term reliability and feasibility. Systems are arranged by region.

Rural Communities: United States and Europe (1892–1920)

1892. Swanson, Louis E.; ed. **Agriculture and community change in the U.S.: the congressional research reports.** Westview Press, 1988. 355 pp., ill., bibl. Based on a 1985 Office of Technology Assessment study of American agriculture. Shows, for five agricultural regions, the connections between farm change and community well-being. Concludes that policies need to take into account regional differences.

1893. Jordan, Terry G.; Kaups, Matti. **The American backwoods frontier: an ethnic and ecological interpretation.** Johns Hopkins University Press, Creating the North American landscape, 1989. 340 pp., ill., bibl., index. Argues that colonial Finnish immigrants shaped the backwoods culture of the American frontier. Discusses techniques of backwoods farming, log construction, folk architecture, and hunting and gathering.

1894. Platt, Rutherford H.; Macinko, George; eds. **Beyond the urban fringe: land use issues of nonmetropolitan America.** University of Minnesota Press, 1983. 416 pp., ill., index. Papers presented at a 1980 symposium. Covers geographic perspectives on nonmetropolitan land-use change, the growth and decline of small towns, floodplain management, and nuclear and toxic wastes.

1895. Building support for conservation in rural areas. Vol. I: Case study summaries. Vol II: Recommendations and conclusions. Quebec Laborador Foundation/Atlantic Center for the Environment, 1986. Bibl. 2 vols. Proceedings of a 1986 workshop. Studies from 19 countries discuss building support among indigenous people, youth, resource users, and the greater community.

1896. Kochanski, Mors. **Bush arts.** Lone Pine, 1989. 62 pp., ill. Manual of crafts and skills of rural Canada. Describes and illustrates how to make bird decoys, willow whistles, cattail dolls, and other items.

1897. Hasselbrook, Chuck; Hegyes, Gabriel. **Choices for the heartland: alternative directions in biotechnology and implications for family farming, rural communities, and the environment.** Iowa State University, Center for Rural Affairs, Technology and Social Change Program, 1989. 113 pp., bibl.

1898. Lee, Robert G.; Field, Donald R.; Burch, William R.; eds. **Community and forestry: continuities in the sociology of natural resources.** Westview Press, Social behavior and natural resources series, 1990. 301 pp., index. Contributed papers explore the relationships of human communities to forests. Includes case studies of communities affected by changes in wood products industries and examples of interactions between forests and communities in an increasingly service-based economy.

1899. Salant, Priscilla. **A community researcher's guide to rural data.** Island Press, 1990. 93 pp., index. Identifies information sources, including the federal population and housing census, population reports and surveys, and labor market data.

1900. Weber, Bruce A.; Howell, Robert E.; eds. **Coping with rapid growth in rural communities.** Westview Press, 1982. 284 pp., ill., bibl., index. Summarizes relevant literature. Discusses the larger sociodemographic context of rapid rural growth in the West and the impacts of growth. Suggests local government response options and ways of enhancing local control.

1901. Green, Bryn. **Countryside conservation: the protection and management of amenity ecosystems.** Allen & Unwin, Resource management series, v. 3, 1985. 253 pp. Comprehensive evaluation of conservation principles applicable to the governing of such amenity lands in the United Kingdom as farmland, grasslands, heathlands, moorlands, woodlands, wetlands, and coastlands. Argues for a coherent, integrated approach toward preservation of the rural environment.

1902. Blacksell, Mark; Gilg, Andrew W. **The countryside: planning and change.** Allen & Unwin, Resource management series, v. 2, 1981. 262 pp. Reviews the relationship between planning policies and their actual effects on England's rural landscape.

1903. Yaro, Robert D.; and others. **Dealing with change in the Connecticut River Valley: a design manual for conservation and development.** Center for Rural Massachusetts, University of Massachusetts–Amherst, 1988. 181 pp. Using aerial and ground-level perspective sketches, site plans, and photographs, compares different kinds of development in rural communities and argues for alternative development scenarios that emphasize community involvement. Provides legal techniques, site plan review standards, and model land-use ordinances. Applicable to any rural community facing growth pressures.

1904. Steiner, Frederick R. **Ecological planning for farmlands preservation.** American Planning Association, 1981. 122 pp., ill., bibl. Case study of preserving agricultural land in Whitman County, Washington. Reviews land classification methods, providing a sample in-

ventory, analysis, and synthesis. Discusses community organization and other means of implementation, including federal, state, and local programs.

1905. Fitchen, Janet M. **Endangered spaces, enduring places: change, identity, and survival in rural America.** Westview Press, 1991. 314 pp., ill., bibl., index. Reviews the declining farm and manufacturing economy, shifting population, increasing poverty, and other factors greatly affecting rural American life. Identifies strategies and government policies and programs to ensure the survival of rural communities.

1906. Rackham, Oliver. **The history of the countryside: the full fascinating story of Britain's landscape.** Dent, 1986. 445 pp. Discusses methods of studying landscape history. Gives examples of the ecology and history of various British landscapes, including woodlands, wood-pasture, dells and pits, and heathland.

1907. Marshall, James M. **Land fever: dispossession and the frontier myth.** University Press of Kentucky, 1986. 239 pp., bibl., index. Life story of dispossessed farmer in frontier Wisconsin and Minnesota. Includes his autobiography and essays on the economic, demographic, and geographic conditions leading to the loss of his homestead.

1908. Collins, Beryl Robichaud; Russell, Emily W. B. **Protecting the New Jersey pinelands: a new direction in land-use management.** Rutgers University Press, 1988. 367 pp., ill., index. Eight experts describe the landscape, biology, and human ecology of the Pine Barrens; state and federal legislation; and the direction of land-use management.

1909. Berg, Peter. **Reinhabiting a separate country: a bioregional anthology of Northern California.** Planet Drum Foundation, 1978. 220 pp., ill., bibl. Eclectic mixture of interviews, poetry, prose, drawings, and photographs by natives of northern California; exemplifies bioregionalism in practice.

1910. Marston, Ed; ed. **Reopening the western frontier.** Island Press, 1989. 324 pp., ill., index. Collection of journalistic essays from writers of *High country news*; analyzes past and present resource management decisions in western states and assesses future challenges.

1911. Detomasi, Don D.; Gartrell, John W.; eds. **Resource communities: a decade of disruption.** Westview Press, 1984. 193 pp., ill., bibl., index. Surveys research and policies on problems faced by resource communities in Canada, Norway, the United Kingdom, and the United States from 1972 to 1982.

1912. Fuguitt, Glenn V.; Brown, David L.; Beale, Calvin L. **Rural and small town America**. Russell Sage Foundation, The population of the United States in the 1980s, 1989. 471 pp., ill., bibl., index. Trends, changes, and fluctuations of the nonmetropolitan population, based on the 1980 census. Traces shifts in age and sex composition, fertility, employment status, and household growth and structure in rural areas. Includes comparison of population and economic characteristics between metropolitan and nonmetropolitan areas.

1913. Sargent, Frederic O.; and others. **Rural environmental planning for sustainable communities**. Island Press, 1991. 260 pp., ill., index. Provides instructions for starting the planning process; establishing committees, time frames, and procedures; and realizing the plans. Emphasis on protecting natural, agricultural, and recreational lands and preserving local culture.

1914. Rural sociology. Rural Sociological Society, 1936 to date. Quarterly. Presents research on the social dimensions of rural life and environment and the relationship of environmental issues to social factors. An early and leading journal for social scientific study of the environment..

1915. Field, Donald R.; Burch, William R., Jr. **Rural sociology and the environment**. Greenwood Press, Contributions in sociology, 74, 1988. 135 pp., ill., bibl. Reviews the literature and changing research directions of rural sociology in relation to environmental problems. In three sections: the domination of nature for food and fiber (concern with agricultural production, land and water, to the 1960s); expanding the domain of nature (in the 1970s); and emergence of nature as a partner (more recent directions).

1916. Stokes, Samuel N.; Watson, A. Elizabeth. **Saving America's countryside: a guide to rural conservation**. Johns Hopkins University Press, 1989. 306 pp., ill., bibl., index. Methods and approaches for initiating and managing a program; inventorying resources and features of the rural community; land-protection techniques suited to local government and volunteer action; federal and state laws regulating water, land, wildlife, and cultural resources; and techniques for effective community education. Several dozen case studies illustrate.

1917. Vale, Thomas R.; Vale, Geraldine R. **U.S. 40 today: thirty years of landscape change in America**. University of Wisconsin Press, 1983. 198 pp., maps, ill., bibl., index. Retraces the journey of George R. Stewart across the United States in 1950 and follows the format of his book *U.S. 40*. Couples 1950 and 1980 photographs

(often from nearly identical perspectives). Interpretive text refers to Stewart's observations and discusses conspicuous and subtle, natural and cultural, intended and unexpected landscape changes.

1918. Berry, Wendell. **The unsettling of America: culture & agriculture**. Avon Books, 1978. 228 pp., bibl. Shows how the current ecological crisis represents a crisis of agriculture, character, and culture. Explores the connections between agriculture and culture, spirit and body, the body and the earth.

1919. Taylor, Christopher. **Villages and farmsteads: a history of rural settlements in England**. Uses radio carbon dating, pollen counts, soil analysis, and aerial photography to document the history of settlement and land use as far back as the Iron Age.

1920. Berger, Jonathan; Sinton, John W. **Water, earth and fire: land use and environmental planning in the New Jersey Pine Barrens**. Johns Hopkins University Press, 1985. 228 pp., ill., bibl., index. Intended as a planning aid. Explains the ecology and land use of the "other New Jersey." Discusses the many uses of water (clamming, crabbing, oystering, drinking water); earth (especially cranberry and blueberry farming); and fire. Proposes several planning approaches.

Urban Communities (1921–1954)

1921. Horowitz, Joel L. **Air quality analysis for urban transportation planning**. MIT Press, MIT Press series in transportation studies, v. 7, 1982. 387 pp., ill., bibl., index. Presents in detail the pollutants associated with urban transportation systems, health effects of the pollutants, changes in transportation to reduce pollution, and techniques to predict the consequences of those changes.

1922. Stilgoe, John R. **Borderland: origins of the American suburb, 1820–1939**. Yale University Press, 1988. 353 pp., index, bibl. A landscape history in the tradition of J. B. Jackson that focuses on visual elements of suburbs, including country homes and grounds, villages, parks, ornamental gardens, transportation and rail lines, planned residential communities, and locales around Philadelphia and Chicago.

1923. Kinkead, Eugene. **Central Park 1857–1995: the birth, decline, and renewal of a national treasure**. Norton, 1990. 257 pp., ill., index. Addresses botanical, geological, architectural, recreational, sociological, and wildlife aspects of Central Park. Recounts in detail the park's design and construction. Describes its changing features, facilities, and patterns of use, briefly reviewing the long periods of neglect, and reporting on the repair and restoration program begun in 1979.

1924. Hough, Michael. **City form and natural process: towards a new urban vernacular.** Croom Helm, 1984. 281 pp., ill., bibl., index. How urban processes affect climate, water, plants, wildlife, and farming. Discusses environmental problems engendered by prevailing urban values. Presents alternative values and design strategies, plus case studies.

1925. Whyte, William H. **City: rediscovering the center.** Doubleday, 1988. 386 pp., ill., bibl., index. Examines what makes cities livable and the dynamics of public places. Discusses the social life of the street, pedestrian flow, the necessity of rich sensory experiences, steps and entrances, blank walls, sun and shadow, and many other components of space. Stresses that cities can be quality environments. Includes abridged text of New York City zoning provisions.

1926. Francis, Mark; Cashdan, Lisa; Paxson, Lynn. **Community open spaces: greening neighborhoods through community action and land conservation.** Island Press, 1984. 250 pp., maps, ill., bibl., index. A multidisciplinary analysis, incorporating landscape architecture, environmental psychology, urban design, and architecture, of ten successful community open space projects in New York City. Introductory chapters provide an overview of the community open space movement in the United States and Europe.

1927. Jacobs, Jane. **The death and life of great American cities.** Vintage Books, 1961. 458 pp. An early and eloquent proponent of the idea that the essence of city life lies in its multiplicity of human activities, not in anonymous new buildings or huge public works. Emphasizes the value of small-scale architecture to promote natural social interactions and foster a sense of community.

1928. Gilbert, Oliver L. **The ecology of urban habitats.** Chapman and Hall, 1989. 369 pp. Describes the characteristics peculiar to urban plants, wildlife, and habitats. Examines urban soils, the effects of air pollution, and the flora and fauna found in industrial areas, city centers, parks, cemeteries, reservoirs, and water mains. Highlights mutually beneficial relationships between people and urban animals.

1929. Cohn, Louis F.; McVoy, Gary R. **Environmental analysis of transportation systems.** Wiley, 1982. 374 pp., ill., bibl., index. Examines the environmental issues involved in highway and airport projects. Covers

federal regulations and legislation. Provides technical discussion of noise pollution, air quality, and effects on terrestrial and aquatic ecology.

1930. Melosi, Martin V. **Garbage in the cities: refuse, reform, and the environment: 1880–1980.** Texas A & M University Press, Environmental history series, no. 4, 1981. 268 pp., ill., bibl., index. Historical analysis of the garbage problem: as a technical issue to be handled by sanitary engineers and as an aesthetic affront to be settled by motivated citizen's groups. Reviews modern management techniques and discusses the perception of solid waste as "land pollution."

1931. Spirn, Anne Whiston. **The granite garden: urban nature and human design.** Basic Books, 1984. 334 pp., ill., bibl., index. Reviews the necessity of incorporating awareness of nature into urban design, specifically focusing on air quality; floods, droughts, and water supply; urban plants, pets, pests, and wildlife; and waste disposal. Provides some case studies and strategies.

1932. Hall, Peter Geoffrey. **Great planning disasters.** University of California Press, California series in urban development, v. 1, 1980. 308 pp., ill., bibl., index. Presents case studies of such disasters as the Anglo-French Concorde, London's third airport, and the San Francisco BART system and analyzes the problems that lie behind them in the interaction of community, bureaucracy, and politicians.

1933. Habitat international. Pergamon Press, 1976 to date. Quarterly. Publishes research on the planning, design, production, and management of housing and human settlements, particularly in developing countries.

1934. Rapoport, Amos. **Human aspects of urban form: towards a man-environment approach to urban form and design.** Pergamon Press, Urban and regional planning series, v. 15, 1977. 438 pp., ill., bibl., index. Brings together ideas and findings from the social sciences that provide a geographic construct of the cultural landscape and a new way of looking at the urban environment and its effects on behavior. Discusses space in the urban environment; evaluating the urban environment; mental maps; sensory perception of urban environment; means of coping with sensory overload; and the cultural, social, and territorial city.

1935. Castells, Manuel. **The informational city: information technology, economic restructuring, and the urban-regional process.** Basil Blackwell, 1989. 448 pp., bibl. Analyzes how socioeconomic restructuring and new information technologies have transformed urban-regional processes; discusses the transition from the welfare state to the warfare state, new capital-labor relationships, the rise of the "dual city," and the internalization of the economy.

1936. Hazlett, Thomas C. **Land form designs.** PDA, 1988. 375 pp., bibl., index. Presents the functional and visual aspects in site design of man-made three-dimensional forms and spaces. Examples display differing features (shape, scale, proportion) and employ varied materials (earth, metal, plastic). Includes over 600 photographs and nearly 175 drawings.

1937. Landscape and urban planning. Elsevier, 1974 to date. Bimonthly. Continues: Landscape planning, Urban ecology. Concerned with conceptual, scientific, and design approaches to land use. Research papers on ecological processes in urban areas, on the relation of those processes to surrounding natural systems, and on specific problems.

1938. Appleyard, Donald; Gerson, M. Sue; Lintell, Mark. **Livable streets.** University of California Press, 1981. 364 pp., ill., bibl., index. Explores traffic's effects on San Francisco residential street life. Describes past attempts to reduce traffic through neighborhoods in England and the Bay Area. Concludes with practical advice on realizing the goal of livable streets.

1939. Payne, Geoffrey K.; ed. **Low-income housing in the developing world: the role of sites and services and settlement upgrading.** Wiley, A Wiley series on public administration in developing countries, 1984. 271 pp., ill., bibl., index. Part I presents eight case studies from Nairobi, El Salvador, Jakarta, and elsewhere. Part II is an analysis of the roles of major actors (communities, multinational organizations) and influential factors (finance, land markets, infrastructure selection) in these and other projects. Makes recommendations for the future.

1940. Rowe, Peter G. **Making a middle landscape.** MIT Press, 1991. 352 pp., ill. Examines American suburbia from a design and physical planning perspective. Includes the house and its garden; roadside franchises, commercial strips, and shopping villages and malls; office parks and corporate estates; and networking roads. Also analyzes accompanying mythic themes, metaphors, and attitudes.

1941. Rapoport, Amos. **The meaning of the built environment: a nonverbal communication approach.** Sage Publications, 1982. 224 pp., ill., bibl., index. Provides examples of small-scale and urban applications of this non-verbal approach.

1942. Alexander Christopher; and others. **A new theory of urban design.** Oxford University Press, 1987. 251 pp., ill. Presents rules for implementing an organic

urban design and uses them to simulate the development of part of the San Francisco waterfront. Final section critiques the results.

1943. Goldstein, Eric A.; Izeman, Mark A. **The New York environment book.** Island Press, 1990. 267 pp., index. Analyzes the successes and failures of the last ten years in cleaning up New York. Surveys five areas: solid waste disposal, hazardous substances, pollution of the waterways, air quality, and the purity of drinking water. Has application to the special environmental problems of all urban areas.

1944. Alexander, Christopher; and others. **A pattern language: towns, buildings, construction.** Oxford University Press, 1977. 1171 pp., ill. Presents an organized structure of 253 guidelines governing the organic design and construction of towns and buildings. Discussion ranges from the distribution of towns and identifiable neighborhoods to bike paths and street cafes, roofs and courtyards, entrances and views, and bed alcoves and shelves.

1945. Emery, Malcolm John. **Promoting nature in cities and towns: a practical guide.** Croom Helm, 1986. 396 pp. Explains formation of a local wildlife group. Provides examples and details of site survey, selection, and design. Reviews ecological principles and practices involved in site creation and management.

1946. Breheny, Michael J.; Hooper, A. J.; eds. **Rationality in planning: critical essays on the role of rationality in urban and regional planning.** Pion, 1985. 247 pp. Essays offer a wide range of opinion on the definition of rational planning and the suitability and feasibility of incorporating rationality in planning.

1947. Mantell, Michael A.; Harper, Stephen F.; Propst, Luther. **Resource guide for creating successful communities: a guide to growth management strategies.** Island Press, 1990. 233 pp., ill., bibl., index. Compendium of techniques developed by the Conservation Foundation. Discusses the tax benefits of private land conservation, ordinances covering all land types, land-use regulations, tax policies, and private voluntary land protection.

1948. Bookchin, Murray. **The rise of urbanization and the decline of citizenship.** Sierra Club Books, 1987. 300 pp., bibl., index. Distinguishes between city and urbanization: the former responds to social needs; the latter is ecologically destructive and dehumanizing. Describes the evolution of both. Suggests ways of viewing cities and politics in ecological terms.

1949. Whyte, William H. **The social life of small urban spaces.** Conservation Foundation, 1980. 125 pp., ill., bibl. Why some city parks and plazas work and others do not. Describes and illustrates the roles of sitting space, sun, wind, trees, water, and food in creating a pleasant environment. Analyzes effective capacity, indoor spaces, concourses and megastructures, and the differences between big and small cities. Most research conducted in New York City.

1950. Van der Ryn, Sim; Calthorpe, Peter. **Sustainable communities: a new design synthesis for cities, suburbs and towns.** Sierra Club Books, 1986. 238 pp., ill., index. Presents case studies in urban and suburban contexts of infilling for urban rehabilitation, rehabilitation of existing structures, and proposals for redesigning the suburban fabric in the context of energy use, employment, housing, and other factors. Emphasis on the need for intelligent planning rather than more resources and on the need for common, public spaces.

1951. Alexander, Christopher. **The timeless way of building.** Oxford University Press, 1979. 552 pp., ill. Companion volume to *A pattern language: towns, buildings, construction.* Presents the theory of making towns and buildings; emphasizes community participation and the use of a commonly understood set of aesthetic and practical considerations in design and construction.

1952. Taylor, Lisa; ed. **Urban open spaces.** Rizzoli, 1981. 128 pp. Originally a catalog for an exhibition on urban spaces at the Cooper-Hewitt Museum in New York. Forty-four brief, illustrated articles by well-known planners and landscape architects.

1953. De Chiara, Joseph; Koppelman, Lee. **Urban planning and design criteria.** Van Nostrand Reinhold, 3d ed., 1982. 723 pp., maps, ill., bibl., index. A reference text that provides general standards for urban planning principles and practices. Explains guidelines and gives examples from airport planning and commercial development to public park expansion. Many drawings, maps, and graphs.

1954. Baines, Chris. **The wild side of town.** BBC Publications, 1986. 186 pp., ill. This accompaniment to a BBC television series describes the wildlife at your doorstep and in gardens, parks, cemeteries, and woodlands, and provides practical advice on how to cultivate disused areas.

Environmental Organizations. Movements (1955–1992)

1955. Meine, Curt. **Aldo Leopold: his life and work.** University of Wisconsin Press, 1988. 638 pp., ill., bibl., index. Full, satisfying biography, based on Leopold papers at the University of Wisconsin and other primary sources. Shows the development of Leopold's ideas on conservation and the environment in the context of his professional and family life.

1956. Tanner, Thomas; ed. **Aldo Leopold: the man and his legacy.** Soil Conservation Society of America, 1987. 175 pp., ill., bibl. Collection of essays, from scholarly to personal.

1957. Moore, N. W. **The bird of time: the science of politics and nature conservation, a personal account.** Cambridge University Press, 1987. 290 pp. British conservationist reflects on changes in British landscapes—particularly heathlands—since World War II; social and political problems in establishing nature reserves; the effects of pesticides on wildlife and their habitats; and public attitudes toward conservation.

1958. Pinchot, Gifford. **Breaking new ground.** Island Press, Conservation classics, c. 1947, 1987. 522 pp., ill., index. Pinchot was the originator of conservation as a government policy and the principal founder of forestry in the United States. His lively and inspiring autobiography, reprinted here, was first published in 1947.

1959. Kipps, Harriet Clyde. **Community resources directory: a guide to U.S. volunteer organizations and other resource groups, services, training events, and courses, and local program models.** Gale Research, 2d ed., 1984. 943 pp., index. Divided into three sections: resource groups and publications, training programs, and local volunteer programs. Gives description, agenda, and location; indexed by name and program emphasis.

1960. Dove, Kent E. **Conducting a successful capital campaign: a comprehensive fundraising guide for nonprofit organizations.** Jossey-Bass, 1988. 292 pp. Key principles and practices by an experienced fundraising executive. Covers key components, preparation, roles of leaders and volunteers, recruiting and motivating volunteers, building the case, the gifts chart, establishing the campaign structure, identifying donors, soliciting major gifts, logistics and operations, and concluding the campaign.

1961. Conservation directory. National Wildlife Federation, 1968 to date, Annual. 37th ed., 1992. Annual guide to U.S. and Canadian government agencies and committees, international and national organizations, and citizen's groups concerned with natural resource use and management. Includes descriptions, contact information, and listings of key individuals.

1962. Muchiru, Simon. **Conservation of species and genetic resources: an NGO action guide**. Environment Liaison Centre, Nairobi, 1985. 76 pp., ill., bibl. Provides names and addresses of nongovernmental organizations (NGOs) and other institutions working on species and genetic resources. Includes practical project ideas for NGOs to pursue.

1963. Borrelli, Peter; ed. **Crossroads: environmental priorities for the future**. Island Press, 1988. 339 pp., index. Environmental activists and leaders assess the successes and failures of the environmental movement.

1964. Directory of environmental NGO's in the Asia-Pacific region. Sahabat Alam Malaysia (Friends of the Earth Malaysia), 1983. 257 pp. Presents profiles of nongovernmental organizations (NGOs) of 14 countries and the Pacific Islands; includes publications, problems, and proposals for future work.

1965. Brainard, John C.; McGrath, Roger N.; eds. **The directory of national environmental organizations**. U.S. Environmental Directories, 3d ed., 1988. 160 pp., index. Contact information and brief descriptions of nearly 400 nongovernmental, environmental, and conservation organizations of national significance; includes organizations concerned with pollution, nuclear power, population, recycling, and other related issues.

1966. Directory of non-governmental development organisations in OECD member countries. Organization for Economic Cooperation and Development, Publications and Information Center, 1990. Index. 2 vols. Provides descriptions to over 2500 nongovernmental organizations, detailing their membership, aims, educational activities, and development actions. Includes full contact information. In French and English; fully indexed.

1967. Encyclopedia of associations. Gale Research, 1961 to date. Annual: 26th ed., 1992. Comprehensive listing of membership organizations, including American, foreign, international, nonprofit, profit, and some nonmembership organizations. Provides contact information and details on size, objectives, and officers.

1968. Langton, Stuart; ed. **Environmental leadership: a sourcebook for staff and volunteer leaders of environmental organizations**. Lexington Books, 1984. 138 pp., bibl. Twelve essays written by and for environmental activists provide advice on fund-raising, proposal writing, community organizing, using the media, and other tactics.

1969. Brower, David R. **For earth's sake: the life and times of David Brower**. Peregrine Smith Books,

1990. 556 pp., ill., bibl., index. Brower reflects on his career as one of this century's most prominent environmental activists. Discusses his years of mountaineering, influential colleagues, victories and defeats, and the value of wilderness and wildlife.

1970. Gale GlobalAccess: associations 1990. Gale Research, 1990. Provides electronic access through compact disc to over 100,000 descriptive entries of national, international, regional, state, and local organizations and associations, as well as association periodicals.

1971. Houle, Cyril Orvin. **Governing boards: their nature and nurture**. Jossey-Bass, The Jossey-Bass management series, 1989. 223 pp., bibl., index. Comprehensive, practical reference on boards and their relations with executives and staff. Chapters on how to think about a board; human potential; structure of the board; board, executive, and staff; operation of the board; external relationships of the board. Author has served on 30 boards. A project of the National Center for Nonprofit Boards.

1972. Manes, Christopher. **Green rage: radical environmentalism and the unmaking of civilization**. Little, Brown, 1990. 291 pp., bibl. Describes the founding of Earth First! and explains its philosophies of deep ecology, civil disobedience, and ecotage. Argues for dismantling of "the culture of extinction" in order to create an ecologically sensitive and harmonious way of life.

1973. Allen, Thomas B. **Guardian of the wild: the story of the National Wildlife Federation, 1936–1986**. Indiana University Press, 1987. 212 pp., ill., bibl., index. Recounts the efforts of the National Wildlife Federation to educate and involve people in the conservation and preservation of America's wilderness and wildlife.

1974. Fox, Stephen R. **John Muir and his legacy: the American conservation movement**. Little, Brown, 1981. 436 pp., ill., bibl., index. Biography of Muir, a history of the conservation movement from 1890 to 1975, and an analysis of themes in the movement, especially the role of the radical amateur and religious aspects of the movement.

1975. Kouzes, James M.; Posner, Barry Z. **The leadership challenge: how to get extraordinary things done in organizations**. Jossey-Bass, 1987. 362 pp., ill., bibl., index. Successful leaders have five things in common: they challenge the process, inspire a shared vision, enable others to act, model the way, and "encourage the heart" of their coworkers. Based on extensive data gathering.

1976. Wolfe, Joan. **Making things happen: how to**

be an effective volunteer. Island Press, 1991. 225 pp., index. Practical recommendations on recruiting and retaining volunteers, plus tips on organizational management, leadership strategies, and communication skills. Emphasizes principles of cooperation, encouragement, and enthusiasm.

1977. Kotler, Philip. **Marketing for nonprofit organizations.** Prentice-Hall, The Prentice-Hall series in marketing, 2d ed., 1982. 528 pp., ill., bibl., index. Provides thorough introduction to marketing for wide range of nonprofit sectors. Discusses organization of marketing, analyzing opportunities, planning the marketing mix, and attracting resources.

1978. Weiner, Douglas R. **Models of nature: ecology, conservation, and cultural revolution in Soviet Russia.** Indiana University Press, Indiana-Michigan series in Russian and East European studies, 1988. 312 pp., ill., bibl., index. Argues that an ecological movement existed before and after the Russian Revolution. Reports on the movement's theories, tactics, and power in the 1920s and 1930s. Examines political, economic, and ideological pressures that led to the discrediting of conservationists and their projects.

1979. National directory of nonprofit organizations. Taft Group, 2d ed., 1991. Index. 3 vols. Lists more than 250,000 nonprofit organizations in the United States, with contact information, descriptions of activities and agenda, estimated annual income, and contribution tax deduction status.

1980. Stroud, Richard H.; ed. **National leaders of American conservation.** Smithsonian Institution Press, 2d ed., 1985. 432 pp., bibl., index. Brief biographies of 500 individuals who have made significant contributions to conservation of natural resources at the national level.

1981. Nicholson, Max. **The new environmental age.** Cambridge University Press, 1987. 232 pp., ill., bibl., index. An informal history of the environmental movement, especially after 1970, informed by the author's extensive involvement in numerous British and international environmental organizations.

1982. Oleck, Howard Leoner. **Nonprofit corporations, organizations, and associations.** Prentice-Hall, 5th ed., 1988. 1274 pp., ill., bibl., index. Authoritative guide to the law and operation of nonprofit enterprises, first published in 1956. Fifty chapters, 1900 topics, hundreds of case references and model forms.

1983. Allard, Denise M.; ed. **Organizations master index.** Gale Research, 1987. 1120 pp. Subtitle: A consolidated index to approximately 50 directories, hand-

books, yearbooks, encyclopedias, and guides providing information on approximately 150,000 national and international associations, government agencies and advisory organizations, foundations, research centers, museums, religious groups, and programs of all kinds in the United States, Canada, and worldwide. Because any given organization may be cited in several different kinds of source, this index gives users several viewpoints. A bibliography describes the sources.

1984. Udall, Stewart L. **The quiet crisis and the next generation.** Peregrine Smith Books, 1988. 298 pp. 25th anniversary edition of *The quiet crisis* takes up the story where its predecessor left off, discussing the individuals and issues that have lately characterized the increasingly complex environmental movement.

1985. McCormick, John. **Reclaiming paradise: the global environmental movement.** Indiana University Press, 1989. 259 pp., bibl., index. Documents the events, organizations, acts, and personalities involved in environmental protection and conservation since 1945. Reviews the Stockholm Conference, the United Nations Environment Programme, growing activism in the North, and increasing development in the South.

1986. Pell, Arthur R. **Recruiting, training and motivating volunteers.** Pilot Books, 1989. 61 pp. Covers interviewing, selecting, and supervising volunteers as well as how to place them in situations where they can do the most good.

1987. Turner, Frederick W. **Rediscovering America; John Muir in his time and ours.** Viking Press, 1985. 417 pp., ill., bibl., index. A vivid portrait of the man, providing historical and cultural perspectives on his life and thought.

1988. Scheffer, Victor B. **The shaping of environmentalism in America.** University of Washington Press, 1991. 249 pp., ill., bibl., index. Anecdotal history of the modern environmental movement. Traces the grass-roots efforts of the 1960s and 1970s to the mainstream cause of the present.

1989. Bryson, John Moore. **Strategic planning for public and nonprofit organizations: a guide to strengthening and sustaining organizational achievement.** Jossey-Bass, The Jossey-Bass public administration series, 1988. 311 pp., ill., bibl., index. Explains the dynamics and key steps of strategic planning. Topics include identifying and clarifying the organization's mandate, mission, and values; assessing the organization's external and internal environments; critiquing strategic issues; developing an effective strategy and a vision of success; and overcoming human, process, structural, and institutional barriers to effective strategic thought and action.

1990. Kipps, Harriet Clyde; ed. **Volunteerism: the directory of organizations, training, programs and publications, 1990–1991.** Bowker, 3d ed., 1990. Previously published as the *Community resources directory*, lists contact information, objectives, services, and publications of volunteer organizations; over 5500 entries.

1991. Trzyna, Thaddeus C.; Childers, Roberta; eds. **World directory of environmental organizations.** California Institute of Public Affairs; Sierra Club; IUCN–World Conservation Union, Who's doing what series, no. 2, 4th ed., 1992. 231 pp. Subtitle: A handbook of national and international organizations and programs—governmental and non-governmental—concerned with protecting the earth's resources. In seven parts: introduction; organizations listed by problem, issue, and biome; overview of world regions; United Nations system; other intergovernmental organizations; other nongovernmental organizations; and country and area listings. An appendix covers directories and databases; there is an index of selected organizations and major programs. Entries include description of organization and its programs; address; and telephone, telex, and fax numbers.

1992. Seredich, John; ed. **Your resource guide to environmental organizations.** Smiling Dolphins Press, 1991. 514 pp., ill., index. Contains 150 selected national and international nonprofit groups. Lists agenda, programs, achievements, publications, and volunteer opportunities in two- to four-page entries that also attempt to convey a group's "personality."

Individuals and Environment (1993–2017)

1993. Seymour, John; Girardet, Herbert. **Blueprint for a green planet: your practical guide to restoring the world's environment.** Prentice-Hall, 1987. 192 pp. Advocates green consumerism with examples of environmentally correct alternatives in daily life.

1994. Corson, Walter H.; ed. **Citizen's guide to global issues.** Global Tomorrow Coalition, 1985. 203 pp., bibl. An overview of major global problems and possible solutions, produced by the Global Tomorrow Coalition.

1995. The compendium newsletter. Educational Communications, Ecology Center of Southern California, 1972 to date. Bimonthly. Activist "guide to the world's environmental crisis." Ecological news and infor-

mation, action alerts, correspondence group targets, calendar of events, special reports, project ideas, merchandise, and audiovisuals.

1996. Monnier, Eric; and others, eds. **Consumer behavior and energy policy: an international perspective.** Praeger, 1986. 344 pp., ill., bibl., index. Papers from a 1985 conference examine the evolution of energy demand and use in Western countries, evaluate energy conservation programs, assess efforts to reduce social inequality in energy use, and review consumers' everyday attitudes and behavior toward energy consumption.

1997. Edelstein, Michael R. **Contaminated communities: the social and psychological impacts of resident toxic exposure.** Westview Press, 1988. 217 pp., ill., bibl., index. Discusses cognitive adjustments; impacts on the individual, family, and community; and the psychological basis for the NIMBY (not in my backyard) syndrome. Based on interviews with victims of toxic pollution.

1998. Narr, John. **Designs for a livable planet: how you can help clean up the environment.** Harper, 1990. 338 pp., ill. Integrated, practical solutions to environmental problems; includes resource lists.

1999. Eckholm, Erick P. **Down to earth: environment and human needs.** Norton, 1982. 238 pp., bibl., index. Prepared for the tenth anniversary of the 1972 Stockholm Conference on the Human Environment. Reviews global environmental problems and solutions, emphasizing connections between environmental degradation and social justice.

2000. Naess, Arne. **Ecology, community, and lifestyle.** Cambridge University Press, 1989. 223 pp., ill., bibl., index. Revised and expanded translation by D. Rothenberg of the author's original work, published in 1976. "Ecosophy" is defined as a whole view of humanity and nature that emerges from the mature, integrated personality. Presents the ecosophical point of view with respect to technology, economics, politics, and all life forms.

2001. Altman, Irwin; Lawton, M. Powell; Wohlwill, Joachim F.; eds. **Elderly people and the environment.** Plenum Press, 1984. 343 pp., ill., bibl., index. Reviews recent research from anthropology, economics, psychology, geography, and urban and regional planning. Most chapters focus on specific environments as experienced by the elderly, from kitchen to large natural settings.

2002. Stern, Paul C.; Aronson, Elliot; eds. **Energy use: the human dimension.** Freeman, 1984. 237 pp., ill., bibl., index. Draws upon behavioral and social science literature related to energy consumption. Examines energy as a commodity, an ecological resource, a social necessity, and a strategic material. Analyzes factors influencing energy-related behavior. Presents 29 policy implications and recommendations involving conservation programs and policies, energy emergencies, and local energy actions.

2003. Hawkins, Keith. **Environment and enforcement: regulation and the social definition of pollution.** Oxford University Press, Oxford socio-legal studies, 1984. 233 pp., bibl., index. Discusses the interplay between criminal law and the personal moral values of individual pollution control officers in the protection of Britain's water quality.

2004. Meadows, Donella H. **The global citizen.** Island Press, 1991. 300 pp., index. Collection of writings relating the interconnectedness of earth and the global impacts of individual and community actions. Clear, brief, and pointed treatments of population, arms control, development, waste disposal, and other environmental issues.

2005. The Global Tomorrow Coalition; Corson, Walter H.; ed. **The global ecology handbook: what you can do about the environmental crisis.** Beacon Press, 1990. 414 pp., maps, ill. General reference book and action guide covers tropical rain forests, global warming, hazardous waste, population growth, agriculture, biological diversity, solid waste management, etc., focusing on practical steps individuals can take to become more informed and effective activists.

2006. Bunyard, Peter; Morgan-Grenville, Fern; eds. **The green alternative: guide to good living.** Methuen, 1987. 368 pp. Poses and answers more than 500 questions on such topics as energy, health, education, and transport from a Green party perspective; suitable as an introduction to Green values.

2007. Vyner, Henry, M. **Invisible trauma: the psychosocial effects of invisible environmental contaminants.** Lexington Books, 1988. 222 pp., index. Analyzes three case studies, including Love Canal, from the point of view of the victim's psychological well-being. Discusses the effects of uncertainty in coping strategies of victims and the role of doctors.

2008. Giono, Jean. **The man who planted trees.** Chelsea Green, 1985. 52 pp., ill. One man reclaims waste area in southern France by planting trees. A simple, touching story that renews faith in humanity.

2009. Rodale, Robert. **Our next frontier: a personal guide for tomorrow's lifestyle.** Rodale Press,

1981. 242 pp. Foresees an evolutionary restructuring of American society to adapt more closely to regional climates and resources.

2010. Gould, Leroy C.; and others. **Perceptions of technological risk and benefits.** Russell Sage Foundation, 1988. 277 pp., ill., bibl., index. Reviews the background and institutions of risk management. Presents and evaluates the results of an opinion survey of the general public and of political activists concerning perceived risks, benefits of technology, and desirable levels of safety regulations.

2011. Geller, E. Scott; Winett, Richard A.; Everett, Peter B. **Preserving the environment: new strategies for behavior change.** Pergamon Press, Pergamon general psychology series, v.102, 1982. 338 pp., ill., bibl., index. Shows the potential of behavioral technology, based on 150 recent studies, to alleviate environmental problems. Chapters on litter control, waste reduction, water conservation, transportation and residential energy conservation.

2012. Lake, Celinda C.; Harper, Pat Callbeck. **Public opinion polling: a handbook for public interest and citizen advocacy groups.** Island Press, 1987. 166 pp., ill., bibl., index. Practical handbook on planning, conducting, analyzing, and interpreting polls.

2013. Douglas, Mary; Wildavsky, Aaron. **Risk and culture: an essay on the selection of technical and environmental dangers.** University of California Press, 1982. 221 pp., bibl., index. Discusses how people decide to take risks and what effect this has on public policy. "An analysis of the arguments connecting technology to environmental decline."

2014. Steger, Will; Bowermaster, Jon. **Saving the earth: a citizen's guide to environmental action.** Knopf, 1990. 352 pp., ill., index. An introduction, through case studies, to successful efforts by citizens and groups to protect the environment and prevent or halt pollution.

2015. Fox, Karl A. **Social system accounts: linking social and economic indicators through tangible behavior settings.** Reidel; Kluwer, Theory and decision library, v. 44, 1985. 221 pp., bibl., index. Proposes that existing data on behavior-setting concepts can be used to create a social system account that incorporates non-market acivities and combines social and economic indicators.

2016. Lorenz, Konrad; and Kickert, Robert Warren, trans. **The waning of humaneness.** Little, Brown, 1st Amer. ed., 1987. 250 pp., ill., bibl. A philosophical essay detailing the harmful effects of civilization, urbanizaton, and the man-made world. Asserts that people must increase their contact with the natural world to regain a proper sense of behavior, perception, and values.

2017. Baldwin, J.; ed. **Whole earth ecolog: tools and ideas for earth-conscious living.** Harmony Books, 1990. Discusses hands-on techniques, including edible landscaping, solar building, energy efficiency, cohousing, bioshelters, appropriate technology, outdoor skills, and recycling.

Education and Communication (2018–2040)

2018. American biology teacher. National Association of Biology Teachers, 1938 to date. 8 issues/yr. Publishes brief articles on topics of interest to high school and college biology teachers. Articles deal with curricula and teaching methods and with how-to-do-it projects.

2019. Audio video review digest. Gale Research, 1989. 350 pp., index. Reviews over 10,000 audio and video materials, drawing on over 600 general and specialized review sources. Covers all formats (records, tapes, compact discs, book-video packages, films, etc.) and provides information on release dates, running times, subject, and suggested audience.

2020. Bowker's complete video directory. Bowker, 1990 to date. Annual. In two volumes. Vol. 2 is Education/special interest. Under 446 subject headings, lists videos available on any format, including VHS, Beta, and laser disc.

2021. Connect. United Nations Environment Programme, 1976 to date. Quarterly. The UNESCO-UNEP environmental education newsletter. Essays on education, news of the International Environmental Education Program (IEEP), and notices of publications.

2022. Greig, Sue; Pike, Graham; Selby, David. **Earthrights: education as if the planet really mattered.** World Wildlife Fund; Kogan Page, 1987. 88 pp. Teachers' guide articulates the need for environmentally literate students with a global perspective. Presents a holistic model of schooling that incorporates personal, local, national, and global concerns. Focuses on four issues: development, the environment, human rights, and peace. Discusses teaching and learning methods for all ages and levels of schooling. Lists organizations, publications, journals, data sources, training opportunities, and classroom activities and resources.

2023. Dasmann, Raymond F. **Environmental conservation.** Wiley, 5th ed., 1984. 486 pp. Introductory

text covers the origins and nature of current environmental problems from economic, historical, sociological, and ecological perspectives; focuses on the United States.

2024. Nowak, Paul F.; and others, eds. **Environmental journalism: the best from the Meeman Archive.** University of Michigan, School of Natural Resources; Scripps Howard Foundation, 1987. 265 pp., ill. Collection of seven award winning newspaper feature stories on environmental topics.

2025. Machlis, Gary E.; ed. **Interpretive views.** National Parks and Conservation Association, 1986. 179 pp. Essays reflect on trends and philosophies of interpretation in the national parks. The perspectives of park management, universities, concessioners, and outsiders are represented.

2026. Journal of environmental education. Heldref, 1970 to date. Quarterly. Reports and research, viewpoints, and program descriptions intended to advance the field of environmental education.

2027. Woodhead, Peter; Stansfield, Geoffery. **Keyguide to information sources in museum studies.** Mansell, 1990. 194 pp., index. Reviews the history, development, and primary literature of museum studies, focusing on Europe and North America. The bibliography, international in scope, is arranged by type of material and includes annotations. Lists selected international and national museum organizations.

2028. Miller, G. Tyler. **Living in the environment.** Wadsworth, 5th ed., 1988. 603 pp., ill., bibl., index. Introductory textbook; begins with basic ecological concepts, then discusses population, resources, pollution, environment, and society.

2029. Nature study: a journal of environmental education and interpretation. American Nature Study Society, 1946 to date. Quarterly. Practical articles and information supporting nature study and environmental education.

2030. New trends in biology teaching. UNESCO, 1966 to date. Irregular.

2031. Our planet. United Nations Environment Programme, 1989 to date. Bimonthly. Popular magazine of the United Nations Environment Programme. Carries features and news of UNEP activities and some editorial comment.

2032. Link, Mike. **Outdoor education: a manual for teaching in nature's classroom.** Prentice-Hall, 1981. 198 pp., ill., bibl. Provides projects, techniques, and ideas. Topics include target audiences, goals and outcomes of environmental education, indoor and outdoor project descriptions, and planning and preparation of guidelines.

2033. Gastel, Barbara. **Presenting science to the public.** ISI Press, The professional writing series, 1983. 146 pp., ill., bibl., index. Discusses general principles, provides specific advice for using the mass media to convey information, then addresses other oral and print communications.

2034. Fazio, James R.; Gilbert, Douglas L. **Public relations and communications for natural resource managers.** Kendall/Hunt, 2d ed., 1986. 399 pp., ill., bibl., index. Textbook introduction to public relations. Discusses tools and communications techniques, including public speaking and the electronic media.

2035. Recent graduate works and programs in environmental education and communications. North American Association for Environmental Education, 1977 to date. Annual. Publishes abstracts of graduate master's and doctoral theses as well as other work and describes graduate programs in the United States. Organized by subject: urban and international environmental education; parks and camps; media communications; student-, teacher-, and citizen-centered studies; and administration and policy.

2036. Resources in education. Department of Education, Office of Educational Research and Development; Government Printing Office, 1964 to date. Monthly. Materials collected by the National Institute of Education, including government-sponsored research. Available as computer database, online or on CD-ROM, with companion file of *Current indext to journals in education.* Primary source of information on research and projects in environmental education.

2037. Science for children: resources for teachers. National Science Resources Center, 1988. 176 pp., ill., index. For teachers of kindergarten through eighth grade. Lists about 300 published lesson plan guides, activity guides, and instructional materials, giving format, grade level, supplier, and cost. Includes annotated lists of science activity books and books and magazines on science for both teachers and students. Directory of museums, professional associations, curriculum projects, and publishers.

2038. Roth, Charles E.; Lockwood, Linda G.; eds. **Strategies and activities for using local communities as environmental education sites.** Eric Clearinghouse on Teacher Education, Ohio State University, 1979. 207 pp., ill. Compilation of practical ideas for teachers and students to become environmentally literate activists.

2039. The video source book. Gale Research, 1979 to date. Irregular: 11th ed., 1989. Describes over 100,000 videotapes, including feature films and instructional films, providing details on age suitability, intended purpose, availability in foreign languages, and subject material.

2040. Sacks, Arthur B.; Burrus-Bammel, Lei Lane; Davis, Craig B.; and others, eds. **The yearbook of environmental education and environmental studies.** Eric Clearinghouse on Teacher Education, Ohio State University, 1980. 387 pp. First section describes a range of environmental programs and experiments. The second section presents research results on the following topics: energy and transportation; environmental action and citizen action; land use; environmental health; attitudes, values, and judgments; and assessing environmental education teachers and curricula.

Behavior and Psychology (2041–2057)

2041. Zube, Ervin H.; Moore, Gary T.; eds. **Advances in environment, behavior, and design.** Plenum Press, 1987 to date. Irregular: vol. 2, 1989. This series examines the relationship between sociophysical environment and human behavior. Articles on theory, place research, user group research, sociobehavioral research, environment-behavior-design methods, and professional applications.

2042. Altman, Irwin; Wohlwill, Joachim F.; eds. **Behavior and the natural environment: advances in theory and research.** Plenum Press, Human behavior and environment, v. 6, 1983. 346 pp., ill., bibl., index. Presents a range of theory and research on people's responses to natural environments.

2043. Wiegele, Thomas C.; ed. **Biology and the social sciences: an emerging revolution.** Westview Press, 1982. 383 pp., ill., bibl., index. Social scientists, biologists, and philosophers assess the implications of recent developments in behavioral biology.

2044. Altman, Irwin; Chemers, Martin. **Culture and environment.** Brooks/Cole, The Brooks/Cole basic concepts in environment and behavior series, 1980. 337 pp., ill., bibl., index. Examines human perceptual responses to the physical environment, behavioral processes in relation to the environment, and reflections of culture found in human-altered environments.

2045. Environment and behavior. Sage Publications, 1969 to date. Bimonthly. Interdisciplinary journal reporting experimental and theoretical work on the influences of physical environments on human behavior at the individual, institutional, and group levels. Publishes papers on the interrelationships of environments and behavioral systems; specific environments; values, beliefs, and meanings attached to environments; and ways of controlling behavior or environments.

2046. Kruse, Lenelis; Arlt, Reiner. **Environment and behavior: an international and multidisciplinary bibliography, 1970–1981.** Saur, 1984. Index. 2 vols. Vol. 1: Alphabetical listing by author and keyword index. Vol. 2: Abstracts.

2047. Kruse, Lenelis; Schwarz, Volker. **Environment and behavior: an international and multidisciplinary bibliography, 1982–1987. Part 2.** Saur, 1988. 2 vols. Titles, listed by author, with abstracts and keyword index. Disciplines represented include sociology, cultural anthropology, ethnology, social medicine, human geography, urban planning, and environmental education. Includes archival data, case and field studies, methodological and theoretical discussions, research reviews, and interviews.

2048. Kaplan, R.; Kaplan, S. **The experience of nature: a psychological perspective.** Cambridge University Press, 1989. 340 pp. Based on 20 years of research into the relationship between people and the natural environment, particularly the effect of nature on people and the preference for some natural settings over others. Part I deals with the preference for and perception of natural settings; Part II, with research on benefits and satisfactions, from wilderness to "nearby nature." Part III develops a synthesis on the "restorative environment." Four appendices summarize studies and procedures in the literature.

2049. Hiss, Tony. **The experience of place.** Knopf, 1990. 233 pp., ill., bibl., index. Discusses the nature of places—countryside, neighborhoods, or cities—and the influence of sunlight, shade, views, niches, resting places, and other factors in determining their character. Draws extensively on knowledge of New York City.

2050. Stokols, Daniel; Altman, Irwin; eds. **Handbook of environmental psychology.** Wiley, 1987. 2 vols. Primary reference to the literature of environmental psychology in its theoretical, empirical, and methodological dimensions.

2051. Man-environment systems. Association for the Study of Man-Environment Relations, 1969 to date. Bimonthly. Forum for communications (short articles) on research in the behavioral sciences as it relates to the design and management of the sociophysical environment.

2052. Bechtel, Robert B.; Marans, Robert W.; Michelson, William.; eds. **Methods in environmental and behavioral research.** Van Nostrand Reinhold, 1987. 415 pp.

2053. Wohlwill, Joachim F. **The physical environment and behavior: an annotated bibliography and guide to the literature.** Plenum Press, 1981. 474 pp., bibl., index. An anotated bibliography aimed at the researcher or advanced student of environmental psychology. Books, articles, book chapters, technical reports, and dissertations are arranged in four parts, each subdivided by chapters: general reference materials; psychological processes (environmental comprehension, stimulation and stress, and sociospatial processes); applied areas and special issues (behavior and natural environment, transportation and travel, housing, institutions, urban areas, and interiors); and related areas of environment and the social sciences.

2054. Levy-Leboyer, Claude; Canter, David, and Griffiths, Ian, trans. **Psychology and environment.** Sage Publications, 1982. 197 pp., bibl. Introduces the relatively new field of environmental psychology. Reviews theories, concepts, and methods. Covers recent research in three areas: the influence of the ordinary physical environment on people, how people understand their physical environment, and what they do to it.

2055. Ulrich, Roger S.; Hygge, Staffan; and others. **Research on environments and people: methods, quality assessment, new directions.** Swedish Council for Building Research, 1987. 148 pp., ill., bibl. Proceedings of a 1985 conference. Research in architecture, geography, medicine, sociology, and psychology organized into sections covering methods and approaches, evaluation of quality, and future needs. Includes a section on practical relevance.

2056. Pick, Herbert L.; Acredolo, Linda P.; eds. **Spatial orientation: theory, research, and application.** Plenum Press, 1983. 378 pp., ill., bibl., index. How do we find our way around? Analyzes this question from a variety of perspectives, including ethology (animal behavior), map reading, linguistics, information processing, and spatial cognition. Based on observations of naturally occurring behavior in the world and in controlled experiments.

2057. Kitcher, Philip. **Vaulting ambition: sociobiology and the quest for human nature.** MIT Press, 1985. 456 pp., bibl., index. Explains sociobiology and its connections to evolutionary theory. Offers a systematic critique of sociobiology's claims about human behavior, with four case studies.

Leisure and Recreation (2058–2076)

2058. Access America: an atlas and guide to the national parks for visitors with disabilities. Northern Cartographic, 1988. 444 pp., maps, ill. Covers 37 national parks. Provides information on weather, altitude, accessible and inaccessible features, and transportation. Includes essays by disabled visitors on their outdoor experiences. Lists nearby hospitals and medical services.

2059. Annals of tourism research. Pergamon Press, 1974 to date. Quarterly. Academic perspectives on tourism tending toward the development of "tourism social science." Articles, commentary, and research notes and reports.

2060. Fishing: an introduction to fishing for fun and food for blind and physically handicapped individuals. National Library Service for the Blind and Physically Handicapped, Library of Congress, 1988. 17 pp. Free booklet includes lists of recorded and braille books and magazines about fishing for children and adults.

2061. Journal of leisure research. National Recreation and Park Association, 1969 to date. Quarterly. Emphasizes original, empirical investigations of outdoor recreation and leisure.

2062. Leisure, recreation and tourism abstracts. Commonwealth Agricultural Bureaux, 1981 to date. Quarterly. Indexes and abstracts publications worldwide on all aspects of leisure, recreation, tourism, sports, and hospitality.

2063. Leisure sciences. Taylor & Francis, 1977 to date. Quarterly. Publishes research on leisure, recreation, and travel and their impacts.

2064. Leisure studies. Leisure Studies Association, 1982 to date. 3 issues/yr. Publishes papers on leisure behavior from social science and professional perspectives.

2065. President's Commission on Americans Outdoors. **A literature review.** Government Printing Office, 1986. Ill., bibl. One of three appendices to the Report of the President's Commission on Americans Outdoors. Essays evaluate such topics related to outdoor recreation as trends and demands, values and benefits, natural resource management, information and communication, financial aspects, special populations, urban recreation, tourism, motivation and barriers to participation, and participation trends.

2066. McMillon, Bill. **Nature nearby: an outdoor guide to 20 of America's cities.** Wiley, 1990. 288 pp., maps, ill., bibl. Covers 20 major cities. Describes and explains how to get to city zoos, parks, botanical gardens, and nearby game preserves and bird-watching sites. Includes directories to local nature and outdoor organizations.

2067. Kochanski, Mors. **Northern bushcraft.** Lone Pine, 2d ed., 1987. 303 pp., ill. Offers practical advice on surviving in the northern forests of Canada with few tools or materials.

2068. Jubenville, Alan; Twight, Ben W.; Becker, Robert H. **Outdoor recreation management: theory and application.** Venture, rev. ed., 1987. 219 pp. Presents an open systems model for recreation management. Focuses on process-oriented management of recreational resources, visitors, and services.

2069. Park practice program. National Recreation and Park Association, 1972 to date. Technical assistance for professionals in parks and recreation. Consists of three publications: 1. *Trends*. Quarterly. Topics of general interest. 2. *Grist*. Quarterly. Practical solutions to everyday problems. 3. *Design*. Quarterly. Quality plans for parks and recreation structures that make intelligent use of materials.

2070. Parks and recreation. National Recreation and Park Association, 1966 to date. Monthly. Illustrated short articles by and for professionals in leisure and recreation: parks, playgrounds, equipment, programs, techniques, and people.

2071. Hultsman, John; Cottrell, Richard L.; Hultsman, Wendy Zales. **Planning parks for people.** Venture, 1987. 310 pp., ill. Provides basic introduction to the practical aspects of planning, designing, and rehabilitating parks and recreation areas. Covers trails, play areas, the needs of special users, and other topics.

2072. Proceedings of the National Outdoor Recreation Trends Symposium II. Vol. 1: General sessions. Vol. 2: Concurrent sessions. U.S. Department of the Interior, National Park Service, 1985. Ill. 2 vols. Papers presented at 1985 symposium on trends in public and private sectors, social indicators, and business, economic, policy, and recreational activities and research related to outdoor education.

2073. Wasserman, Steven R.; ed. **Recreation and outdoor life directory: a guide to national and international organizations.** Gale Research, 2d ed., 1983. 1020 pp., index. A guide to national and international organizations; state, provincial, and territorial agencies; federal grant sources; foundations; consultants; special libraries and information centers; research centers; educational programs; journals and periodicals; speaker bureaus; awards and halls of fame; festivals; and federal, state, provincial, and territorial recreational facilities.

2074. Report of the President's Commission on

Americans Outdoors: the legacy, the challenge, with case studies. Island Press, 1987. 425 pp. Consensus report delivered in 1987 analyzes pressures on park and recreational facilities and examines patterns and trends of use. Includes full text of report, plus edited testimony and research presented to the Commission. Summarizes key issues and makes recommendations for federal, state, and citizen action. Twelve brief case studies illuminate innovative programs and solutions to protect outdoor resources.

2075. Vining, Joanne; ed. **Social science and natural resource recreation management.** Westview Press, 1990. 330 pp. Reflects on key themes of the field: ecology of behavior, social and cultural interactions, values, and social composition and institutional structure of recreational activity. Covers assessment of user experiences, preferences, and values; tourism and marketing; and interactions between agencies, local residents, and recreation seekers.

2076. Manning Robert E. **Studies in outdoor recreation: search and research for satisfaction.** Oregon State University Press, 1986. 166 pp., ill., bibl., index. A review and synthesis of the social science aspects of research-based literature in outdoor recreation. Covers the concept of carrying capacity as an organizational framework for management, the relationship between density and satisfaction, motivations for recreation, and management planning.

Section 9

Ethics. Literature. Arts

This section could have been quite large, given the considerable numbers of publications relating art, architecture, and literature to the natural world. But there already being guides to architecture, landscape architecture, environmental design, and nature writing, less was selected in those areas. More attention was given instead to studies of environmental ethics and philosophy, an area of knowledge that has attracted considerable interest during the past decade.

Ethics. Philosophy. Religion

Topics covered in this group are morality, ethical choices and systems, philosophy of science and technology, environment and religion, rights of nature, and traditions of thought on the natural world.

See also:

- Section 1: Global resources and environment
- Section 8: Society and environment; individuals and environment; behavior and psychology
- Section 10: Law, politics, government
- Section 11: Economy, costs and benefits, valuation; development
- Section 13: Engineering, technology

Nature Writing and Thought. Arts

The literary record of American naturalists and nature writers is quite large. Only a few titles from that literature have been included here, however, because a listing of important works, together with critical comments, is available in a recent anthology (2145). Other titles in this group relate to ideas of wilderness, wilderness values, aesthetics of landscape, nature photography and illustration, and myth.

See also:

- Section 1: Biological systems; ecology
- Section 8: Society and environment; social and human ecology, population; human evolution, history; individuals and environment; behavior and psychology; education and communication
- Section 14: Reference books, journals; guides: writing and illustration

Built Environment. Architecture. Historical Preservation
This group includes works dealing with protection of the built environment, design of solar buildings, historic landscapes, visual elements of landscape, and related topics.

See also:

- Section 2: Weather and life, biometeorology
- Section 4: Landscape ecology; land: terrestrial ecosystems
- Section 8: Social and human ecology, population; urban communities; individuals and environment; behavior and psychology
- Section 11: Economy, costs and benefits, valuation; development
- Section 13: Civil engineering, construction, geotechnology

Ethics. Philosophy. Religion (2077–2116)

2077. Clark, Mary E. **Ariadne's thread: the search for new modes of thinking.** Macmillan, 1989. 584 pp., ill., index. Provocative thinking from a biologist about the economy, human nature, ecology, religion, and other subjects. Points to institutions and ways of living that will save humanity from nuclear war and environmental disaster.

2078. Hargrove, Eugene C.; ed. **Beyond spaceship earth: environmental ethics and the solar system.** Sierra Club Books, 1986. 336 pp., ill., bibl., index. Collection of essays from different perspectives on the moral implications of space exploration and use of space resources.

2079. Tobias, Michael; ed. **Deep ecology.** Avant Books, 1988. 296 pp., ill., bibl. Collection of essays, fiction, poetry, and memoirs offering a humanistic approach to the study of ecological values.

2080. Devall, Bill; Sessions, George. **Deep ecology: living as if nature mattered.** Peregrine Smith, 1985. 267 pp., bibl. Examines philosophical and psychological background of modern environmentalism, revealing an anthropocentric view of nature.

2081. Stone, Christopher D. **Earth and other ethics: the case for moral pluralism.** Harper & Row, 1987. 280 pp., bibl., index. The author of *Should trees have standing?* argues that there may not be one unified ethics applicable to all human experience, but rather that moral acts are partitioned into different ethical frameworks.

2082. Oates, David. **Earth rising: ecological belief in an age of science.** Oregon State University Press, 1989. 255 pp., bibl., index. Describes an ecological world view. Discusses holism, balance, cooperation, cybernetics, and the natural mind. Examines ecological ethics and recent trends in its thought, including ecofeminism and deep ecology.

2083. McCloskey, H. J. **Ecological ethics and politics.** Rowman & Littlefield, 1983. 167 pp., bibl., index. Rejects the idea of intrinsic rights for nature. Argues for an ecological ethics based on obligations and human rights. Addresses practical concerns of preservation and conservation in the context of personal freedom.

2084. Mathews, Freya. **The ecological self.** Barnes & Noble Books, 1991. 200 pp. Develops a new metaphysics of interconnectedness, drawing upon modern physics, Einstein's cosmology, Gregory Bateson's systems theory, and Spinoza. Elaborates on the implications for our conceptions of nature and self.

2085. Sagoff, Mark. **The economy of the earth: philosophy, law, and the environment.** Cambridge University Press, Cambridge studies in philosophy and public policy, 1988. 271 pp., bibl., index. On social regulation and the limitations of economics in the formation of public policies. Bases concept of regulation on shared social and cultural values.

2086. Kohák, Erazim V. **The embers and the stars: a philosophical inquiry into the moral sense of nature.** University of Chicago Press, 1984. 269 pp., ill., bibl., index. Meditations of an academic philosopher grounded in his experiences as a farmer-builder-woodsman on a New Hampshire homestead. The moral sense of nature is that it teaches us to cherish time.

2087. Rifkin, Jeremy; Howard, Ted. **Entropy: a new world view.** Viking Press, 1980. 305 pp., bibl., index. Rifkin formulates a world view based on the second law of thermodynamics, arguing that our present, order-seeking mechanistic world view has only accelerated entropy, especially with respect to agricultural and transportation practices.

2088. Dwivedi, O. P.; Tiwari, B. N. **Environmental crisis and Hindu religion.** Gitanjali, 1987. 202 pp., ill., bibl., index. In-depth interpretation of the Hindu view of the environment. Extensive citation of scriptures demonstrating humans' relationship to the environment.

2089. **Environmental ethics.** John Muir Institute for Environmental Studies, 1979 to date. Quarterly. Intended as a forum for diverse interests, particularly the bringing together of nonprofessional and professional writings on environmental philosophy.

2090. Science Action Coalition; Fritsch, Albert, ed. **Environmental ethics: choices for concerned citizens.** Anchor Press, 1980. 309 pp., bibl., index. Defines the ecological crisis in terms of human failures: greed, waste, shortsightedness, and exaggerated freedom of choice. Discusses theological foundations of environmental ethics and the need to transform reflection into action.

2091. Rolston, Holmes, III. **Environmental ethics: duties to and values in the natural world.** Temple University Press, Ethics and Action, 1988. 391 pp., ill., bibl., index. Examines duties to sentient animals, organisms, species, and ecosystems. Develops a theory of environmental ethics and its applications.

2092. Gunn, Alastair S.; Vesilind, P. Aarne; eds. **Environmental ethics for engineers.** Lewis, 1986. 153 pp. Backgound and fundamental concepts of ethics; excerpts from works on environmental ethics; case studies of environmental tragedies.

2093. Elliot, Robert; Gare, Arran; eds. **Environmental philosophy: a collection of readings.** University of Queensland Press, 1983. 303 pp., ill., bibl. Essays deal with moral consideration of three groups: future generations, nonhuman animals, and nonsentient nature.

2094. Scherer, Donald; Attig, Thomas; eds. **Ethics and the environment.** Prentice-Hall, 1983. 236 pp., bibl. Twenty essays in two parts: Part 1 essays attempt to define the nature of an environmental ethics and examine specific problems in relation to it. Part 2 essays are organized around three topics: land use and property rights; cost-benefit analyses; and individual and collective values in decision making.

2095. Attfield, Robin. **The ethics of environmental concern.** Basil Blackwell, 1983. 220 pp., bibl., index. Reviews moral traditions and principles, mainly of the Judeo-Christian tradition, in the light of ecology. Argues for the concept of stewardship as an appropriate ethical choice.

2096. Singer, Peter. **The expanding circle: ethics and sociobiology.** Farrar, Straus & Giroux, 1981. 190 pp., bibl., index. A sociobiological approach to ethics, based on reason. Seeks to extend moral conduct toward animals and the environment beyond religion and altruism.

2097. Cahn, R. **Footprints on the planet: a search for an environmental ethic.** Universe Books, 1978. 277 pp., bibl., index. Anecdotal account traces the development of an environmental ethics in the United States, from the centers of power (the presidencies of Teddy Roosevelt and Jimmy Carter and the modus operandi of corporate America) to the peripheries (small-scale efforts to create viable alternative lifestyles). Features interviews with presidents of Weyerhaeuser and General Motors, among others.

2098. O'Hear, Anthony. **Introduction to the philosophy of science.** Oxford University Press, 1989. 239 pp., bibl., index. Overview of major topics in contemporary philosophy of science. Focuses on science as intellectual activity, observation and theory, scientific real-ism, probability, scientific reduction, and science and culture.

2099. Margenau, Henry. **The miracle of existence.** Ox Bow Press, 1984. 143 pp., bibl., index. Physics and philosophy professor addresses the mind-body problem and suggests the notion of a universal mind. Introduction has helpful review of several mind-body theories.

2100. Evernden, Lorne Leslie Neil. **The natural alien: humankind and the environment.** University of Toronto Press, 1985. 160 pp., bibl., index. Provocative essay on the nature of environmental thought that probes deeply into concepts of self, being, and other.

2101. Byrne, Peter. **Natural religion and the nature of religion: the legacy of deism.** Routledge, Routledge religious studies, 1989. 271 pp., bibl., index. Traces deism from the eighteenth century, romantic and idealistic reactions to it, and the beginnings of the scientific study of religion.

2102. Callicott, J. B; Ames, Roger T.; eds. **Nature in Asian traditions of thought: essays in environmental philosophy.** State University of New York Press, SUNY series in philosophy and biology, 1989. 335 pp. Scholars in Chinese, Japanese, Indian, and Buddhist thought explore Asian concepts of nature and their use as a conceptual resource in environmental philosophy.

2103. Ash, Maurice. **New renaissance: essays in search of wholeness.** Green Books, 1987. 196 pp. Argues that a dualistic mind-set lies behind our environmental problems. Discusses the roles of language, the division of self and world, and idealism in philosophy. Challenges the doctrines of rational humanism, socialism, capitalism, and the nation-state; also those of ecology, environmentalism, and progressive education and politics.

2104. Prigogine, Ilya; Stengers, Isabelle. **Order out of chaos: man's new dialogue with nature.** Bantam Books, 1984. 349 pp., ill., index. Translation and revision of La nouvelle alliance (1979). Reviews and critiques scientific thought, starting with Newton; explains theories of nonequilibrium thermodynamics, dissipative structures, and self-organizing systems and their relevance to our views of nature.

2105. Rolston, Holmes, III. **Philosophy gone wild; essays in environmental ethics.** Prometheus Books, 1986. 269 pp., ill., bibl., index. Collection of 15 previously published essays on environmental ethics and values.

2106. Berman, Morris. **The reenchantment of the world.** Cornell University Press, 1981. 357 pp., ill., bibl., index. Explores metaphysical presuppositions of the modern era since the 1600s, focusing on the split between fact and value, mind and body, subject and object.

2107. Hargrove, Eugene C.; ed. **Religion and environmental crisis.** University of Georgia Press, 1986. 222 pp. A collection of papers reflecting diverse current thinking about religion and the environment. Protestant Christianity (most papers), Roman Catholicism, Judaism, Islam, Taoism, Native American perspective, and pre-Christian Greek polytheism are all represented.

2108. Taylor, Paul W. **Respect for nature: a theory of environmental ethics.** Princeton University Press, Studies in moral, political and legal philosophy, 1986. 329 pp., bibl., index. Develops a biocentric, as opposed to anthropocentric, theory of environmental ethics, arguing that humans have moral obligations to wild living things.

2109. Kealey, Daniel A. **Revisioning environmental ethics.** State University of New York Press, 1990. 136 pp., bibl., index. Argues that Western mental-rational consciousness is the cause of many current environmental problems and cannot be used in solving them. Explains a different relationship with nature, working toward "integral consciousness" to resolve problems and define a new ethic.

2110. Nash, Roderick Frazier. **The rights of nature: a history of environmental ethics.** University of Wisconsin Press, History of American thought and culture, 1989. 290 pp., bibl., index. Primarily an intellectual history that puts current thinking about environmental ethics in the context of Western philosophy and religion.

2111. Leopold, Aldo. **The river of the mother of god and other essays.** University of Wisconsin Press, 1991. 400 pp., ill., bibl., index. A collection of published and unpublished articles and essays from 1904 to 1947, arranged chronologically; introductions explain circumstances and intended audience for each.

2112. Jantsch, Erich. **The self-organizing universe: scientific and human implications of the emerging paradigm of evolution.** Pergamon Press, 1980. 343 pp., ill., bibl., index. Nontechnical synthesis of scientific concepts develops idea of self-organization as a paradigm for viewing cosmic, biological, and sociocultural evolution.

2113. Shi, David E. **The simple life: plain living and high thinking in American culture.** Oxford University Press, Galaxy book, no. GB 813, 1985. 332 pp., bibl., index. Traces the many ways Americans have pursued the ideal of plain living and high thinking, from the

Puritans and Quakers to Thoreau and modern back-to-the-land philosophies.

2114. Skolimowski, Henryk. **The theatre of the mind: evolution in the sensitive cosmos.** Theosophical Publishing House, 1984. 167 pp. Argues against the one-sided, scientific world wiew of the past several centuries and for intuition, spiritual and mystical experiences, and awareness.

2115. Brennan, Andrew. **Thinking about nature: an investigation of nature, value, and ecology.** University of Georgia Press, 1988. 235 pp., ill., bibl., index. Examines human-centered ethical theory, developments in ecology, and the possibilities of ecohumanism.

2116. Norton, Bryan G. **Why preserve natural variety?** Princeton University Press, Studies in moral, political and legal philosophy, 1987. 281 pp. Philosopher examines arguments and justifications for biological diversity.

Nature Writing and Thought. Arts (2117–2149)

2117. Bourassa, Steven C. **The aesthetics of landscape.** Belhaven Press, 1991. 168 pp., ill., index, bibl. Discussion of general theoretical issues in landscape aesthetics—biological, cultural, and personal. The author contends that the field suffers from lack of theoretical concepts and presents his own aesthetic of engagement.

2118. Jackson, Wes. **Altars of unhewn stone: science and the earth.** North Point Press, 1987. 158 pp., bibl. Eighteen provocative essays by the founder of The Land Institute, an organization that is developing no-till, no-erosion agriculture based on perennial plants. Thoughtful and passionate warnings about the wrongs of contemporary agriculture, especially the loss of species and loss of farmers.

2119. Alinder, Mary Street; Stillman, Andrea Gray; eds. **Ansel Adams: letters and images, 1916–1984.** New York Graphic Society; Little, Brown, 1988. 401 pp., ill., bibl., index. Artistic growth of the noted environmental photographer shown in letters and photos.

2120. Lopez, Barry Holstun. **Arctic dreams: imagination and desire in a northern landscape.** Scribner, 1986. 464 pp., ill., bibl., index. Land, sea, animals, and humans above the Arctic Circle by prize-winning nature writer.

2121. Beebe, William; ed. **The book of naturalists: an anthology of the best natural history.** Princeton University Press, 1988. 499 pp., ill., bibl.

2122. Elbers, Hoan S.; compiler. **Changing wilder-**

ness values, 1930–1990: an annotated bibliography. Greenwood Press, Bibiographies and indexes in American history, v. 18, 1991. 138 pp., index. Surveys the development and diversity of wilderness values found in poetry, fiction, nature writing, history, and scientific writing. Notes content, themes, and key passages for each entry.

2123. Callicott, J. Baird; ed. **Companion to a Sand County almanac: interpretive and critical essays.** University of Wisconsin Press, 1987. 308 pp., ill., bibl., index. The first serious analysis of one of the most influential texts of the environmental movement.

2124. Nasar, Jack L.; ed. **Environmental aesthetics: theory, research and applications.** Cambridge University Press, 1988. 529 pp., ill., bibl., index. Based on a 1983 conference. Papers combine empirical studies of aesthetics and environmental psychology in the search for suitable theories and practical applications.

2125. Terrie, Philip G. **Forever wild: environmental aesthetics and the Adirondack Forest Preserve.** Temple University Press, 1985. 209 pp., ill., bibl., index. Reviews the development of wilderness attitudes and legislation and the role of Adirondack Park in fostering the idea of wilderness preservation.

2126. Pittman, Nancy P.; ed. **From the Land: articles compiled from The Land, 1941–1954.** Island Press, 1988. 478 pp., ill., index. Anthology of writings from *The land*, 1940–1954, founded by Friends of the Land. Essays, fiction, poetry, illustrations and anecdotes by scientists, authors, farmers, artists, and philosophers. Contributors included Gifford Pinchot, Aldo Leopold, Louis Bromfield, E. B. White, Wallace Stegner, and Paul Sears.

2127. Berry, Wendell. **The gift of good land: further essays, cultural and agricultural.** North Point Press, 1981. 281 pp. Exposes through examples the destructive results of agribusiness, modern agricultural techniques, and government aid. Calls for a rethinking of modern notions of progress, development, and success and a return to thrift, subsistence, and the land.

2128. Rue, Leonard Lee, III. **How I photograph wildlife and nature.** Norton, 1984. 287 pp., ill., index. Discusses when and where to find wildlife subjects; appropriate camera and film equipment; use of blinds; what clothing to wear; and when not to disturb animals. Provides species identification information and lists of services and equipment.

2129. Cosgrove, Denis; Daniels, Stephen; eds. **The iconography of landscape: essays on the symbolic representation, design, and use of past environments.**

Cambridge University Press, Cambridge studies in historical geography, v. 9, 1988. 318 pp., ill., bibl., index. Papers of a 1984 conference discuss landscape as image and symbol through history.

2130. Oelschlaeger, Max. **The idea of wilderness from prehistory to the present.** Yale University Press, 488 pp. Argues that the idea of wilderness evolved in conjunction with the transition from hunting and gathering to agriculture and the development of Hellenism and Judeo-Christianity; discusses the rise of classic science and modernism and resulting backlashes to them in the fields of science, philosophy, and literature.

2131. Clewis, Beth. **Index to illustrations of animals and plants.** Neal Schuman, 1991. 220 pp., bibl., index. Six thousand entries cover species from around the world, listed by common and scientific names. Referenced from 140 books, most published in the 1980s.

2132. Munz, Lucile Thompson; Slauson, Nedra G. **Index to illustrations of living things outside North America: where to find pictures of flora and fauna.** Archon Books (dist. by Shoe String Press), 1981. 441 pp., bibl., index. Indexes photographs, paintings, and sketches of over 9000 species in 206 reputable books. Listed by common name, indexed by scientific name; each entry has at least two citations.

2133. Penning-Rowsell, Edmund C.; Lowenthal, David; eds. **Landscape meanings and values.** Allen & Unwin, 1986. 137 pp., ill., bibl., index. Report of a 1989 symposium organized by the Landscape Research Group. Presents papers and discussion on concepts, values, and use of landscapes.

2134. Francis, Mark; Hester, Randolph T., Jr.; eds. **The meaning of gardens: idea, place, and action.** MIT Press, 1990. 283 pp., ill., bibl., index. Contributed essays from garden designers and writers examine the social and philosophical importance of gardens. Organized around the themes of faith, power, ordering, cultural expression, personal expression, and healing.

2135. Jackson, W.; Berry, W.; Colman, B.; eds. **Meeting the expectations of the land: essays in sustainable agriculture and stewardship.** North Point Press, 1984. 250 pp., ill., bibl. Seventeen contributors address the difficulties of making agriculture more ecologically sound. Essays examine soil fertility, energy use, industrial farming, gardening, and other topics.

2136. Rowell, Galen A. **Mountain light: in search of the dynamic landscape.** Sierra Club Books; Yolla Bolly Press, 1986. 224 pp., ill., index. Reproductions of 80 mountain photographs and technical descriptions of how they came to be. Eight sections depict various aspects of light, time of day, figures in the landscape, and other topics. Includes essays on the author's techniques and vision.

2137. Worster, Donald. **Nature's economy: a history of ecological ideas.** Cambridge University Press, Studies in environment and history, c. 1977, 1985. 404 pp., bibl., index. This unique and indispensable history of ecology organizes discussion into five significant periods: ecology in the eighteenth century (Gilbert White and Linnaeus); Thoreau's romantic ecology; Darwinian ecology; ecology on the frontier (Frederick Clements); and the morals of a science (Leopold, Pinchot, the Chicago School, and others).

2138. Jackson, John Brinckerhoff. **The necessity for ruins and other topics.** University of Massachusetts Press, 1980. 129 pp., bibl. In ten essays, geographer and founder of *Landscape* magazine reflects on gardens, the evolution of the street, landscape as theater, historic monuments, and other components of landscape studies.

2139. Orion nature quarterly. Myrin Institute; Conservation International, 1982 to date. Quarterly. Articles, commentary, and photoessays intended to foster humane stewardship, responsiblities toward the earth, and personal connection with the natural world.

2140. Bridson, Gavin D. R.; White, James J. **Plant, animal and anatomical illustration in art and science: a bibliographical guide from the 16th century to the present day.** Saint Paul's Bibliographies; Hunt Institute for Botanical Documentation; Omnigraphics, 1990. 450 pp., ill., index. Lists bibliographies; texts on nature in general, plants, animals, and the human body; artists' biographies; and periodicals. Chapters themselves are divided into drawing and painting, history, and photography. Entries often include a brief annotation and are indexed by title, name, and subject.

2141. Shephard, Paul; Sanders, Barry. **The sacred paw: the bear in nature, myth and literature.** Viking Press, 1985. 243 pp., ill., bibl., index. Discusses the role of the bear in myth, ritual and literature of prehistoric and historical societies.

2142. Leopold, Aldo. **A Sand County almanac and sketches here and there.** Oxford University Press, 1968. 226 pp. Aldo Leopold's celebrated essays, published after his death. In three sections: The first traces the landscape of Sand County, Wisconsin, during the course of a year. The second covers travels through the United States and Canada. The concluding section is a philosophical discussion of wildlife conservation and the need to respect the land, including his most famous essay, "The Land Ethic."

2143. Brooks, Paul. **Speaking for nature: how literary naturalists from Henry Thoreau to Rachel Carson have shaped America.** Houghton Mifflin, 1980. 304 pp., ill., bibl., index. Introduction to the works and lives of some American nature writers. Rescues lesser-known authors from obscurity, including Clarence King, Gene Stratton Porter, and Sidney Lanier.

2144. Waage, Frederick O.; ed. **Teaching environmental literature: materials, methods, resources.** Modern Language Association of America, 1985. 191 pp.

2145. Lyon, Thomas J.; ed. **This incomperable lande: a book of American nature writing.** Houghton Mifflin, 1989. 495 pp., bibl. In three parts: a history of nature writing; an anthology (300 pages); and a bibliography of primary materials and secondary studies. Limited to essays in natural history and experiences in nature, or what the author considers nonfictional.

2146. Muir, John; Engberg, Robert; Wesling, Donald; eds. **To Yosemite and beyond: writings from the years 1863 to 1875.** University of Wisconsin Press, 1980. 171 pp., ill., bibl., index. Begins where Muir left off in his own published autobiographies. Contains letters, journal entries, and articles. Includes writings of people who met him during his years in Yosemite Valley.

2147. Gidley, Mick; Lawson-Peebles, Robert; eds. **Views of American landscapes.** Cambridge University Press, 1989. 227 pp., ill., bibl., index. Contributed essays examine the representation of the American landscape, and hence the meaning of America, in British and American writing, painting, and photography from the American Revolution to 1900. Wilderness, once represented in words or images, is included in the definition of landscape.

2148. Savage, Victor R. **Western impressions of nature and landscape in Southeast Asia.** Singapore University Press, 1984. 456 pp., maps, ill., bibl., index. Surveys European perceptions and writings about Southeast Asia. Identifies sociocultural factors affecting those attitudes and discusses how those attitudes influenced the colonizing process.

2149. Kazin, Alfred. **A writer's America: landscape in literature.** Knopf, 1988. 256 pp., ill., bibl., index. Illustrated book documents the literary phenomenon of wilderness in American literature.

Built Environment. Architecture. Historical Preservation (2150–2169)

2150. Rosvall, Jan; Aleby, Stig; eds. **Air pollution and conservation: safeguarding our architectural her-**

itage. Elsevier, 1988. 427 pp. Proceedings of a 1986 symposium. Papers on the processes and mechanics of building material deterioration; historical trends; and recent conservation and prevention programs involving stone, marble, and ceramics decay.

2151. Lamme, Ary J., III. **America's historic landscapes: community power and the preservation of four national historic sites.** University of Tennessee Press, 1989. 213 pp., ill., bibl. Reviews the literature on landscape-related issues and community power in landscape management. Analyzes community preservation with case studies of St. Augustine, Florida; Colonial National Historic Park, Virginia; Sackets Harbor, New York; and Gettysburg, Pennsylvania.

2152. Ehresmann, Donald L. **Architecture: a bibliographic guide to basic reference works, histories, and handbooks.** Libraries Unlimited, 1984. 338 pp., index. Includes works published in English and western European languages between 1875 and 1980. Organized chronologically and culturally. Landscape architecture and history of gardening are treated together.

2153. Powell, Antoinette Paris. **Bibliography of landscape architecture, environmental design, and planning.** Oryx Press, 1987. 312 pp., index. Includes government documents, dissertations, and journals. Focuses on works with no specific geographic orientation. Includes subject thesaurus and author-title indexes.

2154. Khalili, Nader. **Ceramic houses: how to build your own.** Harper & Row, 1986. 221 pp., ill., bibl., index. Visionary handbook on using earth as building material. Discusses background, materials, and techniques.

2155. Stilgoe, John R. **Common landscape of America: 1580–1845.** Yale University Press, 1982. 429 pp., ill., bibl., index. Investigates the man-made environment in America, using examples of design and construction drawn from cities, towns, farms, transportation, and industries to "delineate the important patterns of common building." Argues that builders, not professional designers, had the most influence because they copied each other and improved upon spaces and structures.

2156. Conservation of historic stone buildings and monuments. National Academy Press, 1982. 365 pp., ill., bibl., index. Proceedings of a 1981 conference. Papers provide a broad introduction to historical preservation and related scientific and engineering disciplines.

2157. Jackson, John B. **Discovering the vernacular landscape.** Yale University Press, 1984. 165 pp., ill., bibl., index. Lectures given to architects and planners on perceiving and understanding landscapes, by the editor of *Landscape* magazine.

2158. Wilkes, Joseph A.; Packard, Robert T.; eds. **Encyclopedia of architecture: design, engineering & construction.** Wiley, 1988–1990. Ill., bibl. 5 vols. Entries address design, laws and regulations, technology, building types and styles, and construction components. Three thousand illustrations, and over 100 biographies of noted professionals.

2159. Butti, Ken; Perlin, John. **A golden thread: 2500 years of solar architecture and technology.** Cheshire Books, 1980. 289 pp., ill., bibl., index. Surveys architecture of the ancient world. Traces mainly European and American development of solar water and house heating and solar motors and engines. Examines future opportunities for solar technology use.

2160. Historic preservation. National Trust for Historic Preservation, 1949 to date. Quarterly. Supports the Trust's mission of encouraging preservation of America's historical and cultural heritage through advocacy, education, technical assistance, and demonstration programs.

2161. Marcus, Clare Cooper; Sarkissian, Wendy. **Housing as if people mattered: site design guidelines for medium-density family housing.** University of California Press, California series in urban development, 1986. 324 pp., ill., bibl., index. Guidelines based on a study of postoccupancy evaluations cover such topics as access to dwellings, private and common open spaces; the needs of children and teenagers; on-site facilities for adults; and landscaping and security.

2162. National Trust for Historic Preservation Library, University of Maryland College Park. **Index to historic preservation periodicals.** Hall, 1988. 354 pp. Some 5000 periodical articles, from 1979 to 1987, on all aspects of historical preservation, mostly without annotations. Arranged alphabetically by subject.

2163. Nabokov, Peter; Easton, Robert. **Native American architecture.** Oxford University Press, 1980. 431 pp., maps, ill., bibl., index. Describes and illustrates architectural structures of nine cultural areas and discusses them in relation to technology, climate, economics, social organization, religion, and history. Based largely on nineteenth- and twentieth-century ethnographic information.

2164. Fathy, Hassan. **Natural energy and vernacular architecture: principles and examples with reference to hot arid climates.** University of Chicago Press; United Nations University, 1986. 172 pp., ill., bibl., index. Master architect demonstrates effectiveness of indigenous architectural form in hot arid climates. Extensive illustrations.

2165. Hough, Michael. **Out of place: restoring identity to the regional landscape.** Yale University Press, 1990. 230 pp., ill., bibl., index. The author is an architect and planner concerned with reestablishing the identity and uniqueness of regional landscapes. The book builds on the premise that the underlying native landscape is the key to regional identity. Has chapters on natural, cultural, utopian, urban, industrial, and tourist landscapes. Concludes by showing how design can create "healthy and clearly identifiable contemporary environments." There are photographs and drawings on every page.

2166. Atkinson, Steven D. **Solar home planning: a bibliography and a guide.** Scarecrow Press, 1988. 343 pp., index. Provides references for directories, articles, monographs, bibliographies, databases, indexes, abstracts, information and research centers, periodicals, software, and film and video material from 1975 to 1986. Topics include architecture, design, legislation, technologies, and education.

2167. Higuchi, Tadahiko; Terry, Charles S., trans. **The visual and spatial structure of landscapes.** MIT Press, 1983. 218 pp., ill., bibl., index. Seeks to under-stand the appearance of any given scene from any chosen observation point. Addresses issues of visual perception of planes, spaces, and space-position relationships. Explains the significance of seven classic types of Japanese landscape and describes their spatial elements and the structures they compose.

2168. Jakle, John A. **The visual elements of landscape.** University of Massachusetts Press, 1987. 200 pp., ill., bibl., index. Historical geographer elaborates on the idea of landscape as visual display, to get beyond the usual preoccupation with form and function, and asks what attracts the eye and what people tend to see. There are chapters on visual composition, character in landscape, cognitive mapping, and prospect and refuge.

2169. Sheppard, Stephen Richard John. **Visual simulation: a user's guide for architects, engineers, and planners.** Van Nostrand Reinhold, 1989. 215 pp., ill., bibl., index. Explains the roles, problems, principles, and effective use of simulation in project planning and review. Wide range of case studies, including a power plant, hospital facilities, and a mixed-use high rise, illustrate simulation in practice. Appendices cover technical aspects of some specific procedures, simulation costs, and a model ordinance and guidelines.

Section 10

Law. Politics. Government

Environmental law is well served with books, periodicals, and information sources prepared for the practicing attorney, legal department, or legal scholar. Consequently, the environmental-legal titles in this bibliography were selected knowing that many comprehensive sources of coverage exist. Note particularly the two encyclopedias opening the section (2170, 2171); the *International Environment Reporter* (2234); *Environment Reporter* (2269); and the *Environmental Law Reporter* (2276).

Entries on politics, policy, and government are scattered throughout the bibliography. In this section, they refer more precisely to political and government processes and actions than do "policy and government" entries in other sections. Also, in this section, regulation by executive agencies of the United States government is emphasized.

The arrangement of the section proceeds from larger political-legal entities to smaller ones: from international and regional to national, state and provincial, and local.

International Law and Policies

Global climate change, transfrontier pollution, protection of marine mammals, and ozone depletion are just a few of the environmental problems currently affecting international law. In this group are negotiations and treaties to deal with these problems and also works on international agencies and cooperation, biosphere politics, Antarctica, multilateral diplomacy, and warfare.

See also:

- Section 1: Global resources and environment; environmental management
- Section 2: Climate change
- Section 4: Land: countries and regions
- Section 8: Society and environment: country studies

Law of the Sea. The most active area of international environmental law is represented in this group, with works on treaties, fisheries, and pollution.

See also:

- Section 1: Global resources and environment
- Section 2: Climate change
- Section 3: Fisheries; marine pollution

National Laws and Policies

Environmental politics and policies and government actions of individual countries are in this group. Included are works on Green politics, natural resource conflicts, administration and bureaucracy, and laws affecting air, water, forests, land regulation, and toxics.

See also:

- Section 1: Global resources and environment; environmental management
- Section 4: Land: countries and regions
- Section 8: Society and environment: country studies

U.S. Politics and Policies

Legal-political surveys of the American environmental situation are presented in this group. Note that works here are broader in scope than those in the groups following, which focus on particular legislation, disputes, and government agencies.

See also:

- Section 2: Air pollution, atmospheric chemistry; acid rain; ozone; climate change
- Section 3: Freshwater; water pollution
- Section 4: Lands, reserves and parks, management
- Section 5: Food and agriculture; atmospheric environment, pollution, pesticides
- Section 6: Forests and forest resources: regions and countries; forest management, silviculture
- Section 7: Wildlife management; animal rights, protection; endangered species, conservation biology
- Section 8: Society and environment: United States
- Section 9: Ethics, philosophy, religion
- Section 11: Economy, costs and benefits, valuation; industry, economic sectors; pollution, industrial wastes; energy
- Section 12: Public health, medicine; toxic threats, hazards; risk assessment; health protection, safety, emergencies
- Section 13: Environmental control technology; biotechnology; energy technology; solid waste, recycling; hazardous wastes; air pollution control; water pollution control, wastewater

U.S. Laws and Legislation. Courts. Disputes

Mediation and dispute and conflict resolution are in this group, along with commentary and analysis of laws and legal reporting services. Note particularly the loose-leaf reporting services, such as the *Environment Reporter* (2269) and *Environmental Law Reporter* (2276), and *CIS Index* (2267). The latter publication provides complete access to bills, laws, committee reports, and hearings of the United States Congress from 1789 to the present. These congressional documents record environmental issues in detail and are widely available through the government's depository library program.

See also U.S. Executive Agencies, Administration and Regulation, below.

U.S. Executive Agencies. Administration and Regulation

Several entries in this group are directories of or guides to agencies of the United States government, beginning with the *United States Government Manual* (2303). Special mention must also be made of the *Monthly Catalog of United States Government Publications* (2296). The published products of government activities, research, and development are prime sources of environmental information. Many thousands of titles are disseminated annually to libraries around the country through the documents depository system. In most of those libraries, laser disk versions of the *Monthly Catalog* are available to provide rapid access to this government information.

Every environmental problem or issue or aspect of resource management is represented in U.S. government documents. In the field of atmospheric sciences, for example, there are publications of the National Oceanic and Atmospheric Administration; in forestry, of the Forest Service experiment stations; in wildlife management, of the Fish and Wildlife Service; and in pollution, of the Environmental Protection Agency.

Other entries in this group refer to the process of regulation, alternative systems of regulation, individual agencies, administration of particular laws, statistics, and published rules and regulations.

See also the remaining groups and subgroups in this section.

Natural Resources: United States. Selections in this subgroup refer to policies and administration affecting the public lands and to soil and water conservation.

See also:

- Section 3: Freshwater
- Section 4: Lands, reserves and parks, management; soils: land degradation, erosion, reclamation
- Section 5: Range management, pastoral systems
- Section 8: Tribal communities; rural communities

Forests, Parks, Wilderness: United States. Titles in this subgroup refer to administration of national forests, national parks, and related categories of United States public lands, such as the Appalachian Trail.

See also:

- Section 4: Lands, reserves and parks, management
- Section 6: Forests and forest resources: regions and countries; forest management, silviculture
- Section 7: Wildlife management; endangered species, conservation biology
- Section 8: Tribal communities; rural communties; leisure and recreation
- Section 11: Economy, costs and benefits, valuation; natural resource industries; agriculture and forest products

Water, Wildlife, Minerals: United States. Entries in this subgroup refer to water, wildlife, and mining uses of United States public lands, such as water rights, endangered species and other wildlife management, wetlands, and oil and gas.

See also:

- Section 1: Geology, earth sciences; energy
- Section 3: Freshwater; marine
- Section 4: Lands, reserves and parks, management; landscape ecology; land: terrestrial ecosystems
- Section 7: Wildlife management; endangered species, conservation biology
- Section 11: Natural resource industries; energy
- Section 13: Energy technology

Pollution Control: United States. This subgroup contains publications on regulation of air and water pollution; chemicals, pesticides, fungicides, and insectides; operations of the Environmental Protection Agency; workings of pollution control laws; principles of protection in regulation and federal law; policy formation; and compensation for injury.

See also:

- Section 1: Chemistry, biogeochemical cycles, pollutants
- Section 2: Air pollution, atmospheric chemistry; ozone; acid rain; climate change
- Section 3: Water pollution; marine pollution
- Section 11: Industry, economic sectors; pollution, industrial wastes
- Section 12: Toxic threats, hazards; health protection, safety, emergencies
- Section 13: Environmental control technology

Pollution Control: Hazardous Wastes, United States. This subgroup is similar to the preceding one except that hazardous wastes and toxic substances are the pollutants regulated.

See also:

- Section 1: Chemistry, biogeochemical cycles, pollutants
- Section 5: Food and agriculture; atmospheric environment, pollution, pesticides

- Section 12: Toxic threats, hazards; health protection, safety, emergencies
- Section 13: Environmental control technology; hazardous wastes

Law and Policies: State and Local. Regional
In this subgroup are entries for laws and regulations of jurisdictions below the national level on such topics as wastes and recycling, development impacts, pollution control, and planning and zoning.

See also:

- Section 2: Air pollution, atmospheric chemistry
- Section 3: Water pollution
- Section 4: Lands, reserves and parks, management
- Section 8: Tribal communities; rural communities; urban communities, individuals and environment
- Section 12: Risk assessment; health protection, safety, emergencies
- Section 13: Environmental control technology

Land Preservation. Trusts. State Parks. Preserving land is an important function of local organizations, public or private. The entries here deal with land trusts, easements, establishment of parks, and other land-saving actions.

See also:

- Section 1: Biodiversity, conservation biology, genetics
- Section 4: Lands, reserves and parks, management
- Section 7: Wildlife management; endangered species, conservation biology
- Section 8: Individuals and environment; leisure and recreation
- Section 9: Built environment, architecture, historical preservation

2170. Wasserman, Paul; McCann, Gary; Tobin, Patricia. **Encyclopedia of legal information sources.** Gale Research, 1988. 634 pp. Subtitle: A bibliographic guide to approximately 19,000 citations for publications organizations, and other sources of information on 460 law-related subjects. Includes: statutes, codes, standards, and uniform laws; annuals and surveys; digests, indexes, abstracts, and citators; online databases, and more.

2171. Wasserman, Paul; Kelly, James R.; Vikor, Desidor L.; eds. **Encyclopedia of public affairs information sources.** Gale Research, 1988. 303 pp. Contains almost 8000 citations of published, electronic, and institutional information sources, emphasizing materials produced since 1980.

International Law and Policies (2172–2206)

2172. Vicuna, Francisco Orrego; ed. **Antarctic resources policy: scientific, legal, and political issues.** Cambridge University Press, 1983. 335 pp., ill., bibl. Papers from the first international conference held in the Antarctic (1982). Covers living and mineral resources; technology; the ecosystem and its fragility; regimes of past and future; the Antarctic Treaty and its relation to international law; the role of the Antarctic in international politics; and the history of its development.

2173. Rifkin, Jeremy. **Biosphere politics: a new consciousness for a new century.** Crown Publishers, 1991. 388 pp. A revolutionary declaration of future politics. Notes that the human quest for security and freedom from the forces of nature has resulted in nature's destruction and a sense of insecurity. Envisions a political and social order incorporating whole earth thinking.

2174. Advisory Committee for the Co-ordination of Information Systems. **Directory of United Nations Databases and information systems.** United Nations, 1984 to date. Irregular. Covers 615 indexing and abstracting services, statistical services, library and documentation services, clearinghouses and referral centers, and information analysis services. Name-acronym and subject indexes in English, French, and Spanish.

2175. Hetzel, Nancy K. **Environmental cooperation among industrialized countries: the role of regional organizations.** University Press of America, 1980. 381 pp., bibl., index. Examines the maze of intergovernmental organizations that has evolved in response to global environmental problems. Looks at functions,

working methods, political problems, interrelationships, and effective cooperation.

2176. Carroll, John E. **Environmental diplomacy: an examination and a prospective of Canadian-U.S. transboundary environmental relations.** University of Michigan Press, 1983. 382 pp., maps, bibl., index. Presents important case studies of oil and the coastline, transboundary toxics and air quality, Great Lakes use and pollution, and acid precipitation. Emphasizes the processes of resolution. Discusses the possibility of more formalized U.S.-Canadian environmental relations.

2177. Westing, Arthur H.; ed. **Environmental hazards of war: releasing dangerous forces in an industrialized world.** Sage Publications, 1990. 96 pp., bibl., index. Examines the effects of conventional war on nuclear power plants, chemical facilities, and dams. Reviews legal, technical, and cultural ways of preventing intentional and collateral ecological damage.

2178. Vieira, Anna da Soledade. **Environmental information in developing nations: politics and policies.** Greenwood Press, Contributions in librarianship and information science, v. 5, 1985. 174 pp., bibl., index. Discusses environmental problems of the Third World in context of information structure and systems and the role of nongovernmental organizations (NGOs) and United Nations–related agencies. Argues for the development of national libraries to guide information systems in developing countries and compares the policies of Egypt, India, Brazil, and Mexico.

2179. Environmental policy and law. IOS Press, 1971 to date. Bimonthly. Sponsored by the International Council of Environmental Law. Multinational environmental law, policy, and administration for pollution, species protection, waste management, land use, and resource conservation.

2180. Westing, Arthur H.; ed. **Environmental warfare: a technical, legal and policy appraisal.** Stockholm International Peace Research Institute; Taylor & Francis, 1984. 107 pp., bibl., index. A broad overview of the ways in which the environment has been and can be manipulated by military activities. Discusses the Environmental Modification Convention of 1977 and formulates policy recommendations.

2181. Tolba, Mostalfa Kamal; ed. **Evolving environmental perceptions: from Stockholm to Nairobi.** Butterworth, 1988. 458 pp., index. Contains edited text of declarations and statements made at the 1972 United Nations Conference on the Human Environment (Stockholm Conference) and its tenth anniversary commemoration in Nairobi in 1982.

2182. Westing, Arthur H.; ed. **Explosive remnants of war: mitigating the environmental effects.** Taylor & Francis, 1985. 141 pp., bibl., index. Overview and case studies, including the aftermath of World War II in Poland and Libya and of the Vietnam War in Vietnam and Laos.

2183. Westing, Arthur H.; ed. **Global resources and international conflict: environmental factors in strategic policy and action.** Oxford University Press, 1986. 280 pp., bibl., index. Analyzes role of natural resources as factors in strategic policy and action, focusing on oil, gas, minerals, fresh water, fisheries, and food crops.

2184. Westing, Arthur; ed. **Herbicides in war: the long-term ecological and human consequences.** Taylor & Francis, 1984. 210 pp., bibl., index. Focuses on the effects of chemical herbicides used during the Vietnam War. On-site research and clinical human studies provide material for examining the delayed consequences of the use of herbicides.

2185. Young, Oran R. **International cooperation: building regimes for natural resources and the environment.** Cornell University Press, Cornell studies in political economy, 1989. 248 pp., bibl., index. Specialized monograph on roles of international organizations, scientists, and "policy entrepreneurs" in building international agreements, using a conceptual approach called "regime theory."

2186. International environmental affairs. University Press of New England, 1989 to date. Quarterly. Seeks to improve knowledge of environmental management at the international level, with emphasis on North America. Articles address such international issues as climate, oceans, Antarctica, desertification, toxic chemicals control, air pollution, and transfrontier management of natural resources. Includes profiles of important international organizations and institutions.

2187. Carroll, John E.; ed. **International environmental diplomacy: the management and resolution of transfrontier environmental problems.** Cambridge University Press, 1988. 291 pp., bibl., index. Fifteen articles on international law, multilateral treaties, and international organizations, with case studies on air and water pollution in North America and Europe.

2188. Caldwell, Layton K. **International environmental policy: emergence and dimensions.** Duke University Press, Duke Press policy studies, 1984. 367 pp., bibl., index. Discusses the events leading to and arising from the Stockholm Conference of 1972. Analyzes how institutional structures and regional arrangements have evolved. Examines the influence of economic and political tensions and reviews efforts to protect the international commons (the atmosphere, outer space, the oceans, and Antarctica).

2189. Middlekauf, R. D.; Shubik, P.; eds. **International food regulation handbook: policy, science, law.** Dekker, 1989. 562 pp. Comprehensive collection of information presenting the current, complex state of national and international approaches to the protection of food. Public policy and scientific considerations in general are treated in Part I; statutes and regulations of selected countries are summarized in Part II.

2190. Kormondy, Edward J.; ed. **International handbook of pollution control.** Greenwood Press, 1989. 466 pp., bibl., index. Experts from 24 countries in the Americas, Europe, Asia, Africa, and Oceania contribute essays on the regulation of air, water, and soil pollution in their countries. Specific issues include the history of pollution control; the role of government and nongovernment agencies in pollution control; and specific implementation practices, including fines, incentives, prohibition, and liability.

2191. Boardman, Robert. **International organization and the conservation of nature.** Indiana University Press, 1981. 215 pp., bibl., index. Examines the origin and changing character of the international conservation movement. Focuses on such organizations as the International Union for Conservation of Nature and Natural Resources (IUCN), the World Wildlife Fund, and United Nations agencies. Studies scientific, political, and network development. Includes case studies on polar conservation, East African wildlife, and migratory bird protection.

2192. Lyster, Simon. **International wildlife law: an analysis of international treaties concerned with the conservation of wildlife.** Grotius, 1985. 470 pp., bibl., index. Comprehensive analysis of the basic principles of international law and how they relate to wildlife treaties. Covers international conventions on wetlands, whaling, endangered species, the Antarctic, and cultural and natural heritage. Gives historical background, analyzes the terms of the treaties, and assesses implementation.

2193. Journal of environmental law. Oxford University Press, 1989 to date. Semiannual. Environmental law in relation to pollution, waste management, habitat protection, biotechnology, and natural resources.

2194. McDermott, Jeanne. **The killing winds: the menace of biological warfare.** Arbor House, 1987. 322

pp., bibl., index. General review of recent biological research and development, focusing on U.S. programs. Reports on several disputed incidents, including "yellow rain," and discusses the interplay of scientists, controversial technology, and the military.

2195. Hancock, Graham. **Lords of poverty: freewheeling lifestyles, power, prestige and corruption of the multi-million dollar aid business.** Macmillan, 1989. 234 pp., ill., bibl. Journalistic review and critique of the costs and benefits of government-sponsored foreign aid programs.

2196. Multilateral treaties in the field of the environment. United Nations Environment Programme; Grotius, 1983–1991. Index. 2 vols. Vol. 1 lists 78 conventions from 1933 to 1979; Vol. 2 contains 54 conventions from the years 1979 to 1989. Provides full texts of conventions and summaries of important provisions, including full title and date of adoption and enforcement.

2197. Register of international treaties and other agreements in the field of the environment. United Nations Environment Programme, 1985. 209 pp. Compiled as an information manual for the United Nations Governing Council and the General Assembly.

2198. Young, Oran R. **Resource regimes: natural resources and social institutions.** University of California Press, 1982. 276 pp., ill., bibl., index. Young pioneered the concept of resource regimes. Argues that these social institutions determine the value of natural resources, the method of valuation, and the resolution of value conflicts. Applies these concepts to a case study of marine fisheries.

2199. Lesser, Ian O. **Resources and strategy.** Macmillan, 1989. 240 pp., bibl., index. Resources and strategic interests of great powers.

2200. Shapley, Deborah. **The seventh continent: Antarctica in a resource age.** Resources for the Future, 1985. 315 pp., ill., bibl., index. Study of Antartica's history, politics, and development prospects.

2201. System-wide medium-term environment programme for the period 1990–1995. United Nations Environment Programme, 1988. 103 pp., bibl. Outlines the United Nations' environmental objectives and strategies to be pursued for 1990–1995 in the areas of the atmosphere, water, terrestrial ecosystems, industry, and human settlement and welfare; addresses issues of improved environmental assessment, management, and awareness.

2202. UNESCO list of documents and publications. UNESCO, 1972 to date. Quarterly, with annual and multiyear cumulations. Covers United Nations General Conference and Executive Board documents, meetings, conferences, working series documents, and others; gives bibliographic information, annotations, keywords, and full indexes.

2203. Castle, Emery N.; Price, Kent A.; eds. **U.S. interests and global natural resources: energy, minerals, food.** Resources for the Future (dist. by Johns Hopkins University Press), 1983. 147 pp., ill., bibl., index. Considers U.S. national interests with respect to energy, minerals, and food.

2204. Westing, Arthur H. **Warfare in a fragile world: military impact on the human environment.** Taylor & Francis, 1980. 249 pp., bibl., index. Describes military impacts on temperate, tropical, desert, Arctic, island, and ocean regions.

2205. Templeton, Virginia Evans; Taubenfeld, Howard J. **World environmental law bibliography.** Rothman, 1987. 480 pp., bibl., index. Subtitle: Nonperiodical literature in law and the social sciences published since 1970 in various languages with selected reviews and annotations from periodicals. Compiles works from governments, international organizations, and commercial sources. Citations include bibliographic information and references to book reviews and annotations.

2206. Schneider, Jan. **World public order of the environment: towards an international ecological law and organization.** University of Toronto Press, 1979. 319 pp., bibl., index. Presents a conceptual framework to identify common human interests and to implement a conserving, economical, and constructive resource policy that advances human dignity and well-being. Studies problems in international environmental law and organizations. Reports and analyzes trends in environmental public order and recommends future policies.

Law of the Sea (2207–2218)

2207. United Nations, Office for Ocean Affairs and the Law of the Sea. **Annual review of ocean affairs: law and policy, main documents, 1985–1987.** UNIFO, 1989. 940 pp. Contains the United Nations' annual report on the law of the sea, plus extracts from related reports, studies, and working papers of other international organizations, grouped by major subject area (maritime safety, offshore structures, pollution from dumping). Articles present main provisions of relevant resolutions and decisions and include additional references.

2208. Krueger, Robert B.; Riesenfeld, Stefan A.; eds. **The developing order of the oceans.** Law of the Sea Institute, University of Hawaii, Sea Grant cooperative report, no. UNIHI-SEAGRANT-CR–85–03, 1986. 749 pp. Proceedings of the eighteenth annual Law of the Sea Institute Conference, held in 1984.

2209. Saetevik, Sunneva. **Environmental cooperation between the North Sea states: success or failure?** Belhaven Press, 1988. 173 pp., maps, ill., bibl. Uses regime theory to explain the results of the Paris Commission's efforts to protect the North Sea environment.

2210. Moore, John Norton; ed. **International and United States documents on oceans law and policy.** Hein, 1986. 5 vols. Compiled by the Center for Oceans Law and Policy, University of Virginia School of Law, for the Virginia Sea Grant College Program.

2211. Timagenis, Gregorios J. **International control of marine pollution.** Oceana, 1980. Bibl., index. 2 vols. Exhaustive treatment of legal and political aspects of marine pollution, especially from ships. First part covers conventions, legislative problems, lawmaking and enforcement, and economic implications. Second and third parts analyze the Oslo and London conventions and the Inter-Governmental Maritime Consultative Organization Convention of 1973. The last part reviews the Third United Nations Law of the Sea Conference, emphasizing aspects pertaining to waste discharge.

2212. Law of the sea: baselines: an examination of the relevant provisions of the United Nations Convention on the Law of the Sea. United Nations, 1989. 70 pp., ill., bibl. Analyzes all provisions of the 1982 convention covering normal baselines, straight baselines, and special local applications. Discusses marking baselines on charts.

2213. Dekker, Lies; Bower, Blair T.; Koudstaal, Rob. **Management of toxic materials in an international setting: a case study of cadmium in the North Sea.** Balkema, 1987. 116 pp., maps, ill., bibl. Uses the Dutch Water Quality Management Plan for the North Sea as a base to examine the kinds of analysis needed to support planning in an international setting. Also studies effects and implementation of regulatory measures.

2214. Charney, Jonathan I.; ed. **The new nationalism and the use of common spaces: issues in marine pollution and the exploitation of Antarctica.** American Society of International Law; Allanheld, Osmun, 1982. 343 pp., bibl., index. Nine essays discuss current and potential uses of oceans and Antarctica. Emphasizes both nationalistic pressures and the lack of scientific data as factors affecting development of international regulation.

2215. Ocean development & international law. Crane Russak, 1973 to date. Quarterly. Articles and legal

commentary on international treaties, institutions, policies, and politics affecting marine resources.

2216. Sanger, Clyde. **Ordering the oceans: the making of the Law of the Sea.** University of Toronto Press, 1987. 225 pp., ill., bibl., index. Discusses seventeenth century sea law and the first two Law of the Sea conferences as precursors to the third conference (1974–1982). Focuses on the negotiations on national jurisdiction, rights of passage, pollution control, seabed mining, fisheries, and marine scientific research. Suggests strategies for future cooperation.

2217. Underdal, Arild. **The politics of international fisheries management: the case of the Northeast Atlantic.** Columbia University Press, 1980. 239 pp., bibl. Argues that fisheries management practices are far more political than scientific or economic. Reviews history of regulations and explains the framework and underlying principles involved in the decision-making process. Illustrates with a case study of North Sea herring and examines effects of maximum sustainable yield and quota distribution from several political perspectives.

2218. Haas, Peter M. **Saving the Mediterranean: the politics of international environmental cooperation.** Columbia University Press, Political economy of international change, 1990. 303 pp., maps, bibl., index. Reviews the development of international and national pollution control measures in the region. Presents interpretations and assessments of international cooperation.

National Laws and Policies (2219–2242)

2219. Schmandt, Jurgen; Clarkson, Judith; Roderick, Hilliard. **Acid rain and friendly neighbors: the policy dispute between Canada and the United States.** Duke University Press, Duke Press policy studies, rev. ed., 1988. 344 pp., ill., bibl., index. Explores the levels of agreement and disagreement between the two countries on the nature and effects of acid rain. Reviews domestic policy developments in both countries and recommends additional steps in the context of past joint measures. Includes discussion of the impact of environmental and economic interest groups on policy.

2220. Bahro, Rudolf. **Building the Green movement.** New Society, 1986. 219 pp., bibl. Collection of essays, articles, and interviews of former Green party builder-fundamentalist on all aspects of the Green movement in West Germany.

2221. Barker, Ivor; Barker, Joan; eds. **Clean air around the world: the law and practice of air pollution control in 14 countries in 5 continents.** International Union of Air Pollution Prevention Associations, 1988. 146 pp. Member associations from 14 countries briefly describe the philosophy underlying their national policies toward clean air and the resulting legislation.

2222. Lowe, Philip; and others. **Countryside conflicts: the politics of farming, forestry, and conservation.** Gower, 1986. 378 pp., ill., index. Examines the cultural, economic, and legislative changes that have influenced the British landscape since 1945, with four case studies. Includes proposals for reform.

2223. Grubb, Michael. **Energy policies and the greenhouse effect.** Dartmouth Publishing, 1990. 2 vols. Vol. 1: Policy appraisal. Argues for increased energy efficiency and fossil fuel abatement policies. Gauges the political and institutional factors to overcome. Vol. 2: Country studies and technical options. Presents case reports from Japan, the United States, China, India, the USSR, and Europe. Discusses issues involved in limiting greenhouse gases. Reviews technical options to reduce carbon dioxide emissions.

2224. Emond, D. Paul. **Environmental assessment law in Canada.** Emond-Montgomery, 1978. 380 pp. Provides a detailed analysis of the Ontario Environmental Assessment Act and a review of the composition and procedures of the assessment board. Examines municipal environmental assessments and evaluates the Federal Environmental Assessment Review process with four case studies.

2225. Kato, Ichiro; Kumamoto, Nobuo; Matthews, William H.; eds. **Environmental law and policy in the Pacific Basin Area.** University of Tokyo Press, 1981. 229 pp., bibl., index. Results of a 1978 conference. Reviews environmental law in Malaysia, Thailand, the Philippines, and Indonesia. Assesses the results of Japan's pollution control efforts. Examines the effects of U.S. environmental regulations and international cooperation.

2226. Ross, Lester; Silk, Michael A. **Environmental law and policy in the People's Republic of China.** Quorum Books, 1987. 449 pp., bibl., index. Translated excerpts from Chinese newspapers and legal and environmental journals. Shows policies and ideologies underpinning environmental protection work in China. Covers air, water, and noise pollution control; solid and toxic wastes; marine resources protection; conservation of land, natural resources, and wildlife; and enforcement means and mechanisms. Includes translations of relevant laws and regulations.

2227. Bhatt, S. **Environmental laws and water resources management.** Radiant, 1986. 355 pp., bibl., index. Survey of environmental legislation in India and analytical review of Indian water resources legislation.

2228. Jancar, Barbara Wolfe. **Environmental management in the Soviet Union and Yugoslavia: structure and regulation in federal communist states.** Duke University Press, Duke Press policy studies, 1987. 481 pp., bibl., index. Notes the similarities between the environmental failures of these two command economies and those of the United States. Suggests that regulation politicizes environmental issues and is therefore not the ideal solution.

2229. European environmental yearbook. DocTer International, 2d ed., 1991. 1100 pp., ill. Analyzes the current status of nature conservancy, town and country planning, and environmental conservation in 12 EEC countries. Includes special surveys of the United States, the USSR, Australia, and Japan. Lists environmental legislation adopted by EEC countries and documents EEC and other multinational environmental protocols and programs.

2230. Hummel, F. C.; ed. **Forest policy: a contribution to resource development.** Nijhoff; Junk; Kluwer, Forestry sciences, v. 12, 1984. 310 pp., bibl. Papers treat the necessity of strengthening forest policies worldwide, emphasizing people's immediate needs, coordinating forestry policy with other government policies, and developing multiple use management.

2231. Irvine, Sandy; Ponton, Alec. **A green manifesto: policies for a green future.** Optima, 1988. 178 pp., ill., bibl., index. Green party manifesto of the United Kingdom delineates specific social and institutional changes to halt environmental degradation.

2232. Hutton, Drew; ed. **Green politics in Australia: a collection of essays.** Angus & Robertson, 1987. 245 pp., bibl. Collection of essays on Australian ecological movements, including a descriptive history of "green bans," an assessment of the ecology-peace connection, a review of ecofeminist thought, and aboriginal perspectives and participation in the Green movement.

2233. Westfall, Gloria; ed. **Guide to official publications of foreign countries.** American Library Association, Government Documents Round Table; Congressional Information Service, 1990. 359 pp. Brief annotations accompany entries of bibliographies, government directories, statistical yearbooks, laws and regulations, legislative proceedings, central bank publications, and economic, budget, health, census, and labor information sources.

2234. International environment reporter. Bureau

of National Affairs, 1978 to date. Biweekly. Loose-leaf legal service on international law and policy in industrial countries.

2235. DeSario, Jack P.; ed. **International public policy sourcebook. Vol. 1: Health and social welfare.** Greenwood Press, 1989. 344 pp., ill., bibl., index. First of two volumes on public policy issues in eight countries—United States, Canada, Israel, Japan, and four European countries. Second volume to address education and environment. Chapters cover the development history of policies, examine and evaluate current strategies, and assess implications for the future.

2236. Feldman, Elliot J.; Goldberg, Michael A.; eds. **Land rites and wrongs: the management, regulation, and use of land in Canada and the United States.** Lincoln Institute of Land Policy, 1987. 326 pp., bibl., index. Explores the planning, handling, and results of comparable land management projects in the United States and Canada. Identifies forces shaping public policy-making. Compares public and private sector performances. Essays include industrial development, siting of toxic waste disposal facilities, and controlling of urban expansion.

2237. Ascher, William; Healy, Robert. **Natural resource policymaking in developing countries: environment, economic growth, and income distribution.** Duke University Press, 1990. 223 pp., bibl., index. Develops a theoretical framework integrating economic production, natural resources, and distribution of wealth. Discusses the failures of well-intentioned economic development projects. Uses case studies of agriculture and forestry modernization, population resettlement schemes, dam construction, and irrigation projects in India, Sri Lanka, Indonesia, Mexico, Brazil, and other countries.

2238. Repetto, Robert; Gillis, Malcolm; eds. **Public policies and the misuse of forest resources.** Cambridge University Press, 1988. 432 pp., ill., bibl., index. Ten case studies of adverse government forest policies involving taxation, credit, investment, concessions, or lease rights. Argues that government incentives are a major cause of deforestation.

2239. Portney, Paul R.; ed. **Public policies for environmental protection.** Resources for the Future, 1990. 308 pp., index. Reviews legislation and regulation applicable to many environmental problems, assesses relevant policy, discusses related economic issues, and recommends policy improvements.

2240. Hurst, Philip. **Rainforest politics: ecological destruction in South-East Asia.** Zed Books, 1990. 303

pp., bibl., index. Documents destruction of rain forests in Indonesia, Thailand, Papua New Guinea, and other countries, describing the roles of politics, economics, and cultural perceptions. Concluding chapter identifies common causes and suggests solutions.

2241. Mellon, Margaret; and others. **The regulation of toxic and oxidant air pollution in North America.** CCH Canada, 1986. 257 pp., ill., bibl., index. Reviews the nature and features of the pollutants, including their "transboundary aspects." Assesses the strengths and weaknesses of domestic and bilateral laws and policies of Canada and the United States. Makes specific recommendations for both countries.

2242. Grindle, Merilee Serrill. **State and countryside: development policy and agrarian politics in Latin America.** Johns Hopkins University Press, Johns Hopkins studies in development, 1986. 255 pp., ill., bibl., index. Reviews the role of the state in supporting capitalist-oriented modernization. Surveys the resulting inefficiency, unproductivity, and poverty. Examines agrarian reform attempts and alternative integrated rural development programs.

U.S. Politics and Policies (2243–2264)

2243. Hays, Samuel P.; Hays, Barbara D. **Beauty, health and permanence: environmental politics in the United States, 1955–1985.** Cambridge University Press, 1987. 630 pp., ill., bibl., index. Focuses on roles of social and government change and the relationship of society and politics.

2244. Comp, T. Allan; ed. **Blueprint for the environment: a plan for federal action.** Howe Brothers, 1989. 335 pp. Over 500 recommendations from leaders of the environmental community. Arranged by responsible cabinet office or administration, then by topic. Recommendations include explanatory paragraphs, expected fiscal savings or costs, sources of expertise, and, where appropriate, explicit implementation steps.

2245. Ophuls, William. **Ecology and the politics of scarcity: a prologue to a political theory of the steady state.** Freeman, 1977. 303 pp., ill., bibl., index. Asserts that there is a global advancement towards scarcity that cannot be checked by technology; states that political democracy and market mechanisms are poorly suited for a world of scarcity; declares that a new consciousness, ethics, and political attitude away from the individual are needed for collective survival.

2246. Environment '90: the legislative agenda.

Congressional Quarterly, 1990. 106 pp. An examination of the pros and cons of numerous environmental issues. Reviews clean air, energy, global warming, solid waste, facilities siting, and other issues. Identifies key congressional aides and special interests.

2247. Adams, John H.; and others. **An environmental agenda for the future.** Island Press, 1985. 155 pp., bibl. Compiled mostly through consensus by executives from major, mainstream groups (Environmental Defense Fund, Sierra Club, etc.). Recommends strategies in 11 areas, such as nuclear issues, energy use, wild living resources, water resources, public and private lands, urban environments, and international responsibilities.

2248. Environmental forum. Environmental Law Institute, 1982 to date. Bimonthly. Publishes diverse points of view and opinion from all sectors to stimulate a creative exchange of ideas and the search for effective solutions to environmental problems. Articles, news, and reviews.

2249. Wenz, Peter S. **Environmental justice.** State University of New York Press, SUNY series in environmental public policy, 1988. 368 pp., bibl., index. Environmental cases and examples are used to illustrate theories and problems of distributive justice. Discusses property rights, human rights, animal rights, utilitarianism, and other topics. Advances and explains his own theory, "reflective equilibrium," which integrates ethical concerns with distributive justice.

2250. Nijkamp, Peter; and others. **Environmental policy analysis: operational methods and models.** Wiley, 1980. 283 pp., ill., bibl., index. Presents several multidimensional models and theoretical constructs that integrate economics, physics, regional science, ecology, and social and political science.

2251. Vig, Norman J.; Kraft, Michael E.; eds. **Environmental policy in the 1990s: toward a new agenda.** CQ Press, 1990. 418 pp., bibl. Reviews past policy developments and notes potential new sources for initiatives. Studies public policy dilemmas and assesses resolution methods. Reports on environmental policies internationally and examines the future role of environmental politics in a democratic society.

2252. Rosenbaum, Walter A. **Environmental politics and policy.** CQ Press, 2d ed., 1991. 336 pp., ill., bibl., index. Argues that the environmental situation is growing worse and that purely national approaches will not work. Reviews major developments in environmental politics over the last 20 years and identifies challenges for the future.

2253. Lester, James P.; ed. **Environmental politics and policy: theories and evidence.** Duke University Press, 1989. 405 pp., ill., bibl., index. Synthesis of nearly three decades of research on environmental policy from a political science perspective. Examines the conservation and environmental movements and federalism. Analyzes policy with respect to public opinion, interest groups, party politics, Congress, bureaucracy, the courts, and elites. Covers international environmental policy and categorizes the literature, predicting future directions in the field.

2254. Forum for applied research and public policy. Tennessee Valley Authority, 1986 to date. Quarterly. Brief articles by academics and government officials on environmental policy and protection, energy policy, and economic development.

2255. Zorack, John L. **The lobbying handbook.** John Zorack (dist. by Beacham), 1990. 1118 pp., bibl., index. Functions as both a "how-to" and a quick-reference text. Contains advice on how to gain access to the executive and legislative branches and how to manage a poltical action committee. Explains the committee system, the budget process, and House and Senate procedures.

2256. Major studies & issue briefs of the Congressional Research Service: 1916–1989 cumulative index. University Publications of America, 1989. 2 vols. Microfilm compilation of 5000 monographs and issue briefs produced on matters of interest to Congress by the Congressional Research Service, 1916–1989, with two-volume index. Biennial supplements.

2257. Henning, Daniel H.; Mangun, William R. **Managing the environmental crisis: incorporating competing values in natural resource administration.** Duke University Press, 1989. 377 pp., ill., bibl., index. Examines the differing forces and concerns involved in environmental policy and administration. Discusses renewable and nonrenewable resource management, wilderness and outdoor recreation management, pollution control, and urban, regional, and international environmental policy.

2258. National news report: a summary of news concerning the nation's environment. Sierra Club, 1969 to date. Semimonthly. Provides brief summaries and commentary on legal, legislative, and scientific developments. Provides names and telephone numbers for more information.

2259. Natural resources journal. University of New Mexico, School of Law, 1961 to date. Quarterly. International, interdisciplinary forum for the study of natural and environmental resources, with emphasis on research directed toward public policy.

2260. Henderson, Hazel. **The politics of the solar age: alternatives to economics.** Anchor Press, 1981. 433 pp., ill., bibl., index. Explains the "failures" of our falsely apolitical and pseudo-objective economics and suggests alternatives.

2261. Fernie, John; Pitkethly, Alan. **Resources: environment and policy.** Harper & Row, 1985. 338 pp. Contends that resource problems require institutional solutions. Discusses resource management as a political activity and proposes management techniques with respect to population, energy, commodities, food, forestry, and wilderness, using examples from the United Kingdom and North America.

2262. Nichols, Albert L. **Targeting economic incentives for environmental protection.** MIT Press, MIT Press series on the regulation of economic activity, v. 8, 1984. 189 pp., bibl., index. Based on the author's work on benzene emissions regulation. Shows how the choice of target—the specific point at which standards or incentives are imposed—interacts with the choice of instrument to determine the efficiency of environmental regulations. Argues the need for strategies sensitive to wide variations in mariginal costs and benefits.

2263. Baumol, William J.; Oates, Wallace E. **The theory of environmental policy.** Cambridge University Press, 2d ed., 1988. 299 pp., ill., bibl., index. Part I examines the theory of externalities, presenting a formal analysis and reviewing market imperfections, price versus quality control, and optimal pricing of exhaustible resources. Part II discusses the design of environmental policy, including marketable emission permits, the charges and standards approach, and national versus local environmental quality standards.

2264. Buck, Susan J. **Understanding environmental administration and law.** Island Press, 1991. 224 pp., bibl., index. Explains the factors, processes, and politics involved in the creation and application of environmental law.

U.S. Laws and Legislation. Courts. Disputes (2265–2283)

2265. Boston College environmental affairs law review. Boston College Environmental Law Center, 1971 to date. Quarterly. Continues: Environmental affairs.

Multidisciplinary forum for the analysis of a broad range of environmental issues.

2266. Susskind, Lawrence; Cruikshank, Jeffrey. **Breaking the impasse: consensual approaches to resolving public disputes.** Basic Books, 1987. 276 pp., bibl., index. The authors advocate consensus building as a viable alternative to political stalemates, particularly at the local level. Discusses the pros and cons of consensus building, unassisted and assisted negotiation, and the theory and practice of dispute resolution.

2267. CIS index/annual. Congressional Information Service, 1970 to date. Monthly. Indexes and abstracts documents of the U.S. Congress: hearings, reports, and laws, from 1789 to date. A critically important source for data on environmental problems, given the number of Congressional hearings held, the volume of testimony, and the number of supporting documents submitted by those testifying. Available as a computer database, online and on CD-ROM.

2268. Ecology law quarterly. University of California, Berkeley, School of Law, 1971 to date. Quarterly. In-depth articles address application and intricacies of varied environmental laws and regulations, often with detailed discussion of particular cases.

2269. Environment reporter. Bureau of National Affairs, 1962 to date. Weekly: loose-leaf service. One of two main sources for current developments in U.S. environmental law. In several sections: current developments, federal laws and regulations, mining, state air laws, state water laws, state solid waste and land-use laws, court decisions, and cumulative index.

2270. Morse, C. W. **Environmental consultation.** Praeger, 1984. 193 pp., index. Argues for an environmental regulatory system based on consultation and mediation.

2271. Wenner, Lettie M. **The environmental decade in court.** Indiana University Press, 1982. 211 pp., ill., bibl., index. Examines major role of the courts in development and implementation of environmental policy in the 1970s.

2272. Carpenter, David, A.; Roznowski, Bruce; Cushman, Robert F. **Environmental dispute handbook: liability and claims.** Wiley, 1991. Ill., index. 2 vols. Examines the basis for liability for manufacturers, property owners, insurers, engineers, and others. Reviews damages and explores ways to resolve environmental disputes, including nonlitigation options such as CERCLA enforcement actions.

2273. Bacow, Lawrence S.; Wheeler, Michael. **Envi-**

ronmental **dispute resolution**. Plenum Press, 1984. 372 pp., ill., bibl., index. Original case studies prepared for the Environmental Protection Agency on bargaining and negotiation between government, environmental advocates, and regulatees. Supplemented with essays, notes, and additional readings.

2274. Crowfoot, James E.; Wondolleck, Julia M. **Environmental disputes: community involvement in conflict resolution**. Island Press, 1990. 278 pp., ill., index. Seven case studies illustrate when and how citizen groups should employ techniques of environmental dispute resolution without litigation.

2275. Environmental law deskbook. Environmental Law Institute, 1989. 764 pp., bibl. Compendium of frequently needed information on environmental matters such as hazardous wastes, air and water pollution, and environmental impact statements and related legal procedures.

2276. Environmental law reporter. Environmental Law Institute, 1971 to date. Monthly: loose-leaf service. One of the two main sources for current developments in U.S. environmental law. Issued in separate volumes covering news and analysis; litigation; pending litigation; statutes; administrative materials; and indexes.

2277. Federal environmental laws: amended through April 1, 1988. West, 1988. 1053 pp. Listed with their title and section classifications of the United States Code Annotated and their Congressional Act and section designations. Individual sections are followed by references to assist in research.

2278. Rose, Jerome G. **Legal foundations of environmental planning: textbook-casebook and materials on environmental law**. Rutgers University, Center for Urban Policy Research, 1983. 537 pp. Presents cases and materials on legal theories and procedures. Covers air pollution, water pollution, control of population growth, and distribution.

2279. Brower, David J.; Carol, Daniel S.; eds. **Managing land-use conflicts: case studies in special area management**. Duke University Press, Duke Press policy studies, 1987. 323 pp., bibl., index. Case studies detail methods and means useful in resolving conservation and development conflicts involving complex ecological and administrative factors. Summarizes common elements and seeks to define a process of special area management to resolve conflicts, provide greater predictability, identify management strategies, and allow varying judgments and outcomes based on the particular features of a case.

2280. Amy, Douglas J. **The politics of environmental mediation**. Columbia University Press, 1987. 255 pp., bibl., index. Critical review of the politics inherent in mediation. It is not necessarily cheaper, faster, or less confrontational than litigation, and less-experienced negotiators run the risk of making concessions too easily.

2281. Bingham, Gail. **Resolving environmental disputes: a decade of experience**. Conservation Foundation; Ford Foundation, 1986. 284 pp., bibl., index. Documents the history and growth of mediation. Chapters on success rate, factors influencing success, and overall efficiency of the process. Based on 161 cases.

2282. Talbot, Allan R. **Settling things: six case studies in environmental mediation**. Conservation Foundation: Ford Foundation, 1983. 101 pp., maps. Describes in detail six diverse cases involving hydroelectric power, highway extensions, garbage disposal, and park access. Evaluates the success of negotiated settlements and identifies difficulties in implementation.

2283. Bureau of National Affairs. **U.S. environmental laws**. BNA Books, 1988. 665 pp. Complete texts of the principal federal laws and helpful summaries of related laws through 1987. Section-by-section finding list.

U.S. Executive Agencies. Administration and Regulation (2284–2305)

2284. Zwirn, Jerrold. **Access to U.S. government information: guide to executive and legislative authors and authority**. Greenwood Press, Bibliographies and indexes in law and political science, no. 12, 1989. 158 pp. Guide to U.S. government publications. Lists executive and legislative jurisdiction by specific subject category, plus parent agencies, congressional committees, and appropriations subcommittees. Provides useful bridge to *CIS index/annual* (2267) and other works that cite individual publications.

2285. Baram, Michael S. **Alternatives to regulation: managing risks to health, safety, and the environment**. Lexington Books, 1982. 245 pp., bibl., index. Addresses alternatives to conventional government regulation in common law; industrial self-regulation; insurance, bonding, escrow, and restoration funds; government procurement; information and publicity; and threats to regulate. Three case studies.

2286. Frick, G. William; ed. **Environmental glossary**. Government Institutes, 3d ed., 1984. 325 pp. Over 3000 definitions gathered from EPA regulations, federal statutes, and government agencies. Focuses on the more legalistic, technical, and bureaucratic terms.

2287. EPA journal. U.S. Environmental Protection Agency; Government Printing Office, 1975 to date. Bimonthly. Official publication of the Environmental Protection Agency offers nontechnical summaries of developments in air and water, solid wastes, hazardous materials, Superfund, pesticides, and other topics. Covers regulations and standards, new technologies, and environmental management.

2288. Federal executive directory. Carroll, 1980 to date. Provides contact information for cabinet and administrative agencies and other quasi-governmental organizations (such as National Academy of Science and International Bank for Reconstruction and Development). Includes members of Congress, committees and subcommittees. Alphabetical listing of executives and keyword index.

2289. Federal information sources and systems. Government Printing Office, Congressional sourcebook series, 1976 to date. Annual. Directory issued by the comptroller general that describes federal sources and information systems maintained by executive agencies, which contain fiscal, budgetary, and program-related data and information. Includes subject, agency, and budget indexes.

2290. Federal register. National Archives and Records Administration, General Services Administration; Government Printing Office, 1936 to date. Daily. The official record of U. S. government environmental regulations and policy statements.

2291. Federal regulatory directory. Congressional Quarterly Books, 1979–1980 to date. Annual: 6th ed., 1990. Describes the activities and responsibilities of executive and independent regulatory agencies; provides biographies of heads of major agencies, plus organizational, personnel, and contact information.

2292. Federal staff directory. Congressional Staff Directory, 1982 to date. Annual. Provides 30,000 individual names, job titles, addresses, and telephone numbers; also 2000 biographies of top-level civilian and military authorities.

2293. Federal yellow book. Washington Monitor, 1976 to date. Quarterly. Directory of federal departments and agencies. Provides full contact information for over 35,000 top people in the executive branch.

2294. Government assistance almanac, 1989–90: the guide to all federal financial and other domestic programs. Foggy Bottom, 1989. 759 pp., index. Covers over 1100 programs and lists over 4000 addresses and telephone numbers: research grants, subsidies for non-profit organizations, fellowships, scholarships, technical information and advisory services, etc.

2295. Abramovitz, Janet N.; Baker, Douglas S.; Tunstall, Daniel B. **Guide to key environmental statistics in the U.S. government.** World Resources Institute, 1990. 167 pp., bibl., index. Lists programs that develop and distribute environmental statistics. Entries provide information on background of program, statistical coverage, data collection, recent publications, and availability of databases; organized by department and agency.

2296. Monthly catalog of United States government publications. Government Printing Office, 1895 to date. Monthly. Official listing. Premier source of environmental information because of government operations and research and because government publications are widely accessible through the documents depository system. Available as a computerized database, online and on CD-ROM.

2297. Murthy, Keshava S. **National Environmental Policy Act (NEPA) process.** CRC Press, 1988. 215 pp. Reviews the technical aspects of environmental laws, standards, and regulations, the Nuclear Waste Policy Act, and the National Environmental Policy Act (NEPA) process. Offers advice on how to incorporate NEPA into the early design stages of a project, how to select control technologies, and how to write environmental documents.

2298. NEPA deskbook. Environmental Law Institute, 1989. 438 pp. Helpful analysis and reference tool for the National Environmental Policy Act; includes glossary.

2299. Sayre, Kenneth M.; and others. **Regulations, values, and the public interest.** University of Notre Dame Press, 1980. 207 pp., bibl., index. Investigates the bias of utility regulators in favor of the utility industry. Examines in particular the role of initial value orientations in determining the ultimate stance of regulators with respect to the industry they are regulating.

2300. Magat, Wesley A.; Krupnick, Alan J.; Harrington, Winston. **Rules in the making: a statistical analysis of regulatory agency behavior.** Resources for the Future, 1986. 182 pp., ill., bibl., index. Demonstrates the strengths and weaknesses of using statistics to determine what factors influence the establishment of government regulations. Uses a case study of the EPA's establishment of effluent standards. Concludes that the size, structure, and lobbying power of an industry greatly influence the stringency of standards imposed.

2301. Caldwell, Lynton Keith. **Science and the National Environmental Policy Act: redirecting policy through procedural reform.** University of Alabama Press, 1982. 178 pp., bibl., index. Argues that the environmental impact statement was an effective procedural function by which the National Environmental Policy Act reoriented public policy and administration. Explores the role of science in decision making.

2302. Superfund manual: legal and management strategies. Government Institutes, 4th ed., 1991. 320 pp. Written by attorneys specializing in Superfund cases. How Superfund works, what it requires, and how it is implemented. Covers hazardous substance release reporting, government response, liability and enforcement, response strategies, natural resource damages, role of the states, and other topics.

2303. United States government manual. Office of the Federal Register, National Archives and Records Service; Government Printing Office, 1935 to date. Annual. Official handbook of the federal government, widely available. Sections for legislative, judicial, and executive branches; independent establishments and government corporations; boards, committees, and commissions; quasi-official agencies; and selected multilateral and bilateral organizations. Appendices contain abbreviations and acronyms; map of federal regions; and list of agencies terminated and transferred. Indexes by name and subject. Contains 800 numbers to clearinghouses of the Federal Information Centers Program. The information centers are staffed by specialists who can provide telephone numbers, contact points, and other information about the federal government.

2304. Washington information directory. Congressional Quarterly Books, 1975–1976 to date. Maps, ill., index. Annual. Lists information sources in government agencies, Congress, and nongovernment organizations with offices in Washington. Organized by subject area, such as "Agriculture, Environment, and Natural Resources." Includes several ready reference lists, schematic diagrams illustrating the structure of departments and agencies, and maps of downtown Washington.

2305. Who knows: a guide to Washington experts. Washington Research, Business research series, v. 5, 8th ed., 1986. 440 pp., index. Presents title, area of expertise, and contact information for more than 11,000 federal experts providing free or low-cost information, arranged by office; also indexed by 12,000 subject headings.

Natural Resources: United States (2306–2321)

2306. Arrandale, Tom. **The battle for natural resources.** Congressional Quarterly Books, 1983. 230 pp., ill., bibl., index. Traces federal public land policy and the trend toward conservation and preservation. Outlines controversies over leasing and selling of federally owned resources for mining, oil drilling, and grazing. Looks at regional tensions over federal policies on water, land, and other resources.

2307. Fairfax, Sally K.; Yale, Carolyn E. **Federal lands: a guide to planning, management, and state revenues.** Island Press, 1987. 252 pp., maps, bibl., index. Reviews legal history. Details over 20 acts regulating minerals, geothermal energy, oil and gas, timber, coal, and rangelands. Discusses fair market value, preference right leasing, and below-cost timber sales.

2308. Foss, Phillip O. **Federal lands policy.** Greenwood Press, Contributions in political science, v. 162, 1987. 205 pp., bibl., index. Research papers and essays on various aspects of public land policy, including ideological impacts on policy, institutional structures involved in policy-making, and wilderness preservation.

2309. Clawson, Marion. **The federal lands revisited.** Resources for the Future; Johns Hopkins University Press, 1983. 302 pp. A re-examination of federal land policy by an economist and policy analyst with 45 years of professional experience and study. Reviews the history and status of federal lands and argues in favor of retention and disposal. Evaluates five alternatives for managing federal lands: full federal retention, transfer of rights to states, sale to the private sector, and leasing of land for both commercial and conservation purposes. Focuses on Forest Service and Bureau of Land Management lands.

2310. Coggins, George Cameron; Wilkinson, Charles F. **Federal public land and resources law.** Foundation Press, 2d ed., 1987. 1066 pp., bibl., index. Casebook. Reviews history, constitutional underpinnings, and relevant administrative systems of public land policy. Covers water, minerals, timber, range, wildlife, recreation, and preservation.

2311. Mandelker, Daniel R. **Land use law.** Michie, 2d ed., 1988. 551 pp., bibl., index. Reviews principal federal and state court decisions. Notes trends in state case law and statutes. Surveys constitutional arguments against land-use laws.

2312. Halbach, Daniel W.; Runge, C. Ford; Larson, William E.; eds. **Making soil and water conservation work: scientific and policy perspectives.** Soil Conservation Society of America, 1987. 174 pp. Papers from a 1986 conference assess federal conservation efforts; examine the role of the states, given budget constraints; and suggest innovative approaches to soil and water conservation.

2313. Dysart, Benjamin C., III; Clawson, Marion; eds. **Managing public lands in the public interest.** Praeger, Environmental regeneration series, 1988. 144 pp., bibl., index. Collection of short essays from a diverse group, including a policy analyst, a conservation group lobbyist, an industry planner, an environmental lawyer, and a research ecologist; addresses such aspects of land-use planning as private use of public lands, obstructionism, multiple use, and public participation in planning; suggests additional background readings.

2314. Churchman, C. West; Rosenthal, Albert H.; Smith, Spencer H.; eds. **Natural resource administration: introducing a new methodology for management.** Westview Press, Westview special studies in natural resources and energy management, 1984. 228 pp., bibl., index. Emphasis on fish and wildlife management and the impact of human values. Presents a methodology of resource management based on studies of public participation and political and economic factors.

2315. Natural resources law handbook. Government Institutes, 1991. 375 pp. Written by 15 attorneys and government experts. Covers public land rights-of-way; minerals and mining; oil and gas; coal; national forests; water rights; federally protected areas; wildlife and fisheries; and wetlands.

2316. Coggins, George C. **Public natural resources law.** Clark Boardman, Environmental law series, 1990 to date. Annual. Discusses laws pertaining to individual resources, in their historical, constitutional, and administrative contexts. Sections on the frameworks of public natural resource law; mechanisms and overlay doctrines; federal land and resource preservation management; multiple-use and sustained-yield management of surface resources; and mineral resources management.

2317. Brubaker, Sterling; ed. **Rethinking the federal lands.** Resources for the Future; Johns Hopkins University Press, 1984. 306 pp., bibl., index. Papers from a 1982 workshop. Presents diverse views on appropriateness of management and land tenure policies.

2318. Short, Brant C. **Ronald Reagan and the public lands: America's conservation debate, 1979–1984.** Texas A & M University Press, The environmental history series, no. 10, 1989. 178 pp., bibl., index. Case study of Reagan administration public land policy. Describes the

events and politics involved. Notes the increased emphasis on economics and human use in valuing wilderness. Identifies various proponents and opponents of administration policies and interprets their motives.

2319. Ferguson, Denzel; Ferguson, Nancy. **Sacred cows at the public trough.** Maverick, 1983. 250 pp., ill., bibl., index. Reviews the history and politics of cattle raising on public lands. Documents the detrimental effects, focusing separately on soils, streams, plant life, and wildlife. Examines the politics of cattle ranchers and Bureau of Land Management officials.

2320. Soil and Water Resources Conservation Act: 1980 appraisal: soil, water and related resources in the United States. U.S. Department of Agriculture; Government Printing Office, 1981. 2 vols. Part I: Status, condition, and trends. Part II: Analysis of resource trends. Projects resource demands to the year 2030. Examines impacts on soil, water, fish and wildlife habitat, flood damage, energy, and organic waste management. The second RCA appraisal was published in 1989.

2321. Clarke, Jeanne Nienaber; McCool, Daniel. **Staking out the terrain: power differentials among natural resource management agencies.** State University of New York Press, SUNY series in environmental public policy, 1985. 189 pp., bibl., index. Using a synthesis of policy analysis, historical development, case study, and budgetary analysis, formulates a model of agency power, focusing on the ability of agencies to expand resources and jurisdiction for environmental control. Case studies include the Army Corps of Engineers, the Forest Service, the Bureau of Reclamation, the National Park Service, and the Fish and Wildlife Service.

Forests, Parks, Wilderness: United States (2322–2351)

2322. Foresta, Ronald A. **America's national parks and their keepers.** Resources for the Future; Johns Hopkins University Press, 1984. 382 pp., ill., bibl., index. Analytic study of the National Park Service's bureaucracy; examines its lack of a sense of mission in the context of tradition, precedence, and political power. Discusses the Service's role in natural and historical preservation, urban parks, and land beyond park boundaries.

2323. Foster, Charles H. W. **The Appalachian National Scenic Trail: a time to be bold.** Appalachian Trail Conference, 1987. 232 pp., maps, bibl., index. Comprehensive history of the institutions involved in the trail's development, particularly the Appalachian National Scenic Trail Advisory Board.

2324. Hartzog, George B. **Battling for the national parks.** Moyer Bell, 1988. 284 pp., index. Memoirs of former director of the National Park Service provide an inside look at the turbulent 1960s.

2325. Dilsaver, Lary M.; Tweed, William C. **Challenge of the big trees: a resource history of Sequoia and Kings Canyon national parks.** Sequoia Natural History Association, 1991. 379 pp., maps, ill., bibl., index. A general history of the parks from their founding to the present. Bibliography includes brief annotations and evaluations.

2326. The complete guide to America's national parks, 1990–1991. National Park Foundation; Viking Press, 6th ed., 1990. 349 pp., maps, index. Lists over 300 areas in the National Park System. Provides maps, directions, and information on fees, facilities, accommodations, and attractions.

2327. Deacon, Robert T.; Johnson, M. Bruce; eds. **Forestlands: public and private.** Pacific Research Institute for Public Policy; Ballinger, Pacific studies in public policy, 1985. 332 pp., ill., bibl., index. Contributed chapters examine such controversial subjects as regulation of logging practices; management objectives and timber harvest strategies of public land agencies; and the economics of federal timber sales and exports. Argues that private ownership of federally managed forestlands is justified.

2328. Sedjo, Roger A.; ed. **Governmental interventions, social needs, and the management of U.S. forests.** Resources for the Future (dist. by Johns Hopkins University Press), 1983. 300 pp., ill., bibl. Surveys U.S. forest resources and land use; explains the rationale for public intervention on private forestlands; reviews techniques and strategies for national forest system planning and management.

2329. Alston, Richard M. **The individual vs. the public interest: political ideology and national forest policy.** Westview Press, 1983. 250 pp. On resolving ideological conflicts over uses of natural resources. Rejects management based on economic analyses in favor of holistic view and solutions based on compromise, bargaining, and arbitration.

2330. Investing in park futures: the National Park System plan—a blueprint for tomorrow. National Parks and Conservation Association, 1988. 9 vols. The Association's plan to guide the National Park System. The nine volumes contain plans for protection, research, visitors, interpretation, boundaries, public involvement,

constituency building, land acquisition, acquisition of new parks, and the National Park Service.

2331. Wilkinson, Charles F.; Anderson, H. Michael. **Land and resource planning in the national forests.** Island Press, 1987. 396 pp., bibl., index. Details the history, development, and legal basis of land and resource planning. Chapters focus on range, timber, water, minerals, wildlife, recreation, and wilderness. Names and explains statutory and policy mandates for forest planning and management.

2332. Opie, John. **The law of the land: two hundred years of American farmland policy.** University of Nebraska Press, 1987. 231 pp., ill., bibl., index. Emphasizes the tendency of land laws and farm policies to benefit speculative private enterprise more than farmers.

2333. Lime, David W.; ed. **Managing America's enduring wilderness resource.** Tourism Center, Minnesota Extension Service; Minnesota Agricultural Experiment Station, 1990. 706 pp. One hundred eighteen papers from a 1989 conference, organized into four sections: 1. Managing one wilderness system (papers from the Forest Service, the Bureau of Land Management, the National Park Service, and the Fish and Wildlife Service). 2. Managing resources and people within wilderness (includes fire, interagency coordination, access to wilderness by the disabled, visitor education). 3. Managing lands adjacent to wilderness (boundaries; roads; trails; air, sound, and water quality impacts; recreation facilities). 4. Linking tourism, wilderness, and economic development (measuring social and economic impacts of wilderness, marketing, case studies of successful programs).

2334. Sax, Joseph L. **Mountains without handrails: reflections on the national parks.** University of Michigan Press, 1980. 152 pp., bibl., index. What should the national parks be for? Lawyer-preservationist argues for public policies that promote distinctive recreation, parks where individuals can encounter nature intensively.

2335. National parks. National Parks and Conservation Association, 1919 to date. Monthly. Continues: National parks and conservation magazine. Illustrated popular articles on individual parks, plant and animal species, and conservation issues. The Association is dedicated to defending, promoting, and improving the national parks.

2336. National parks for a new generation: visions, realities, prospects: a report from the Conservation Foundation. Conservation Foundation, 1985. 407 pp., ill., bibl., index. Report addresses the existing

National Park System and National Park Service, stewardship of resources, and private sector involvement. Proposes measures for developing a park system of the future.

2337. Connally, Eugenia Horstmann; ed. **National parks in crisis.** National Parks and Conservation Association, 1982. 220 pp. Twenty-one essays concerned with threats to the parks from within and without. Addresses overcrowding, air and water pollution, politicization of the National Park Service, and the growing influence of concessioners. Recommendations include increasing preservation efforts, discouraging motorized recreation, and further regulating concessioners.

2338. Runte, Alfred. **National parks: the American experience.** University of Nebraska Press, 2d ed., 1987. 335 pp., ill., bibl., index. History of the National Park System that emphasizes the relation of parks to the formation of a distinctive national character. Discusses the perennial difficulty of preserving and using the parks.

2339. Simon, David J.; ed. **Our common lands: defending the national parks.** Island Press, 1988. 567 pp., bibl., index. Essays discuss federal legislation designed to protect and preserve publicly owned land, including the Endangered Species Act, the Clean Water Act, the Wild and Scenic Rivers Act, and many others. Explores the roles of various federal agencies in implementing these laws. Discusses attempts to use the various laws and interpretations by the courts.

2340. Allin, Craig Willard. **The politics of wilderness preservation.** Greenwood Press, Contributions in political science, no. 64, 1982. 304 pp., ill., bibl., index. Narrative history of the wilderness issue in American politics through the 1970s. Emphasizes the period since 1955. Summaries at the end of each chapter.

2341. Preserving our natural heritage. Nature Conservancy; U.S. Department of the Interior, 1977 to date. 383 pp., bibl., index. Provides summaries of private, academic and federal, state, and local government activities geared toward protecting natural areas and systems.

2342. Wondolleck, Julia M. **Public lands conflict and resolution: managing national forest disputes.** Plenum Press, 1988. 263 pp., bibl., index. Applies experiences from several federal natural resource management agencies to explain the procedures used in handling national forest disputes. Indicates shortcomings and suggests alternative methods for conflict resolution.

2343. Culhane, Paul J. **Public lands politics: interest group influence on the Forest Service and the Bureau of Land Management.** Johns Hopkins University Press; Resources for the Future, 1981. 398 pp., ill., bibl., index. Contests the popular "capture thesis," which holds that certain interest groups have disproportionately influenced Forest Service and Bureau of Land Management policies, backing the conclusions with empirical data.

2344. O'Toole, R. **Reforming the Forest Service.** Island Press, 1988. 249 pp., ill., bibl., index. Critique of the Forest Service alleges financial mismanagement (below-cost timber sales, grazing), environmental damage (clear-cutting, herbicides), and poorly designed legislation. Proposes major structural reforms and budgetary incentives to improve management.

2345. Zaslowsky, Dyan. **These American lands: parks, wilderness and the public lands.** Holt; Wilderness Society, 1986. 404 pp., ill., bibl., index. Comprehensive review of history and future of U.S. public lands. Chapters discuss the particular problems and prospects of national parks, forests, resource lands, scenic rivers, trails, and Alaskan lands. Appendix collects statistical information on these lands and provides chronological history of major legislation.

2346. Clary, David A. **Timber and the Forest Service.** University Press of Kansas, Development of western resources, 1986. 252 pp., ill., bibl., index. Examines the culture of the Forest Service bureaucracy, explaining the Service's history in terms of its unswerving commitment to timber production.

2347. Rowley, William D. **U. S. Forest Service grazing and rangelands: a history.** Texas A & M University Press, Environmental history series, no. 8, 1985. 270 pp., ill., bibl., index. Narrative analysis of issues facing the Forest Service on protecting and regulating grazing. Reviews controversy over grazing permits and fees, guaranteed use of land, and assessment of range conditions. Examines effects of social change on policy.

2348. Wilderness. Wilderness Society, 1936 to date. Quarterly. Continues: Living wilderness. Illustrated articles on wilderness areas, principally in the United States and wilderness policy.

2349. Graf, William L. **Wilderness preservation and the sagebrush rebellions.** Rowman & Littlefield, 1990. 329 pp., bibl., index. Documents federal initiatives toward public land preservation and western rebellions against them, explaining the legislation, issues, and actors central to the controversies. Covers episodes involving irrigation, forest, grazing, and wilderness lands.

2350. Wellman, J. Douglas. **Wildland recreation policy: an introduction.** Wiley, 1987. 284 pp., ill., bibl., index. Documents key events in the history of wildland recreation policy. Includes chapters on intellectual origins of policy in utilitarian conservation and romantic preservation; institutional origins in the Forest Service and National Park Service; and policy developments since the 1930s.

2351. Runte, Alfred. **Yosemite: the embattled wilderness.** University of Nebraska Press, 1990. 271 pp., maps, ill., bibl., index. Narrative history illustrating the conflict between preservation and use. Emphasizes philosophies of management and use, including Yosemite's role as a training ground for park managers and its embodiment of the national park idea.

Water, Wildlife, Minerals: United States (2352–2371)

2352. Lund, Thomas Alan. **American wildlife law.** University of California Press, 1980. 179 pp., bibl., index. Traces the development of American wildlife law to its roots in English law. Emphasizes historical aspects of current issues. Discusses federal and state law, the constitutional limits of wildlife law, and the changing focus of preservation.

2353. Favre, David S.; Loring, Murray. **Animal law.** Quorum Books, 1983. 253 pp., bibl., index. Collects decisions and writings from eight representative states. Chapters cover the sale of animals, bailment of animals, property rights over animals, and humane and wildlife laws.

2354. Kohm, Kathryn A.; ed. **Balancing on the brink of extinction: the Endangered Species Act and lessons for the future.** Island Press, 1991. 318 pp., index. Contributed essays discuss legal, political, and philosophical ramifications of the Endangered Species Act. Notes the strengths and weaknesses of interagency cooperation and international implementation. Raises issues of invertebrate conservation, predator protection, water rights, and pesticide regulation. Explores the necessity of moving toward an ecosystem-based approach.

2355. Maxfield, Peter C.; Houghton, James L.; Garr, James R. **Cases and materials on the federal income taxation of oil and gas and natural resources transactions.** Foundation Press, 1990. 337 pp. Addresses topics of depletion; lease, sale, and exchange of mineral properties; and expenses of mineral operations. Employs a transactional approach to explain sharing arrangements, pooling, and unitization.

2356. Endangered species technical bulletin. U. S. Department of the Interior, 1976 to date. Monthly. Records news of the Department of the Interior's endangered species program, particularly recovery plans; government actions and regulations; and related international activities. Includes plants and animals, but animals predominate.

2357. Endangered species update. University of Michigan, School of Natural Resources, 1985 to date. Monthly. Reprint of the *Endangered species technical bulletin* with additional, related material.

2358. Bean, Michael J. **Evolution of national wildlife law.** Praeger, rev. ed., 1983. 449 pp., bibl., index. Detailed analysis of legal framework and major themes of wildlife law. Examines three comprehensive federal wildlife programs.

2359. Tarlock, A. Dan. **Law of water rights and resources.** Clark Boardman, 1988 to date. Irregular: looseleaf service. Covers western and eastern water law doctrines; acquisition of proprietary water rights for Indian tribes and public land management agencies; groundwater conservation, regulation and allocation; public trust doctrine; interstate allocation; and litigation strategies.

2360. Want, William L. **Law of wetlands regulation.** Clark Boardman, Environmental law series, 1989 to date. Annual. Covers federal and state law, programs, and jurisdiction. Details judicial decisions and agency regulations. Topics include regulation exemptions, the role of the EPA, mitigation enforcement, and the Coastal Zone Management Act; also includes addresses and phone numbers of regulatory offices and state agencies around the country.

2361. Leshy, John D. **The mining law: a study in perpetual motion.** Resources for the Future, 1987. 521 pp., bibl., index. Discusses problems and successes of free access and reviews the evolution and application of the law of discovery. Addresses the challenges facing the Mining Law, including multiple claims, environmental protection, and federally owned minerals under privately owned land. Explores the relationship and roles of the judiciary and executive branches in administering the law.

2362. National wetlands newsletter. Environmental Law Institute, 1979 to date. Bimonthly. Covers wetland science, management, and policy. Discusses legislative, administrative, and judicial developments; state and local activities; and private sector initiatives. Occasional special issues devoted to particular topics.

2363. Yaffe, Steven Lewis. **Prohibitive policy: implementing the federal Endangered Species Act.** MIT Press, MIT studies in American politics and public policy, v. 9, 1982. 239 pp., bibl., index. Social scientist examines the Endangered Species Act as an instance of prohibitive policy-making. Five cases illustrate the many social, legal, and political complexities.

2364. Sly, Peter W. **Reserved water rights settlement manual.** Island Press, 1988. 259 pp., index. By the director of the Conference of Western Attorneys General. How to settle conflicts between federal, state, and tribal jurisdictions over water rights. Focuses on settlement agreements, quantification standards, administrative and legislative implementation, and judicial finality of settlement.

2365. Uslaner, Eric M. **Shale barrel politics: energy and legislative leadership.** Stanford University Press, Stanford studies in the new political history, 1989. 241 pp., ill., bibl., index. Case study of barriers to U.S. energy policy. Chapters on synthetic energy development, natural gas deregulation, and Canadian energy policy. Argues that government and private institutions matter less than social norms and congressional unwillingness to offend constituents.

2366. Goldfarb, William. **Water law.** Lewis, 2d ed., 1988. 284 pp., bibl., index. Explains regulations, legal terms, and issues pertaining to all water law, including water diversion and distribution, development and protection, and treatment and pollution.

2367. Getches, David H. **Water law in a nutshell.** West, 1984. 439 pp., index. Concise review of water law in the publisher's "nutshell" series.

2368. Ingram, Helen. **Water politics: continuity and change.** University of New Mexico Press, 1990. 158 pp., ill., bibl., index. Presents a 1968 case study of New Mexico's role in passing the Colorado River Basin Act, which authorized the Central Arizona Project, last and biggest of western water projects. Discusses changes in water politics and policies since that time.

2369. Anderson, Terry L.; ed. **Water rights: scarce resource allocation, bureaucracy, and the environment.** Ballinger, 1983. 348 pp., ill., bibl., index. Papers provide an overview and historical background for water policy, focusing on the inherent waste of rent seeking; suggest possible improvements in restructuring water allocation institutions; and advocate tradable pollution rights and the privatization of local irrigation facilities.

2370. Tober, James A. **Wildlife and the public interest: nonprofit organizations and federal wildlife policy.** Praeger, 1989. 220 pp., bibl., index. Reports on the make-up, constituents, budgets, tactics and means used by various organizations to influence federal wildlife policy. Emphasizes activities in the late 1970s and

1980s and presents case studies of preserving the California condor and the bobcat.

2371. Smeltzer, John F. **Wildlife law enforcement: an annotated bibliography.** Colorado Division of Wildlife, Research Center Library, Divisional report, no. 13, 1985. 139 pp., ill., index. Almost 600 entries, arranged by author, annotated, with keyword index, on nonforensic wildlife law.

Pollution Control: United States (2372–2399)

2372. Rothenberg, Eric B.; Van Voorhees, Robert F.; eds. **The 1989 environmental yearbook.** Executive Enterprises, 1989. 597 pp. Environmental statutes; Clean Water Act, Superfund, energy developments; toxic substances; regulation of storage tanks; environmental claims in bankruptcy; OSHA hazard communication; FIFRA; RCRA; groundwater; safe drinking water; Clean Air Act; insurance for environmental loss; risk financing; international environmental law; SARA Title III; CERCLA; private cost recovery; criminal enforcement; asbestos; PCBs; underground injection.

2373. Office of Technology Assessment, U.S. Congress. **Acid rain and transported air pollutants: implications for public policy.** Unipub, 1985. 323 pp., ill., bibl., index. Outlines scientific aspects of sulfur dioxide, nitrogen oxides, and hydrocarbon pollutants. Examines the risks of damage versus the risks of control. Suggests steps to turn strategies into legislative proposals. Contains technical appendices studying emission control, effects of transported pollutants, and atmospheric processes. Final section contrasts North American experience with the situation in Europe.

2374. Van Strum, Carol. **A bitter fog: herbicides and human rights.** Sierra Club Books, 1983. 288 pp., bibl., index. An autobiographical account of a rural Oregon community's battle with the Forest Service to prevent the spraying of herbicides into the local watersheds. Includes many anecdotal accounts and testimonies from farmers, parents, Vietnam veterans, and others affected by Agent Orange and other herbicides.

2375. Clean Air Act: law and explanation. Commerce Clearing House, 1991. 536 pp. Reproduces full text, with the 1990 amendments, of the Clean Air Act. Reviews specific provisions and discusses aspects related to nonattainment areas, motor vehicles, air toxics, acid rain, permits, and EPA enforcement.

2376. Brownell, F. William; Zeugin, Lee B. **Clean air handbook.** Government Institutes, 1991. 336 pp. How the 1990 Clean Air Act amendments fit into the regulatory framework. Covers air quality regulation, control technology regulation, permits, acid deposition control, hazardous air pollutants, fuels regulation, enforcement and judicial review, and other topics.

2377. Frye, Russell S.; and others. **Clean Water Act permit guidance manual.** Executive Enterprises, 1984. 644 pp., ill., index. Explains how National Pollutant Discharge Elimination System permits work. Summarizes regulations and provides strategies for obtaining or modifying permits.

2378. Frye, Russell S.; and others. **Clean Water Act update.** Executive Enterprises, 1987. 198 pp. Reviews changes in the federal Clean Water Act of 1987. Discusses water quality standards and criteria, new permit regulations, and judicial-regulatory developments.

2379. Kovalik, Joan; ed. **The Clean Water Act with amendments.** Water Pollution Control Federation, 1982. 132 pp. Includes a historical overview of the act and a user's guide for those unfamiliar with legal terms. Written by a former deputy director of the EPA.

2380. Clean water deskbook. Environmental Law Institute, 1988. 521 pp., maps, ill. Presents the statutes and their legislative history, reviews the policies and agendas of relevant agencies, and analyzes important major acts, including the Clean Water Act and the Water Quality Act of 1987.

2381. Arbuckle, J. Gordon; Randle, Russell V.; and others. **Clean water handbook.** Government Institutes, 1990. 321 pp. How clean water laws and regulations work. Covers enforcement, water quality standards for industrial toxics, effluent limitations, national pollutant discharge system, control of storm water and nonpoint sources, monitoring, reporting and cleanup requirements, oil spill liability, and special issues affecting publicly owned treatment works.

2382. Brickman, Ronald; Jasanoff, Sheila; Ilgen, Thomas. **Controlling chemicals: the politics of regulation in Europe and the United States.** Cornell University Press, 1985. 344 pp., index. Systematically compares toxic chemical regulation in the United States, Great Britain, France, and Germany, based on research into four areas: food additives; pesticides; chemicals in the workplace; and industrial chemicals requiring premarket testing and notification. Final chapter includes cross-national analysis and suggestions for regulatory reform.

2383. Dunlap, Thomas R. **DDT: scientists, citizens, and public policy.** Princeton University Press, 1981. 318 pp., bibl., index. Case study places the DDT controversy in historical perspective. Covers evolution of knowledge and policy regarding pesticides, early regulations of DDT, and legal challenges in 1968–1969.

2384. The environmental compliance handbook series. Executive Enterprises, 1989. 4 vols. Volumes include The TSCA compliance handbook, The RCRA compliance handbook, The Clean Water Act compliance handbook, and The Clean Air Act compliance handbook.

2385. Rodgers, William H., Jr. **Environmental law.** West, 1986–1988. Index. 3 vols. Vols. 1 and 2: Air and water. Vol. 3: Pesticides and toxic substances. Provides an overview of the factors, forces, and parties involved in environmental law, regulations, and judicial decisions. Reviews legislative and regulatory changes, predicts future courses, and suggests strategies to maneuver successfully within the laws.

2386. Arbuckle, J. Gordon; and others. **Environmental law handbook.** Government Institutes, 11th ed., 1991. 666 pp., index. A reference text for the nonlegal community. Discusses the fundamentals of environmental law and common law. Covers broad issues (toxic substances, pesticide regulation) and specific acts (OSHA, NEPA, FIFRA, Clean Air Act, Clean Water Act). Discusses underground storage tanks, asbestos, and the Emergency Planning and Community Right-to-Know Act. Companion volumes are *Environmental regulatory glossary* and *Environmental statutes*.

2387. Tolley, George S.; and others, eds. **Environmental policy.** Ballinger, 1980–1981. Ill., bibl., index. 5 vols. Comprehensive review of what had been learned in the previous ten years about the formulation and analysis of environmental policies. Examines problems, control measures and costs, and analytic methods. Suggests improvements. Vol. 1: Elements of environmental analysis. Vol. 2: Air quality. Vol. 3: Water quality. Vol. 4: Solid wastes. Vol. 5: Recreation and aesthetics.

2388. Landy, Marc K.; Roberts, Marc J.; Thomas, Stephen R. **The Environmental Protection Agency: asking the wrong questions.** Oxford University Press, 1990. 309 pp., bibl. Seeks to ask the right questions: how technical issues of policy analysis are connected to the managerial and political problems faced by government officials. In three parts: origins and development of the EPA; studies of regulation in ozone, solid waste (RCRA), Superfund, cancer, and clean air; and the EPA during the Reagan years. Provides information on agency activities: setting standards, writing regulations, working in a legislative role, devising policy in concert with other agencies, and enforcing regulations.

2389. Anderson, Frederick R. **Environmental protection: law and policy.** Little, Brown, 1990. 914 pp., ill., index. Legal issues and precedents associated with air and water quality protection, toxic and hazardous waste control, and NEPA. Also covers the relationship between the environment and the common law, such as common law damages for environmental harm.

2390. Cross, Frank B. **Environmentally induced cancer and the law: risks, regulation, and victim compensation.** Quorum Books, 1989. 229 pp., ill., bibl., index. Discusses the difficulties of applying traditional judicial rules and procedures in cases of environmentally induced cancer (statute of limitations, linking the incidence of disease with exposure to a specific chemical). Suggests available avenues for successful regulation.

2391. Freedman, Warren. **Federal statutes on environmental protection: regulation in the public interest.** Quorum Books, 1987. 174 pp., bibl., index. Briefly summarizes 69 federal statutes. Emphasizes those relevant to hazardous waste disposal.

2392. Novick, Sheldon M.; Stever, Donald W.; Mellon, Margaret G.; eds. **Law of environmental protection.** Clark Boardman, Environmental law series, 1987 to date. Irregular: loose-leaf service. Identifies general principles in environmental law and summarizes statutory and case law in relation to them. Evaluates laws and policies, exposing conflicts and inconsistencies, and suggests improvements and clarifications.

2393. Yeager, Peter Cleary. **The limits of law: the public regulation of private pollution.** Cambridge University Press, 1991. 369 pp., bibl., index. Analytic history of industrial water pollution control. Reviews pre-1970 control efforts, passage of the Water Pollution Control Act in 1972, and the constraints that have shaped its implementation. Seeks to understand the limits to law's effectiveness, which are institutionalized in social, economic, and political relations.

2394. Conner, John D., Jr.; and others, eds. **Pesticide regulation handbook.** Executive Enterprises, 1987. 480 pp., bibl., index. Text and analysis of Federal Insecticide, Fungicide, and Rodenticide Act (FIFRA). Includes also laws regulating sale, application, and disposal; tolerances and food additives; biotechnology products; risks and benefits.

2395. Bosso, Christopher John. **Pesticides and politics: the life cycle of a public issue.** University of Pittsburgh Press, Pitt series in policy and institutional studies, 1987. 294 pp., bibl., index. Follows the development of the Federal Insecticide, Fungicide, and Rodenticide Act (FIFRA) to study the interactions of popular values and political structures and their influence on public policy-making.

2396. Yandle, Bruce. **The political limits of environmental regulation: tracking the unicorn.** Quorum Books, 1989. 180 pp., bibl., index. Investigates important elements in the EPA's regulatory decisions over the last 20 years. Argues that the agency's decisions have been strongly influenced by industry lobbyists and special interest groups.

2397. Wolf, Sidney M. **Pollution law handbook: a guide to federal environmental laws.** Quorum Books, 1988. 282 pp., index. Detailed summary of eight major federal statutes controlling pollution. Covers air and water pollution, toxic and solid waste, pesticides, Superfund, and community right-to-know laws.

2398. Liroff, Richard A. **Reforming air pollution regulation: the toil and trouble of EPA's bubble.** Conservation Foundation, An Issue report, 1986. 186 pp., ill., bibl., index. Reviews evolution of the bubble policy and its application to existing, new, and modified sources, using many specific examples. Recommends tightening trading rules, clarifying risks and actual results of trading to the public, and improving monitoring of emissions and state trading activity.

2399. Regulating pesticides in food: the Delaney paradox. National Academy Press, 1987. 272 pp., bibl., index. Prepared by the National Research Council. Report examines the EPA's methods for setting pesticide tolerances. Reviews legal framework and administrative system, potential cancer risks from current tolerance levels, alternative methods for establishing tolerances, and potential pesticide innovations.

Pollution Control: Hazardous Wastes, United States (2400–2419)

2400. Danford, Howard H.; ed. **The AHERA compliance manual: a guide to EPA's 1987 asbestos-in-schools rule.** SourceFinders; Center for Energy and Environmental Management, 1988. 518 pp. Covers every aspect of the Asbestos Hazard Emergency Response Act (AHERA) and how school officials can comply with the law. Includes a guide to technical assistance and loan and grant programs.

2401. Asbestos compliance encyclopedia. SourceFinders; Business and Legal Reports; Bureau of Law and Business, 1988. 2 vols. Guide for industrial managers. Explains OSHA's separate asbestos standards for industry and the construction trade. Includes information on how to set up an in-house asbestos orientation program, how to document compliance, and how to hire a consultant.

2402. Mendeloff, John M. **The dilemma of toxic substance regulation: how overregulation causes underregulation at OSHA.** MIT Press, MIT Press series on the regulation of economic activity, v. 17, 1989. 321 pp., ill., bibl., index. Using toxic substance regulation at OSHA for illustration, asserts that both over- and underregulation exist at OSHA. Examines reasons, noting judicial effects on both the slow pace and the strictness of regulation setting. Presents solutions involving procedural reform and alternatives to legislative reform.

2403. Davis, Charles E.; Lester, James P.; eds. **Dimensions of hazardous waste politics and policy.** Greenwood Press, Contributions in political science, no. 200, 1988. 256 pp., ill., bibl., index. Addresses the political issues of hazardous waste management policy creation and implementation in the 1980s, from the local to the international level.

2404. Quarles, John. **Federal regulation of hazardous wastes: a guide to RCRA.** Environmental Law Institute, 1982. 229 pp., bibl., index. An overview of RCRA, its regulatory specifics, and its enforcement and potential liabilities. Each chapter begins with a summary page, and key sentences and phrases are highlighted throughout.

2405. Haun, J. William. **Guide to the management of hazardous waste: a handbook for the businessman and the concerned citizen.** Fulcrum, 1991. 212 pp., bibl., index. Provides advice to the businessman on waste laws, regulations, risk assessment, cleanup, and liability. Supplies the citizen with suggestions on influencing public policy. Explains ways for both to reduce waste generation.

2406. Dominguez, George S.; ed. **Guidebook: Toxic Substances Control Act.** CRC Press, 1977–1983. 2 vols. Includes complete text and analysis of the Toxic Substances Control Act (TSCA). Reports on the EPA's implementation plan, steps for corporate preparedness, and recent litigation involving testing, PCBs, and health and safety issues. Assesses economic impacts of TSCA.

2407. Stensvaag, John-Mark. **Hazardous waste law and practice.** Wiley, 1986–1989. Index. 2 vols. Explains complex regulatory procedures of Subtitle C of the Resource Conservation and Recovery Act. Vol. 1 shows how to determine whether materials are hazardous. Vol. 2 discusses commercial chemical products, specific and non-specific source wastes, derivative wastes, delisted wastes, exclusions, and other topics.

2408. Briggum, Sue M.; and others. **Hazardous waste regulation handbook: a practical guide to RCRA and Superfund.** Executive Enterprises, 1986. 440 pp., ill., bibl., index. Obligations and requirements under RCRA and Superfund. Includes checklist of compliance obligations, EPA action deadlines, determination of hazardous materials, PCB regulations, and other topics.

2409. Stever, Donald W. **Law of chemical regulation and hazardous waste.** Clark Boardman, Environmental law series, 1986 to date. Ill., index. Annual: loose-leaf service. Chapters on the Toxic Substances Control Act (TSCA), pesticides, and hazardous waste describe major aspects of federal regulations, their implementation and their interpretation. Less-specific chapters treat food, air, water, and workplaces.

2410. Burns, Michael E.; ed. **Low-level radioactive waste regulation: science, politics, and fear.** Lewis, 1988. 311 pp., ill., bibl., index. Nineteen professionals in waste management, public health, law, medicine, and radiation chemistry reflect on the politics of disposal, cancer risk assessment, and other topics. Includes case histories involving disposal by the nuclear power industry and medical centers and ocean disposal.

2411. Lester, James P.; Bowman, Ann O'M.; eds. **The politics of hazardous waste management.** Duke University Press, Duke Press policy studies, 1983. 315 pp., bibl., index. Examines economic, technical, political, and perceptual factors shaping government responses to hazardous waste management at the national and subnational levels. Discusses the relative importance of bureaucratic infighting, public sector–private sector disputes, state versus local disagreements in the implementation of RCRA, and other topics.

2412. Lipschutz, Ronnie D. **Radioactive waste: politics, technology, and risk.** Ballinger, 1980. 247 pp., bibl., index. Reviews the nature and hazards of radioactivity; how radioactive wastes are produced, managed, stored, and disposed of; and the history and current (1980) state of waste management programs. Discusses the requirements for a successful program.

2413. Lewis, Richard J.; Sweet, Doris; eds. **Regulations, recommendations, and assessments extracted from the Registry of Toxic Effects of Chemical Substances.** U.S. Department of Health and Human Services, Public Health Service, Centers for Disease Control, 1986. 416 pp. Provides selected data on almost 5000 hazardous chemicals.

2414. Fire, Frank L. **SARA Title III: intent and implementation of hazardous materials regulation.** Van Nostrand Reinhold, 1990. 279 pp. Describes the background, provisions, and intent of SARA Title III; intended to to help industry and local communities implement it successfully. Covers emergency response plans at the state and local levels and training. A final chapter provides an overview of hazardous materials and their classification.

2415. SARA Title III law and regulations. Government Institutes, 3d ed., 1989. 310 pp. Written by attorneys specializing in SARA cases. Explains and analyzes the Emergency Planning and Community Right-to-Know Act. Covers emergency planning and notification, reporting requirements, and general provisions. Appendix includes relevant regulations.

2416. Needham, Helen Cohn; Menefee, Mark; eds. **Superfund: a legislative history: the evolution of selected sections of the comprehensive Environmental Response, Compensation and Liability Act.** Environmental Law Institute, 1982. 2130 pp., index. Presents all relevant congressional documents and covers many topics: liability, government abatement authority, federally permitted release, victim compensation, and others.

2417. Superfund deskbook: an ELI deskbook. Environmental Law Institute, 1989. 411 pp. A guide to changes in the Superfund Amendments and Reauthorization Act of 1986, prepared by the staff of the *Environmental law reporter*.

2418. Toxic substances and hazardous wastes. American Law Institute–American Bar Association Committee on Continuing Professional Education; Environmental Law Institute, 1980. 1036 pp. Presents articles, briefs, pleadings, and excerpts from proposed, pending, and existing federal and state legislation. Analyzes recent legal developments and identifies new issues and trends.

2419. TSCA handbook. Government Institutes, 2d ed., 1989. 490 pp. Written by attorneys engaged in Toxic Substances Control Act (TSCA) practice. Covers activities subject to TCSA, the TCSA inventory, new chemical review, regulation of new chemicals, testing under TCSA, reporting, TSCA inspections and enforcement, internal audits, asbestos hazard, radon, and other topics.

Law and Policies: State and Local. Regional (2420–2450)

2420. Hall, Bob; Kerr, Mary Lee. **1991–1992 Green index: A state-by-state guide to the nation's environmental health.** Island Press, 1991. 168 pp., index.

Charts compare the status of states with respect to air and water pollution, energy, hazardous waste, workplace health, and more. Describes, contrasts, and analyzes state policies; identifies regional environmental strengths and problems; and indicates areas for improvement.

2421. Acid rain 1986: a handbook for states and provinces: research, information, policy. Acid Rain Foundation, 1986. 610 pp. Proceedings of a 1986 conference. Covers scientific and legislative activities at local, state or provincial, national, and international levels.

2422. Allan, Theresa; Platt, Brenda; Morris, David. **Beyond 25 percent: materials recovery comes of age.** Institute for Local Self-Reliance, 1989. 134 pp., bibl. Answers questions on how to gain citizen support and modify existing collection processes. Describes specific strategies and programs of communities in the United States that have achieved 25 percent recovery.

2423. Institute for Local Self-Reliance. **Beyond 40 percent: record-setting recycling and composting programs.** Island Press, 1990. 270 pp., ill. Reviews successful recycling programs around the country. Discusses equipment, costs, collection and processing facilities, and methods. Includes contact information for recycling program officials in featured cities.

2424. Stewart, Lynn. **California hazardous waste enforcement: a practical guide.** Environmental Law Institute, 1989. 169 pp. Intricate set of laws and regulations explained.

2425. Smith, Herbert H. **The citizen's guide to zoning.** Planners Press, 1983. 242 pp., ill., bibl., index. Uses straightforward, informal approach to discuss basic principles of zoning, process of developing zoning regulations, zoning administration, and variances.

2426. Community right-to-know deskbook. Environmental Law Institute, 1988. 407 pp. How to fulfill reporting requirements under SARA Title III, with statutory and regulatory deadlines.

2427. Nelson, Arthur C.; ed. **Development impact fees: policy rationale, practice, theory, and issues.** Planners Press, 1988. 396 pp. Evaluates the theory, application, and results of impact fees. Addresses economic, public finance, incidence, equity, social, and ethical issues. Includes advice on how to implement and administer a program and examines alternatives to excise taxes and linkage fees.

2428. Directory of state environmental agencies. Environmental Law Institute, 1977 to date. Describes the structure, jurisdiction, responsibilities, and programs of each state's environmental agency. Each entry has a general section on primary responsibilities of agencies and a section on specific program areas. Includes addresses and telephone numbers.

2429. Moskowitz, Joel S. **Environmental liability and real property transactions: law and practice.** Wiley, 1989. 384 pp., bibl. Explains environmental aspects of real estate transactions. Suggests methods of gathering and assessing information and ways to lessen liabilities. Reviews related laws, regulations, and cases.

2430. Committee on Ground Water Quality Protection. **Ground water quality protection: state and local strategies.** National Academy Press, 1986. 309 pp., ill., index. Briefly reviews state and local groundwater programs in ten states. Discusses groundwater protection strategies, such as classification systems, water quality standards, and control of contamination sources.

2431. Henderson, Timothy R.; Trauberman, Jeffrey; Gallagher, Tara. **Groundwater strategies for state action.** Environmental Law Institute, 1984. 353 pp. Reviews the nature of groundwater. Explains why some state programs are successful and how they can be adapted for use in other states. Covers policy goals, management techniques, enforcement methods, and funding sources.

2432. Jessup, Deborah Hitchcock. **Guide to state environmental programs.** BNA Books, 2d ed., 1990. 700 pp. Explains the organization and agendas of each state's environmental programs. Lists addresses, phone numbers, and recommended contacts. Includes directories of related federal, state, and local agencies.

2433. **Journal of the American Planning Association.** American Planning Association, 1925 to date. Quarterly. Continues: Journal of the American Institute of Planners. Articles for and by academics and practitioners in urban and regional planning, with emphasis on legal, policy, and economic aspects.

2434. **Monthly checklist of state publications.** Library of Congress; Government Printing Office, 1955 to date. Monthly. Records states' publications received by the Library of Congress. Since 1987 contains monthly and annual subject indexes. A significant source of information on obscure but valuable publications, on topics from air quality to zoning law.

2435. Kusler, Jon A. **Our national wetland heritage: a protection guidebook.** Environmental Law Institute, 1983. 167 pp., ill., bibl. Intended for local governments, conservationists, and landowners interested in wetland protection. Identifies management principles and standards, protection techniques, and proposal evaluation procedures. Assesses federal, state, and local reg-

ulatory efforts. Addresses private sector roles and alternative, nonregulatory methods.

2436. Dandekar, Hemalata C.; ed. **The planner's use of information: techniques for collection, organization, and communication.** Planners Press, 1988. 224 pp., ill., bibl. Advice and techniques for determining the most appropriate method for handling planning problems. Chapters include applications and bibliographies to facilitate understanding.

2437. **Planning.** American Society of Planning Officials, 1969 to date. Monthly. Articles, news, and commentary on the professional activity of planning in the United States, with emphasis on planners, projects, and programs.

2438. Thompson, Paul. **Poison runoff: a guide to state and local control of nonpoint source water pollution.** Natural Resources Defense Council, 1989. 484 pp., ill. A manual for controlling pollution runoff from agriculture, grazing, urban development, construction, logging, and mining.

2439. Popper, Frank J. **The politics of land-use reform.** University of Wisconsin Press, 1981. 321 pp., bibl., index. Discusses the political, social, environmental, and economic dimensions of land-use reform in the United States since the 1960s. Focuses on six state-level programs.

2440. So, Frank S.; Getzels, Judith; eds. **The practice of local government planning.** International City Management Association, 2d ed., 1988. 554 pp., ill., bibl., index. New and revised chapters on district, environmental, and transportation planning; urban design; zoning; subdivision regulation; and economic development.

2441. So, Frank S.; Hand, Irving; McDowell, Bruce D.; eds. **The practice of state and regional planning.** American Planning Association, Municipal management series, 1986. 653 pp., ill., bibl. Part I examines the context and process, evolution, practice, techniques, and administration of state and regional planning. Part II discusses impact and policy analysis and techniques of information collection and management. Part III focuses on urban, rural, and economic development. Part IV features major state and regional plans, including discussion of such elements as housing, transportation, energy, environmental protection, and solid waste management.

2442. **Resource guide to state environmental management.** Council of State Governments, 2d ed., 1990. 198 pp., ill. Directory of some 3800 state environmental contacts. Information on environmental spending, bureaucracies, and programs.

2443. Colman, William G. **State and local government and public-private partnerships: a policy issues handbook**. Greenwood Press, 1989. 437 pp., bibl., index. Encyclopedic reference and guide to management and policy in state and local government.

2444. Balachandran, M.; Balachandran, S.; eds. **State and local statistics sources, 1990–1991**. Gale Research, 1990. 1124 pp. Arranged in 54 state and territorial sections. Some 40,000 entries refer to sources of business, social, educational, and economic data for states, cities, and localities.

2445. Selmi, Daniel P.; Manaster, Kenneth A. **State environmental law**. Clark Boardman, Environmental Law Series, 1989 to date. Annual: loose-leaf service. Covers the common law, state regulatory requirements, environmental impact assessment, and environmental litigation. Includes issues of pesticide regulation, coastal zone and wetlands management, and forestry and mining practices. Guide to state agencies gives contact information and agency policy and authority.

2446. Gill, Kay; Tufts, Susan E.; eds. **State government research directory**. Gale Research, 1987. 349 pp. Subtitle: A descriptive guide to basic and applied research and data collection programs and activities sponsored and/or conducted by the government agencies of the 50 states, the District of Columbia, and the U.S. territories. Includes contact information, staff size and composition, special facilities, and publications. Indexed by subject, keyword, master name, and agency. Some topics covered: energy and natural resources, conservation and wildlife, parks and recreation, environment, education, public utilities, business and industry, and agriculture.

2447. **State information book**. Potomac Books, 1975 to date. Maps. Continues: *State information and federal region book*. Continued by *State yellow book*. Collects data on each state's demographics, geography, administration, government, judiciary, legislature, economy, and education; includes contact information for state organizations and officials.

2448. Salvesen, David. **Wetlands: mitigating and regulating development impacts**. Urban Land Institute, 1990. 120 pp. Examines issues involved in wetland regulation, conservation, and development and describes federal and state wetland regulations. Focuses on six progressive, tough state programs and discusses mitigation strategies.

2449. Babcock, Richard F. **The zoning game: mu-** nicipal practices and policies. University of Wisconsin Press, 1966. 202 pp., bibl. Identifies the players in zoning regulation and disputes—city planners, lawyers, judges, developers, and local legislators—and the rules, purposes, and principles of zoning.

2450. Babcock, Richard F.; Siemon, Charles L. **The zoning game revisited**. Lincoln Institute of Land Policy, 1985. 304 pp., ill., bibl., index. Self-described "brazenly anecdotal" companion to *The zoning game* (1966). Chronicles land-use disputes in eight states, from the rich and very rich in Palm Beach, Florida, to a shopping center in Sioux City, Iowa.

Land Preservation. Trusts. State Parks (2451–2462)

2451. Keller, Jane Eblen. **Adirondack wilderness: a story of man and nature**. Syracuse University Press, 1980. 241 pp., ill., bibl., index. Recounts the history of Adirondack State Park, composed of both private and public land. Focuses on how evolving American attitudes toward nature have affected its formation and use. Explains the complex decisions and compromises in the management and preservation of its resources.

2452. Hoose, Phillip M. **Building an ark: tools for the preservation of natural diversity through land protection**. Island Press, 1981. 221 pp., ill., bibl., index. Handbook of techniques for protecting privately held land, aimed primarily at professionals. Discusses heritage programs, notification of landowners of ecological resources on their land, registration and dedication, designation of public lands, management agreements, acquisition of fee title, conservation easements, and lobbying.

2453. Foster, Charles H. W. **The Cape Cod National Seashore: a landmark alliance**. University Press of New England, Experiments in bioregionalism, 1985. 125 pp., bibl., index. Narrative history and analysis examines the first 20 years of the Cape Cod National Seashore Advisory Commission in the context of bioregional conservation efforts. Includes a record of Commission meetings, the text of the law creating the national seashore, and numerous references.

2454. Diehl, Janet; Barrett, Thomas S. **The conservation easement handbook: managing land conservation and historic preservation easement programs**. Land Trust Exchange, 1988. 269 pp., ill., bibl., index. Based on a survey of more than 200 easement programs. Explains the management of a program, from development and promotion to monitoring and enforcement. Discusses easement termination and valuation. Includes two model easements for land conservation and historical preservation.

2455. Barrett, Thomas S.; Livermore, Putnam. **The conservation easement in California.** Island Press, 1983. 173 pp., bibl., index. Authoritative legal guide discusses historical and legal background, tax implications, and problems in drafting easements.

2456. Exchange. Land Trust Alliance, 1982 to date. Quarterly. Practical articles on land conservation. The Alliance promotes expansion of the land trust community and provides services and programs to support land trusts.

2457. Small, Stephen J. **The federal tax law of conservation easements.** Land Trust Alliance, 1990. 437 pp. Interprets IRS regulations on gifts of conservation easements. Discusses related income and estate tax considerations, historic preservation easement, and other topics.

2458. Brenneman, Russell L.; Bates, Sarah M.; eds. **Land-saving action.** Island Press, 1984. 249 pp., bibl., index. Thirty-five articles contributed by 29 experts cover all aspects of private land conservation. Includes creating and managing a land-saving organization, initiating and completing conservation transactions, applicable portions of the federal tax code, and options and procedures for the private landowner interested in saving land.

2459. Cox, Thomas R. **The park builders: a history of state parks in the Pacific Northwest.** University of Washington Press, 1988. 248 pp., ill., bibl., index. Institutional and administrative history. Focuses on politics and key individuals. Explains factors contributing to successful state park systems.

2460. Montana Land Reliance, Land Trust Exchange. **Private options: tools and concepts for land conservation.** Island Press, 1982. 292 pp., bibl., index. Proceedings of two 1981 conferences. Presents issues facing local land preservation organizations and the tools and methods they use. Reviews estate-planning laws and relevant tax laws. Advises on managing conservation easements, interacting with landowners and public agencies, and assessing land for preservation.

2461. Starting a land trust: a guide to forming a land conservation organization. Land Trust Alliance, 1990. 184 pp. Covers articles of incorporation and by-laws, financial management, liability and insurance, building public support, membership and fund-raising, getting and keeping tax exemption status, and land protection tools. Includes case studies, a resources list, and sample documents.

2462. Myers, Phyllis; Green, Sharon N. **State parks in a new era.** Conservation Foundation, 1989. Ill., bibl. 3 vols. Growth, management, and direction of state parks since 1955, in three volumes. Vol. 1: A look at the legacy. Vol. 2: Future directions in funding. Vol.3: Strategies for tourism and economic development.

Section 11

Economy. Economics. Business and Industry

To many in the business world, environmental laws and policies discourage or reduce economic activity and render companies less competitive. Costs of regulation seem out of touch with "bottom line" business realities. To environmental advocates, on the other hand, economic activity usually threatens life support systems. Regulation never seems to go far enough, and arguments about costs are seen as excuses to do nothing.

The entries in this section record these conflicting interactions of economics, economic activity, and environmental conservation, with special reference to sustainable development. The entries cover economies as a whole, development, and industrial sectors. They also introduce the study of environmental economics.

As with law and politics, titles having to do with economics or economic activity appear in many sections of the bibliography. What distinguishes titles in this section is their closeness to economics as a field of study.

Economy. Costs and Benefits. Valuation
This introductory group has entries that refer to whole economies or political economy and also to methods, techniques, and concepts of environmental economics, particularly cost-benefit analysis and valuation.

See also:

- Section 1: Global resources and environment; environmental management
- Section 2: Climate change
- Section 8: Society and environment
- Section 9: Ethics, philosophy, religion
- Section 10: Law, politics, government
- Section 12: Public health, medicine; toxic threats, hazards; risk assessment; health protection, safety, emergencies
- Section 14: Quantification, measurement, statistics

Development. In this subgroup are titles on development, economic growth, and sustainable development that tend more toward economic aspects.

See also:

- Section 1: Global resources and environment; environmental management; biodiversity, conservation biology, genetics
- Section 2: Climate change
- Section 3: Freshwater; marine
- Section 4: Lands, reserves and parks, management
- Section 5: Food and agriculture
- Section 6: Forests and forest resources: regions and countries
- Section 7: Wildlife management; endangered species, conservation biology
- Section 8: Society and environment: country studies; social and human ecology, population
- Section 9: Ethics, philosophy, religion; built environment, architecture, historical preservation
- Section 10: Law and policies: state and local, regional
- Section 14: Modeling and simulation

Industry. Economic Sectors

The whole economy having been introduced, this group presents entries dealing in more detail with business and industry. Most of the entries are in the subgroups that follow.

See also:

- Section 1: Environmental management
- Section 8: Society and environment: country studies; individuals and environment; behavior and psychology
- Section 10: U.S. executive agencies, administration and regulation
- Section 13: Environmental control technology

Natural Resource Industries. This subgroup deals with economic sectors based completely on natural resources, whether products or services, and the study of them in natural resource economics. Topics include wildlands, nonrenewable resources and mining, fisheries, protected areas, tourism, and others.

See also Agriculture and Forest Products, below.

Agriculture and Forest Products. An even more narrowly defined group of entries on natural resources economics deals with farms and forests. There are titles on land, agricultural, and forestry economics; on agribusiness, forest products industries, timber sales, timber supply, and on property and tenure issues.

See also:

- Section 1: Global resources and environment; environmental management
- Section 3: Freshwater; marine; fisheries

- Section 4: Land degradation, erosion, reclamation
- Section 5: Food and agriculture; range management, pastoral systems
- Section 6: Forests and forest resources: regions and countries
- Section 8: Rural communities
- Section 10: U.S. executive agencies, administration and regulation; natural resources: United States; water, wildlife, minerals: United States; forests, parks, wilderness: United States
- Section 13: Water engineering; civil engineering, construction, geotechnology

Pollution. Industrial Wastes. Here are works detailing cost-benefit analyses of air and water pollution; emissions trading; environmental audits; workplace hazards; waste minimization; and industrial disasters.

See also:

- Section 2: Climate change; air pollution, atmospheric chemistry; acid rain; ozone
- Section 3: Water pollution
- Section 4: Land degradation, erosion, reclamation
- Section 5: Atmospheric environment, pollution, pesticides
- Section 10: U.S. executive agencies, administration and regulation; pollution control: hazardous wastes, United States
- Section 12: Toxic threats, hazards; health protection, safety, emergencies
- Section 13: Environmental control technology; hazardous wastes

Energy. As with pollution, entries referring to energy are found in almost every section of the bibliography. Here the entries deal with the production and economics of energy: coal and oil, renewable sources, demand, policy, and statistics.

See also:

- Section 1: Global resources and environment; environmental management; chemistry, biogeochemical cycles, pollutants; energy
- Section 2: Air pollution, atmospheric chemistry
- Section 3: Freshwater; water pollution
- Section 4: Land degradation, erosion, reclamation
- Section 5: Food and agriculture
- Section 8: Society and environment; social and human ecology, population; individuals and environment; behavior and psychology
- Section 10: Law, politics, government
- Section 12: Toxic threats, hazards; risk assessment
- Section 13: Water engineering; energy technology; radioactive, nuclear

2463. Berle, G. **Business information sourcebook.** Wiley, 1991. 400 pp. Collects "the most important references" among currently available business directories, indexes, books, periodicals, electronic sources, and government printings. Provides annotations and bibliographic information.

2464. Daniells, Lorna M. **Business information sources.** University of California Press, 1985. 673 pp., index. Provides bibliographic information on basic business reference sources, including bibliographies, indexes, directories, and statistical and financial reports. Later chapters focus on specific business functions, covering banking, insurance, marketing, international, and human resources management.

2465. Strauss, Diane Wheeler. **Handbook of business information: a guide for librarians, students and researchers.** Libraries Unlimited, 1988. 537 pp., ill., bibl., index. Reviews the many formats of business information, including directories, periodicals, government reports, and databases. Covers ten business fields, such as marketing, banking, and stocks. Introduces basic concepts and key vocabulary and identifies and describes important information sources.

Economy. Costs and Benefits. Valuation (2466–2487)

2466. Freeman, A. Myrick, III. **The benefits of environmental improvement: theory and practice.** Johns Hopkins University Press; Resources for the Future, 1979. 272 pp., ill., bibl., index. Examines concepts and practical considerations of measuring pollution control benefits. Attempts to assess the value of an improved environment in terms of longevity, recreational use, and productivity.

2467. Dasgupta, Partha. **The control of resources.** Basil Blackwell, 1982. 223 pp., ill., bibl., index. Presents mathematical models linking common features of environmental pollution and overexploitation of resources. Discusses welfare economics, use of accounting prices, irreversibility, and uncertainty.

2468. **Ecological economics.** Elsevier, 1989 to date. Quarterly. Journal of the International Society for Ecological Economics. Publishes research papers concerned with extending and integrating the subjects of ecology and economics. Valuation principles and uses, modeling methods, alternative approaches to economic theory, case studies of ecological-economic conflict, methods of implementing efficient environmental policies, and other research areas.

2469. Hufschmidt, Maynard M.; Hyman, Eric L.; eds. **Economic approaches to natural resource and environmental quality analysis.** Tycooly International, 1982. 333 pp., ill., bibl. Proceedings and papers of a 1979 conference on extended cost-benefit analysis.

2470. Pearce, David W.; Turner, R. Kerry. **Economics of natural resources and the environment.** Harvester Wheatsheaf, 1990. 378 pp., ill., bibl. Applies conventional economics to environmental concerns. Considers sustainable economies; the economics of pollution (markets, taxation, permits, valuing damage, costs of control); renewable and nonrenewable natural resources; and ethics and future generations.

2471. Faber, M.; and others. **Entropy, environment and resources: an essay in physio-economics.** Springer-Verlag, 1987. 205 pp., ill., bibl., index. Analyzes the interrelationship of environment, resources, and economics using theromodynamic concepts and methods. Theoretical in approach; addressed primarily to social scientists.

2472. Tietenberg, Thomas H. **Environmental and natural resource economics.** Scott, Foresman, 2d ed., 1988. 559 pp., ill., bibl., index. Introductory textbook covers renewable and nonrenewable resources, stationary and mobile source air pollution, toxic substances, water scarcity, forest resources, and regional and global air pollutants. Includes problem sets.

2473. Daly, Herman E.; Cobb, John B., Jr. **For the common good: redirecting the economy toward community, the environment, and a sustainable future.** Beacon Press, 1989. 482 pp., bibl., index. Critique of neoclassical economics and its destructive effects by an economist and theologian. Proposes to integrate economics with public policy and social ethics. Illustrates ideas with specific recommendations in the areas of population, land use, agriculture, industry, labor, and income and tax policies.

2474. Goldsmith, Edward. **The great U-turn: de-industrializing society.** Green Books, 1988. 217 pp., ill., bibl. Shows how current trends in education, unemployment, health, pollution, and war reflect modern society's overreliance on technology and economic progress. Only a "great U-turn" can prevent modern industrial societies from going the way of the Roman Empire.

2475. Kneese, Allen V.; Sweeney, James L.; eds. **Handbook of natural resource and energy economics.** Elsevier, Handbooks in economics, v. 6, 1985 to date. Ill., bibl., index. 3 vols. Examines current theory and application methods. Volumes I and II cover environmental and renewable resources, including assessing benefits of environmental programs, national input-output models, the economics of outdoor recreation, and case studies of resource management in the Soviet Union and China; Volume III addresses energy and minerals, including chapters on the economics of environmental policy.

2476. Journal of environmental economics and management. Academic Press, 1974 to date. Quarterly. Presents theoretical and empirical papers in economics that link economic and natural systems. Mathematical and statistical analyses predominate.

2477. Johnston, George M.; Freshwater, David; Favero, Philip; eds. **Natural resource and environmental policy analysis: cases in applied economics.** Westview Press, 1988. 282 pp., ill., bibl., index. Eleven case studies examine political institutions and economic outcomes, economic efficiency in policy analysis, and mathematical models useful to policy analysis. Each case study addresses relevant biological, physical, social, and institutional aspects. Some examples include agricultural land policy, nuclear waste disposal, below-cost timber sales, and Columbia River water management.

2478. Rees, Judith. **Natural resources: allocation, economics, and policy.** Routledge, 1990. 499 pp., ill., bibl., index. Analyzes the spatial distribution of resource availability, development and consumption, and distribution of wealth and welfare derived from global resources. An interdisciplinary consideration of the interactions between economic forces, administrative structures, and political institutions.

2479. Neary, J. Peter; van Wijnbergen, Sweder; eds. **Natural resources and the macroeconomy.** Centre for Economic Policy Research, 1986. 352 pp., ill., bibl., index. Using several models, examines the often negative effects of natural resource booms. Describes the experiences of Colombia, Nigeria, Egypt, the Netherlands, and other countries.

2480. Murdoch, William W. **The poverty of nations: the political economy of hunger and population.** Johns Hopkins University Press, 1980. 382 pp., ill., bibl., index. Integrates our understandings of world hun-

ger and its causes, covering human fertility, constraints on food production, origin of the dual economy, and causes of deteriorating environments.

2481. Hirschhorn, Joel S.; Oldenburg, Kirsten U. **Prosperity without pollution: the prevention strategy for industry and consumers.** Van Nostrand Reinhold, 1990. 386 pp., bibl., index. Calls for pollution prevention rather than control. Encourages consumers to demand research and incentives to lessen pollution. Case studies illustrate effective and ineffective methods and strategies.

2482. Dryzek, John S. **Rational ecology: environment and political economy.** Basil Blackwell, 1987. 270 pp., ill., bibl., index. Evaluates social choice mechanisms such as markets, persuasion, and legal systems in terms of their ecological rationality. Concludes that radical decentralization is more ecologically rational than prevailing social choice mechanisms.

2483. Coombs, H. C. **The return of scarcity: strategies for an economic future.** Cambridge University Press, 1990. 230 est. pp. Collected essays of an economist specializing in resource use and allocation. Some topics include the changing role of governments in preservation and development; environmental law; quality-of-life assessment; and the interplay of economic and ecological issues.

2484. Daly, Herman E. **Steady-state economics.** Island Press, 2d ed., 1991. 300 pp., index. Revised edition of an influential text first published in 1977, arguing that unbridled growth and development are not the solution to all economic and social problems and in fact damage the global environment and system.

2485. Turner, R. Kerry; ed. **Sustainable environmental management: principles and practice.** Belhaven Press; Westview Press, 1988. 292 pp., ill., bibl., index. Identifies basic principles and approaches and their implementations in cases of pollution control, new agricultural and biological techniques, and wildlife valuation.

2486. Mitchell, Robert Cameron; Carson, Richard T. **Using surveys to value public goods: the contingent valuation method.** Resources for the Future, 1989. 463 pp., bibl., index. Provides a theoretical basis for the contingent valuation method and discusses its advantages and the circumstances in which it works. Addresses such topics as the honesty and meaning of respondents' answers, enhancing reliability, and measuring bias.

2487. Valuing health risks, costs, and benefits for environmental decision making: report of a confer-

ence. National Academy Press, 1990. 244 pp. Reviews philosophical, political, administrative, economic, and scientific aspects of cost-benefit analysis. Recommends improvements of the analysis used for regulation.

Development (2488–2509)

2488. Spooner, Brian; Mann, H. S.; eds. **Desertification and development: dryland ecology in social perspective.** Academic Press, 1982. 407 pp., ill., bibl., index. Notes the major roles economic and political forces play in desertification, often manifested in poorly planned development programs. Reports on work done at two regional programs, the Turan Programme in Iran and the Central Arid Zone Research Institute in India.

2489. Sachs, Ignacy; Fawcett, Peter, trans. **Development and planning.** Cambridge University Press; Editions de la Maison des Sciences des Hommes, 1987. 134 pp., bibl., index. A collection of articles meant to challenge "a rigid, technocratic, economist view of development." Topics include planning and local autonomy, ecodevelopment, anthropological economics, and the crisis of the Welfare State.

2490. Mabogunje, Akin L. **The development process: a spatial perspective.** Unwin Hyman, 1989. 399 pp., maps, ill., bibl., index. Notes the imbalance between rural and urban development in many tropical African countries. Presents specific strategies for achieving integrated development based on reduced population growth, population mobility, improved information flow, and internal trade.

2491. Welsh, Brian W. W.; Butorin, Pavel; eds. **Dictionary of development: Third World, economy, environment, society.** Garland, Garland reference library of social science, v. 487, 1990. 2 vols. Defines and describes facts, concepts, events, and issues pertinent to the development process. A country indicator chart provides economic and social statistical data on developing countries. Essays evaluate issues and policies in development. Includes an annotated listing of nongovernment organizations, national and international periodicals, and newsletters.

2492. Leonard, H. Jeffrey; ed. **Divesting nature's capital: the political economy of environmental abuse in the Third World.** Holmes & Meier, 1985. 299 pp., bibl., index. Examines how various natural resource and environmental constraints affect contemporary economic development strategies and prospects of the developing nations of the world.

2493. Collard, David; Pearce, David; Ulph, David; eds. **Economics, growth, and sustainable environments.** Macmillan, 1988. 205 pp., ill., bibl., index. Essays attempting to deal with the "greening" of economics. Topics include the compatibility of economic growth and environmental sustainability, the validity of gross national product as a measure of welfare, and the role of risk analysis in policy evaluation.

2494. Barbier, Edward B. **Economics, natural-resource scarcity and development: conventional and alternative views.** Earthscan, 1989. 223 pp., ill., bibl., index. Demonstrates that conventional economic theory does not properly address "nonproductive" environmental values. Posits an alternative view with greater emphasis on environmental protection and sustainability.

2495. Hufschmidt, Maynard M.; and others. **Environment, natural systems, and development: an economic valuation guide.** Johns Hopkins University Press, 1983. 338 pp., ill., bibl., index. Surveys techniques to quantify environmental impact of development projects in monetary terms. Emphasizes cost-benefit analysis and reviews alternative input-output and mathematical programming strategies. Gives examples from developed and developing nations.

2496. The environment, public health, and human ecology: considerations for economic development. World Bank, 1985. 294 pp., ill., bibl. Provides basic guidance in identifying, detecting, measuring, and controlling effects of projects that impact environment, health, and human ecology. Summarizes the World Bank's environmental guidelines and considers problems and issues associated with tropical agriculture development, industrial development, energy projects, and urban and regional development. Includes a checklist of considerations, a 75-page bibliography, and a discussion of information sources.

2497. Ives, Jack D.; Messerli Bruno. **The Himalayan dilemma: reconciling development and conservation.** Routledge, 1989. 295 pp., ill., bibl., index. Environmental and socioeconomic analysis of the Himalayan area challenges many perceptions and assumptions about the causes of mountain deforestation, soil erosion, and downstream destruction.

2498. Leonard, H. Jeffrey. **Natural resources and economic development in Central America: a regional environmental profile.** Transaction, 1987. 279 pp., ill., bibl., index. Produced by the International Institute for Environment and Development. Focuses on problems of development assistance policies.

2499. Steidlmeier, Paul. **The paradox of poverty: a reappraisal of economic development policy.** Ballinger, 1987. 318 pp. Presents an analytic framework that explicitly recognizes population and resources, technological innovation, social organization and power, and cultural values and preferences as inseparable components of the development process.

2500. Luten, Daniel B. **Progress against growth: Daniel B. Luten on the American landscape.** Guilford Press, 1986. 366 pp., ill., bibl., index. Compilation of articles and papers by a research chemist, environmental activist, and academic geographer. Divided into sections on population, food and agriculture, energy, water as a resource, wild nature, and conservation.

2501. Goodland, Robert; ed. **Race to save the tropics: ecology and economics for a sustainable future.** Island Press, 1990. 219 pp., bibl, index. Contributors address a broad range of issues related to development projects in the tropics and the application of ecological principles. Practical examples, broad coverage, concise presentations, and numerous references.

2502. Kneese, Allen V.; Brown, F. Lee. **The Southwest under stress: national resource development issues in a regional setting.** Johns Hopkins University Press; Resources for the Future, 1981. 268 pp., ill., bibl., index. Examines effects of economic development on water, air quality, and other environmental factors. Analyzes resulting distribution of benefits, with special attention to the Navajo Indians.

2503. Berg, Robert J.; Whitaker, Jennifer Seymour; eds. **Strategies for African development: a study for the Committee on African Development Studies.** University of California Press, 1986. 603 pp., bibl., index. Contributed papers present specific strategies for African governments and their collaborators in such fields as agriculture, protection of renewable resources, population growth, public health, small-scale industry, and human resources development.

2504. Tri, H. C.; and others. **Strategies for endogenous development.** Oxford & IBH, 1986. 309 pp., bibl. Examines factors encouraging development from within and in service of a society.

2505. Tolba, Mostafa Kamal. **Sustainable development: constraints and opportunities.** Butterworth, 1987. 221 pp., index. Thirty-five statements and speeches made between 1982 and 1986 by the executive director of the United Nations Environment Programme supporting sound environmental management and long-term development.

2506. Pearce, David; Barbier, Edward; Markandya, Anil. **Sustainable development: economics and environment in the Third World.** Elgar (dist. by Gower), 1990. 217 pp., ill., bibl. Discusses principles of ecology and economic progress, "discounting the future," and economic appraisal with respect to the natural environment. Case studies of Indonesia, the Sudan, Botswana, Nepal, and Amazonia apply these concepts, provide valuable data, and offer policy strategies for sustainable development.

2507. Redclift, Michael R. **Sustainable development: exploring the contradictions.** Methuen, 1987. 221 pp., ill., bibl., index. Explores the contradictory relationships of development, environment, and the international economy. The success of "sustainable development" will depend on a redefinition of "development."

2508. Southgate, Douglas D.; Disinger, John F.; eds. **Sustainable resource development in the Third World.** Westview Press, Westview special studies in natural resources and energy management, 1987. 177 pp., ill., bibl., index. Selected papers from a 1985 symposium call for analysis of market and institutional forces influencing natural resource use and local values and traditions. Case studies, mostly from Africa, are also presented.

2509. Bunker, Stephen G. **Underdeveloping the Amazon: extraction, unequal exchange and the failure of the modern state.** University of Illinois Press, 1985. 279 pp., ill., bibl., index. Argues that extractive economies have degraded and continue to damage the human and ecological environments of the Amazon basin.

Industry. Economic Sectors (2510–2523)

2510. Leonard, H. Jeffrey. **Are environmental regulations driving U.S. industries overseas?** Conservation Foundation, 1984. 155 pp., ill., bibl., index. Not in industries where product demand is strong and technology superior, as in mineral processing, chemical production, and pulp and paper. Industries that have relocated abroad have done so in response to several factors or because they use extremely hazardous chemicals.

2511. Gilbreath, Kent; ed. **Business and the environment: toward common ground.** Conservation Foundation, 2d ed., 1984. 533 pp., bibl. Illustrates the interrelationship between the economy and the environment. Highlights the views of leading businessmen and environmentalists and points out ways that they can reach a middle ground.

2512. Wasserman, P.; Morgan, J.; eds. **Consumer sourcebook:.** Gale Research, 1974 to date. Irregular: 7th ed., 1992–1993. A directory and guide to government organizations, associations, centers, and institutes; media services; company and trademark information; and bibliographic material relating to consumer topics, sources of recourse, and advisory information.

2513. Pearson, Charles S. **Down to business: multinational corporations, the environment, and development.** World Resources Institute, 1985. 107 pp., bibl. Explores the characteristics and roles of multinational corporations (MNCs) in developing countries. Discusses sustainable development and the possibility of establishing environmental standards. Puts forth principles and recommended actions for MNCs, and host and home governments.

2514. Johnson, Terry L. **ECO: the national directory of environmental consulting organizations.** T. L. Johnson, Chicago, IL, 1989. 134 pp. Provides contact information and a corporate profile for 248 organizations, listing primary service area, available services, year founded, and size.

2515. Elkington, John. **The ecology of tomorrow's world: industry's environment.** Associated Business Press; Halsted Press, 1980. 311 pp. Reports on industry's gradual accommodation, since 1960, to growing public and government pressure for pollution control.

2516. Bennett, Steven J. **Ecopreneuring: the complete guide to small business opportunities from the environmental revolution.** Wiley, 1991. 320 pp. Gives information on market size, growth potential, capital requirements, overhead, special equipment, insurance, regulations, competition, and marketing and public relations for dozens of opportunities, including recycling, food packaging, and environmental publishing.

2517. DiMento, Joseph F. **Environmental law and American business: dilemmas of compliance.** Plenum, 1986. 228 pp., ill., bibl., index. Seeks to explain why many businesses fail to comply with environmental regulations. Presents the advantages and disadvantages of many kinds of sanctions. Discusses the characteristics of public agencies and businesses and how agencies communicate the law.

2518. Anderson, Terry Lee; Leal, Donald R. **Free market environmentalism.** Westview Press, 1991. 192 pp., bibl., index. Compares the incentives and costs found in an environmental free market system with those under government regulation. Examples from land and water management, energy development, recreation, ocean management, and pollution control both support the free market solution and illustrate problems and difficulties with it.

2519. Elkington, John; Burke, Tom. **The green capitalists: industry's search for environmental excellence.** Gollancz, 1988. 258 pp., bibl., index. Documents the movement of environmentalism into the corporate world, from "corporate chameleons" to environmental entrepreneurs. Includes "10 steps to environmental excellence," a how-to for industry.

2520. Industry and environment. United Nations Environment Programme, 1978 to date. Quarterly. Aims to promote faster dissemination of topical information on protection technologies, environmentally sound development, standardization, and monitoring and assessment techniques. Each issue has a theme based on a topic or industrial sector. News of legislation and international programs.

2521. Connor, Richard A., Jr.; Davidson, Jeffrey P. **Marketing your consulting and professional services.** Wiley, 2d ed., 1990. 256 pp., ill., bibl., index. Practical advice on implementing a client-centered, client-leveraged approach, which holds that servicing fewer clients or markets can yield greater profits. Explains how to use a personal computer to achieve these ends.

2522. Gordon, Deborah. **Steering a new course: transportation, energy, and the environment.** Island Press, 1991. 244 pp., ill., bibl., index. Addresses the link between traffic congestion, dependence on foreign oil, and pollution. Gives overview of transportation development in the United States and discusses such policy options as alternative fuels, mass transit and freight vehicle improvements, fuel efficiency, telecommuting, and staggered work schedules.

2523. Kelman, Steven. **What price incentives? economists and the environment.** Auburn House, 1981. 170 pp., bibl., index. Develops a theory to explain why economists support using economic incentives to control pollution, while noneconomists generally do not. Based on survey of industrialists, environmentalists, and congressional staff members.

Natural Resource Industries (2524–2541)

2524. Peterson, George L.; Driver, B. L.; Gregory, Robin; eds. **Amenity resource valuation: integrating economics with other disciplines.** Venture, 1988. 260 pp. Applies techniques from economics, psychology, social psychology, and other disciplines to determine the value of such amenity uses as outdoor recreation, wildlife, and scenery.

2525. Bohi, Douglas R.; Toman, Michael A. **Analyzing nonrenewable resource supply.** Resources for the Future; Johns Hopkins University Press, 1984. 159 pp., bibl., index. Offers unified treatment of theoretical and empirical issues in analysis of supply behavior.

2526. McNeely, Jeffrey A. **Economics and biological diversity: developing and using economic incentives to conserve biological resources.** International Union for Conservation of Nature and Natural Resources, 1988. 236 pp., bibl., index. Describes the use of economic incentives to promote conservation at the community, national, and international levels. Discusses the funding of such incentives and provides guidelines for central government planners and resource management agencies. Includes 25 case studies.

2527. Anderson, Lee G. **The economics of fisheries management.** Johns Hopkins University Press, 1986. 296 pp., ill., bibl., index. Basic introduction to fishery economics. Proceeds from simple models to more complex and realistic models. Includes discussion of fishery regulation. No economic background assumed.

2528. Krutilla, John V.; Fisher, Anthony C. **The economics of natural environments: studies in the valuation of commodity and amenity resources.** Resources for the Future; Johns Hopkins University Press, 1985. 300 pp., maps, ill., bibl., index. Presents analytical framework for evaluating amenity resources. Argues that development activities often receive incentives and subsidies, and preservation is often the better option after a true cost-benefit assessment.

2529. Dixon, John A.; Sherman, Paul B. **Economics of protected areas: a new look at benefits and costs.** Island Press, 1990. 234 pp., maps, ill., bibl., index. Geared toward planners and analysts. Part I addresses theoretical economic issues associated with establishing and maintaining protected areas, especially in developing countries, and provides a methodology for assigning monetary values to nature. Part II examines the application of this approach in Thailand, the Virgin Islands, Australia, and Cameroon.

2530. Dovring, Folke. **Land economics.** Breton, 1987. 532 pp. Survey textbook in the tradition of the historical-institutional school of land economics.

2531. Land economics. University of Wisconsin, 1925 to date. Quarterly. Continues: Journal of land and public utility economics.

2532. Dawson, Andrew H. **The land problem in the developed economy.** Barnes & Noble Books, Croom Helm series in geography and environment, 1984. 265 pp., ill., bibl., index. Case studies from Britain, Japan, the United States, and eastern Europe are used to analyze land-use planning. Introductory chapters discuss Malthusian and neo-Malthusian theories and review the participants common to many planning situations, such as landowners, interest groups, professional advisors, and governments.

2533. Smith, Duane A. **Mining America: the industry and the environment, 1800–1980.** University Press of Kansas, 1987. 210 pp., ill., bibl., index. Examines the evolution of the mining industry's attitude toward the environment and mining practices.

2534. Whelan, Tensie; ed. **Nature tourism: managing for the environment.** Island Press, 1991. 223 pp., index. Describes pros and cons of ecotourism with examples from Kenya, Costa Rica, Yellowstone Park, and the western United States. Five chapters in Part Two present a framework for developing successful and environmentally beneficial tourism.

2535. Keen, Elmer A. **Ownership and productivity of marine fishery resources: an essay on the resolution of conflict in the use of ocean pastures.** McDonald & Woodward, 1988. 122 pp. Describes negative effects of current common ownership of fishery resources. Proposes "full ownership" as a means of discouraging exploitation and enhancing productivity. Examines arguments against full ownership and reviews expected reactions of consumers, fishing communities, resource managers, and legislators.

2536. Resources policy. Butterworth-Heinemann, 1976 to date. Quarterly. The international journal of minerals policy and economics. Articles (full-length or shorter "works in progress") aimed at economists and decision makers. Regional and global reports on minerals availability; exploration and development; markets, trade, and prices.

2537. Hite, James C. **Room and situation: the political economy of land-use policy.** Nelson-Hall, 1979. 340 pp., bibl., index. Probes the fundamental causes of land-use problems: speculation, common law, administrative markets, government fiscal policies, and poor information used in planning.

2538. Inskeep, Edward. **Tourism planning: an integrated and sustainable development approach.** Van Nostrand Reinhold, 1991. 508 pp., maps, ill., bibl., index. For both developed and developing nations, suggests techniques for tourism planning, taking into account environmental, social, economic, and institutional considerations.

2539. Peterson, George L.; Randall, Alan; eds. **Valuation of wildland resource benefits.** Westview Press, A Westview special study, 1984. 258 pp., ill., bibl. Essays discuss general theories, methods, and problems in several kinds of benefit valuation, focusing on the valuation of specific resources (timber, minerals, scenic sites, and recreation areas); refers primarily to public lands.

2540. Decker, Daniel J.; Goff, Gary R.; eds. **Valuing wildlife: economic and social perspectives.** Westview Press, 1987. 424 pp., ill. Examines ecological, aesthetic, educational, economic, and recreational values of wildlife. Case studies of managing private lands for wildlife, damage control, and evaluating direct economic benefits. Also addresses methods of value determination, applications for environmental impact assessment, and strategies in wildlife planning.

2541. Tilton, John E.; Eggert, Roderick G.; Landsberg, Hans H.; eds. **World mineral exploration: trends and economic issues.** Resources for the Future, 1988. 464 pp., ill., bibl., index. Assesses the state of mineral exploration, reviewing efforts in New Guinea, South Africa, the USSR, Canada, the United States, and Australia. Attempts to identify and understand the factors influencing the level and direction of exploration, including mineral prices, government policies, and exploration and extraction technologies.

Agriculture and Forest Products (2542–2560)

2542. Sutton, John D.; ed. **Agricultural trade and natural resources: discovering the critical linkages.** Rienner, 1988. 245 pp. Papers from a 1987 workshop seek to provide a conceptual framework for describing relations between trade and resources that will aid policy formation and economic analysis. Sections on developing a theoretical framework, implications of natural resource policies for agricultural trade, and implications of trade policy for natural resources. Includes formal mathematical models.

2543. American journal of agricultural economics. American Agricultural Economics Association, 1968 to date. 5 issues/yr. Publishes research on the economics of agriculture, natural resources, and rural and community development.

2544. Appropriate forest industries. Food and Agriculture Organization of the United Nations, FAO forestry paper, no. 68, 1986. 426 pp., maps, bibl. Topics include features of forest industry projects, rural enterprise, institutional requirements, people and industry,

education and training, and the definition of appropriateness.

2545. LeMaster, Dennis C.; and others, eds. **Below-cost timber sales.** Wilderness Society, 1987. 266 pp., maps, ill. Proceedings of a 1986 conference on the economics of national forest timber sales. Ten papers discuss the economics and effects of the timber sales program, examining future timber supplies, timber-dependent communities, forest protection, recreation and tourism, and fish, wildlife, and species diversity.

2546. Dean, Warren. **Brazil and the struggle for rubber: a study in environmental history.** Cambridge University Press, Studies in environment and history, 1987. 234 pp., ill., bibl., index. Presents the history of rubber cultivation in a global context, in particular, the failure in Brazil of cultivating rubber on a large scale.

2547. Sedjo, Roger A. **Comparative economics of plantation forestry: a global assessment.** Resources for the Future, 1983. 161 pp., ill., index. Analyzes the economic feasibility of plantation forestry in 12 areas of the world and concludes that major expansion is feasible in tropical areas.

2548. Johansson, Per-Olov; Lofgren, Karl-Gustav. **The economics of forestry and natural resources.** Basil Blackwell, 1985. 292 pp., ill., bibl., index. Focusing mostly on forestry, chapters address optimal rotation, the theory and modeling of timber supply, and welfare aspects. Technical discussion assumes previous knowledge of quantitative techniques, economics, and modeling.

2549. Kula, Erhun. **The economics of forestry: modern theory and practice.** Timber Press, 1988. 185 pp. Reviews forestry policy and practices in several Western countries. Analyzes costs and benefits of public sector forestry using ordinary and modified discounting. Addresses private sector forestry and the problem of optimum rotation.

2550. Fenton, Thomas P.; Heffron, Mary J.; eds. **Food, hunger, agribusiness: a directory of resources.** Orbis Books, 1987. 131 pp., ill., index. Annotated entries of organizations, books, periodicals, articles, and audiovisuals dealing with the role of agribusiness and the political and economic origins of Third World hunger.

2551. Buongiorno, Joseph; Gilless, J. Keith. **Forest management and economics: a primer in quantitative methods.** Collier Macmillan, 1987. 285 pp., bibl., index. Covers simulations and linear, integer, goal, and dynamic modeling; network modeling and ecometric analysis. Applies methods to practical management problems.

2552. Granger, A. **The future role of the tropical rain forests in the world forest economy.** Oxford Academic, 1991. 350 pp. Detailed overview of the tropical hardwood trade. Analyzes the causes and trends of deforestation. Includes a global computer simulation model of the world's rain forest resources and the tropical hardwood trade.

2553. Kallio, Markku; Dykstra, Dennis P.; Binkley, Clark S.; eds. **The global forest sector: an analytical perspective.** Wiley, 1987. 706 pp., ill., bibl., index. Offers comprehensive background on forest sector. Reviews forest sector modeling to provide detailed economic analysis.

2554. Raintree, John B.; ed. **Land, trees and tenure.** International Council for Research on Agroforestry; University of Wisconsin, Land Tenure Center, 1987. 412 pp., ill., bibl., index. Proceedings of a 1985 workshop. Papers summarize the experience of tenure issues in agroforestry projects in Africa, Asia, and Latin America. Includes summaries of related issues, such as technology-tenure interactions, women and tenure, and agroforestry project design.

2555. Blaikie, Piers. **The political economy of soil erosion in developing countries.** Longman, Longman development studies, 1985. 188 pp., ill., bibl., index. Argues that conservation programs fail because they assume erosion is a purely environmental issue brought about by farmer ignorance and apathy. Asserts that soil use and erosion can be understood only in the context of political and economic relations among land users and the state.

2556. Gregory, C. Robinson. **Resource economics for foresters.** Wiley, 1987. 477 pp., ill., bibl., index. Textbook covers price theory, wood-based industries, timber production, economic guide to investment decisions, nontimber goods and multiple use, and international aspects of forest economics. Includes problems and questions.

2557. Hyde, William F. **Timber supply, land allocation, and economic efficiency.** Resources for the Future; Johns Hopkins University Press, 1980. 224 pp., bibl., index. Applies economic efficiency criteria to forest management, arguing for the maximization of economic land rent. Uses case studies.

2558. Sanderson, Steven, E. **The transformation of Mexican agriculture: international structure and the politics of rural change.** Princeton University Press, 1986. 324 pp., ill., bibl., index. Combines empirical case study and analysis of global economy to examine prob-

lems and politics of Mexico's rural development and food production.

2559. Oldeman, Roelof A. A.; ed. **Tropical hardwood utilization: practice and prospects.** Nijhoff; Kluwer, Forestry sciences, v. 3, 1981. 584 pp., ill., bibl., index. From a 1979 seminar. Summarizes forest resources and the socioeconomic pressures on them. Gives commercial statistics for producer and consumer nations and major end uses in Europe and North America. Addresses the need for standardized nomenclature and increased international cooperation.

2560. Fortmann, Louise; Bruce, John W.; eds. **Whose trees? proprietary dimensions of forestry.** Westview Press, 1988. 341 pp., bibl. Forty-one international contributors discuss trees and land tenure, communities and trees, tenure and deforestation or afforestation, effects of gender on tenure rights, and the role and past performances of governments in forest conservation. Alternate approaches are proposed.

Pollution. Industrial Wastes (2561–2596)

2561. Freeman, A. Myrick, III. **Air and water pollution and control: a benefit-cost assessment.** Wiley-Interscience, Environmental science and technology, 1982. 186 pp., ill., bibl., index. Reviews benefits of air pollution control on health, vegetation, and aesthetics and of water pollution control on recreation and commercial water uses. Evaluates costs and results and makes recommendations.

2562. Morehouse, Ward; Subramaniam, M. Arun. **The Bhopal tragedy: what really happened and what it means for American workers and communities at risk..** Council on International and Public Affairs, 1986. 190 pp., ill., bibl. Examines what happened, who was responsible, health and environmental impacts, and legal and compensation processes. Explores implications for U.S. communities.

2563. Liberman, Daniel F.; Gordon, Judith G. **Biohazards management handbook.** Dekker, Occupational safety and health, v. 17, 1989. 439 pp., ill., bibl., index. In three parts: facility considerations; biosafety principles and practices; regulatory agency considerations.

2564. Sontag, James M.; ed. **Carcinogens in industry and the environment.** Dekker, Pollution engineering and technology, v. 16, 1981. 761 pp. Analyzes and evaluates the relationship of environmental and industrial carcinogens to humans.

2565. Scott, Ronald McLean. **Chemical hazards in**

the workplace. Lewis, 1989. 196 pp., ill., bibl., index. Concise introduction to industrial toxicology, in three sections: vocabulary and practices, hazards of specific compounds, and regulatory compliance.

2566. Sarokin, David J.; and others. **Cutting chemical wastes: what 29 organic chemical plants are doing to reduce hazardous wastes.** INFORM, 1985. 535 pp., ill., bibl. Uses case studies to explore industry initiatives to reduce waste generation. Describes 44 waste reduction practices.

2567. Duerksen, Christopher J. **Dow v. California: a turning point in the envirobusiness struggle.** Conservation Foundation, 1982. 151 pp., ill., bibl. Case study of Dow Chemical's 1977 decision to halt plans for a $500 million petrochemical facility near San Francisco, citing environmental regulatory roadblocks.

2568. EI environmental services directory. Environmental Information, 1983 to date. Annual. Organized by service (low-level nuclear wastes, PCBs, underground tanks, etc.). Profiles over 4500 firms, including consulting firms, spill response firms, transporters, laboratories, and others. Details their service areas, capabilities, and size. Also provides information on state regulatory programs. Both national and regional editions available.

2569. Tietenberg, T. H. **Emissions trading: an exercise in reforming pollution policy.** Resources for the Future, 1985. 222 pp., bibl., index. Evaluates economic theory behind transferable permit systems and assesses implementation. Finds that current policies, though superior to conventional regulation, fall short of maximum cost efficiency; offers suggestions for reform.

2570. Environmental aspects of aluminium smelting: a technical review. United Nations Environment Programme, Industry & Environment Office, UNEP industry & environment technical review series, v. 3, 1981. 167 pp., ill., bibl. Concise review discusses pollution production, fume collection, cleaning and emission, liquid and solid residue treatment, and worker protection.

2571. The environmental audit handbook series. Executive Enterprises, 1989. 5 vols. Reviews basic principles of environmental compliance auditing: quality management; planning, staffing, and contracting for an environmental audit; and preparing for a government inspection of facilities.

2572. Environmental auditor. Springer-Verlag, 1990 to date. Quarterly. Publishes informational articles and research on activities and techniques used to determine whether a facility or operation meets environmental requirements, including compliance, risk assessment, and resource management.

2573. Cahill, Lawrence B.; Kane, Raymond W. **Environmental audits.** Government Institutes, 6th ed., 1989. 592 pp.

2574. Environmental guidelines. World Bank, Office of Environmental Affairs, 1984. 422 pp., ill., bibl. Designed for the use of the World Bank in assessing industrial projects. Covers most commonly encountered industries and pollutants. Presents environmental factors, permissible pollutant levels, and primary control measures.

2575. Lindgren, Gary F. **Guide to managing industrial hazardous waste.** Butterworth, 1983. 287 pp., ill., bibl., index. Introduces the hazardous waste management system, explains federal regulations, and supplies practical information on disposal site selection, insurance options, legal liabilities, and good management practices.

2576. Dyer, Jon C.; Mignone, Nicholas A. **Handbook of industrial residues.** Noyes, 1983. 453 pp. Provides the data and concepts necessary for municipal and industrial managers to cooperate in handling residuals left over from pretreatment and treatment of industrial wastes.

2577. Cherniack, Martin. **The Hawk's Nest incident: America's worst industrial disaster.** Yale University Press, 1986. 194 pp., ill., bibl., index. Recounts story of deaths from silicosis in excavation of 1930s road tunnel in Appalachian Virginia. Conditions of the Hawk's Nest disaster resemble those in developing countries, where work forces are mostly unorganized, intimidated, and impoverished.

2578. Schwartz, Seymour I.; Pratt, Wendy B. **Hazardous waste from small quantity generators: strategies and solutions for business and government.** Island Press, 1990. 266 pp., ill., bibl., index. Assesses the extent and severity of pollution from small businesses. Examines liability issues, regulations, and national, state, and local programs for small quantity generators in California. Suggests policy steps to encourage legal, regulated disposal.

2579. Freeman, Harry; ed. **Hazardous waste minimization.** McGraw-Hill, 1990. 343 pp., ill., bibl., index. Provides specific advice on how industry and local governments can sell, promote, and institute waste minimization programs. Reviews reduction techniques, including recycling, inventory planning, and production adjustments. Includes case studies of successful programs.

2580. Higgins, Thomas E. **Hazardous waste minimization handbook**. Lewis, 1989. 228 pp., ill., bibl., index. Defines waste minimization and outlines specific techniques and treatments, applicable to many industries, to reduce the quantity and toxicity of waste generated. Discusses industrial processes most often responsible for producing hazardous waste.

2581. Wang, Charleston C. K. **How to manage workplace derived hazards and avoid liability**. Noyes, 1987. 335 pp.

2582. **ICC guide to effective environmental auditing**. International Chamber of Commerce Publishing, Publication no. 483, 1991. 87 pp. Provides practical advice on designing an effective audit program, reviews actual audit activities step by step, and goes over presentation and analysis strategies.

2583. Cralley, Lester V.; Cralley, Lewis J.; eds. **Inplant practices for job related health hazards control**. Wiley, 1989. 2 vols.

2584. Davidson, Art. **In the wake of the Exxon Valdez: the devastating impact of the Alaska oil spill**. Sierra Club Books, 1990. 333 pp., maps, bibl. Recounts the spill and the immediate response in detail. Studies the methods and ways that Exxon, Alaska, and the federal government attempted to contain the oil and protect wildlife, fisheries, and communities. Assesses economic, social, and ecological effects of the spill and the steps taken to repair the damage.

2585. Schelling, Thomas C.; ed. **Incentives for environmental protection**. MIT Press, 1983. 355 pp., bibl., index. Uses in-depth case studies of aircraft noise regulation, airborne benzene regulation, and air quality under the Clean Air Act to examine the effectiveness of pricing systems in environmental protection.

2586. Kleindorfer, Paul R.; Kunreuther, Howard C.; eds. **Insuring and managing hazardous risks—from Seveso to Bhopal and beyond**. Springer-Verlag, 1987. 534 pp., bibl., index. Reviews different approaches to risk assessment, alternative mechanisms for determining acceptable risk, risk communication, and methods of handling compensation. Includes case studies of crisis management.

2587. Buttel, Frederick H.; Geisler, Charles; Wiswall, Irving W.; compilers. **Labor and the environment: an analysis of and annotated bibliography on workplace environmental quality in the United States**. Greenwood Press, 1984. 148 pp., bibl., index. Documents with analysis and bibliographic references the interaction of environmental and labor concerns. Provides a cost-benefit analysis of workplace environments.

2588. Lindgren, Gary F. **Managing industrial hazardous waste: a practical handbook**. Lewis, 1989. 389 pp., ill., bibl., index. Examples and practical applications using such common activities as storage of wastes pending shipment, on-site treatment, and solvent distillation. Gives overview of hazardous waste management system and explains federal regulatory standards.

2589. Harrison, Lee L.; editor-in-chief. **The McGraw-Hill environmental auditing handbook: a guide to corporate and environmental risk management**. McGraw-Hill, 1984. 428 pp., ill., index. A compilation intended to increase public and private understanding of environmental auditing. In five parts: introduction to auditing, with one case history; detailing your risks (air, water, toxic wastes, underground tanks, occupational health and safety, product liability, and others); performing an audit (includes perspectives of auditor, engineer, and insurance broker, case histories, report of findings, alternative approaches, and managing data); cautionary notes (on confidentiality of data and evaluating the program); and, finally, the EPA's perspective.

2590. Kneese, Allen V. **Measuring the benefits of clean air and water**. Resources for the Future; Johns Hopkins University Press, 1984. 159 pp., ill., bibl., index. Describes the results of the EPA's research on the economics of environmental protection.

2591. Leonard, H. Jeffrey. **Pollution and the struggle for the world product: multinational corporations, environment, and international comparative advantage**. Cambridge University Press, 1988. 254 pp., bibl., index. Does environmental regulation affect the location of industrial production? Examines siting decisions in four countries.

2592. Campbell, Monica E.; Glenn, William M. **Profit from pollution prevention: a guide to industrial waste reduction and recycling**. Pollution Probe Foundation, 1982. 404 pp., ill., bibl., index. Geared for small- and medium-sized businesses trying to minimize their generation of hazardous wastes. Discusses dry cleaning, electroplating, food processing, photography, printing, tanning, and many other processes.

2593. Huisingh, Donald; and others. **Proven profits from pollution prevention: case studies in resource conservation and waste reduction**. Institute for Local Self-Reliance, 1986. 316 pp. Forty-six case studies from a wide range of industries, including agriculture, forestry, paper and printing, and electronic equipment. Documents successful methods of recycling, reuse, recovery, distillation, and filtration which paid for themselves.

2594. Bartlett, Robert V. **The Reserve Mining controversy: **science, technology, and environmental quality.** Indiana University Press, 1980. 293 pp. In-depth examination of the corruption and controversy surrounding Reserve Mining Company's dumping of millions of tons of mining wastes into Lake Superior.

2595. Seldman, Neil. **Waste to wealth: a business guide for community recycling enterprises.** Institute for Local Self-Reliance, 1984. 121 pp. Techniques and concepts of recycling.

2596. Lake, Elizabeth E.; Hanneman, William M.; Oster, Sharon M. **Who pays for clean water: the distribution of water pollution control costs.** Westview Press, An urban systems research report, 1979. 244 pp., ill., bibl. Examines industrial responses and changes in public sector budgets resulting from the Water Pollution Control Act. Assesses the equity of cost distribution in the population if clean water is paid for by public agencies or by industry.

Energy (2597–2611)

2597. Gever, John; and others, eds. **Beyond oil: the threat to food and fuel in the coming decades.** Ballinger, 1986. 304 pp., ill., bibl., index. Computer analysis of U.S. energy and agricultural resources extending past 2000.

2598. Ramsay, W. **Bioenergy and economic development: planning for biomass energy programs in the Third World.** Westview Press, CSIS energy policy series, v. 1, no. 1, 1985. 291 pp., bibl., index. Examines both positive and negative aspects of bioenergy development. Discusses potential crops, their environmental impacts, and the required technological conversion; costs and financing; and local versus national planning and control.

2599. Office of Technology Assessment, U.S. Congress. **The direct use of coal: prospects and problems of production and consumption.** Government Printing Office, 1979. 411 pp., ill., bibl. Explains the coal process from extraction to combustion. Studies the impacts of increased coal use on health, the environment, employment, and communities. Assesses new technology, discusses federal coal policy, and suggests legislative and policy options.

2600. Dicks, Brian; ed. **Ecological impacts of the oil industry.** Wiley, 1989. 316 pp., ill., bibl. Proceedings of an international meeting organized by the Institute of Petroleum and held in 1987. Discusses survey and monitoring techniques, environmental impacts on intertidal and subtidal rock and sediment communities, and the

fate of oil in sedimentary systems. Most of the research was conducted at an oil port in Wales.

2601. Lee, Thomas H.; Ball, Ben C., Jr.; Tabors, Richard D. **Energy aftermath.** Harvard Business School Press, 1990. 274 pp., ill., bibl. Critizes U.S. energy policy since 1945, particularly in the 1970s. Attributes mistakes to an overreliance on analytic models. Includes a case study of the electric utility industry. Discusses the requirements of successful energy systems for the twenty-first century.

2602. Hall, Charles A. S.; Hall, A. S.; Cleveland, Cutler J.; and others. **Energy and resource quality: the ecology of the economic process.** Wiley, 1986. 577 pp., ill., bibl., index. Economics from a physical point of view—the meaning of resource scarcity and its ultimate impact.

2603. Morovic, T.; and others. **Energy conservation indicators.** Springer-Verlag, 1987. 333 pp., ill., bibl. Presents data on energy consumption in ten member states of the European Community in the residential, agricultural, commercial, public, industrial, and transportation sectors. Useful background information for comparing the intensity of energy use in the members of the European Community.

2604. Chateau, B.; Lapillonne, B. **Energy demand: facts and trends: a comparative analysis of industrialized countries.** Springer-Verlag, Topics in energy, 1982. 280 pp., ill., bibl., index. Analyzes energy demand in the three major energy-consuming sectors: residential and tertiary, transport, and industry. Emphasizes, where appropriate, technological and socioeconomic aspects and historical perspectives. Reviews energy demand forecasting models and methods.

2605. Energy economics. IPC Science and Technology Press, 1979 to date. Quarterly. A forum for papers concerned with economic analysis of energy issues, including economic theory and application, methods, statistics, and modeling.

2606. Energy policy. IPC Science and Technology Press, 1973 to date. Quarterly. Appraises and analyzes the economic, planning, social, and environmental aspects of energy supply and utilization.

2607. Energy statistics of OECD countries, 1987–1988. Organization for Economic Cooperation and Development; International Energy Agency, 1990 to date. Annual. Provides statistics on the production, trade, and consumption of oil, natural gas, solid fuels, manufactured gas, and electricity of OECD countries.

2608. Arrow, Kenneth J.; et al. **Energy, the next**

twenty years. Ballinger, 1979. 628 pp., ill., bibl., index. Somewhat out of date but provides a useful look back as a guide to future issues. Discusses energy demand and conservation; regulation of crude oil prices; international resources, trends, and policies; coal production, supplies, and health hazards; fossil fuel alternatives; nuclear power and solar energy; and issues in jurisdiction, regulation, and decision making.

2609. Spreng, Daniel T. **Net energy analysis and the energy requirements of energy systems.** Praeger, 1988. 289 pp. Compares different ways in which strategies for energy conservation are evaluated.

2610. Stevens, Paul; ed. **Oil and gas dictionary.** Nichols, 1988. 270 pp., ill. Designed for government officials, businessmen, bankers, and others outside the industry proper. Explains technical terms to economists and financiers, economic terms to engineers, and industry terms to nonspecialists.

2611. World energy statistics and balances, 1985–1988. Organization for Economic Cooperation and Development; International Energy Agency, 1990. 407 pp., bibl. Compiles data on the production and consumption of coal, oil, gas, electricity, and heat in over 80 developing countries, eastern Europe, and the Soviet Union.

Section 12

Health. Medicine. Human Biology

The section for health and medicine in this bibliography is relatively small because so many excellent sources of medical information are already available. Note particularly, *Index Medicus* (2621) and *Information Resources in Toxicology* (2686).

Environmental health, like public health itself, is about protection, prevention, and dealing with epidemics. Specifically, environmental health deals with protecting the public from pollution and toxic substances by means of risk assessment, understanding of toxicology, and implementation of safety and emergency practices.

The first group in the section presents reference books and other sources of public health and medical information. The environmental health entries are in four categories: toxic threats and hazards, which give a general picture of what faces us; risk assessment, which shows how risks are calculated; toxicology, which documents methods of testing pollutant effects on living systems; and finally health protection, which has works on safety, emergencies, disasters, and other aspects of immediate protection.

Public Health. Medicine

Titles in this group are mainly reference books and textbooks on medicine, human anatomy and biology, public health practice, and sciences.

See also:

- Section 1: Global resources and environment; biological systems
- Section 8: Society and environment: country studies; social and human ecology, population; rural communities; urban communities
- Section 10: Law, politics, government

Toxic Threats. Hazards

General and persistent problems of toxics or hazards in the environment and their relation to human health are addressed here.

See also:

- Section 1: Chemistry, biogeochemical cycles, pollutants
- Section 2: Air pollution, atmospheric chemistry
- Section 3: Water pollution
- Section 4: Land degradation, erosion, reclamation
- Section 5: Food and agriculture; atmospheric environment, pollution, pesticides
- Section 8: Society and environment: country studies; individuals and environment; behavior and psychology
- Section 10: U.S. laws and legislation, courts, disputes; U.S. executive agencies, administration and regulation
- Section 11: Industry, economic sectors; pollution, industrial wastes
- Section 13: Environmental control technology; hazardous wastes; radioactive, nuclear
- Section 14: Assessment and monitoring; testing and analysis

Risk Assessment. There are many entries on risk scattered throughout the bibliography. Here, the emphasis is on formal procedures and methodologies, dealing more particularly with human health.

See also:

- Section 8: Social and human ecology, population; individuals and environment; behavior and psychology
- Section 10: U.S. laws and legislation
- Section 11: Industry, economic sectors; pollution, industrial wastes
- Section 13: Environmental control technology, hazardous wastes; nuclear, radioactive
- Section 14: Quantification, measurement, statistics

Toxicology. This subgroup includes handbooks and works dealing with testing and analytical methods and procedures, mechanisms of action, and lists and descriptions of toxic compounds.

See also:

- Section 1: Biological systems; chemistry, biogeochemical cycles, pollutants
- Section 2: Air pollution, atmospheric chemistry
- Section 3: Water pollution
- Section 7: Animal biology, zoology; animal rights, protection
- Section 10: U.S. laws and legislation, courts, disputes; U.S. executive agencies, administration and regulation
- Section 14: Quantification, measurement, statistics; assessment and monitoring; testing and analysis

Health Protection. Safety. Emergencies. In this last subgroup are entries referring to medical-environmental emergencies and protection—at home, in the workplace, in the community, and outdoors.

See also:

- Section 8: Social and human ecology, population; individuals and environment, behavior and psychology
- Section 10: U.S. politics and policies; U.S. executive agencies, administration and regulation
- Section 11: Industry, economic sectors; pollution, industrial wastes
- Section 13: Environmental control technology; hazardous wastes

Public Health. Medicine (2612–2633)

2612. Annual review of public health. Annual Reviews, 1980 to date. Annual. Topical reviews of research in public health.

2613. Netter, Frank H.; Colacino, Sharon. **Atlas of human anatomy.** CIBA-Geigy Corporation, 1989. 514 pp., ill., bibl. Illustrates male, female, infant, and aged anatomy. Color-coded drawings clearly indicate specifics and details. Includes cross-sectional, topographic, and medial views; cross-referenced to other relevant drawings and sections.

2614. Dulbecco, Renato; ed. **Encyclopedia of human biology.** Academic Press, 1991. Ill., bibl., index. 8 vols. Covers all aspects of human biology, including neurosciences, biochemistry, anthropology, pharmocology, immunology, behavior, genetics, physiology, cytology, and toxicology. Includes glossary and subject index.

2615. Murray, Michael T.; Pizzorno, Joseph E. **An encyclopedia of natural medicine.** Prima; St. Martin's Press, 1991. 622 pp., ill., index. Basic principles of health and therapies for more than 50 health problems by accredited practitioners of naturopathic medicine.

2616. Cairncross, Sandy; Feachem, Richard G. **Environmental health engineering in the tropics: an introductory text.** Wiley, 1983. 283 pp., ill., bibl., index. Presents engineering technologies appropriate for poor countries; covers health and pollution, water supply, human waste disposal, environmental modification, and vector-borne disease.

2617. Brown, Sanford M.; Clark, Wayne N.; Zuieback, Steven L. **Environmental health field practice.** Praeger, 1983. 288 pp. Spiral-bound manual of procedures, forms, records, and sampling protocols for inspection and consultation on health aspects of wastewater, solid waste, swimming and bathing, food and consumer affairs, housing and residential areas, and institutions.

2618. Bruce-Chwatt, Leonard Jan. **Essential malariology.** Heinemann Medical Books, 2d ed, 1985. 452 pp. Examines the most pervasive and crippling disease of humans in the tropics, if not the world. Practical methods of prevention, diagnosis, and treatment and control in the context of an overall health care policy; relationship of research to application.

2619. Chitty, Mary Glen; compiler. **Federal information sources in health and medicine: a selected annotated bibliography.** Greenwood Press, Bibliographies and indexes in medical studies, v. 1, 1988. 306 pp. Index. Twelve hundred publications and 100 databases from 90 U.S. federal agencies.

2620. Hall, Ross Hume. **Health and the global environment.** Polity Press; Basil Blackwell, 1990. 214 pp., index. Argues that personal health depends on environmental health. Critique of existing health care systems. Presents preventive approach to health care.

2621. Index medicus. National Library of Medicine; Government Printing Office, 1960 to date. Monthly. Indexes the world journal literature of biomedicine. Available as an online computer database, (*Medlars,* and its main component, *Medline*).

2622. Becker, E. Lovell; and others, eds. **International dictionary of medicine and biology.** Wiley, A Wiley medical publication, 1986. Index. 3 vols. Over 150,000 entries cover medical sciences and medically related areas of biological sciences; includes both current and obsolete terms. Detailed introduction explains organization and cross-referencing formats.

2623. Journal of environmental health. National Environmental Health Association, 1938 to date. Bimonthly. Publishes articles on occupational health, health effects of waste disposal, contaminated foods, and similar topics related to environmental health.

2624. Kruzas, A. T.; ed. **Medical and health information directory.** Gale Research, 1977 to date. 3 vols. Irregular: 6th ed., 1992–1993. "A guide to more than 46,000 associations, agencies, companies, institutions, research centers, hospitals, clinics, treatment centers, educational programs, publications, audiovisuals, data banks, libraries, and information services in clinical medicine, basic biomedical sciences, and the technological and socio-economic aspects of health care."

2625. The Merck manual of diagnosis and therapy. Merck, 1899 to date. Irregular: 15th ed., 1988. Standard physician's handbook.

2626. Hope, R. A.; Longmore, J. M.; Moss, P. A. H.; and others. **Oxford handbook of clinical medicine.** Oxford University Press, 2d ed., 1989. 796 pp. Standard guide to clinical and surgical procedures.

2627. Oxford textbook of public health. Oxford University Press, Oxford Medical Publications, 2d ed., 1991. 3 vols. Articles by more than 160 leaders in the field of public health. Vol. 1: Influences of public health.

Chapters on the development of public health, determinants of health and disease, policies and strategies, financing, services, and ethics. Vol. 2: Methods of public health. Chapters on information systems and sources, epidemiological approaches, social science techniques, and field investigation of hazards. Vol. 3: Applications in public health. Chapters on interventions, planning and evaluation, major problems, needs of special clients, and performance of the public health function.

2628. Greenberg, Michael R.; ed. **Public health and the environment: the United States experience.** Guilford Press, 1987. 395 pp., maps, bibl., index. Combining environmental health science and environmental policy, reviews health risk appraisal; life-style and chronic disease; worker health; and the relationship between water, air quality, solid waste, and public health. Part 2 discusses choices and solutions in environmental health policy.

2629. Haselbauer, Kathleen J. **A research guide to the health sciences: medical, nutritional, and environmental.** Greenwood Press, Reference sources for the social sciences and humanities, no. 4, 1987. 655 pp., ill., index. Provides full annotations to more than 2000 sources of information. Environmental health, occupational health, and nutrition each have one chapter. Divided into four parts: general works (including dictionaries, encyclopedias, and other reference works); basic sciences; social aspects; and medical specialties. Has numerous cross-references and author, title, and subject indexes.

2630. McWhinney, Ian R. **A textbook of family medicine.** Oxford University Press, 1989. 380 pp., ill., bibl., index. Discusses the nature and philosophical and scientific basis of family medicine. Chapters examine common complaints, illnesses, and chronic problems encountered in family practice. Addresses prevention and family influences on sickness and health.

2631. Basch, Paul F. **Textbook of international health.** Oxford University Press, 1989. 544 pp., ill. Examines the major factors affecting health in all regions of the world; assesses international campaigns to combat disease and improve health. Describes intervention efforts at community, national, and international levels.

2632. Hatt, John. **The tropical traveller: an essential guide to travelling in hot climates.** Hippocrene Books, 1984. 253 pp., ill., bibl., index. Presents useful advice on equipment, preparation, and hazards of travel, based largely on the author's experience. Particularly useful for first-time travelers.

2633. Johns, Timothy. **With bitter herbs they shall eat it: chemical ecology and the origins of the human diet and medicine.** University of Arizona Press, Arizona studies in human ecology, 1990. 356 pp., ill., bibl., index. Examines the methods humans have used both biologically and culturally to maneuver around the many toxins in the plant world.

Toxic Threats. Hazards (2634–2661)

2634. Regenstein, Lewis. **America the poisoned: how deadly chemicals are destroying our environment, our wildlife, ourselves and how we can survive!** Acropolis Books, 1982. 414 pp., ill., bibl., index. Describes the prevalence in modern society of toxic chemicals from pesticides, herbicides, toxic waste, and other sources. Maintains that there has been a deliberate policy to continue and increase the sale of toxic chemicals. Offers the reader practical suggestions for improving the situation.

2635. Archives of environmental health. American Medical Association, 1960 to date. Bimonthly.

2636. Smith, Kirk R. **Biofuels, air pollution, and health: a global review.** Plenum, 1987. 452 pp., ill., bibl., index. Discusses the nature and possible health effects of indoor air pollution in less-developed countries caused by the combustion of wood, crop residues, dung, and other low-grade fuels.

2637. Gandhi, Om P.; ed. **Biological effects and medical applications of electromagnetic energy.** Prentice-Hall, 1990. 573 pp. Explores thermophysiological, cellular, teratogenic, and behavioral effects of electromagnetic radiation exposure, as well as reported links with cancer. Also covers auditory perception of pulsed fields, epidemiological studies, and common misperceptions.

2638. Wang, Rhoda G. M.; Franklin, Claire A.; Honeycutt, Richard C.; and others, eds. **Biological monitoring for pesticide exposure: measurement, estimation, and risk reduction.** American Chemical Society, ACS symposium series, v. 382, 1989. 387 pp., ill., bibl., index. Twenty-eight papers discuss monitoring methods, percutaneous absorption after exposure, chemical analysis, risk assessment, and regulation.

2639. Coffel, Steve. **But not a drop to drink: the life-saving guide to good water.** Rawson, 1989. 323 pp., bibl. Describes the origins and nature of water pollution, consequent health risks, and strategies to save water at the household and community levels. Appendices list toxic substances and water conservation citizen organizations.

2640. Searle, Charles E.; ed. **Chemical carcinogens.** American Chemical Society, ACS monograph, no. 182, 2d ed., 1984. Bibl., index. 2 vols. Twenty-two chapters detail knowledge and research developments in many fields of carcinogen study. Updated text includes new chapters on cancer epidemiology, inorganic carcinogens, halogenated organic compounds, and more.

2641. Lappe, Marc. **Chemical deception: the toxic threat to health and the environment.** Sierra Club Books, 1991. 360 pp., index. Disputes ten myths of the "chemical revolution," including those asserting that tap water is safe, the environment is resilient, low doses of toxins are not harmful, and the body's defenses are adequate.

2642. Tollison, Robert D.; ed. **Clearing the air: perspectives on environmental tobacco smoke.** Lexington Books, 1987. 148 pp., bibl. Collection of articles deals with scientific, economic, legal and social aspects of environmental tobacco smoke, all leading to the conclusion that government regulation of smoking is inappropriate.

2643. Gough, Michael. **Dioxin, Agent Orange: the facts.** Plenum Press, 1986. 289 pp., ill., bibl., index. Reviews what is known about the nature, use, and effects of dioxin in Agent Orange and in other herbicides. Explains controversial exposure incidents (Times Beach, Missouri; industrial exposure; the Vietnam War) and the results of animal and epidemiology studies.

2644. Drinking water and health. National Academy of Science Press, 1977–1987. Bibl., index. 8 vols. Prepared by the National Research Council, Safe Drinking Water Committee. Series of reports cover drinking water contaminants, health effects, drinking water distribution systems, and disinfection methods.

2645. Kryter, Karl D. **The effects of noise on man.** Academic Press, 2d ed., 1985. 688 pp., ill., bibl., index. Evaluates and interprets the effects of noise on people and animals, positing a theory for predicting health effects and other results. Examines social, legal, and government regulations and problems resulting from these concerns.

2646. Environment and health. Congressional Quarterly Books, 1981. 227 pp., maps, ill., bibl., index. Discusses health impacts of all forms of environmental pollution and includes relevant legislation from 1970 to 1980.

2647. Goldsmith, John R.; ed. **Environmental epidemiology: epidemiological investigation of commu-**nity environmental health problems. CRC Press, 1986. 296 pp., ill., bibl., index. Results of symposium convened by the EPA and the American Chemical Society. Covers use of biological monitoring to assess exposure data and methods of relating exposure to contaminants in air, water, and workplaces.

2648. Environmental health perspectives. National Institute of Environmental Health Sciences; Government Printing Office, 1972 to date. Bimonthly. Publishes original research, toxicological summaries, overviews, and reviews concerning health hazards of particular pollutants. Many issues contain proceedings of conferences and workshops.

2649. Draggan, Sidney; Cohrssen, John J.; Morrison, Richard E.; eds. **Environmental impacts on human health: the agenda for long-term research and development.** Praeger, 1987. 228 pp. Papers on genetic and molecular epidemiology, the use of epidemiological data to show disease causation, the value of health registries, and the health hazards of biotechnology.

2650. Kumar, R.; ed. **Environmental pollution and health hazards in India.** Ashish, 1987. 292 pp., ill., bibl., index. Collection of 24 articles, covering range of topics; authors from fields of medicine, public health, sociology.

2651. Environmental research. Academic Press, 1967 to date. Bimonthly. Publishes research on the causes and origins of environmentally induced illness. Fields covered include pathology, pharmacology, molecular and cellular biology, epidemiology and risk analysis, and environmental and occupational medicine.

2652. Committee on Passive Smoking Surveys, National Research Council. **Environmental tobacco smoke: measuring exposures and assessing health effects.** National Academy Press, 1986. 337 pp., ill., bibl., index. Reviews physicochemical and toxicological studies of environmental tobacco smoke and methods of assessing exposure. Surveys health effects possibly related to environmental tobacco smoke.

2653. Legator, Marvin S.; Harper, Barbara L.; Scott, Michael J.; eds. **The health detective's handbook: a guide to the investigation of environmental health hazards by nonprofessionals.** Johns Hopkins University Press, 1985. 256 pp., ill., bibl., index. Manual guides reader step by step through the process of formulating and carrying out a descriptive epidemiological study; discusses the nature of experimental design, data gathering, community organization, sources of assistance, and legal aspects.

2654. Wilson, Richard; and others. **Health effects of fossil fuel burning: assessment and mitigation.** Ballinger, 1980. 392 pp., ill., bibl., index. Focusing on sulfur oxides, nitrogen oxides, and particulates, examines trends in emissions, health effects at high concentrations, efforts to study low-level effects, and control options.

2655. Gammage, Richard B.; Kaye, Stephen V.; eds. **Indoor air and human health.** Lewis, 1985. 430 pp. Examines the following pollutants from the perspectives of measurement and source characterization, habitat studies, health effects, risk analysis, and future needs: radon, microorganisms, passive cigarette smoke, combustion products, and organics.

2656. Steneck, Nicholas H. **The microwave debate.** MIT Press, 1984. 279 pp., ill., bibl., index. Well-documented analysis covering the debate from its beginning in the 1930s, to the military interest in the thermal effects in the 1960s and the controversy when environmentalists and consumer activists joined the debate. Explores the roles of government, scientists, mass media and the courts in the debate.

2657. Perrow, Charles. **Normal accidents: living with high-risk technologies.** Basic Books, 1984. 386 pp., ill., bibl., index. Argues that accidents are inevitable and presents a theory of accidents that draws from both engineering and social science. Concentrates on the properties of systems rather than on human error, faulty equipment, or underfinanced mismanagement. Based on findings, recommends abandoning nuclear weapons and power.

2658. Benarde, Melvin A. **Our precarious habitat: fifteen years later.** Wiley, 1989. 636 pp., ill., bibl., index. Marshals impressive array of epidemiological evidence to examine such environmental issues as air, water, and noise pollution, sanitary sewage and wastewater treatment, occupational health, pesticides, and others.

2659. D'Itri, Frank M.; Kamrin, Michael A.; eds. **PCBs, human and environmental hazards.** Butterworth, 1983. 443 pp., ill., bibl., index. Examines scientific, social, and political issues; analysis and monitoring; metabolism and toxicity; and human health effects and regulation.

2660. Tweety, B. G.; and others, eds. **Pesticide residues and food safety: a harvest of viewpoints.** American Chemical Society, ACS symposium series, v. 446, 1990. 360 pp., index. Developed from a special conference sponsored by the Division of Agrochemicals, American Chemical Society, in 1990.

2661. Lave, Lester B.; Upton, Arthur C.; eds. **Toxic chemicals, health, and the environment.** Johns Hopkins University Press, 1987. 304 pp., ill., bibl., index. Discusses problems of monitoring chemicals; measuring quantity, exposure, dose, and physiological effect; and cleaning up toxic waste sites.

Risk Assessment (2662–2675)

2662. **Asbestiform fibers: nonoccupational health risks.** National Academy Press, 1984. 334 pp. Prepared by the Committee on Nonoccupational Health Risks of Asbestiform Fibers Commission on Life Sciences, National Research Council. Reports on assessing exposure levels, effects on human health, and laboratory studies. Provides risk assessment of nonoccupational exposure, concluding that extent of risk is highly uncertain.

2663. Travis, Curtis C.; ed. **Carcinogen risk assessment.** Plenum Press, Contemporary issues in risk analysis, v. 3, 1988. 210 pp., ill., bibl., index. Fifteen papers provide overview of risk assessment, examine use of scientific data in assessment, and discuss exposure assessment and risk management.

2664. Whipple, Chris; ed. **De minimis risk.** Plenum Press, Contemporary issues in risk analysis, v. 2, 1987. 208 pp., ill., bibl., index. Proceedings of a 1985 workshop. Explores incentives, obstacles, applications, and quantitative aspects of the de minimis risk concept.

2665. Krimsky, Sheldon; Plough, Alonzo. **Environmental hazards: communicating risks as a social process.** Auburn House, 1989. 333 pp., ill., bibl., index. Five case studies illustrate the social, political, and cultural dimensions of risk and the difficulty of predicting public response to technical information. Case studies document the controversies surrounding pesticide residues in food, the release of genetically engineered organisms into the environment, radon gas, point source pollution, and a toxic waste site.

2666. Whyte, Anne V.; Burton, Ian. **Environmental risk assessment.** Wiley, SCOPE, v. 15, 1980. 157 pp., ill., index. Based on a 1977 international working seminar. Examines the social evaluation of risk and application of risk assessment to environmental management.

2667. Graham, John D.; Green, Laura C.; Roberts, Marc J. **In search of safety: chemicals and cancer risk.** Harvard University Press, 1988. 260 pp., ill., bibl., index. Examines the role of science in policy-making, using case studies of attempts to regulate benzene and formaldehyde. Looks at scientific evidence of risk, and political and judicial reactions to scientific disagreement.

2668. Viscusi, W. Kip; Magat, Wesley A.; Huber, Joel; and others. **Learning about risk: consumer and worker responses to hazard information.** Harvard University Press, 1987. 197 pp., ill., bibl., index. New field studies of consumer and worker behavior use economic models and economic behavior hypotheses to assess the impact and effectiveness of labeling hazardous substances. Research on effective label design is still needed.

2669. Ricci, Paolo F.; ed. **Principles of health risk assessment.** Prentice-Hall, 1985. 417 pp., ill., bibl., index. Focuses on measures and methods for making cost-benefit analysis and evaluation.

2670. Lave, Lester B.; ed. **Quantitative risk assessment in regulation.** Brookings Institution, Studies in the regulation of economic activity, 1982. 264 pp., bibl., index. Presents case studies analyzing the role of quantifying risk assessment in six regulatory decisions involving the ozone standard, benzene, coke oven emissions, ionizing radiation, chlorobenzinate, and food additives and contaminants. Also describes different methods of quantifying risk assessment.

2671. Cohrssen, John J.; Covello, Vincent T. **Risk analysis: a guide to principles and methods for analyzing health and environmental risks.** Council on Environmental Quality, 1989. 407 pp., bibl. Includes case studies and examples, explaining the issues through both technical and nontechnical sources.

2672. Paustenbach, Dennis J.; ed. **The risk assessment of environmental hazards.** Wiley, 1989. 1155 pp., ill., bibl., index. Twenty-two case studies demonstrate techniques and approaches for assessing environmental and occupational health hazards. Addresses hazardous waste sites, radon and radioactive waste, risk management, and risks to wildlife.

2673. Wynne, Brian; ed. **Risk management and hazardous waste: implementation and the dialectics of credibility.** Springer-Verlag, 1987. 447 pp., index. Discusses such issues as risk perception, risk assessment of technological systems, and risk assessment and hazardous waste regulations. Also presents case studies of hazardous waste management in Germany, the United Kingdom, the Netherlands, and Hungary.

2674. Crandall, Robert W.; Lave, Lester B.; eds. **The scientific basis of health and safety regulation.** Brookings Institution, 1981. 309 pp., ill. Fifteen conference papers on the role of scientific data in regulation. Five topics are considered: passive restraints in automobiles, cotton dust in manufacturing, sulfur dioxide standards,

saccharin as a food additive, and waterborne carcinogens. On each topic, there are papers by a scientist, an economist, and a regulator, which reveal quite different approaches to regulation.

2675. Tardiff, Robert G.; Rodricks, Joseph V.; eds. **Toxic substances and human risk: principles of data interpretation.** Plenum Press, Life science monographs, 1987. 445 pp., ill., bibl., index.

Toxicology (2676–2690)

2676. Alternative methods in toxicology series. Liebert, 1983–1991. 8 vols. to date. Volumes contain symposium presentations, poster presentations, and workshop reports. Addresses product safety evaluation, alternatives to acute toxicology and acute ocular irritation testing, and progress in in vitro toxicology.

2677. Lundy, Paul. **A cancer primer.** National Audubon Society, 1984. 156 pp., ill., bibl. A general overview providing factual, clear information on cancer biology, incidence, causes, determinants, and identification.

2678. Amdur, Mary O.; Doull, John; Klaassen, Curtis D.; eds. **Casarett and Doull's toxicology: the basic science of poisons.** Pergamon Press, 4th ed., 1991. 1033 pp., bibl., index. Authoritative reference and textbook arranged in five sections: general principles, systemic toxicology, toxic agents, environmental toxicology, and applications.

2679. Gosselin, Robert E.; Smith, Roger P.; Hodge, Harold C. **Clinical toxicology of commercial products.** Williams & Wilkins, 5th ed., 1984. Various paging, index. Lists commercial products ingredients, estimated toxicity, and recommended treatment, and provides manufacturer contact information. Case reports and related research papers are also included.

2680. Sax, Newton Irving; Lewis, Richard J., Sr. **Dangerous properties of industrial materials.** Van Nostrand Reinhold, 7th ed., 1989. Bibl. 3 vols. Details physical and toxic properties, chemical aspects, synonyms, exposure standards, and regulations pertaining to over 20,000 chemicals.

2681. Hodgson, Ernest; Mailman, Richard B.; Chambers, Janice E. **Dictionary of toxicology.** Van Nostrand Reinhold, 1988. 395 pp., bibl. More than 60 experts have submitted brief definitions of toxicological, anatomical, biochemical, pathological, and physiological terms. Intended as a bridge between specialties, not an exhaustive listing.

2682. Fawell, J. K.; Hunt, S. **Environmental toxi-**

cology: **organic pollutants**. Halsted Press, 1988. 440 pp. Emphasizes chronic toxicity and carcinogenicity in relation to long-term exposure to low levels of contaminants. Presents data on the occurrence of mammalian toxicity of more than 200 contaminants based on a study of raw and treated drinking waters.

2683. Milman, Harry A.; Weisburger, Elizabeth K.; eds. **Handbook of carcinogen testing**. Noyes, 1985. 637 pp., ill., bibl., index. Examines developments in the identification and prediction of carcinogenicity. Topics include in vitro testing, limited and long-term animal bioassays, and bioassays for insoluble materials; also assesses risk estimation models.

2684. Tu, Anthony T.; ed. **Handbook of natural toxins**. Dekker, 1983–1986. Ill., bibl., index. 6 vols. to date. A complete guide to the chemistry and mechanisms of action of poisons obtained from plants, animals, and microorganisms. Vol. 1: Plant and fungal toxins. Vol. 2: Insect poisons, allergens, and other invertebrate venoms. Vol. 3: Marine toxins and venoms. Vol. 4: Bacterial toxins. Vol. 5: Reptile venoms and toxins. Vol. 6: Toxicology of plant and fungal compounds.

2685. Sittig, M. **Handbook of toxic and hazardous chemicals and carcinogens**. Noyes, 2d ed., 1985. 950 pp., ill., bibl., index. Information on 950 chemicals arranged alphabetically. Each one is identified as a carcinogen, hazardous substance, hazardous waste, or priority toxic pollutant.

2686. Wexler, Philip. **Information resources in toxicology**. Elsevier, 2d ed., 1987. 510 pp., index. Essential, comprehensive sourcebook provides annotated listings of texts, journals, databases, and organizations from the United States, distinguishing particularly important and noteworthy references. Includes discussion of legislation, regulation, and hazard communication compliance. Reviews international resources as well as those from 16 other countries.

2687. **The Merck index**. Merck, 1889 to date. Irregular: 11th ed., 1989. An essential reference for chemists, biochemists, pharmacists, biologists, pharmacologists, and health practitioners; provides concise descriptions of chemicals, drugs, and biological substances. Gives properties; trivial, generic, and chemical names; structures, trademarks, and company affiliations; and use, principal pharmacological action, and toxicity.

2688. Eller, Peter M.; ed. **NIOSH manual of analytical methods**. U.S. Department of Health and Human Services, Centers for Disease Control, National Institute for Occupational Safety and Health, Division of Physical Sciences and Engineering; Government Printing Office,

3d ed., 1984. Ill., bibl., index. 2 vols. Reviews air and biological analytic methods, examining sampling and measurement techniques. Views methodologies for the study of more than 200 toxic substances.

2689. Clayton, Florence E.; Clayton, George D.; eds. **Patty's industrial hygiene and toxicology**. Wiley, 4th ed., 1991. Ill., bibl., index. 2 vols. Classic reference text covering the recognition, evaluation, and control of environmental factors and hazards in the workplace. Reviews current regulations, science, technology and methods. New sections on pollutants in the home and workplace, the design of analytical laboratories, worker right-to-know programs, hazardous waste, video display terminals, asbestos, and man-made mineral fibers.

2690. Steering Committee on Identification of Toxic and Potentially Toxic Chemicals for Consideration by the National Toxicology Program. **Toxicity testing: strategies to determine needs and priorities**. National Academy Press, 1984. 382 pp., ill., bibl. Assesses the status of toxicology test information on potentially toxic substances. Develops criteria to set research priorities for these substances.

Health Protection. Safety. Emergencies (2691–2711)

2691. Lampe, Kenneth F.; McCann, Mary Ann. **AMA handbook of poisonous and injurious plants**. Chicago Review Press, 1985. 432 pp., ill., bibl., index. Quick-reference handbook gives broad information about species (genera and family), toxic parts, toxins, symptoms, management of poisoning, and literature references.

2692. **American Industrial Hygiene Association journal**. Williams & Wilkins, 1958 to date. Monthly.

2693. Altman, Roberta. **Complete book of home environmental hazards**. Facts on File, 1990. 304 pp., index. Focuses on environmental hazards inside the house. Explains why and how certain substances (radon, lead, asbestos) are dangerous, how they can be detected, and which federal and state agencies can help, with contact information. Also reviews hazards outside the house and what to look for in purchasing an environmentally safe house.

2694. Lunn, George; Sansone, Eric B. **Destruction of hazardous chemicals in the laboratory**. Wiley-Interscience, 1990. 271 pp., ill., bibl., index. Descriptions detailing steps to degrade and decontaminate over 40 hazardous chemicals at the laboratory scale.

2695. **Emergency response planning and pre-**

paredness for transport accidents involving radioactive material. International Atomic Energy Agency, Safety series. Recommendations (IAEA), v. 87, 2d ed., 1987. 103 pp., ill., bibl. Guide for safety officials; some topics include emergency response planning, transport regulations, and the consequences of transport accidents.

2696. Cohen, Gary; O'Connor, John. **Fighting toxics: a manual for protecting your family, community, and workpalce.** Island Press, 1990. 346 pp., index. A guide for citizen activists. Part I focuses on strategies of community organizing, influencing corporate business practices, accessing information about potential threats, and using the media effectively. Part II, Toxics and the law, is a legal guide. Part III discusses reducing the use of toxic materials. Includes reading lists and useful contacts.

2697. Fire/emergency services sourcebook 1990–91. Specialized Publication Service, 2d ed., 1990. 650 pp., index. Covers books, periodicals, audiovisuals, associations (local, state, and national), and schools and courses on all aspects of emergency prevention, response, and research. Includes comprehensive list of commonly used abbreviations and acronyms.

2698. National Fire Protection Association. **Fire protection guide on hazardous materials.** National Fire Protection Association, 10th ed., 1991. Various paging. Identifies fire hazards of different materials, including sections on the hazard properties of flammable liquids, gases, and volatile solids; reviews hazardous chemicals and their reactions.

2699. Lefevre, Marc J.; Conibear, Shirley; eds. **First aid manual for chemical accidents.** Van Nostrand Reinhold, 2d ed., 1989. 262 pp., index. Provides first aid information for over 600 chemicals. Covers poisoning, inhalation, ingestion, skin contact, and eye contact. Shows how to interpret Department of Transportation codes on shipping labels to identify unknown substances.

2700. Plog, Barbara A.; ed. **Fundamentals of industrial hygiene.** National Safety Council, 3d ed., 1988. 915 pp.

2701. De Zuane, John. **Handbook of drinking water quality: standards and controls.** Van Nostrand Reinhold, 1990. 523 pp., index. Introductory reference work reviews physical and chemical parameters of water and details potential contaminants including inorganics, organics, radionuclides, and carcinogens. Discusses standards for water analysis and treatment.

2702. Waugh, William L., Jr.; Hy, Ronald John; eds. **Handbook of emergency management: programs and policies dealing with major hazards and disasters.**

Greenwood Press, 1990. 336 pp., maps, ill., bibl., index. Arranged by disaster type; reviews manner in which people address each hazard and assesses efforts in disaster preparation, mitigation, response, and recovery for each case.

2703. Koren, Herman. **Handbook of environmental health and safety: principles and practices.** Lewis; National Environmental Health Association, 2d ed., 1991. Bibl., index. 2 vols. Updates current concerns, issues, and regulations.

2704. Lewis, Richard J. **Hazardous chemicals desk reference.** Van Nostrand Reinhold, 2d ed., 1991. 1579 pp., index. Denotes poisonous, irritant, corrosive, explosive, and carcinogenic properties of 5000 hazardous chemicals; notes general physical properties and standards for exposure limits.

2705. Schoemaker, Joyce M.; Vitale, Charity Y. **Healthy homes, healthy kids: protecting your children from everyday environmental hazards.** Island Press, 1991. 221 pp., bibl., index. Practical advice for preventing, removing, and reducing threats from radon, lead, food additives, air pollutants, and yard chemicals. For each problem, reviews possible solutions and their related costs and lists sources for additional information and professional assistance.

2706. Lowry, George G.; Lowry, Robert C. **Lowry's handbook of right-to-know and emergency planning: handbook of compliance for worker and community, OSHA, EPA, and the states.** Lewis, 1988. 421 pp., ill., bibl., index. Among other features, this handbook explains how to identify hazardous materials, plan for emergencies, and comply with reporting requirements.

2707. NIOSH pocket guide to chemical hazards. U.S. Department of Health and Human Services, Public Health Service, Centers for Disease Control, National Institute for Occupational Safety and Health; Government Printing Office, 1990. 245 pp. Presents information on exposure limits, incompatibilities, personal protection, and health hazard data for almost 400 work environment chemicals covered by specific federal regulations.

2708. Kavianian, H. R; Wentz, C. A. **Occupational and environmental safety engineering and management.** Van Nostrand Reinhold, 1990. 383 pp., index. Focuses on the chemical industry. Reviews newly emerging safety laws, compliance requirements, hazard analysis methodology, and safety analysis in process design.

2709. Zenz, Carl; ed. **Occupational medicine: principles and practical applications.** Year Book Medical Publishers, 2d ed, 1988. 1273 pp., ill. Covers administrative and clinical aspects of occupational medicine, including the physical and chemical environment; particular work categories; psychological and social considerations; and epidemiology. Thoroughly revised, with 30 new chapters.

2710. Bechdel, Les; Ray, Slim. **River rescue.** Appalachian Mountain Club Books (dist. by Talman), 2d ed, 1989. 238 pp., ill, bibl., index. Trip planning; organization and leadership; reading the river; rescue techniques (including self-rescue and ropework); patient care and evacuation; CPR, first aid, and hypothermia.

2711. Harte, John; and others. **Toxics A to Z: A guide to everyday pollution hazards.** University of California Press, 1991. 479 pp., bibl., index. Comprehensive presentation in two parts: Part 1, "All About Toxics," provides a general overview of toxic hazards, reviewing sources of exposure, toxics movement through the environment and the food chain, 14 major groups of toxics, and toxics regulation. Part 2, "Guide to Commonly Encountered Toxics," is an alphabetical listing of 100 toxics, telling what they are, how they are measured, where they are found, symptoms of exposure, known risks, and lessening and avoidance of risks.

Section 13

Engineering. Technology

The engineering and technology of this section have to do with pollution control and civil engineering. There are also references to engineering for power production and energy conservation, to nuclear engineering and radioactive waste, and to sources of engineering and technical information.

The world often seems divided into those who are technically illiterate and fearful and those who are technically arrogant. Desperately needed are individuals with a knowledge of engineering, to provide balance and intelligent criticism. Improper use of technology is plentifully documented in our bibliography. But the titles in this section convey another message: that applied science and engineering can be used to overcome major problems, right past wrongs, and build a world according to environmental principles.

Environmental Control Technology
Under this heading are titles dealing with air, water, and land engineering, whether for pollution control or for other structures and processes of civil engineering, such as dams, power plants, and buildings. The entries in this group complement and supplement Sections 2, 3 and 4 on air, water, and land.

See also:

- Section 1: Global resources and environment; environmental management
- Section 8: Social and human ecology, population
- Section 10: National laws and policies; U.S. politics and policies; U.S. executive agencies, administration and regulation
- Section 11: Industry, economic sectors; pollution, industrial wastes
- Section 12: Toxic threats, hazards

Solid Waste. Recycling. Entries in this subgroup cover domestic and municipal wastes, garbage, materials recovery, recycling, composting, and solid waste management.

See also:

- Section 4: Land degradation, erosion, reclamation
- Section 8: Urban communities
- Section 10: Law and policies: state and local, regional

Biotechnology. In this subgroup are titles on genetic engineering, biological waste treatment, status of biotechnology, microbiological control of pollution, and more.

See also:

- Section 1: Biological systems; biodiversity, conservation biology, genetics; physical and chemical systems
- Section 5: Plants, agriculture; endangered plants, genetic resources; diseases and pests
- Section 6: Trees, forests, forestry; species, genetic resources

Hazardous Wastes. The technology of controlling hazardous wastes is represented in this subgroup, including asbestos; chemical fixation; handling, storage, transportation, and disposal; site problems; and innovative solutions.

See also:

- Section 1: Chemistry, biogeochemical cycles, pollutants
- Section 5: Food and agriculture; atmospheric environment, pollution, pesticides
- Section 10: U.S. executive agencies, administration and regulation; pollution control: hazardous wastes, United States
- Section 11: Industry, economic sectors; pollution, industrial wastes
- Section 12: Toxic threats, hazards; health protection, safety, emergencies

Air Pollution Control. The air pollution titles in this subgroup deal with technologies of emission reduction; operation of control systems; principles of design and engineering; incineration of municipal and hazardous wastes; and radon.

See also:

- Section 2: Air pollution, atmospheric chemistry
- Section 10: U.S. executive agencies, administration and regulation; pollution control: United States
- Section 11: Industry, economic sectors; pollution, industrial wastes; energy
- Section 12: Toxic threats, hazards; health protection, safety, emergencies
- Section 14: Modeling and simulation; assessment and monitoring; testing and analysis

Water Engineering
Both freshwater and marine structures are treated in this group. Channels, dams, water supply, coastal engineering, water quality monitoring systems, and water conservation are some of the topics covered.

See also:

- Section 3: Marine: physical aspects; water: physical aspects, hydrology
- Section 4: Soils; land degradation, erosion, reclamation
- Section 14: Assessment and monitoring

Water Pollution Control. Wastewater. Most entries in this subgroup deal with freshwater pollution and its control. There are titles for appropriate technology, biological treatment, water chemistry, constructed wetlands, urban wastewater and runoff control, wastewater analysis, operational management, septic systems, and sludge management and disposal.

See also:

- Section 1: Chemistry, biogeochemical cycles, pollutants
- Section 3: Water pollution
- Section 14: Assessment and monitoring; testing and analysis

Civil Engineering. Construction. Geotechnology
The selections on civil engineering here include bioengineering, landfills, construction and buildings, engineering geology, site remediation, land disposal of wastes, underground storage tanks, surveying, transportation, and wind engineering.

See also:

- Section 1: Geology, earth sciences
- Section 3: Water: physical aspects, hydrology
- Section 4: Land degradation, erosion, reclamation
- Section 8: Rural communities; urban communities
- Section 9: Built environment, architecture, historical preservation
- Section 11: Economy, costs and benefits, valuation; development; industry, economic sectors

Radioactive. Nuclear
In this group are entries for environmental radioactivity, geological disposal, high-level and low-level radioactive wastes, nuclear power technology, and Three Mile Island.

See also:

- Section 1: Geology, earth sciences; energy
- Section 4: Soils; land degradation, erosion, reclamation

- Section 10: International law and policies; national laws and policies; U.S. politics and policies; pollution control: hazardous wastes, United States
- Section 11: Industry, economic sectors; pollution, industrial wastes
- Section 12: Toxic threats, hazards; risk assessment; health protection, safety, emergencies

Energy Technology

Works on energy transmission, coal technologies, energy management and control systems, energy research and development, production technologies, and fuels are in this group.

See also:

- Section 1: Global resources and environment; environmental management; geology, earth sciences; energy
- Section 8: Society and environment
- Section 10: Law, politics, government
- Section 11: Industry, economic sectors; energy

Renewable Energy. Unconventional energy and power sources are entered in this last subgroup, including bioenergy and biomass, solar power, geothermal energy, methane, energy conservation techniques, fuel reduction, refuse-derived fuels, and hydroelectric power.

See also:

- Section 1: Global resources and environment; environmental management; energy
- Section 5: Plants, agriculture
- Section 6: Forests and forest resources: regions and countries
- Section 8: Tribal communities; rural communities
- Section 11: Industry, economic sectors; energy

2712. Bever, Michael B.; ed. **Encyclopedia of materials science and engineering.** Pergamon Press; MIT Press, 1986. Ill., bibl., index. 8 vols. Contains over 1500 articles explaining materials science and engineering, from basic theories to specific engineering practices. Overview articles introduce subject areas and provide guidance and reference to particular topics.

2713. Engineering index. Engineering Index, 1906 to date. Monthly. Indexes and abstracts the world literature of engineering—books, journals, technical reports, patents, and other publications. Available online and on CD-ROM as *Compendex.*

Environmental Control Technology (2714–2731)

2714. Wann, David. **Biologic: environmental protection by design.** Johnson Books, 1990. 284 pp., ill., bibl., index. Presents strategies and suggestions to balance current "throwaway" society with its environment, ranging from recycling to improved airport design.

2715. Cheremisinoff, Paul N.; Cheremisinoff, Nicholas P.; Cheng, Su Ling; eds. **Civil engineering practice.** Technomic, 1987–1988. Ill., index. 5 vols. Reviews the theory and practice of structures, hydraulics and mechanics, geotechnical and ocean engineering, surveying, construction, transportation, economics and government, the use of computers, water resources, and environmental engineering.

2716. Porteous, Andrew. **Dictionary of environmental science and technology.** Taylor & Francis, 1991. 399 pp., bibl. Supplements definitions and reviews of current issues with addresses of information sources and further readings.

2717. Cheremisinoff, Paul N.; Alves, S. S.; eds. **Encyclopedia of environmental control technology.** Gulf, 1989–1991. Ill., bibl., index. 4 vols. to date. Information source for specialized topics in pollution control. Each volume provides an overview of technology and research trends. Vol. 1: Thermal treatment of hazardous wastes. Vol. 2: Air pollution control. Vol. 3: Wastewater treatment technology. Vol. 4: Hazardous waste containment and treatment.

2718. Vesilind, P. Aarne; Peirce, Jeffrey J. **Environmental pollution and control.** Butterworth, 3d ed., 1990. 416 pp., ill.

2719. Environmental science and technology. American Chemical Society, 1967 to date. Monthly. Features peer-reviewed research reports; articles on new materials and engineering approaches; and news of emerging issues, changes in regulations, and events significant to environmental science.

2720. de Waal, K. J. A.; van den Brink, W. J.; eds. **Environmental technology.** Nijhoff, 1987. 826 pp., ill., bibl. Proceedings of the Second European Conference on Environmental Technology in 1987. Aims to show the state of the art and the wide range of possibilities in environmental technology, defined as techniques to identify, quantify, and reduce environmental problems. Sections on raw materials and energy; clean technology; industrial emissions and waste recycling; product design; remediation techniques; incentives and attitudes.

2721. Bower, Cynthia E.; Rhoads, Mary L.; eds. **EPA index: a key to U.S. Environmental Protection Agency reports and Superintendent of Documents and NTIS numbers.** Oryx Press, 1983. 385 pp. Lists reports by EPA report number and by title, with corresponding Superintendent of Documents classification numbers or National Technical Information Service report numbers.

2722. Wang, Lawrence K.; Pereira, Norman C.; eds. **Handbook of environmental engineering.** Humana Press, 1979–1986. Ill. 4 vols. Vol. 1: Air and noise pollution control. Vol. 2: Solid waste processing and resource recovery. Vol. 3: Biological treatment processes. Vol. 4: Water resources and natural control processes. Basic text and reference. Gives scientific background, design concepts, and applications.

2723. Journal of environmental engineering. American Society of Civil Engineers, 1956 to date. Bimonthly. Environmental, social, and health aspects of sanitation, public water supplies, and waste management engineering.

2724. Journal of the Air and Waste Management Association. Air and Waste Management Association, 1951 to present. Monthly. Continues: Journal of the Air Pollution Control Association. Covers air, water, and solid waste. Feature articles, reports of new research, and in-depth reports and commentary on government regulations and policies.

2725. Reed, Sherwood C.; Middlebrooks, E. Joe; Crites, Ronald W. **Natural systems for waste management and treatment.** McGraw-Hill, 1988. 288 pp., ill., bibl., index. Covers use of plants, soils, and aquatic and terrestrial organisms to treat wastes. Includes planning, design, and site selection.

2726. Kates, Robert W.; Hohenemser, Christopher;

Kasperson, Jeanne X.; eds. **Perilous progress: managing the hazards of technology.** Westview Press, Westview special studies in science, technology, and public policy, 1985. 489 pp., ill., bibl., index. Contributors with backgrounds ranging from physics and geochemistry to law and psychology discuss conceptualizing, assessing, and managing hazards and measuring consequences; specific topics reviewed include economic and noneconomic losses, airborne mercury, nuclear power, PCBs, contraceptives, and television as a social hazard.

2727. Pollution abstracts. Cambridge Scientific Abstracts, 1970 to date. Bimonthly. Abstracts and indexes worldwide technical information on air, water, solid waste, and toxic pollution. Includes measuring and monitoring techniques, statistics, treatment and control, recovery and recycling, standards and criteria, socioeconomic and legal aspects, and effects of contaminants on animal and plant species in nature and in controlled laboratory experiments. Also covers environmental policies, programs, legislation, and education. Available as a computer database, online and on CD-ROM.

2728. Pollution technology review series. Noyes, 1974 to date. Several volumes/yr. Reference series brings together relevant technical reports, government studies, standards, and patents on the technology of different kinds of pollution, from sick building syndrome to ocean dumping. Intended for managers and engineers.

2729. Straub, Conrad P.; ed. **Practical handbook of environmental control.** CRC Press, 1989. 537 pp. Includes descriptions of many types of air pollution control measures and water quality treatments; covers the collection, treatment, recycling and reuse, bioassay, and toxicity of wastewater; studies the handling and disposal of solid wastes; and includes a section on the human sector: ventilation and air conditioning, noise production and control, safety concerns, and general sanitation.

2730. Corbitt, Robert A.; ed. **Standard handbook of environmental engineering.** McGraw-Hill, 1990. 1281 pp., ill., bibl. Comprehensive reference on principles and practice of environmental engineering. Covers, in part, air quality control, water supply, wastewater disposal, solid waste management, storm water, and hazardous waste management. Additional chapters focus on the history and fundamentals of legislation, quality standards, and environmental assessment procedures.

2731. Ausubel, Jesse H.; Sladovich, Hedy E.; eds. **Technology and environment.** National Academy Press, 1989. 221 pp., ill., bibl., index. Contributed papers examine the paradoxical nature of technology as both a source of and a solution to environmental damage. Examples of potential technological solutions; discussion of social and institutional aspects.

Solid Waste. Recycling (2732–2749)

2732. BioCycle: journal of waste recycling. JG Press, 1960 to date. Monthly. Continues: Compost science, Compost science/Land utilization. Short articles (up to 20 per issue) and news on all aspects of recycling, solid waste, composting, and waste-to-energy, national and international. Sponsors conferences.

2733. Disposal of industrial and domestic wastes: land and sea alternatives. National Academy Press, 1984. 210 pp., ill., bibl. Report from the Board on Ocean Science and Policy, Commission on Physical Sciences, Mathematics, and Resources, National Research Council. Discusses alternative solutions to the disposal of industrial and domestic wastes. Presents results, with qualifications, of several modeling exercises assessing the results and consequences of disposal alternatives.

2734. Facing America's trash. What next for municipal solid waste? Office of Technology Assessment; Government Printing Office, 1989. 385 pp., ill., index. Thorough review of municipal solid waste (MSW) situation, trends, immediate problems, and policy options. Chapters on MSW system; generation and composition; prevention; recycling; incineration; landfilling; and government planning and programs.

2735. Garbage: the practical journal for the environment. Old House Journal, 1989 to date. Bimonthly. Feature articles, news, commentary, letters, and advertisements on reducing and managing wastes, trash, sewage, and toxics.

2736. Holmes, John R.; ed. **Managing solid wastes in developing countries.** Wiley, 1984. 304 pp., ill., bibl., index. Examines solid waste collection, disposal and reclamation problems in developing countries. Cautions against indiscriminant use of Western technology and emphasizes differences in climate and socioeconomic conditions.

2737. Alter, Harvey. **Materials recovery from municipal waste: unit operations in practice.** Dekker, Pollution engineering and technology, 24, 1983. 264 pp. Principles and operation of tested methods for recovering glass, magnetic metals, aluminum, and combustible materials from municipal solid waste.

2738. Polprasert, Chongrak. **Organic waste recycling.** Wiley, 1989. 357 pp., ill., bibl., index. Contains laboratory, pilot-scale, and field data from developed and developing countries on characteristics of organic wastes, composting, biogas production, algae production, aquatic weeds and their utilization, land treatment of wastewater, and planning and institutional development.

2739. Denison, Richard A.; Ruston, John. **Recycling and incineration: evaluating the choices.** Island Press, 1990. 322 pp., index. Scientific, legal, and economic aspects of waste disposal. Part I compares recycling and incineration from an economic perspective and discusses waste generation and reduction. Part II covers the health and environmental risks of incineration and their control. Part III discusses strategies for citizen involvement in planning, implementation, and environmental review.

2740. Resource recycling: North America's recycling journal. Resource Recycling, 1982 to date. Monthly. Short articles (10 to 15), features, news, and departments.

2741. Resources, conservation and recycling. Elsevier, 1988 to date. Quarterly. Continues: *Resources conservation* and *Urban ecology*. Publishes research and reviews on management of renewable and nonrenewable natural resources, emphasizing the efficient use of materials and energy. Includes institutional, political, and legal aspects.

2742. Rush to burn: solving America's garbage crisis? Island Press, 1989. 269 pp., maps, ill., index. Report of a team of six reporters from *Newsday* on a six-month investigation. Chapters on the impact of incinerators, debate over landfills, solid waste management abroad, recycling and other alternatives, and the impact of fast-food containers.

2743. Robinson, William D.; ed. **The solid waste handbook: a practical guide.** Wiley, 1986. 811 pp., ill., index. Encyclopedic coverage by 36 authors of legislation, regulation, planning, finance, technologies, operations, economics, administration, and public perception of future trends.

2744. Neal, Homer A.; Schubel, J. R. **Solid waste management and the environment: the mounting garbage and trash crisis.** Prentice-Hall, 1987. 240 pp., ill., bibl., index. An assessment of the problem and options for handling solid wastes. Discusses constituents and amounts of trash produced, impacts of landfills and ocean dumping, and recovery and disposal technologies. Provides a comparative analysis of disposal methods.

2745. Suess, Michael J.; ed. **Solid waste management: selected topics.** World Health Organization, 1985. 210 pp. Presents a model code of practice for the disposal of solid waste on land. Reviews and evaluates compost systems and incineration and their roles in modern solid waste management. Discusses treatment and disposal of animal waste.

2746. Blumberg, Louis; Gottlieb, Robert. **War on waste: can America win its battle with garbage?** Island Press, 1989. 301 pp., ill., index. On the causes of the solid waste crisis and the conflict between environmentalists and the waste industry. Analyzes incineration policies; the role of advertising and packaging; alternatives to incineration, notably the LANCER project in Los Angeles; and the politics of garbage.

2747. Waste management and research. Academic Press (London), 1983 to date. Quarterly.

2748. Wastes and their treatment: information sources and bibliography. United Nations Environment Programme, 1986. 334 pp., index. Listing of sources worldwide. Organizations (sources) are arranged by country and indexed by subject codes. Alphabetical indexes to these subject codes are given in English, French, Spanish, and Russian. Includes annotated bibliography of over 500 items.

2749. Vogler, Jon. **Work from waste: recycling wastes to create employment..** Intermediate Technology; Oxfam, 1981. 396 pp., ill., bibl., index. Provides details on recycling various waste products and starting a small waste-recycling business.

Biotechnology (2750–2763)

2750. Bioresource technology. Elsevier, 1969 to date. Monthly. Continues: Biological wastes (incorporates Biomass). Publishes original research, critical reviews, and case studies on biomass biological waste treatment, bioenergy, and biotransformation.

2751. Sasson, Albert. **Biotechnologies and development.** UNESCO; Technical Centre for Agriculture and Rural Cooperation, 1988. 361 pp., bibl. Discusses developments in various biotechnology fields. Reports on opportunities to transfer these technologies to developing nations.

2752. Biotechnology and bioengineering. Wiley, 1962 to date. Monthly. Publishes research on applied biotechnology, covering animal cell, environmental, plant cell, and mineral biotechnology; applied genetics, enzyme systems, and more.

2753. Gibbs, Jeffrey N.; Cooper, Iver P.; Mackler, Bruce F. **Biotechnology and the environment: international regulation.** Stockton Press, 1987. 375 pp., bibl., index. Reviews U.S. biotechnology policy, examining the roles and responsibilities of regulatory agencies. Discusses biotechnology regulatory status in 11 other developed nations.

2754. Fiksel, Joseph; Covello, Vincent T.; eds. **Biotechnology risk assessment: issues and methods for environmental introductions.** Pergamon Press, 1986. 174 pp., ill., bibl., index. Discusses adequate evaluation of microorganisms to be genetically modified, effects of human exposure to viruses and genetically modified bacteria, the fate and dispersal of bioengineered microorganisms in the environment, and analysis of ecosystem structure and function.

2755. Antébi, Elizabeth; Fishlock, David. **Biotechnology: strategies for life.** MIT Press, 1986. 239 pp., ill., bibl., index. Reviews developments in various aspects of biotechnology. Examines various biotechnologies that will prevent birth defects, defeat diseases, improve food supply, and create energy.

2756. Arestam, M.; Forti, G.; eds. **Carbon dioxide as a source of carbon: biochemical and chemical uses.** Kluwer, NATO ASI series, Series C, Mathematical and physical sciences, v. 206, 1987. 441 pp., ill., bibl., index. Explains chemical and biological aspects of the carbon cycle. Examines and assesses industrial uses of carbon dioxide and ecological consequences.

2757. Critical reviews in biotechnology. CRC Press, 1983 to date. Quarterly. Reviews scientific research and developments in all areas of biotechnology, many of which are either environmental problems or solutions.

2758. Forster, Christopher F.; Wase, D. A. John. **Environmental biotechnology.** Horwood; Halsted Press, Ellis Horwood series in chemical engineering, 1987. 453 pp., ill., bibl., index. Review of current status and developments and prediction of future trends.

2759. Suzuki, David T.; Knudtson, P. **Genethics: the clash between the new genetics and human values.** Harvard University Press, 1989. 384 pp., ill., bibl., index. Discusses ethical issues raised through genetic screening, biological weapons, crossing of evolutionary boundaries, and genetic diversity. Explains genes, their processes, and selected aspects and techniques of genetic engineering.

2760. Crafts-Lighty, Anita. **Information sources in biotechnology.** Macmillan; Nature Press, 1983. 306 pp., bibl., index. Guide to biotechnology serials, trade magazines, newsletters, proceedings, and databases. Focuses on modern application areas. Covers biochemical engineering, applied microbiology, genetic engineering, cell

culturing, and enzyme immobilization. Biomechanics and biomaterials are not included.

2761. Dart, R. K.; Stretton, R. J. **Microbiological aspects of pollution control.** Elsevier, Fundamental aspects of pollution control and environmental science, v. 2, 2d ed., 1980. 265 pp. Explains use of microorganisms in removing pollutants from the environment. Topics range from currently practical (wastewater treatment) to theoretical (pesticide biodegradation).

2762. Marx, Jean L.; ed. **A revolution in biotechnology.** Cambridge University Press, 1989. 227 pp., ill., index. Contributions from experts working in such areas as crop improvement by gene transplants, production of feedstock chemicals, monoclonal antibodies, and diagnosis of genetic diseases.

2763. Fiksel, Joseph; Covello, Victor T. **Safety assurance for environmental introductions of genetically-engineered organisms.** Springer-Verlag, NATO ASI series, Series G, Ecological sciences, v. G18, 1989. 282 pp., ill., bibl. Inventories and evaluates risk assessment methods available for determining human and ecological risks involved in the release of genetically modified microorganisms. Identifies research needs in biology, ecology, and other disciplines.

Hazardous Wastes (2764–2787)

2764. Piasecki, Bruce, W.; Davis, Gary A.; eds. **America's future in toxic waste management: lessons from Europe.** Quorum Books, 1987. 325 pp., ill., bibl., index. Reviews legal, technical, and planning strategies for hazardous waste management in ten European countries. Examines successful and unsuccessful programs. Contends that the United States has much to learn from Europe.

2765. D'Angelo, William Chip; Spicer, R. Christopher; Mease, Michael J. **Asbestos removal in occupied buildings: sophisticated procedures for structures with operating HVAC systems.** SourceFinders, 1987. 42 pp. Step-by-step explanation of planning and procedures involved in minimizing airborne asbestos contamination during asbestos removal when a building cannot be evacuated. Includes checklists and discussions of how to isolate, monitor, and modify heating, ventilating, air-conditioning (HVAC) systems.

2766. Conner, Jesse R. **Chemical fixation and solidification of hazardous wastes.** Van Nostrand Reinhold, 1990. 692 pp. General reference work covers the history and background of chemical fixation and solidification (CFS) technology, particularly as influenced by the Resource Conservation and Recovery Act (RCRA). Discusses principles of leaching, fixation of organic and inorganic constituents (including metal), waste and waste sources, and determination of appropriate technology.

2767. Crowl, Daniel A.; Louvar, Joseph F. **Chemical process safety: fundamentals with applications.** Prentice-Hall, 1990. 426 pp., ill., bibl., index. Reviews principles of toxicology, industrial hygiene, and toxic dispersion models. Discusses the nature of such industrial accidents as fires and explosions and provides specific guidelines for preventing them. Covers hazard identification and risk assessment and presents case histories.

2768. Kokoszka, Leopold C. **Environmental management handbook.** Dekker, 1989. 656 pp., ill. Reviews toxics management regulatory programs and examines handling, sampling, storing, and transportation requirements. Assesses treatment and disposal options. Gives other information on state and federal agencies, vendors and services, toxics identification, and compliance deadlines.

2769. Schumacher, Aileen. **A guide to hazardous materials management: physical characteristics, federal regulations, and response alternatives.** Quorum Books, 1988. 288 pp., ill., bibl., index. Explains and reviews regulations for air and water, toxic and hazardous materials, asbestos, and radioactive materials. Recommends management techniques and alternative handling strategies; discusses emergency procedures.

2770. Allegri, Theodore H. **Handling and management of hazardous materials and waste.** Chapman and Hall, 1986. 458 pp., ill., bibl., index. Explains federal regulations on the handling of PCBs, asbestos, pesticides, heavy metals, oil spills, and radioactive waste. Offers ideas on the best ways of disposing of hazardous materials.

2771. Saxena, Jitendra; Fisher, Farley; eds. **Hazard assessment of chemicals: current developments.** Academic Press, 1981 to date. Ill., bibl., index. Irregular. Ongoing series that gathers together comprehensive and authoritative reviews of new and significant developments in the hazard assessment of chemicals. Topics include databases and information sources, exposure assessment, health and environmental effects, risk assessment, monitoring and analysis, and case studies of chemicals and chemical spills.

2772. Coleman, Ronny J.; Williams, Kara Hewson. **Hazardous materials dictionary.** Technomic, 1988.

176 pp., ill. Identifies unique terms that apply to hazardous waste emergencies. Defines 916 terms, including acronyms, symbols, and slang.

2773. Hazardous waste and hazardous materials. Liebert, 1983 to date. Quarterly. Publishes research and technical papers in four categories: technology (treatment, storage, disposal), health effects, environmental effects, and policy.

2774. Harris, Christopher; Want, William L.; Ward, Morris A. **Hazardous waste: confronting the challenge.** Quorum Books, 1987. 255 pp., bibl., index. Provides historical overview of hazardous waste production and disposal since 1945. Reviews the 1976 RCRA and its 1980 amendments. Focuses on the origins, evolution, rationale, and legislative history of the Hazardous and Solid Waste Amendments of 1984.

2775. Epstein, Samuel S.; Brown, Lester O.; Pope, Carl. **Hazardous waste in America.** Sierra Club Books, 1982. 593 pp., bibl., index. Thorough discussion of politics, economics, and history of hazardous waste disposal for the general reader. Includes five case studies, extensive appendices on Superfund and potentially hazardous sites, sources and composition of hazardous waste, and more.

2776. Wentz, Charles A. **Hazardous waste management.** McGraw-Hill, 1989. 461 pp., ill., bibl., index. Comprehensive review. Discusses scientific and engineering principles and summarizes relevant legislation. Covers such concerns as groundwater contamination, landfill disposal, injection well disposal, process selection and facility siting, and site remediation.

2777. Maltezou, Sonia P.; Biswas, Asit K.; Sutter, Hans; eds. **Hazardous waste management.** Tycooly International, 1989. 344 pp., ill. Selected papers from an International Expert Workshop in 1987. Discusses waste management and reduction technology. Addresses economic, environmental, institutional, and legal factors that influence adoption of technology. Reviews developing nations' policies, problems, and experiences.

2778. Harthill, Michalann. **Hazardous waste management: in whose backyard?** Westview Press, AAAS selected symposium, v. 88, 1984. 205 pp., ill., bibl., index. Based on a 1981 symposium. Topics include site selection, site cleanup, alternative disposal methods, and the role of the public in hazardous waste disposal problems.

2779. Goldman, Benjamin A.; Hulme, James A.; Johnson, Cameron. **Hazardous waste management: reducing the risk.** Island Press, 1986. 316 pp., ill., bibl., index. Results of a study to evaluate the commercial hazardous waste industry. Studies eight leading publicly owned companies and ten facilities. Discusses federal and state regulations, evaluates hazardous waste strategies and technologies, and makes recommendations to minimize dangerous disposal methods.

2780. Kiang, Yen-Hsiung; Metry, Amir A. **Hazardous waste processing technology**. Ann Arbor Science, 1982. 549 pp., ill., index. Covers thermal incineration fundamentals and equipment, heat recovery and air pollution control, developing technologies, selection of treatment processes and land disposal sites, and physical, chemical, and biological treatment.

2781. Hazardous waste site management: water quality issues. National Academy Press, 1988. 212 pp., ill., bibl., index. Report of a 1987 colloquium; papers address the problems of defining cleanup levels and examine current approaches from the views of scientists, regulators, and impacted parties.

2782. Freeman, Harry M.; ed. **Innovative hazardous waste treatment technology series.** Technomic, 1991. 3 vols. Reports on innovative technologies in use or in development. Vol. 1, Thermal processes, contains 20 reports on incineration or pyrolysis. Vol. 2, Physical and chemical processes, includes 24 technical overviews of physiochemical treatment methods. Vol. 3, Biological processes, contains 21 reports on biodegradation techniques.

2783. Wu, Yeun C.; ed. **Physiochemical and biological detoxification of hazardous wastes.** Technomic, 1989. Ill. 2 vols. Over 60 reports on current and potential technology and processes for treating hazardous waste.

2784. Griffin, Roger D. **Principles of hazardous materials management.** Lewis, 1989. 207 pp., ill., bibl., index. Emphasizes health, transportation, regulation, and management aspects of hazardous materials as a framework for understanding. By registered professional engineer, consultant in field for 12 years.

2785. Freeman, Harry M.; ed. **Standard handbook of hazardous waste treatment and disposal.** McGraw-Hill, 1989. 1051 pp., ill., bibl., index. Exhaustive treatment of alternative technologies (104 contributors). Covers waste minimization, recycling, thermal processes, biological treatment, waste characteristics, health effects, risk assessment, sampling and analysis techniques, and other topics. Summarizes current legislation that encourages "cradle-to-grave" approach.

2786. Webster, James K.; ed. **Toxic and hazardous materials: a sourcebook and guide to information sources.** Greenwood Press, Bibliographies and indexes in science and technology, no. 2, 1987. 431 pp. Contains over 1600 annotated entries, including books, periodicals, indexes, audiovisual material, databases, government agencies, research organizations, and more. Emphasis on information released after 1980.

2787. Krueger, Raymond F.; Seiber, James N.; eds. **Treatment and disposal of pesticide wastes.** American Chemical Society, ACS symposium series, v. 259, 1984. 368 pp., ill., bibl., index. Based on a symposium sponsored by the American Chemical Society in 1983. Papers examine federal regulations, demonstration technologies, and other developments.

Air Pollution Control (2788–2797)

2788. Licht, William. **Air pollution control engineering: basic calculations for particulate collection.** Dekker, 1988. 477 pp., ill., bibl., index. Reference and textbook presents fundamental principles and engineering calculations. Emphasizes modeling of centrifugal collectors, electrostatic precipitation, filtration, and wet scrubbing.

2789. Theodore, Louis; Buonicore, Anthony J.; eds. **Air pollution control equipment: selection, design, operation, and maintenance.** Prentice-Hall, 1982. 429 pp., ill., bibl., index. Describes absorbers, adsorbers, incinerators, condensers, mechanical collectors, baghouses, wet scrubbers, electrostatic precipitators, flue gas desulfurization systems, and other devices. Provides information on design, installation, operation, and maintenance, as well as methods of improving operation and performance.

2790. Bretscheider, Boris; Kurfurst, Jiri. **Air pollution control technology.** Elsevier, Fundamental aspects of pollution control and environmental science, no. 8, 1987. 296 pp. Emphasizes the importance of sources. Develops realistic possibilities for emission reduction. Stresses that even small amounts of pollutants can have concentrated spatial and temporal effects. Provides an economic analysis of pollution control.

2791. Hesketh, Howard. **Air pollution control: traditional and hazardous pollutants.** Technomic, 1991. 475 pp., index. Reviews basic principles of air pollution control and the common technologies among control systems; discusses and compares design and operating aspects of different systems, examining mechanisms and devices for particulate and gas control.

2792. Dravnieks, Andrew. **Atlas of odor character profiles**. American Society for Testing and Materials, ASTM data series, v. DS 61, 1985. 354 pp. Odor characteristics of 150 chemicals and mixtures.

2793. Brunner, Calvin R. **Handbook of hazardous waste incineration**. TPR, 1989. 388 pp., ill., bibl., index. Details on design and operation of current systems (rotary kiln, liquid waste, waste sludge). Covers site cleanup, industrial processes, incineration at sea, materials handling, and European technology. Provides calculations for design parameters, government regulations, classification of hazardous wastes, and energy recovery. By a registered professional engineer.

2794. Bonner, T.; and others. **Hazardous waste incineration engineering**. Noyes, Pollution technology review, v. 88, 1981. 432 pp. A collection of information, guidelines, and requirements for hazardous waste incineration, useful for both operational decisions and permit application preparation.

2795. Freeman, Harry M.; ed. **Incinerating hazardous wastes**. Technomic, 1988. 375 pp., ill., bibl. Based on the EPA's thermal destruction research since 1975. In five parts: facilities, incineration processes, boilers and industrial processes, newer thermal processes, and laboratory or pilot-scale research.

2796. Theodore, Louis; Reynolds, Joseph. **Introduction to hazardous waste incineration**. Wiley, 1987. 463 pp., ill., bibl., index. Textbook covers technical and engineering aspects. Topics include thermodynamic considerations, thermochemical applications, equipment, and facility design.

2797. **The radon industry directory, 1990–1991**. Radon Press, 2d ed., 1990. 660 pp., ill. Annual guide. Lists radon detection and mitigation firms; radon product manufacturers and research facilities; federal, state, and local agencies involved in radon-related activities; and special interest groups. Discusses radon legislation, publications, and conferences.

Water Engineering (2798–2820)

2798. Jansen, Robert B.; ed. **Advanced dam engineering for design, construction, and rehabilitation**. Van Nostrand Reinhold, 1988. 811 pp. Leading authorities provide engineering instruction on every aspect of dam design and analysis. Five hundred drawings and photographs.

2799. Fingas, Merv; ed. **Arctic and marine oil spill technology**. Technomic, 1989. 519 pp. Proceedings of a 1988 conference. Technical reports on early detection, treating agents and countermeasures, modeling, and monitoring.

2800. Le Moigne, Guy; and others, eds. **Dam safety and the environment**. World Bank, World Bank technical paper, no. 115, 1990. 174 pp., bibl. Collection of technical papers in three sections: overview of dams, dam safety, and environmental problems of dam construction. Strong on engineering and design principles.

2801. Ward, Robert C.; Loftis, Jim C.; McBride, Graham B. **Design of water quality monitoring systems**. Van Nostrand Reinhold, 1990. 231 pp., index. Provides updates on current sampling, laboratory analysis, data handling, and reporting methods; discusses information utilization, design documentation, and case studies of design projects.

2802. Schoenen, D.; Schoeler, H. F. **Drinking water materials: field observations and methods of investigation**. Halsted Press, 1985. 195 pp. Comprehensive review of the materials used to store and transport drinking water, with microbiological implications. Compares field observations with laboratory tests.

2803. Mitsch, William J.; Jorgensen, Sven Erik; eds. **Ecological engineering: an introduction to ecotechnology**. Wiley, 1989. 472 pp. Reviews ecological modeling plus economic and educational aspects of ecological engineering. Case studies illustrate applications in aquatic ecosystems, pollution control, wetland management, and restoration of lakes, reservoirs, and streams.

2804. Rice, Leonard; White, Michael D. **Engineering aspects of water law**. Wiley, 1987. 206 pp., ill., bibl., index. Discusses historical aspects of water rights, including the riparian appropriation doctrines. Examines federal, state, and local roles. Reviews groundwater resource development and engineering-based information applicable to water rights issues. Includes case studies and examples of documents and forms typical of water rights law.

2805. Herbich, John B.; ed. **Handbook of coastal and ocean engineering**. Gulf, 1990–1991. Ill., index. 3 vols. Comprehensive reference to theories and practices. Vol. 1 covers wave phenomena and coastal structures; Vol. 2, offshore structures, marine foundations, and sediment processes; Vol. 3, harbors, navigational channels, estuaries, and environmental effects.

2806. Novotny, Vladimir; Chesters, Gordon. **Handbook of nonpoint pollution: sources and management**. Van Nostrand Reinhold, Van Nostrand Reinhold environmental engineering series, 1981. 555 pp., ill., bibl., index. Discusses surface water problems caused by nonpoint source pollution, precipitation and runoff, and associated hydrologic considerations. Reviews methods of quantifying pollution from various nonpoint sources. Also covers the transport and fate of pollutant materials from surface soils into groundwater, simulation models, and management practices and planning.

2807. Linsley, Ray K., Jr.; Kohler, Max A.; Paulhus, Joseph L. H. **Hydrology for engineers.** McGraw-Hill, McGraw-Hill series in water resources and environmental engineering, 2d ed, 1975. 482 pp., ill., index. Presents basic hydrologic data regarding weather, precipitation, stream flow, evaporation and transpiration, and subsurface water. Describes basic concepts and their application to solving hydrologic problems in such areas as stream flow routing, sedimentation, stochasticity, and river basin morphology.

2808. Journal of water resources planning and management—ASCE. American Society of Civil Engineers, 1983 to date. Quarterly. Contains research papers on planning and management of water projects, with emphasis on modeling and statistical analyses.

2809. Crawford, J. **Offshore installation practice.** Butterworth, 1988. 389 pp., ill., bibl., index. Provides practical information for construction of installations in accordance with national and international regulations. Discusses general requirements, flare systems, fuel gas and crude oil burning, and fire protection, detection, and extinction.

2810. Barcelona, Michael J.; and others. **Practical guide to ground-water sampling.** Illinois State Water Survey, SWS contract report, no. 374, 1985. 94 pp. Development of a cost-effective monitoring system, given local hydrogeologic conditions and water quality considerations. Recommendations on procedures for site characterization, water-sampling methods, and selection of materials and equipment.

2811. Hamphill, R. W.; Bramley, M. E. **Protection of river and canal banks: a guide to selection and design.** Butterworth, CIRIA water engineering report, 1989. 200 pp., ill., bibl., index. Discusses erosion processes and ways to minimize erosion damage. Explains how to do site surveys and preliminary design studies. Evaluates effectiveness of natural and artificial bank protection methods in light of engineering, environmental, and economic constraints. Covers natural bank protection, vertical bank protection, and revetments, from loose stone to concrete or masonry structures. Glossary, line drawings, and photographs.

2812. Responding to changes in sea level: engi-

neering implications. National Academy Press, 1987. 148 pp., ill., bibl., index. Prepared by the National Research Council. Reviews methods of measuring mean sea level and projects relative change over the next 100 years. Describes potential effects on both natural shoreline and man-made structures. Examines general response strategies and assesses plans for specific facilities and systems. Recommends future strategies.

2813. Safety of dams: flood and earthquake criteria. National Academy Press, 1985. 276 pp., ill., bibl., index. Prepared by the Committee on Safety Criteria for Dams, Water Science and Technology Board, Commission on Engineering and Technical Systems, National Research Council. Reviews present practices on dam safety standards, critiques design of flood and earthquake estimates, discusses importance of risk calculation and legal issues and proposes hydrologic and earthquake criteria for dam construction.

2814. Hofkes, E. H.; Huisman, L.; and others, eds. **Small community water supplies: technology of small water supply systems in developing countries.** International Reference Centre for Community Water Supply and sanitation; Wiley, 1983. 442 pp., ill., bibl. Provides a broad introduction to planning and management, water sources, water tapping, and treatment and distribution techniques.

2815. Schwab, Glenn O.; and others. **Soil and water conservation engineering.** Wiley, 3d ed., 1981. 525 pp., ill. Comprehensive treatment of engineering principles and practices. Includes water and wind erosion control; terracing and embankments; flood control, drainage, and open channels; pumps, pumping, and irrigation works; and water supply and quality. Eight appendices provide data, design criteria, and specifications.

2816. Stahre, Peter; Urbonas, Ben. **Stormwater detention: for drainage, water quality, and CSO management.** Prentice-Hall, 1990. 338 pp., ill., maps, indexes. Proven strategies and designs for planning and constructing storm water detention basins. Considers alternatives of local disposal, inlet control at source, on-site detention, in-line detention, off-line storage, and storage at treatment facilities. Covers types of storage facilities, flow regulation, estimation of storage volumes, and storm water quality enhancement.

2817. Schulz, Christopher R.; Okun, Daniel A. **Surface water treatment for communities in developing countries.** Wiley, 1984. 299 pp., ill., bibl., index. Topics include pretreatment, chemicals, rapid mixing, flocculation, sedimentation, and filtration.

2818. Lloyd, Barry; Helmer, Richard. **Surveillance**

of drinking water quality in rural areas. Wiley, 1991. 171 pp., maps, ill., index. Assesses the human and technical requirements for monitoring, protecting, and improving rural water supplies. Focuses on cost-effective methods and the essential minimum required for reliable monitoring.

2819. Water environment and technology. Water Environment Federation, 1990 to date. Monthly. Continues: Journal of the Water Pollution Control Federation. Publishes current, relevant, and practical information on every aspect of the water quality profession.

2820. Waterlines. Intermediate Technology, 1982 to date. Quarterly. Appropriate technologies for water supply and sanitation. Reports technical developments and programs and projects. Provides communication with development workers and practical help for those in the field (technical briefs).

Water Pollution Control. Wastewater (2821–2847)

2821. Reid, George W.; ed. **Appropriate methods of treating water and wastewater in developing countries.** Ann Arbor Science (dist. by Butterworth), 1982. 392 pp., ill. Addresses technology transfer and utilization, prediction methodologies for water and wastewater processes, water supply and treatment in developing countries, wastewater disposal and treatment, prediction of water demand, and management concerns. Includes case study of Indonesia.

2822. Haenel, Klaus. **Biological treatment of sewage by the activated sludge process.** Horwood; Halsted Press, 1988. 299 pp. Discusses theoretical, technical, and management aspects of sewage treatment using the activated sludge process.

2823. Horan, N. J. **Biological wastewater treatment systems: theory and operation.** Wiley, 1990. 310 pp., ill., bibl., index. Reviews wastewater characteristics, the engineering and processes involved in treatment systems, microorganisms used in wastewater treatment, microbial growth, and the importance of organic, nutrient, and pathogen removal.

2824. L'Hermite, P.; Otto, H.; eds. **Characterization, treatment, and use of sewage sludge.** Reidel; Kluwer, 1981. 803 pp. Proceedings of a 1980 symposium. Evaluates research conducted from 1977 to 1980. Topics include sludge processing, chemical and biological pollution of sludge, and environmental effects of sludge.

2825. Faust, Samuel D.; Aly, Osman M. **Chemistry of water treatment.** Butterworth, 1983. 723 pp. Use of chemical reactions to purify water, with emphasis on activated carbon and removal of bacteria and viruses.

2826. Hammer, Donald A.; ed. **Constructed wetlands for wastewater treatment: municipal and agricultural.** Lewis, 1989. 831 pp., ill., index. Provides advice on siting, regulation, and management of constructed wetlands systems, including an introduction to wetlands ecology and processes. Includes case studies of treatments for municipal waste, urban storm waters, livestock waste, and chemical waste.

2827. Curds, C. R.; Hawkes, H. A.; eds. **Ecological aspects of used water treatment.** Academic Press, 1975–1983. Ill., bibl., index. 3 vols. Responds to recent growth of interdisciplinary cooperation between engineers, chemists, and biologists in the improvement of used-water treatment technology. Vol. 1 of this series was published in 1975. Vol. 2: Biological activities and treatment processes. Presents existing engineering processes for water treatment and the activities, physiology, and habitats of the organisms present. Vol. 3: The processes and their ecology. Focuses on biological filters, mathematical modeling, and the applied significance of ecological studies of aerobic processes.

2828. Patterson, James William. **Industrial wastewater treatment technology.** Butterworth, 2d ed., 1985. 467 pp. Standard reference, first published in 1975. Reviews pollutants and treatment technologies; suitable as a basic textbook.

2829. Eckenfelder, W. Wesley, Jr. **Industrial water pollution control.** McGraw-Hill, 2d ed., 1989. 400 pp., ill., bibl., index. Discusses in-plant control, water reuse, and by-product recovery. Stresses application of principles specific to industrial situations. Chapter topics include coagulation and precipitation, aeration and mass transfer, biological oxidation, biological wastewater treatment, ion exchange, chemical oxidation, and sludge handling and disposal.

2830. Kawamura, Susumu. **Integrated design of water treatment facilities.** Wiley, 1991. 658 pp., index. Practical manual. Covers the project process in sequence from initial design to planning, construction, and plant management. Includes planning steps to achieve maximum efficiency at minimum cost.

2831. Novotny, Vladimir; and others, eds. **Karl Imhoff's handbook of urban drainage and wastewater disposal.** Wiley, 1989. 390 pp., ill., bibl. Topics include calculation of drainage systems; overflow management; mechanical, chemical, and biological treatment of wastewater; urban nonpoint sources and abatement of pollution from urban runoff; sludge handling; planning and design of treatment plants; protection of receiving waters, and more.

2832. Clark, Douglas W. **Microbiological skills for water and wastewater analysis.** New Mexico Water Resources Research Institute, Report, no. M16, 1985. 70 pp. Training manual covers the proper and safe use of microbiological equipment and procedures, including basic aquatic analyses regardless of the water source.

2833. Korbitz, William E. **Modern management of water and wastewater utilities.** Garland, 1981. 261 pp. Defines and discusses management techniques and problems associated with utility administration; identifies management responsibilities and constraints; analyzes relevant legislation and legal aspects; and covers specific management concerns such as public and employee relations, the use of consultants, and adequate contract administration.

2834. Kemmer, Frank N.; ed. **NALCO water handbook.** McGraw-Hill, 2d ed., 1988. 530 pp. Intended to help managers optimize water usage and treatment processes for each class of water usage; includes glossary.

2835. Dinges, Ray. **Natural systems for water pollution control.** Van Nostrand Reinhold, 1982. 252 pp., ill., bibl., index. Case histories of pilot- and full-scale natural systems—stabilization ponds, aquatic vegetation (water hyacinth), aquatic animals, and land treatment.

2836. Beck, M. B. **Operational water quality management: beyond planning and design.** International Institute for Applied Systems Analysis, Executive report, no. 7, 1981. 74 pp. Focuses on often-neglected operational problems of treating wastewater. Discusses water quality management in context of changing institutions, pollution problems, monitoring and instrumentation techniques, and economic conditions.

2837. Kaplan, O. Benjamin. **Septic systems handbook.** Lewis, 1987. 290 pp., ill., bibl., index. Examines engineering, soil science, geology, and public health aspects. Topics include degradation of groundwater by septic systems, factors affecting leach line failures, and the perk test. Shows how county or state officials and consultants can use basic principles creatively to solve practical problems.

2838. Winneberger, John H. Timothy. **Septic-tank systems: a consultant's toolkit.** Butterworth, 1983. 2 vols. Vol. 1: Subsurface disposal of septic tank effluents. Covers site evaluation; techniques for percolation tests and soil permeability assessment; public health concerns; and sanitary surveys and survival curves of septic tank systems. Vol. 2: The septic tank. Covers sludge

gases; nitrogen removal; atmosphere, venting, and disease vectors; dissolved oxygen, suspended solids removal, and scum accumulation.

2839. Fox, J. Carl; Fitzgerald, Paul R.; Lue-Hing, Cecil. **Sewage organisms: a color atlas.** Metropolitan Sanitary District of Greater Chicago, 1981. 116 pp., ill., bibl., index. Three hundred twenty-six full-color photomicrographs depict 136 organisms living in sewage. Describes concentration methods, counting techniques, staining and filtration methods, and isolation of parasites from sewage samples.

2840. Vesilind, P. Aarne; Hartman, Gerald C.; Skene, Elizabeth. **Sludge management and disposal for the practicing engineer.** Lewis, 1986. 341 pp., ill., bibl., index. Discusses sludge disposal alternatives, available technologies, and regulations. Presents a case study of evaluating disposal options based on cost effectiveness, reliability, flexibility, technology, environmental impact, and public acceptance. Describes a methodology for quantitatively ranking alternatives.

2841. Vesilind, P. Aarne. **Treatment and disposal of wastewater sludges.** Ann Arbor Science, rev. ed., 1979. 323 pp., ill., bibl., index. Discusses the characteristics, stabilization, pumping, thickening, dewatering, conditioning, drying, and combustion of sludge; examines its disposal on land and in water; covers regional sludge management.

2842. Adams, V. Dean. **Waste and wastewater examination manual.** Lewis, 1990. 247 pp., bibl., index. Practical laboratory work guide and reference to procedures, standards, and parameters used in water quality analysis.

2843. Laak, Rein. **Wastewater engineering design for unsewered areas.** Technomic, 2d ed., 1986. 171 pp. Explores in detail the steps involved in investigating and designing an on-site disposal system. Discusses soil evaluation and the differing qualities and characteristics of business and household wastewater; examines pretreatment methods (including lagoons, septic tanks, sand filters, and oxidation ditches); contains examples of innovative designs.

2844. Metcalf & Eddy, Boston. **Wastewater engineering: treatment, disposal, reuse.** McGraw-Hill, McGraw-Hill series in water resources and environmental engineering, 3d ed., 1991. 920 pp., ill., index. Standard source on wastewater treatment objectives and methods. Describes physical unit operations, chemical and biological unit processes, and sludge and effluent disposal. Covers small and independent wastewater treatment systems and composting and land application of sludge.

2845. Water research. Pergamon Press, 1967 to date. Monthly. Journal of the International Association on Water Pollution Research and Control. Original research papers on collection and treatment of municipal and industrial wastewaters, nonpoint pollution sources, analytic and monitoring techniques, sludge treatment and disposal, and water pollution and its control.

2846. Water science and technology. Pergamon Press, 1969 to date. Monthly. Published for the International Association on Water Pollution Research and Control. Papers emphasize the engineering and technical aspects of water pollution control and treatment. Numerous special issues with proceedings of meetings. Worldwide in scope.

2847. Viessman, Warren, Jr.; Hammer, Mark J. **Water supply and pollution control.** Harper & Row, 4th ed., 1985. 797 pp. Updated information on the treatment of toxic substances, sedimentation, filtration, pressure filtration of sludges, wastewater reclamation and reuse, and water quality modeling. Also covers groundwater, toxic water pollutants, suspended solids removal, and centrifugation.

Civil Engineering. Construction. Geotechnology (2848–2873)

2848. Schiechtl, Hugo M. **Bioengineering for land reclamation and conservation.** University of Alberta Press, 1980. 404 pp., ill., bibl., index. Covers methods and techniques for wide range of projects, including technical site preparation (drainage, gully and bank constructions, rockfall protection, and contouring works), earthworks, and waterway projects. Also discusses the use of plant materials. Reviews the most frequent mistakes and how to avoid them and areas with special problems.

2849. Bagchi, Amalendu. **Design, construction, and monitoring of sanitary landfill.** Wiley, 1990. 284 pp., ill., bibl., index. Reviews both theory and practice of landfill technology, studying siting, leachate and gas, and hazardous waste. Examines modeling to estimate construction, operation, closure, and monitoring costs.

2850. Stern, Peter; and others, compilers and eds. **Field engineering: an introduction to development work and construction in rural areas.** Intermediate Technology, 1983. 251 pp., ill., bibl. From an original work by F. Longland. Handbook gives practical advice on

surveying, engineering, materials, building, sanitation, roads, bridges, and power.

2851. Thumann, Albert; Miller, Richard K. **Fundamentals of noise control engineering.** Fairmount Press, 2d ed., 1990. 295 pp., ill., index, tables. Describes regulations, noise measurement, engineering for noise reduction, and commercial products that reduce noise. Many tables, charts, and drawings.

2852. Oweis, Issa S.; Khera, Raj P. **Geotechnology of waste management.** Butterworth, 1990. 273 pp., index. Eleven chapters review principles important in waste disposal, including applicable regulations, characteristics of waste materials, site selection and investigation, soil properties and behavior, design considerations of waste disposal facilities, and the use of waste deposits as foundations for new construction.

2853. Bell, F. G.; ed. **Ground engineer's reference book.** Butterworth, 1987. 1160 pp., bibl., index. Surveys all aspects of engineering related to the ground, covering engineering geology, surveying and exploration, soil mechanics and improvement, dams and foundations, and numerical methods and modeling.

2854. Rettinger, Michael. **Handbook of architectural acoustics and noise control: a manual for architects and engineers.** Tab Books, 1988. 247 pp., ill., index, tables. Reviews the physics of sound, noise sources, noise transmission, and room acoustics. Numerous tables, graphs, and figures facilitate its use as a reference.

2855. Bellandi, Robert. **Hazardous waste site remediation: the engineer's perspective.** Van Nostrand Reinhold, 1988. 422 pp. Practical information on remediating and restoring hazardous waste sites; includes case studies.

2856. Carra, Joseph S. **International perspectives on municipal and solid wastes and sanitary landfilling.** Academic Press, 1990. 256 pp., ill., tables. Fifteen countries report on the composition, quantities, and management of solid wastes.

2857. Novak, J. D.; Loehr, Raymond C.; and others, eds. **Land application of wastes.** Van Nostrand Reinhold, Van Nostrand Reinhold environmental engineering series, 1979. 308 pp., ill., bibl., index. Uses self-contained modules to explain design procedures for land application of wastes; treatment systems, effluent qualities, and costs; the role of vegetative cover; site evaluation; costing of land application systems; societal constraints, and legal aspects. Also reviews 13 case studies of land application systems. Applicable to municipal, industrial, and agricultural wastes and residues.

2858. Parr, James F.; Marsh, Paul B.; Kla, Joanne M.; eds. **Land treatment of hazardous wastes.** Noyes, 1983. 422 pp. Addresses the processes that influence the fate and effects of wastes, reviewing volatization, degradation, advection, diffusion, plant uptake of inorganic pollutants, potential effects of waste on the food chain, the fate of pathogens, and the role of composting in stabilizing biodegradable organic municipal sludges. Discusses 11 waste types and treatment experience where applicable. Does not provide design, siting, construction, or operational considerations for land treatment systems.

2859. Crawford, John Faulds; Smith, Paul G. **Landfill technology.** Butterworth, 1985. 159 pp., bibl., index. Concise text covers site selection, preparation and operation, landfill biochemistry, and leachate contamination and treatment.

2860. Landphair, Harlow C.; Klatt, Fred. **Landscape architecture construction.** Elsevier, 1988. 431 pp., ill., bibl., index. Provides guidelines in the areas of grading and earthwork, circulation, storm water management and drainage design, statics and mechanics, carpentry and design with wood, concrete and masonry design, and the design of irrigation, lighting, fountains, and pools.

2861. Lu, James C. S.; Eichenberger, Bert; Stearns, Robert J. **Leachate from municipal landfills: production and management.** Noyes, Pollution technology review, no. 119, 1985. 453 pp., ill., bibl., index.

2862. Kittel, J. Howard. **Near-surface land disposal.** Harwood Academic, Radioactive waste management handbook, v. 1, 1989. 440 pp., ill. Covers incipient planning, site closure, and subsequent monitoring. A primary and secondary reference for the technical community.

2863. Remedial technologies for leaking underground storage tanks. Lewis, 1987. 216 pp., ill., bibl., index. Prepared by Roy F. Weston, Inc., and the Environmental Science Program, University of Massachusetts. Surveys and evaluates technology for cleaning soil and groundwater contaminated from underground tanks; provides information to help those responsible operate within the new legal requirements.

2864. Clayton, C. R. I.; Simons, N. E.; Matthews, M. C. **Site investigation.** Halsted Press, 1982. 424 pp., maps, ill., bibl., index. Intended for civil engineers with limited background in geotechnology. Describes advantages and disadvantages of available techniques of site investigation, including preliminary desk studies, subsurface methods, undisturbed sampling techniques, drilling, and laboratory studies.

2865. Head, K. H. **Soil technician's handbook.** Pentech Press; Wiley, 1989. 158 pp., ill. Materials testing of soils. Provides a concise and accessible summary of the data required when carrying out tests on soils for civil engineering purposes.

2866. Hughes, John R. **The storage and handling of petroleum liquids.** Wiley, 1987. 332 pp., ill., bibl., index. Explains technical aspects of the risks and dangers of petroleum liquids. Reviews regulations and delineates procedures to handle petroleum and store it safely, focusing on practice in the United Kingdom.

2867. Brinker, Russell C.; Minnick, Roy; eds. **The surveying handbook.** Van Nostrand Reinhold, 1987. 1270 pp. Guide to such techniques of surveying as triangulation, field astronomy, and photogrammetry. Includes details on construction, hydrographic, and topograpic surveys; covers legal and business aspects of surveying.

2868. Nelson, P. M.; ed. **Transportation noise reference book.** Butterworth, 1987., Various paging, ill., bibl., index. Covers the effects of transportation noise on people, including community and health effects and sleep disturbance. Studies the characteristics of road traffic, train, and aircraft noise. Reviews control methods and legal information, using international examples. Examines environmental and economic aspects of noise control.

2869. Schwendeman, Todd G.; Wilcox, H. Kemdall. **Underground storage systems: leak detection and monitoring.** Lewis, 1987. 213 pp., ill., bibl., index. For installers, users, and owners of underground tanks. Explains what is available and how to design a system appropriate to needs and location. Sections on construction, location, and sampling of observation wells; types of leak detectors; methods of interstitial monitoring; and testing and monitoring of piping systems.

2870. Rizzo, Joyce A.; and others. **Underground storage tank management: a practical guide.** Government Institutes, 4th ed., 1991. 420 pp. Covers the regulatory and technical picture, with chapters on inventory control, leak prediction, tank closure, testing, tank design, secondary containment, tank installation, maintenance, storage of hazardous substances, remedial action, liabilities, financial responsibility, and other topics.

2871. Coppin, N.; and others. **Use of vegetation in civil engineering.** Butterworth-Heineman, 1990. 292 pp., ill., bibl., index. Reviews plant biology and the physical effects of vegetation on surface water movement, soil properties, and air flow; discusses the selection, establishment, and management of plants and their integration into a variety of civil engineering projects. Technical specifications geared toward Britain.

2872. Utilization, treatment, and disposal of waste on land. Soil Science Society of America, 1986. 318 pp., ill., bibl., index. Papers from a 1985 workshop cover land treatment of sewage with minimal pretreatment, on-site and clustered systems, land applications of municipal sludge, and hazardous waste in soil.

2873. Liu, Henry. **Wind engineering: a handbook for structural engineers.** Prentice-Hall, 1991. 209 pp., index. Explains basic characteristics of wind, pressures exerted on structures by wind, and structural responses to them. Reviews scale model testing, plus building codes and standards. Focuses primarily on weather conditions in the United States.

Radioactive. Nuclear (2874–2889)

2874. Eisenbud, Merril. **Environmental radioactivity: from natural, industrial, and military sources.** Academic Press, 3d ed., 1987. 475 pp., ill., bibl., index. Basic facts and principles; provides current and historical view of the use of nuclear energy; focuses on artificial radioactivity; includes discussion of Chernobyl.

2875. Chapman, Neil A.; McKinley, Ian G. **The geological disposal of nuclear waste.** Wiley, 1987. 280 pp. Overview of scientific rationale for radioactive disposal in geological formations. Describes processes of waste handling, biological hazards, and problems of the leading geological waste disposal technologies. Occupies a middle ground between caution and optimism.

2876. Roxburgh, I. S. **Geology of high-level nuclear waste disposal: an introduction.** Chapman and Hall, 1987. 229 pp., ill., bibl., index. Discusses the sources and nature of high-level nuclear waste and describes major rock types in terms of their suitability as repositories for such waste. Reviews the design and construction of repositories and methods of assessing their safety. Uses case studies from Europe and North America.

2877. Journal of environmental radioactivity. Elsevier, 1984 to date. Bimonthly. Covers occurrence of man-made and natural radioactivity in oceans, sediments, rivers, lakes, groundwater, soil, and atmosphere.

2878. Gershey, Edward L.; and others. **Low-level radioactive waste: from cradle to grave.** Van Nostrand Reinhold, 1990. 212 pp., index. Explains how criteria for defining low-level radioactive waste were determined. Reviews burial sites, disposal techniques, risk management assessment techniques, and public perceptions.

Emphasizes the needs for waste reduction and for planning that begins at the time of production.

2879. Wolfson, Richard. **Nuclear choices: a citizen's guide to nuclear technology.** MIT Press, The new liberal arts series, 1991. 467 pp., ill., bibl., index. Explains the basic concepts and workings of nuclear energy and radiation, nuclear power, and nuclear weapons, noting both the benefits and the dangers of the technology. Illustrates the connections and relationships among nuclear technologies and issues.

2880. Carter, Luther J. **Nuclear imperatives and public trust: dealing with radioactive waste.** Resources for the Future; Johns Hopkins University Press, 1987. 473 pp., bibl., index. Argues that for now, reprocessing and recycling of nuclear waste are not technically or economically viable. Dangers of radioactive waste are overestimated by the public in comparison with such dangers as the proliferation of nuclear warheads. Uses case studies from the United States, Europe, and Japan.

2881. Glasstone, Samuel; Jordan, Walter H. **Nuclear power and its environmental effects.** American Nuclear Society, 1980. 395 pp., ill., bibl., index. Describes the siting, licensing, and operation of nuclear power plants. Explains the creation, handling, transportation, and disposal of radioactive nuclear materials, addressing potential biological and environmental effects.

2882. Katz, James Everett; Marwah, Onkar S.; eds. **Nuclear power in developing countries: an analysis of decision making.** Lexington Books, 1982. 372 pp., bibl. Presents case studies of the nuclear power programs of 15 less-developed nations. Illustrates how numerous factors, including politics, population pressure, and national prestige, can influence nuclear decision making processes, often overriding scientific and economic concerns.

2883. Marshall, W.; ed. **Nuclear power technology.** Clarendon Press, 1984. Ill., bibl., index. 3 vols. Vol. 1: Reactor technology. Discusses the workings and physics of nuclear reactors, including gas-cooled, light- and heavy-water, and fast breeder reactors. Vol. 2: Fuel cycle. Covers fuel topics, from uranium mining to the decommissioning of nuclear facilities. Vol. 3: Nuclear radiation. Reviews the production, measurement, control, biological effects, risk assessments, and medical and archaeological uses of nuclear power.

2884. Pochin, Edward Eric. **Nuclear radiation: risks and benefits.** Oxford University Press, Oxford science publications; Monographs on science, technology and society, 1983. 197 pp., ill., bibl., index. Discusses history, artificial radionuclides, use of nuclear fission, radiation measurement, sources and exposure, cellular and genetic effects, protection, safety and risks.

2885. Berlin, Robert E.; Stanton, Catherine C. **Radioactive waste management.** Wiley-Interscience, 1989. 444 pp., ill., bibl., index. Reviews the sources and nature of radioactive waste. Uses case studies to illustrate various techniques of waste management, focusing on the role of government agencies.

2886. Simon, R.; ed. **Radioactive waste management and disposal.** Cambridge University Press, 1986. 734 pp., ill., bibl., index. Proceedings of the Second European Community Conference in 1985. Main topics include treatment and conditioning technology, barrier systems, geological disposal, modeling, and evaluation.

2887. Wood, M. Sandra; Schultz, Suzanne M. **Three Mile Island: a selectively annotated bibliography.** Greenwood Press, Bibliographies and indexes in science and technology, no. 3, 1988. 309 pp., bibl., index. Includes articles and editorials from journals in the humanities, and social and natural sciences; books and monographs; federal and Pennsylvania state government documents; and congressional hearings. Journal articles and government documents are annotated and arranged by broad subject category and issuing agency, respectively. Cutoff date is July 1986, though some items after that are included.

2888. Moss, Thomas H.; Sills, David L.; eds. **The Three Mile Island nuclear accident: lessons and implications.** New York Academy of Sciences, Annals of the New York Academy of Sciences, v. 365, 1981. 343 pp.

2889. Walker, Charles A.; Gould, Leroy C.; Woodhouse, Edward J.; eds. **Too hot to handle? social and policy issues in the management of radioactive wastes.** Yale University Press, 1983. 209 pp., ill., bibl., index. Seven chapters cover management problems, science and technology, human health, public attitudes, perceived and acceptable risks, politics, and value judgments.

Energy Technology (2890–2903)

2890. Carstensen, Edwin L. **Biological effects of transmission line fields.** Elsevier, 1987. 398 pp., ill., bibl. Reviews the properties and nature of electrical fields, including magnetically induced fields, and their effects in the body. Examines the electrical properties of biological materials. Reports on surface effects, long-term biological effects, acute responses of tissues to extremely low frequency (ELF) electromagnetic fields, the relationship of magnetic fields to cancer, and other topics.

2891. Spaite, Paul W. **Emerging clean coal technologies.** Noyes, 1986. 293 pp. Describes and rates 13 technologies.

2892. Glasstone, Samuel. **Energy deskbook.** Van Nostrand Reinhold, 1983. 453 pp. Over 400 entries, arranged alphabetically, explain energy materials, technology, and processes, covering both current and potential resources. Emphasizes basic and general principles.

2893. Payne, F. William; McGowan, John J. **Energy management and control systems handbook.** Fairmont Press; Prentice Hall, 2d ed., 1988. 399 pp. Describes three levels of control systems: remote controllers; central monitoring with manual or mostly manual control; and direct digital control (DDC). Discusses installation, fine-tuning, and maintenance.

2894. Lee, Kaiman; Masloff, Jacqueline. **Energy oriented computer programs for the design and monitoring of buildings.** Environmental Design & Research Center, 1979. Ill., bibl. 2 vols. Contains over 150 abstracts of computer programs for the analysis, design, and energy monitoring of buildings. Topics include energy analyses and cost; heating and cooling design; ventilation; solar design; system evaluation; and automated environmental control. Abstracts include information on program title, author, objective, and limitations; input requirements; software and hardware; and availability.

2895. Energy research abstracts. U.S. Department of Energy, Technical Information Center; Government Printing Office, 1977 to date. Semimonthly. Indexes and abstracts scientific and technical reports and patent applications originated by the U.S. Department of Energy and its contractors, by federal and state governments, and by foreign government and nongovernment organizations. Five indexes: corporate author, personal author, subject, contract number, and report number.

2896. Viola, John; Mack, Newell B.; Stauffer, Thomas R.; eds. **Energy research guide: journals, indexes, and abstracts.** Ballinger, 1983. 284 pp. Describes 500 periodicals, indexes, and abstracting publications dealing with energy. In three sections: an alphabetical master list of periodicals, a subject list, and a description of each periodical.

2897. Energy: the international journal. Pergamon Press, 1976 to date. Monthly. Multidisciplinary journal covering activities relating to the development, assessment, and management of energy-related programs. Includes material that correlates energy and other factors, such as population, agriculture, and commerce. Articles cover input-output analyses relating to energy-consuming systems, resource or reserve assessments of all kinds, energy conservation measures and their imple-mentations, evaluation of energy systems management, environmental impact assessments, and policy alterna-tives.

2898. Harder, Edwin L. **Fundamentals of energy production.** Wiley, Alternate energy, 1982. 368 pp., maps, ill., index. Discusses the technology, status, and economics of oil, coal, gas, hydroelectric, nuclear, solar, geothermal, and wind energy. Reviews principles of en-ergy chemistry and physics, and nuclear physics. Ad-dresses energy transportation and storage.

2899. Meyers, Robert A.; ed. **Handbook of synfuels technology.** McGraw-Hill, 1984. 906 pp., ill., index.

2900. Supp, Emil. **How to produce methanol from coal.** Springer-Verlag, 1990. 201 pp., ill. Most methanol is derived from natural gas. Reviews promising technol-ogies to extract methanol from coal, the world's largest source of fossil fuel.

2901. Elliott, Thomas C.; and others, eds. **Standard handbook of powerplant engineering.** McGraw-Hill, 1989. Various paging, ill., bibl., index. Guide to improv-ing plant operation, choosing equipment, and selecting designs for new facilities. Sections on steam generation, turbines and diesels, fuels and pollution control, plant electrical systems, and instrumentation and control.

2902. Crow, Michael; and others. **Synthetic fuel technology development in the United States: a ret-rospective assessment.** Praeger, 1988. 175 pp., index. Examines the development of direct coal liquefaction (DCL) from technological, public policy, and economics perspectives. Assesses the effects of inconsistent and un-even public and private support for DCL.

2903. Probstein, Ronald F.; Hicks, R. Edwin. **Syn-thetic fuels.** McGraw-Hill, McGraw-Hill chemical engi-neering series, 1982. 490 pp., ill., bibl., index. Discusses the methods and processes involved in converting coal, oil shale, tar sands, and biomass into liquid, gaseous, or solid fuels; also covers environmental and economic as-pects.

Renewable Energy (2904–2926)

2904. Rabl, Ari. **Active solar collectors and their applications.** Oxford University Press, 1985. 503 pp., maps, ill., bibl., index. Technical overview. Topics in-clude the optics of solar collectors and of nontracking collectors; solar collector efficiency and testing; optical analysis and optimization of parabolic reflectors; and system optimization. Assumes knowledge of calculus.

2905. Pasztor, Janos; Kristoferson, Lars A. **Bioe-**

nergy **and the environment.** Westview Press, Westview special studies in natural resources and energy manage-ment, 1990. 410 pp., ill., bibl. Examines the impacts of bioenergy systems (wood, animal and crop wastes, and alcohols) compared with those of fossil fuels, using ex-amples from bioenergy-dependent countries. Stresses the importance of bioenergy as a renewable, inexpensive, and benign resource for developing countries.

2906. Braunstein, Helen M.; and others. **Biomass energy systems and the environment.** Pergamon Press, 1981. 182 pp., ill., bibl., index. Reviews methods of bio-mass production, harvest, and conversion. Assesses en-vironmental, social, and economic implications of large-scale biomass energy programs.

2907. Simonson, John R. **Computing methods in solar heating design.** Macmillan, 1984. 340 pp., ill., bibl., index. Brings together existing solar energy litera-ture on water and space heating for domestic and com-mercial purposes. Emphasizes the use of computers for solving problems in the design of solar heating installa-tions. Ten full FORTRAN listings.

2908. Zackrison, Harry B., Jr. **Energy conservation techniques for engineers.** Van Nostrand Reinhold, 1984. 332 pp., ill., index. Presents cost-effective tech-niques for conserving power, focusing on lighting. In-tended for engineers and architects; applicable to new construction and renovation.

2909. Vimal, O. P.; Tyagi, P. D. **Energy from bio-mass: an Indian experience.** Agricole, 1984. 440 pp., bibl., index. Examines biomass availability, production, conversion, and utilization in India. Includes extensive bibliography arranged by subject areas and accessed by author, geographic, botanical, keyword and source in-dexes.

2910. Energy technologies for reducing emis-sions of greenhouse gases. Organization for Economic Cooperation and Development, 1989. Ill., bibl. 2 vols. Proceedings of an experts' seminar in 1989. Seventy-two papers and keynote addresses cover such topics as coal conversion technologies, technology strategies for the energy sector, possible courses of action in national and regional contexts, prospects for international coopera-tion, and technology options and systems for immediate or short-term action.

2911. Bungay, Henry R. **Energy: the biomass op-tions.** Wiley, Alternate energy, 1981. 347 pp., ill., bibl., index. Evaluates methods and procedures for obtaining energy through biomass fuels and chemicals. Addresses anaerobic digestion, fractionation and pretreatment, and thermochemical and photobiological processes.

2912. Butler, Edgar W.; Pick, James B. **Geothermal energy development: problems and prospects in the Imperial Valley of California.** Plenum Press, 1982. 361 pp., ill., bibl., index. Assesses the social, economic, and environmental effects of developing geothermal energy sources in this stable, agricultural county; reviews projected population, employment, and displacement; surveys public opinion and local government actions.

2913. Hobson P. N.; Bousfield, S.; Summers, R. **Methane production from agricultural and domestic wastes.** Applied Science, Energy from wastes series, 1981. 269 pp., ill., bibl., index. Covers microbiology and biochemistry of anaerobic digestion, types of digesters, construction and operation, uses of sludge, laboratory and pilot plant experiments, and energy production by practical scale digesters.

2914. Jacques, J. Keith; Lesourd, Jean-Baptiste; Ruiz, Jean-Michael; eds. **Modern applied energy conservation: new directions in energy conservation management.** Halsted Press, Ellis Horwood series in applied science and industrial technology, 1988. 405 pp., ill., bibl., index. Extensive mathematical, statistical, and computer modeling presentations of energy-saving technology. Emphasizes financial projections. Case studies of corporations and energy conservation.

2915. Bleviss, Deborah Lynn. **The new oil crisis and fuel economy technologies: preparing the light transportation for the 1990s.** Greenwood Press, 1988. 268 pp. Examines technologies in reducing fuel consumption and designing fuel-efficient cars. Addresses the problems with such technologies (safety, performance, cost). Discusses the leaders in innovation, the role of the market in assisting widespread use of alternative fuel technologies, and global and national policy implications.

2916. Pryde, Philip R. **Nonconventional energy resources.** Wiley, Environmental science and technology, 1983. 270 pp., maps, ill., bibl., index. Explains and assesses ocean, geothermal, solar, wind, and biofuel energy options. Notes cost, technical restraints, and environmental consequences. Factors in geographic and regional considerations in its evaluations.

2917. Mazria, Edward. **The passive solar energy book: a complete guide to passive solar home, greenhouse and building design.** Rodale Press, expanded, professional ed, 1979. 687 pp., ill., bibl., index. Describes and illustrates, for the nonarchitect, various types of passive systems. Discusses many design patterns and how to calculate their performance. Numerous appendices provide data on the insulating values of construc-

tion materials, average daily solar radiation in the United States, and other topics.

2918. Hasselriis, Floyd. **Refuse-derived fuel processing.** Butterworth, 1986. 360 pp., ill., index. Based on a decade of experience in the processing of municipal waste for extracting recyclables and producing fuel. Sections include transport, storage, and handling; size reduction; metals recovery; air classification; and size separation.

2919. Blackburn, John O. **The renewable energy alternative: how the United States and the world can prosper without nuclear energy or coal.** Duke University Press, 1987. 201 pp. Economist advocates the use of solar, wind, geothermal, biomass, and hydroelectric energy sources; proves his case with many U.S. and international examples.

2920. Kristoferson, Lars A.; Bokalders, K. **Renewable energy technologies: their applications in developing countries.** Pergamon Press, 1986. 319 pp., ill., bibl. A study of the more viable energy options suitable to developing countries, taking into account socioeconomic and environmental consequences. Explains the workings of bioenergy production, biomass engines, solar energy technology, and hydroelectric, wind, and water power.

2921. de Winter, Francis; ed. **Solar collectors, energy storage, and materials.** MIT Press, Solar heat technologies: fundamentals and applications, v. 5, 1991. 1104 pp., ill. Assesses the materials and equipment needed for solar thermal energy systems; reviews successful and failed designs; and examines promising technology, focusing more on performance than on cost or application.

2922. Pleskov, Yuri V. **Solar energy conversion: a photoelectrochemical approach.** Springer-Verlag, 1990. 163 pp. Presents fundamentals of converting solar energy into electrical and chemical energy using semiconductor electrodes and reviews the operating principles of different kinds of photoelectrochemical cells.

2923. Hulstrom, Roland L. **Solar resources.** MIT Press, Solar heat technologies, v. 2, 1989. 408 pp., ill., bibl., index. Second volume in a series intended to distill the results of research on solar energy conducted since the 1973 oil crisis. Detailed analysis of the sun's contribution to the heating of the earth. Topics include insolation models and algorithms, solar radiation monitoring networks and instrumentation, spectral terrestrial solar radiation, and insolation forecasting. Assumes strong background in physics and math.

2924. Milne, T. A.; Brennan, A. H.; Glenn, B. H.

Sourcebook of methods of analysis for biomass and biomass conversion processes. Elsevier; Solar Energy Research Institute, 1990. 440 pp., index. Presents titles and abstracts of sources detailing industry standards and techniques. Topics addressed include elemental analyses, enzymatic assays, feedstock sampling and preparation, and chromatography.

2925. Garg, H. P. **Treatise on solar energy. Vol. 1: Fundamentals of solar energy.** Wiley, 1982. 587 pp. Presents case for solar energy. Discusses solar radiation availability and measurement, heat transfer, optical properties and radiation characteristics of materials, and liquid flat plate and flat plate air collectors.

2926. Gipe, Paul. **Wind energy: how to use it.** Stackpole Books, 1983. 400 pp., ill., tables. Practical information from consultant and installer that describes the technology and tells the prospective builder how to evaluate what is available. Includes tips, advice, and recommendations from leaders in the field. Many drawings, photographs, and tables of data.

Section 14

Science. Research. Methods

This section comes last to emphasize that environmental studies and practice rest primarily on foundations of science and mathematics. Beginning the section are general works on research and scientific activity, followed by groups of entries on scientific organizations and information services, reference books and general scientific journals, and guides to writing and presentation of results.

Most of the section contains entries on quantitative measures of the environment: modeling and simulation, assessment and monitoring, and testing and analysis. Environmental sciences are becoming ever more sophisticated in their use of mathematics, statistics, computers, and remote sensing. Entries on the environmental sciences occur throughout the bibliography, but in this section, the emphasis is on techniques and methods.

Information Sources
Included here are entries for clearinghouses, research centers, technical and scientific organizations, computer databases, libraries and information centers, information services, United Nations sources, computer networks, graduate degree programs, faculty in U.S. universities, and learned societies.

See also:

• Section 8: Education and communication
• Subject Index

Reference Books. Journals
This group has the essential reference works that guide one to the results of scientific research throughout the world, such as general science journals and indexes; handbooks, dictionaries, and encyclopedias; sources of maps, books, technical reports, and dissertations; and literature searching. Many such reference works are found elsewhere in the bibliography. The criterion for inclusion here is science in its most general aspects.

See also the Subject Index.

Guides: Writing and Illustration. Complementing the preceding group are these works on scientific presentations, writing, style guides, and illustration.

See also:

- Section 8: Education and communication

Quantification. Measurement. Statistics

In this group are entries for standard and specialized works on statistics and biometry, data analysis and interpretation, experimental design and measurement, sampling, measurement and relative sizes, and units of measurement.

See also Testing and Analysis, below.

Modeling and Simulation. Powerful, inexpensive computers have given new impetus to the use of simulation and modeling techniques, as the entries in this subgroup show. They deal with ecological modeling, principles and design of models, simulation, systems analysis, and mathematical programming.

See also Testing and Analysis, below.

Assessment and Monitoring. These are the most familiar techniques associated with environmental management. This subgroup has entries dealing with remote sensing, biomonitoring, chemical sensing, impact assessment, aerial photogrammetry, geographic information systems, and instrumental analysis.

See also Testing and Analysis, below.

Testing and Analysis. New equipment and techniques are revolutionizing the way the environment is tested and sampled. Entries in this subgroup introduce methods, techniques, and equipment for analyzing data from air, water, and land sources.

See also:

- Section 1: Global resources and environment; chemistry, biogeochemical cycles, pollutants; biological systems; ecology; biodiversity, conservation biology, genetics
- Section 2: Atmosphere, climate, weather; climate change; air pollution, atmospheric chemistry
- Section 3: Water pollution
- Section 4: Landscape ecology; soils; land degradation, erosion, reclamation
- Section 5: Plant sciences; plant ecology; endangered plants, genetic resources; atmospheric environment, pollution, pesticides
- Section 6: Forests and forest resources: regions and countries; tree and forest sciences; forest ecology, ecosystems; air, soil, and water relations, pollution

- Section 7: Animal biology, zoology; animal ecology, species; endangered species, conservation biology
- Section 11: Industry, economic sectors; pollution, industrial wastes
- Section 12: Toxic threats, hazards; risk assessment; toxicology
- Section 13: Environmental control technology

Information Sources (2927–2950)

2927. Canadian sources of environmental information. Environment Canada, Document and Library Services, 1989. 457 pp. Lists specialists from government, industry, universities, and the public sector. Entries include brief accounts of their work, experience, or specialty, plus contact information. Subject index groups sources by their expertise; bilingual.

2928. Batten, Donna; ed. **The clearinghouse directory: a guide to information clearinghouses and their resources, services, and publications.** Gale Research, 1991. 429 pp., index. Describes over 600 information clearinghouses, listing contact information, background summary, primary clientele, publications and materials, and services of these often hard to find organizations.

2929. Marcaccio, Kathleen Y.; ed. **Computer-readable databases: a directory and sourcebook.** Gale Research, 7th ed., 1991. 1646 pp. Profiles over 6000 publicly available databases, listing subjects, data elements, availability and rates, and contact information. Includes online, CD-ROM, and electronic bulletin boards. Separate section for database producers and vendors.

2930. Lehmann, Edward J.; ed. **Directory of federal laboratory & technology resources: a guide to services, facilities, and expertise.** National Technical Information Service, 1988. 191 pp., index. Provides information on over 1000 federal agencies, laboratories, and engineering centers willing to aid researchers; arranged by 32 subject areas; fully indexed.

2931. Directory of online databases. Gale Research, 1991 to date. Semiannual. Lists some 4900 databases accessible from 700 online services. Covers reference and source databases—bibliographic, referral, numeric, textual-numeric, full-text, and software. Descriptions include contents, geographic coverage, time span, and frequency of updating. Indexes by subject, database producer, online service, telecommunications network, or vendor's geographic location. Lists addresses of database vendors and gateway organizations.

2932. Federer, Anne; and others, eds. **Directory of periodicals online, indexed, abstracted and full-text: science and technology.** Info Globe, 2d ed., 1991. 1098 pp., index. Lists North American and English-language online journals. Describes database contents and vendors. Indexed by subject and database.

2933. Directory of portable databases. Gale Research, 1991 to date. Semi-annual. Gives summaries of some 1900 databases on CD-ROM, diskette, and tape. Information includes content description, format, system requirements, and software used by the product.

2934. Directory of special libraries and information centers. Gale Research, 1963 to date. 3 vols. Annual: 15th ed., 1992. Alphabetically lists special and research libraries, archives, information centers, and other specialized information collections maintained by public, private, and nonprofit agencies, institutions, and organizations. Notes services, facilities, holdings, availability, contact information, and staff. Covers Canada and the United States, plus major special libraries in over 80 countries.

2935. Advisory Committee for the Co-ordination of Information Systems (ACCIS) **Directory of United Nations databases and information services.** United Nations, 1990. 484 pp., index. Provides information on 872 databases and information systems and services; arranged by subjects, which include natural resources and the environment, social conditions and equity, agriculture, economic development and development finance, and science and technology.

2936. Encyclopedia of information systems and services. Edwards Brothers, 10th ed., 1990. Index. 2 vols. Comprehensive international coverage; 4300 citations provide details on 30,000 information providers and sources and access and support services. Separate index volume contains master, geographic, and subject indexes.

2937. Wasserman, Steven; Smith, Martin A.; Mottu, Susan; eds. **Encyclopedia of physical sciences and engineering information sources.** Gale Research, 1989. 736 pp. Subtitle: A bibliographic guide to approximately 16,000 citations for publications, organizations, and other sources of information on 425 subjects relating to the physical sciences and engineering. For each of the subjects, citations are arranged by format: abstract services and indexes, associations and societies, directories and biographical sources, general works, databases, periodicals, and research centers.

2938. Lesko, Matthew. **The federal data base finder: a directory of free and fee-based data bases and files available from the federal government.** Information USA, 3d ed., 1990. 571 pp., index. Entries contain description of database content, contact information, technical requirements, and price information where applicable. Grouped by government department or agency.

2939. Orenstein, Ruth M.; ed. **Fulltext sources online.** BiblioData, 1989 to date. Semiannual. Covers periodicals, newspapers, newsletters, and news wires reporting on science, technology, medicine, law, finance, business, industry, and more. Guide to some 1000 databases providing full-text coverage; revised every six months.

2940. Government research directory: 1985 to date. Annual: Gale Research, 6th ed., 1991–1992. Lists more than 3700 research programs and facilities operated by or for the U.S. government. Arranged by federal office or department; includes contact, organizational, research area, publication, and service information.

2941. Hurt, Charlie Deuel. **Information sources in science and technology.** Libraries Unlimited, Library science text series, 1988. 362 pp., index. Organized by topic; provides comprehensive coverage of databases and recent titles; includes annotations.

2942. Piatetski-Shapiro, Gregory; Frawley, William; eds. **Knowledge discovery in databases.** MIT Press, 1991. 540 pp. Technical guide to optimal use of databases. Topics include discovery of quantitative and qualitative laws, use of knowledge in discovery, data summarization, domain-specific discovery methods, integrated and multiparadigm systems, and methodology and application issues.

2943. Quarterman, John S. **The matrix: computer networks and conferencing systems worldwide.** Digital Press, 1990. 719 pp., ill., bibl., index. Thorough guide and roadmap for those who have wanted to know what computer networks and conferencing systems are used for, how they are constructed and connected, and how to use them. Part I contains introductory material on user services, protocols, management, administration, and standards. Part II describes specific systems, like Usenet, Internet, and Econet; commercial systems; and public data networks. "Matrix" refers to these networks considered as a connected whole.

2944. National faculty directory. Gale Research, 1970 to date. 3 vols. Annual. Lists the names, addresses, and department affiliations of almost 600,000 faculty members in United States and Canadian colleges and universities.

2945. Kelly, R. **Natural resources and environmental management at North America universities: a guide to training opportunities.** RARE, 1985. 306 pp. Guide to 92 North American programs providing training in sustainable natural resource management. Intended primarily for students from developing countries.

2946. Peterson's guide to graduate programs in the biological and agricultural health sciences. Peterson's Guides, Peterson's annual guides to college study, v. 3, 1967 to date. Annual: 26th ed., 1992. Annual guide to over 5000 programs in several dozen academic areas in the United States and Canada.

2947. Research centers directory: a guide to over 12,000 university-related and other nonprofit research organizations. Gale Research, 1965 to date. 2 vols. Annual: 16th ed., 1992. Provides contact information and details on research facilities working in agriculture, biological sciences and ecology, business and economics, engineering and technology, government and public affairs, behavioral and social sciences, and other fields.

2948. Young, Margaret Labash; ed. **Scientific and technical organizations and agencies directory.** Gale Research, 2d ed., 1987. 2 vols. A guide to some 15,000 organizations and agencies providing information in the physical sciences, engineering, and technology. Has sections on associations, computer information services, consulting firms, educational institutions, global science information networks, libraries and information centers, patent sources, science and technology centers, standards organizations, federal agencies, federal research centers, and others. Contains master name and keyword indexes.

2949. Sachs, Michael; ed. **World guide to scientific associations and learned societies.** Saur, Handbook of international documentation and information, v. 13, 5th ed., 1990. 702 pp., indexes. Contains over 17,000 associations from 132 countries involved in all areas of culture and academic and scientific study. Provides full contact information and lists areas of activity. Indexed by country, subject, name (second names, variations, abbreviations, translated names), and publication.

2950. Lengenfelder, Helga; and others, eds. **World guide to special libraries.** Saur, Handbook of international documentation and information, v. 17, 2d ed., 1990. Index. 2 vols. Lists over 32,000 libraries under 1000 subject terms; entries include full contact information and report on collection size and composition, special collections and departments, accessible data banks, and interlibrary loan program participation.

Reference Books. Journals (2951–2971)

2951. Academic press dictionary of science and technology. Academic Press, 1991. 2176 pp., ill. Over 100,000 entries cover terminology from 122 fields of science and technology: computer science, veterinary science, ecology, biotechnology, and others.

2952. Bibliography of reports by the National Academy of Sciences, 1945–1985. Government Printing Office, Science policy study. Background report, no. 2, pt. B, 1986. 149 pp. Prepared for the Task Force on Science Policy, Committee on Science and Technology, House of Representatives, Ninety-Ninth Congress, Second Session, 1986.

2953. Powell, Russell H.; Powell, James R., Jr. **Core list of books and journals in science and technology.** Oryx Press, 1987. 134 pp., index. Lists 700 books and 800 periodicals in English published since 1980. Topics covered are agriculture, astronomy, biology, chemistry, computer science, engineering, geology, mathematics, physics, and reference.

2954. Current contents. Institute for Scientific Information, 1955 to date. Weekly. Provides current awareness of the latest scientific developments by printing the contents pages of leading journals throughout the world, as determined by the institute and its advisors. Presently issued in seven weekly editions, one of which is *Current contents: agriculture, biology, and environmental sciences.* Each weekly edition has a title word index, an author index and address directory, and a publisher's address directory. Weekly editions are cumulated and upgraded to create the annual *Science citation index,* described in this section. Available online and on computer diskette.

2955. Dissertation abstracts international. University Microfilms, 1938 to date. Monthly. Indexes and abstracts doctoral dissertations produced in the United States and in some universities in other countries.

2956. Geo-Katalog. Geo Center Verlagsauslieferungen und Barsortiment, Stuttgart, 1972 to date. Annual. Catalogs publicly available, in-print, quality maps of more than local interest. Entries, organized by geographic region and then grouped thematically, provide title, date, scale, subject, and scope. Text in German only, with French, English, and German forewords.

2957. Government reports announcements & index. National Technical Information Service, 1975 to date. Biweekly. Record of U.S. government-sponsored research and development. Available online and on CD-ROM.

2958. Cobb, David A.; compiler. **Guide to U.S. map resources.** American Library Association, 2d ed., 1990. 495 pp., index. Covers academic, geoscience, private, public, and state and federal libraries. Gives information on holdings, personnel, collection focus, hours, use statistics, equipment, classification and preservation methods, size of facility, and access facilities.

2959. Powell, Russell H.; ed. **Handbooks and tables in science and technology.** Oryx Press, 2d ed., 1983. 297 pp., index. Covers both generalized and specialized handbooks in many fields, from agriculture to zoology; gives full bibliographic information and details of contents.

2960. Interciencia: journal of science and technology of the Americas. Interciencia Association, 1976 to date. Bimonthly. Publishes scientific and technological research of Latin America and the Caribbean, emphasizing the social context. Many articles on the regional impact of human activities (deforestation, coral reefs). Articles in English, Spanish, and Portuguese.

2961. Pritchard, Eileen; Scott, Paula R. **Literature searching in science, technology, and agriculture.** Greenwood Press, 1984. 174 pp., ill., bibl., index. Basic introduction to library research. Discusses search strategy, using abstracts and indexes, computer retrieval, and specialized reference sources.

2962. Thompson, Morris M. **Maps for America: cartographic products of the U.S. geological survey and others.** U.S. Department of the Interior, Geological Survey, Federal Center, 1987. 265 pp., maps, ill., bibl., index. Promoting better understanding of maps and map content, explains the meaning of lines, colors, symbols, and other notations found on maps produced by public and private U.S. organizations. Reviews various map types and information and the sources of that information and notes possible errors and inconsistencies affecting map interpretation.

2963. Parker, Sybil P.; ed. **McGraw-Hill concise encyclopedia of science and technology.** McGraw-Hill, 2d ed., 1989. 2222 pp., maps, ill., bibl., index. A condensed version of the McGraw-Hill *Encyclopedia of science and technology.* Over 7000 cross-referenced articles supply information on a wide range of technical and scientific topics.

2964. Nature. Macmillan Press, 1869 to date. Weekly. "International weekly journal of science." Includes news, correspondence and letters, book reviews, review articles, and original research on all aspects of science.

2965. New Scientist. New Scientist, 1971 to date. Weekly. Environmental issues are well represented among the scientific topics covered by this British weekly. Four or five features and many shorter articles. Investigative reporting style. News of scientific and technological developments.

2966. Northwest science. Washington State University Press, 1927 to date. Quarterly. Publishes original research by members of the Northwest Scientific Association in the basic, applied, and social sciences; research often concerns the Pacific Northwest.

2967. Science. American Association for the Advancement of Science, 1883 to date. Weekly. What is happening in science each week. The frontiers of research in articles and reports; the latest trends, issues, and programs in the letters, news, and comment sections. Global and environmental issues are regularly reported.

2968. Science citation index. Institute for Scientific Information, 1961 to date. An international, interdisciplinary index to the literature of science, medicine, agriculture, and technology. The social and behavioral sciences are covered in the *Social science citation index.* In three parts: source index (articles published under an author's name in any of the journals covered); citation index (titles of articles cited by each author appearing in the source index); and Permuterm subject index (each significant word in a title paired with every other significant word in that title). Annual and five-year cumulations. Available online and on CD-ROM. By 1991, the ISI database had 13 million source items and 191 million cited references.

2969. Scientific American. Scientific American, 1845 to date. Monthly. Illustrated, comprehensive features on scientific topics, environmental problems among them, as articles or special issues.

2970. Considine, Douglas M.; Considine, Glenn D.; eds. **Van Nostrand's scientific encyclopedia.** Van Nostrand Reinhold, 7th ed., 1989. 3180 pp., Ill., index. 2 vols. Concise definitions of scientific terms and concepts. Topics include animal life, energy sources and power technology, and plant sciences.

2971. Maizlish, Aaron; Hunt, William S. **The world map directory, 1989.** Map Link, 1988. 278 pp., index. Entries, organized geographically using the Library of Congress numbering system, list map title, publisher, scale, and date; includes topographic, regional, country, city, and specialty maps.

Guides: Writing and Illustration (2972–2979)

2972. CBE style manual: a guide for authors, editors and publishers in the biological sciences. Council of Biology Editors, 1983. 324 pp., ill., bibl., index. Handbook covers manuscript preparation, editorial review, copyright, publishing, and other topics.

2973. Tufte, Edward R. **Envisioning information.** Graphics Press, 1990. 126 pp., maps, ill., bibl., index. Illustrates design strategies for charts, diagrams, graphs, tables, guides, instructions, directories, and maps. Examines what works and what does not in conveying complex data intelligibly. Considers elements of color, contrast, detail, typography, and layout.

2974. Hodges, Elaine R. S.; ed. **The Guild handbook of scientific illustration.** Van Nostrand Reinhold, 1989. 575 pp. Discusses tools, materials, techniques, and innovative applications for scientific illustrations of all kinds. Covers the illustration of plants, animals, and anthropological and archaeological artifacts; the use of microscopes and cartography; and operation of a freelance business.

2975. Day, Robert A. **How to write and publish a scientific paper.** Oryx Press, 3d ed., 1988. 211 pp., ill., bibl., index. Concepts and mechanics of organizing, editing, and publishing scientific writing.

2976. Illustrating science: standards for publication. Council of Biology Editors, 1988. 296 pp., ill., bibl., index. Expert illustrators, photographers, editors, publishers, and printers contribute standards and guidelines for preparing artwork, graphs and maps, computer graphics, camera-ready copy, continuous tone photographs, halftone printing, and color illustration. Discusses quality criteria and instructions to authors and legal and ethical considerations. Contains glossary of graphic arts terms.

2977. Woodford, F. Peter; ed. **Scientific writing for graduate students: a manual on the teaching of scientific writing.** Council of Biology Editors, 1986. 187 pp., bibl., index. Chapters provide step-by-step instructions, with suggested time allotments, for writing a journal article. Includes material on the design of tables and figures, and doctoral thesis and research proposal preparation. From a biological and biochemical perspective, but principles are widely applicable.

2978. Tufte, Edward R. **The visual display of quantitative information.** Graphics Press, 1983. 197 pp., ill., bibl., index. Examines principles of graphical excellence, integrity, and sophistication, and illustrates with examples from the eighteenth century to the present.

Shows how to improve all kinds of graphs (time series graphs, thematic maps, scatterplots, relational graphs, multivariate designs, and high-density displays) by eliminating clutter. Also shows how graphs can be used to distort data.

2979. Booth, Vernon. **Writing a scientific paper and speaking at scientific meetings.** Biochemical Society, 5th ed., 1981. 48 pp., bibl, index. Succinct advice on avoiding problems of style and punctuation most common in scientific writing.

Quantification. Measurement. Statistics (2980–2995)

2980. Biometrics. Biometric Society, 1945 to date. Quarterly. Papers on mathematical and statistical methods in pure and applied biological sciences.

2981. Sokal, Robert R.; Rohlf, F. James. **Biometry: the principles and practice of statistics in biological research.** Freeman, 1981. 859 pp., ill. Revised edition of a leading text directed at the academic biologist. Develops subject from elementary introduction to advanced application. Numerous boxes and special tables in the text give examples of computational methods from the literature. Covers distribution, estimation, variance (six chapters), correlation, linear and multiple regression, analysis of frequencies, and others. The authors are strong advocates of quantitative methods and assert that biometry can be learned and used by those with "very limited mathematical backgrounds."

2982. Jongman, R. H.; ter Braak, C. J. F.; van Tongeren, O. F. R. **Data analysis in community and landscape ecology.** PUDOC, 1987. 299 pp., ill., bibl., index. Intended for researchers using computers to analyze field data on plant and animal communities. Includes chapters on data collection, regression analysis, calibration, ordination, cluster analysis, and spatial analysis.

2983. Mead, R. **The design of experiments: statistical principles for practical applications.** Cambridge University Press, 1988. 620 pp., ill., bibl., index. Extensive text emphasizes logical principles of statistical design, examining unit variation and control, treatment questions, and structure. Includes problems and examples from a wide range of disciplines.

2984. Hairston, Nelson G. **Ecological experiments: purpose, design, and execution.** Cambridge University Press, 1989. 370 pp., bibl., index. Intended to instruct researchers on the good and bad points of experiments that have been carried out. Discussion of these experi-ments is arranged by type of environment: forests, terrestrial successional environments, arid lands, freshwater, and marine. Discusses experimental design on the basis of conclusions drawn from the examples.

2985. Barford, N.C. **Experimental measurements: precision, error, and truth.** Wiley, 2d ed., 1985. 159 pp., ill., bibl., index. Laboratory workbook. Provides an understanding of random experimental errors and the proper presentation of results. Develops the necessary mathematical principles; discusses a theory and model of errors.

2986. Pielou, E. C. **The interpretation of ecological data: a primer on classification and ordination.** Wiley, 1984. 263 pp., ill., bibl., index. Provides an introduction to the most popular techniques for analyzing multivariate data; demonstrates and explains the techniques used.

2987. Asimov, Isaac. **The measure of the universe.** Harper & Row, 1983. 339 pp., ill., index. An attempt to render the variety of sizes in the universe comprehensible. Looks at increments of measurement of length, area, volume, mass, density, pressure, time, speed, and temperature.

2988. Doebelin, Ernest O. **Measurement systems: application and design.** McGraw-Hill, 3d ed., 1983. 876 pp., ill., bibl., index.

2989. Digby, P. G. N.; Kempton, R. A. **Multivariate analysis of ecological communities.** Chapman and Hall, Population and community biology, 1987. 206 pp., ill., bibl., index. Succinctly describes techniques of multivariate analysis suitable for ecological data, including ordination and classification, the analysis of asymmetry, and computing; includes examples.

2990. Morrison, Philip; Morrison, Phylis; Office of Charles and Ray Eames. **Powers of ten: a book about the relative size of things in the universe and the effect of adding another zero.** Freeman, 1982. 150 pp., ill., bibl., index. Features a set of 42 color plates illustrating the orders of magnitude in the observable world, ranging from the universe as a whole at the largest down to the smallest, a subnuclear haze of quarks within the nucleus of an atom. Accompanied by fascinating supplementary reading.

2991. Keith, Lawrence H.; ed. **Principles of environmental sampling.** American Chemical Society, ACS professional reference book, 1988. 458 pp., ill., bibl., index. Describes basic principles and considerations for planning and sampling design and quality control. Addresses sampling of water, air, biota, and wastes.

2992. Drazil, J. V. **Quantities and units of measurement: a dictionary and handbook.** Mansell (dist. by Wilson), 1983. 313 pp., bibl., index.

2993. Cormack, Richard M.; Patil, Ganapati P.; Robson, Douglas S.; eds. **Sampling biological populations.** International Co-operative Publishing House, Statistical ecology, v. 5, 1979. 392 pp., ill., bibl., index. Addresses problems of designing and estimating sample selection probabilities for line and strip transects and mark and recapture. Develops techniques for ecological sampling on land and at sea.

2994. Mason, Robert L.; Gunst, Richard F.; Hess, James L. **Statistical design and analysis of experiments: with applications to engineering and science.** Wiley, Wiley series in probability and mathematical statistics, 1989. 692 pp., index. Intended for readers with limited mathematical backgrounds. In three parts: descriptive measures and graphical techniques; design; and data analysis.

2995. Ludwig, John A.; Reynolds, James F. **Statistical ecology: a primer on methods and computing.** Wiley-Interscience, 1988. 337 pp., ill., bibl., index. Designed for college courses; covers spatial patterns analysis, species abundance relations, species affinity, community classification, ordination, and interpretation. Includes 21 programs on IBM-PC disk.

Modeling and Simulation (2996–3023)

2996. Marani, A.; ed. **Advances in environmental modelling.** Elsevier, Developments in environmental modelling, v. 13, 1988. 691 pp. Proceedings of a 1987 symposium address systems theory and modeling techniques. Papers focus on terrestrial ecosystems; marine and coastal ecosystems; and lakes, lagoons, and wetlands.

2997. Lauenroth, William K.; Skogerboe, Gaylord V.; Flug, Marshall.; eds. **Analysis of ecological systems: state-of-the-art in ecological modelling.** Elsevier, Developments in environmental modelling, v. 5, 1983. 992 pp., ill., bibl. Papers discuss theory, methods, and applications with respect to animals, land resources, water resources, and energy development. A final section summarizes findings.

2998. Basta, Daniel J.; Bower, Blair T.; eds. **Analyzing natural systems: analysis for regional residuals—environmental quality management.** Resources for the Future, 1982. 546 pp., ill., bibl. Discusses applications and principles of environmental residuals models. Reviews appropriate methods to employ in modeling residuals dispersion in surface runoff, rivers and lakes, and the atmosphere.

2999. Starfield, Anthony M.; Bleloch, Andrew. **Building models for conservation and wildlife management.** Macmillan, Biological resource management, 1986. 253 pp., ill., bibl., index. Addresses conceptual questions of how to build and use models; uses specific cases to illustrate development of different types of models.

3000. Harte, John. **Consider a spherical cow: a course in environmental problem solving.** University Science Books, 1988. 283 pp. Designed to help students transform qualitatively described problems into quantifiably solvable form, uniting mathematical and environmental concepts. Presents 44 problems and their solutions that illustrate how to invent models, define variables, establish system boundaries, and select tools to derive information from models. Problems involve such topics as assessing a polluted lake, determining the warming impact of the greenhouse effect, and building a model for China's population-planning efforts.

3001. Legendre, Pierre; Legendre, Louis; eds. **Developments in numerical ecology.** Springer-Verlag, NATO ASI series, Series G: Ecological sciences, v. 14, 1987. 585 pp., ill., bibl., index. Presents theories on scaling techniques, clustering with models, fractal theory, qualitative path analysis, and spatial analysis. Working group reports assess applicability to microorganisms, benthic communities, and other fields of specialization.

3002. Ecological modelling. Elsevier, 1975 to date. 20 issues/yr. International journal on ecological modeling and engineering and systems ecology. Covers mathematical models and systems analysis applied to ecosystems, pollution, environment, population dynamics, and natural resources. Contains state-of-the-art reviews of global modeling.

3003. Swartzman, Gordon L.; Kaluzny, Stephen P. **Ecological simulation primer.** Macmillan, 1987. 370 pp. Reviews the justifications for and methodologies of developing ecological models and illustrates with examples for several aquatic and terrestrial ecosystems. Topics include stochastic methods and sensitivity analysis techniques.

3004. Bennett, Robert John; Chorley, R. J. **Environmental systems: philosophy, analysis and control.** Princeton University Press, 1978. 624 pp., ill., bibl., index. Attempts a unified treatment of ecological, economic, social, psychological, and physical systems based on control theory. Reference book, requiring mathematical background.

3005. Salthe, Stanley N. **Evolving hierarchical systems: their structure and representation.** Columbia University Press, 1985. 343 pp., ill., bibl., index. Biologist concerned with evolutionary theory presents a metatheory of science based on hierarchical organization of the natural world's complexity. Focus is on hierarchical structure of organic evolution.

3006. Swann, Robert L.; Eschenroeder, Alan; eds. **Fate of chemicals in the environment: compartmental and multimedia models for predictions.** American Chemical Society, ACS symposium series, v. 225, 1983. 320 pp., ill., bibl., index. Based on a 1982 symposium. Papers discuss chemical release, environmental and multimedia models, model validation and parameters, and human risk assessment.

3007. Straskraba, Milan; Gnauck, Albrecht H. **Freshwater ecosystems: modelling and simulation.** Elsevier, Developments in environmental modelling, v. 8, 1985. 309 pp., ill., bibl., index. The authors link stochastic, simulation, and cybernetic methodologies with experimental limnology to develop a single method for modeling freshwater ecosystems. Part I introduces principles of systems theory, their application, and a summary of systems analysis methods. Part II emphasizes the pelagic processes in standing water from which models can be developed. Part III cites examples of applying such models, and Part IV looks at recent developments in ecosystem modeling.

3008. Smardon, Richard C.; ed. **The future of wetlands: assessing visual-cultural values.** Allanheld, Osmun (dist. by Rowman & Allanheld), 1983. 226 pp., maps, ill., index. Presents a comparative approach for developing models to establish priorities for wetland preservation and protection, taking into account recreational, aesthetic, social, and educational values.

3009. Tomlin, Dana C. **Geographic information systems and cartographic modeling.** Prentice-Hall, 1990. 249 pp., ill., index. Introduction to cartographic modeling, the aspect of geographic information systems (GIS) that focuses on the use of data. The book is intended particularly for those with some experience in GIS data storage and handling. In three parts: cartographic modeling conventions, cartographic modeling capabilities, and cartographic modeling techniques.

3010. Ripple, William J.; ed. **Geographic information systems for resource management: a compen-**

dium. American Society for Photogrammetry and Remote Sensing, 1987. 288 pp. Twenty-two papers culled from 11 publications on geographic information systems (GIS). Topics include creating a computerized spatial database; capabilities of computer-based GIS; GIS for land suitability studies; urban studies; water, soil, and vegetation resources; and global studies.

3011. Jeffers, John N. R. **An introduction to systems analysis, with ecological applications.** University Park Press, A series of student texts in contemporary biology, 1978. 198 pp., ill., bibl., index. Explains modeling process and demonstrates five mathematical models used in systems analysis: dynamic, matrix, stochastic, multivariate, and optimization.

3012. Clark, Colin Whitcomb. **Mathematical bioeconomics: the optimal management of renewable resources.** Wiley, Pure and applied mathematics, 2d ed., 1990. 352 pp., ill., bibl., index. Presents a basic dynamic fishery model. Discusses optimal control theory and discrete-time models. Examines more complex models involving age structure and multispecies systems.

3013. Dyskstra, Dennis P. **Mathematical programming for natural resource management.** McGraw-Hill, 1984. 318 pp., ill., bibl., index. Introduces concepts and techniques of mathematical programming, emphasizing linear programming. Provides review of literature related to applications; college-level algebra assumed.

3014. Kingsland, Sharon E. **Modeling nature: episodes in the history of population ecology.** University of Chicago Press, 1985. 267 pp., ill., bibl., index. Presents the gradual progress of population ecology theory, identifying seeming patterns, connecting ideas, and explaining variations; emphasizes animal ecology.

3015. Smith, John Maynard. **Models in ecology.** Cambridge University Press, 1974. 145 pp. Covers mathematical and laboratory models, with emphasis on the forms. Includes topics such as predator-prey systems, competition, migration, stability, and complexity.

3016. Legendre, Louis; Legendre, Pierre. **Numerical ecology.** Elsevier, Developments in environmental modelling, v. 3, 1983. 419 pp., ill., bibl., index. Designed as a handbook for ecologists, emphasizing biological interpretation of each topic. Covers matrix algebra, dimensional analysis, multidimensional data, measures of ecological resemblance, cluster analysis, ordination, structure analysis, ecological series, Markov process, and Leslie matrix.

3017. Jeffers, J. N. R. **Practitioner's handbook on**

the modelling of dynamic change in ecosystems. Wiley, SCOPE, v. 34, 1988. 181 pp., ill., bibl., index. Surveys modeling techniques, including systems analysis, and dynamic, Markov, and multivariate models. Assesses each method's requirements, limitations, and means of application.

3018. Jørgensen, S. E.; ed. **State-of-the-art in ecological modelling.** Pergamon Press, Environmental Sciences and applications, v. 7, 1979. 891 pp., ill., bibl. Papers deal with theoretical mathematical problems of modeling and present examples of aquatic, atmospheric, and lithospheric ecological models; emphasis is on aquatic ecosystems.

3019. Grant, William Edward. **Systems analysis and simulation in wildlife and fisheries sciences.** Wiley, 1986. 338 pp., ill., bibl., index. Graduate-level textbook explains conceptual model formulation, quantitative specification of the model, and model validation, and use. Uses one hypothetical case to illustrate concepts. Includes exercises and solutions.

3020. Gordon, Robert B.; Koopman, Tajaling, C.; Nordhaus, William, B.; and others. **Toward a new iron age? quantitative modeling of resource exhaustion.** Harvard University Press, 1987. 173 pp., ill., bibl., index. An analysis of the long-term future use of the most widely used of the geochemically scarce metals—copper—based on an economic model, data of available resources, and opportunities for substituting alternative materials and/or recycling.

3021. Macdonald, Norman. **Trees and networks in biological models.** Wiley, 1983. 215 pp., ill., bibl., index. First half uses graph theory terminology to describe abstract networks, characterizing them in terms of numerical indexes and covering steady states and oscillations. Second half reviews the descriptions, biophysics, and simulation of branching structures, using examples from botany and zoology.

3022. Mitsch, William J.; Straskraba, Milan; Jorgensen, Sven E.; eds. **Wetland modelling.** Elsevier, Developments in environmental modelling, v. 12, 1988. 227 pp. Discusses several types of wetlands and presents ecological modeling as an appropriate management tool.

3023. Verner, Jared; Morrison, Michael L.; Ralph, C. John; eds. **Wildlife 2000: modeling habitat relationships of terrestrial vertebrates.** University of Wisconsin Press, 1986. 470 pp., ill., bibl., index. Based on a 1984 symposium. Discusses development, testing and application of models predicting wildlife responses to habitat change.

Assessment and Monitoring (3024–3061)

3024. Paine, David P. **Aerial photography and image interpretation for resource management.** Wiley, 1981. 571 pp., ill., bibl., index. Covers geometry and photographic measurements, mapping, photograph interpretation, forest inventory, and nonphotographic remote sensing. College-level text with questions, problems, and laboratory exercises.

3025. AI applications in natural resource management. AI Applications; University of Idaho, Department of Forest Resources, 1987 to date. Quarterly. Describes developments in artificial intelligence research and applications appropriate to natural resources, agriculture, and environmental science. Evaluates specific models and systems, reports on works in progress, and identifies and discusses areas of future application.

3026. Gruber, David; Diamond, J. **Automated biomonitoring: living sensors as environmental monitors.** Horwood; Halsted Press, 1988. 208 pp., ill., bibl., index. Papers in Part I review basic concepts of automated biological systems to monitor drinking water, industrial effluents, and wastewaters. Part II papers present case studies of the use of fish as biological monitors. Part III papers focus on other kinds of biological sensors.

3027. Worf, Douglas L.; ed. **Biological monitoring for environmental effects.** Lexington Books, 1980. 227 pp., ill., index. Reviews federal, industrial, and academic development and application of biomonitoring methods to assess the effects of water, air, and soil pollutants; essays evaluate techniques and identify issues and priorities.

3028. Cass, A. E. G.; ed. **Biosensors: a practical approach.** IRL Press at Oxford University Press, Practical approach series, 1990. 271 pp., ill., bibl., index. Describes the design, construction, and use of many kinds of biosensors, emphasizing electrochemical methods. Includes chapter on the theoretical analysis of biosensors in order to optimize their performance.

3029. Hollenberg, C. P.; Sahm, H.; eds. **Biosensors and environmental biotechnology.** Gustav Fischer Verlag; Biotec, v. 2, 1988. 149 pp., ill., bibl. Reviews development of different types of biosensors used for detection and treatment of gaseous pollutants, wastewater and metal-contaminated materials.

3030. Edmonds, T. E.; ed. **Chemical sensors.** Chapman and Hall, 1988. 326 pp., ill., bibl., index. Individually authored chapters address molecular and ionic recognition by biological systems and chemical methods. Examines factors and techniques involved in recognition. Covers electrochemical and nonelectrochemical transduction.

3031. Hyman, Eric L; Stiftel, Bruce. **Combining facts and values in environmental impact assessment: theories and techniques.** Westview Press, Social impact assessment, v. 16, 1988. 304 pp. Reviews and assesses methods of placing social and economic values on the environment, including cost-benefit analysis; land suitability analysis; checklists, matrices, and networks; modeling, simulation, and resource management approaches; and multiple-objective analysis. Examines common pitfalls in environmental assessment.

3032. Westman, Walter E. **Ecology, impact assessment and environmental planning.** Wiley, 1985. 532 pp., maps, ill., bibl., index. This synthesis of methods and concepts discusses the ecological constraints on environmental law and decision making, reviews quantitative and economic approaches to impact assessment, and examines prediction of the effects of impacts on the physical environment and biological communities.

3033. EIS: digests of environmental impact statements. Information Resources Press, 1970 to date. Bimonthly. Abstracts and indexes government-released environmental impact statements.

3034. Cheremisinoff, Paul N. **Environmental assessment & impact statement handbook.** Ann Arbor Science, 1977. 438 pp., ill., bibl., index. Explains the principles and methods involved in the preparation and development of an environmental impact statement. Reviews the informational requirements for assessing impacts from solid wastes, petroleum refineries, nuclear power and radioactive wastes, and the rubber industry.

3035. Cairns, John, Jr; Patil, Ganapati P.; Waters, William E.; eds. **Environmental biomonitoring, assessment, prediction, and management: certain case studies and related quantitative issues.** International Co-operative Publishing House, Statistical ecology, v. 11, 1979. 438 pp., ill., bibl., index. Discusses biological assessment methods in various settings, using case studies to demonstrate applications, difficulties, and areas needing greater research and understanding.

3036. Rau, John G.; Wooten, David C.; eds. **Environmental impact analysis handbook.** McGraw-Hill, 1980. 642 pp., maps, bibl., index. In-depth guide to the development and preparation of an environmental impact statement.

3037. PADC Environmental Impact Assessment and Planning Unit, University of Aberdeen. **Environmental impact assessment.** Nijhoff; Kluwer, NATO ASI series, Series D, Behavioural and social sciences, v. 14, 1983. 439 pp., ill., bibl., index. Papers discuss environmental impact assessment in the United States and Canada, its role in the planning process, methods, and assessments of specific impacts.

3038. Clark, Brian D.; Bisset, Ronald; Wathern, Peter. **Environmental impact assessment: a bibliography with abstracts.** Bowker, 1980. 516 pp. Lists over 1000 books and articles concerned with environmental impact assessment (EIA); critiques and reviews of EIA; EIA and other aspects of planning, EIA in selected countries, (United States, Canada, U.K. and Australia); and information sources. Many entries include detailed abstracts.

3039. Environmental impact assessment review. Plenum Press, 1980 to date. Quarterly. Intended to give multiple insights into the problems and processes of environmental assessment, dispute resolution, and decision making.

3040. Golden, Jack; and others, eds. **Environmental impact data book.** Ann Arbor Science, 1979. 864 pp., ill., bibl., index. Collects sources used frequently in the preparation of environmental impact statements, including databases, law books, textbooks, technical papers, the *Federal register*, and government publications. Also presents technical data on air quality, water and physical resources, noise, toxic chemicals, energy, and ecosystems.

3041. Environmental monitoring and assessment. Kluwer, 1981 to date. Quarterly. Contains original research pertaining to the scientific basis for monitoring and the design and development of monitoring systems. Also covers sampling techniqes, data handling, exposure assessment, and pollution risk assessment.

3042. Draggan, Sidney; Cohrssen, John J.; Morrison, Richard E.; eds. **Environmental monitoring, assessment, and management: the agenda for long-term research and development.** Praeger, 1987. 128 pp., bibl., index. Discusses research needs in the following areas: database development, industrial pollution control, risk analysis and its role, ecological modeling, and the role of interdisciplinary research in natural resource management.

3043. Culhane, Paul J.; Friesema, H. Paul; Beecher Janice A. **Forecasts and environmental decisionmaking: the content and predictive accuracy of environmental impact statements.** Westview Press, Societal impact assessment series, v. 14, 1987. 306 pp., ill., bibl. Assesses the analytic quality of environmental impact statements, comparing the accuracy and descriptions of the forecasts with the actual impacts of 29 projects.

3044. Cornillon, Peter. **Guide to environmental satellite data.** University of Rhode Island, University of Rhode Island marine technical report, v. 79, 1982. 469 pp., ill., bibl. Presents overview of environmental satellites and sensors, including a general survey of where their data are stored. Second section details each satellite and its particular sensors and abilities, with contact information for data requests.

3045. Drury, Stephen A. **A guide to remote sensing: interpreting images of the earth.** Oxford University Press, 1990. 199 pp., ill., bibl., index. Aerial photographs and satellite images illustrate both the problems and the potentials for remote sensing of the earth. Includes discussion of theories and processes involved in planning and interpreting remote sensing.

3046. Jorgensen, S. E.; ed. **Handbook of environmental data and ecological parameters.** Pergamon Press, Environmental sciences and applications, v. 6, 1979. 1162 pp., ill., bibl., index. Reference book of the parameters needed to assess many biological systems, such as equilibrium constants, uptake rates, growth rates, diffusion coefficients, and others. Sections include the ecosphere and chemical compounds, toxicological effects, and equations for biological and physiochemical processes.

3047. Avery, Thomas Eugene; Berlin, Graydon Lennis. **Interpretation of aerial photographs.** Burgess, 1985. 554 pp., ill., bibl., index. Broad introduction to aerial photography and its applications in land cover mapping, archaeology, agriculture, soils, forestry, engineering, and mining.

3048. Hyatt, Edward. **Keyguide to information sources in remote sensing.** Mansell, 1988. 274 pp. A guide to sources for both researchers and educators. Covers journals, dissertations and theses, textbooks, reports, bibliographies, patents, images, audiovisual products, and organizations.

3049. Cowell, Robert N.; ed. **Manual of remote sensing.** American Society of Photogrammetry, 2d ed., 1983. Maps, ill., bibl., index. 2 vols. Vol. 1: Theory, instruments, and techniques. Vol. 2: Interpretation and applications. Comprehensive, concise presentation of principles, equipment, and applications of remote sensing.

3050. Moore, James W.; Ramamoorthy, S. **Organic chemicals in natural waters: applied monitoring and impact assessment.** Springer-Verlag, Springer series on environmental management, 1984. 289 pp., ill., bibl.,

index. Focuses on organic compounds from EPA priority pollutant list. Reviews chemistry, production, use, discharge, behavior in natural waters, residues, and toxicity.

3051. Clark, Brian D.; Gilad, Alexander; Bisset, Ronald; and others, eds. **Perspectives on environmental impact assessment.** Reidel; Kluwer, 1984. 520 pp., ill., bibl., index. Reviews the objectives and procedures of environmental impact assessment (EIA) in the United States, Canada, France, the Netherlands, and developing countries. Discusses health and medical aspects of EIA. Examines developments in methods, techniques, and applications. Includes case studies involving oil, gas, water, and tourism development.

3052. Burrough, P. A. **Principles of geographical information systems for land resources assessment.** Clarendon Press, Monographs on soil and resource surveys, no. 12, 1986. 193 pp., ill., bibl., index. Presents the general principles behind systems now in use. Covers data structures, digital elevation models, data quality and handling, classification methods, and spatial interpretation.

3053. Skoog, Douglas A. **Principles of instrumental analysis.** Saunders College Publishing, 3d ed., 1985. 879 pp., ill., bibl., index. Complete introduction to the principles and practical aspects of scientific measuring devices and methods. Addresses optical spectroscopy, nuclear magnetic resonance, chromatography, and electrochemistry.

3054. Eden, M. J.; Parry, J. T. **Remote sensing and tropical land management.** Wiley, 1986. 365 pp., ill., bibl., index. Explains the technology of remote sensing, including aerial photography, side looking airborne radar (SLAR), and satellite imaging systems. Essays discuss their application to classifying and evaluating land resources, surveying land use, and monitoring vegetation cover and crops through northern Australia, Africa, South America, and the Pacific Islands. Evaluates problems and promises of future technology and its uses.

3055. Damen, M. C. J.; Smit, G. Sicco; Verstappen, H. Th.; eds. **Remote sensing for resources development and environmental management.** Balkema, 1986. Ill., bibl., index. 2 vols. Proceedings of a 1986 symposium. Topics include visible, infrared and microwave data; spectral signatures; renewable and nonrenewable resources; hydrology; human settlement; and geoinformation systems.

3056. Cracknell, A. P.; ed. **Remote sensing in meteorology, oceanography and hydrology.** Halsted Press, Ellis Horwood series in environmental sciences, 1981.

542 pp., maps, ill., index. Twenty-six papers from a 1980 meeting cover atmospheric, marine, and terrestrial applications of remote sensing.

3057. Hobbs, R. J.; Mooney, H. A.; eds. **Remote sensing of biosphere functioning.** Springer-Verlag, Ecological studies, v. 79, 1990. 312 pp., ill., bibl., index. Reviews current methods, technology, and research problems. Covers the remote sensing of carbon, water, trace gas exchange, and the processes and structural changes of vegetation and landscape. Argues that it is becoming possible to make global assessments of the earth's changing structural and functional properties.

3058. Remote sensing of environment. Elsevier, 1969 to date. Monthly. Articles report on advances in and applications of remote-sensing technology. Topics range from modeling of surface temperatures to population estimation.

3059. Carter, D. J. **The remote sensing sourcebook: a guide to remote sensing products, services, facilities, publications and other materials.** McCarta, 1986. 175 pp. Intended for the educational community. Covers the history of remote sensing and provides data sources, a list of textbooks, and a guide to technical literature. Also discusses the organizational structure of remote-sensing activities in the United Kingdom.

3060. Szekielda, Karl-Heinz. **Satellite monitoring of the earth.** Wiley, Wiley series in remote sensing, 1988. 326 pp., ill., bibl., index. Reviews platforms and sensors, atmospheric considerations, spectral characteristics of natural systems, and concepts in data processing and interpretation. Illustrates and explains observations over oceans and land.

3061. Harris, Ray. **Satellite remote sensing: an introduction.** Routledge & Kegan Paul, 1987. 220 pp. Introductory chapters cover definitions and history, the physics of remote sensing, satellite sensors, and significant satellites. Discusses digital image processing. Covers application areas: land cover and vegetation, geology and soils, the atmosphere, and the hydrosphere.

Testing and Analysis (3062–3084)

3062. Afghan, B. K.; Chau, Alfred S. Y.; eds. **Analysis of trace organics in aquatic environment.** CRC Press, 1989. 384 pp. Reviews the practical aspects of analytic methodology. Discusses the occurrence, distribution, fate, effect, and environmental impact of such classes of compounds as PCBs, phenols, phthalate esters, humic acids, and organometallics.

3063. Albaiges, J.; ed. **Analytical techniques in environmental chemistry.** Pergamon Press, Pergamon series on environmental science, v. 3, 1980. 646 pp., ill., bibl., index. Proceedings of a 1978 conference. Individual papers present both data and methods in environmental chemistry, including case history information.

3064. Sheehan, Patrick; and others, eds. **Appraisal of tests to predict the environmental behavior of chemicals.** Wiley, 1985. 380 pp. Presents detailed evaluations of specific and general test procedures for chemicals in the atmosphere, water, sediments, and soils. Also studies the prediction, transformation, degradation, and accumulation of chemicals in biota and their movement between environmental compartments.

3065. Lodge, James P., Jr.; Chan, T. L.; eds. **Cascade impactors: sampling and data analysis.** American Industrial Hygiene Association, 1986. 170 pp. Discusses commonly used instruments in aerosol science, air pollution, and atmospheric chemistry. A practical and theoretical guide for experimental practitioners.

3066. Kalvoda, Robert; ed. **Electroanalytical methods in chemical and environmental analysis.** Plenum Press, 1987. 237 pp., ill., bibl., index. Discusses methods for monitoring substances polluting or otherwise affecting the environment.

3067. Conway, Richard A.; ed. **Environmental risk analysis for chemicals.** Van Nostrand Reinhold, 1981. 558 pp. Covers wide range of testing procedures and methods for determining the risk of any chemical.

3068. Ramamoorthy, S.; Baddaloo, E. **Evaluation of environmental data for regulatory and impact assessment.** Elsevier, Studies in environmental science, v. 41, 1990. 466 pp., index. Reviews models common to current environmental impact and risk assessment. Discusses methods to ensure quality biological and analytic data. Shows how to evaluate testing procedures for toxic chemicals screening. Describes public involvement and participation in regulatory decision making.

3069. Suess, Michael J.; ed. **Examination of water for pollution control: a reference handbook.** Pergamon Press, 1982. Maps, ill., bibl., index. 3 vols. Compilation of research from 31 countries. Vol. 1: Sampling, data analysis, and laboratory equipment. Vol. 2: Physical, chemical, and radiological examinations. Vol. 3: Biological, bacteriological, and virological examinations.

3070. Simmons, Milagros S.; ed. **Hazardous waste measurements.** Lewis, 1991. 315 pp., ill., index. Updates methods in field testing and quality assurance; specific topics include soil sample homogenization techniques, air monitoring, gas chromatography, infrared spectroscopy, X-ray fluorescence, and toxicity screening of complex matrices.

3071. Moore, James W.; Ramamoorthy, S. **Heavy metals in natural waters: applied monitoring and impact assessment.** Springer-Verlag, 1984. 268 pp., ill., bibl., index. Focuses on eight most common heavy metals, providing information on chemistry, production, use and discharge, residues, and toxicity impact assessment methods; recommends an interdisciplinary approach.

3072. McDowall, Michael E. **The identification of man-made environmental hazards to health: a manual of epidemiology.** Macmillan, 1987. 140 pp., ill., index. Addresses the following: analytic problems of specific types of environmental hazards; mechanisms and outcomes of environmentally linked health afflictions, including carcinogens; descriptive and analytic methods of epidemiological investigation; statistical evaluation procedures; and causality, proof, and probability.

3073. de Kruijf, H. A. M.; and others, eds. **Manual on aquatic ecotoxicology.** Kluwer, 1988. 332 pp. Produced from a joint venture between the Netherlands and India. Describes simple, reliable laboratory protocols intended for use in India.

3074. Vouk, Velimir B.; and others, eds. **Methods for estimating risk of chemical injury: human and non-human biota and ecosystems.** Wiley, SGOMSEC, v. 2; SCOPE v. 26, 1985. 680 pp., ill., bibl., index. Based on a 1982 workshop. Reviews and evaluates methods for measuring chemical exposure, risk, and injury.

3075. Austin, B.; ed. **Methods in aquatic bacteriology.** Wiley, Modern microbiological methods, 1988. 425 pp., ill., bibl., index. Detailed introduction to practical methods. Presents basic techniques, approaches for specialized environments and taxonomic groups, and techniques to measure bacterial activity.

3076. Lodge, James P., Jr.; ed. **Methods of air sampling and analysis.** Lewis, 1989. 763 pp. Describes and evaluates hundreds of methods of measuring air contaminants. Discusses ambient air sampling and analysis (carbon, halogens and their compounds, metals, inorganic nitrogen compounds and oxidants, particulate matter, radioactivity, sulfur compounds). Assesses chemicals in the air in the workplace. Provides state-of-the-art reviews. Covers conversion factors.

3077. **OECD guidelines for testing of chemicals.** Organization for Economic Cooperation and Development, 1981. 700 pp. Reference work details the guidelines accepted by all OECD countries for the testing of

the physiochemical properties, effects on biotic systems, degradation and accumulation, and health effects of chemicals.

3078. Ram, Neil M.; Calabrese, Edward J.; Christman, Russell F.; eds. **Organic carcinogens in drinking water: detection, treatment, and risk assessment.** Wiley, 1986. 542 pp. Integrated, broad treatment includes an overview of the problem and data on the nature and extent of pollutants, detection and treatment methods, health assessment, and regulatory aspects. Discusses the significance of microorganic contamination and evaluates methods of concentrating, separating, identifying, and quantifying microorganics.

3079. Suffet, I. H.; Malaiyandi, M.; eds. **Organic pollutants in water: sampling, analysis, and toxicity testing.** American Chemical Society, Advances in chemistry series, v. 214, 1987. 707 pp., ill., bibl., index. Thirty-six papers cover protocols, reverse osmosis for pollutant isolation, synthetic polymers for pollutant concentration, comparison of isolation methods for removing pollutants, toxicity testing and analysis, and case histories of biological testing.

3080. Johnson, Ted R.; Penkala, Stanley J.; eds. **Quality assurance in air pollution measurements.** Air Pollution Control Association, 1985. 850 pp. Transactions of 1984 conference. Explores recent advances in techniques for data validation and analysis. Covers application of procedures used in air quality, meteorological source emissions, and personal monitoring programs. Additional sections on regulatory and health implications of assurance methods in relation to pollution measurements.

3081. Boyle, Terence P.; ed. **Validation and predictability of laboratory methods for assessing the fate and effects of contaminants in aquatic ecosystems.** American Society for Testing and Materials, ASTM special technical publication, no. 865, 1985. 233 pp. Papers compare laboratory tests and microcosms to outdoor mesocosms, relate laboratory methods and results to field techniques and measurements, and examine differing complexities of microcosms. Includes discussion of the importance of prognostic over diagnostic models in assessing chemical effects on a large scale.

3082. Minear, Roger A.; Keith, Lawrence H.; eds. **Water analysis.** Academic Press, 1982. 287 pp., ill., bibl., index. Detailed text covers origin and nature of inorganics in natural waters, redox potential, pH, conductance, and turbidity. Surveys analytical procedures.

3083. Fresenius, W.; Quentin, K. E.; Schneider, W.;

eds. **Water analysis: a practical guide to physico-chemical, chemical and microbiological water examination and quality assurance.** Springer-Verlag, 1988. 804 pp., ill., bibl., index. Comprehensive work covers sampling, local testing, classic and instrumental water analysis methods, organic and inorganic parameters, biological analysis, and the evaluation of data.

3084. Krajca, Jaromil M.; ed. **Water sampling.** Wiley, Ellis Horwood series in water and wastewater technology, 1989. 212 pp., ill., bibl. Reviews atmospheric sampling, groundwater sampling, and surface and soil water sampling. Explains the appropriate equipment, sampling techniques, transport and handling procedures, and hygiene and safety concerns. Describes the effects climate and hydrologic conditions can have on sampling.

Part III

APPENDICES

Appendix 1

Author-Title Index

Appendix 2

Subject Index